Perspectives in American History

VOLUME III

Essay Reviews

A TRANSCENDENTALIST FATHER: THE CHILD-REARING PRACTICES OF BRONSON ALCOTT

Charles Strickland

A TRANSCENDENTALIST FATHER: THE CHILD-REARING PRACTICES OF BRONSON ALCOTT

1. Introduction*

O N March 16, 1831, Anna Bronson Alcott was born in German-town, Pennsylvania, and welcomed with warm enthusiasm by her parents, Mr. and Mrs. Amos Bronson Alcott. One hour after the birth, her father recorded his feelings: "How delightful were the emotions produced by the first sounds of the infant's cry—making it seem that I was, indeed, a father! Joy, gratitude, hope and af-fection were all mingled in our feeling."[1] Mrs. Alcott was in no condi-tion to write about her feelings just then. It had been a difficult preg-nancy, casting her often into periods of gloom and anxiety, and she had endured thirty-six hours of labor in giving birth. Nevertheless, eleven days after Anna's arrival, she proved no less ecstatic than her husband. Writing her brother, Mrs. Alcott was eager to convey her joy, and to assure him it made not the least difference that her first child had not been a boy. Anna was in good health and perfectly quiet, while nursing and caring for her was delightful. "I would not," she said, "delegate it to an angel. I am at times most impatient to dismiss my nurse, that not even she should participate with me in this pleasure."[2]

* The author wishes to thank the U.S. Office of Education and the Emory University Research Committee for grants enabling him to undertake the work on which the pres-ent paper is based. Gratitude should also be expressed to Mrs. F. Wolsey Pratt and the Harvard College Library for permission to quote at length from the Alcott Family Man-uscripts deposited by Mrs. Pratt in Harvard's Houghton Library. During early stages of the writing, valuable suggestions were supplied by Erik Erikson, William Harrison, Boyd McCandless, G. Alexander Moore, James Jordan, Robert Wheeler, R. Jackson Wilson, Richard Ward, and, especially, Kai Erikson. My wife, Eycke M. Strickland, not only transformed Alcott's child diaries into a legible typescript, she also shared her hard-won insights into the nature of family life.

1. Bronson Alcott Journals, March 16, 1831, Alcott Family Manuscripts (Houghton Library, Harvard University). All citations of manuscripts refer, without further desig-nation, to this collection.
2. Abigail Alcott to Samuel May, March 27, 1831, Family Letters, 1828–1861.

The joy that the Alcotts found in their first-born was, perhaps, common enough, but Anna's birth meant far more to her father than the usual delights of parenthood. He had in mind nothing less than an experiment in perfecting mankind. "We do not yet know," he wrote, "what favorable influences, from birth, will do for the infant. . . . It is reserved for some individual, who . . . shall take the infant, from the beginning, and paying due respect to his whole nature, shall cooperate with it, in due accordance and harmony with the laws of its constitution, and suggest to the world, both by success and failure, what the human being may become."[3]

An experiment should, of course, be recorded. Consequently, on March 25, just nine days after Anna's birth, Alcott began his "Observations on the Phenomena of Life, as Developed in the Progressive History of an Infant, during the First Year of its Existence." The record was fully worthy of the impressive title. It was, for one thing, one of the first infant diaries kept by an American, although Alcott had been inspired to undertake the work by the example of similar records left by Europeans.[4] The other remarkable thing about Alcott's manuscript was its volume and scope. When Anna's first year was completed, he began another series of observations, and ultimately the record swelled to cover Anna's development until she was five, spilling over to include the early experience of Louisa, born in 1832, and of Elizabeth, born in 1835. When Alcott laid down his pen in 1836, he had filled nearly 2500 manuscript pages with observations on the behavior of his young daughters and with reflections on the significance of the early years of human life.

Alcott's awesome industry was the product of professional ambition, as well as paternal love and scientific curiosity. Born in 1799, the son of an impecunious Connecticut farmer, Alcott spent much of his youth engaged in farming and peddling, acquiring more formal learning only through primitive rural schools and by dint of his efforts at self-educa-

3. Bronson Alcott, Observations on the Life of My First Child (Anna Bronson Alcott) during Her First Year, p. 27.

4. The articles that prompted Alcott's interest were two brief letters by a certain "R.B." appearing in Nicholson's Journal of Natural Philosophy, Chemistry and the Arts, 15 (September–December, 1806), 42–50, 181–187. See Alcott, Journals, March 25 and July 16, 1831.

tion.[5] At the age of 23 he became a district school teacher, which in itself was not so unusual. What else could a young man with bookish inclinations and no advantages aspire to? But Alcott, though poorly educated, possessed both intelligence and demonic energy, and he began to think of himself as a Messiah, come to save the world through reforming education. He also made two discoveries during his years as a Connecticut schoolmaster: first, that he had a way with children, especially with the little ones, and, secondly, that his talent was appreciated. His impressive work in the schools of Bristol and Cheshire, Connecticut, won him no friends in the local districts, to be sure, but he did manage to attract the attention of Boston's avant-garde, who proved willing to tolerate an educational Messiah. In 1828, Alcott accepted an invitation to conduct an "infant" school in America's intellectual capital and within two years he had acquired a reputation as a reformer of schools for young children.

Convinced that a good family provided the model for a good school, he also began speaking out on the reform of family life. He hoped to write a book on nurture that would be welcomed by mothers anxious to do well by their children, as well as one that would place him in the front rank of American sages. In either case, Alcott reasoned, his conclusions should be based on a thorough understanding of child development, secured through the painstaking observation of an infant.[6] His marriage to Abigail May, in 1830, held out, therefore, not only the usual marital joys but also an opportunity for scientific research.

Mrs. Alcott, far from resenting his curiosity about their offspring, did all within her power to encourage her husband's plans and ambitions.[7] Contrary to legend, she was not a long-suffering wife who merely out of love for her husband tolerated his idealism. From the date of their first meeting she was fully taken with his ideas, and she had good reason to believe she understood what he was talking about. Com-

5. The essential facts of Alcott's career are drawn from Odell Shepard's excellent biography, *Pedlar's Progress: The Life of Bronson Alcott* (Boston, 1937), and from Bronson Alcott's *New Connecticut: An Autobiographical Poem*, ed. F. B. Sanborn (Boston, 1887). Dorothy McCuskey has dealt explicitly with Alcott's school career in *Bronson Alcott, Teacher* (New York, 1940).

6. Bronson Alcott, "Maternal Instruction," *Unitarian Advocate*, 1 (1828), 304–308; Journals, January 17, October 3, 1830, February 20, March 25, 1831.

7. Abigail Alcott to Samuel May, March 27, 1831, Family Letters, 1828–1861.

ing from a respectable family, she was a highly perceptive and intelligent woman, who defied the conventions of her age and read widely in
philosophy and history. Before making Alcott's acquaintance, she acquired decided opinions on a variety of subjects, including a leaning toward liberalism in theology and convictions about the necessity of providing freedom for the slaves, equal rights for women, and reform of
the school and the home.[8]

Abigail was not, however, cut out for the career of a militant spinster.
When she met Alcott she was already twenty-six, and she apparently
decided immediately that they should join their lives together. For two
years she pressed the shy, doubting, and hesitant Alcott toward a marital
decision. Some of her relatives wondered if she should marry a man of
Alcott's doubtful origins, and she was fully aware that he would never
become a pecuniary success, but, swept by a tide of affection and idealism, she regarded such considerations as unimportant. Like so many
who knew Alcott well, she was awed by his apparent serenity of spirit,
which, she thought, would provide a beneficial check on her own vola-
tile temperament.[9] In any event, her faith overcame his doubts, and the
way was prepared for an experiment in ideal domesticity. Seven months
after their marriage, Alcott accepted an invitation from Reuben Haines,
a wealthy Quaker farmer, to open a school in Germantown, Pennsylvania. Accompanied by his pregnant wife, Alcott sailed in December,
1830 for Philadelphia, where they spent the winter preparing for the
new ventures in school and home, both of which Alcott trusted would
launch a reputation among men of influence. Specifically, he hoped that
the detailed observations of his infant would find a publisher.[10]

Unfortunately for Alcott's ambitions, his voluminous notes on the
children held little interest either for scientists or for mothers. His journals were far too abstruse in content and turgid in style to be of help to

8. Bronson Alcott, Journals, August 2, 1828; Bronson Alcott to William A. Alcott,
December 21, 1829, Letters, 1828–1834; Abigail Alcott to Samuel May, August, 1828,
Family Letters, 1828–1861; Shepard, *Pedlar's Progress*, p. 107; Sandford Salyer, *Marmee:
The Mother of Little Women* (Norman, Okla., 1949), chaps. i, ii.

9. Abigail Alcott to Samuel May, August, 1828; Abigail Alcott to Lucretia May, June
15, 1830. Family Letters, 1828–1861; Bronson Alcott, Journals, December 19, 1829, January 25, 1830.

10. Bronson Alcott, Journals, November 5, December 14, December 18, 1830, June 23,
June 24, 1831.

harassed housewives. As a practical book of advice, his luxuriant record would require considerable pruning; it is obvious that Louisa did not inherit her writing gift from her father. His observations also had failings as a scientific work. Alcott himself put his finger on the difficulty when he commented in 1834 that

I am carried away from the individual, however much I seek to fasten my observations upon detailed exhibitions of life. The finite runs into the infinite by imperceptible gradations. The individual and the personal connects itself by some subtle tie to the general and universal. I sit down to make some remarks on the lives and circumstances of my children, but, ere I am aware, I have left the considerations of them as individuals, and have merged their existence into the common life of the spirit.[11]

He resolved to do better by way of recording more factual detail, but Alcott's account unmistakably reveals an impatience with fact and a preoccupation with abstraction. Emerson, who shared Alcott's yearnings for the infinite, nevertheless found portions of the manuscript painful to read, and he had the courage to tell his friend not to think of publication. Emerson pointed out that the writing was diffuse and disjointed, while its chief fault was a "want of compression."[12] Alcott sadly acknowledged the justice of Emerson's remarks and put the observations away. For the next century his record of infancy and childhood remained only of sentimental value to the immediate family and of cursory interest to a few writers who investigated the Alcott clan, or aspects of transcendentalism.[13]

Nevertheless, Alcott's record possesses a value that neither he nor his contemporaries could have anticipated. His efforts clearly mark the be-

11. Bronson Alcott, Observations on the Spiritual Nurture of My Children, p. 146. This manuscript is bound with another entitled, Researches on Childhood. For the sake of clarity, the two manuscripts will be cited as separate volumes.

12. Ralph Waldo Emerson to Bronson Alcott, February 27, 1836, Bronson Alcott, Autobiography, 1834.

13. Only within the past decade have scholars begun to appreciate the historic value of Alcott's observations. To date, Barbara Garlitz has made the best use of the material as a basis for a chapter in her unpublished dissertation, "The Cult of Childhood in Nineteenth-Century England and America" (Radcliffe, 1959), portions of which have appeared in her article, "The Immortality Ode: Its Cultural Progeny," *Studies in English Literature*, 6 (1966), 639–649. Brief portions of Alcott's child-rearing journals are included in Honoré Willsie Morrow's *The Father of Little Women* (Boston, 1927), pp. 111–117, 148–160; in Kenneth W. Cameron's *Emerson the Essayist* (Raleigh, N.C., 1945), II, 101–125; and in Sherman Paul's "Alcott's Search for the Child," *Boston Public Library Quarterly*, 4 (April 1952), 88–96.

ginnings of child psychology in America, a full half-century before G. Stanley Hall launched the "child-study" movement with his well-known investigation of Boston kindergarten children.[14] Moreover, whatever his failings as a scientist, Alcott was actually a much more accurate and conscientious observer of children than Hall, and his work deserves a much larger place in the history of American psychology than he has been accorded. Then again, the fact that his daughters became the prototypes of the characters in *Little Women* lends a certain interest to his record. Those concerned, for example, with Louisa's career as a writer can discover in her father's infant journals early but clearly recognizable portraits of "Meg" and "Jo," which suggest the type of literary realism that Louisa's astoundingly popular novel attempted to convey.

In the end, however, the most valuable revelations in Alcott's manuscript do not concern his daughters, contrary to his intentions. He set out to note the details of child development, and the focus was to be on Anna, and then on Louisa and Elizabeth, but he actually disclosed much more about himself than about his children. Through a veil of vague mysticisms and philosophic abstractions emerges a rare historic glimpse of a father, and of the way he thought about his children, felt about them, and treated them.

Alcott's thinking and feeling about his children were largely a compound of the philosophic idealism, romantic imagery, and native religious sentiment that was to become known as American transcendentalism. In 1831, before transcendentalism had become a self-conscious intellectual movement, Alcott had already arrived, by dint of his strenuous self-education, at the faint outlines of the persuasions that Emerson would expound five years later in his seminal essay "Nature." Alcott was not, by any means, a systematic philosopher, but he read widely and thoughtfully, and one can detect in his early journals the beginnings of a rebellion against materialism—both as a philosophy and as a way of life. He was also speaking of a universal order, embracing both man and nature, but transcending both, to which men can refer their aspirations

14. See "G. Stanley Hall: Prophet of Naturalism," *Health, Growth and Heredity: G. Stanley Hall on Natural Education*, eds. Charles E. Strickland and Charles Burgess (New York, 1965), pp. 1–26.

for the ideal. Above all, one can see Alcott groping for a belief in man's essential divinity, which consists in the power to transcend the limitations of human nature and human society.[15]

For Alcott, as later for Emerson, it was important to point to a concrete symbol to represent the possibilities of human nature, and, thanks to the tuition of romantic literature, the child sprang readily to mind. If one perceived aright, the child represented human nature uncorrupted by false philosophy and constricting institutions. The image of the child —simple, innocent, and idealistic—could serve as a kind of moral standard against which to measure and condemn the sophistication, hypocrisy, and materialism of adults. It was to be expected that this vision of childhood would readily join with Alcott's programmatic emphasis on educational reform, for if the child were uncorrupted, then it was incumbent upon adults to protect the child from the world in order to help him realize the future possibilities for human perfection.

As Alcott's transcendentalism matured, however, he began to think that he could learn as much from the child as he could teach him. Through association with the young, the adult could recapture from his own childhood a quality of innocence and idealism to sustain him amid the temptations of Jacksonian America. "Childhood hath *Saved* me!" Alcott exclaimed after a period of intensive association with his daughters, and it was, in fact, Alcott's musings about the spirit of childhood that led Emerson to remark:

Infancy is the perpetual Messiah, which comes into the arms of fallen men, and pleads with them to return to paradise.[16]

15. Shepard, *Pedlar's Progress*, pp. 145–160. Shepard has accurately dated the period of Alcott's most rapid intellectual development toward transcendentalism from August, 1832, when he read Coleridge; but Alcott's Journal for 1831 records several assaults on materialism. On September 24, 1831, Alcott wrote: "Thus man's duty is within him. It is his apprehension of his own nature which gives him the idea of a divinity. It is his nobler part which he adores. The deity within him is more excellent than any which is revealed to him from without, for his senses, holding communion only with the external world, can never bring to him those views of divine truth and beauty which it is the peculiar province of the reflective powers to appreciate. Without is but the resemblance of God. Within, He dwells and reveals Himself." This is not, however, the place to enter into the vexing question of whether the transcendentalism of Alcott and Emerson was the only version available in the early eighteen-thirties. See Joel Porte, *Emerson and Thoreau: Transcendentalists in Conflict* (Middletown, Conn., 1965), esp. pp. 8–10.

16. Ralph Waldo Emerson, "Nature," in *Emerson on Education*, ed. Howard Mumford

When Emerson published these lines, they may have had for him no more than a poetic significance, for he himself was not yet a father. His first child, Waldo, was born one month after "Nature" was published. But five years earlier, in Germantown, Alcott faced not only the image of an infant, but also a living, breathing fact. How did one go about the business of rearing a demigod? The romantic conception would seem to impose on parents a staggering obligation to protect the children from the world and at the same time to help the child realize his spiritual potential. As Alcott's diaries demonstrate, he and his wife took their obligations seriously, but even they encountered finite limits to their energy and dedication. Mrs. Alcott was often stricken with illness, and she missed some of the finer points of her husband's child-rearing theories. Alcott himself, after an initial enthusiasm for the domestic experiment, began to chafe under the restrictions of family life, longing for somewhat broader intellectual horizons. Always the threat of poverty hovered over the family. Evidently the world was jealous of a transcendentalist household, while, alas! parents were not themselves always what they should be.

Transcendentalist expectations were no less trying for the children. It was not that joy was absent from the Alcott household. For all his seriousness of purpose in child-rearing, Alcott believed in gentle means. The "rod and its appendages" were banished, and there is in Alcott's extensive record no hint of deliberate cruelty or neglect. Moreover, the father's theories led him to grasp that play and imagination are the roads to a child's heart, and his record produced the kind of vignettes out of which are woven fond memories of childhood—Anna and her father romping about his study, imitating the letters of the alphabet; Anna engaged in sober conversation while sitting on her father's lap; Anna listening with wonder to her father's stories. There is a point, if a somewhat exaggerated one, to Lewis Mumford's comment that the major legacy of transcendentalism was the belief that childhood could be happy.[17]

But Alcott never confused happiness with hedonism. If he tried to see

Jones (New York, 1966), p. 72; Paul, "Alcott's Search for the Child," pp. 88–96. Paul's observation that Alcott was seeking in the image of the child an image of his own "untarnished self" anticipated the view elaborated upon in the present article.

17. Lewis Mumford, *The Golden Day; A Study in American Experience and Culture* (New York, 1926), p. 163.

to it that his daughters were happy, he also expected a great deal from the children in the way of conscientious self-control at a very early age. The major point of transcendentalist child-rearing, as practised by Alcott, was that gentle means must be used to promote ascetic ends, a view which made the burdens of childhood peculiarly intense. If a child is a demigod, then he should try to act like one. And, when he falls short, he should have the decency—perhaps one should say the divinity —to feel badly about it. Consequently, by the time she was four, Anna had often experienced a troubled spirit, while even Louisa had felt the lash of conscience. In this sense, at least, Alcott's child-rearing was a resounding success.

In 1831, however, the joy and sorrow of Alcott family life lay in the future. The father had an ample supply of theories about children, but he had not yet encountered the experience of dealing with his own, nor had he learned that the world, as one historian has put it, "has many ways of defeating those who try to stand too far from it."[18]

II. Anna's First Year: the "Little Paradise"

ANNA'S first residence in Germantown was a boarding house belonging to a Mrs. Stuckart.[19] The Alcotts had lived in such establishments since their marriage, and they would do so again, but it was hardly the place Alcott would choose for his experiment in child-rearing. Required was something ideal, which meant in this instance something antiseptic. He could imagine the setting, far removed from the corrupt world. It would be a cottage set in a "romantic" valley, beside a bubbling brook, and surrounded by steep precipices and lofty mountains. Here, under the supervision of a mother who had renounced fash-

18. Edmund S. Morgan, *Visible Saints: the History of a Puritan Idea* (Ithaca, N.Y., 1963), p. 112.
19. Bronson Alcott, Journals, February 18, 1831.

ionable society and of a father who had repudiated worldly ambition, children would be reared as they ought.[20]

Germantown fell short of the ideal, but it was still much better than either Philadelphia or Boston, and for that Alcott was grateful. Meanwhile, Reuben Haines, chief patron of Alcott's school, had promised to do his part by getting the family out of Mrs. Stuckart's boarding house, and he kept his promise. On May 13, nearly two months after Anna's birth, the Alcotts moved into a cottage, recently painted, neatly furnished, and provided rent-free by Haines.[21] Situated on a main road, with more than an acre of grounds and garden, the setting was very close to ideal, in Mrs. Alcott's opinion. She reported to her brother that the home was a "little paradise." The house would vie with her father's residence in Boston for neatness and order, while the garden was charming, lined with raspberry, currant, and gooseberry bushes. The grounds featured also a lovely walk shaded with pine, fir, cedar, apple, pear, peach, and plum trees. Completing the picture was an efficient housekeeper, and, of course, "the mild, constant and affectionate sympathy" of her husband. "With good health, clear head, grateful heart and ready hand, what can I not do when surrounded by influences like these?" she asked. "What can I leave undone with so many aids?"[22]

It was Alcott's opinion that she should leave precious little undone, in so far as Anna was concerned. Success with Anna required that her care be completely under parental control, for the family was to be a fortress from which worldly incursions would be vigorously repelled. Relatives would present no threat; the move from New England to Pennsylvania ensured little interference from that quarter. Servants might, however, become a problem, for Alcott thought too many parents failed by consigning their infants to the care of a nurse, who was usually ignorant, selfish, and lazy.[23] It seems the Alcotts could not do without household assistance, and the record reveals that a servant usually worked in the home during these early years, but the danger was kept within bounds. The Alcotts insisted that the domestic take care of the house, while they

20. *Ibid.*, July 8, 1831.
21. *Ibid.*, May 10 and May 13, 1831.
22. Abigail Alcott to Samuel May, May 22, 1831, Family Letters, 1828–1861.
23. Bronson Alcott, First Child, First Year, pp. 75, 78.

kept Anna to themselves. With the exception of the first four weeks, therefore, Anna remained under the sole charge of her mother and father during her first year, as reported by Mrs. Alcott in August and as confirmed by her husband later in the year. Mrs. Alcott rarely left the house without Anna on her arm, and she even developed the habit of retiring with Anna in the evening, holding the infant until she fell asleep in her arms.[24]

Alcott himself revolved in a slightly larger orbit of concern, busy with his school, attending professional meetings, and engaged in one or another writing project, but he also hovered about Anna a good deal.[25] As Mrs. Alcott noted in March, "my husband has not left my room many hours since my illness and though employed principally at his table with his manuscript, his presence has shed tranquillity on the scene."[26] Alcott's school opened in May, but even then he was still much in evidence, since the pupils came to the Alcott home for instruction.[27] Always, of course, his "observations" kept him preoccupied with the infant, and during the first twelve months of her life, he managed to put down an average of one page of notes daily.

The unflagging attention bestowed by the Alcotts was meant to ensure that little Anna would dwell securely in an atmosphere permeated by warmth, affection, and extraordinary permissiveness. This, it might be thought, was only the usual reaction of parents, especially older parents (he was thirty-one and his wife thirty), to the arrival of their first child. But Alcott himself was rarely casual about anything, and least of all about the crucial matter of a parent's relationship with his child. In the first place, physical affection was not a thing that Alcott displayed easily. He did not think of himself as possessing great warmth and affection, and he believed in fact that it was a man's task to provide some check on feminine emotion.[28] It was undoubtedly this view that led Mrs. Alcott to remark to a friend, shortly after her marriage, that with

24. Ibid., pp. 167, 194, 232, 308; Abigail Alcott to Samuel May, August 11, 1831, Family Letters, 1828–1861.

25. Bronson Alcott, Journals, March 21, April 10, April 15, July 25, September 15 and November 19, 1831.

26. Abigail Alcott to Samuel May, March 27, 1831, Family Letters, 1828–1861.

27. Bronson Alcott, Journals, June 24, 1831.

28. Ibid., December 19, 1829; First Child, First Year, p. 11.

her and Mr. Alcott "love was a principle and not a passion."[29] As far as Anna was concerned, some "passion" was doubtless involved, and there is no reason to suspect that Alcott's outburst, on learning that he was a father, was anything but genuine. But in this instance, passion was reinforced by principle. He gave way to affection because he had first persuaded himself that infants are in fact lovable and that loving them would do no harm. His *Observations on the Principles and Methods of Infant Instruction*, published just the preceding year, had already laid down the general idea, drawn from sources in romantic literature and idealistic philosophy, that infants are worthy of affection and reverence.[30] Wordsworth's "Ode on Intimations of Immortality," which Alcott had first read five years earlier, had made him, as well as generations of romantics, familiar with the notion of infant purity:

> Our Birth is but a sleep and a forgetting:
> The Soul that rises with us, our life's star,
>   Hath had elsewhere its setting,
>   And cometh from afar;
>   Not in entire forgetfulness,
>   And not in utter nakedness,
> But trailing clouds of glory, do we come
>   From God who is our home.
> Heaven lies about us in our Infancy.

When Alcott viewed his first-born, he exclaimed, with less poetry but equal enthusiasm:

Could we but descend into this little world—the infant mind—could we behold the first-forming thoughts, the young affections, the dimly-perceived anticipations, the remembered joys, which dwell there, should we not find all that is elevated in intellect, pure in affections, lofty in anticipation, and happy in remembrance! Should we not find the newly-born soul, entering upon its new relations, full of all that is noble, sweet, and pure and happy!—imaginations, whose forms are all glorious, visions of bliss, which bring before the mind the remembrance of the joys of previous existence and the whole intellectual principle full of the divine life![31]

The enemy, in Alcott's view, was the orthodox Calvinist position

---

29. Abigail Alcott to Lucretia May, June 15, 1830, Family Letters, 1828–1861.
30. Bronson Alcott, *Observations on the Principles and Methods of Infant Instruction* (Boston, 1830), p. 9.
31. Bronson Alcott, First Child, First Year, p. 23; Shepard, *Pedlar's Progress*, pp. 80–81.

that the infant is depraved by the taint of original sin. He himself owed little to this view, since at the age of sixteen, he had become an Episcopalian, thus joining, as he later put it, the "signers-off from Calvin's colder creed."[32] By 1831, his opposition to Calvinism was becoming violent:

Of all the impious doctrines which the dark imagination of man ever conceived, this is the worst. This is, indeed, the sin, which is unpardonable—the belief in the original and certain depravity of infant nature. If man had set himself down to contrive an agency which would . . . most effectually degrade human nature, he could not have accomplished his foul purpose so effectually as by this. Happy is it for the world that the progress of our race has outdistanced this debasing doctrine; that nobler views are gaining currency. Infancy is beginning to be respected.[33]

His major objection to the orthodox position rested on psychological rather than on theological grounds. He accused the Calvinists of blasphemy for labelling God's creatures corrupt, but his greater concern was with the effect that such parental views would have on the children. Alcott feared that the belief in infant depravity would encourage parents either to neglect their children or to treat them with brutality. If parents believed children are tainted by original sin, they might argue that they are powerless to shape the character of their offspring. And, if parents believed infants are depraved, they might, as a consequence, treat children with cruelty. Addressing himself to the orthodox, he accused them of robbing "the author of the infant mind of all his glory, and this mind itself of all its loveliness, that ye may find an excuse for your indifference and impiety in guiding it as you ought. Ye would stamp upon the infant the seal of sin that ye may find an excuse for your own sin." Thus, by Alcott's reasoning, the orthodox view was a self-fulfilling prophecy. By acting toward children with cruelty and neglect, orthodox parents succeeded in corrupting their offspring. He put it aptly: "Having made the child perverse by inheritance, ye contrive, upon principle, to make him so by education."[34]

There is reason to doubt that Calvinist parents loved their children less than transcendentalists, or, if they did treat their children with

32. Bronson Alcott, *New Connecticut: An Autobiographical Poem*, ed. F. B. Sanborn (Boston, 1887), p. 53.

33. Bronson Alcott, First Child, First Year, p. 24.

34. *Ibid.*, p. 24.

cruelty and neglect, that they were prompted to do so by their theological views.[35] Moreover, Alcott's romantic opposition to Calvinist views of man can be easily misinterpreted. His high estimate of child-like virtue was not intended to license indiscriminate toleration of childish foibles, which would have struck him as smacking of parental indifference. If not a Calvinist by persuasion, he was nonetheless a New Englander by birth, and he recalled that he had acquired early in life a notion of the importance of putting duty above pleasure. He was regarded by schoolmates as somewhat peculiar in this regard, and they made him the object of ridicule for his extremely serious demeanor. Dedication to a life of duty was confirmed, he recalled, when at the age of sixteen he read a copy of *Pilgrim's Progress*, which he thereafter believed had been the most important book in his life.[36]

He had, it was true, sometimes forgotten the call of duty during his youthful years of peddling in the South. Alcott managed to retain his chastity amid divers temptations, but he found poverty galling. Despite the fact that his father had gone deeply into debt to finance Bronson's peddling ventures, the son indulged in "fashion and improvidence," dressed himself in finery he could not afford, evaded a hotel bill by fleeing like a thief in the night, and returned home to face the disapproval of his parents. When he learned that his frugal father had to sell part of his small farm to pay the creditors, Bronson was truly penitent, and resolved he would turn to a life of "moral sentiment." His resolve was heightened when, during his final peddling trip to the South, he made the acquaintance of the Quakers, whose simplicity, gentle manners, and notions of the "inner light" may well have set Alcott's thinking in the direction of transcendentalism.[37]

Calvinist theology, then, Alcott understood only at second-hand, but

35. See chapter III for a comparison of Alcott's practices with a popular treatise on child-rearing, *The Mother at Home*, written by an orthodox clergyman, The Reverend John S. C. Abbott.

36. Bronson Alcott, Journals, December 4, 1828, April 29, 1834; *New Connecticut*, pp. 27, 36, 173.

37. Bronson Alcott, *New Connecticut*, pp. 77–101, 241–242. Alcott's cousin, William Andrus Alcott, accompanied him on one of his peddling trips and later published his account under the name "Father William." William recalls that he and Bronson sternly resisted many temptations, but, unfortunately, William's good influence was not always available. See *Recollections of Rambles at the South* (New York, 1854), pp. 46–47, 91–100.

the threat of hedonism to his integrity had been a matter of painful personal experience.[38] Men, if not fatally corrupt, were at least weak, and he regarded the age in which he lived as one well calculated to exploit that weakness in himself and in others. Only a heroic conquest of self and a repudiation of worldly temptation would enable a man to save his purity and integrity. By 1831 he was prepared to announce that virtue, by its very definition, is the "supremacy of the higher over the lower" in man's nature, while the chief purpose of education is to instill virtue.[39] Thus, when Alcott observed three-month-old Anna screaming and flailing her arms and legs from frustration, he did not perceive the beginnings of sin, but neither did he think he was witnessing the perfection of human nature. For all his reading of Wordsworth, Alcott frankly admitted that the infant was necessarily "selfish." He explained that

Infancy is the period of animal activity. The appetites and passions are then most supreme; the mind, in its weakness, has not assumed control over them; happiness is identified with the gratification of senses.[40]

Moreover, despite his Wordsworthian sentiments, Alcott advised the parent, when confronted by the animal nature of the infant, to express toleration rather than unrestrained admiration. Parents should, in their treatment of the very young, exercise "charity for its failings, pity for its weaknesses, forbearance with its errors."[41]

In the light of these views, one wonders what is to be made of Alcott's celebrated opposition to Calvinist theories of infant depravity? Were Alcott's opinions nothing but a ludicrous and bewildering collection of contradictions? There was, doubtless, considerable ambivalence in Alcott's attitude toward infancy, and, later, toward childhood, and he sometimes imposed more restrictions on his children than his theories would seem to justify. But in this instance, Alcott could reconcile his various attitudes toward infants, and at the same time set his position off as distinct from that held by Calvinists. The chief fault of their view, he thought, was not that they made so much of man's potential for sin,

38. Three years after his return home in disgrace, Bronson wrote his brother, Chatfield, still expressing his regret for having given his parents such pain by his extravagance: *New Connecticut*, p. 245.

39. Bronson Alcott, Journals, July 7, September 24, 1831.

40. Bronson Alcott, First Child, First Year, pp. 37–38, 95.

41. *Ibid.*, pp. 95–96.

but that they made so little of man's power to transcend his weaknesses. The infant might be largely a bundle of appetites and passions, but at a very early age the infant also possesses higher faculties which hold great promise for spiritual perfection. From the day of Anna's birth, her father searched eagerly for the appearance of "mind," "soul," "spirit," or the "internal principle." For weeks his search was in vain, and he admitted that Anna's "internal principle" lay effectively hidden somewhere in the center of her being.[42] But, on May 13, when Anna was nearly two months old, Alcott was delighted to report that he detected the beginnings of a "conscious and intelligent soul." As proof he cited something like a smile crossing Anna's face as she gazed on a vase of wild violets resting on the mantel. This episode, minor though it might seem to the insensitive parent, provided Alcott with evidence that Anna was no mere animal being, but also a soul capable of recognizing and responding to beauty![43]

Parents must, through an exercise of faith in the infant's spiritual potential, bring to the surface its capacity for affection, reason, and conscience. Success in drawing out the operation of the higher faculties would, Alcott admitted, require a "generous indulgence" of the infant's desires, even to the point of tolerating behavior that a Calvinist might regard as willful.[44] At the heart of Alcott's child-rearing theories was the belief that the conquest of the lower nature by the higher must be in some sense voluntary. A virtue imposed from without was no virtue at all, and Alcott had little patience for popular biographies of saintly prodigies, not because the subjects were so young, but because their piety was too perfect and their character was so drained of willfulness. Virtue was not a gift of birth, but a quality acquired through heroic struggle, and for this an indomitable will was essential.[45]

The question is, of course, just how far Alcott was willing to take these theories. To use his own terms, just how was he to exercise a "generous" but not a "reckless" indulgence of his infant daughter?[46] The record reveals that during Anna's first six months, the Alcotts were

42. *Ibid.*, p. 2.
43. *Ibid.*, p. 10.
44. *Ibid.*, p. 39.
45. *Ibid.*, p. 197; *Principles and Methods*, p. 15.
46. Bronson Alcott, First Child, First Year, p. 96.

generous to the point of recklessness. The father's conviction and, doubtless, the mother's instincts produced something like a paradise for little Anna during her first year. The picture was often idyllic. Anna was permitted to spend many hours in her mother's lap after nursing at the breast, and she was the recipient of innumerable caresses.[47] The parents made every effort, moreover, to ensure that she was protected from "distorted faces" and "harsh sounds." Always she was addressed in "cheerful countenance, with soft tones and deep interest."[48] On the theory that too much movement disturbed Anna's tranquillity, the Alcotts even banned a rocking cradle,[49] and they would not permit their daughter to be treated as a plaything by well-intentioned but ignorant visitors. Specifically banned were sudden movements, loud voices, baby talk, and "incessant prattle." These "may excite surprise and thus gain the child's momentary attention," Alcott commented, "yet by their excess, they soon weary and irritate."[50]

Anna must also be protected from fear, a stricture that Alcott himself once violated in his eager quest for information. When Anna was a little more than two months old, he made faces at her to see how she would react:

She seemed impressed by them all, and especially by that which embodied the emotion of fear, so much so that terror was manifested by loud cries, and the desire of seeking protection in the presence of her mother; and it was with difficulty that she could erase the idea of this . . . from her mind and restore herself to her accustomed tranquillity. The vision would reappear before her imagination, and produce the recurrence of the feeling for some time after its first entrance; and tears would flow.

Alarmed, Alcott resolved that he would never again frighten her. "The influence of fear, even in its milder forms, upon the mind of infancy must be unfavorable to its improvement and happiness."[51]

Above all, Alcott and his wife made every conceivable effort to see to it that their daughter should neither be frustrated nor coerced. He was perfectly delighted when Anna loudly protested something that displeased her. Like any proud father, Alcott was prone to make invidious

47. *Ibid.*, pp. 7, 10, 17, 25, 40, 57, 113, 170–171.
48. *Ibid.*, p. 26.
49. *Ibid.*, pp. 69–70.
50. *Ibid.*, p. 70.
51. *Ibid.*, p. 17.

comparisons between his own offspring and other children, to the advantage of the former, and he noted with satisfaction that Anna was not so "passive" as other infants.[52] Consequently, when he observed Anna, at three months, crying from frustration, he refused to become alarmed:

> To some these might seem like indications of passion, to which criminality is attached. They might regard them as the beginnings of anger, and think it their duty to check and overcome them in their early weakness. The will, they might believe, should be only subjected to their own; and thus obedience, that virtue so often imposed on infancy, be made habitual from the beginning.
>
> But this view of infant nature, seems to me essentially erroneous and the consequences which flow from it, in education, most injurious to the mind and character. Liberty is a primary right of all created natures, and the love of it inherent in all. . . .

Underscoring his words for emphasis, Alcott declared:

> The *child* must be *treated* as a *free*, self-*guiding*, self-*controlling* being. He must be allowed to feel that he is under his own guidance, and that all external guidance is an injustice which is done to his nature unless his own will is intelligently submissive to it. . . . He must be free that he may be truly virtuous, for without freedom there is no such thing as virtue.[53]

Whether Anna as yet possessed a free will may be subject to debate, but there is no doubt that she made demands, which the parents pledged themselves to obey. "Her nature has been watched and interrogated," Alcott wrote during the third month, "and its answers regarded, as far as they could be ascertained. She has not been permitted to cry, as is too often the case, for long periods, but her wants have been anticipated, and the occasions for tears have been few."[54] Writing to her brother during the fifth month, Mrs. Alcott assured him, "I have no rules. I am one great one to do what she [Anna] indicates to have done and she is so reasonable that I find no difficulty." The trick, she explained, was to satisfy the baby's "real wants" so quickly that she did not have time to generate artificial ones.[55] With regard to dress, this liberal program meant that Anna would be dressed warmly but not so as to check the freedom of moving her hands and legs.[56] As for feeding, it appears that

52. *Ibid.*, pp. 73–74.
53. *Ibid.*, pp. 45–46.
54. *Ibid.*, pp. 25–26.
55. Abigail Alcott to Samuel and Lucretia May, August 11, 1831, Family Letters, 1828–1861.
56. Bronson Alcott, First Child, First Year, p. 170.

Mrs. Alcott nursed the infant frequently and on demand. When Anna was six months old, Alcott reported that she was "partaking at regular intervals of an hour or an hour and half."[57] When Anna was nine months old, the loving father would even permit the baby to pull his hair.[58]

On one occasion at least, the Alcotts momentarily overlooked their permissive principle. Five-month-old Anna suffered some minor ailment in July and worked herself into a bad temper, which appeared at intervals for several weeks. At last it occurred to the parents that she was chafing under confinement to the house. Someone—it may have been her father—built a small "waggon" designed expressly to take her for a daily outing, and after a few days her clamour subsided. The parents were to blame, he confessed, for their inattention. Observe Nature and heed her signs![59]

There were limits, however, to the tolerance of even such fond parents. Anna evidently disliked washing and dressing from her earliest hours and continued to register protest for months and even years thereafter, but to no avail. In November of Anna's first year Alcott noted her dissatisfaction and even suggested that "a good temper is of more importance than a clean frock; an amiable disposition and docile will more to be regarded than a face always without spot or blemish."[60] Mrs. Alcott evidently did not share her husband's tolerance in this matter, and the washing and dressing continued, with some signs, at least, that Anna was submitting with less reluctance to the daily routine.[61]

On the whole, the Alcotts were pleased with the results of their program of warmth, affection, and indulgence. When Anna was five months old, Mrs. Alcott stated proudly that she was reaping the reward of constant attention to the infant. "She has no bad habits. I keep no light at night. She sleeps tranquilly till morning and retires regularly at about eight o'clock."[62] Two months later Alcott found his daughter happy and healthy and still sleeping the night through, and without a

57. *Ibid.*
58. *Ibid.*, p. 231.
59. *Ibid.*, pp. 93, 104.
60. *Ibid.*, p. 252.
61. *Ibid.*, p. 251. Alcott's mention of washing and dressing is the only reference, and an oblique one at that, to matters involving toilet training.
62. Abigail Alcott to Samuel and Lucretia May, August 11, 1831, Family Letters, 1828–1861.

lamp burning.[63] By the end of Anna's first six months, the Alcotts could congratulate themselves on having created, by dint of constant effort, an Eden for their offspring.

During Anna's second six months the permissive regime continued with some modification, but with increasing signs that all was not serene in Anna's world. For one thing, the parents learned they could not protect their infant from all discomfort. Anna's paradise was rudely shattered on September 26, during her seventh month, with the appearance of a first tooth. Heretofore a "stranger to pain," according to her father, Anna was a stranger no longer. The parents could only relieve the discomfort she suffered by making an incision in the gum to ease the passage of the tooth. The operation, Alcott said, gave immediate relief.[64]

It was a pity, Alcott reflected, that physical pain could be relieved more readily than mental anguish, for it appeared to him that Anna was now becoming querulous and unhappy.[65] Anna's loud protests, which a few months previously had pleased him, now appeared to be getting out of hand, and he was becoming a bit uneasy. There seemed a danger that her will, in itself so admirable, might fall under the reign of her "passions." By Anna's seventh month, he thought the danger had become real. She was attempting to move a book too heavy for her, and the frustration produced an expression of "passion" that alarmed her father. He acknowledged he had witnessed "decided tones" before, but nothing to match this! "This expression was so strong as to induce movements of the hands forcing the book away from her with tears and all the manifestations of anger."[66] Was it possible that a generous indulgence had indeed become reckless?

Soon afterward, Alcott found it necessary to speak sharply with Anna, his first recorded use of a reprimand. It seems that Mrs. Alcott had been in the habit of allowing the infant to sleep in the parents' bed-room, and, in fact, the mother retired at night herself when she put the baby down to sleep. For several days, however, Mrs. Alcott could not go to bed at

63. Bronson Alcott, First Child, First Year, p. 171.
64. *Ibid.*, pp. 186, 190.
65. *Ibid.*, p. 186.
66. *Ibid.*, p. 174.

the usual hour, and rather than putting Anna to sleep, she allowed her to remain in the lighted parlor. When at last Anna was taken to bed, she cried because, in Alcott's opinion, she missed the light. The mother at last yielded, returned Anna to the parlor, where she enjoyed herself for a time, but on being returned to bed, she once again wailed. After this drama was repeated several more times, Alcott decided that indulgence had gone too far. Entering the room, he spoke to his daughter in a "kind though decided tone," attempting to make her understand "by the peculiarity of this tone that it was not his wish that her wants, in this case, should be gratified." Alcott thought she understood him. At any event she left off crying and not long after fell asleep.[67]

Alcott's treatment of Anna in this instance came perilously close to intimidation, when viewed in the light of his own theories. And, in fact, he had in mind a much more subtle campaign to handle Anna's growing obstreperousness. It consisted of an attempt to weaken the "animal" side of her nature, which her father regarded as the source of her discontent, and to strengthen the "spiritual" forces of reason, affection, and conscience. As part of his campaign against the animal nature, Alcott sought to weaken the flesh by depriving it, quite literally, of its nourishment. One of Alcott's more exotic notions stemmed from his growing vegetarianism. He believed that eating meat strengthened the animal faculties and led to the development of a brutish character. Although his vegetarian convictions reached their height in later years (he had not yet himself forsworn meat), he revealed when Anna was four months old that he had doubts about feeding meat to infants, or, for that matter, to adults.[68] He dismissed the doubts for a time, and we discover Anna, in her tenth month, enjoying a diet including meat.[69] But, when Anna was one year old, Alcott had reverted to his earlier doubts. Finding that his daughter was more difficult to please and easily irritated when fed animal food, Alcott dictated that she be limited to "vegetable and natural substances."[70] It was also Alcott's view that too much sleep strengthened the animal faculties unduly, and he noted with satisfaction that his

67. *Ibid.*, pp. 194–195.
68. *Ibid.*, pp. 35–36.
69. *Ibid.*, p. 258.
70. *Ibid.*, p. 337.

daughter, at nine months, limited herself to a half-hour nap during the day. Better still, she sometimes dispensed with it altogether.[71]

An even greater threat to Anna's development than either meat or mid-day naps was sheer boredom. The solution was simply to keep her busy. Here, Alcott's New England heritage seems again to reveal itself, and there was a sense in which he would subscribe to the dictum that idleness is the devil's workshop. But, as far as the infant Anna was concerned, Alcott meant only that she should be preoccupied with play and other diversions. Already, from the day of Anna's birth, her father had spent countless hours with his daughter—talking to her, offering his finger to be seized, allowing her to pull his hair, and surrounding her with all manner of colorful objects. A rocking cradle was banned, but Alcott thought some motion was not harmful, and he introduced a small swing, which would occupy the six-month-old infant for as much as a half-hour at a time.[72]

Since the Alcotts kept Anna pretty much to themselves, the necessity of stimulating her through play must have placed a large burden on the parents. As always, too little is known of Mrs. Alcott's dealing with the infant, but the record makes clear that the father was giving her still more attention during the second six months. Moreover, the games he initiated with Anna had a point beyond simply preventing boredom. Alcott aimed at developing her infant reason through establishing what he called "associations" in her experience. The first lesson to be learned was the connection between cause and effect. He noted that nine-month-old Anna was greatly attracted by the lamp and even put her hand very near the flame. Her father was content for the present to forbid her to touch it.[73] Several weeks later, he judged that the time had arrived for the lesson:

Delighted with the brilliant light and anxious to seize it, she was permitted gently to place her hand within the flame, and experience the pain thus produced. At first she seemed greatly disappointed that an object so beautiful to her imagination should conduce to her pain, and obviously doubted the correctness of her sensations, for she put her hand again within the blaze in order to satisfy herself, but immediately withdrew

71. *Ibid.*, p. 255.
72. *Ibid.*, pp. 17, 33, 34, 62, 64, 89, 183, 185.
73. *Ibid.*, p. 245.

it, her eyes suffused with tears, and her whole countenance assuming the appearance of chagrin and disappointment.

Never again, Alcott claimed, could Anna be induced to put her hand in the flame.[74]

He employed similar means to put an end to Anna's hair-pulling, which heretofore he had tolerated. Now, when she pulled his hair, he pulled hers, although very gently. Thereafter, when he presented his head for her amusement, she would only pat it and smile pleasantly. With the help of reason, her father explained, she was coming to exercise power over her own desires, which gave her as much pleasure as the power she had formerly exercised over her father. Thus, the incident supplied an example of transferring pleasure from an improper to a proper act.[75] The success of the lessons led Alcott to similar experiments. When Anna began playing with sharp objects, her father pricked her finger with a pin. Again Anna learned the lesson perfectly.[76]

Anna's father was inordinately pleased with the success of these little experiments, for they beautifully illustrated one of his major contentions about child-rearing. As he interpreted the episodes, Anna had learned a connection between cause and effect, and, through an act of free-will, had subjugated her desire to touch the flame, to pull her father's hair, or to play with pins. And it had all come about without the forcible imposition of parental authority! Through the use of her infant reason, Anna was making contact with universal, natural law and behaving herself accordingly.[77]

But could Anna order her conduct in the light of her reason alone, insufficiently developed as her intellect was? After all, her father had been able to protect her from the flame only by his fatherly command until he judged she was prepared to obey a higher law. Moreover, Alcott acknowledged, there are some lessons that cannot be learned under the tutelage of reason alone. For these the faculty of conscience must be brought into play, which would reveal to Anna not alone the natural laws of physics, but also the natural laws of ethics. Alcott admitted that

74. *Ibid.*, p. 259.
75. *Ibid.*, pp. 258–259.
76. *Ibid.*, p. 288.
77. *Ibid.*, p. 325.

Anna did not as yet exhibit a conscience, but he understood that the conscience, though divine in origin, depended for its full development upon a child's relations with his parents. The chief prerequisite was that there be a strong bond of affection between parent and child.[78]

Alcott saw evidence that Anna was strongly attached to her mother. Such attachment is, of course, not surprising during an infant's first year, but, to judge by Alcott's comments, it seems that Anna could not bear to let her mother out of her sight. He noted that at six months Anna required constant attention and became very unhappy when left alone. With the appearance of teething and other minor ailments, Anna's clinging increased. At times her demands could be inconvenient. Her father noted she cried bitterly when Mrs. Alcott, deprived of domestic help for a few days, left her on the bed in order to take care of household duties. Four months later Anna shed jealous tears when an infant, somewhat older than herself, came under the mother's care for a few days.[79]

Despite his praise of self-reliance, Alcott was delighted. He took Anna's querulous demands for attention as simply a demonstration of affection. She was, he said, learning how to love. Even her illnesses were welcomed by the father, provided they were not too severe, for they opened the springs of gratitude and affection toward her parents.[80] It was evident that Alcott did not really admire the kind of self-reliance that arises from emotional detachment. At the end of Anna's first year, he found her still impatient of all restraint, but he also noted with pleasure that she was strong and ardent in her affections. By means of these affections Anna could be brought to the desired restraint.[81]

The difficulty here, as even Alcott himself suspected, was that a child's affection for his parents, no less than his fear of them, could run counter to the inner voices of reason and conscience. Alcott insisted therefore, that parents must faithfully reflect—in the models they present, in the commands they issue, and in the approvals they dispense—the universal, natural laws of ethics. Their role is to illuminate, not to obscure, the

78. *Ibid.*, pp. 292–293.
79. *Ibid.*, pp. 146, 167, 182, 272, 308, 316.
80. *Ibid.*, pp. 146, 182.
81. *Ibid.*, p. 289.

transcend laws of being that the infant contains within his own breast.[82] Only by governing themselves could the Alcotts bring Anna to govern herself in the light of reason and conscience.

III. Anna's Second and Third Years: Paradise Lost

DURING the spring and summer of 1832, Anna continued to enjoy considerable attention, relatively light discipline, and increasing liberty of movement. She was beginning to creep about and walk with the aid of furniture. A renewed bout with teething and an attack of measles reduced her mobility for a time, but restored health in the summer enabled her to toddle out into the yard, where she watched the passage of horses, wagons, and people. Her success at opening a gate meant that someone would have to accompany her on daily walks along the road, for it was her father's conviction that health and growth depended on her liberty to explore at will.[83]

Anna may, however, have begun to detect that her mother seemed troubled. For one thing, Mrs. Alcott was pregnant, which seemed again to throw her into periods of depression.[84] Pregnancy was in those times also referred to as "confinement," and for good reason. Women were expected to confine themselves to their homes when it became all too apparent they were expecting a child. Mrs. Alcott, although obedient to the fashion, suffered under it. Her Boston family had been an extremely sociable one, and Mrs. Alcott liked to get about. She could invite persons to her home, but there was in the Germantown community a lack

82. *Ibid.*, pp. 298–299, 322–325.

83. Bronson Alcott, Observations on the Life of My First Child [Anna Bronson Alcott] during Her Second Year, pp. 1, 5, 8, 11, 16–18. This item in the Alcott Family Manuscripts is bound with another concerning Anna's third year, but the two manuscripts will here be cited as separate volumes.

84. Bronson Alcott, Observations on the Life of My Second Child [Louisa May Alcott] during the First Year, pp. 1–4.

of "congenial society," as her husband admitted.[85] She was getting a bit bored with her rural paradise.

More disturbing than either confinement or boredom was the fact that the Alcott family was hovering between genteel poverty and outright destitution. In October, 1831, just six months after Alcott opened his school, Reuben Haines died. Not only had the rich farmer provided a rent-free cottage and a direct subsidy to Alcott, it also turned out that he had given money to parents to pay their children's tuition. Now, with Haines's support withdrawn, parents began removing their children from Alcott's school. Alcott began to speak of leaving for Boston, but for some reason he could not bring himself to abandon the failing venture, perhaps as a matter of pride.[86]

As a partial solution, Mrs. Alcott began to take in pupils as boarders. The first to invade the intimacy of the family was an eight-year-old girl, Elizabeth Lewis, who appeared during Anna's second summer. Anna may, in fact, have enjoyed the girl's company, while Mr. Alcott admired her remarkable facility at metaphysical discussions.[87] But the boarder must have added a considerable burden to the cares of the pregnant wife. Soon, four other youngsters had arrived in the Alcott home, and their behavior was not so exemplary. Although their education may not have been neglected, as Alcott charged, nonetheless they were having a bad effect on Anna, by leading her into unspecified bad habits. Moreover, the quarreling that erupted over playthings put Anna in a bad temper and, doubtless, proved hard on parental nerves.[88] By winter, Alcott was hoping the children would soon be gone, but spring saw the youthful boarders still present in the family circle, exuding their "ungenial influences."[89] Mrs. Alcott, too, was complaining. In a letter to her brother she commented that "it is a thankless employment to take care of other people's children." She longed for the intimacy of "as

85. *Ibid.*, p. 2.

86. Bronson Alcott, Journals, November 7 and December 24, 1831, June, September, 1832.

87. Bronson Alcott, Journals, October, 1832; Second Child, First Year, p. 3.

88. Bronson Alcott, First Child, Second Year, p. 41; Observations on the Experience of a Child during the Third Year of Its Existence, p. 2; Abigail Alcott to Samuel May, August 24, [1832], Family Letters, 1828–1861. This letter is incorrectly dated "1831," for it refers to the death of Reuben Haines.

89. Bronson Alcott, First Child, Second Year, p. 47.

small a circle as possible," and resolved someday to reside in a house with only three rooms, just enough for herself, her husband, and her children.[90]

Although the parents were disturbed by boarders, the most unhappy event for Anna occurred on November 29, 1832, when Louisa May was born. Her father now transferred the bulk of his attention, along with his recorded "Observations," to the new baby.[91] Her mother was even more preoccupied with Louisa, who soon showed herself as demanding of her mother's attention as Anna had been. Soon Alcott was noting that Louisa seemed always in the arms of her mother, whether she was nursing or not.[92] The Alcotts were determined that the infant Louisa should be as happy during her first year as Anna had been during hers.

Mrs. Alcott's preoccupation with Louisa May put Anna under the care of a succession of domestics for a period of a year. During this time, when, her father admitted, she should ideally have been around her parents a good deal, she spent most of her time with servants, taking meals with them and even sleeping with them.[93] To make matters worse for Anna, many of the servants were unable to satisfy Alcott's rigid standards and thus did not remain long with the family. The first unsatisfactory nurse was a fourteen-year-old girl, who appeared shortly after Louisa's birth. She possessed "an agreeable countenance and an interesting manner of address," Alcott admitted, but she was otherwise unsatisfactory. In the place of Mrs. Alcott's "judicious and timely management," Anna was now subject to the girl's "jarring" and "hasty" ways, which had the effect of destroying Anna's peace of mind and her good behavior, or so her father thought.[94]

Deprived of her mother's attention and subjected to incompetent nurses, Anna's reaction was, perhaps, predictable. At twenty-two months of age she was becoming unusually obstinate and aggressive. She manifested her feelings frequently by striking both her mother and

90. Abigail Alcott to Samuel and Lucretia May, February 20, 1833, Family Letters, 1828–1861.

91. Alcott's observations on Anna, which occupied more than 300 manuscript pages during her first year, dwindled to only 120 pages for both her second and third years. His "observations" of Louisa's first year, largely of a speculative sort, filled nearly 300 pages.

92. Bronson Alcott, Second Child, First Year, pp. 45–46, 58.

93. Bronson Alcott, Experience of a Child, p. 62.

94. Bronson Alcott, First Child, Second Year, pp. 27–29.

her little sister.[95] Mrs. Alcott believed—or said she believed—that the blows were delivered out of "pure affection."[96] But her husband was not at all persuaded that affection had been the motive. A crisis had arrived in Anna's development.

Alcott assumed that his daughter, now nearly two years old, was capable of sympathy and remorse, and he intended to bring these sentiments to the surface by deliberately withholding physical punishment, and employing instead the withdrawal of parental approval and affection. A dramatic sample of this treatment occurred one day after Anna had once again assaulted her infant sister. Alcott delivered a lecture, warning Anna of possible physical punishment and speaking to her of the effect of her blows on Louisa's feelings. He then left the room whereupon Anna struck her sister again. Mrs. Alcott, loyal to her husband's theories, gave only a reprimand and pointedly sympathized with the baby, prompting Anna to run out of the room and down the stairs, saying, "Father, punish; Father, punish," while making gestures of striking someone. Rather than fulfilling her wish, Alcott explained to Anna once again the nature and consequences of her aggression. "She seemed sorry for it," he reported, "sympathized with her sister and returned to her play again."[97]

There are at least two ways to interpret little Anna's feelings as she ran down the stairs, asking for punishment. One is that she felt no genuine remorse for her behavior, but, instead, was simply trying to find out if her father really meant what he said when he warned of a possible spanking, thus testing and discovering the limits of permitted behavior. If this were the case, a sound spanking then and there might have checked the problem. The other view—and the one to which Alcott seemed to subscribe—was that Anna, in asking for punishment, was seeking relief for pangs of conscience. In sparing her bottom, Alcott deliberately sought to trouble her spirit. According to this view, the withdrawal of approval, so apparent in the above incident, would prove unbearably painful to a girl already suffering doubts about her parents' love.[98]

95. *Ibid.*, pp. 31–32.
96. Abigail Alcott to Samuel and Lucretia May, February 20, 1833, Family Letters, 1828–1861.
97. Bronson Alcott, First Child, Second Year, pp. 33–34.
98. *Ibid.*, pp. 34–38, 42–43.

It was with some puzzlement, therefore, that Alcott noted the recurrence of Anna's aggressions and jealousy. She continued to strike her sister when the opportunity presented itself. Consistent with his view of Anna's feelings, Alcott suspected that withdrawal of affection could be effective only if there were affection to be withdrawn. From Anna's point of view, it may have appeared that she had lost her mother's attention forever, and the only way to get it back was to strike someone, preferably, of course, the sister who was the cause of the deprivation. Her father reasoned that Anna was suffering from a lack of attention. The teen-age nurse was still not working out to his satisfaction, and the only solution seemed to be Anna's return to the care of her mother, or to secure an "attendant of cheerful habits, judicious management and long-tried experience"—in short, a substitute for the mother.[99] But Mrs. Alcott was still preoccupied with Louisa; and, where could such a superb domestic be found?

Alcott began to believe that a change of scene might do everyone some good. A move to the city of Philadelphia would relieve his wife's boredom, and it might be easier to secure an experienced attendant for Anna. As for himself, Alcott had in mind that Philadelphia boasted a good library, which he was now eager to exploit. Finally, there was the fact that he could not operate a school without pupils. In Germantown, only eight children remained in his school, and he calculated that he required at least twenty, at a tuition of eighty dollars each, in order to provide a "barely adequate" livelihood for himself and his family. At the urging of friends, he decided that Philadelphia might provide a larger clientele for his teaching services, and by February, 1833, the decision had been made to move.[100]

On April 10, the family left Germantown, with "few regrets," according to Alcott, and moved to the city, taking lodgings at a boarding house. Despite his earlier preference for isolated rural cottages, he now attempted to persuade himself that boarding would give Mrs. Alcott more time for the children, since she would not be required to prepare meals, and there was also the inescapable advantage that lodgings were cheaper than paying rent on a house. His school, which opened on April

99. Bronson Alcott, Experience of a Child, pp. 2–4.
100. Bronson Alcott, Journals, January, February, 1833.

22, fell short of the ideal enrollment, but still provided nearly twice as many pupils as at Germantown. Philadelphia also offered the inestimable advantages of the Loganian Library, while there was ample opportunity to meet more men of intellect and influence. Now also the Alcotts acquired a housekeeper who could meet even the father's exacting standards, a woman he described as possessing "good sense, aimable manners, and long-tried experience in the care of children." Finally, Alcott felt that Anna was happy with the change, being deeply interested in the greater variety of objects, and finding delight in walking the streets.[101] Cities, it seems, were not so bad after all.

Within a month, however, his doubts about urban life returned. Philadelphians, for all their urbanity, proved thick-headed when it came to grasping Alcott's idealistic views of education, and he once again thought how much more sympathetic patrons would be in Boston.[102] The city was also bad for his daughters. It was impossible to allow Anna to roam as freely as she had done in Germantown:

She suffers . . . from confinement. Denied the free, unrestrained range afforded her while in the country, she sometimes finds it difficult to content herself with the few objects of the nursery and the attentions of her mother and nurse.[103]

Their father was reminded of his earlier convictions that the city, artificial and conventional as it is, has little to offer the simple, docile mind of the child. It was so difficult to protect children under such conditions! One had to be with them every minute, unless one was content, like too many parents, to allow them to run in the streets and there encounter heaven knows what kinds of experience. Then, too, Anna's health was suffering. By June it was necessary to call in a physician, always a risky, distasteful, and expensive matter.[104]

Proof that Anna was in a bad state lay in the fact that she continued to strike or scratch Louisa, but now with more frequency. Anna would approach her younger sister, giving every indication that she was delighted to see her, and then, suddenly, lash out at her. Alcott had not,

101. Bronson Alcott, Journals, March, April, 1833; Experience of a Child, pp. 3, 9; Second Child, First Year, p. 215.

102. Bronson Alcott, Journals, April, 1833.

103. Bronson Alcott, Experience of a Child, p. 28.

104. *Ibid.*, pp. 31–32, 33.

however, surrendered his conviction that he should, on these occasions, appeal to Anna's conscience, in spite of the fact that Anna still *asked* to be punished physically:

> Having been told that this hurts her sister, she seems sorry, sympathizes with her, and, sometimes, asks to be punished for the act. The sense of opinion seems awake—the consciousness of incurring the displeasure of her parents is obvious, and yet she seems to have too little power over her will to desist from the act when her sister's face is within her reach.[105]

The problem, Alcott still felt, was that Anna needed more attention from her mother. Louisa had fallen into a period of ill health, meaning that Anna was handed over more exclusively to the care of the house-keeper. Writing in July Alcott commented:

> She does not see her mother often enough; she is not under her influence enough to make her feel its continuous power, to form those habits of obedience . . . necessary to the happiness of the young. . . . She expects the constant attention of her mother and loses her temper if this be withheld and vents her displeasure upon her little sister, who is sharing her mother's attention.[106]

Mrs. Alcott was distraught. She had never openly challenged her husband's child-rearing theories, and she did not do so now. But she found it difficult to translate his ideas into practice without more help. Writing to her brother she complained that her husband was so engrossed in his work and writing that he was unable to lend practical assistance. "Mr. A. aids me in general principles, but nobody can aid me in the detail," she mourned. Finding herself once again in bad health, she feared that the children might, despite the assistance of the housekeeper, prove too much for her. Moreover, her husband's views kept her constantly wondering if she were doing a good job. "Am I doing what is right? Am I doing enough? Am I doing too much?" She found herself so easily discouraged if everything did not go well, and, just now, Anna was ailing, irritable, and demanding.[107]

Whether or not life in Philadelphia was responsible for this deplorable state of affairs, Alcott decided a vacation in New England would do

---

105. *Ibid.*, pp. 29–30.
106. *Ibid.*, p. 43.
107. Abigail Alcott to Samuel and Lucretia May, June 22, 1833, Family Letters, 1828–1861.

the family some good, and besides, he wished to attend an educational convention in Boston, discuss with Boston publishers the prospects of issuing books written for children, and sound out prospects for opening a school.[108] Consequently, on July 29 Alcott and family left Philadelphia and arrived in Wolcott, Connecticut, where he deposited wife and children with his mother. As for himself, he journeyed on to Boston to take care of business, feeling some pangs at this, his first separation from the family. Three weeks later he returned to Wolcott, lacking prospects for a school but encouraged by the publishers and feeling that both he and his family had benefited by the vacation.[109]

By September 1, the Alcotts were back in Philadelphia, "fitted," as Mr. Alcott put it, "for the duties of life in the city."[110] He believed that the country air had worked wonders for his daughters, although he had to admit that Anna was still inclined to strike her sister on occasion. Incredibly enough, her father chose once again to take an indulgent view: this was merely a stage that would soon pass.

The habit of *striking* her sister still continues to operate on her organism. This is obviously instinctive and habitual. It is periodical in all its appearances; seldom appearing when all exterior influences favour her tendencies. It will leave her in due time, as her system attains vigour, and her instincts are subjected to the power of her volitions. As yet she is not accountable for these aberrations. Time will correct the nervous and instinctive impulse.[111]

Alcott always believed that his child-rearing theories were well ahead of current opinion, and his awesome patience in the face of Anna's aggression would seem to provide evidence of it. Even as Alcott was indulging Anna, in the hopes of an appeal to her conscience, the pastor of the Central Calvinist Church of Worcester, Massachusetts, published a book that proved to be the first really popular treatise on child-rearing to appear in America.[112] The Reverend John S. C. Abbott's *The Mother at Home* points up the differences between Alcott's practices and what

108. Bronson Alcott, Journals, July–August, 1833.
109. *Ibid.*
110. *Ibid.*
111. Bronson Alcott, Experience of a Child, p. 50.
112. John S. C. Abbott, *The Mother at Home: or, The Principles of Maternal Duty Familiarly Illustrated* (Boston, 1833). Frank Luther Mott estimates that Abbott's book sold more than 125,000 copies, in several editions, making it a "best-seller" for the times: *Golden Multitudes: The Story of Best Sellers in the United States* (New York, 1947), p. 303.

was probably fairly widespread opinion in 1833. There were, to be sure, similarities between the clergyman and the transcendentalist heretic. Abbott was no less concerned than Alcott with parental neglect of children (else he would not have written the book), and he prescribed large doses of maternal sympathy and love. He even acknowledged that during the first year of an infant's life, a mother was perfectly justified in indulging the infant's desires.[113] In this respect, at least, he was as liberal in theory as the Alcotts had been in practice. Evidently Calvinists were not quite as benighted as Alcott had assumed they were.

But the over-all tone of *The Mother at Home* was decidedly somber. Through a variety of examples Abbott made perfectly clear his conviction that the major causes of sin in Jacksonian America were mothers who indulged their offspring. He portrayed the typical American child of his era as a spoiled brat, and, like two centuries of Calvinist clergymen before him, he believed that nothing short of stern measures could put down the little tyrants. Whenever the child is old enough to understand an order, which Abbott thought was usually during the second year, he must obey. It was, he argued, a mistake to reason much with children—something Alcott never tired of doing with Anna. According to the Reverend Abbott, parents should give absolute commands, insist that they be obeyed without fail, and if the child refuses compliance, the parents should punish promptly and severely, including the infliction of "real pain."[114] The desire to be tender could be disastrous, Abbott warned, and he pointed with relish to Napoleon turning his artillery on the mobs of Paris. Parents must be domestic Napoleons, as ready as Bonaparte to invoke decisive measures in putting down childish rebellion. After the child's resistance is shattered, there is then occasion to speak to him of repentance. The success of these tactics, combined, to be sure, with kindness and love, would be recorded in the creation of a child who thereafter remains above temptation, a pale counterpart, indeed, to Alcott's vision of the child heroically transcending his passions through an act of will.[115]

---

113. Abbott, *Mother at Home*, pp. 50, 60–62.

114. *Ibid.*, chap. ii.

115. *Ibid.*, pp. 71–77. Abbott's boundless admiration of Napoleon led him, in 1850, to publish *A History of Napoleon Bonaparte*.

Alcott nowhere records that he read Abbott's popular treatise, although he would not have had much praise for it if he had, but Mrs. Alcott was evidently beginning to feel some sympathy for the point of view which the clergyman expressed. In the fall of 1833, Alcott noted euphemistically that a great deal of "power and pain" had suddenly appeared in Anna's experience. We may surmise that Mrs. Alcott, out of concern for Louisa's safety, had tired of waiting on the development of her elder daughter's volitions and administered instead some sound spankings. This treatment, in Alcott's opinion, only made Anna's behavior worse.[116]

The question of Anna's discipline must have produced tense moments between the parents, but a favorable change of situation fortunately provided relief. Louisa, now a year old, was requiring less of her mother's attention, and Anna began to spend more time with her parents. For the first time in twelve months, she was permitted to sleep in the same room with them. Her father noted a striking change for the better in Anna's temper and behavior. She was now happier, more obedient, and more affectionate, both to her mother and sister. By December, her father's descriptions of her character and conduct were approaching something like rapture, although there is no way of knowing if the improvement resulted from his patience, Mrs. Alcott's spankings, or, what is more likely, Anna's restored intimacy with her mother.[117]

And then, without warning, Alcott's record of his children came to an abrupt end. It is not known if the observations were lost, destroyed, or simply never made, but a sudden gap in Alcott family records usually suggests trouble so painful that someone could not bear the memory of it. Alcott's personal diary for the winter of 1833–1834 gave no hint of domestic difficulty, revealing only that he was busily engaged in preparing children's books for publication.[118] But in reflecting back on the period he admitted, indeed, that all had not been well in the Philadelphia boarding house. The principal problem, he thought, had been lack of space. Unable to rent a house of their own in the city, the family had

116. Bronson Alcott, Experience of a Child, pp. 56–57.
117. *Ibid.*, pp. 62–63, 66–70.
118. Bronson Alcott, Journals, January, February, March, 1834. At the end of his record for Anna's third year there stands a laconic note: "January and February, to complete the round of this year, are wanting . . . ," Experience of a Child, p. 70.

been thrown too close together in their small apartment without even a study for the father, a convenience he had enjoyed in Germantown:

It is absolutely necessary to the natural unfolding of the infant mind, as well as the tranquillity and progress of the parent, that *Space* should be enjoyed. . . . Before this, both myself and companion got time for reflection and study. This is of the first importance to us both. To me, it is a positive want of my being. I pine, and lose my Spirits, my hopes and aspirations without it. During the last few months, our arrangements were such that opportunity for free, uninterrupted thought, was almost impossible. My companion suffered from the same cause. We were thrown in *each other's* way. The children were thrown in *our way*. The effect on all was depressing. Life was rendered too monotonous. *Proximity* was too large an element in our experience. The space and freedom . . . we ought to have had, was denied us. Intellectual progress was retarded, and health prostrated thereby.[119]

Had Alcott lived in a later age, he might have been given the opportunity to train himself for a post as a professor of philosophy in some college, and thus supported his family comfortably, if not handsomely, while pursuing his spiritual and scholarly ambitions. As it was, however, his domestic ideals and his professional aspirations were painfully in conflict. In early April, therefore, he made what was for him an agonizing decision, removing his family from the city, and extracting himself from the family, except for periodic visits. He packed his wife and children off to a cottage in Germantown, where he intended they should remain through the spring and summer.[120] As for himself, he took a sparsely-furnished attic room across from the library, and began taking advantage of the leisure and quiet now available to him to read German literature and philosophy in translation, and to work on his writing style, which he admitted was abominable:

Here I am, removed from the third to the fourth story—blessed at last with my one little window fronting the City Library and the Athenaeum, with a bed, a trunk for my clothes, a wash-stand, two chairs, and my books. On these I am to feed and content myself during the summer.

Well, it matters little, after all, what surrounds us, how few are the things in which we feel a property and to which we attach ourself, if the mind have wherewith to feed and the heart to comfort itself. Man can live on his own faith, if his faith be fastened on Love and Wisdom. 'Tis not necessary that external goods should enter largely into the supply.[121]

119. Bronson Alcott, Journals, April 23, 1834.
120. *Ibid.*, April 13, 1834.
121. *Ibid.*, April 28, 1834.

These ascetic sentiments might do very well for Alcott, holed up in his scholarly cell, but what of his family in Germantown? Was there not some disparity between his ideals in 1831, and the actual state of affairs three years later? Would not model child-rearing require the presence of the father?

Despite the evident pleasure Alcott took in his monkish cell, he was troubled by the question of his family responsibilities and not a little of his personal diary, now swelling as a result of the new-found leisure to write, was devoted to mulling over the decision to send his family away. He did miss the "little prattlers." No question about that.[122] But he suspected that distance had lent some enchantment, which, indeed, was one of the advantages of the separation:

> It will test my affection, reveal to me more fully the true value of those treasures which I call my own, by giving me an opportunity of surveying them from a new point of view. For when valued objects are removed from their accustomed nearness, and we can no longer commune with them in bodily forms, the imagination, idealizing their presence, invests them in all the charms of the heart.[123]

He persuaded himself, moreover, that the separation was a positive good for the family as well as for himself. Mrs. Alcott would now have more quiet also, and, reverting to a familiar theme, Alcott had great hopes for the country's beneficial effect on the health and morals of the children. Besides, he pointed out to himself, he intended to pass the weekends with them, and on occasion, he would even stay overnight in Germantown in the middle of the week.[124]

Blessed now by the absence of his children in their concrete form, Alcott was free to contemplate the significance of their "idealized presence" for his life and work. Just why, he asked himself, was he so interested in children? As a professional educator, he had, of course, asked the question before, and he thought he had arrived at a satisfactory answer. He conceived it his mission to teach children, to protect them from corruption and to help them achieve spiritual perfection. But now, as he thought about it, children seemed to have a deeper significance,

122. *Ibid.*, April 21, 1834.
123. *Ibid.*, April 21, 1834. See also entries for April 14, April 22, April 27, and April 30, 1834.
124. *Ibid.*, April 13, 1834.

related to his own past. Reflecting on his childhood, he recalled that he had been pure and idealistic as a child, although he had not been really happy. Too many in his acquaintance had failed to lead him by kindness and encouragement, not out of cruelty, but simply because they failed to grasp his sensitivity. It had been a lonely time on the Connecticut farm, for only his mother had given him genuine affection. Even she, a barely-literate housewife, had failed to perceive his idealistic yearnings. Her affection—Alcott refused to call it "love"—had sprung more from an "affinity of disposition" and from her preference for the first-born than from a "sympathetic perception of the high purpose which then slept in my unfolded being." But, he admitted, there was something motherly about her feeling for him, and, imperfect as it was, her affection nourished his purity and idealism, inspiring his ambition to learn and to serve.[125]

Referring no doubt to his youthful escapades while peddling in the South, Alcott thought his child-like ideals had, for a time, been obscured during adolescence. Even now, he sometimes wondered if he had not forever lost the "vision," the "bright ideal" of his childhood:

How little of this fairy land do we know—we whose early associations have all been swept from the heart by the foul currencies of adult life—over whose spirits have passed the cold winds and pelting storms, withering and destroying the heart's young freshness and verdure, nipping its promises in the very bud, and shrouding us in the atmosphere of winter! What bond of sympathy is there to unite us, either in thought or sentiment, with the spirit of a child! What have we in common with it? Where is its joyous yearning for the beautiful in nature's liberal array, its young trustingness in human sayings, its deep love for those on whom it relies for attention and support, its vivid picturing of ideal life, and exhaustless Providence, its guileless simplicity . . . its freedom from prejudice and false sentiment. Where are these to be seen in the outbreaking of our dimmed natures! Alas! they are lost and gone; the early brilliancy of the Soul is faded; and in its place, we find the morbid indifference to the beautiful. A suspicion has crept around the Soul like the coiled Serpent, hissing and stinging its loves and joys to death.[126]

Catching himself taking a nap after lunch, Alcott thought remorsefully that his torpor symbolized the adult, who sleeps even when awake and who has lost the vigor and faith of childhood![127]

125. *Ibid.*, April 28, 1834.
126. *Ibid.*, May 29, 1834.
127. *Ibid.*, June 17, 1834.

Alcott's gloomy comparisons between his childhood and the present may have been prompted by the fact that the Philadelphia school was going from a failure to a disaster. Parents began withdrawing their children until he was once again facing only a handful of pupils, a situation trying both for the spirit and the pocketbook. Alcott thought the parents were unhappy because he emphasized moral above intellectual education, but had he not warned them, before they enrolled their children, that he intended to weed out their offspring's bad habits and to produce in his pupils a "moral regeneration"? Indeed he had, but it was becoming evident that Philadelphians liked their children much the way they were. The parents even ridiculed his "simplicity of character" and passed along rumors that he had lost his sanity. Alcott tried to console himself by considering the source, but still the accusations hurt, and he found himself increasingly cast into gloom and doubt about his ideals. When, if ever, would the rewards of his idealism appear?[128]

But he would not lose faith. However trying the parents, his association with children restored at times his memory of his own childhood and consequently his faith in himself.

Blessed be the memory of childhood. . . . May the sacred light of childhood continue to be both a remembrance and a hope. . . . Looking ever into the past for young images of life and beauty and into the future for their realization.[129]

Somehow a man must retain child-like virtues, shaking off fear, shame, sorrow, and "ungovernable and vexing thoughts." What, indeed, would the future be if it were not illuminated by the faith of one's childhood.[130]

Seeking to restore the faith of his early years, was he not neglecting the childhood of his daughters? Mrs. Alcott thought so, notwithstanding the advantages Alcott professed to see in the separation. While he hovered between faith and doubt in Philadelphia, she was enduring loneliness and anxiety in Germantown. Faithful to his promise, Alcott spent virtually every weekend for three months with his family, and frequently made visits in the middle of the week, but, unfortunately for

128. *Ibid.*, April 29, May 5, May 10, May 13, May 14, May 15, May 16, June 6, June 9, June 14, 1834.
129. *Ibid.*, April 28, 1834.
130. *Ibid.*, April 28, May 29, June 21, 1834.

his peace of mind, Mrs. Alcott usually took advantage of the visits to remind him that she was not at all happy about the arrangements. For one thing, she was having difficulty making ends meet, due to his apparent indifference to the question of making money. Alcott admitted that he might seem "unkind, indifferent, improvident" but he refused to be deflected from his study and writing:

My family must feel the evil of this in some degree, but this should not deter one from striving to effect what has been attempted in conceptions of duty and right. I shall never acquire external goods in large measure. It cannot be made an object of ambition.[131]

Mrs. Alcott might have endured the poverty, but the separation from her husband she found terribly trying. She simply missed having him around the house.[132] Her desire that the family be reunited became insistent, however, after his absence nearly took her life. On May 20, he received an urgent message that his wife was ill. He hurried home to discover that she had experienced difficulty in summoning a physician. Whatever the cause of the malady, Alcott acknowledged that a delay of a half hour more in securing medical aid would have proved fatal.[133] Six days later she had recovered, and Alcott returned to his duties at the school, but he now admitted that the separation from the family, whatever its advantages for his work, must come to an end.[134] As for Philadelphia, he could no longer survive there with his ideals intact.

On July 3, having fulfilled his obligations to the remaining pupils, he closed the school and one week later gathered up his family for a visit to Boston to explore once again the possibility of launching a school there.[135] Thanks largely to the efforts of his old friend, Elizabeth Peabody, he met this time with success. On September 22, he opened the Temple School, which proved for a time his most successful venture. As for his family, which he idealized but which he at times found so difficult to live with, Alcott resolved he must do better by his wife and daughters. In October, he resumed once more his "observations" and with them, his attempts to be a model father.

131. *Ibid.*, April 27, 1834. See also entries for April 30 and May 1.
132. *Ibid.*, April 25, 1834.
133. *Ibid.*, May 20, 1834.
134. *Ibid.*, May 22, May 29, June 6, June 7, June 14, 1834.
135. *Ibid.*, June 29, July 3, 1834.

IV. The Renewed Campaign

O N September 22, 1834, Alcott opened the Temple School in Boston, a project that conveyed fresh hope to him. Not for two years had he felt the excitement that always came when he believed he was making a contribution to the welfare of mankind; and not until two years later would he publish *Conversations with Children on the Gospels*, which would enrage influential Bostonians and result in the closing of the experimental school. For the time being, prospects looked favorable for his latest venture in educational reform. Important people had gathered more than thirty pupils from some of Boston's leading families. Elizabeth Peabody, herself a reformer of no mean repute, was present to assist in the school and to make a remarkable record of the proceedings. Altogether, great things were expected of Alcott, and he expected much of himself. Although he noted in his journal that some of the school children seemed undisciplined and indulged, he had no doubt he could bring out the best in the youngsters. In fact, he felt himself to be on the verge of a great discovery about man, and that discovery had to do with the "redemption of infancy and childhood." Alcott himself would be the Redeemer.[136]

Mrs. Alcott, practical woman that she was, was a bit cautious about the worldly success of the venture. Writing her brother early in September, she admitted that her husband's prospects were never brighter, "but I try to suppress all emotion but that of hope," she confided, "for I have always been woefully disappointed in my expectations and I mean this time to keep on the safe side."[137] Despite the memory of trying days in Philadelphia, however, she entertained no doubts about the worth of Alcott's mission. "I believe there will be a great educational regeneration and I believe that my husband is to be the Messiah to announce to the world a new revelation."[138]

As Alcott poised on the brink of this new educational venture, he

136. Bronson Alcott, Journals, October 11, October 12, October 27, 1834. For a portrait of the Temple School see Elizabeth Peabody's *Record of a School: Exemplifying the General Principles of Spiritual Culture*, 2nd ed. (Boston, 1836).

137. Abigail Alcott to Samuel May, September 1, 1834, Family Letters, 1828–1861.

138. *Ibid.*, September 7, 1834.

realized he had not been doing well by his family. It would never do for childhood's Messiah not to have his domestic affairs in order. He admitted neglect of the family's financial needs and hoped that the income from the Temple School would be more than enough to free him from debt and to support the family comfortably. His anticipated salary constituted, in fact, a veritable "pot of gold," as Alcott put it, and he felt positively embarrassed by these unaccustomed riches.[139]

But there was also the matter of personal neglect. His desperate attempts at self-education had kept him too much from the domestic circle. At ten o'clock in the evening of October 19, as a church bell tolled and he looked out on the darkened city, Alcott reflected with no little guilt on his role as a father:

Am I a *husband* and *father* in very deed? For I have a kind, loving wife, and two sweet little ones, whose outward image reminds me of their terrestrial parent and guide. I am a husband, but mingle too little of exposed sentiment in my daily manners and demeanor perhaps. I am a *father*, but pass too little time with the children, whose characters are being shaped under my eye. I am absorbed in the things belonging to my profession . . . while those at home are deprived of their just claims.

The proof of his neglect, he thought, lay not so much in outward complaints but in the undisciplined character of his children. Louisa May, now two years old, presented the most dramatic and pressing problem. By her father's account, she was obstinate, ungovernable, rude, aggressive and—at times—even violent. Anna, now three and one-half years old, suffered from more subtle difficulties. She had, it was true, become obedient and docile, but she was also timid and fearful.[140]

Consequently, after Alcott had safely launched the Temple School, he turned attention to his daughters. On Sunday, October 26, he wrote:

Some habits, I regret to say, have been permitted to attain a strength and fixity that will require no small degree of skill, delicacy, and yet force of discipline to remove— more than the mother will be able to put forth, in the fondness and timidity of her heart. . . . I have left the mother to shape her methods to herself; but I find that without something more than this theoretical influence my duties as a father will be imperfectly discharged, and my relations as a husband be feebly met. It is my duty to act in the way of example. My speculations, however true, must be actualized to the observation in practical methods under the eye of the mother, or a part of their value will be

139. Bronson Alcott, Journals, September 22, 1834.
140. *Ibid.*, October 19, 1834.

lost, or misunderstood by her—to say nothing of the consequences that must result to the children.[141]

Alcott resolved that he could no longer delay so important a work: he would enter upon the task the very next morning. And so, on Monday, October 27, he rose earlier than usual in order to undertake both the disciplining and the observations of his children from the moment when they opened their eyes.[142] The observations were not new, but it was the first time that Alcott would be personally responsible for the discipline of the children for much of the day. Previously, he had been content to supervise Mrs. Alcott's handling of their daughters, but now he would be frequently rising before daybreak with the children and spending all but the school hours in domestic concerns. By the end of the following February he would have filled more than five hundred manuscript pages with observations and would have helped, he believed, Anna and Louisa weather a crisis in their coming-of-age.[143]

The circumstances and setting for the domestic campaign were less than ideal. No more than Philadelphia was Boston a good place to rear children, in Alcott's opinion, but at the same time, he obviously had no intention of surrendering the advantages of living in the city. The only solution seemed to be close supervision of Anna's movements. She could not be allowed to roam freely, nor was she permitted to play with youngsters other than those in Alcott's school. She required outings, to be sure, but this meant that adults would have to take her and her sister for walks in the streets or on the Boston Common.[144]

The home itself presented still another difficulty. After spending the summer in a boarding house on Morton Place, the family moved into a similar establishment on Bedford Street.[145] Neither Mr. nor Mrs. Alcott was entirely satisfied with the arrangement. As she told her mother-in-law in November, she was "tired of living about in other people's

141. *Ibid.*, October 26, 1834.

142. *Ibid.*, October 27, 1834.

143. The record of this four-month period is contained in two manuscripts by Alcott entitled, Observations on the Spiritual Nurture of My Children, and Researches on Childhood. Although bound together, the manuscripts will be cited separately, the first as: Spiritual Nurture, and the second as: Researches.

144. Bronson Alcott, Spiritual Nurture, p. 14; Researches, pp. 87, 191.

145. Bronson Alcott, Journals, October 13, 1834; Memoir, 1878, entry on fly-leaf.

houses."[146] Her husband also noted once again the problem of space. Lacking freedom to play outside of the house, his daughters would also lack room inside. The girls were allowed in the common rooms only for their dinner meal, and even then, they usually were not permitted to eat with adults. They were, moreover, confined in their play to the Alcott suite—a nursery, one bedchamber, and a study, when these rooms were not occupied by adults.[147] On the other hand, Mrs. Alcott's health was still far from robust, and in a boarding house she would be relieved of the burden of preparing meals. Moreover, she seemed at times to enjoy the sociability of a boarding house after three months of isolation in the Germantown cottage.[148]

Ideal child-rearing required also ideal personnel, and here Alcott felt he had ample cause for complaint. Mrs. Alcott was again pregnant and suffering the attendant ailments, and, though the Alcotts could once again afford servants, they were to prove no more satisfactory in Boston than in Pennsylvania. "Mary," the first in a line of Boston women to eserv the family, proved to be "stupid" and was dismissed late in 1834. There followed another woman who, according to Alcott, lacked imagination and failed to evoke the affections of the children. After only four weeks of service, she too left the household.

We require an Ideal person. . . . She must have retained the purity, the innocence, the spirituality, the humble wisdom and seraphic love of infancy, and, at the same time, have suffered the trials of terrestrial existence, to bring forth and render hardy and vigorous the virtues of fortitude, self-dependence, self-control. An angel is, indeed, wanted.

Unfortunately, angels were in short supply in Boston, and Alcott entertained the thought of giving up on servants altogether.[149]

Even Mrs. Alcott lacked the angelic qualifications. As Alcott viewed more closely the way his wife handled Louisa and Anna, the greater his dissatisfaction grew. She was far too indulgent with Louisa, and she

146. Abigail Alcott to Mrs. Anna Alcott, November, [1834], Memoir, 1878. This letter appears to be incorrectly dated "1835,"; for it refers to Anna's sprained ankle, which she suffered in 1834, and it speaks of the family's recent arrival in Boston.

147. Bronson Alcott, Spiritual Nurture, p. 14.

148. Abigail Alcott to Samuel May, September 1, 1834, Family Letters, 1828–1861.

149. Bronson Alcott, Spiritual Nurture, pp. 28, 61, 81, 137, 239; Researches, pp. 5, 21–24.

really did not understand Anna. Moreover, she felt harassed by the children, often lost her temper with them and at times sought only escape from the burdens of motherhood. To her physical ailments were added frequent periods of melancholy, brought on in part, one suspects, by the difficulties of being the helpmate to childhood's Messiah.[150]

Nevertheless, Alcott expected nothing less than moral perfection from his daughters, and to this end the child-rearing must go forward under perfect parental control.

Vain is the hope of confirming a child in good habits, while he is the subject of various influences over which the parent has no control. . . . The parent, like the Divinity, should exert a special oversight over all the relations of the sphere in which he moves; he should be the Providence that fills, sustains and protects every member of his domestic creation.[151]

Considering the circumstances and Alcott's high expectations, it was perhaps well that he intended to spend much of his day in the home.

He began by drawing up an orderly schedule, and adhered to it more or less faithfully. The schedule called for him to rise at six a.m. with the children. He washed and dressed them, frequently over their protest, although the nursery was kept warm during the night to make the task a bit more pleasant. The girls were then permitted to play in the nursery until seven o'clock, when the maid brought in breakfast. Afterward they spent some time with their father in the study, or resumed play in the nursery.[152]

At eight-thirty the girls separated, Louisa to spend the morning with her mother, until lunch at eleven o'clock and a nap at twelve. Anna would pass the morning at the school with her father from nine o'clock until two, playing with the children, looking at pictures, listening to stories, and marking letters on her slate. By two-thirty, Anna and her father had returned to the boarding house, where Anna and Louisa would have dinner together, and afterward take a walk, either with their father or with the maid. The remainder of the afternoon they spent playing in the nursery, taking a light supper at six o'clock, followed by

150. Bronson Alcott, Spiritual Nurture, pp. 67–68; Researches, pp. 37–38, 103–105.
151. Bronson Alcott, Spiritual Nurture, p. 69.
152. Ibid., pp. 82–83.

more play in the nursery, or, perhaps, by conversation with their father in the study. At seven-thirty they were put to bed.[153]

One of the chief benefits of the schedule was that it kept the sisters apart for much of the day, an essential for Anna's safety and for their mother's peace of mind. Anna had developed a mortal fear of her younger sister and often ran to her mother for protection. Her fear did not, however, bar a good deal of quarreling between the girls, which often shattered the calm of the Alcott apartment. It was evident that Anna and Louisa betrayed as yet no signs of sisterly love. Seemingly the wisest course was to leave Louisa with her mother while Alcott took his elder daughter to school. Except for a period of several weeks, when a sprained ankle kept Anna at home, the separation was enforced, and with encouraging results. Louisa played happily when alone with her mother, while Anna seemed to enjoy the company of her friends at school.[154]

Still, they could not be kept apart always, and Alcott believed he must play a larger role in Louisa's discipline. She possessed a "deep-seated obstinacy of temper" that could be eradicated only by a firm hand. She puzzled her father by an almost total lack of remorse. She was, Alcott said, a creature of "instinct." Once, after Anna had sprained her ankle, Alcott observed that Louisa seemed to take cruel delight in having her sister under her power:

She seems practicing on the law of *might*—the stronger and colder has the mastery over the weaker and more timid. She is still the undisciplined subject of her *instincts*, pursuing her purpose[s] by any means that will lead her to their attainment. Anna suffers a good deal from this temper of her sister's. She bears the mark of her sister's *hand*, at present, on her cheek. The sentiment of *love* is as yet too weak to regulate the appetites and desires.[155]

Louisa was young, and her father made allowances for that fact—although not as many allowances as he had made for Anna when she was two years old—but Alcott was convinced that Louisa was not too young to behave in a more seemly manner. The source of her difficulty, he felt, lay in inherited temperament, heightened by her mother's indulgence. For one thing, Mrs. Alcott insisted on giving Louisa meat.

153. *Ibid.*
154. *Ibid.*, pp. 37, 39, 133, 161.
155. *Ibid.*, pp. 21, 161.

I am not sure but that her untameable spirit derives something of its ferocity from the nature of her diet. The Spirit is, perhaps, clogged in its functions, from having to dispose of so much animal matter, in the way of organic association, digestion, etc. . . . Think of a young being, compelled to lug about, in the very seat of its Spiritual life, a burden of flesh![156]

Beyond the matter of diet, Alcott noted that Louisa was, after all, very much like her mother. In both mother and daughter, "the will is the predominating power."[157] Little wonder, then, that Mrs. Alcott seemed to indulge her daughter in a way that Alcott could only regard as reckless.

His immediate prescription for Louisa was to put an end to indulgence. Ten days after Alcott instituted his regime, an incident occurred that revealed both Louisa's temperament and her father's way of dealing with it. Mother, father, and daughter were seated at the dining table, waiting for their food to be served, when Louisa began teasing for a place on her mother's lap. Noting perhaps her husband's disapproval, Mrs. Alcott refused, prompting loud protests from Louisa. Her father then took a hand, "requesting" her to stop. He put Louisa's chair by her mother's place and invited her to be seated. She refused. There followed still another request and another refusal.

I told her that I should place her in the chair if she did not get in herself. She refused saying, "No! No!" with her usual force of expression, raising her tones and giving me to understand that the decision was made in her mind. I placed her in it, notwithstanding her struggles. The cry was heightened and prolonged; the persistance more decided and obstinate. I told her she must stop crying and sit in the chair, or I should punish her —hurt her—for she "must mind *father*." "No! No!" she exclaimed with more decided vehemence than before. I said, "Father must *spank* Louisa if she does not do as he says. Will she?" "No! No! Sit with mother," she reiterated. I *spanked her*. She cried the louder. I then told her that she must sit on her little chair by the side of her mother, and be still, or I should punish her more. She was unwilling to give up her purpose, and set up crying again. I repeated the punishment, and did not attain peace and quiet for her, till I had repeated it again. She then became quiet and continued talking with me and her mother till her supper was brought in, when, as I had promised her, she . . . sat at the table to eat it.[158]

156. *Ibid.*, pp. 25–26. Despite Alcott's reference to his wife's indulgence, she recognized that Louisa was then a "noisy, boisterous child": Abigail Alcott to Mrs. Anna Alcott, November, [1834], Memoir, 1878.
157. Bronson Alcott, Researches, p. 105.

During this period, Alcott was not consistent in his treatment of Louisa. On occasions such as the above, he disciplined her with a severity and firmness that would have delighted the Reverend John Abbott, but at other times he permitted the most outrageous behavior, usually with the explanation that she was not yet responsible for her conduct. Once, the two-year-old actually had the temerity to pinch her father, but he restrained himself:

> Sitting with me today, she held my hand in hers and while enjoying the sense of contact, she seemed to be instinctively tempted to *pinch* me. She actually seized the skin of my hand, pressed her finger nails into the flesh, and with not a little muscular irritation awaited the result. I paid no attention to it and she soon ceased the pressure. A little reaction, on my part, would doubtless have led to a scene of violence.[159]

Clearly, Louisa baffled her father, and he could not quite fit her into his child-rearing scheme. He did not like to spank her, for it contradicted one of his most characteristic rules. He still felt it was a "brutal" and "barbarous" method, resting on "false and impious views of human nature—denying it faith, spirituality, power of self-guidance and self-reliance." The problem with spanking was that it appealed to the animal, rather than the spiritual side of a child's nature. Parents who relied on it were employing an animalistic, pleasure-pain psychology.[160] On the other hand, what was one to do with a creature who acted like a devil?

Alcott defended his frequent departures from theory, in Louisa's case, as a measure of last resort, made necessary by her mother's indulgence. Somewhat testily he remarked that "had the children been under my supervision continually, had the principles of prevention been carried out in the nursery, I do not believe that it would have been necessary to have resorted to such methods."[161] However distasteful Alcott found his conflicting methods, they seemed to work, at least as far as bringing Louisa under some semblance of control, although Alcott was not satisfied that he was reaching the source of her difficulty.[162]

In dealing with Anna, Alcott found himself on much firmer ground,

158. Bronson Alcott, Spiritual Nurture, pp. 109–110.
159. *Ibid.*, p. 232. See also pp. 21, 37, 133, 136, 152.
160. *Ibid.*, pp. 111–112.
161. *Ibid.*, p. 112.
162. *Ibid.*, pp. 141, 153.

and he could resort to more congenial tactics. He decided that Anna was much like himself—sentimental where Louisa was direct; idealistic and theoretical where Louisa was crude and practical; timid and inhibited where Louisa was aggressive and impulsive:

> Anna is apt to *theorize* both for herself and for Louisa, whereas Louisa, intent solely on *practice*, is constantly demolishing Anna's ideal castles and irritating her Spirit with a gothic rudeness. The one builds; the other demolishes; and between the struggle of contrary forces, their tranquillity is disturbed. Anna seldom provokes her sister intentionally and seems sorry when she does; whereas Louisa, from the mere love of action, often assaults her sister and looks on to see what will be the result of her temerity.[163]

Not that Anna was perfect, for all her quiet ways. Her father noted with disapproval a certain "indolence of will," and "imbecility of purpose," and an "extreme susceptibility of sentiment" that made her less than ideal. Although she was not cursed with Louisa's animal ferocity, still Anna could benefit by some of her sister's force and energy.[164] Anna's timidity sometimes took forms that her father thought "peculiar." She was, unlike Louisa, very neat and orderly, and she often rebuked her younger sister for disorderly ways. Anna was "very careful of her playthings, books and clothes," Alcott commented proudly, and he never knew her to break a toy intentionally, to tear a book or to injure her dress. At the same time, he admitted her passion for order could go to extremes. He noticed that for Anna a door opened in a certain way must always be opened just that way or it was not opened correctly. On one occasion, while visiting friends, she would not leave until the chair in which she had been sitting was replaced and the toys she had been playing with had been put back in good order.[165]

In search for explanations of Anna's peculiarities, Alcott fastened on her native temperament and once again, on her mother's incompetence. Alcott contended that Anna was a child who required an utterly different discipline than Louisa. A timid, fearful child responded to encouragement rather than reproof. She should at all times be treated with "great delicacy."[166] Unfortunately, Mrs. Alcott seemed to lack both

---

163. *Ibid.*, pp. 37–38.
164. Bronson Alcott, Researches, pp. 80–81.
165. Bronson Alcott, Spiritual Nurture, pp. 94–95, 258.
166. *Ibid.*, pp. 59–60, 210.

delicacy and patience where Anna was concerned. At least the mother did not exhibit enough of these qualities to satisfy her husband:

Anna's extreme susceptibility is rendered more acute by the want of entire sympathy between herself and her mother. Of somewhat different dispositions, they do not, at once, fall into the current of each other's feelings and associations. The mother does not comprehend Anna's *wants*. Neither does she seize the happiest moment or the best means of allaying them. The subtle associations that move Anna's spirit are not employed by the mother; she has lost the freshness that once invested her spirit; she does not readily enter into the simple wants of childhood. Anna asks her many questions, answers to which are of the greatest importance to her happiness, and yet the mother, from her want of comprehension of Anna's train of ideas, or from the deep absorption of her mind in domestic concerns, cannot think it a matter of much importance to answer them; and so Anna is thrown back upon her own susceptible nature, and seeks relief in tears or in silence. Or when the questions are responded to by the mother, the answer is oftentimes too vague to be satisfactory, and, not doubting her mother's ability to vouchsafe a satisfactory reply, Anna repeats the question, and, sometimes, in a tone of impatient entreaty, until her mother, irritated by the repetition, replies in a similar tone, setting down the young inquirer as a querulous, captious spirit, and deigns no further reply. This is unfortunate, as it operates against both: increases Anna's susceptibility and disturbs the mother's repose.[167]

As Alcott perceived, Anna's behavior was more than a matter of intellectual curiosity; she craved attention. Repelled by his wife's example and inspired by his theories, Alcott set out to lavish on Anna—and on Louisa also if she could benefit by it—all the affection, gentleness, and attention he could command. Since Alcott had a decade of teaching experience behind him, much of the time spent with his daughters involved educational pursuits. He stressed that he was not attempting to rush Anna's development as a scholar—she need not learn to read until she was five—but a leisurely time-table did not exclude large attention to plays and games of an educational import.[168] When, for example, Anna became interested in the alphabet, her father devised a game of imitating the letters with the body. One is quite prepared to believe Alcott's report that Anna was "much amused" by these carryings on.[169]

On still another occasion, Alcott brought home an educational game, made in England. The game was a simple one, consisting of circular

167. Bronson Alcott, Researches, pp. 104–105. See also Spiritual Nurture, pp. 67–68.
168. Bronson Alcott, Spiritual Nurture, p. 80; Researches, p. 191.
169. Bronson Alcott, Spiritual Nurture, p. 91.

pieces of pasteboard, with a letter drawn on one side and an appropriate animal picture on the other, together with a box into which the discs could be placed. Her father asked Anna to select from the letters those she knew and arrange them in a row. Alcott thought the toy an excellent one, and he was pleased that it absorbed Anna's attention for an entire afternoon.[170] Louisa was not excluded from such pastimes altogether. She frequently joined her sister and father in the study after supper to enact little dramas, adapted from stories they knew, with a bit of music and dancing added for good measure. On another occasion, Alcott proposed to his daughters that they build a tower out of books, which occupied them for an hour.[171]

Louisa enjoyed one game especially. The Alcotts permitted the girls to run about the room naked for a time before they were dressed for bed. Anna, of course, was awkward and inhibited in her enjoyment, but Louisa let herself go, "running riot," as her father put it.[172] It was rare indulgence in New England, and somewhat curious in view of Alcott's pronounced antipathy to the things of the flesh. Under his prompting Anna had told him that naughtiness came "from the body," and he filled his record with remarks on the unremitting warfare between the "lusts" and the "spirit."[173] Never in these militant tirades, however, did he refer explicitly to sexual lust, perhaps because he supposed children innocent of this particular impulse. How else can one explain his naive assurance when, in 1835, he instituted a series of discussions with his school pupils both male and female on the significance of birth? Proper Bostonians, more sensitive to the taboo than Alcott, were scandalized, but they did not realize the depths of innocence in a man who sincerely believed that sexual matters could be discussed with children in a purely symbolic way. It had not occurred to him that anyone would think children might approach the subject on any but the loftiest of planes.[174]

He chose to view the nightly romp of his daughters in the same light. He argued that the body, after all, is a symbol of the spiritual. When the girls view their naked bodies, "they dwell on the shape, as did the won-

170. *Ibid.*, pp. 177–179.
171. *Ibid.*, p. 170; Researches, p. 247.
172. Bronson Alcott, Researches, p. 258.
173. Bronson Alcott, Spiritual Nurture, p. 162; Researches, p. 121.
174. Shepard, *Pedlar's Progress*, pp. 180–197.

dering disciples, and the voice cometh to them, even the voice of the Spirit within, saying 'It is I, be ye not afraid.' " Alcott recognized there were other, less spiritual ways to regard the body, but he thought children at least are innocent of corrupt attitudes. "The celestial Personage inspireth an awe that charmeth into respect, and even while it familiarizes, checks all unworthy ideas."[175] In this oblique way Alcott recorded his sole observations on the question of sexual modesty.

Romps and games were good fun and could be instructive, but it was through his conversations and stories that Alcott attempted to address the spirit of his daughters most directly. The conversations were restricted for the most part to Anna, for only she seemed to have the patience for them. She sometimes spent a half hour in sober discussion and affectionate interchange with her father:

I had an interesting interview with Anna at twilight, the hour when my own mind is most self-reposing and when, amid the blendings of light and shadow, by the glowing grate of coals, ere the lamp is lighted, the imagination shapes outward things into correspondences adapted to its own ideal. . . . I assisted her to come to me, for she had not the full use of her foot, and took her on my knee. She listened to what I was saying, and after I had finished, putting her arms around me, she says [sic] "Father, I like you," repeating the caress, with great ardour of feeling.[176]

On some occasions the conversations approached the metaphysical. Once Anna told her father she had dreamed she was up in the sky and had tumbled out of it. Alcott responded that she had tumbled down from the sky when she was born; if she were good she would go back there someday. Anna said she did not wish to go to the sky, but she was curious as to how precisely she would get there. Alcott explained that one of these days she would "shake off her body—her head and feet— and that her mind—where she knew God was—would then be *above* the world that she saw with her eyes, and that she would not then want a body." Noting Anna's puzzlement, he then asked her if she had not gone up to the sky when she was dreaming. "So I did," she said, but repeated that she did not wish to go above the world. "But," her father said, "would you not if father and mother were to go with you?" "Oh, yes," she said, "but not without [you]."[177]

175. Bronson Alcott, Researches, p. 258.
176. Bronson Alcott, Spiritual Nurture, pp. 122–123.
177. *Ibid.*, pp. 213–214.

The theme of separation entered frequently into the conversations between father and daughter. While looking at a picture of a daughter supporting her aged mother, Alcott said, "Anna, when you grow to be a woman, as this girl has, then your mother will also grow to be an old woman as this girl's mother has. Shall you take good care of her as this good woman does of her mother?" Anna promised she would. Looking at the picture a moment, tears came to her eyes, and she said, "Father, I don't want to have mother go away where I can't see her anymore. Mother must not die. No, Father, she shall not die, for I will give her some medicine and that will make her well again, won't it?" Seizing the opportunity to drive home a lesson, Alcott replied, "Yes, Anna, Mother will never leave you if you are *good*; for the same good feelings that you now have will always keep her alive, and you can love her always, in your *heart*, as you do now."[178]

In the conversations, as in all his dealings with Anna, he aimed only incidentally at the intellect. His primary purpose was to strike at Anna's emotions until she had learned to suppress every disagreeable association connected with duty. The child will have mastered himself only when "his will is the ready servant of his heart and, under all conditions of his nature, yields itself to the dictation of conscience—the law of the spirit."[179]

Story-telling provided Alcott with the surest avenue to the conscience. He prepared the evening hour with great care and surrounded his little narratives with caresses and kisses, taking pains to associate the stories with frequent demonstrations of parental warmth and affection. Quickly, the tales became something of a bedtime ritual, enjoyed not only by Anna, but also by Louisa, who could summon a patience for stories that she could not command for her father's conversations. As with the games and discussions, the stories aimed at a serious purpose. Anna and Louisa would plead with their father to provide "something to make us laugh," but their father insisted that the stories be more than "merely humorous or ludicrous." They must be "beautiful," "pure," and always present a moral. Alcott, for all of his stress on play, utterly lacked a sense of humor. Anna, at least, began to share her father's preferences. "Well, Anna," he once asked her, "shall I tell you stories to

178. Bronson Alcott, Researches, pp. 54–55.
179. Bronson Alcott, Spiritual Nurture, pp. 61–62.

make you laugh or to make you cry?" Anna replied that she liked best the stories that made her cry. Among her favorites was the tale of a little boy whose mother died under unspecified but heartrending circumstances. It never failed to prompt Anna to tears. Still another story providing a good cry told of a little boy and girl who stole birds out of a nest and then plucked the feathers from their wings.[180]

Striking for Anna's emotions through imaginative devices was still, in Alcott's time, a bold strategy. More orthodox parents had not yet surrendered their hostility toward the "fancy," which they regarded as the realm of the devil. Alcott had joined a vigorous minority who were arguing that the imagination could be the ally as well as the enemy of morality. They observed that children might endure the catechism, but that they loved a good story. True, many evil "romancers" had produced tales that lured children from the paths of virtue, but the obvious solution was not to ban fiction, but rather to create a literature especially for children that could lay hold of their affections and lead them toward moral perfection. Viewing the issue from a psychological perspective, Alcott pointed out that fanciful tales could nurture the development of conscience by providing models of moral behavior that the real world so sadly lacked. Even the best of parents—even an Alcott—fell short of excellence. Hence, one must turn to the arts, where few limits were imposed on the artist's imagination in his portrayal of perfection. Fiction enabled the child to measure himself against the ideal.[181]

Alcott preferred to tell stories of his own invention, since there was not yet a sizeable body of literature suitable for children, but he did allow that Maria Edgeworth, a pious English gentlelady, had provided eminently suitable models for Anna's edification.[182] Indeed, there seemed no limit on Miss Edgeworth's ability to imagine perfection. How must Anna have felt when she compared herself with "Frank," a six-year-old boy conjured out of the fancy of this prolific writer of children's tales?[183] Miss Edgeworth's stories have long been forgotten by literary histor-

180. *Ibid.*, pp. 45, 124–125; Researches, pp. 53–54.

181. Spiritual Nurture, p. 124; Researches, pp. 66–67.

182. Elizabeth Inglis-Jones, *The Great Maria: A Portrait of Maria Edgeworth* (London, 1959).

183. Maria Edgeworth, *Frank: The Sixth Part of Early Lessons* (Philadelphia, 1808).

ians, but a child might have found it difficult to dismiss Frank from
memory. Frank was the very model of obedience. He loved his parents
dearly and liked nothing better than to do what he was told. When his
father or mother said, "Frank, shut the door," Frank directly ran to the
door and shut it. When they said, "Frank, do not touch that knife,"
Frank would not touch the knife. Frank was also extremely careful of
the feelings and rights of others. Accompanying his mother for a visit to
a neighbor's garden, Frank looked at the flowers but he did not touch
any. When invited by the gardener to walk down a path to see some
flowers, Frank answered, "I should like to come down the narrow path;
but I am afraid of coming because the skirts of my coat, I am afraid, will
brush against the flowers." Frank was also scrupulously honest. When a
little boy inadvertently dropped some nuts on the ground, Frank asked
his mother, "May I pick them up and run after the little boy and give
them to him?"

Anna proved to be "deeply interested" in this curious youngster,
asked many questions about Frank's character and about the incidents
portrayed. Alcott, who was reading the story to his school pupils, noted
that Anna grasped the story more readily than most of the older children.
She was particularly intrigued by Frank's honesty in admitting to his
mother, without prompting, that he had broken a window pane while
throwing a horse chestnut. She resolved to be more like Frank. Upon
one occasion, after confessing one of her misdeeds, Anna explained to
her father that Frank always told the truth voluntarily. "I will do as
Frank did," Anna promised.[184]

Try as she might, Anna had difficulty being as good as Frank. She
sometimes fussed when being dressed in the morning, cried at bedtime,
and, for all her timidity, often disobeyed her parents. At times Anna
could be as aggressive as Louisa. She once attacked a schoolmate who
irritated her, sometimes responded to Louisa's blows in kind, and—despite her father's remark that she never destroyed her things—deliberately tore one of her schoolbooks. She had also invented a misdeed that
seemingly had not yet occurred to her younger sister. Anna had taken

184. Bronson Alcott, Researches, pp. 51, 126; Spiritual Nurture, p. 211. Five years
later, Anna was still reading Miss Edgeworth's story. See entry for November 23, 1839,
in Anna's diary, Family Letters and Diaries from 1837 to 1850.

to telling lies and practicing little deceptions—stealing cookies or writing on her father's papers when he was absent.[185]

In keeping with his theories and out of respect for Anna's delicacy, Alcott did not usually respond to misbehavior with physical punishment. He claims to have spanked Anna only twice between October, 1834 and March 1835, on both occasions for unspecified demonstrations of "querulousness" and "excessive sensibility."[186] As punishment, he preferred rather to ration the warmth and affection he otherwise lavished on the girls. On occasion, he would shut off contact altogether. The usual punishment for misdeeds was to eliminate the bedtime story hour, and with it the kisses and other little demonstrations of affection. He would also shut the door to their bedroom, which ordinarily was left open to admit some light. "They are left in darkness," he explained, "without the conscious presence of their parents—a natural consequence of naughtiness and a means of quickening the sentiment of conscience." With Anna the punishment usually brought expressions of repentance and promises of better behavior.[187]

Even Anna was crude enough, her father admitted, to prize rewards more tangible than parental affection and approval. Both she and Louisa were inordinately fond of apples, and it occurred to their father to appeal to Anna's appetite for apples in the hopes of associating it with more worthy motives. Anna, whose sprained ankle kept her at home, was sitting one day in a rocking chair. Louisa wanted the chair and used tears, pleas, and blows to make her point. Alcott intervened and suggested that Anna, because she was older, should give in to Louisa's demands, Anna promised to try, but an hour later fresh outcries brought Alcott back to the nursery where he discovered Anna sitting in the chair once again and Louisa standing beside her in tears.

"Anna, what is the matter with Louisa?"

"She wants to sit in the rocking chair, where mother told me I might sit because I am lame, while she puts the room in order."

"But will you not let her sit in it, if it will stop the tears from running so down her cheeks. Will you not get up to make your sister happy?"

"I want to sit here. Mother said I might."

185. Bronson Alcott, Spiritual Nurture, pp. 10, 155, 208; Researches, pp. 15, 199, 273.
186. Bronson Alcott, Researches, pp. 250, 273.
187. Bronson Alcott, Spiritual Nurture, pp. 10, 20, 83, 97.

"So does your sister. And don't you know that you said you would give up your wants to Louisa's. And now you can do so. Mother is willing that Louisa should sit in the chair. Are *you*, Anna?"

"I want to sit in it."

"Well, Anna, I see you do not mean to be *very good*. Very good little girls give up their own wants to the wants of their little sisters whom they *love*. Love makes us give up our own wants. If you love your little sister, you will give up the chair to her."

"I love her but I want to sit in the chair."

Alcott then asked Anna to go down with him to the study. When she refused he turned to Louisa and asked her to go. Louisa agreed, and he picked her up in his arms, but as he was leaving the room, he said to Anna:

"Now, you are not a *very good* girl. If you were, you would give up the chair to Louisa. I shall not give you the apple that you were to have if you [had been] good, when I come up again.

"I will let her sit in the chair," Anna said, moving herself to the floor to make room for Louisa.

"Now, Anna, did you give up the chair because you *loved* your sister, or because you wanted the apple?"

"Because I *wanted* the *apple*." After a reflective pause, she added, "and I like sister too."

It was, Alcott admitted, not a "perfect" example of self-sacrifice but he hoped that Anna would soon perceive the superiority of acting out of love for Louisa than out of love for apples.[188] His comment points up the value of the incident not only in illustrating his techniques, but also in underscoring the high expectations he entertained. In this instance he demanded that Anna, who had suffered a sprained ankle, give up the chair to Louisa, who was apparently in perfectly good health. His rule rested on no concept of equity, despite his reference to the fact that Anna was older. The rule, as he told Anna, was that "very good little girls give up their own wants to the wants of their sisters whom they *love*. Love makes us give up our own wants." The principle here was one of ascetic self-sacrifice for the sake of sacrifice, resting on the commands of love. It was also clear that love, as Alcott used the term, was no spon-

188. *Ibid.*, pp. 200–202. In extracting Alcott's lengthy conversations with his daughters, the author has taken some liberties with the form of capitalization, paragraphing, and punctuation. Punctuation and appropriate capitalization have been supplied where wanting, while explanatory phrases, such as "she said," etc., have been omitted where they seem superfluous.

taneous impulse but rather the result of an heroic exercise of will-power.

To those who might believe that Anna was too young for such ex-alted feelings, Alcott had a firm reply. A child of Anna's age was just as capable of self-sacrifice for the sake of principle as an adult. His theories of childhood compelled him, in fact, to go even further and assert that a child might well be superior to adults in this respect, having not yet developed a worldly wisdom that could circumvent the clear demands of conscience.[189] No, Alcott could not believe he was asking too much of Anna. Did she not, after all, have within her a spark of divinity? He must forge ahead, training her conscience, subjecting it to many trials of strength, and engaging Anna in conversations to probe the true nature of her motives.

v. The Trials Of Conscience

THE discipline Alcott instituted in the Bedford Street boarding house during the fall and winter of 1834–1835 falls clearly within that mode of child-rearing that subsequent students would call "love-oriented," as opposed to "object-oriented." Object-oriented discipline is a dimension of treatment that includes the granting and withholding of tangible rewards and privileges and the administering of physical punishment. Alcott did, it was true, spank Louisa and, less frequently, Anna, and he even offered them apples, but his emphasis was rather on reasoning with his children, giving praise and affection as a reward, and practicing isolation and withdrawal of affection as forms of punishment. He already sensed what later investigations would make clear, that a love-oriented discipline is usually associated with the early appearance of conscientious behavior. Alcott's approach was, therefore, well calcu-lated to produce his transcendentalist objectives.[190]

189. *Ibid.*, pp. 58, 156–158.
190. See Robert R. Sears, *et al.*, *Patterns of Child Rearing* (Evanston, Ill., 1957), pp. 387–388.

Alcott's judgments about the effectiveness of his technique is, of course, suspect, since it was important for him to believe that he understood children, but, in any event, he was pleased when he observed the changes overcoming Anna. Her father thought she was becoming very sensitive to the matter of parental approval and could not bear to be regarded as bad. Her father noted also that she often averted her face and blushed, sure signs of the struggle within. Noteworthy too was the fact that she was beginning to confess her little sins, having been assured by her father that he would love her even more for doing so. Shortly after her first such confession, she began telling her father, "You make me good, Father," and "Good Father, I love you," or asking repeatedly, "I am good, am I not, Father?"[191] Even her lies were taken as encouraging signs. Anna had lost that candor with which Louisa still confronted her parents, but deplorable as her deceptions were, they suggested that she was vexed at being accused of faults and took to denying them.[192]

Anna not only displayed the effects of a conscience, she even managed to locate it physiologically, or so her father maintained. During one of their metaphysical conversations, Anna informed him that God was in her, and He told her when she was naughty and when she was bad. Alcott then asked her just *where* it was that she was told. She laid her hand on her heart. "There, there!" she said. Surely, Alcott thought, she could not have learned this connection through mere experience. On the following evening, at bedtime, father and daughter were discussing voices when Anna announced that there was something that spoke to her sometimes, and asked her father if he knew what it was. Alcott told her he supposed she meant her conscience. "Yes," Anna replied, something *here* that says 'naughty girl—good girl.' Father, can you hear it when it speaks to me?" Putting her head down on the pillow, she listened for a moment and said, "I think it will say 'good girl, good girl,' for I have been good today." Alcott admitted to himself that Anna might have picked up the ideas from him. Certainly it was clear that he had supplied the words "conscience," "good girl," "bad girl," but he was convinced that in this instance he had witnessed the "senti-

191. Bronson Alcott, Observations on the Spiritual Nurture of My Children, pp. 56–57, 77–79.
192. *Ibid.*, pp. 56, 155–156.

ment of self-approval" itself springing from an "inward, spontaneous conviction."[193]

But how could one always be certain that Anna's behavior sprang from the correct motive? Alcott's characteristic way of answering this question consisted of lengthy conversations similar to those with his pupils, which he later made famous—and infamous—through the publication of *Conversations with Children on the Gospels*. As he explained in the preface to that book, he assumed children of Anna's age were sources of divine revelation, provided only that the adult is skillful in his probing.[194] Elizabeth Peabody, who was already busy recording Alcott's school talks, later came to have her doubts, fearing that the questioning might injure the children, especially the good ones, by making them reflect too much on their imperfections.[195] Harriett Martineau, after visiting Alcott's school, expressed her objections in stronger terms. She agreed with Miss Peabody that the interrogation might "over-stimulate the consciences," but her major complaint sprang from doubts that children were really as sagacious in moral questions as Alcott assumed. She thought Alcott was merely "offering them every inducement to falsehood and hypocrisy," for the youngsters would be tempted, in response to his questions, to express sentiments they did not feel.[196] Miss Martineau had touched on a point to which Alcott himself was already sensitive. He admitted that he sometimes led the children by the tenor of his questions and by his method of disposing of their replies, but he thought he had fallen into this error only seldom. He was, he said, a "simple Analyst of the consciousness of the children, and, having no opinions of his own to establish against their common convictions, he treated with reverence whatever he found within it."[197]

At home, in his dealings with Anna and Louisa, Alcott took the same position. He simply wished the girls to tell him the truth about their own feelings, and one is bound to be impressed by the extent to which this stern father was able to put off the mantle of adult authority and

193. *Ibid.*, pp. 92–93, 99–100.
194. *Conversations with Children on the Gospels*, ed. A. Bronson Alcott (Boston, 1836–1837), I, xi–xii.
195. Bronson Alcott, Journals, October 8, 1835.
196. Harriett Martineau, *Society in America*, 4th ed. (New York, 1837), II, 277–278.
197. Bronson Alcott, *Conversations*, I, xv.

treat the children as if they were his intellectual and moral equals. It was an unusual quality for the time, one that attracted Emerson and even Elizabeth Peabody, for all her doubts. The result was that Alcott elicited from his daughters some remarkably candid statements, not all of which he expected or desired, but which, nevertheless, he faithfully recorded. But it is difficult for a child to respond to an adult on terms of equality, much as an adult might wish it. Anna's replies to her father were often ambiguous, a product perhaps of a certain ambivalence in her father's questions. On the one hand he wished her to be entirely honest in reporting her feelings. On the other hand he could not quite disguise his preference for the correct answers. Hence a conversation between father and daughter could become a subtle duel of wits.

An illustration of this mixture of candor and conformity on Anna's part is provided by lengthy conversations that ensued between father and daughter on the question of her feelings about punishment. Alcott had begun to worry that Anna feared him and, it was true, he sometimes forgot his serenity and shouted at her. As Anna reminded him:

Father, when I am good, how kindly you speak to me; but when I am naughty I do not like the way you speak; you speak loud to me and make me afraid.[198]

It is noteworthy that Anna felt free to make this confession to him, but her candor did nothing to still his concern. Not only on theoretical but also on deeply personal grounds, it was important to him that he not lose the affection he had so carefully cultivated. His worry was increased by Mrs. Alcott's distressing habit of leaving punishment to him. He could, to be sure, console himself with the thought that Mrs. Alcott appealed only to the children's pleasure, whereas he addressed himself to their higher nature:

They have associated *pleasure*, I think, with the idea of her, and *happiness* with the idea of me. We are thus the representatives and Symbols of *Pleasure* and *Happiness* to them. The *Spirit* and the *Flesh* receive an objective life from our mutual influence. The defect of the mother's influence lies, mainly, I think, in her limiting her agency within the body, the pleasures of which she imparts alone to the children. They linger around her in expectation of physical enjoyment, and oftentimes lose the spiritual quietude that results from the possession of happiness.[199]

198. Bronson Alcott, Spiritual Nurture, p. 160.
199. Bronson Alcott, Researches on Childhood, p. 89.

Still, it was just possible that Anna did not understand the matter this way. A bit of conversation was in order. Alcott asked Anna if he made her happy.

"Yes, Father, you do."

"Now, by making you give up your want to mine or Mother's, or by letting you do as you please?"

"By making me give up."[200]

A few days later, Anna was not so sure. "Father," she said, "I don't love you as well as I do Mother."

"Aye, I should like to be loved as much as Mother. I suppose when I am as good as Mother, you will love me as much? Don't you think you shall?"

"Yes, Father, I think I shall."

"But Anna, *why* am I not as good as Mother? What have I done? I wish you would tell me so that I may try to make you love me as much as you do her. Do you think you can tell me?"

"You punish me, Father, and Mother does not."

"Aye, that is the reason then. Well, should not naughty girls—naughty children—be punished to make them better?"

"Yes, Father."

"And is not Anna naughty, sometimes, and does her father punish her then to make her better and make her *love* to be good?"

"Yes, Father."

"Well, then, cannot you love Father, though he does punish you sometimes? For he punishes you to make you love him and to *dislike* your naughtiness that makes you feel so bad."

"Well, Father, I like you both sometimes and sometimes I do not like you both. But you are both good."[201]

Anna seemed to agree, verbally at least, with Alcott's opinion that a worthy father could be a punishing father, but she had not yet grasped the point that she should control her loves and likes, directing them only to worthy objects. After a particularly severe punishment for some undesignated misbehavior, Anna confessed she understood a bit better. Her father asked her if she knew why she had been punished.

"Yes, for being cross."

"How do you feel now?"

"Pleasant."

200. *Ibid.*, p. 90.
201. *Ibid.*, pp. 117–119.

"What made you feel cross?"

"I was naughty."

"What did you do?"

"Troubled sister."

"Did that make you cross?"

"I believe so."

"Could you have helped being cross?"

"Yes."

"How?"

"By trying to be."

"Did you try?"

"Not much."

"Why?"

"I believe I did not want to."

"What! Not want to be good?"

"I believe not."

"Do you want to be good now?"

"Yes, I do."

"What made you?"

"Being punished, I believe."

"Do you think the punishment made you feel as you now feel?"

"Yes; you made me want to be good."

"Was I good for wanting to make you good? You think I punished you to make you better, don't you?"

"Yes, you punished me to make me better."

"Can you love me after I have punished you?"

"Yes."

"Do you love me now?"

"Oh, yes; I love you."

"Should you love me as much as you do now if I did not try to make you good by punishing you when you are naughty?"

"I love you, though you do punish me."

"Does my punishment make you love me?"

"I believe it does."

"You mind me better after I have punished you, don't you?"

"Yes."

"Do you mind me because you love me?"

"I think I do."

"Are [you] afraid of me?"

"A little."

"Don't you sometimes mind me because you are *afraid* of me—afraid I shall punish you if you do not?"

Anna smiled her agreement.

"Then you do sometimes mind me because you are afraid of me. Do you mind me more because you love me, or more because you are afraid of me?"

"Because I love you."

"I want to have you love me enough to mind me always, and then you would never be afraid of me—of punishment. Do you think you can love me so well?"

"I should like to."

"Well, you can. Give up your want to Father's, and then you will begin to love me *more*. And the more you do so, the more you will go on to love me, till, by and by, you will love me well enough to *give up* your want always."[202]

Though Alcott succeeded in securing Anna's agreement to his beliefs, still he understood that she would fall short of true virtue if she did not behave well, and, moreover, behave in obedience to conscience. By January, 1835, Alcott judged that the time had arrived to subject Anna's conscience to a trial.

The first opportunity presented itself while father and daughter were visiting the office of a physician, where Anna was to have her ankle treated. Anna spotted a neatly rolled bandage lying on the floor and asked for it. Alcott explained that it was not hers, but the explanation did not prevent her from asking for it again. Alcott gave the bandage to her. Holding it in her hand, Anna said, "Father, I am going to have this." Alcott replied, "Anna, it is not yours. Ask the doctor for it, and if he says you may have it, I am willing." Anna said she did not want to ask him. She then put the bandage under her cloak, saying, "Father, I am going to put it here a little while." Fascinated by the little drama in temptation which he was sure would unfold, Alcott agreed and waited. Anna then put the bandage in her apron pocket and sat, evidently deliberating her next move. Looking at her father, her face "suffused with the doubtfulness of the act," she said, "Father, I am going to do a little thing."

Alcott replied, "Yes, Anna, I know you are. You have put the bandage into your pocket. You did not like to ask the man for it, and so you put it first under your apron, where you thought he would not see it, and when you had done this, you slipped it into your pocket, where you thought Father would not see it. And when you had done this, you went on thinking of what you had done, and something within you

202. *Ibid.*, pp. 273–276.

seemed to tell you that you had done wrong to put the thing away so, and to make yourself feel better, you said to me, 'I am going to do something,' hoping that I should ask you what you meant to do and let you do it. . . ." Anna's father reported she looked "much abashed," and said, "Yes, Father, so I did." Alcott made clear that he loved Anna for admitting her guilt, but he explained again the rights of property. What she was in fact doing was stealing. "Is it?" she asked. "I will not steal. . . . I will take the things out of my pocket." And so she did.[203]

The exercise of conscience in the physician's office was fortuitous, but the next trial came about as the result of deliberate planning. Moreover, Anna would be on her own this time, without her father's presence to strengthen her resolves. As Alcott was leaving school with his daughter, he made a point of calling her attention to an apple he had not eaten at lunchtime. Instead, he was taking it home with him. After arriving home, he left Anna and Louisa in the nursery, first taking care to put his apple in full view on a wardrobe. Without referring to the apple directly, he asked, "Anna, should little girls take things that do not belong to them without asking their fathers or mothers?"

"No, they should not."
"Do you think you shall ever do so—take an apple, or such thing if you should see one, without asking for it?"
"No."
"And shall you, Louisa?"
"No, Father."

When Alcott returned from dinner, Louisa had the apple core before her on the table, and Anna was standing near. Their father asked Louisa what was lying before her plate.

"Apple."
"Where did you get it?"
"By the fire."
"Yes," said Anna, "I put it there. Louisa and I took it from the wardrobe. We both got up to get it at the same time. Louisa took it before I could get it. I told her she must not, but she did, and then we eat [sic] some of it, and then I threw the rest into the grate, but Louisa took it from the grate and bit some more from it. I was naughty. I *stole*, didn't I? I did not ask you, as I ought to. Shall you punish me, Father, for it?"

203. *Ibid.*, pp. 7–10.

Her father explained he would not punish her, but he added, "I put the apple there on purpose to *try* you, and I rather thought that you *would* take it, but I hoped you would *think* of what I had said, and that you *would not* take it. Did you think you were doing right when you took it?"

"No. My *conscience* told me I was not."

"And shall you mind it next time?"

"Yes, I think I shall."

"Well, Anna, always *mind* that, and then you will do right, whether Father or Mother be by or not."[204]

Even Louisa benefited somewhat by the trial, or, at least, she provided a good imitation of her sister's behavior. Taking Louisa on his knee, Alcott asked, "Louisa, you eat [*sic*] some of the apple, did you?"

"Yes I did."

"Why did you take it before Father said you might have it?"

"I wanted it," she said with a grin, but catching the expression in her father's face, she added, "but I was naughty."

On the following day still another apple was left on the wardrobe in Louisa's sight. Mrs. Alcott reported that Louisa went to it several times during the morning, took it in her hands, looked at it wistfully, and seemed on the point of biting it, but each time she said, "No. No. Father's. Me not take Father's apple. Naughty! Naughty!" The temptation proved too much, however, and when her mother left the room, she devoured the apple. When her mother returned, she exclaimed, "Me could not help it. Me *must* have it."[205]

On the whole, their father was pleased. Both Anna and Louisa had done extremely well, for though they had succumbed to temptation, they had resisted for a time. They had fallen short of perfection, but at least they were beginning to grasp, however faintly, the idea of perfection, to measure themselves against it, and to struggle for its attainment.[206] Anna must, however, have felt discouraged at times, especially when her father commented that he "rather thought" she would take the apple, although he "hoped" she would not.

204. *Ibid.*, pp. 156–159.
205. *Ibid.*, pp. 159, 164.
206. *Ibid.*, p. 164.

Mrs. Alcott hinted that her husband's expectations might be much too high. She loved him deeply and still stood in awe of his convictions, but she managed on occasion to register mild dissent to some of his ways. She remarked with amusement to her brother that Alcott did not always enjoy as much success in disciplining Anna and Louisa as he did in dealing with other children.[207] Alcott's own record betrays a more pointed conflict between the parents. If his barbed remarks about his spouse can be trusted, it seems she frequently undermined the carefully prepared domestic campaign, giving way to sheer impulse in dealing with the children. She often indulged her daughters when she felt like indulging them, and spanked them when they annoyed her. Alcott believed the sabotage sprang from his mate's indifference and incompetence.[208] Perhaps it did. But Mrs. Alcott was no fool and she loved her daughters. It was just possible that she felt uneasy as she sensed the pace and intensity of her husband's child-rearing program. On one occasion, at least, she openly disagreed. During a conversation between Anna and her father, Mrs. Alcott interrupted with the remark that the discussion was far too difficult for the child, being "too metaphysical." Alcott recorded the comment only to refute it. "Nothing," he rejoined, "is too metaphysical for the mind of a child."[209]

VI. Conclusion

THOSE who are wise in the ways of the world—or those who are merely cynical—may suspect that Alcott was embarked on a dangerous course with his daughters. Even as he liberated childhood from barbarity and indifference, he sought to impose a burden that could prove more crushing to the human spirit. He asked of the girls nothing less than moral perfection. The expectations were doubly severe in that

207. Abigail Alcott to Lucretia May, April 12, 1835, Family Letters, 1828–1861.
208. Bronson Alcott, Researches, p. 280.
209. Bronson Alcott, Spiritual Nurture, p. 214.

the model of perfection was essentially an ascetic one. Human maturity was seen by Alcott as a gradual escape from entanglement in the world, not as a growing wisdom in dealing with it. Consequently he held up models of other-worldly perfection and then asked Anna to engage in a voluntary act of self-renunciation—"by and by you will love me well enough to give up your want always." There could be no escape from this expectation. It was the price of parental approval. And, if Alcott succeeded in his training of the conscience, it would also prove to be the price of self-approval. Confronted by his stern expectations, Anna might be tempted to simulate attitudes she did not feel—"I love you, though you punish me." Ultimately she might become the self-sacrificing saint her father desired, but she could also become a precious prig.

It is well, to remember, however, the kind of man Alcott was. He is an easy target for criticism, for in family life, as in all his projects to save the world, he exposed himself recklessly. Even many of his contemporaries thought him ridiculous. Nevertheless, deep conviction can give a certain dignity and meaning to the most bizarre of practices. Alcott may have asked much of Anna, but he also asked much of himself. Ascetic renunciation of the world was for him a way of life, not a merely sentimental gesture. Boston merchants might despise his innocence of worldly values, but Thoreau thought him one of the sanest men in Jacksonian America. Anna paid her tribute by observing—without prompting—that she thought her father nearly as good as Jesus.[210] He did shout at her occasionally, and he often provoked her to anger and resentment, but by practicing what he preached he may have invested his stern demands with sufficient meaning to save Anna from hypocrisy. Only the future would tell.

In later years, Alcott thought Anna and Louisa had turned out well, and it was true that they both displayed a keen sense of putting duty above pleasure, which was consistent with their father's early stress on the importance of self-sacrifice. It is well known that Louisa nourished a fierce loyalty to the welfare of the family, especially to her mother and sisters, and, during her early career, wrote juvenile potboilers to keep the family afloat. Less well known is Anna's devotion. She left home at

210. Bronson Alcott, Researches, p. 52.

sixteen to work, and until her marriage thirteen years later she sent most of a small salary home for the support of her family.[211]

It can be argued, of course, that Alcott's dealings with Anna and Louisa during their early years had little to do with their displays of self-sacrifice. Their father's later refusal, on principle, to engage in lucrative employment gave them little choice, after all, while it is quite possible that Mrs. Alcott exerted far more influence on the daughters through her own sacrificial example. Moreover, if Anna and Louisa did their duty, they were frequently unable to find in it the contentment that their father had always promised as the reward of sacrifice. Neither took his more exotic principles seriously after they reached adolescence. They began to treat him as if he were a lovable though difficult child—responding, it seems, to that quality of childlike innocence which he struggled all his life to retain, through many utopian adventures and in the face of monumental financial difficulties. At the age of twenty-one, when the family was destitute, Anna wrote a letter to her father (in which she enclosed some money) gently teasing him about building "such beautiful castles" for making the world better.[212] Louisa, at twenty-four, displayed a similar tone:

I know you were a serene and placid baby when you began your wise meditations in the quiet little Spindle Hill farm house (I believe that is where you descended from on high) looking philosophically out of your cradle at the big world about you . . . . Surely, dear father, some good angel, an elf, dropped a talisman in your cradle that gave you power to walk through life in quiet sunshine while others groped in the dark.[213]

Whatever the subsequent effect of the child-rearing experiment on his daughters, Alcott was certain that the consequences for himself had been wholly beneficial. As if in anticipation of the end of the recorded experiment, he reflected on the significance of the venture which had begun in Germantown four years previously. He found himself, in January, 1835, more interested in his family than ever before:

Life is fuller of serene joy and steady purpose. I am happier—have more of the faith that reposes on Providence and the love that binds me to human nature, more of the assurance of progression than I have been wont to enjoy.

211. Abigail Alcott, Fragments of Diaries, March 16, 1856.
212. Anna Alcott to Bronson Alcott, July 1, 1852, Family Letters, 1850–1855.
213. Louisa May Alcott to Bronson Alcott, November 28, 1855, Correspondence by Various Hands.

As he looked back it seemed to him that he had once wandered from this child's "kingdom of heaven," a reference perhaps to the period of discouragement and familial separation in Pennsylvania. He had come very near to losing his "innocence," he said, but thanks to the association with his children, he had regained it. He did not dare think what his life might have been had he not been a father:

Verily, had I not been called to associate with children, had I not devoted myself to the study of human nature, in its period of infancy and childhood, I should never have found the tranquil repose, the steady faith, the vivid hope, that now shed a glory and a dignity around the humble path of my life. Childhood hath *Saved* me![214]

Alcott's exclamation marked a depth of feeling that he was unable to sustain over long periods. Seven months later he found himself overwhelmed by the responsibility of caring for Anna and Louisa (Mrs. Alcott being preoccupied with the infant Elizabeth born in June), and he was even plagued by heretical doubts concerning the divinity of his daughters. He also found them suffering from a want of sympathy, and he was disturbed that he could not give them the love they seemed to need.[215]

But Alcott's worship of the idea of the family, erratic though it might prove in practice, reflected an emotion that was gaining force, even outside Transcendentalist circles. The family was no longer to be seen as a mere legal convenience for passing along life, names, and property. Neither was the family alone a device to protect children from the corruptions of society, although that essential function had been in Alcott's mind when he undertook his experiment in domesticity. What he had discovered, both in his successes and his failures as a father, was that the family should also serve the parent—as a refuge from the world, as a compensation for worldly frustrations, and as a means of renouncing worldliness within one's self. By the agency of Louisa's books, this was the message Alcott left to later generations of American women.

214. Bronson Alcott, Journals, January 21, 1835.
215. Bronson Alcott, Psyche, or, The Breath of Childhood, pp. 63, 157–160; Journals, August 17, 1835. The volume entitled: Psyche, or, The Breath of Childhood, contains observations from June, 1835, to June, 1836, and reveals that Alcott's child-rearing tactics remained essentially unchanged. It reveals also that his attention was gradually drifting away from the concrete life of the family into the realm of the empyrean. A subsequent volume, entitled Psyche, an Evangel, was exclusively speculative.

THE "COUNTRY BOY" MYTH AND ITS PLACE IN AMERICAN URBAN CULTURE: THE NINETEENTH-CENTURY CONTRIBUTION

R. Richard Wohl (1921-1957)

EDITED BY MOSES RISCHIN

THE "COUNTRY BOY" MYTH AND ITS PLACE IN AMERICAN URBAN CULTURE: THE NINETEENTH-CENTURY CONTRIBUTION

[EDITOR'S NOTE: R. Richard Wohl (1921–1957) died on the threshold of an outstanding career as a historian and social scientist. "The kind of general scholar seldom found in this age of specialization,"[1] Wohl did not live to complete a single major work or project. Yet he left behind a resonance, a sense of intellectual excitement, and a memory of magnificent strivings for wider intellectual horizons that are the hallmarks of the innovator in any field. The study printed here blends urban history, popular culture, and the Protestant ethic, with a rare freshness.

A native New Yorker, Wohl completed his undergraduate work at New York University. There he came under the influence of Thomas C. Cochran, then at work in the interdisciplinary study of problems in history and the social sciences. Following a year of course work in economics at Yale, Wohl was invited to Harvard because his interests and those of Professor Arthur H. Cole's newly established Research Center in Entrepreneurial History were so closely akin. There, along with Cole and Hugh J. G. Aitken, he helped edit a new landmark journal, *Explorations in Entrepreneurial History*, and was especially influenced by Leland H. Jenks and his role theory. His doctoral dissertation in economic history, "Henry Noble Day: The Development of an Entrepreneurial Role," a model of scholarly craftsmanship, reflects Wohl's enduring fascination with classic New England entrepreneurship, the interplay between business practice and ideology.[2]

In 1951, upon completing his work at Harvard, Wohl went as an assistant

* Mr. Rischin wishes to thank Professor Anselm Strauss of the University of California Medical Center, San Francisco, who brought Wohl's essay to his attention; Professor William Lawton, of California State College, Hayward, who owns the original manuscript; and Mrs. Rhoda L. Holzman, widow of Professor Wohl, for their cooperation and permission to publish this essay.

1. Thomas C. Cochran, "R. Richard Wohl," *Economic Development and Cultural Change*, 6 (April, 1958), 256.

2. See R. Richard Wohl, "Henry Noble Day: A Study in Good Works, 1808–1890" in *Men in Business*, ed. William Miller, 2nd ed. (New York, 1962) for an elegant summary.

professor in the social sciences to the University of Chicago, where he was to remain, except for a one-year lectureship at Harvard, until his premature death six years later. In addition to teaching in an unusually stimulating circle that included Everett Hughes, David Riesman, and Anselm Strauss, Wohl helped found and edit a second pioneer scholarly journal, *Economic Development and Cultural Change*. More important, he became the guiding spirit in the History of Kansas City Project, sponsored by the Committee on Human Development at the University of Chicago, a venture in group and interdisciplinary research financed by the Rockefeller Foundation.

Had Wohl lived he would probably have made his most enduring contribution in the field of urban history.[3] Two significant books dedicated to him and the two published volumes in the Kansas City series by his younger associates testify to the great impact he made upon his immediate circle in the few years that were given him.[4] Vast and unstructured, urban history lent itself to the interdisciplinary range characteristic of Wohl's work. His broad interests, fertilized by a fusion of the resources and techniques of both the humanities and the social sciences, presented opportunities for a relevant new scholarship uninhibited by the constraints of the established disciplines. The urban story, of necessity ill-suited to more formal traditions of scholarship, required just the program of speculative and freewheeling research that Wohl envisioned. Regrettably, he never spelled out, in writing at least, a comprehensive intellectual framework for the study of American urban history. Perhaps he was too prudent to do so. But in an unpublished manuscript prepared for the Kansas City project, Wohl hinted at the exciting horizons he saw:

> The founders of cities, the pioneers who open up unsettled regions, bring with them not only the physical equipment which they will need to work the land, build homes, and establish communities. They come bearing an invisible intangible baggage as well; a system of preconceptions about their new country which is borrowed and imported from the homes they left to make the trek. These misplaced metaphors and outworn images (for the most part, they are nearly all inappropriate to the new locale) are one of the chief handicaps to be overcome by the pioneer, and turn out to be as threatening to him as the physical dangers that he braves.

> Thus, every fresh wave of pioneer settlers finds itself shocked and sobered into an

3. See R. Richard Wohl, "The History of Kansas City: The Earliest Years to 1860" (first draft, property of Anselm Strauss); R. Richard Wohl, "Urbanism, Urbanity and the Historian," *University of Kansas City Review*, 22 (Autumn, 1955), 53–61; R. Richard Wohl and A. Theodore Brown, "The Usable Past: A Study of Historical Traditions in Kansas City," *Huntington Library Quarterly*, 23 (May, 1960), 236–259.

4. Anselm M. Strauss, *Images of the American City* (New York, 1961) and Charles N. Glaab and A. Theodore Brown, *A History of Urban America* (New York, 1967); Charles N. Glaab, *Kansas City and the Railroads* (Madison, Wis., 1962) and A. Theodore Brown, *Frontier Community Kansas City to 1870* (Columbia, Mo., 1963).

humble recognition of the *genius loci* of its new home. Chastened by failure, they learn its vagaries at the price of pain, terror and great hardship; and this forms the chief drama of pioneering. In time, their bits of knowledge and the special insights into the place they have so painfully gathered are diffused and become the common property of their successors. Gradually, too, the first errors are forgotten and wiped from memory. Those who come later find that not only is the physical challenge smaller but they can profit from the sophistication of their predecessors; and the "tenderfeet" and "greenhorns" are gradually and with sarcastic casualness instructed in the known right way.[5]

Intimately associated with Wohl's interest in American urban history was his interest in the common mind. His first published article essaying intellectual history reflected his obsession with popular culture as well as his gifts for charting imaginative new channels of understanding and research. In appraising the shortcomings of what he called the "plebeian school" of intellectual history in contradistinction to what he termed the "aristocratic school," he called for a revitalized intellectual history that would cast a wide interdisciplinary net and be especially sensitive to the problems and moods of the mind of everyman. Study, he said, of "the purveyors of stock ideas and clichés, the popularizers and vulgarizers, the creators of the ephemeral, casual, and fugitive productions with which each age is littered and which later are dismissed when times and tastes have changed as 'worthless' or 'trash' " had generated little more than "mechanical, misdirected and faintly archaic" responses by intellectual historians. Wohl countered with a problem and a plan for fruitful investigation that would show the way. The problem was no mean one: it concerned "the common and generally accepted belief that the United States is, and has been in the past, a land of great opportunity." The design for its productive investigation was outlined to meet the requirements of the so-called "plebeian school" of intellectual history. Wohl wrote:

It deals with an item dredged up from the popular culture of the country; it requires explicit and definable contributions from the social sciences; it has need, for instance, of a theory of social mobility; some underlying conceptions of what social classes are and how they are recognized; a notion of social morale to account for the effective impact of the ideas being discussed; and many other helps which the full course of investigation would rather readily disclose. Last, but by no means least, this example demonstrates the great impact that an item from the common, popular culture can have on higher, academic intellectuals and their professional work.[6]

5. R. Richard Wohl, "The History of Kansas City: The Earliest Years to 1860," pp. 6–7; see also R. Richard Wohl, "Urbanism, Urbanity, and the Historian," *The University of Kansas City Review*, 22 (Autumn, 1955), 53–61.

6. R. Richard Wohl, "Intellectual History: An Historian's View," *Historian*, 16 (Autumn, 1953), 64–65, 68–69.

Onward and Upward: American Ideologies of Success, the title of Wohl's projected work, based on an analysis of fifty-five Horatio Alger novels, apparently was not completed, so we cannot measure Wohl's grasp as against his reach, execution as against concept. We have, however, in "The 'Country Boy' Myth and Its Place in American Urban Culture: The Nineteenth-Century Contribution" an example of the kind of history that Wohl advocated, as well as an exploration of the success theme grounded in the social realities and ideological sentiments of nineteenth-century urban America.

In this monograph, first presented in briefer form to The Seminar on Urbanization and Cultural Change at the University of Chicago, Wohl probes the background, changing character, and persistence of the country boy myth in an era of emergent urbanism that acutely challenged the American yeoman verities and seemingly the whole American system, with its self-fulfilling pastoral stereotypes. "Fact and symbol, symbol and fact; it is as if the United States had developed an urbanized economy without developing a thoroughly urbanized citizen," Wohl wrote elsewhere. "America entered a great period of city building during the nineteenth century protestingly, metaphorically walking backward. . . ."[7] The hallowed tradition of rural origins and a country upbringing, Wohl reminds us, was a part of this protest, and was not perceptibly weakened by the fact that most Americans lived in cities and gathered most of their impressions of the country from the mass media. And clearly Americans still express this protest, if somewhat less shrilly and self-consciously.

Curiously, Wohl does not explicitly address himself to the meaning and place of the Protestant ethic in nineteenth-century urban America. Even in his well-known Alger essay and in his study of Henry Noble Day,[8] Wohl appears committed to a pragmatic empiricism in which the interaction between religious ideology and economic action is boldly and picturesquely laid out but never conceptualized. Nowhere is there a mention of Max Weber or a suggestion that Weber's grand intuition demands explicit confrontation in the urban milieu. Yet clearly throughout the nineteenth century, the spirit of capitalism was not quite divested of its religious motivation. Henry Noble Day, as Wohl has written, "phrased business activity in terms of theological field work" and identified business projects with a symbol, "militant Christian awareness." Indeed, if Alger, unlike Day, felt no need to apologize for a business career, both stood closer to the Protestant ethic than they did to the spirit of capitalism. The city induced ideological shock and a sense of moral

---

7. Strauss, *Images of the American City*, 123.

8. R. Richard Wohl, "The 'Rags to Riches Story': An Episode of Secular Idealism," in Reinhard Bendix and Seymour Lipset, eds., *Class, Status, and Power* (New York, 1953), pp. 388–395; Wohl, "Henry Noble Day."

peril. In Alger's case, it led "Holy Horatio" to provide literary guidance and therapy for youngsters by the millions not quite prepared to bridge the gap between rural traditions and urban realities. It is fitting that Wohl should have seen the matter in popular rather than in purely intellectual terms. By avoiding the overarching theme of the Protestant ethic and the spirit of capitalism he may have diminished the conceptual grandeur of his design. But in so doing he proved truer to his theme and to the nineteenth-century urban life and literature from which it derived.]

In the tangle of human beliefs, as conventionally expressed in talk and in literature, it is easy to distinguish a compulsory factor called facts or things from a more optional and argumentative factor called suggestion or interpretation; not that what we call facts are at all indubitable, or composed of immediate data, but that in the direction of fact we come much sooner to a stand, and feel that we are safe from criticism. To reduce conventional beliefs to the facts they rest on—however questionable those facts themselves may be in other ways—is to clear our intellectual conscience of voluntary or avoidable delusion. If what we call a fact still deceives us, we feel we are not to blame; we should not call it a fact, did we see any way of eluding the recognition of it. To reduce conventional belief to the recognition of matters of fact is empirical criticism of knowledge.

George Santayana, *Scepticism and Animal Faith*

I N 1954, the *Saturday Evening Post* published a long article on the Congressional activities of Senator William Langer of North Dakota. The article itself, a straightforward piece of political reporting, need not detain us; more to our present purpose are the editorial remarks about it, which were tucked away in a column among the advertisements in the back pages. Here we were told that Senator Langer left North Dakota when little more than a boy to begin his studies at Columbia University. He was a brilliant and successful student, rising to become the president of his class, its valedictorian, and, most fatefully, chairman of the Junior Prom.

This last distinction proved to be a piece of potential political dynamite for the future senator. It might be mistaken to mean that, during his sojourn in New York, he had become a city "slicker," a sophisticate, that he had somehow been alienated from the local, rural genius of the North Dakota prairies. The senator's campaign biographer, using the most delicate tact, exorcised this ominous implication. "He led the Prom," the voters were informed, "in a rented dress suit, remaining, as he is, the North Dakota country boy."[1]

The point of this story lies not so much in the campaign biographer's sensitive caution before the threat of the senator's urbanity; but rather in the jocular, rather playful spirit with which the anecdote was shared with the millions of largely urban readers of the magazine. But in making something of a joke of the symbolic country boy and the implica-

1. "Keeping Posted," *Saturday Evening Post*, 226 (January 23, 1954), 130.

tion of his unspoiled, original innocence, this political reporter seriously misread the signs of the times. Had he looked about him he would soon have seen that such pieties were no laughing matter; that even a college-trained, citified country boy turned politician could ill afford to disclaim or disregard his rural roots.

Even Dean Acheson, that model of urbane polish and diplomatic suavity, protested that he was only a "simple country boy," invoking thereby what he felt sure was an established touchstone of political sincerity and fitness for public office. Former President Truman was proud, and indeed careful, to call himself a "plain old country boy," an insistence he varied only by stressing that he was also "just a farmer from Missouri."[2] He blended in these attributions two streams of agrarian idealism which have always figured largely in appealing to American voters. It is a tradition almost as hallowed as the presidency itself that candidates for that office should claim rural origins and a country upbringing, a tradition that has not been perceptibly weakened by the fact that most Americans now live in cities and probably gather most of their impressions of the country from advertisements and the movies.

This hardy tradition has admitted of only minor variations, and only briefly, when it was garnished by further supporting ornament. It was the custom, for a time, for presidential candidates to claim not only a country boyhood, but the moral advantages of birth in a log cabin as well.[3] With the disappearance of log cabins, however, the formula reasserted its pristine simplicity; and the appeal that quickened hearts in the days of Jefferson is still found stirring in the days of Eisenhower.[4]

2. These with other similar illustrations are cited in an excellent article on this theme in American politics by Roger Butterfield, "The Folklore of Politics," *Pennsylvania Magazine of History and Biography*, 74 (1950), 164–165. Cf. Frank McNaughton and Walter Hehmeyer, *This Man Truman* (New York, 1945), pp. 13–37; Jonathan Daniels, *The Man of Independence* (New York, 1950), pp. 75–88.

3. The last use of this token of special rectitude appears to have been made during Garfield's campaign of 1880.

4. "The abiding faith in country boys is one of the oldest and most persistent components of our political folklore . . . . Although it has been submerged at times by other issues —and other forms of folklore—it has never died out, and it has had a lusty renewal since April 25, 1945 [with Mr. Truman's accession to the Presidency]." Butterfield, "Folklore of Politics," p. 165. Cf. Kevin McCann, *Man from Abilene* (New York, 1952), esp. p. 15. For a more comprehensive survey of this political tradition cf. Edward Townsend Booth, *Country Life in America as Lived by Ten Presidents of the United States* (New York, 1947).

But, it may be thought, politicians choose their symbols with calculation, and the rest of the community is relatively free from this insistent anachronism. Who can believe this when so much stylized rusticity confronts us on every side, especially in the mass media?

For decades now, the moviemakers have ground out film after film exalting the country boy and life on the farm until the theme has been worn threadbare. So much so that, in the end, rural audiences rebelled against this steady diet of synthetic sentimentality. "STICKS NIX HICK PIX," *Variety*'s classic headline warned the trade in 1935;[5] but Hollywood has still to surrender this darling cliché. Such opposition has only served to challenge its ingenuity, and the same formula is still served up with new trimmings.

Scriptwriters now regularly disguise the country boy by costuming him in evening clothes and send him to disport himself in night clubs, but even completely urban audiences see through the masquerade. His tow hair, his freckled face, his frank stare of astonishment at his gilded surroundings, and his good-natured grin, give him away; indeed, we almost expect him to ask the supercilious headwaiter for a glass of milk instead of for the standard tot of champagne. And the film reaches a climax of sorts when this hero persuades the heroine to decamp with him for a walk in the park and a feast of peanuts under the trees—which is as close to the countryside as the hero can get and still remain in the plot.

The country boy, and the dream of "going back to the farm"—from the wicked city presumably—have had an uncanny fascination for the song writers of Tin Pan Alley. City-born and city-bred almost to a man, these composers and "lyricists" have produced an enormous literature on both these themes which is so superbly stereotyped and mechanical as to render quotation from it almost incredible.[6] I have room only for one choice example, Richard Jerome's *Country Boy*, which begins:

5. This front-page story carried a sub-head which stressed that country audiences were "not interested in Farm Drama," and the body of the article expatiated at length on the losses that theater owners were suffering from lack of attendance when such films were shown. *Variety*, 114 (July 17, 1935), 1.

6. Sigmund Spaeth has examined this literature with devastating precision. "One of the recent bucolics," he writes, "has the title *The Old Farm House on the Hill*, and it contains all the regular fixin's, including a mill that 'creaks.' . . . Sam Lewis did one about the *Old Farm House in New Hampshire*, possibly influenced by Harry von Tilzer's successful

Little man with cheek of tan, whistling down the country lane
Barefoot lad, my heart is glad, when I hear your sweet refrain.

"The words grow Whittier and Whittier," Sigmund Spaeth observes maliciously, and the song concludes "with a surprise punch that the author of the *Barefoot Boy* would scarcely have recognized: 'Gee! You make me feel life out here is real!' "[7]

Radio and television, too, boast numerous homely, ruralized philosophers and homebodies who, in effect, are country boys full-grown. They roam the soap operas, helpful and cheery, inhabiting a world in which "Just Plain Bill's" hearty lovableness mocks the presumed superficiality of big city manners and big city relationships. Even the comedy shows share in this theme by amiably matching "corny" jokes with a "corny" outlook in a favorable, if implicit, contrast to cultivated urbanity.[8]

Old New Hampshire Home. A slangier version of the same old emotion is *I Wanna Go Back to the Farm* (without any obeisance to Berlin), reaching a nice climax in the line 'and shyly she whispered gosh darn.' There are chickens and a milk pail for good measure." Sigmund Spaeth, *The Facts of Life in Popular Song* (New York, 1934), pp. 54–55.

7. "Of course, it is argued," Spaeth continues in his comment on this song, "that the country boy has a far better time than city folks, 'fishin', pickin' raspberries an' cherries, swimmin', hitchin' horses, an' pitchin' hay.' Well, Mr. Jerome, you may call it gladness, but I call it hard work." *Ibid.*, pp. 55–56.

8. A classic exponent of this genre of humor is Herb Shriner, the Hoosier, who recently acted out his rusticity in a picture story in which he portrays the country boy taking a typical sight-seeing tour of New York City. The text which accompanies the pictures states the classic elements of the country boy outlook on the city, city people, and city manners. "Herb Shriner's New Home Town," *Pageant*, 10 (November, 1954), 12–19. When Shriner left for his 1955 summer holiday he was replaced by Sam Levenson, an urban comedian who specializes in humorous anecdotes about Brooklyn "neighborhoods." When asked about his plans for the summer series of TV programs Levenson confided to a newspaper reporter that "now the city boy will have a chance" on the program. (*New York Times*, June 26, 1955). Upon Shriner's return in the fall, the network advertisements read: "Herb Shriner with cracker-barrel quiz fun on 'Two for the Money.' Television's country boy returns tonight to CBS television . . . ." (*Chicago Daily News*, September 10, 1955).

1. The Urban Pastoral

BY now, as these illustrations suggest, the country boy as a symbol has evolved into an intricate tradition, a truly "urban pastoral."[9] Country boys come in all ages; for the beneficial attributes which flow from rural boyhood are supposed to design a character which lasts a lifetime. And we have become so adept in distinguishing the cues of country boyhood that we can easily detect them in the full-grown man. At bottom, as everywhere within the limits of this span of folklore, an invidious distinction between "country" and "city" is stressed. The tacit contrast is between the presumably artificial and superficial (hence morally dangerous) childhood in the city, and the deep-seated virtues and sturdy manliness infused in the countryside.

Nor, indeed, is the "country" a place any more but rather, and quite literally, a state of mind. It represents an idyllic ideological universe in which plain speech, simple emotions, and the direct and immediate appreciation of men and things is the rule. It is, in a word, the very opposite of urbanity—the schooled sophistication, the tangled motives, and the ambiguous sincerity—which is supposedly characteristic of the city. Sophistication is recognized as subtle and condemned as subtile. It may be used to manipulate, possibly to exploit, those who are exposed to it. According to this special usage, sophistication reverts to an eighteenth-century meaning when it connoted an attempt to spoil and adulterate.

Human relationships in this expressive country world are remarkably transparent. They are alleged to take place in an atmosphere in which norms and motives are standardized, universally known, and unanimously acknowledged. Within this unruffled consensus, social roles are carried through in an equally stable routine. People in this world are steady, moral, and honest. They make promises slowly, adhere to them without reserve, and fulfill them without fail. All else—especially urban

---

9. I owe this felicitous phrase to David Riesman, who coined it and explored some of its many meanings very trenchantly in his *Thorstein Veblen, A Critical Interpretation* (New York, 1953), pp. 170–193; and in his "The Study of Kansas City: An Informal Overture," *University of Kansas City Review*, 20 (1953), 15–22.

complexity, explicit self-interest, and heightened self-consciousness—is, in effect, a subterfuge, if not deliberate deceit.[10]

Stated most generally, it is in the country that things and people are what they seem, but in the city appearances are dangerously deceiving. Friends may turn out, in reality, to be bitter enemies; great fortunes may vanish like fairy gold in the wink of an eye; and the people in the milling crowd are strangers given to "soft soap" and slick tricks.[11] The evolution of these special images of city and country, and particularly the elaboration of the image of the legendary country boy, can be credited mainly to certain persuasive publicists of the nineteenth century, whose works and methods we will examine a little later. Their lurid and simplified portrayal of the city's meaning and influence stemmed from contemporary pressures and contemporary fears: for many who lived in them, cities were then ugly danger-spots to which these writers drew attention by crying out in alarm.

10. An interesting shift in the meanings of rurality is to be observed over the years. The "countryside," through an extension of analogy with the farmstead, widens and diffuses its associations to comprehend the village and the small town as affording the type of gratifyingly intimate and trustworthy social relationships which, formerly, were imputed to the cluster of farmsteads in open country. This widening of meanings is not at all surprising with the decline of the relative isolation of the farm, especially since the advent of the automobile and the influx of mass media.

11. The polarity between city and country is steadfastly maintained in a continuing literature of urban derogation. *The Reader's Guide to Periodical Literature* keeps a standing rubric, "city and country," under which the latest contributions to this polemic appear. The titles which follow are only a limited selection from this vast mass of writings. Nino and Irene R. LoBello, "City vs. Country," *The Rotarian*, 83 (July 1953), 42–43, 58–59; W. Wollerman, "No More Cities for Me!" *Saturday Evening Post*, 225 (February 28, 1953), 17–19; [Unsigned] "Why Live in New York?" *Commonweal*, 154 (June 1, 1951), 18; E. W. Smith, "We Escaped to Reality," *Reader's Digest*, 160 (February 1952), 129–132.

11. Arthur in Babylon

LEST it be thought that this picture is overdrawn, we may examine, with some profit, the tragic history of Arthur, a country boy who came to the city in the 1850's, at the height of the urban boom, with disastrous consequences to his good name, his peace of mind, and in the end, to his life. I choose this tale because it is typical of the stories which filled the "conduct of life" books—the popular philosophy—of the nineteenth century.[12] In many respects, modern versions still preserve many of its classic features. It is especially suitable for our purposes because it is more compact than most, denser with the minatory warnings of the time against the evils of the city. It is, furthermore, a version which is singularly free from the exculpatory complications which embroidered later variants of the same theme. Arthur was no poor boy, cast adrift in the city without friends or funds. On the contrary, he is represented a being "nineteen years of age, educated, handsome, of fascinating manners, and manly spirit," almost a spoiled darling of fortune until he "visited a certain city in search of business."[13]

Despite his maturity and good breeding Arthur was, it turned out, wholly unprepared to resist the city's wiles. Once there, "he unhappily fell into dissolute society, and began to run the giddy rounds of deep dissipation. A few months served to exhaust his finances and run him into debt. A bill lay upon his table, one day, which he was required to pay the next morning."

Like a good country boy, Arthur made no attempt to evade or postpone his obligation; instead "he took the fatal step of selling an opera-

12. Cf. *Hints to Tradesmen* (Boston, 1838), pp. 73–77; H. Winslow, *The Young Man's Aid* (Boston, 1839), pp. 76–82, 93–94, 182–204; Charles Quill, *The American Mechanic* (Philadelphia, 1838), pp. 69–79; [R. W. Pomeroy?], *The Young Merchant* (Boston, 1841), pp. 61–69; John Mather Austin, *A Voice of Youth* (New York, 1847), pp. 117–135.

13. Rev. Daniel Wise, *The Young Man's Counsellor* (New York, 1852), p. 196. The belief that undertaking a business career in the city was fraught with grave moral peril was by no means an uncommon opinion in the early nineteenth century. All the prudential manuals of the time warn against the dangers attendant on such a decision. "I consider you going to such a city as New York," wrote President Jeremiah Day, of Yale University, to his son, "for the purpose of going into mercantile business like a young physician going into the midst of pestilence to become proficient in the art of healing." Jeremiah Day to Sherman Day, October 12, 1826, Jeremiah Day Papers, Yale University.

glass, which he had borrowed from a gay friend; and thus paid his bill."
Even if we were not admonished that this was a "fatal" decision, we
would know that Arthur had now embarked on a course from which
there was no turning back. According to the rhetorical conventions of
the time, the implication is perfectly plain. Arthur had snatched at the
poisoned bait of urban pleasure unaware that it would be his undoing.
And the symbolic significance of the "opera-glass" as the instrument of
his ruin, we may be sure, was not lost on contemporary readers.

Arthur, undeceived too late about the dubious delights of urban fun,
had yet to come to an equally crushing awareness of the duplicity that
lurks behind the mask of friendship in the city:

His friend called for the glass. Arthur, though much confused, frankly confessed his
fault, and promised to obtain funds from home to remunerate the loser. But his quondam friend had the heart of a Shylock, and hurried the astonished and mortified young
man to the police court, charging him with the crime of stealing the opera-glass. After
a summary hearing, he was committed for trial, and immured in jail.

Having passed into the hands of the police and terrified by the inevitable
publicity which will follow on his trial, Arthur is utterly unmanned by
grief and shame. He concludes that he can only redeem his disgrace by
death. "Casting himself on the ground," before his cell-mate, he exclaims "in tones of utter anguish":

"Cut my throat! kill me! trample me to death! My parents! How
can I ever look them in the face again?"

Arthur then begins to beat his head against the stone floor of his cell
with such violence that his cell-mate becomes alarmed. He calls a turn-
key who supposes that Arthur is delirious. A physician is summoned
who, after examining the raving boy, pronounces him "to be in immi-
nent danger of dying."

While Arthur hovered on the brink of death, a "distinguished philanthropist" was sent for, who "bailed the young man out and conveyed
him to his own residence."[14] This benevolent man immediately dis-
patches a letter to Arthur's father, bidding him hurry to his stricken

14. This detail is another instance in which some of the fell consequences of the perils
of the city are mitigated for Arthur. He finds a friend and supporter rather promptly.
Contemporary writers were not always so accommodating to their heroes, and the terror
of being friendless in the city was often exploited for dramatic effect.

son's bedside. When Arthur is told of this development, he becomes hysterical once more:

"O, no! Let me die rather—kill me! I have brought dishonor to his gray hairs, and how can I look in his face again? Let me die, but have pity on my poor father!"

At last, Arthur's father arrives and the boy is told that he is on his way up to see him, whereupon Arthur emits a "piercing groan," muffles his face in the covers, repeating:

"I can't see him! I can't—I can't! Speak to him for me, tell him I died—"

As these words are spoken, the "venerable father entered and stood transfixed with agony beside his dying son." Rather unnecessarily, the author allows himself one final exclamation. "What a scene!" he interjects awesomely.[15]

This brutal little yarn, so equally devoid of mercy and moderation, was printed as a true story; and was intended, and surely was accepted by some, as an edifying and moral tale. Arthur's reckless hysteria, his pathological sense of guilt, his panic, and his egregious moral vanity, are blandly recounted by the author as something just and genteel. The story's excessive melodrama is in itself revealing. The fear and hatred of urban demoralization was so great that its condemnation was correspondingly enormous. The story serves well to polarize city and country, stigmatizing the one and, by implication, unreservedly approving the other. Arthur's downfall commences from the day he comes to the city; in the country he was happy, useful, and ornamental. The city is the villain and Arthur is its victim.[16]

---

15. Wise, *Counsellor*, pp. 196–199.

16. The city as a Moloch has been an endlessly suggestive theme to those who have written more recently to condemn city life, in some cases with little more restraint than Reverend Wise showed in his book. "A recent study of the second largest city in the United States," a recent article praising rurality asserts, "shows that the rate of insanity in the center of the city is nearly double that in suburban areas. I am writing from a place some 500 miles southwest of those suburbs and thus *still* saner. I am writing from the country!" LoBello "City vs. Country," p. 43. (Italics in original.)

III. Perils of the City

ALL exaggeration to one side, there were good and sufficient reasons for a revulsion against city life in many quarters, in 1852, when Arthur's sad history was published. In that same year, Charles Loring Brace was making a horrified exploration of living conditions in New York City. Large parts of the city, he found, were huge slums in varying stages of demoralization and decrepitude. New York was filling up at a furious rate, wearing out houses and neighborhoods very quickly, adding little more than jerry-built, stop-gap construction.

Slum life at the time was no marginal urban fringe; it was the collecting point for the new arrivals in the city. The most unfortunate never managed to leave these slums, and it was the mark of a rising man that he progressed outward from them as his circumstances improved. Manhattan Island was shaped like a bottle, but it was a bottle into which a tight cork had been driven, sealing off the lower portion to form a continuously deteriorating slum. "Being hemmed in on either side by water," contemporary observers complained, "the only direction in which it [the city] can be extended is rapidly filling up with places of business and residences of the opulent."[17]

The already great overcrowding, it was expected, would continue unchecked by reason of that inhumane economic quirk which rendered slum property so greatly remunerative to its owners. Each accession of urban population made houseroom more valuable and, proportionally, more expensive. It was not long before slum housing was returning profits ranging between fifteen and fifty percent on capital each year, with the costs of maintenance very nearly nil.[18]

The chief outcome of this overcrowding resulted, as might be expected, in alarming social disorganization. And the first casualty which

17. New York Association for Improving the Condition of the Poor, *First Report of a Committee on the Sanitary Condition of the Laboring Classes in the City of New York with Remedial Suggestions* (New York, 1853), p. 6. This is an exact, factual report written after careful observation in the areas discussed, and was compiled by an extremely conservative group from an extremely conservative welfare organization. One of the charter aims of the Association was to help the poor help themselves by discouraging the "impulsive" giving of alms, and extending aid only after the most careful preliminary investigation.

18. *Ibid.*, pp. 7–14.

fell before the onslaught of slum conditions was the integrity of family life. "Every honest, sober, industrious resident should at least have it in his power to procure a decent and healthy home for himself and his family," ran the blameless assumption of the New York Association for Improving the Conditions of the Poor; and it should be noted that they were not speaking of the underprivileged or the indigent, but of anyone who came to a city to live. "This is now impossible," they saw, "for multitudes who dwell in this City."[19] As the family and home life deteriorated, the children (like their parents) were forced to find society and sociability on the streets. The home became a dormitory and the gutters a classroom.

In one New York ward, the eleventh, Brace found 12,000 children between the ages of 5 and 16, eloquent testimony to slum overcrowding. These children, for the most part, seemed to be as much beyond the reach of society at large as they were beyond the control of their own parents. There appeared to be no social institution which concerned itself with their fate, barring the marginal control of an inadequate police force. A great many were illiterate and godless (only 7,000 were in some kind of school, only 2,500 confessed some kind of religious affiliation), they were for the most part unemployed, or given to the most casual and uncertain street trades.

Crime flourished, and these children all stood excellent chances of falling foul of the law sometime during their minority. The warden of the City Prison told Brace that one in every two arrests for petty crimes in the city was charged against criminals who had not reached their twenty-first birthdays. With a morbid fascination, Brace calculated that this worked out to one arrest for every fourteen New York inhabitants.[20]

For very many, life in the city must surely have approximated Hobbes's conception of savagery: a life that was nasty, brutish, and short.[21] It was, for many more, a life in which decency and upright-

19. *Ibid.*, p. 6.

20. Charles Loring Brace, "The Children's Aid Society of New York: Its History, Its Plan, and Results," *History of Child Saving in the United States*, ed. C. D. Randall (Chicago, 1893), pp. 3ff.

21. The threat of demoralization was so strong in New York City at this time, that a special section of the *First Report* of the Association for Improving the Condition of the Poor was set aside to discuss the psychological aspects of the depression and apathy produced by slum life. Although a strongly temperance-minded group, the Committee re-

ness were balanced with terrible uneasiness on a job, a wage, on the
maintenance of health and strength. Unemployment and temporary
illness were the workingman's twin nightmares. A few weeks of enforced idleness might well turn a respectable workman (and his family)
into derelicts. Nor was there any reason to be solaced by the thought
that the conditions that Brace (and similar contemporary investigators)
turned up were atypical: the eleventh ward was a cross section, not an
exception.[22]

These problems and these conditions were not merely temporary
ones arising from a momentary defect in the circumstances of city life.
They were concomitants of rapid urbanization in which the inflow of
newcomers regularly outstripped the capacity of the social arrangements available for dealing with them. If this could be called a problem
—it might be better to recognize it for a large-scale social upheaval—it
was one which continued with undiminished force throughout the
whole of the nineteenth century and well into the twentieth, and we
have probably not seen the end of it even now.

The horrified response of many contemporary publicists to the conditions of much of urban life was not altogether a cheap bid for vicari-
ous melodramatic thrills for their readers. In good part—perhaps to a
greater degree than it is easy to imagine now—what they described was
straightforward reporting colored perhaps by rather stagy narration.

---

ported that it could understand, and almost sympathize with, some of the prevailing ad-
diction to drink in these areas. "I must confess," they quoted one of their informants as
saying rather sadly, "that the wonder to me is, not that so many of the laboring classes
crowd to the liquor shops, but that so many may be found struggling to make their
wretched abodes a home for their family." New York Association for Improving the
Condition of the Poor, *First Report*, pp. 20–29. (The material quoted above appears at
page 21.)

22. *History of Child Saving*, pp. 3ff. This volume, which contains reports from a number of cities, shows that these problems were not local and exceptional to New York
City, but were the rule everywhere that rapid urbanization was making headway. Very
detailed and circumstantial evidence of the conditions which prevailed among the urban
"poor" of the time will be found in the annual reports, especially the first ten issued, of
the New York Association for Improving the Condition of the Poor, published by the
Association between 1843 and 1852 in New York. For material with a special emphasis
on the state of urban youth see the annual reports of the New York Children's Aid Society for the first decade of its operation, published by the Society, New York, 1853–
1862. For further discussion of the situation outside New York City see Robert A.
Woods, *et al.*, *The Poor in Great Cities* (New York, 1895), which also contains valuable
material concerning contemporary conditions in a number of European cities.

Nor were the "perils of the city" the clumsy invention of hack writers and excitable preachers. The social workers of the time, as we shall see, frequently proclaimed their inability to portray adequately the hideous conditions they uncovered when they ventured into the slums. The hardships and demoralization they discovered among city people, especially in the slums, were to provide a continuous theme for shocked and angry "human interest" journalism right into the twentieth century, as the drama of rapid American urbanization continued to unfold.

In 1800, as the nineteenth century opened, only 1 in every 25 Americans lived in a city, a ratio that was to grow increasingly favorable to urban communities in the decades which followed. By 1850, 12 out of every 100 Americans were city dwellers and fifty years later in 1900, one in every three: all this in a country which increased vastly in numbers and in size throughout the period. Not only did urban populations increase in absolute numbers but cities grew at a rate which steadily outstripped that of country districts throughout the century; and in only one decade, 1810–1820, did both increase at the same rate. By 1840–1850, cities were growing three times as quickly as rural places were expanding, and the high point for the century had not yet been reached. The centennial crest came between 1880 and 1890, when cities increased more than four times as rapidly as did country areas.[23]

This urban growth was recruited, in no small measure, from an exodus out of the countryside, whence poured a steady stream of farm-born youth for whom there was no longer any place on the land.[24]

23. These are census figures, and it should be noticed that they are subject to two kinds of sustained error. For one thing, these figures have a downward bias in reporting the number of the urban population within any one decade, since the census until 1900 defined an urban place as consisting of 8,000 or more inhabitants. Throughout this period many communities which were urban according to many other criteria fell outside this limit and were counted as rural. There is, furthermore, an upward bias in reporting the rate of urbanization in a given decade. Many communities barely short of the 8,000 minimum abruptly became urban, according to the census, when they reached it, although they may have been urban in character long before. All the relevant figures, including data processed for a lower population limit of urbanization than the census allowed, are given in David Kinley, "The Movement of Population from Country to City," in Cyclopedia of American Agriculture, ed. L. H. Bailey (New York, 1909), II, 113–115.

24. It is difficult to trace this farm-to-city migration with any very great statistical precision. "However, when all allowance is made for the increase due to the excess of city births over city deaths, and to the influx of immigrants, there still remains a considerable

Farm boys, as a class, were caught in the interplay of two fields of force. The opening up of new, fertile lands had made farming uneconomic in some of the older sections of the country and drove out some of the farm population to the cities. Furthermore, the productivity of farm labor was increasing steadily throughout the century, so that in the 1890's only a fifth of the work force needed in the 1830's could bring in even larger crops of many of the main agricultural outputs, like corn, wheat, cotton, hay, and others. All these forces freed large numbers from a rural life and pushed them off the land. To these pushes away from the farm were added the pulls exerted by commercial and industrial demands for ever-larger labor forces in the cities. Quondam farmers and their sons were tempted with promises of steady work, regular cash wages, and the attractions of an exciting city life. These lures proved so effective, and the pressures to leave the land so inexorable, that the slums were soon teeming.[25]

iv. The Model American Boy

THESE new city boys, so recently and so obviously country boys, provided substantial inspiration for the nostalgic, imaginative creation of the country boy of legend. Intellectuals of the day casting about for a figure on which they could pin their hopes and their message found, as we shall see, in country boys the most likely candidates out of which to fashion heroes and good examples. The city afforded them with plenty of object lessons in what needed mending, shortcomings from which, with a willing imagination, it was easy for them to believe that the country boy was wholly free.

In the eyes of such an urban observer, these youngsters stood out in favorable contrast to the slum boy and the immigrant lad recently ar-

---

part of the growth to be explained by a direct draft on the country population. That this is the case is shown by the fact that the cities to which most of the immigrants go are few in number, but that the growth of the cities to which they do not go is as marked as that of those in which they are found." *Ibid.*, p. 116.

25. Cf. *Ibid.*, pp. 116–117.

rived from Europe. The country boy seemed healthier, and his pink cheeks, bright eyes, and broad biceps soon became the trade-mark of his mythical counterpart. Real country boys might be rude and crude, but they were engagingly ebullient and brisk, vigorous and enterprising; all these were the hallmarks of a sound boy in a culture which worshipped work and energy. They seemed unspoiled, full of pent-up hope, and brimming with optimism. Wastrels and loafers were exported from the country to the city, too, but these were soon lost in the maelstrom of the slum; only the energetic and self-reliant showed, even if only briefly, above the surface of city life.[26]

The comparison with the immigrant boys was even more favorable to American eyes. Unlike the American country boy, immigrant boys very likely could not speak English or speak it well, seemed strange, and had literally outlandish tastes. Ethnocentricism and parochial narrowness both combined to prevent a sympathetic and realistic appraisal of their worth. The cream of the rural crop of youth easily achieved a position of ideological prominence; they were chosen to be models by the mentors of the American boy.

It is remarkable to observe how rapidly this image was translated into a literature of exhortation. By the early 1860's and for long decades thereafter, the country boy of legend displaced the real country boy in the minds of millions of Americans, especially in boys' books. The country boy "and the lure of the city supplied literature with one of its legendary figures. Knapsack in hand, clothing coarse and homespun, the bloom of outdoor health on his cheeks, the rustic hero entered New York to seek fame and fortune."[27]

26. On the character of the migrants from country to city, see *ibid.*, p. 117.

27. Eugene Arden, "The Evil City in American Fiction," *New York History*, 25 (1954), 261. Arden's conclusion compels agreement from anyone who has attempted to wade through this mass of literature. There is, however, some further evidence to support it as well. The Huntington Library possesses 1,531 dime novels published by Beadle & Adams between the summer of 1860 and the firm's dissolution in 1898. An analysis of the themes of these novels, most of which were Western stories, shows that 6 per cent deal with this aspect of city life. "The setting of these novels," it is reported, "is generally New York City, but it can also be Philadelphia or San Francisco, and occasionally a continental capital. Theme situations develop around 'poor but honest' girls, bootblacks, and messenger boys, as they seek 'true love' and suffer poverty and misfortune, only to find success and wealth in the end." Philip Durham, "A General Classification of 1,531 Dime Novels," *Huntington Library Quarterly*, 17 (1954), 289.

Against the country boy, there was no highly esteemed competing image of the well-bred, urbane city boy. Almost all attempts to portray virtuous sophistication in the city were choked off. In 1860, for example, Oliver Wendell Holmes made a foray for such a type in his *Atlantic Monthly* serial, *The Professor's Story*. Wittily, but with underlying seriousness, he disclosed the existence of a New England "Brahmin Caste," leisured, cultivated, and sophisticated, whose children were being advantageously placed in strategic posts in the nation's schools and colleges. These few, Holmes argued, were developing a sensitive and urbane canon of taste and tradition: they were a group to be watched. His report, disguised though it was in a novel, raised an immediate outcry, and he was soon answered by a New England clergyman with the astonishingly Puritan name of Increase Tarbox, who angrily denounced Holmes's description as an inaccurate, sinister, and effete misrepresentation of the facts.

Our "great men" come from the country, Tarbox argued, and far-sighted benevolence has even provided college scholarships for the needy country boy who often turned out to be a better scholar, as well as a better man, than his city cousin. Although there was something in what Holmes was saying, Tarbox thought the trend pointed to was a lamentable one. The country boy's mind and morals, he felt were better than the city boy's, and in and out of college he should be championed.[28]

On the other side of the continent, in the fast-growing city of San Francisco, another futile attempt was made to bring the city boy into favorable notice. The Reverend Dr. W. A. Scott's arguments in favor of city life and urban nurture were almost as defeatist as they were passionate, for the tide of rural bias was so strong he was forced to concede his case almost before he began to present it. "The country and village may be the best place for the birth and early training of youth," he admitted, "but it is for the excitement of the city that the highest developments of mind are made."

It was not in the country that the greatest cultivation and civilization were bred. "The newspapers, teachers and books, and professional skill

28. Oliver Wendell Holmes, "The Professor's Story," *Atlantic Monthly*, 5 (1860), 88–99; Rev. Increase N. Tarbox, "Where Do Our Scholars and Great Men Come From?" *Congregational Quarterly*, 3 (1861), 158–168.

which our towns and remote neighborhoods enjoy are the products of city institutions." Besides, he urged despondently, not all of us should or could be farmers, and surely there was a state of grace that could be earned in the city as well. "If all the world were farmers," he argued, "they might have bread and beef enough, but the mass of mankind would be idle, untaught, and narrowminded." The obvious benefits of a complex division of labor, of rich intellectual variety, and the cultivation of elegance and subtlety would die out, he seems to be saying, and such sophistication is badly needed in American society.[29]

In these remarks, the Reverend Dr. Scott has, all unwittingly, touched one of the central, but subterranean, issues which have persistently colored the controversy between town and country: the suspicion, of urban and rural people both, that urbanity was something intellectually and emotionally treacherous. The very things Dr. Scott was calling for were being defined away for the most part and by most teachers and preachers of the day as idleness, wickedness, sinful indulgence. Those who felt called upon to nourish and praise these elegant ideals felt themselves then, as many of their counterparts so often do now, to be an alienated minority, a choice but unhappy few.

Nearly twenty years before the doctor's impassioned lecture, the scion of a rich, socially prominent Connecticut family was bemoaning the fact that even the sons of the wealthy and well-born were not permitted to indulge in urbane refinements and in the careful cultivation of their leisure. It was, he protested, "one of the strangest misconceptions" of American culture

which blinds us to the policy, as well as the duty, of educating in the most finished manner our youth of large expectations, expressly to meet the dangers and fulfill the duties of *men of leisure*. The mischievous, and truly American notion, that to enjoy a respectable position, every man must *traffic*, or *preach*, or *practise*, or *hold an office*, brings to beggary and infamy, many who might have lived, under a juster estimate of things, usefully and happily, and cuts us off from a needful, as well as ornamental, portion of society.[30]

29. Rev. Dr. William Anderson Scott, *On the Influence of Great Cities* (San Francisco, 1854), pp. 30, 28, 25. This essay was originally read as a lecture before the Mercantile Library Association of San Francisco, on June 16, 1854.

30. James A. Hillhouse, "The Relations of Literature to a Republic: The Education of Men of Leisure," *Cyclopedia of American Literature*, ed. E. and G. Duyckinck (New York, 1855), II, 121. (Italics in original.)

A few percipient observers of the day, however, were already wondering whether such total commitment to work was wise; whether it was healthy to stress so severely that life was real and earnest. A slim, questioning literature was beginning to appear expressing anxiety over obsessive industry; cautiously advising husbands to find time enough to converse casually with their wives, to play with their children, to create and cultivate their leisure. These special pleadings for even a rudimentary urbanity—if I may call it that—were a minority report on the state of American civilization.[31]

v. The Persistent Rural Idyl

THESE straws in the wind were easily scattered by the steady gusts of praise for rurality with its hard work and unadorned life-style. In great part, American culture in the nineteenth century was saturated with bucolic imagery and with an insistence on the special moral significance of country life in a democracy. This was the message of the most sober and learned treatises and of McGuffey's Readers, too. Little Rollo, the nineteenth century's "good boy" *par excellence*, might visit London and Paris with his parents and acquire some of the polish that comes with foreign travel, but the lessons which formed his character and set the cast of his personality were acquired on the farm and in the country in the company of Jonas, the hired man.[32]

The popular writers and pundits of the day, not unexpectedly, slipped

31. S. Teackle Wallis, *Leisure: Its Moral and Political Economy* (Baltimore, 1839), pp. 1–52, is a sustained attack on excessive work and its consequent impoverishment of leisure, the author arguing very eloquently that if industry is admired so unreflectively it will produce a dull and stultified national character. On the nature of the home life of the too-busy man, cf. Josiah Gilbert Holland, *Timothy Titcomb's Letters to Young People*, 40th ed. (New York, 1866). Cf. esp. "Special Duties of the Husband," pp. 177–187; "The Institution of Home," pp. 219–228.

32. For a very thorough compilation of American ideological pronouncements in favor of country life and in praise of country nurture, with very full citations of nineteenth-century material, see John G. Thompson, *Urbanization* (New York, 1927), pp. 3–23.

into the vein of this rich rural vocabulary when they came to confront the social problems posed by rapid urbanization. But cities, after all, were crucially different from the country, and the best they could do was to color and adapt the rural tradition to new purposes. The manner in which they did so was conditioned by two important considerations: the threat offered by the relatively new scale of urban misery and, from another standpoint altogether, the special position imputed to youth, particularly boys, in this greatly optimistic era. In the nineteenth-century United States, progress had ceased to be a doctrine and had become a dogma, and youth was elevated to a position of special significance because the future belonged to it, and it must not, in good conscience, waste a single golden opportunity to make a better world.[33]

Agrarian idealism had solidly entrenched itself around the human and social benefits which, it was claimed, accrued to the country household and to the typically large farm family. And it was precisely the urban changes in both home and family life that evoked so much anxious concern in the nineteenth century. What was particularly noticeable, and especially menacing, were the great, new hordes of urban poor. A few middle-class observers watched the disorganization and the demoralization in the slums with utter dismay, fearful that at some unexpected moment the limit of endurance would be reached and the poor would degenerate into anarchy. From this standpoint, it is not surprising, nor was it unfeeling, for Brace to think, after more than twenty years' work in the slums, that these people made up New York's "dangerous classes," ripe for riot and revolution. Especially disconcerting to this worried handful was the neglect, debasement, and wastage of the children of the poor, to whom Brace, incidentally, devoted a lifetime of anxious and improving effort, lest they become a lost generation.[34]

33. On the special position of young men and boys as the coming generation see Rev. W. F. Crafts, *The Coming Man is the Present Child* (Chicago, 1878), esp. "Homes, Streets and Fields," pp. 417–500. For earlier specimens see "Claims on Youth," in Austin, *Voice to Youth*, pp. 17–26; and Winslow, *Young Man's Aid*, pp. 13–31, esp. "The Responsibilities of Young Men," pp. 29ff.

34. "In the view of this book," he wrote in his best-known work, "the class of a city most dangerous to its property, its morals, and political life, are the ignorant, destitute, and abandoned youth: the outcast street-children grown up to be voters, to be the implements of demagogues, the 'feeders' of the criminals, and sources of domestic outbreaks and violations of law." Charles Loring Brace, *The Dangerous Classes of New York* (New York, 1872), p. ii.

Overcrowding and the breakdown of the most elementary arrangements for privacy and sanitation had produced the classically wretched conditions of slum life which, in turn, brought about the very nearly complete collapse, in many cases, of the basic routines and sanctions of family life. There were many families who lived dignified and rewarding lives even in the slums, but there were even more who gave way before their forbidding environment, and their condition was glaringly obvious to those who cared to look into it.[35]

For this great group, the main problem of their everyday lives was to work out the rehabilitation or the restoration of a semblance of viable home life. These people, however, were too absorbed in their daily concerns to be approached directly by the writers and preachers who glorified the country boy. The message reached them, as we shall see, through the agency of middle-class social workers who were pondering the amelioration of their plight. And it was Charles Loring Brace, to choose one example, who saw in the legend of the country boy a kind of symbolic past which needed to be recalled to the urban poor to inspire them to work toward a way of life in which the usual amenities and decencies of civilization prevailed.

The middle classes, generally, did their very best to stay away from the slums so that they would not see, and would not be involved in, what was going on there.[36] A guide book to New York warned its

35. It would be difficult to exaggerate the miseries of slum life during the period, especially during the latter half of the nineteenth century in most big cities, and notably in the biggest, New York. This degradation, in addition to all else, constituted a public menace of the first order, most obviously, of course, in the matter of public health. Within one seventeen-year period, New York was subjected to four epidemics which can be traced, in great part, to the filthy slums of the time: cholera (1832, 1834, 1849), typhus (1847). *The Great Metropolis: or the New York Almanac* (New York, 1852), 95. I have no room here to dilate on the many detailed descriptions of conditions in the slums which are available for this period. One of the best of these descriptions based on a careful house-by-house, street-by-street survey conducted by a New York State Legislative committee will be found in New York State, *Report of the Select Committee Appointed to Examine into the Condition of the Tenement Houses in New York and Brooklyn* (Albany, 1857), *passim*. (This report is Assembly Document No. 205.) Reporting on slum conditions and on related aspects of city life continued unbroken throughout the nineteenth century. See, for example, Jacob Riis, *How the Other Half Lives* (New York, 1890), on New York at the end of the century, and on Chicago, see W. T. Stead, *If Christ Came to Chicago!* (London, 1894).

36. A Southern visitor to New York in 1852, the year of Brace's survey of the Eleventh

readers, in 1873, to "beware the purlieus of the city. They are to be visited under the escort of a police officer."[37] It is not likely that many middle-class folk were eager to make the trip even under these conditions; and aside from such sightseeing there was an effective, if not a literal, segregation of classes and masses.

The upper class of New York, the old-line aristocracy of the city, was aloof and isolated in its ancient houses, and in its close ties, from the rest of the city; fearful only that a rich and ambitious *parvenu* might try to invade their citadel.[38] For the rest, the cost of rent or the price of a good city house served to draw the lines within the middle class itself.[39] The richest in this group lived sumptuously. The brownstone was then in the zenith of its glory, servants and wages were cheap, and profits, if one was lucky enough to make them, were likely to be plump. The lower layers of the middle class, however, faced a housing shortage which, in its own way, was probably as acute as that which festered in the slums, although less drastic in its social consequences. They solved it by moving into boarding houses, sometimes for years at a time, until they could afford to establish an independent household. Family life, in such circumstances, was strained and, according to contemporary reports, the coterie life of such boarding houses was both comical and wearing. By the standards of the time, however, the family and the

---

Ward and of Arthur's downfall, makes a penetrating observation on this point in which he reflects middle-class attitudes of the time. He is speaking of dispossessed slum dwellers. "To be sure there are not a few of the most abject and wretched sent away by some cold and heartless landlord, but you hardly ever see them in our streets. Go to the hospital, the poorhouses, and there you may be gratified with a sight of the picture you desire (no, I believe not, you will say, and you are right). It is no pleasure to look upon the misery of our fellow-creatures. I do wish I had never left my country home." "A South Carolinian," *Glimpses of New York City* (New York, 1852), p. 181.

37. *Wood's Illustrated Handbook of New York* (New York, 1873), p. 28.

38. A good description of upper class life of the period will be found in K. J. Van Rensselaer, *The Social Ladder* (London, n.d.), see esp. chap. ii, "The Age of Innocence," pp. 55–63. The remainder of the book deals with the competition of the new rich with old families and the gradual victory of new wealth over old blood.

39. The guidebook cited earlier makes an unintentionally revealing comment on this point. Under the heading, "Unfurnished Apartments," the author observes: "These are abundant for the lower and working classes in what are called 'tenement houses.' For the higher classes they are not so common, the latter finding their homes in hotels, boarding-houses, and in a whole private house. A new class of fashionable lodging houses is, however, being introduced, but their success is still to be proved." *Wood's Handbook*, p. 178.

home held together nicely even under the frictions of such relative overcrowding.[40]

The pressures that the middle class—to lump them all together—felt on their home life, and to which the country boy legend offered relief and solace, were not those arising chiefly from the corruptions of unwholesome living conditions. Their dangers were more subtle, but just as real. They saw in the city a nest of wonderful opportunities, a continually self-renewing El Dorado, in which a careful and assiduous man might nurse a piece of luck into lasting fame and fortune. A worthwhile boy, therefore, kept his ear cocked to hear opportunity knocking and was ready, when good fortune beckoned, to accept the burdens and rewards of a lifetime of work and winning.[41] Within their homes, and with their children, the middle classes stressed ambition, the virtues of sustained application, and the uncomfortable but necessary discipline of principled inhibition. Composure and control were their watchwords.[42]

But this was only one side of the city and of middle-class behavior. The same parents who in one context urged frugality and abstinence, in other moments taught their children the virtues of conspicuous con-

40. Almost all contemporary travel books comment on this phenomenon. The peculiar social milieu of the boarding house and the pressures of its coterie life on the individual family were also the subject of much contemporary wit. See, for example, Thomas Butler Gunn, *The Physiology of New York Boarding Houses* (New York, 1857). Behind many of Gunn's jibes at boarding house inmates there is much serious but good-natured criticism of their plight. It should be noticed, too, that there were many varieties and types of boarding houses offering accommodations to the poor, the rich, and the moderately well-off.

41. The middle classes were always eager to learn about and to celebrate the lives of city boys who made good. This preoccupation, as a matter of fact, even invaded their commercial reference books. In 1852, Moses Yale Beach, a New York journalist, published a directory of "wealthy" New Yorkers with inspiring biographies appended in each case. New, expanded editions appeared in 1845, 1846, and 1855. See Moses Yale Beach, *Wealth and Biography of the Wealthy Citizens of the City of New York* (New York, 1846). A personal fortune of $100,000 was the smallest Beach could admit into his list; but even the almanacs of the time carried lists of those who had succeeded more modestly. *The Great Metropolis*, p. 89, has a table listing persons in the city with fortunes of $17,000 and more, thus cutting deeper into the middle-class sector. Long lists with biographies were also compiled for Philadelphia, Brooklyn (and other cities). See esp. Abner Forbes, *Rich Men of Massachusetts* (Boston, 1857) in which the author segregates in a final table those who married money, were self-made, were farmers.

42. A very thoughtful contemporary discussion of these points can be found in A. D. Mayo, *The Symbols of the Capital; or, Civilization in New York* (New York, 1859), cf. esp. chap. i, "The Hudson; or, Life in the Country," and the contrasting ch. ii, "The Capital City; or Society in Town," pp. 7–64.

sumption, their solemn duty to keep up with the Joneses, and to enjoy (sometimes with an uneasy conscience) all the good things that life afforded. This counsel was not easy to understand or to absorb; in many respects it was contradictory to the other parental injunctions.[43] In addition to the temptation to be weak there were the external dangers of being led astray. The city abounded in low company, tricksters, and criminals, who were always offering abundant lures to the unwary. These had to be avoided or else a boy might be "ruined," that is to say, distracted, and his morale broken for the high-minded and sustained pursuit of worldly success.[44]

The villains in the novels of Horatio Alger, one of the architects of the country boy legend whose work we will examine at length and who addressed himself to this particular dilemma, are of these two kinds: the out-and-out criminal who rejoices in his evil ways, and the little boy-snobs who try, without lifting a finger to earn the right, to pass themselves off as privileged characters because their parents are rich and well-known. In both cases, we see mirrored the failure according to middle-class standards. For by its canon only one right is recognized: the right, which is a duty too, of each man to earn his own money, his own distinction, and his own claims to deference. The criminals, by this logic, stand condemned by law and man; the little boy-snobs are ridiculous, for after all, in their weakness, they are only so many crows tricked out in borrowed plumage.

To accommodate this tension in middle class life in the city, the country boy myth had to be modified from its traditional forms to incorporate clear-cut imperatives to social mobility. On this score, the prevailing image of the country boy and the tradition of rural moral

43. Preachers in middle-class urban churches regularly pointed out this discrepancy, and tirelessly explored the dangers to a Christian life in this antithesis. For full discussion of this point by a minister who used his personal experience among the urban poor to guide his remarks, see, for example, the writings of E. H. Chapin, *Moral Aspects of City Life* (New York, 1853); *Humanity in the City* (New York, 1854). For the context in which Chapin's views have a place see Henry F. May, *Protestant Churches and Industrial America* (New York, 1949), pp. 26–36.

44. Guidebook advice to new arrivals in the city sheds some light on prevailing middle-class ideas on this point. "On approaching the city," the newcomer is warned to beware "the goodnatured civilities of persons you have never seen before. Gratuitous offers of assistance or advice, or good fellowship, are suspicious, to say the least. Do not be persuaded to go anywhere with these casual acquaintances." *Wood's Handbook*, p. 27.

superiority lay at hand ready for adaptation. The country boy was famous for being inured early to hard work (life on the farm was never easy); and for his singleminded devotion to making a place (for which read, a farm) for himself in the world or so, at least, the existing literature of bucolic nostalgia claimed. He was described as abstemious (life in the country was simpler than in the city), steady and saving (cash was always scarce in the country), he mastered depression and defeat (living close to nature gave him spiritual and psychic resources unknown to the city boy), he was—in the slogan Horatio Alger was to make famous—"bound to rise."

I do not mean to leave the impression that the country boy legend neatly divided itself along class lines. For one thing, the myth remained in the custody of middle-class intellectuals who dispensed it either as missioners to the urban poor, or else as the exhorters of the uncertain and ambitious within the wide range of the middle-class itself. Moreover, all variants of the myth were essentially the same, different elements being stressed to suit particular purposes. All versions, furthermore, were focused on a common concern to make the mushrooming urbanization of the day comprehensible to the people caught up in it.

A mature man considering the rapid growth of American cities in 1850 or 1860, like A. D. Mayo whose views we now turn to examine, had been born into an unmistakably rural America; and had been caught off guard in his own lifetime by a great, seemingly unprecedented, social convulsion. Nor did it seem that the example and history of European cities could guide and inform the American experience. As Mayo saw it (and his sentiments are typical for the period) "an American city is essentially a different thing from an European capital."[45] Continental cities, viewed from a long retrospect, seem to have enjoyed long periods of slower, more organic growth; they had historic roots as centers of civil or ecclesiastical administration; and, Mayo reflected, in their time they had even served the cause of progress by forming themselves into a vanguard to wrest political liberty from feudal overlords. None of these circumstances paralleled recent American urban history.[46]

45. Mayo, *Civilization in New York*, p. 40.
46. This was not so unnatural a view to hold as might at first appear. It would have been difficult, to choose one example, to think of Italian cities in 1859 which, by then,

These new cities seemed rather to be great disorderly camps thriving on a fantastic commerce which was fed people and goods from a broad, outlying agricultural base. To Mayo, writing in 1859, it appeared that "an American city is only a convenient hotel, where a free country people come up to tarry and do business. . . . It is not the deep, firm root out of which rises the trunk and foliage of a great nationality; rather a boat tossed on the billows of American enterprise and emigration."[47]

Into this turbulent and eccentric community the country boy arrives a stranger, to confront an inevitably unhappy fate. "The quiet, affectionate youth comes from the congenial atmosphere of the rural neighborhood, and finds himself struggling with a rushing crowd of adventurers, each bent on success." If he fails, he is cast aside without compunction. "There is no long suffering, pitiful [pitying?] community behind the combatant to receive him, wounded and weary in defeat; he must leave the pavement for the country if he fails, and too often there is no home among the fields; and the deep vault which runs under every drawing-room and counting-room, claims him at the end." Even success and victory are mockeries:[48]

... through what prolonged and withering toils, amid what dangers of health and life, and sanity of soul, does the prosperous citizen approach his reward. The majority of successful dwellers in town are scarred in body and twisted in mind by their prolonged stimulation of all the powers of life and in grasping the prize of ambition have lost their own best resources of enjoyment.

"*Happiness does not depend so much on what we have*," runs the inevitable conclusion, "*as on a certain freshness of nature which illuminates every corner of our life from within. . . .*"[49] And it is precisely because the city is destructive of this interior cultivation—and of the original simplicities of human nature—that it is a dangerous and unwholesome place in which to live. "All the dangers of the town," Mayo concludes, "may be

---

were not at least one thousand years old. And Mayo in stressing the comparison between American and European experience is reflecting the imaginative burden of his contemporaries in taking in so rapid a rate of urbanization as was then going forward in the United States. It is hardly surprising that American cities appeared to such observers to be culturally anomalous and socially untenable.

47. Mayo, *Civilization in New York*, pp. 42–43.
48. *Ibid.*, pp. 49–50.
49. *Ibid.*, p. 50. Italics in original.

summed up in this: that here, withdrawn from the blessed influence of Nature, and set face to face against humanity, man loses his own nature and becomes a new and artificial creature—an inhuman cog in a social machinery that works like a fate, and cheats him of his true culture as a soul."[50]

Here then, in summary, are the representative attitudes and beliefs which formed the background and the continuing context for the emerging legend of the country boy. This background was modified, in time, and the elements in the image of the country boy were artfully reshuffled until the nineteenth-century version of this pastoral myth gradually established itself. This process of conversion and redefinition proceeded so slowly, and with such apparent fidelity to the forms of the past that, finally, it still seemed to be clothed with traditional sanctions and traditional endorsement.

vi. Charles Loring Brace:
Reclaimer of Tenement Youth

IT may seem strangely inadequate to summon only two from the great cloud of witnesses who testified to the merit of the country boy in the nineteenth century. I have chosen to dwell on the work of Charles Loring Brace and Horatio Alger because these two men, among the thousands who unwittingly collaborated to enlarge and enforce this myth, built almost the whole of their life-work on the development and exploitation of a new version of the country boy legend.

In tracing the flow and influence of ideas from the documents that remain there is always the temptation to overstress the importance of an occasional book, a stray statement of attitudes and beliefs, without much assurance of how representative or widespread such feelings were. In the work of Brace and Alger we escape this pitfall and go on to surer ground. They had audiences of millions who responded to the effects of their work. They spoke for and to a majority, if not for all, of the grow-

50. *Ibid.*, p. 51.

ing American cities. Let no one think, however, that I am gainsaying in any way the work of those many others who contributed indispensably to the development of the legend, or even that I am imputing any major innovative role to Brace and Alger. They both ran deep furrows in an already well-ploughed field.

Of the two, Brace was the man of action. The policy he developed of exporting urban waifs from New York to the West to turn them, as it were, into country boys and girls by main force was his major contribution to the further growth of the country boy legend. What the motives and methods of this policy were will be explained later. Suffice it to say now that he, perhaps more than any other individual of his time, tried to carry into action the dicta of this legend and in order to do so he created and inspired a whole network of institutions to help serve this purpose.

As much as any institution can be said to be the work of one man, the Children's Aid Society of New York was Brace's creation. And from his lead followed the inauguration of similar societies in most of the nation's major cities.[51]

By the end of the nineteenth century, a web of such benevolent enterprises, in which Brace's ideas and policies were flattered by almost slavish imitation, criss-crossed the nation. It would be idle to speculate on the total number of children whose lives were affected by these social service agencies, but some indication of the scope of the work can be inferred from the fact that, by 1892, Brace has succored some 300,000 children through the New York organization alone.[52]

51. Organizations corresponding to the New York Children's Aid Society in New York were established in Brooklyn (then an independent city), Philadelphia, Washington, Chicago, St. Louis, Cleveland, San Francisco, Toronto, and other cities. Howard Potter, who delivered a eulogy on Brace in 1890, pointed to "the influence of such a life in setting in motion, whether from motives of imitation or opposition, benevolent enterprises for the help of children everywhere, and among all sects and denominations of Christian people. Indeed, he may be said, in the latter sense, to have even originated (in the sense that apprehension of the effect of what the Children's Aid Society was doing incited them) the greater or the better part of the Roman Catholic charities for street-boys of their religion in New York." Howard Potter, *Charles Loring Brace* (New York, 1890), pp. 11, 13. Potter's eulogy was privately published by the Children's Aid Society of New York.

52. This estimate was made by Professor Herbert B. Adams, of Johns Hopkins University, and is cited in Emma Brace, *The Life of Charles Loring Brace* (New York, 1894), p. 503.

Alger, on the other hand, was the man of words and ideas. I have said before that in the course of time the country boy legend was refashioned into something new from its traditional forms. It is in Alger's novels that we trace the transformation to a new formula: one which deftly blends old and new and contrives a specious continuity with the past. Just how many novels Alger wrote we shall probably never know. The latest count comes to 135 titles, but the country's untouched library stacks and neglected attics will probably yield up further additions in time.[53] As a matter of fact—and this is a tribute to Alger's historical significance—some of the books now labelled with his name may never have been written by Alger at all. After his death, some New York publishers hired hacks to duplicate the typical Alger story for a market which demanded yet still more of these stories, and not all of these bibliographical fakes have been uncovered.[54]

Alger commands our attention in the present discussion not only because he was so prolific but because his audience was so vast, and his work, presumably, so relatively influential. We can no more know now how many people read Alger's novels in his own lifetime—he died in 1899—than we can discover how many he wrote.[55] The very extravagance of some of the estimates of his audience is an indirect tribute to the pervasiveness of his influence. It has been said, with obvious exaggeration, that as many as 200 million people read these books in the nineteenth century. This figure need hardly be taken seriously, but a con-

53. In 1928, Herbert R. Mayes compiled what he believed was a nearly complete list of the Alger corpus, which totalled 118 titles. Since then, and up to 1945, 17 new titles have been uncovered. Alger, however, was so stereotyped a writer, and his formula varied so little, that these newly uncovered volumes add nothing to what was already known of his technique or themes. Cf. Herbert R. Mayes, *Alger, A Biography Without a Hero* (New York, 1928), pp. 240–241. The most recent list is printed in *Struggling Upward*, ed. Russel Crouse (New York, 1945).

54. See the discussion of this point, and the evidence for it, in Malcolm Cowley, "The Alger Story," *New Republic*, 113 (September 10, 1945), 319.

55. His books fell off in popularity and in sales in the first two decades of the twentieth century, despite a lingering market for these stories immediately after his demise. In April 1906 C. L. Munger in an interview with another writer of boys' books ("A Talk with Henry Castleman," *American Boy*, April, 1906) reported the editor of a juvenile magazine remarking: "We want such stories as Horatio Alger . . . used to write." In the twentieth century new versions of the Alger success story were being developed, and his archaisms of style and type were being gradually abandoned. In this instance, as so often later, the adult editor was lagging behind his young readers in judging taste.

servative estimate would go no lower than to give him 50 million readers between 1868—when he published his first best-selling novel—and
1900.[56]

Indeed, Alger's influence—the identification of his name with the
"rags to riches story" of which the country boy myth is a principal ornament—had long outlasted even his popularity as a writer. His name
and what it stands for has become proverbial, and we are hardly permitted to forget it. When, in 1945, Russell Crouse republished a one-
volume edition of several of Alger's novels as a kind of literary souvenir,
he wrote an acid introduction "exposing" Alger's faults as a writer and
concluding comfortably that his book was in the nature of an exhuma-
tion. But in 1955 Crouse's teasing boomeranged: the whole body of
Alger's works are being reissued for a new generation which it is presumed will relish the same old stories.[57]

In the hands of both Brace and Alger, the country boy legend was
manipulated by two conservative intellectuals—men whose hearts and
eyes were on an imagined past—into an instrument meant to accommodate newly urban people to life in the city. Both felt—like so many of
their contemporaries—that increasing urban numbers and the advancing complexity of urban existence represented a sharp break with the
recent American past which had to be explained and mitigated for their
generation. And in the contrast between Brace's despair of the city as a
humane and decent social entity and Alger's increasing admiration and
enthusiasm for New York's glamour, we can observe the changing
and significance of the legend of the country boy.

Charles Loring Brace was an easily recognizable man of his time: a
lean, determined, Connecticut Yankee who had come to New York to
decide his future. He left Yale to continue his theological education in

56. Frank Luther Mott estimates, in his study of American best-sellers, that 17 million
copies of the Alger books were sold. Calculating most conservatively that each volume
bought had at least three readers gives me the total I have cited above. If anything, this
figure may underestimate Alger's total readership. Frank Luther Mott, *Golden Multitudes*
(New York, 1947), p. 159.
57. These books are appearing as twenty-five cent paperbacks, and are published by
Value Books Company of Quincy, Massachusetts. The assumption that there is still a
mass market for these stories appears to be borne out by the fact that they move quickly
enough to be disposed of in Boston's supermarkets, where they are prominently displayed
for sale.

the big city.[58] In New Haven, where he had begun his studies, he had been vaguely repelled by the abstract, rather cerebral theology which constituted the professional preparation of ministers in his day. If Brace had a talent, it was a talent for action, a practical aptitude for organization; the metaphysical disputes he studied about the essential nature of good and evil, about fundamental ethical imperatives, left him cold. But, at 22, when he got his first look at New York City, he had not formalized his antipathy. He felt it, characteristically for an intending minister, as a set of "religious doubts."[59] The plain fact—which he came to see in time—was that he could not perceive any worthwhile relation between the ordinary conduct of a middle-class pastorate and an essentially Christian life. He wanted to dedicate himself to helping a suffering mankind, to bring the solace of Christianity to oppressed and deeply troubled people.[60]

In our own time, such an ambition might be received sceptically and psychiatrically, but Brace never doubted his motives for a moment. He was chafing for lack of an outlet for a large fund of unexpended zeal; and his last student years were devoted to trying to find an appropriate niche for himself. "I only wait to see where I shall certainly be most useful," he wrote his father at twenty-three,

and to carry on well my training. I must give my life to make men happy—in weakness and worldliness perhaps—but still such I am. Whatever I shall be, teacher or preacher, the brightest of all visions before me is a humble, self-controlled life, all devoted, all given up, to working for human happiness. But it is very easy to *dream*. May God help me to *do*![61]

58. The fundamental source for Brace's life is his sister's biography cited earlier. For his early history and family background, see Emma Brace, *Life of Brace*, pp. 1–73.

59. *Ibid.*, pp. 62–70.

60. "But, after all, the inefficiency of religion," he wrote his father, "doesn't strike me so much in such places [as Blackwell's Island Alms-House] as in what I see every day, and what I realize constantly of our New England religion. It's affecting so sadly little of our practical business relations . . . so seldom inspiring men with genial kindness and charity towards one another; no, never, hardly, entering the least in a politician's duties, or influencing his operations. There's so much of the dogma—Calvin piety—and so little which makes better men. I am almost hopeless sometimes, and I fully believe that New England piety, if it doesn't change considerably very soon, will, in the course of two or three generations, run out. This may sound extravagant. But do think of it." *Ibid.*, pp. 76–77, 62–76.

61. *Ibid.*, p. 71.

We may take these words at their face value. Once his decision was made, Brace devoted thirty-eight years of life to his self-chosen task of saving children in New York. In the meantime, as he had written, he was preparing himself for his yet undetermined profession, following as by instinct on to his yet unseen goal. How well he studied the city and the life of urban people of all classes may be judged from the fact that when he was ready to begin the work of the Children's Aid Society he had a program ready which became the organization's standing agenda for the next four decades.[62]

The highlights of his self-education are marked out in three special ventures which Brace undertook to improve his qualifications. First, he attempted to reach the miserable and unchurched adult poor in the city and, particularly, those unfortunates who had fallen foul of the law. He preached, as he himself recognized, without any discernible improving effect to the fallen men and women on Blackwell's Island; but these people were too brutalized by their past, too sunk in apathy, to be moved by even the most earnest eloquence. From this experience Brace concluded, at first perhaps unconsciously, that the poor had to be caught young if they were to be salvaged.[63]

Brace's second venture—a European journey—was begun in a restless dissatisfaction with his own progress toward a settled profession. He went abroad in the familiar hope that a change of scene might induce a changed perspective on his future. Ostensibly, this was to be a trip devoted to both recreation and education; instead, his travels turned out to be a field trip for a social worker in the making.

In Germany, especially in middle-class Hamburg, Brace was impressed and delighted with the amiable and sunny quality of the "home-life" he found there. Family life in these ample and comfortable German houses seemed rewarding, genial, humane, and moral: a happy blend, it seemed to Brace, of good sense and good feeling. All this was a far cry from both the austerities of Brace's own New England upbringing and the degradation of family life which had so recently shocked him in

62. "It is worthy of remark," Brace's sister and biographer observes, "that all the distinctive features of the society as it developed later . . . are found in outline in the society's first circular." *Ibid.*, p. 158. The circular itself, which was probably written for the most part by Brace, is reprinted in the same volume, pp. 489–492.

63. *Ibid.*, p. 75, cf. p. 78.

New York.[64] Here was a range of social possibilities in the organization of life in the city which he had hardly suspected could exist. With absolutely innocent delight Brace informed his American friends that the Germans he encountered had discovered how to transform even an ordinary meal into an occasion for "sociality."[65]

In Hamburg, where the memories of 1848 were still fresh, Brace also learned of the emergence of a new Protestant social work movement which was beginning to sweep Germany: the Inner Mission.[66] The recent revolutionary wave which had paused in Germany in its course across the continent had alarmed German religious circles. Much as they abhorred revolution, which was little less than blasphemous in their eyes, these religious leaders nonetheless recognized that the revolutionary social protest was solidly grounded in real grievances which enabled it to draw on the support of the country's poor. And, to prevent revolution and to relieve existing hardships, they joined together to promote a religious awakening among the poor and to create social service agencies to palliate urban misery.

The Inner Mission developed, therefore, as a loosely articulated, decentralized movement which energetically created hospitals, orphanages, city missions, and other similar institutions, always drawing on the initiative and support of aroused local groups of middle-class people.[67] To

64. Brace was under no sentimental illusions about what he was observing. "It will be seen that my facts and experiences are mostly gained from association with the middle classes. These—the men of business, the farmers, the merchants, the lawyers and scholars —are the influential portion of a People, who stamp especially its social character. It is their habits and manners we mean, when we speak of the social life of the Germans." Charles Loring Brace, *Home Life in Germany* (New York, 1853), p. iv; cf. also chaps. ii and iii. Brace was not only convinced of the essentially middle-class cast of American culture which, he felt, made his remarks on the Germans apt and instructive; but he felt, too, that middle-class life set the pattern for those social ideals which ought to be propagated throughout American society, and especially among the lower classes. On this latter point cf. Emma Brace, *Life of Brace*, p. 149, where Brace discusses his reasons for writing his book on Germany, and what he hopes his countrymen will learn from it.

65. See Brace's letter to J. H. Olmsted, written from Berlin on December 13, 1850, in Emma Brace, *Life of Brace*, p. 104.

66. The movement had been founded in 1848 and styled itself the Centraler Ausschuss für die Innere Mission der Deutschen Evangelischen Kirche.

67. Unhappily, there is no work in English on the operations of the Inner Mission or on the life of Wichern, the leader of this movement. The best work in German is Friedrich Oldenburg's *Johann Hinrich Wichern: Sein Leben und Wirken* (Hamburg, 1884–1887). Cf. also Martin Porksen, *Johann Hinrich Wichern und die sozialen Fragen* (Rendsburg, 1932)

Brace this work seemed a perfect model for the career toward which he had been groping at home. He arranged to meet the leader of the Inner Mission, Johann Hinrich Wichern, and to discuss the movement's progress with him.

To Brace, Wichern expounded the notion that modern industrialization and urbanization had created a dense city proletariat which posed new problems and challenges to modern Protestantism. Brace could understand this well enough, he had seen these things happening all around him in New York and had been especially chagrined by the flight of the Protestant Churches from the slums, where the poor were, to all intents and purposes, unchurched.[68]

Furthermore, Wichern told his American visitor, these neglected urban masses, if left without the counsel and consolation of their church, could become reckless revolutionaries and, through the mists of 1848, Brace began to discern the "dangerous classes" of New York City. According to Wichern, desperation and hopelessness encouraged demagoguery, and demagoguery, in turn, led to dictatorship and absolutism.

So far, Brace had discovered a philosophical and emotional basis for his formerly vague yearnings for a humanitarian career. His own future was foreshadowed in his admiration of German *gemütlichkeit* and in the practical, systematic philanthropy of the Inner Mission. Not long after, he got a frightening and instructive taste of authoritarianism. While in Hungary, one of the stops on his European tour, he had been summarily seized by the Austrian police and flung, *incommunicado*, into prison as a suspected agent of the Hungarian rebels. The astonished Brace was baffled and outraged by this highhandedness but, always of a practical turn of mind, he adapted himself quickly to the conspiratorial atmosphere in which he found himself. With brisk efficiency he smuggled out a message to the American *chargé d'affaires* in Vienna and, after repeated dip-

---

for a discussion of Wichern's work in the context of Germany's contemporary social problems and social history. For material on Wichern's collaborators cf. "Der Begründer der Inneren Mission," *Süddeutsche Monatshefte*, 26 (1928 /1929), 174–179.

68. For a full discussion of urban Protestantism at the time cf. A. I. Abell, *The Urban Impact on Protestantism, 1865–1900* (Cambridge, 1943); and for similar material relating to the earlier part of the nineteenth century cf. Henry F. May, *Protestant Churches and Industrial America* (New York, 1949), esp. pp. 91–162.

lomatic protests, was released and made his way home.[69] "Tyranny" which, until then, had been a rather academic shibboleth with Brace, was now a piece of his own experience and his detestation of it was reinforced.[70]

When, therefore, Brace returned to the United States he was ready to begin the orderly development of his life work. There remained only the essential preparatory task of getting precise professional knowledge of the nature and incidence of urban poverty. This he accomplished by his methodical survey of the eleventh ward in New York in 1852, to which I have already alluded. Almost immediately thereafter, he was approached by a philanthropic group of affluent and influential New Yorkers to begin the organization of the Children's Aid Society.[71] And, as I said, the program he drafted was, and remained, a finished and exact statement of the Society's policy to the very end of the century.

Brace was a versatile and indefatigable organizer and executive and in his long lifetime he developed a host of social service programs. Of all of these, I shall address myself to only one aspect of his work, which reflects a central tenet of his philosophy of social work and which bears very closely on Brace's contribution to the legend of the country boy. Brace's initial reaction to the effects of urban life on the urban poor was to conclude that the city was no place in which they could reform their present mode of life, and he felt that this was especially true for the children of the poor. He was insistent, from the very first, that these unfortunate youngsters had to be "drained from the city" and restored to

69. "Mr. Brace had found, soon after entering prison, that a priest was to be immediately released, [by whom he proposed to send a message to Vienna.] How could they exchange the necessary words! The ingenious priest surmounted the difficulty by mingling questions with his 'Ora pro nobis' in a most amusing way. As they passed and repassed in their walk, 'What did you say is his name?' (In louder tones from his prayer book) 'O! Maria beatissime!' Then as he passed again, 'Ora pro nobis! *MacCurdy*, did you say? . . .' Thus his letters were taken to Mr. MacCurdy, American Charge d'Affaires at Vienna." Emma Brace, *Life of Brace*, pp. 139–140.

70. For a full account of his Hungarian experiences cf. Charles Loring Brace, *Hungary in 1851* (New York, 1853). A briefer account can be found in Emma Brace, *Life of Brace*, pp. 133–143.

71. This group formed itself into the Board of Trustees of the Children's Aid Society, a list of their names and the background of circumstances which led to the organization of the Society can be found, *ibid.*, pp. 492 and 156–157 respectively.

country life and country manners.[72] It was only in the rural areas that they could find decent homes and become economically useful. And, for Brace, the "family was God's reformatory."[73] The family farm, with its happy coincidence of an intimate household united with a viable, supporting economic enterprise, provided both the social and economic basis for a coherent and rewarding kind of family life. The grand object of his work, therefore, was to arrange for the exportation of poor young people from the city to rural areas.[74]

Brace had been prepared, by long experience, for his admiration of the countryside. He himself was a city boy, but the Hartford in which he had been raised was a small countrified city. Within easy range of his boyhood home there was free access to the "countryside": to long sylvan walks, open stretches of pretty wildflowers, even nearby farms which might supply produce for the Brace kitchen.[75] But, it must be remembered, Brace was never a farmer himself; his perspective was that of a city man enjoying a romantic contrast between town and country. Characteristically, when Brace first came to New York he found his greatest pleasure in visiting—not working on—his friend Olmsted's farm on Staten Island, in those days a delightfully rural enclave in the midst of New York's urban hustle. All through his life, although his work confined him to the city, he arranged matters so that he could have his home in country surroundings—more properly in suburban

72. "We hope, too," the Society's first circular announced, "especially to be the means of draining the city of these homeless children, by communicating with farmers, manufacturers, or families in the country who may have need of such employment." *Ibid.*, p. 491.

73. This apothegm, his biographer remarks, "is in accord with a great natural principle that the Christian's Aid Society is aiming at the removal of the children from the city streets to farmers' homes in the West. This solution seems doubly natural, owing to the unusual advantages of the United States in having a vast area of arable land in the cultivation of which the farmers need help." *Ibid.*, p. 171.

74. The most complete exposition of Brace's ideas on the subject can be found in Brace, *Dangerous Classes*, chap. xix, "The Best Remedy for Juvenile Pauperism," pp. 223–233. To Brace the solution offered by emigration to the countryside was compellingly self-evident, "it was but a natural inference from the important movement now inaugurating for the benefit of the unfortunate classes of New York, [that I] should at once strike upon a plan of emigration."

75. "His home in Hartford was in a suburb, and within easy reach of streams and country walks . . . ," his biographer reminds us, adding, ". . . in addition to boys' games and plays, he loved rambles in the country." Emma Brace, *Life of Brace*, p. 5.

neighborhoods—away from the noisier, dirtier, and more obvious side of city life.[76]

Brace's confidence in the intrinsic merits of country life was so great that he very soon abandoned any attempt to regulate the placement of city children too closely. At the very outset, some attempt had been made to try to match families with the children who were placed in their homes, but this was expensive and time-consuming and, so it seemed to Brace,[77] really unnecessary. A decent trust in human nature and in the wholesome effects of farm life should, he felt, make both parties to the bargain content. In the end, a simple procedure was worked out. Children were made up into parties and sent out with an escort—often a clergyman—to some "western state." The communities which were visited had been warned in advance by special announcements and newspaper advertisements of the arrival of the party. When a town on the itinerary was reached, the children were lined up on the railroad platform, or else displayed in the local church, and selections were made by the local farmers.

A child taken by a family was not adopted by that family. It was simply received into the home as a sort of quasi-kinsman—or at least so Brace hoped—and was to be given a common-school education, taught to work and cultivate a farm; and then at twenty-one the protégé was to receive $100 and be sent into the world to establish himself. Presumably, and this would have coincided with Brace's dearest wishes, such a boy would thereupon stake out a farm of his own or, if a girl, would marry some sturdy yeoman, and recapitulate the happy family life which he or she had learned to appreciate as transplanted children.[78]

This attempt to create country boys and girls by an act of transportation was, as might have been foreseen, only successful in part. Too little provision was made for adjusting children fresh from a city slum to some of the harder realities of farm life: the loneliness, drabness, con-

76. See Brace's sentimental comments on Olmsted's place, *ibid.*, p. 59. His passionate fondness for the country was a lifetime habit and interest with Brace, and is specifically mentioned even in the brief eulogy referred to in footnote 51 of this paper.

77. On this point cf. Emma Brace, *ibid.*, p. 173.

78. Brace was fond of printing the histories of successful emigrations in the annual reports of the Children's Aid Society, and he reported an especially fortunate case in Brace, *Dangerous Classes*, pp. 228–229.

tinuous hard work, and enforced simplicities. Slum children sent out to live on farms often reacted violently and bitterly against the change. They mustered the resourcefulness they had learned on the city streets to run off and to follow vagrant lives until they found some other place more suitable to their taste. Even those children who took more kindly to their new environment were frequently aggrieved at finding themselves no more than unpaid hired hands in the farm family, who remained permanently outside the inner circle of family intimacy and family affection.[79]

For a variety of reasons, and the two I have cited were among the most prominent and most usually mentioned, great disillusionment with the scheme became manifest after only a few years. Anxious "westerners" complained that Brace's plan was "poisoning" their communities with young criminals and juvenile delinquents from city slums.[80] Other social service workers complained about the casual placement procedures under which children were sent into foster homes.[81] All in all, and for decades after the plan was set in operation in the 1850's, Brace conducted investigations to support his views and poured out an undiminishing stream of rebuttals to criticisms of his work.[82] For nearly thirty years at its height and with diminishing emphasis as the nineteenth century drew on, each National Conference of Charities and Correction filled its proceedings with disputes over the merits of the emigration scheme.[83] But with the passing of the years and the increasing professionalization of social work, the controversy

79. Hastings W. Hart, "Placing Out Children in the West," *Proceedings of the National Conference of Charities and Correction*, 11 (1884), 171–177. (Hereafter cited as *PNCCC*.)

80. These complaints and their justifications are discussed in a survey of the results of the "placing-out" covering many years' practice by Boston Children's Aid Society, Ruth W. Lawton and J. Prentice, "A Study of Results of a Child-Placing Society," *PNCCC*, 42 (1915), 164ff.

81. Robert W. Hebberd, "Placing Out Children: Dangers of Careless Methods," *PNCCC*, 26 (1899), 171–177.

82. A typical explanation and defense of the plan can be studied in Charles Loring Brace, "The 'Placing Out' Plan for Homeless and Vagrant Children," *PNCCC*, 3 (1876), 135–150.

83. The literature of this controversy is listed and analyzed in the *Proceedings of the National Conference of Social Work, Index 1874–1933* (Chicago, 1935) under the relevant rubrics. It should be noted that after 1916 the National Conference on Charities and Correction was renamed the National Conference of Social Work.

ground to a halt. Not that there was any lack of direct, affirmative evidence that in many cases the scheme was spectacularly successful. Brace never tired of telling of New York urchins who had found affectionate foster parents, who were redeemed to independence and respectability by life on the farm. Even as recently as 1953, the *Christian Science Monitor* had no difficulty in collecting such testimonies from living men and women who attributed their success to just such a transplantation.[84]

In time, however, Brace came to see that the increase in the city's numbers and the corresponding increase in the clientele of the Children's Aid Society could not be accommodated simply by shipping children back to the farms.[85] Slowly but surely he retreated from his original plan: he built more and more schools, industrial training centers, lodging houses, and the like in New York City, and increasingly geared his activities to the assumption that underprivileged city children would remain permanently in the city. The empty agricultural West into which he had hoped to transplant them was vanishing under his very eyes, and within only a few years of his death the Census Bureau was formally to abolish the frontier.[86] But his ideological convictions in favor of rural nurture were never completely surrendered. If he could not send his boys and girls away to spend their youth in country surroundings, they might still reap some of the intended benefits by taking a vacation in the countryside. Toward the end of his life, Brace accordingly agitated for such inspiring and healthy holidays for poor children in the city; and to

84. These testimonies were collected in an article on the centennial celebration of the founding of the New York Children's Aid Society, Gratia L. Snider, "Flood of Gratitude Hits Children's Aid Society," *Christian Science Monitor*, May 5, 1953, 3. Brace also has a lasting place, and a measure of fame, in the history of the development of American social work, cf., for example, Jean Charnley, *The Art of Child Placement* (Minneapolis, 1955), pp. 72, 74.

85. After thirty years of experience with "placing-out" in the New York Children's Aid Society, by 1884 that organization was dispatching only 3,500 children to new western homes each year. Hastings H. Hart, "Placing Out Children," p. 143.

86. Brace believed that the "Empty West" was an inexhaustible reservoir of space and opportunity for depressed city populations, a true safety valve, in Turner's sense, for the crowded cities. In this respect he once again proved himself to be an authentic carrier of the ideas of his time. Much of his lifework was built around Horace Greeley's slogan: "Go West, young man!" His views on this subject are most systematically expressed in his report of a journey to California and the far West at the end of the Civil War, Charles Loring Brace, *Our New West, or California in 1867–1868* (New York, 1869).

this very day, that side of his work and that aspect of his predisposition are still kept up in a lively fashion by Fresh Air Funds.[87]

In compiling records of his experience with slum children in the country, Brace scrupulously included statements from those of his young clients who opposed his views as well as those who throve under them. One of the best examples of the mordant wit of a slum boy evaluating the "country boy" stress has been preserved for us in an extemporaneous speech by an Irish street-boy who was mimicking Brace's pep-talk to emigrants before a crowd of his fellows:[88]

Boys, gintlemen, chummies: Praps you'd like to hear summit about the West, the great West, you know, where so many of our friends are settled and growin' up to be great men. . . . Do you want to be newsboys always, and shoeblacks, and timber merchants in a small way selling matches? If ye do you'll stay in New York, but if you don't you'll go out West, and begin to be farmers. . . .

You haven't any idear of what ye may be yet, if you will only take a bit of my advice. How do you know but honest, good, and industrious you may get so much up in the ranks that you won't call a gineral or judge your boss. . . .

Brace read no irony into these words; he took them as an awkward quizzical endorsement of his preachments. He was, indeed, so much a hostage to the legend of the country boy that he neatly parried reality with his zeal. The street-boy, he might have seen, was no displaced future farmer. He was, instead, an urban gamin, wise in the ways and dodges of surviving in the naked struggle to get along on nothing every day. He was disenchanted in self-protection, from bitter experience. If he was willing to go West it was because he had nothing to lose; a change of scene might change his luck, and the venture was taken on as a gambler's chance.

Often enough, as Brace's critics were not slow to point out to him, the experiment did not produce the expected transformation of an urchin into a contented plough-boy. But Brace indefatigably sought out the successful cases, rooted out the particular reasons for the failures but never seems to have summed them up in a generalized evaluation and criticism of his policy. Indeed, he went further than most panegyrists of

87. Charles Loring Brace, "Child Saving as Shown in Summer Homes and Sanatoria near Large Cities," *PNCCC*, 11 (1884), 150–158.
88. Brace, *Dangerous Classes*, p. 111.

country life in overlooking, as many of them did not, the vulnerability of the "bound boy's" position and the exploitation to which his helplessness exposed him.[89] Strictly speaking, Brace's boys were not "bound" to their new homes and could leave them if they were not satisfied. In practice this meant that the successfully placed-out were traceable and reportable, while the unsuccessful cases drifted out of sight and out of the tabulations. Superficially, therefore, the emigration scheme could appear to its sponsors to be working, while in fact, and except for a relatively few cases, it had failed.

For Brace, the country boy legend exhausted itself under the pressure of the practical details involved in his work of ministering to the ever-increasing swarms of needy children in New York City. His sympathies never abandoned it, but the changing character of his duties forced him to leave it behind as a sentimental souvenir, an episode, of his professional beginnings as a social worker.

VII. Horatio Alger:
The Legend Transformed

BY dint of a most inartistic coincidence, Horatio Alger was drawn into the orbit of Brace's social service empire to revise and reshape the country boy legend into a new form which would be compatible with the needs of a permanently urban age. In 1854 Brace had established a hotel for newsboys. Always on the lookout for industrious and not-yet-wholly-corrupted children who could be lured back to a life of useful work and rectitude, he had spotted newsboys as likely candidates for moral improvement.

It is typical of the man that he treated them as so many little entrepreneurs in a world of petty commerce and was, with mock solemnity,

89. The unhappy condition of the "bound boy" was the only blemish which the anonymous urban author of *Country Scenes* (Boston, 1850) could find in the sunny country culture he was eulogizing, cf. pp. 88–90. This source—one especially revealing of the urban bias for rurality—is characterized in detail in footnote 96 of this paper.

as businesslike and as matter-of-fact about his benevolence as these newsboys wished him to be. He was shrewd enough to realize that unguarded charity would be scorned by these proud and poverty-stricken boys. Brace therefore sold them beds for six cents a night and, in time, tried subtly to win them as permanent recruits to respectability.[90] Since Brace gave a fine bargain in shelter the house was soon full and the establishment enjoyed the steady patronage of the newsboys. A savings bank was begun for them, improving conversation and wholesome sociability was provided, and the newsboys discovered a taste for hymns. ("There's a Light in the Window for Thee, Brother," ranked as a prime favorite, but it contested for honors for first place with "There's a Rest for the Weary.")

This good work continued uninterrupted until the end of the Civil War, when New York was invaded by a rough crowd of former drummer boys who had seen service in the Union Army. These new clients wholly disrupted the ameliorative decorum of the lodging house with their barracks manners and brawls. The Superintendent, Mr. O'Conner, was routed by these juvenile veterans. These boys argued only with their fists and yielded only before superior prowess. O'Conner thereupon summoned Everett Jansen Wendell, a once famous Harvard athlete, to share command with him over his new charges. It was a wise choice.

Wendell made short work of rowdyism and insubordination. Although he was really a very gentle man and felt great sympathy and affection for the newsboys under him, he could put on a front of convincing ferocity. He took charge by arming himself with a barrel stave and bawling commands in a hearty bass voice in fine imitation of a sergeant-major. Rebellion melted in the Newsboys' Lodging House. The boys were commanded to bathe once a week, and they submitted tamely. Wendell organized classes and ordered them to attend; they went without a murmur. So great was his influence over these boys that he even commandeered their blood-and-thunder novelettes as unfit lit-

90. "The first thing to be aimed at in the plan was, to treat the lads as independent little dealers, and give them nothing without payment, but at the same time to offer them much more for their money than they could get elsewhere. Moral, educational, and religious influences were to come in afterward. Securing them through their interests, we had a permanent hold of them." Brace, *Dangerous Classes*, pp. 100–101.

erature, and they surrendered them. It was difficult, however, to replace these unworthy books, Wendell found, with others which the street boys would consent to read. The acceptable literature of the day, which Wendell would have liked to put in their hands, was too didactic and mawkish for this tough-minded audience. One day, while leafing through a juvenile magazine, *School and Schoolmate*, he came on an installment of *Ragged Dick*, Horatio Alger's first major novel, and knew he had found his man.

Wendell sought Alger out and introduced him to the Newsboys' Lodging House, inviting him to use that institution as a source of inspiration for his future books. Alger, who had all along been planning to write a series of novels on the same theme as *Ragged Dick*—the life of a street boy—felt he had stumbled upon an inexhaustible mine of material for his future novels. For the rest of his working life as a writer of children's books, the Lodging House was a second home to him. He befriended the boys, lived and played with them, and used them as a perfectly representative audience on which to test his stories. Wendell had been the author of an historic confrontation: he brought Alger face to face with his audience and his literary material.[91]

The fiction formula which Alger evolved out of this favorable opportunity was a version of the even then familiar success story—but with a new twist. Traditionally, these stories had been model biographies, lives with a lesson. Benjamin Franklin's exemplary life was a favorite, and the young reader was invited to read the hero's success backward in time, from the vantage point of his ultimate eminence. These were necessarily tame stories, generally without credible climax or conflict, their drama undermined by the fact that the outcome was repeatedly announced in advance. Few boys, especially those who were poorly circumstanced, could easily identify with a hero who, unlike themselves, seemed marked out by fate for glory. Neither could they be persuaded by the tacit admonitions in these stories to be patient and persevering, that success was inevitable if only a boy maintained virtuously high morale.[92]

91. The circumstances surrounding Alger's introduction to the Newsboys' Lodging House are described in Mayes, *A Biography*, pp. 99–102.

92. This type of success story was written over and over again by William Makepeace

The ordinary city boy, whether fresh from the country or a veteran of the slum, was easily sceptical of such fine promises. His life and his surroundings taught him to expect much less from life, and he countered with good-humored fatalism. Such a boy's tutelary deity was Lady Luck. If he had savings he invested them in a lottery ticket. If he lost, he forfeited a trifle, not enough, even if compounded many times over, to change his circumstances; if he won, he might get a sufficient grubstake to change his standards and his style of life. In these circumstances and by these standards, gambling rather than saving made sense.[93] Nor was it easy for such a boy to adopt, or believe in, middle-class precepts which urged a thrifty postponement of gratification, or in their companion philosophies which urged that abstinence built sound character. He often enough did without and discerned no improvement in either body or mind in consequence. Life was hard and he took his pleasure as it came, feast and famine by turns.[94] The future, as hope deferred, was too vague for him to grasp, too far away to be a matter of immediate concern.

Alger took his audience more fully into account than did his predecessors, and wrote a new kind of success story intended to enthrall the poor and friendless city boy. His stories dramatized the city as a place of infinite, unsuspected promise, and he wove the theme of random luck

---

Thayer, whose most successful juvenile biography was *How Benjamin Franklin, The Printer Boy, Made his Mark. An Example for Youth*, ed. var. Cf. Morrison Heady, *The Farmer Boy and How He Became Commander-in-Chief* (New York, 1863), a life of George Washington which was edited by Thayer as a sequel to his Franklin biography.

93. On the function of gambling and lotteries among street-boys cf. Brace, *Dangerous Classes*, pp. 100–102.

94. Alger recognized this tendency to immediate gratification among poor boys and commented on it quite soberly in his first important novel. "Another of Dick's faults was his extravagance. Being always wide-awake and ready for business, he earned enough to have supported him comfortably and respectably. There were not a few young clerks who employed Dick from time to time in professional capacity, who scarcely earned as much as he, greatly as their style and dress exceeded his. But Dick was careless of his earnings. Where they went he could hardly have told himself. However much he managed to earn during the day [as a bootblack], all was generally spent before morning. He was fond of going to the Old Bowery Theatre, and to Tony Pastor's and if he had any money left afterwards, he would invite some of his friends in somewhere to have an oyster stew; so it seldom happened that he commenced the day with a penny." Horatio Alger, *Ragged Dick; or, Street Life in New York with the Boot-Blacks* (Boston, 1868), p. 16.

into the fabric of his tales. Alger heroes might be picked troops in the battle for success, but they were ambushed by good fortune. And their good luck was enticingly delayed for long enough to make a really absorbing story.

The reader's attention was first engaged by an alluring description of the city in which Alger laid on, realistically and with elaborate detail, broad patches of local color. Indeed, Alger novels can be read as a guidebook to large sections of the New York City of his day. To be sure, it is the city that the slum boy knows: at one end, in Park Row, is the center of the world of slums and the culture of street-life; at the other is the empyrean of the Astor House, the opulent reaches of Fifth and Madison Avenue, the glory to which his fortunate heroes are ultimately translated. Between the two the city pulses with life: the streets are there, humming with traffic, spotted with landmarks, full of the noise and verve of hurrying people and traffic. An endless urban panorama, a continuous show and field of contrasts, unrolls for the reader. But this is not all.

The city has a fascinating seamy side as well. His readers are faithfully given the "inside dope" on the confidence men and their "bunco" games, which constituted the specifically urban hazard to which the new or the trusting city boy was likely to fall victim. And Alger's disquisition on how to avoid being fleeced as a "sucker" was as much fundamental guidance for his readers as were his careful budgets for new city boys, his lists of prices for their necessities, his sage advice on how to choose a meal or a boarding-house in New York. Each engrossing Alger story had a didactic, bread-and-butter side to it in which his readers were carefully taught the mechanics of living and working in a city.

Alger's heroes were poor, stranded boys adrift in the city; and he built a nice climax into his stories by realistically stressing how hard their plight really was. An Alger hero saves for the good of his soul, not because he has any realistic hope of accumulating capital. He is frugal both because he has to be and because he hopes—on undisclosed philosophic grounds—that his thriftiness will make him a better man. He works hard not because his labors are interesting or well-paid, but because he fears if he is idle he will starve, or become demoralized, perhaps even drift into crime. An Alger hero is heroic in only one respect: he displays a superb self-confidence that somehow, somewhere, he will succeed despite his inauspicious prospects.

Nor, indeed, does the Alger hero earn his success when, at last, it does come to him. It is not the fruit of hard-work, thrift, or high-minded moral attitudes. It is a freak as unearned as it is unanticipated. Typically, Alger arranges a rather painfully contrived *mise en scène* to snatch his hero from what seems his settled and lowly fate. The boy happens to capture a thief or to save a child from drowning, and by that noble deed finds a patron who gives him a job "with a future," makes him a protégé, and at once rewards him with a handsome gift of money to finance his first steps upward to fame and fortune.[95] If anything puzzled Alger's readers it surely must have been his strange insistence on the stern morality and austerity of his heroes. These highly vaunted attributes seemed beside the point of the story he was telling. But Alger, as a writer and a thinker, ventured only so far with innovations of the success story. Perhaps he hoped that he could edify his readers, in this indirect manner, into becoming better boys. In any case, the boys who read his books did not engage to chop logic with Alger; they delighted in them so much that his name is, even now, a by-word for the American success story. Some even think he invented it.

Alger's most ingenious, and from our standpoint most interesting, manipulations of the traditional country boy legend arose from his experiments in designing a stock hero for his stories. As a popular writer hoping to win and keep a large juvenile audience, he retained, as we shall see, the accumulated good will of the mock-bucolic country boy tradition but fused it with a novel, citified urbanity to create the Alger hero. These heroes were good boys, improved by their country beginnings as of old, but they were also competent and resourceful youths who could meet and cope with the challenge of the city.

Alger did not devise his standardized protagonist as a self-conscious propagandist trying to lure an audience to his message, but as a writer led by, as well as leading, the tastes of a fickle and exacting group of

95. I have treated the Alger version of the success story elsewhere and traced changes in it through to the present day, cf. R. Richard Wohl, "The 'Rags to Riches Story': An Episode of Secular Idealism," *Class, Status and Power,* eds. Reinhard Bendix and S. M. Lipsett (Glencoe, Illinois, 1953), pp. 388–395.

bookbuyers and readers. In his first efforts his conception of a hero proved too impoverished to sustain the staple melodrama of his stories. And since he was more concerned with the entertainment of his readers than with their education he had to ginger up the central figures in his stories so that they could bear the burden of new and different kinds of adventures in the culture of the cities.

From the very beginning of his writing career Alger seems to have sketched out the main outlines of his story formula: a boy's dramatic journey from country to town, his tribulations as a newcomer to the city, and finally his struggle for fame and fortune in his new home. At first he tried to adapt the existing country boy tradition to these new purposes, but with little success. The essence of the country boy tradition, especially in the form in which it was exploited by nostalgic city folk, was that the country boy was not mobile: he remained on the farm, was content at home, and did not aspire to any great measure of worldly success or a fancy style of life.[96] Alger, therefore, as he tried to work within this canon, had to find some way to dislodge this kind of country boy from the farm and send him on an urban quest.

In one of his earliest magazine pieces, a dialogue typically entitled *Seeking His Fortune*, Alger tried to reconcile his formula with a modifi-

---

96. A fair sample of how the country boy legend was manipulated by urban writers of the day can be found in the children's book *Country Scenes*, which was cited earlier in footnote 89 of this paper. The anonymous author of this volume prefaces his sketches with the observation that these are "every day scenes and characters to be met with in the rural districts of our widespread country. The city boys will learn from it many things which are new and interesting, and the country boys will recognize some of their old acquaintances among our country characters. . . ." *Country Scenes*, p. 3. At a later place (pages 33–34) the author characterizes the country boy with full fidelity to the traditional stereotype. "He works hard to assist his father upon the farm. You never find him yawning in bed after the sun is up, nor whining because he has nothing to do, nor wishing, when allowed to attend school in the winter, that there was no school, nor teasing the persons around him for something new. . . . Hard labour makes him strong and healthy. He does not fear the rain, the heat, or the frost. When the day is over, he enjoys play as well as other boys; but it is, like his work, manly and healthful. Perhaps to a child who has always lived in the city, the farm boy seems rude or vulgar. His disposition is frank and noble, and he finds pleasure in being useful." The whole of this book is in this vein: quite obviously written from the city man's standpoint and addressed, as the internal emphasis repeatedly shows, to urban readers. It is, in its own way, a model of the kind of literature which, throughout this essay, we have identified with the traditional country boy legend. Cf. Uncle Frank [Francis Woodward], *The Boy's and Girl's Country Book* (New York, 1852), chap ii, "The City Boy in the Country," pp. 15–35.

cation of the prevailing tradition and signally failed in the attempt.[97]
The plot of this brief story involves Deacon Elnathan Peters, a farmer;
Mrs. Almira Peters, his wife; and most especially, Jonathan Peters, their
son. The plot revolves, in typical Alger fashion, about Jonathan's decision to go to the city—Boston—to seek his fortune.

Unlike the country boy of legend, Jonathan is bored and dispirited by
life on the farm. "I aint goin' to stay here all my life, raisin' cabbages,
and hoin' taters," he announces to his parents one day. "I'm fit for
somethin' better." This declaration startles the napping Deacon Peters
awake, and the following revealing exchange takes place:

Jonathan:	I might as well tell you fust as last, Dad. I'm goin' to Bostown.
Mrs. Peters:	Massy sakes! Bostown's a hundred miles off. What you goin' there for?
Jonathan:	To make my fortin.
Deacon Peters:	'Taint so easy as you think for, Jonathan. You'd a plaguy sight better better stay round here and help me.

But Jonathan has no illusions about work on the farm or about the en-
nobling effect of country surroundings. He is tired of the monotonous
and hard work, and his ambition has been pricked by the snobbery of a
summer visitor.[98]

Jonathan:	I can't do nothin' here, dad. I have to work till I get all tuckered out, just to make a livin' and can't never wear nothin' better than overalls. Now, if I was in the city, I could wear store clothes all the time, like that are fellow that boarded up at the tavern last summer.
Mrs. Peters:	I'm afraid, Jonathan, you're gettin' proud. You ain't no call to be ashamed of wearin' overalls. They're what me and your father always wear.
	. . . .
Jonathan:	Can't help it marm. When that feller passed me in the field last summer, he turned up his nose at me, and I aint goin' to stand it. I'm as good as he is, any day.

97. Horatio Alger later reprinted this early effort in a book which, except for this one
dialogue, was made up entirely of his sister's stories. He was apparently using the commercial value of his name to sponsor his sister's efforts. In the preface he identifies his dialogue as an early magazine contribution adding that, as far as his sister's stories are concerned, his part in producing the book was "merely that of an editor." Horatio Alger
and O. Augusta Cheney, *Seeking His Fortune and Other Dialogues* (New York, 1882), pp.
11–26.

98. Alger and Cheney, *Seeking his Fortune*, p. 12.

When Jonathan's father continues to try to dissuade him from leaving the farm, the boy forces him to admit that his last trip to the big city was made thirty-one years before and that his judgment of Boston, therefore, is hopelessly out of date.

Mrs. Peters, however, still has an arrow in her quiver. "The city is a wicked place, Jonathan," she reminds her son. "Who knows but you'd get to drinkin' and swearin'." But Jonathan has no false views of the moralities of country life and beats down this argument, too. "I tasted some whiskey, the other day, down to Hiram Johnson's and it most turned my stummik. I shan't drink anything stronger than cider." This turn in the conversation reminds Jonathan's parents—and alerts the readers of this dialogue—that drunkenness is common in the country as well as in the city. The Deacon recalls that only the other day a cider-drinking neighbor became so exhilarated on this innocent beverage that he "smashed forty panes of glass in the meetin' house."[99]

Finally thrown back on her last reserves of argument, Jonathan's mother tries to convince him that he is unprepared to go off to live alone in the big city. He has no job and no plans. Jonathan is unimpressed. Unlike later Alger heroes he has a tidy inheritance in hand— two hundred and fifty dollars—that he plans to take along for investment and to live on until he finds work. His ambition is to get a comfortable job working behind the counter in a store. "Lazy business, Jonathan," his father murmurs deprecatingly. "That's what I like it for," his son replies candidly, "I've had hard work enough, and I want to take it easy awhile."[100]

Jonathan is so eager to find a soft berth that he falls easy prey to a glib confidence-man as soon as he arrives in Boston. He is easily convinced by this plausible swindler that if he invests only $225 he can be guaranteed an annual income of $2,000. Jonathan, who has come to the city prepared to be overtaken by just such financial miracles, parts with his money gladly.

He is soon disillusioned when the rightful owner of the business in which he has just "bought" a partnership returns and discloses the swindle to him. At this crisis, Jonathan shows neither reticence nor courage:

99. *Ibid.*, p. 14.
100. *Ibid.*, pp. 14–15.

he is furious and dismayed. But the good merchant takes pity on him, summons the police, who capture the swindler and restore Jonathan's money to him. This chastening experience dampens all of Jonathan's dreams of glory and easy money. And the boy who so confidently dreamed of spending two thousand a year now settles for a two-dollar a day grocery clerk's job which his mentor thoughtfully finds for him.[101] He then settles down in Boston, a self-conscious greenhorn, awaiting the gradual sophistication that will familiarize him with urban customs and city-bred caution.[102]

It is not difficult to see why Alger rapidly abandoned such a character as a candidate for the hero's role in his stories. Jonathan, the country boy, acted the fool in the city, and his clumsiness and ignorance were more farcical than tragic, and therefore completely undermined the reader's sympathy. Besides, in order to motivate Jonathan into mobility Alger was compelled to paint a rather devastating picture of country life in which rural people were portrayed as dull and crude, their lives stagnant and toilworn. Such a picture might be factually accurate but it clearly ran counter to the urban bucolic prejudice. And it was important to please urban parents who chose their youngsters' books and who might not patronize an author who did not pamper their preconceptions.[103]

Alger next experimented with making the city boy—or, more exactly, the streen urchin—into a hero. He was probably led to make this attempt by noticing the increasing popularity of journalistic accounts of slum children and their peculiar way of life which were creeping into

---

101. *Ibid.*, pp. 19–25.

102. Throughout this story Jonathan is portrayed as a clumsy country bumpkin with a ridiculous naiveté about city life. For example, he registers in a Boston hotel under the impression that the daily charge covers a week's board and lodging. The differences between town and country are patiently explained to him by his merchant friend. "Beanville [Jonathan's home town] and Boston are two different places," he is cautioned with great understatement, "and differ greatly in some important respects." *Ibid.*, p. 26. Because he does not anticipate these differences, Jonathan is transformed into a rather comic yokel toward the end of the dialogue.

103. On Alger's relations with his publishers, who guided him in finding his formula, see Mayes, *A Biography*, pp. 43–45. As we shall see later, Alger's portrayal of country life was just in both detail and tone. City folk, especially urban social workers, when they went into the countryside after 1900 were to be surprised and shocked to find real country boys talking about their lives and prospects in much the same way as Jonathan does in this dialogue.

the newspapers and magazines of his day. These writings were a sensational and sentimental kind of social anthropology practiced by newspaper reporters who made literary capital of discovering and describing subcultures in the slums. Since middle-class city dwellers had little actual knowledge of what went on in the slums, they read these accounts eagerly, enjoying vicariously, as it were, the pathos and scandal of low life.[104]

This new departure, enhanced by the inspiration Alger received from the inhabitants of the Newsboys' Lodging House, produced his first best-seller, *Ragged Dick*.[105] Despite the book's reassuring success, Alger did not find a model hero in the characters in this story. The personality of Ragged Dick, the street urchin, seems to have got out of control as he was writing the book. Dick turns out to be a delightful, authentic personality whose vitality and integrity shine out all the more brightly because the other personages in the story are so wooden and uninspired. Dick has no parents, no family, not even a fixed residence. He sleeps away the nights in boxes and in doorways like thousands of other homeless New York waifs. But poverty has not been able to break his spirit nor undermine his manliness.

He accepts his destitution cheerfully and feels no false shame about his condition. If he is taunted about it, he laughs good naturedly and joins in the fun. On the whole, despite his outcast condition, he is independent, resourceful, and quite a happy boy, all middle-class notions about his presumptive misery notwithstanding.

Thus one of Ragged Dick's rather tactless customers teases him about his shabby clothes and is firmly put in his place by gamin wit:

104. One of the finest examples of this kind of special reporting, one which illuminates the whole genre, is George C. Needham's, *Street Arabs and Gutter Snipes. The Pathetic and Humorous Side of Young Vagabond Life in the Great Cities, with Records of Work for Their Reclamation* (Boston, 1884). Needham's book after giving a careful description of the street-life of these children goes on to discuss—and to publicize—the emigration policy established by Brace, cf. esp. pp. 280–312. For an example of this kind of writing more nearly contemporary with Alger's earliest literary efforts, cf. Junius Henri Browne, *The Great Metropolis: A Mirror of New York* (New York, 1869), esp. "The Gamins," pp. 424–433.

105. Alger specifically acknowledged the help he had received from the patrons of the Newsboys' Lodging House in his introduction to *Ragged Dick*. Alger, *Ragged Dick*, pp. vii–viii.

"What tailor do you patronize?" asked the gentleman surveying Dick's attire.

"Would you like to go to the same one?" asked Dick shrewdly.

"Well, no; it strikes me that he doesn't give you a very good fit."

"This coat once belonged to General Washington," said Dick comically. "He wore it all through the Revolution, but got it torn some, 'cause he fit so hard. When he died he told his widder to give it to some smart young feller that hadn't got none of his own; so she gave it to me. But if you'd like it, sir, to remember General Washington by, I'll let you have it reasonable."

"Thank you, but I wouldn't want to deprive you of it. And did your pants come from General Washington, too?"

"No, they was a gift from Lewis Napoleon. Lewis had outgrown 'em and sent 'em to me—he's bigger than me, and that's why they don't fit."

"It seems you have distinguished friends. Now, I suppose, my lad, you would like your money."

"I shan't have any objection," said Dick.

"I believe," said the gentleman, examining his pocket-book, "I haven't got anything short of twenty-five cents. Have you any change?"

"Not a cent," said Dick. "All my money's invested in the Erie Railroad."

All this is rather superb panache from an urchin who has wakened only a little while ago from sleeping out-of-doors all night and who is hungry for his long-delayed breakfast.[106]

Despite his hard life and small means, Dick is a loyal and steadfast friend and he shares what little he has with his friends and, particularly, with his special friend, a smaller and weaker boy, Johnny Nolan. Just after he has finished with his first customer of the day, with whom he exchanged the pleasantries just mentioned, he meets Johnny hiding in an alley. Johnny is dodging the well-intentioned but unwanted benevolence of a social worker.[107]

"Has he gone," asked Johnny his voice betraying anxiety.

"Who gone, I'd like to know?"

"The man in the brown coat."

"What of him. You aint scared of him, are you?"

"Yes, he got me a place once."

. . . .

"What if he did?"

"I ran away."

"Didn't you like it?"

106. *Ibid.*, pp. 13–14.
107. *Ibid.*, pp. 23–24.

"No, I had to get up too early. It was on a farm, and I had to get up at five to take care of the cows. I like New York best."

. . . .

"Why didn't you stay?" [if you had good food and a good bed in the country.] "I felt lonely," said Johnny.

Dick understands this perfectly; like Johnny he is a city boy firmly committed to the city, and life on the farm—all comforts notwithstanding—has no attractions for him. Alger, by coming into intimate contact with street boys, had come to understand their point of view with a thoroughness and sympathy whose subtleties seem always to have eluded the well-intentioned determination of Brace, forever busy with the organization and direction of his welfare enterprises. Dick seems so well-adjusted to his substandard existence and able to cope with hardship so graciously that Alger is put to really desperate straits to motivate him in some way to ambition and social mobility. Dick has no great ambitions and no illusions about his future.[108]

Having run out of plausible incident to carry his story along, Alger invokes coincidence. Dick overhears a visiting country boy, Frank, tell his uncle, a Mr. Whitney, that he wishes he could see the sights of New York. His uncle regrets that he is too busy and promises Frank that on his next trip to the city he will escort him on a tour of New York. Dick, ragged and dirty as he is, volunteers to be Frank's guide, boasting that he knows New York well. Strangely enough, this offer is accepted and thereupon Dick is taken to Frank's hotel, where he is bidden to wash and where he is provided with one of Frank's suits so that he will be a seemly companion for the visitor. Both boys then set out on a tour of New York in which Dick explains life and work on Manhattan Island to Frank.

At large in the city, Dick is in his element and appears to know everything and everyone, and is always ready to explain to Frank what these

108. Later in the story, when Ragged Dick is escorting Frank Whitney, a visitor, around New York, they pause to admire the Fifth Avenue Hotel. Frank tells Dick that his uncle always stops there when he comes to New York. "I once slept on the outside of it," Dick observes. "They are very reasonable in their charges and told me that I might come again." "Perhaps some time you'll be able to sleep inside," Frank suggests hopefully. "I guess that'll be when Queen Victoria goes to the Five Points [a notorious New York slum] to live," Dick replies cheerfully. *Ibid.*, p. 72.

novel sights and sounds stand for.[109] But Dick is not only a walking guide-book, he is a skilled city dweller, too, and quickly initiates Frank into some of the hazards of city life. They have not gone far when they encounter a "bunco" man who tries to trick them. With effortless ease, Dick exposes the game, drives off the confidence man, and invites Frank to take up their perambulation. "You were too smart for him," Frank observes admiringly. "Yes," answers Dick rather matter-of-factly, "I aint knocked around the city streets all my life for nothin'."[110]

But Frank's role in this walk through the city is not a passive one. He cannot understand Dick's complacency with his mean estate and keeps preaching to him that he ought to strive to improve himself, that he ought to cultivate lofty ambitions. Throughout their walk he plies Dick with little success stories—and in this respect Alger's novel has a plot within a plot—hoping to fire the boot-black to emulation with choice examples of men who have risen from the ranks. Dick, however, accepts class differences and inequality of opportunity as a fact of life and does not rise to the bait.[111]

Frank then tells him the story of Dick Whittington and his cat, trying to prove that the lowliest can rise high: that in an earnest urchin lurks a potential Lord Mayor of London, or possibly an American millionaire. "That's a pretty good story," Dick admits, "but only a story after all. . . . I don't believe all the cats in New York will ever make me mayor."[112] Frank, however, does not abandon this tack. When he learns a little more about Dick's early life—he is an abandoned orphan—he tries to prompt his zeal with the tale of A. T. Stewart's rise from a poor teacher to a great department-store owner and millionaire. Dick, who is barely literate, sees no parallel to his own hard case. "He knowed enough to be a teacher, but I'm awful ignorant," he remarks.[113] At this point, on the level of practical policy, Frank breaks through Dick's reserve. He concretely offers to help Dick with his education. Dick has a

---

109. For a good example of Dick's tourist guide patter, cf. *ibid.*, pp. 61–71.

110. *Ibid.*, p. 83.

111. "Some boys," he tells Frank, "is born with a silver spoon in their mouth. Victoria's boys is born with a gold spoon, set with di'monds; but gold and silver was scarce when I was born, and mine was pewter." *Ibid.*, p. 67.

112. *Ibid.*, p. 69.

113. *Ibid.*, p. 90.

gamin's seasoned practicality, and this is the only suggestion Frank has made so far that seems to him he can turn to good purpose. He accepts the offer and then, in a fashion that is really out of character with the firm personality we have been shown so far by Alger, he becomes more and more committed to middle-class proprieties. He works hard, studies long, watches his diction and his manners, and achieves a standard of personal cleanliness which heretofore was unknown to him. But all along the reader entertains an uneasy suspicion that this is no permanent reform, that after the first flush of fervor, Dick will relapse into the happy-go-lucky, catch-as-catch-can existence he followed before he met Frank.

Alger, in what is probably the most painfully contrived *deus ex machina* in nineteenth-century American literature, settles this disturbing doubt for his readers once and for all. Dick, after more than nine months of hard work, decides to take a brief holiday to refresh himself for further effort, and with his friend Henry Fosdick, another industrious apprentice, he takes a ferry-boat ride. A gentleman with two children, a little boy and a little girl, are fellow passengers; as both these small children are playing near the railing the little boy loses his footing and falls screaming into the bay. Unhappily, the father cannot swim and there appears to be no one in sight to save his son.

"My child," he exclaims in anguish, "who will save my child? A thousand—ten thousand dollars to any one who will save him."[114] Dick leaps into the bay to save the child.[115]

When the little boy is safely restored to his father Dick's happy fate is sealed. "My brave boy," he is gratefully assured, "I owe you a debt I can never hope to repay. But for your timely service I should now be plunged into an anguish which I cannot think of without a shudder."[116] Mr. Rockwell, whose son has so narrowly escaped drowning, turns out

114. *Ibid.*, p. 283.
115. This is a necessary but embarrassing contretemps for Alger. He wishes to show Dick to be animated by high moral purpose, but he also needs to find some way to subsidize his permanent improvement and further ambition. He therefore explains that Dick "no sooner saw the boy fall than he resolved to rescue him. His determination was formed before he heard the liberal offer made by the boy's father. Indeed, I must do Dick justice to say that, in the excitement of the moment, he did not hear it at all, nor would it have stimulated the alacrity with which he sprang to the rescue of the little boy." *Ibid.*, p. 284.
116. *Ibid.*, p. 291.

to be a rich merchant, and he becomes Dick's sponsor in the struggle for success. He rewards him, outfits him with an even more dashing outfit than he has been able to afford so far, and gives him a fine job in his "counting-house" at ten dollars a week. Poverty, street-life, and the perils of destitution are now things of the past for our hero, and the novel ends as he adopts a new name: no longer Ragged Dick, but Richard Hunter, Esq. "A young gentleman on the way to fame and fortune," his friend Fosdick carefully explains in the book's last words.[117] The further adventures of Ragged Dick, a model boy, are continued in the sequel, *Fame and Fortune*.

The vein of narrative Alger had tapped in *Ragged Dick* was mined to fill out a whole series of books which bore the name of the first successful story. The Ragged Dick series was followed by another, the Luck and Pluck Series, which was a close imitation; then this particular format seemed to be played out. Alger was driven back to trying to utilize the country boy legend as inspiration for the further multiplication of his stories. *Bound to Rise* exemplifies his further efforts with the same old theme.

Harry Walton, the hero, is a country boy who has been reared on an impoverished New England farm. By the time he has come to adolescent years, the family farm is bankrupt, producing little more than a small garden crop and the milk required to feed the family. Then, catastrophe: the cow dies, and Hiram Walton, Harry's father, is forced into a hard bargain with the avaricious local squire in order to get a new one. Without a cow, the family and the farm both collapse completely. "Yes, I must have a cow," Mr. Walton explains to the squire. "My children live on bread and milk mostly. Then there's the butter and cheese, that I trade off at the store for groceries."[118] Under the pressure of this need, Mr. Walton contracts what is for him a heavy debt, uneasily aware that if he fails to repay principal and interest punctually the squire will foreclose on his farm.

Life on the farm and the conditions of country living again appear in a wholly unfavorable light in this story. Mr. Walton's dearest ambition

---

117. *Ibid.*, p. 296.
118. Horatio Alger, Jr., *Bound to Rise, or Up the Ladder* (New York, 1908), p. 11. I have used a reprint of this popular book. This novel appeared in numerous editions.

is to preserve his son from a farmer's life and to keep him in school long enough to be able to make some other career. The level of living on the Walton farm is desperately low. The Waltons are no happy yeomen; they live as poor peasants in a rural slum. When disaster overtakes the family, Harry, a good son, leaves home to try and earn enough to recoup the family's meager fortunes. And the further he gets away from the farm—he does not go very far cityward in this novel—the less and less he insists on his identity as a country boy. His first major stop on the way to the city is a New England industrial village where he adopts the classic occupation of the mobile New England farm boy who has left home: he becomes a shoe-pegger. And Alger allows his hero to adjust so perfectly to this trade that he has to invent a traveling magician who makes Harry a handsome offer to get him out of this little shoe-shop with its meager opportunities for getting ahead.

Harry takes to the road and keeps on traveling until he decides that the city is the place for him. His further career, after this long prefatory explanation, is carried on in a second volume, *Risen from the Ranks, or, Harry Walton's Success*. Harry, who in the later story is destined to become a successful and affluent printer, returns to the farm for only one purpose. He brings home the earnings of his *Wanderjahr* to pay off the squire, in high triumph, and to rescue the wreckage of the family farm.[119] The country, all legend notwithstanding, is as hard and unfeeling a place as the city, and the returns for hard work and high ambition there are trifling in comparison.[120]

Alger found the country and the qualities imputed to it so unpromising for his success melodramas that he progressively dropped it, except as a sort of ceremonial vestige, from his stories. The country is the place his heroes leave; it is the place in which, perhaps, the source of their virtue is found, but where they learn nothing that is vital for the main point of his tales: the struggle to succeed, to find fame and wealth in an urban setting. As a matter of fact, it is a tribute to the commitment of city folk to a vision of country life and nurture that Alger had to include

119. The last chapter of this novel is especially rewarding reading in the context of the issues raised in this paper. Cf. "Settled," Alger, *Bound to Rise*, pp. 157–162.

120. None of Mr. Walton's neighbors can or will help him in his trouble. And the squire is merciless. When Mr. Walton complains at the squire's sharp dealing he is told: "A contrack's a contrack. It's the only way to do business." *Ibid.*, p. 161.

this troublesome and—for his purposes—rather irrelevant element in his stories at all.

In the end, he simply begged the whole question of the acculturation of the country boy to the city scene. He assumed it, and sent his boys off from the farm or the rural village fully equipped, even before they left home, with all the necessary attributes to get along in the city. In this way he avoided the problem, which had plagued him for so long, of writing a long preliminary background story—usually a whole volume—in order to get his central figure into the city and into what he considered the important story of social mobility.

In his later works and after the attenuation of the country boy story in dozens of Alger's own novels, the issue of adjusting to city life is no longer raised. As if by instinct, the hero knows how to get along in town: the country boy has subtly and completely been transformed into the city boy *par excellence*; although, with a bow to the past, Alger is careful to mention his rural origins and country nurture.

In his later novels, Alger's heroes have lost nearly every trace of rusticity, even on their first arrival in the city. Thus in *The Store Boy*, the hero, Ben Barclay, enters New York trained to a fine hair to pick up social distinctions and is already prepared with an initial urbanity to cope with any urban adventures he might have. In the first hour of his arrival in New York he manages not only to foil a pickpocket (always a sign of urban sophistication in an Alger novel), but he also manages coolly and shrewdly to appraise city people with a carefully calculating eye. "Ben regarded his fellow passengers with interest," we are told.

In Pentonville he seldom saw a new face. Here all were new. Our hero was, though he did not know it, an embryo student of human nature. He liked to observe men and women of different classes and speculate upon their probable position and traits.[121]

Ben Barclay, therefore, is no longer a "hick," he comes to the city fully prepared for his main business, which is to succeed and to lay the foundations of a comfortable fortune. He does not dally gawking at the sights; he is polite and polished, eager and ready, single-mindedly concerned with getting ahead and with nothing else. Not many pages after his first introduction to New York, he calmly undertakes, despite his

121. Horatio Alger, Jr., *The Store Boy* (Philadelphia, 1887), p. 83.

youth, to become the agent for a wealthy lady in disposing of a farm. When he investigates and finds that there is oil on the land, he maneuvers a cheating speculator out of the way and disposes of the land to a corporation at a handsome profit, like any bright young modern executive. Ben Barclay, as Alger's final version of the hero figure he sought for so long, is a young, budding entrepreneur and as urbane as any city boy could be, despite his country beginnings.

In transforming the legend of the country boy, as I already have had occasion to say, Alger was no ideological iconoclast. He was merely translating into the rhetoric of boys' books the obvious fact that the cities were filling up and that the sentimentalization of the country boy was a false panegyric. The legend tried anachronistically to circumvent the tensions created by the physical hardships, the race for success, and the relative impersonality of city life, by creating an imaginary Arcadia, where a rural idyll produced a perfectly harmonious and completely rewarding childhood free from all that was troubling and unsettled in the city.

On the positive side, Alger was directly instructive and suggestive to city boys and to country boys who yearned to come to the city. He taught them, sometimes clumsily but always within an exciting melodramatic context, a sensitivity to status differences, the moral urgency of striving for success, and the proper decencies of desiring and competing for an ample material standard of living. In his own way he provided an ideological solution for the problems which vexed new city boys. He gave them, so to speak, high hopes and visible inspiration in a time when they might be tempted to complacency and possibly to despair. In doing so, he glorified the city and continually stressed its opportunities for glamour and gratification. New York, for example, might be a dangerous place even in Alger's stories, but it was a wonderful and exciting city, too, full of hope and reward for the deserving.

VIII. The Myth in Eclipse

B Y the end of the nineteenth century and in the first decades of the
twentieth, the country boy legend passed into the hands of its
critics.[122] The reasons for this new assessment are not far to seek. The
legend had become clumsy, and even its adherents found it difficult to
use to channel the feeling and enthusiasm of city people. Brace surrendered it reluctantly because it interfered with the progress of his social
service work, Alger found it an embarrassing bit of ideological baggage
which unnecessarily complicated his stories. Their reactions are portents
of the more general malaise which overtook this tradition.

The chief difficulty with the legend was that its very success had served
to screen it from the crucial realities of rural as well as urban life. The
growth of cities could not be turned back by determined social work,
nor could the model country boy function in his new environment with
the competence that the developing ideals of city life demanded. Most
grievous of all for the tradition, was the fact that city life and the increase
of city numbers were firmly established as fixed trends by the end of the
century. The incompatibilities of fact and feeling that the legend
prompted by insisting on a vanished past were increasingly onerous
even to willing believers.

In the earlier years of the nineteenth century the country boy legend
was honestly believed by some city people, like Brace, to be a fair description of life in the countryside. For such spokesmen, what I have
called the legend was, at its rosiest, merely an enthusiastic but fair picture of how they imagined rural people lived and reared their children.
If that picture was touched up here and there, it was only in the interest
of pointing a devastating contrast to the miseries of urban life. Furthermore, enthusiastic exponents of the legend, like A. D. Mayo, whom I
cited earlier, were convinced that cities were somehow anomalous in
the United States, and represented a break with a national tradition tied
to the land and agrarian values. This break, many hoped—how literally

122. For a very judicious summary of the re-evaluation of agrarian life and ideals during this period cf. Richard Hofstadter, *The Age of Reform* (New York, 1955), esp. "The
Agrarian Myth and Commercial Reality," pp. 23–59.

we may judge from Brace's work—might be repaired by timely policies and a rebirth of agrarian fervor. And since the development of the country boy legend in this latter phase was in the hands of city folk—writers, preachers, and social service workers—their practical experience was never able to disabuse them of the fact that their assumptions about the realities of country life were becoming more and more unfounded in the years after the Civil War. The happy yeoman, like the model country boy, existed more and more in their imaginations and in their affections, not on the farms and in the villages of the agricultural hinterland.[123]

This discrepancy offered purchase for a debunking attack, and journalists were not slow in capitalizing on the opportunity to contrast fact with fiction. At its gentlest, this criticism confined itself to pointing out that the country boy of legend was no longer representative of contemporary rural youth, that the traditional country boy has vanished in the reorganization of the nation's economy and in the transformation of American agriculture itself. "The old sort of country boy," a leading periodical editorialized as late as 1911,

went out just before the Civil War, that is about 1850. There were some genuine specimens that went into the army, and they did good fighting. They were a simple-

123. It is difficult now to mark out just how difficult it was for city people to grasp the magnitude of the social and cultural changes which were involved in the growth of American cities. By 1871, even in such a thoughtful, indeed determinedly high-brow, journal as the *North American Review* a comparison between country and city was still restricted to the description of a few gross and rather obvious differences, their implications barely explored. "The city differs from the country in these, among other respects: 1st. Fewer of its people own real estate. 2d. A great proportion of them live in crowded tenements, which is not the case in the country of course. 3d. A far greater proportion of them live from hand to mouth, and lay by little or nothing. 4th. The distinctions between wealth and poverty are far more marked in the city than in the country; and 5th. The relations between the wealthy and the poor or humble citizens are less intimate . . . . In New York the public schools form now almost the only common meeting-ground for the rich and poor . . . ." Charles Nordhoff, "The Misgovernment of New York—A Remedy Suggested," *North American Review*, 113 (1871), 323. The tendency of urban people to sentimentalize country life and a rural childhood did not escape the notice of clear-eyed observers of the rural scene. "Persons in middle life," Dean L. H. Bailey of the Cornell University Agricultural College pointed out, "who are now deeply immersed in affairs are too far away from the farm to be trusted to give an account of the methods which guided them in their youthful choice [to leave the farm]; I have usually found that such persons are likely to unconsciously color their replies by the experience of later years. . . . I have, therefore, chosen to inquire of students why they leave the farm, if at all, with a definite purpose, and they are still near the point of departure." Henry Israel, "Why Do Boys Leave the Farm?" *Rural Manhood*, 1 (October, 1910), 18.

hearted lot, but loved their country home, and didn't care to be millionaires. A home in the country at that time took in everything that could be conceived of as desirable; but the factories were already whistling very loudly to attract the boys and girls town-ward.[124]

But many of the debunkers were more scathing. They systematically examined all the doctrines and images that had gone into the making of the legend and exposed them as complacent fictions which ignored the realities of country life. One of these critics, John M. Welding, was per-haps the most thoroughgoing. He began by stating the main outlines of the legend, and then turned to attack one of its main assertions—that the country produces more "great men" than the city—as a statistical fal-lacy.

Some years ago, an article published—if I remember rightly in the *Youth's Companion* —was extensively copied and circulated by the press of the country. The writer had sent one hundred postal cards to as many men prominent in politics, education, litera-ture, commerce, arts and sciences. Upon these cards were printed inquiries as to the place of birth and circumstances of boyhood. The answers showed that but ten per cent of these leading men had been born and reared in large cities, while the other ninety per cent had come either from the country, or from *towns of less than five thou-sand inhabitants.*[125]

Such data, Welding points out rather contemptuously, have been used to buttress the legend, but the significance claimed for them disappears under close examination. The article being quoted was published in 1882, and its author stated that his respondents were, for the most part, over sixty at the time of writing. This meant, Welding points out, that in 1830—to choose a conservative date for their childhood years—they represented a population in which only one person in thirty-two lived in a city of five thousand inhabitants or more. And Welding is insistent —the Census Bureau notwithstanding—that a place with five thousand or more inhabitants is a *city*. Even as late as 1880, only two years before the article was written, the urban population of the country amounted to only eighteen per cent of the whole.

Now, what else do these figures show but a complete victory of the much traduced city-bred boys, who, starting in the race numbering less than three per cent of the con-

124. "The New Country Boy," *The Independent*, 70 (June 22, 1911), 1382.
125. John M. Welding, "The Country Boy versus Town Boy," *Social Economist*, 3 (1892), 15–16. (Italics in original.)

testants, came out in the end with ten per cent of the prizes! And then, we may inquire, why should boys belonging to towns of *less than five thousand inhabitants* be ranked with the country boys?

If anything, he concludes, his conservative recalculation underestimates the city boy's superiority in achieving success.

As a matter of fact, he argues, there has been an ideological overstress on rural social origins which tends falsely to claim as country boys men who owe their eminence to urban advantages and opportunities. "Henry Clay, for instance," he observes, "acquired his title as 'Mill-boy of the Slashes' before he was nine years of age. The really formative period of his life was the time from that early age to manhood spent in Richmond, Va."[126] And he then goes on to sharpen his argument by calling the roll of city boys—pure and simple—who have made good but whose urban origins are not singled for approving recollection: Franklin, Sumner, Poe, Parkman, Emerson, John Jay, Washington Irving, and so on, for a solid page of names to form a remarkable roster of American notables.

From this vantage point, Welding's argument continues until every article of faith in praise of the legendary country boy is taken up and demolished. The countryside, he points out, contains tenants as well as owners, and the lot of these tenants is often as hard and as stultifying as that of any underprivileged urban proletarian. All pretensions to the contrary, farming areas are not made up only of solid, prosperous yeomen.[127] But leaving this important qualification aside, what of those who own their acres and live independent lives?

The whole basis of country life, in Welding's eyes, is built on the subordination of the farm family to the land it owns and works; this onerous tie is strengthened by a generally avid land hunger which eats up savings and opportunities for ease and culture, in order to get more land to work and worry over.

And though he owns hundreds of acres, lives in a brick house and has a fine equipage, the farmer and his family are about as poor in their secret family life as most of his

126. *Ibid.*, p. 17.
127. *Ibid.*, p. 98. "The wretched tenant," Welding remarks, "is kept so poor he has no chance to 'go to the city.'" And the tenant's loyalty to the soil, often claimed for him in rural panegyrics, is nothing more than an inability to leave it.

tenants. He will labor and scrimp and save to buy another piece of land; labor and scrimp and save to pay for one recently purchased, and sell the best of the farm produce and live upon the refuse.

Work is the rule of the farmer's life, but work in which he spends himself and his family in a fierce obsession with a material greed for property.

These are the maxims of economy among the great mass of farmers. The farmer is a slave, and his wife (alas for the farmer's wife) is the slave of a slave . . . Now, harp all you will about the pure air and free sunshine of the country life, but account, if you can, for the generally stunted physical and mental growth of country children.[128]

Not least disadvantaged in the farmer's family and in the family's total mobilization for farm work, was the country boy himself. His education, already handicapped by poorer rural resources in schools and teachers, was further undermined by competition with his chores.[129] Instead of having greater stamina than the city boy, the reverse was likely to be the case, and experience had shown that the country boy did not stand up to physical strain and hardship as well as the city boy does. Welding quotes with great relish General Sherman's verdict on the soldiers who made the grueling march through the South with him to the effect that "city soldiers far excelled those from the country in enduring the hardships of the march, the privations of the siege, and the assaults of diseases."[130] The country boy was not only overworked and likely to be at his labors in all weathers, but his family life had certain peculiar stressful aspects. A country boy's father was usually loath to acknowledge the maturity, independence, and judgment of his son. He tried, as long as possible and often by means of uncloaked domination, to keep his son under his full control. This, naturally, produced resentment on both sides and, frequently, the boy fled the family farm in order to testify to his independence and to devise a life in which his own choices and judgments would prevail. Even those observers who were

128. *Ibid.*, p. 99.

129. *Ibid.*, pp. 101–102. One of the tenets of the country boy legend was that limited educational opportunity contributed to the physical healthiness of the country boy. Welding points out, in another place (*ibid.*, p. 11) that "the short school terms of the country at once afford the youth opportunity to develop his physical powers by labor, and this, in its turn, gives him a zest for study." Such at least was the conventional claim.

130. *Ibid.*, p. 100.

friendliest to the traditional claims of the moral superiority of the country boy, confessed that this was an abiding fault in farm families.[131] One journal which was trying to promote a "back to the farm" movement and consistently touted the virtues of the country boy, printed a bitter poem stressing this very point.[132]

> Why did you leave the farm, my lad?
> Why did you bolt and leave your dad?
> Why did you beat it off to town
> And turn your poor old father down?
>
> . . . . . .
>
> We're all agreed the farm's the place,
> So free your mind and state your case.
> Well, stranger, since you've been so frank
> I'll roll aside the hazy bank
> The misty cloud of theories,
> And tell you where the trouble lies.
> I left my dad, his farm, his plow,
> Because my calf became his cow.
> I left my dad—'twas wrong, of course—
> Because my colt became his horse.
> I left my dad to sow and reap
> Because my lamb became his sheep.
>
> . . . .
>
> It is not the smoke in the atmosphere,
> Nor the taste for life that brought me here.
> Please tell the platform, pulpit, press,
> No fear of toil or love of dress
> Is driving off the farmer lads,
> But just the methods of their dads.

Quite aside from the struggle to declare his personal independence of parental authority, the daily facts of the country boy's life were, in fact, anything but inspiring. His work was as routine as it was demanding, his perspective on the world limited and drab; even his diet was dull and

131. "Father, generally speaking, is slow to recognize the fact that his sons have grown to man's stature and have brains of their own. He still wants to do their thinking for them, although he is glad of their help with the rough work. The boy wants to get away from the everlasting sameness of things he has known and done always. He wants to try out his own brain and body and find out if he can fend for himself." Philip L. Barker, "Shall Farm Boys Find Fortune in the City?" *Rural Manhood*, 6 (May, 1915), 214.

132. "Why Boys Leave the Farm," *Rural Manhood*, 2 (January, 1920), 2.

poorly cooked.[133] As nearly as Welding could detect, this kind of life bred neither nobility nor enterprise in the boy who remained in it, and if a country boy was venturesome at all he signalized this trait by leaving the farm and going off to the city. As a matter of fact, Welding thought that, in his time, drafts were being made on the city to contribute both pluck and imagination to the agricultural community. "The mines and homestead claims of the West," he remarked, "tell the tale of the pluck and enterprise of town-bred boys. Some of the great wheat farms of Dakota and cattle ranches of Montana are owned and operated by men born in the cities and educated in the public schools."[134]

133. One of the favorite fantasies of urban people about rural life was to imagine that country food was especially opulent and sumptuous, that the farmer subsisted off his choicest crops, and that farm cookery was traditionally excellent. Welding, who seems to have had considerable experience with the ordinary varieties of country fare, is especially bitter on this point. "Greasy biscuit, fat pork swimming in gravy, and the everlasting pie are the main items of the farmer's bill of fare. Strange as it may seem, it is a fact that there is a greater variety of viands on the mechanic's table than on that of the farmer. The writer has spent months in farmhouses where fresh beef or mutton is almost an utter stranger . . . Chickens are eaten only for the regalement of company, or when the market for poultry is low . . . The mechanic or merchant can enjoy all the luxuries of garden, orchard, and dairy at moderate cost, the year round. His wife cooks only for her own family, and usually possesses a fair share of culinary skill." Welding, "The Country Boy," pp. 99–100.

134. Ibid., pp. 17–18. One of the most persistent claims of the legend is that country boys, by reason of the seasoning of farm life, are especially favored in becoming business leaders. This claim has been so insistent that it still occupies a large share of the attention of scholars who are investigating the social origins of successful business men. William Miller, who studied the careers of the country's senior business leaders between 1900 and 1910, points out that "poor immigrant and poor farm boys make up no more than 3 per cent of the business leaders who are the subject of this essay. . . . More likely, poor immigrant boys and poor farm boys who became business leaders have always been more conspicuous in American history books than in the American business elite." "American Historians and the Business Elite," Journal of Economic History, 8 (1948), 199, 208. In 1928, F. W. Taussig and C. S. Joslyn, in their study American Business Leaders (New York, 1932), commented on "the surprisingly poor showing of the farmer class in respect to productivity of business leaders. Its position in this respect is lower than that of any other class, save only that of unskilled and semi-skilled labor." In 1955, W. Lloyd Warner and James Abegglen published a replication of the Taussig and Joslyn study which confirmed these findings. "There are fewer social differences between rural and urban populations as a result of this much greater social interaction [between town and country]. It was therefore to be expected that these forces would have worked to increase the participation of the sons of farmers in vertical social mobility in American business and industry. This is not the case. The low level of representation of farmers' sons in 1928 business leadership continues in 1952. . . . Technological and demographic revolutions have not changed the fact that the farmer's son has very limited access to mobility into the business elite." Occupational Mobility in American Business and Industry (Minneapolis, 1955), p. 50.

Welding's critical observations were fierce and polemical but they were not atypical of the reporting of rural life as the nineteenth century wore on. Observers who were far less aggrieved at the country boy legend than he reluctantly admitted the truth of his statements and tried, rather ruefully, to moderate them with nostalgia for the tradition.[135] The cumulative effect of this debate was a gradual and perhaps rather grudging admission that a fundamental change had overtaken both American agriculture and American society, and that the claims which had been made for the country boy as exemplar of an ideal of American character no longer referred to a believable reality.

The half century between 1850 and 1900 produced several city-bred generations who had come to maturity in the full tide of rapid urban growth. They had no memories, harsh or sentimental, of life on the farm, nor did the surging expansion of the cities startle them. The world they had been born into was one in which urban populations swelled rapidly, real estate was always booming, and the complexities of a new technology and an increasing economic interdependence between town and country were usual. These new generations were increasingly confident, too, that the city offered a manageable and rewarding way of life. And it was from these completely urban generations that a counter-statement to the agrarian tradition issued. These new views by these new men were crystallized in such manifestoes as Frederic C. Howe's *The City, The Hope of Democracy*,[136] in which the title itself was a fighting summary of the position being taken.

Howe proudly proclaimed the city the great social innovation of the modern age. "The modern city marks an epoch in our civilization," he announced,

135. Welding wrote three articles altogether, of which only portions have been mentioned and discussed here. Since his criticism was the most systematic, all three articles are worth reading to discern the critical temper of late nineteenth-century writing on the subject of the legend, *ibid.*, pp. 11–22; 98–107; 179–184. For writings friendlier to the tradition but reaching substantially the same conclusions as Welding, see T. N. Carver, "Why Young Men Leave the Country for the City," *Rural Manhood*, 1 (October, 1910), 3; T. N. Carver, "An Appreciation of Country People," *ibid.*, 7–10; Henry Israel, *Rural Manhood*, 1 (October, 1910), 18–20; L. K. Hall, "The Rural Boy," *Rural Manhood*, 10 (May, 1919), 203; John M. Gillette, "The Drift to the City in Relation to the Rural Problem," *Rural Manhood*, 2 (March, 1911), 18–82; Guy D. Gold, "The Psychology of the Country Boy," *Rural Manhood*, 2 (April, 1911), 107–109; "What is a Rural Community?" *Rural Manhood*, 10 (February, 1919), 56–58.

136. New York, 1905.

through it, a new society has been created. Life in all its relations has been altered. A new civilization has been born, a civilization whose identity with the past is one of historical continuity.[137]

The new city, in his view, was connected with what had preceded it only in time, not in temper or in tone. In these latter respects it was a critical discontinuity, not only with the American past but with the fundamental social organization—the rural based past—of Western civilization. The modern city

marks a revolution—a revolution in industry, politics, society, and life itself. Its coming has destroyed a rural society, whose making has occupied mankind since the fall of Rome . . . man has entered an urban age.

This new pride in the city was taken seriously enough—although Howe is cited here only to exemplify an increasingly articulate urban viewpoint—to be made part of the frame of reference for a large-scale reassessment of the quality of rural life and work.

In the early months of 1909, little more than three years after Howe's book appeared, the Report of the Commission on Country Life was presented to Congress by President Theodore Roosevelt.[138] The findings of this Commission confirmed many of the criticisms of country life that had been made by previous observers, adding to them only by the wider coverage of the study, which was more comprehensive than any preceding inquiry. American agriculture, and its supporting communities, were described as being in dire straits with little or none of the special cultural vitality that had been imputed to them by such doctrines as the country boy legend. In particular, the report highlighted the diminishing esteem in which country life was held in the United States. "It would be idle to assert," President Roosevelt said bluntly,

that life on the farm occupies as good a position in dignity, desirability, and business results as the farmers might easily give it if they chose. One of the chief difficulties is the failure of country life, as it exists at present, to satisfy the higher social and intellectual aspirations of country people. Whether the constant draining away of the best elements in the rural population into the towns is due chiefly to this cause or to the su-

137. *Ibid.*, p. 9.
138. This document was published as "The Report of the Country Life Commission," *Senate Report*, 60 Cong., 2 Sess., no. 705 (1909). Subsequent citations of President Roosevelt's Special Message which accompanied the report are from pp. 3–9 of this publication.

perior business opportunities of city life may be open to question. But no one at all familiar with farm life throughout the United States can fail to recognize the necessity for building up the life of the farm upon its social as well as upon its productive side.[139]

What was particularly striking about this report, written as it was by experts on the nation's agricultural community, was the indirect endorsement of the primacy of city life and urban culture in the country. "It is true that country life has improved greatly," the President admitted, "in attractiveness, health, and comfort, and that the farmer's earnings are higher than they were. But city life is advancing even more rapidly, because of the greater attention which is being given by citizens of the towns to their own betterment. . . . The Commission has tried to help farmers to see their own problem and to see it whole . . . and it wishes to bring not only the farmers but the Nation as a whole to realize that the growing of crops, though an essential part, is only a part of country life. . . . it is no less essential that the farmer shall get an adequate return for what he grows, and it is no less essential—indeed it is literally vital—that he and his wife and his children shall lead the right kind of life."[140]

This acknowledgment of urban values and the increasing cultural reciprocities between town and country was not, however, wholly unqualified. "I warn my countrymen," the Presidential message continued,

that the great recent progress made in city life is not a full measure of our civilization; for our civilization rests at bottom on the wholesomeness, the attractiveness, and the completeness, as well as the prosperity, of life in the country. The men and women on the farms stand for what is fundamentally best and most needed in our American life.[141]

Nor was this injunction simply the prudent caveat of a politician anxious to retain the loyalty and the votes of rural constituents. The legend of the country boy and the tradition of the special moral excellence of country life was still lively and defended, most strongly perhaps, by urban people. The Country Life Commission Report produced a brisk debate in the urban press on the needs and prospects of country life and,

139. *Ibid.*, p. 5.
140. *Ibid.*, p. 57.
141. *Ibid.*, p. 9.

in addition, added fresh enthusiasm for a special crusade by urban social workers to penetrate the countryside and to rescue and reinvigorate the country boy.[142]

The Young Men's Christian Association, which now began earnestly its own "county" work, had participated in the investigations which produced the Report of the Country Life Commission.[143] The findings of that report pointedly stressed the need for the rehabilitation of country life, a task in which such an organization as the YMCA might achieve in the country the kind of brilliant results already produced by its efforts in the city. The YMCA, so far, had been an unmistakably urban organization, operating with greatest success in the larger cities. Rural work, on the scale on which it now embarked, was a new departure for the organization, and one in which it was hoped that urban models and methods might be adapted to rural needs and conditions.[144] To this newly developing work the organization brought characteristic determination, and by 1920 had at its disposal more than two hundred local organizations to carry out its programs. In judging the outcome of these efforts, therefore, it cannot be held against them that they lacked energy or resources or that serious and sustained attempts were not made to achieve success. But the program failed, and its failure, in great part, was due to the fact that its urban leadership, bred in the tradition of the city man's view of country life, could not penetrate or decisively in-

142. For specimen discussions of the Report with special reference to the country boy cf. "What the Country Life Commission Had to Say Regarding Personal Ideals and Local Leadership," *Rural Manhood*, 1 (August, 1910), 17–18; Henry Wallace, "Country Life Commission," *Rural Manhood*, 1 (January, 1910), 5–6. Cf. "The Country Life Commission," *The Outlook*, 95 (July 23, 1910), 601–602 and Theodore Roosevelt, "Rural Life," *The Outlook*, 95 (August 27, 1910), 919–922.

143. Owen Earle Pence, *The Y.M.C.A. and Social Need, a Study of Institutional Adaptation* (New York, 1939), p. 116.

144. Although by 1900, YMCA Associations had been organized in most cities with over 25,000 in population, "Similar growth did not typically take place in much more numerous smaller communities. There were Associations in about one-half of the cities of 10,000 to 25,000; one-fourth of those 5,000 to 10,000; one-eighth of those under 5,000. But the cities listed by the 1900 census then included only 40.0 per cent of the population; only 8.3 per cent of the people lived in the 8,930 incorporated villages under 2,500; and 51.7 per cent still lived in smaller unincorporated villages or in the open country. Despite some promising beginnings, it was still problematic in 1900 how far the Y.M.C.A. could adapt itself to the rural field. It had become established in the city environment, and correlated with the complexity of life there." *Ibid.*, p. 53.

fluence the realities of country life in America at the turn of the twentieth century. This verdict was reached reluctantly but inevitably; and the rural work of the YMCA is particularly germane to our present study because its emphasis was on assisting and influencing the country boy.[145] Its relative failure, in effect, represents the tradition's last stand as a basis for policy and organized action; thereafter the legend was no longer to be treated as a description of reality but as an organization of sentiments.

The work of the YMCA in the nation's rural areas produced many beneficial results, not the least of which was to bring some urban amenities into the countryside and to advertise widely the merits of many others.[146] Altogether, its work—and especially its programs of organized sociability—served to awaken and reinforce new interests and aspirations in the country. The irony of these very successes, however, was that they served to bring the thought and tone of city life into country communities, rather than to enliven latent, or quiescent, tendencies in rural life itself to greater vitality. From the first, YMCA workers were caught up in a puzzling question: what is a rural community and how can we best serve it?[147] The answer more often than not—and in conformity with the suggestive findings of the Country Life Commission Report—was to try to narrow the gap in style of life between town and country. Country life and country boyhood, which tradition

145. "Yet in its efforts to work realistically toward a solution of the rural problem," Pence concludes, "[urban] institutional patterns dominated in organization and method. Its leaders were not adequately trained to meet the technical problems of an unhealthy rural culture." *Ibid.*, pp. 116–117. Part of the inadequacy of this leadership, as we shall see, and perhaps not the smallest part, lay in their conception of what was problematical in the rejuvenation of country life, a conception which was rooted in traditional agrarian idealisms despite the instructive findings and data contained in the Country Life Commission Report.

146. In this connection, see the arguments for the founding of free libraries in rural areas. M. S. Dudgeon, "The Rural Book Hunger," *Rural Manhood*, 6 (September, 1915), 303–307.

147. This tendency to try and amalgamate town and country, and tacitly to blur rural-urban distinctions, may be discerned in an operating definition of community which was ultimately offered to guide YMCA county workers. "It is recommended," they were advised, "that the term 'community' when construed in a technical sense with reference to farm populations, be employed to designate *the population group which is formed by a village or small city, together with all the farm families making this village or city their regular business center.*" "What is a Rural Community?" *Rural Manhood*, 10 (February, 1919), 56. (Italics added.)

argued had intrinsic merit, were defined, over the years, as an as yet undetermined reciprocity between the country and the city.[148]

The ambiguities of the rural community and rural culture were not the only ones which divided thinking on how to dispose of the country boy. One of the main considerations which affected YMCA policy was a rather undecided outlook on the means of coping with the drift of young people from town to country. Here, too, contradictory inclinations were in evidence. Thomas Nixon Carver, who was to achieve his greatest fame as a professor of economics at Harvard, pointed out that sentiment alone could not anchor the farm boy to the soil. It should be understood, he warned, that while "the cry 'back to the farm' may possibly check the migration from country to city, it will not be able to stop it completely. We must expect, as far in the future as anyone is able to see, that the stream of migrating youths will continue to set cityward."[149] Yet, while Professor Carver was willing to admit the economic realities which were reducing labor requirements in agriculture, another side of his mind clung fast to the legendary sublimities of a life of active husbandry. "There are, of course, greater opportunities for excitement and amusement which the city affords;" he conceded reluctantly, "but this can only appeal to more or less depraved human nature, and is a most discouraging feature of the whole problem."[150]

Depraved or not in their inclinations, the city lured country boys with its glamour as well as its cash, and YMCA workers were as anxious

148. It is interesting to observe that the term "rural sociology" now begins to creep into the social work literature dealing with such problems as these, and is being defined to express the ambiguity stressed above. "It is recommended that cooperative research in rural sociology be directed primarily to the social problems of farm populations. This limitation, however, is not to be construed as shutting out treatment of the relations of farm populations either to village populations or to city populations." *Ibid.*, p. 56.

149. T. N. Carver, "Why Young Men Leave the Country for the City," *Rural Manhood*, p. 3.

150. *Ibid.*, p. 3. In another article, in the same vein ("An Appreciation of Rural People," *Rural Manhood*, 10) Carver more fully explains his commitment to this line of thought. "The differences between country life and city life are so wide as to produce inevitable divergences of great width in their ideals, their manners and their outlook on life were it not that nature has a way of exterminating city people when they get too far away from the rural point of view. If we may assume that nature knows what she is about it is safe to conclude that the rural point of view is the correct one. It therefore behooves us to ponder seriously what seems to be the maturer preference before we affect to despise the homely virtues of rural people."

to try to accommodate the newcomer to the city as they were to provide for the increasingly fewer stay-at-home country boys. Nor was this a small task. One rural economist estimated that no fewer than 25,000 country boys came each year to New York City alone, and that altogether the drift to the cities from farms and small towns aggregated no less than "several hundred thousand annually."[151] From the very beginning of its work—and despite serious professions that its main interest was in the country boy and his life on the farm—plans were made and proposals canvassed for dealing with the country boy at home and abroad.[152] It was not long before the long reach of urban influence was felt, ever more strongly, in the intended reawakening of country life.

The principal difficulty which these YMCA workers faced, it seemed, was in conceiving programs which might correspond to the sentimental outlines of the legend of country boyhood and the traditional folklore of country life. The nearest they could come to establishing congruence between the two was in the literal enactment of the urban version of country life in the rural areas themselves. For example, they organized and built a camp, in one instance, where country boys might take country holidays and indulge in such appropriate exercises as "nature study" and the cultivation of those handicrafts which urban social workers thought might suit young people brought up in the country.[153] These matter-of-fact ventures into nostalgia did not have, and perhaps did not deserve, lasting success. The greatest efforts, however, were devoted to a purely symbolic reinforcement of the legend through propaganda. Within the framework of a "back to the farm" crusade facts and fantasies about country life and country boyhood could be blended together

151. This estimate is given in Fred M. Hill, "City Hospitality for the Country Boy," *Rural Manhood*, 1 (October, 1910), 5.

152. The original aims of YMCA country work were plainly stated at the outset of its operations. "The County Work of the Young Men's Christian Association, as the custodian of the trust funds placed in its hands to aid the maximum development of country life, deliberately proposes to use the larger part of its resources in work with boys between the ages of eighteen and twenty-five, with the emphasis on the former class." "The Boy First," *Rural Manhood*, 1. That same year, six months later, it was pointed out in the same journal that "the country boy is a national figure." It was observed, however, that "comparatively little attention is being given the native stranger whose coming and reception and assimilation [into the city] is so significant . . . ." Hill, "City Hospitality," p. 1.

153. See for example the recital of experiences in one such camp in W. B. Holliday, "A Camp That Failed," *Rural Manhood*, 10 (June, 1919), 251–253.

without fear—at least in the short run—of an unkind censorship by experience.

We can best judge the firm grip of the legend of the country boy on the minds of urban people by consulting the intense, always fervid literature which celebrated the return of the country boy from the city to his rural home. This literature was unvarying in form and emphasis. It recited the disillusionment of the country boy with the city, the hardships he had suffered there, and his ultimate recollection of the simple beauty and the homely charm of country life.[154] And this literature reached a full circle when a city newsboy left his paper stand and his streetcorner to head out into the countryside because he had been converted by the legend. This particular story concerns the change which came over Isadore Greenberg, who for thirteen years had sold newspapers on the northeast corner of Broadway and Fulton Street, in New York. His testimony repays extended quotation:

> I've watched the faces of thousands of men and women who passed me in the crowds, and it struck me that a lot of them were playing a losing game. They were prisoners of the city serving a life sentence.
>
> I knew the day would come when I'd have to quit the game on the corner, and I kept wondering what I'd do. The outdoor life has made me hard as nails. I wanted to find something that would keep me in God's fresh air—something that I like and that would be a paying proposition.
>
> And then it all came on me in a flash. People have forgotten that all the wealth in the world comes out of the ground. They've left the open places of the earth and have crowded into the markets in the cities, and they are stepping on each other and narrowing themselves, mentally and physically, while they grub for pay dirt.
>
> Pretty soon, some day, they are going to go back home—home to the forest and the farms . . .[155]

It should perhaps be mentioned that this is the speech of a newsboy who has just entered Cornell to study scientific agriculture in college before he migrates to the country and the good life. There is a kind of poetic

154. For a sample account in this vein cf. D. C. Vandercook, "The Boy Who Came Back Home," *Rural Manhood*, 6 (May, 1915), 211–212. This literature was buttressed by more generalized discouragements about the life of the country boys in the city as compared with life on the farm. Cf. Philip L. Barker, "Shall Farm Boys Find Fortune in the City?" *Rural Manhood*, 6, pp. 213–215, and Theodore Temple, "The Country Boy Who Goes to a Great City," *The Chatauquan*, 13 (1891), 322–326.

155. "Newsie Quits New York Street Corner," *Rural Manhood*, 6 (May, 1915), 210–211.

justice in this incident: the myth had come home to roost. The legendary country boy, tended and nourished by urban intellectuals, could not move true country boys who knew life on the farm but it could and did fire the romantic imagination of a city boy. One wonders if he found his dream of happiness on a scientifically-cultivated farm.

IX. The Myth Lives On

IT is easy, indeed too easy, to mock the legend of the country boy, but debunking stops short of measuring its true significance. One might as well mock Virgil's *Georgics* and their evocation of the Roman rural past and ancient Roman virtue. It is said that Virgil was led to writing the poem by the encouragement of Maecenas, who wanted not only to patronize a great poet but, in a lively conservative concern, wanted to recall a vision of a noble past in which his city's glory had been forged. The impulse, it is true, was born in the greatest city of ancient times, not on a farm; but the city man's nostalgia for the country was ancient even then and Virgil, no doubt, recalled Hesiod's *Works and Days*. In the same spirit, Oliver Goldsmith, millennia later, conjured up his Sweet Auburn and mourned the *Deseretd Village* while he heard the rumbling of the Industrial Revolution in the distance. So, too, although in a much less distinguished literature, the legend of the American country boy was created and propagated: there is a lasting style in sentiment.

But a cliché does not become trite inadvertently; a platitude is repeated because it is serviceable. In the thundering rush which filled up American cities, urban life was too complex, too difficult, and too hazardous to be easily grasped and readily understood. To make it intelligible and to give it ideals to strive for, men like those discussed here searched for a formula which could encompass a worthy code of conduct and a durable philosophy of life. Coming as they did, in the beginning, from a rural tradition and background, it is not surprising that they chose what they had known to guide them. The dilemmas of the myth and its increasingly unreal sentimentality emerged as the stereotype of rurality became more and more divorced from the realities of both urban and rural life. Then it became more unreal, but it did not, as we saw, relinquish its grip on the imagination. As so often before and since, that strange but characteristically human attempt was made to preserve the growing fiction from the assaults and criticism of reality. Nor, indeed, was the myth ever wholly vanquished. To be sure, it is no longer believed as a description of the real world—rural or urban—but it remains an enclave of secret feeling and sentiment embedded in our popular songs and stories, living, like all traditions, on its past.

THE SOCIAL ORIGINS OF AMERICAN LEADERS: THE DEMOGRAPHIC FOUNDATIONS

P. M. G. Harris

THE SOCIAL ORIGINS OF
AMERICAN LEADERS: THE
DEMOGRAPHIC FOUNDATIONS

Introduction

WAS America a more open, a more equal, society in 1950, in 1850, in 1750, or in 1650? This question and its correlates have intrigued scholars and ideologues alike, and suggested answers have provided the backbone for fundamental commentaries on the character and meaning of American history.

To what extent did the mere fact of migration to a new land create a new kind of society? Some interpretations of the American experience imply that those who chose in the seventeenth century to leave their European homes for permanent settlement in the New World at once established social conditions that differed from the Old World. With respect to a later stage of American development, much controversy of a similar sort revolves about the issue of how the Revolution and the founding of the republic generated a different type of social structure. Some scholars have argued that the War of Independence reflected and sought to preserve an existing social order though the latter had already departed substantially from the early colonial model of its European antecedents. There follows the issue of whether early nineteenth-century Jacksonianism entailed a major increase in various forms of opportunity, especially greater access by the common man to political power. Some writers have maintained that the impact of this era upon the actual social structure—as distinct from the growth of an American ideology and self image—has been exaggerated.

In addition, seventy-five years after the initial exposition of Turner's thesis, many crucial problems remain about the relationship of the frontier to American life at various points in our history. Bound up with this are the social ramifications of the demise of a frontier society. Has twentieth-century industrialism made our social structure more open by fostering widespread education, a stream of new occupational roles and rewards, a melting-pot labor force, and the breakdown of old-fashioned restraints upon the individual? Or has it generated class distinctions in the New World Eden? In generation after generation of literature about our society—by historians, political theorists, sociologists, and economists alike—so many of the galvanizing conclusions, the absorbing issues, and the irresistible challenges to further inquiry have turned upon facts or opinions concerning which citizens at various times in our history have enjoyed economic opportunity, have had a say in political decision-making, or have had the freedom of action and the self-respect associated with a relatively flexible and generous social order.

One strategy for bringing the social sciences to bear on these questions has been to examine the kinds of men who became leaders at different points in the past. A sizeable literature on the origins of American businessmen, for example, has accumulated over the last generation of scholarship. This corpus now reaches—with a few chronological gaps and some variation in the degree of systematic quantification—from the beginnings of colonial trade to the present time.[1] The desire to understand the backgrounds from which political leaders or public officials were derived at various points in history has also produced a growing list of

---

1. Some of the key studies are, for early America: Bernard Bailyn, *The New England Merchants in the Seventeenth Century* (Cambridge, 1955); Bernard and Lotte Bailyn, *Massachusetts Shipping, 1697–1714: A Statistical Study* (Cambridge, 1959); Arthur M. Schlesinger, *The Colonial Merchants and the American Revolution, 1763–1776* (New York, 1917), lxviii, Virginia D. Harrington, *The New York Merchant on the Eve of the Revolution* (New York, 1935); and Samuel Eliot Morison, *The Maritime History of Massachusetts, 1783–1860* (Boston, 1921); and for the period since the Civil War: F. W. Taussig and C. S. Joslyn, *American Business Leaders* (New York, 1932); C. Wright Mills, "The American Business Elite: A Collective Portrait," *The Task of Economic History*, supplementary issue of the *Journal of Economic History* (December, 1945) pp. 20–44; William Miller, *Men in Business: Essays in the History of Entrepreneurship* (Cambridge, 1952); Suzanne Keller, "The Social Origins and Career Lines of Three Generations of American Business Leaders" (unpub. PhD diss., Columbia, 1953); Mabel Newcomer, *The Big Business Executive* (New York, 1955); W. Lloyd Warner and James C. Abegglen, *Occupational Mobility in American Business and Industry* (Minneapolis, 1955); and Reinhard Bendix and Frank W. Howton, "Social Mobility and the American Business Elite," *Social Mobility in Industrial Society*, ed. Seymour Martin Lipset and Reinhard Bendix (Berkeley, 1959), ch. IV.

investigations.[2] Other studies of professionals or eminent men in arts or letters have also tried to say as much as possible about the origins of these men.

One can of course argue that changes in opportunity at the lower end of the social scale directly affected the personal lives of many more individuals than any change in the recruitment of leaders. Any effort to document social change from the bottom up, however, is plagued by the difficulty of obtaining data about ordinary people and generalizing from what initially has to be local information. The under-privileged, traditionally, are also the under-reported. Nevertheless, in the last few years, we have begun to enjoy the benefits of historical inquiries that tell much about who voted and held local or lesser offices, who invested in trade, how much land was typically held by farmers, how inheritance worked in agricultural society, what was the ownership of urban property, who opened new settlements or speculated in their acreage, and how industrial workingmen acquired and used various forms of life chances.[3] Starting from views of contemporary America, meanwhile, sociologists—in addition to contributing to the analysis of elites—have been pushing back studies of more general social structure to include comparisons of the social origins of present-day adults with the back-

2. Of special value are these recent studies: Sidney H. Aronson, *Status and Kinship in the Higher Civil Service* (Cambridge, 1964); David J. Rothman, *Politics and Power: The United States Senate 1869–1901* (Cambridge, 1966); Robert Emmet Wall, Jr., "The Membership of the Massachusetts General Court, 1634–1686" (unpub. PhD diss., Yale, 1965); and Jackson Turner Main, *The Upper House in Revolutionary America, 1763–1788* (Madison, 1967).

3. In particular, Robert E. Brown, *Middle-Class Democracy and the Revolution in Massachusetts, 1691–1780* (Ithaca, 1955); Wall, *Massachusetts Court*; Bailyn and Bailyn, *Massachusetts Shipping*; Charles S. Grant, *Democracy in the Frontier Town of Kent* (New York, 1961); Kenneth A. Lockridge, "Land, Population, and the Evolution of New England Society, 1630–1790," *Past and Present*, 39 (1968), 62–80; James A. Henretta, "Economic Development and Social Structure of Colonial Boston," *William and Mary Quarterly*, 3rd ser., 22 (1965), 75–92; Philip J. Greven, Jr., "Family Structure in Seventeenth-Century Andover," *William and Mary Quarterly*, 3rd ser., 23 (1966), 234–256; also Prof. Greven's dissertation, which I had the privilege of reading while still under restriction: "Four Generations: A Study of Family Structure, Inheritance, and Mobility in Andover, Massachusetts, 1630–1750" (unpub. PhD diss., Harvard, 1965); Stephan Thernstrom, *Poverty and Progress: Social Mobility in a Nineteenth Century City* (Cambridge, 1964); some very interesting research is currently being finished and reported by Eugene Harper of Morris Harvey College on western Pennsylvania in the late eighteenth century.

grounds of their fathers earlier in the twentieth century.[4] The fruits of these chronologically converging inquiries about the life of ordinary citizens provide the stuff from which the rising edifice of our understanding must eventually be constructed if we are ever to say with general assurance whether or not America was a more open, egalitarian society in 1850 than it had been in 1750, and to specify what we mean within the boundaries of that broad conclusion.

Meanwhile, further systematic analysis of the origins of leadership at various points of history may at least suggest how opportunity changed across the society as a whole even though decades of work on local data remain. Moreover, to study the backgrounds of more eminent and well-known Americans is to study the origins of those who possessed the greatest leverage for shaping our society. At the same time one is studying those whose personal histories have frequently symbolized—whether in approval or in reproach—what contemporaries thought was happening to the American way of life. Within fairly large and varied samples of leadership, moreover, there is material for an encouraging amount of regional, even local, comparison and not a little insight into the opportunities of more ordinary young persons. We can observe in part the ease of access to the preliminary advantages in education, the early career stages, and the wealth or connections which made possible for some of them a subsequent advancement to exceptional levels of attainment and influence.

Two parallel and overlapping studies of the origins, education, career patterns, migration, and families of American leaders which this writer has been conducting[5] throw fresh light upon approaches to the question of whether America was a more open or a less open society at one time or another in our past. The first inquiry covers all the Harvard and Yale graduates from 1642 through 1745, and most of the Harvard students who did not graduate—some 2,500 individuals, or virtually the universe

4. For references to these studies see Lipset and Bendix, *Mobility in Industrial Society* chap. iii; Thernstrom, *Poverty and Progress*, pp. 218–219.

5. For the Center for the Study of the History of Liberty in America, Harvard University. The writer is deeply indebted to the Center and to Oscar Handlin, its director, for eight years of sustained research support. This is a first and partial presentation of the results of those inquiries.

of college men in the northern colonies for most of the colonial period.[6] The second involves all the 15,000 men and women for whom sketches were incorporated in the *Dictionary of American Biography*. Each of these investigations has opened up an intricate set of problems about how family, property, ability, education, and other factors worked to shape American leadership, to determine who rose to the top in specific fields of endeavor, in particular political institutions, economic enterprises, arts and professions. The more detailed information from the two inquiries is assembled and presented separately elsewhere. Yet throughout the material of these two distinct and predominantly independent samples of life histories of American leaders, there runs a common central phenomenon—a way in which the number of leadership places, and the social openness or equality of access to them for men from different types of background, each changed in step with certain largely recurrent variations in the rate of growth of the American population and of particular age groups within the society. It seemed worthwhile to set forth here in summary or overview—drawing upon the two separate studies in support of each other—the fundamental findings about how the origins of those who did most to shape our society varied over given periods of time; and to indicate the explanation that seems to account best for the way in which opportunity varied.

In answer to the sweeping question used to introduce the discussion, the following exposition will demonstrate that differences in the degree to which America was an open society between 1750 and 1760, or, for example, 1840 and 1850, were greater in certain crucial respects than those between 1750 and 1850. Over and over again, fairly predictably patterned changes within the span of a decade or so exceeded the effect of trends lasting a century or more. Past generalizations in the literature which have noted or implied shifts in the social structure from one broad conventional era of our history to the next, or as the immediate results of particular crises, appear to have been overstated. Yet significant differences in opportunity *have* existed at various times in the Amer-

---

6. John Langdon Sibley, *Biographical Sketches of Graduates of Harvard University* (Cambridge, 1873–85), I–III; Clifford K. Shipton, *Sibley's Harvard Graduates* (Cambridge, 1933, in progress), IV and continuing; Franklin B. Dexter, *Biographical Sketches of the Graduates of Yale College, with Annals of the College History* (New York, 1885), I.

ican past. These real variations in opportunity have come about, however, for reasons which have more to do with relatively short-term demographic and economic processes than with macroscopic political events, ideological movements, or cultural developments.

Section I begins the discussion by illustrating how the problems of varying sources of American leadership and broader social change have usually been handled in the literature. The quite different pattern of chronologically fluctuating opportunity that has actually kept cropping up again and again in several forms of data is described in Section II. These historical variations back and forth in the openness of opportunity, as Section III indicates, have been associated with parallel swings in the rate of growth of the American population, in migration and the numbers of new settlements or communities being established, and in the resulting numbers of new places for various kinds of leadership. In addition, as demonstrated in Section IV, the changes of pace in several forms of economic development which scholars have been exploring in the period since the Civil War, and have recently linked more and more closely to demographic processes, can be identified as far back—following surprisingly standard intervals—as the earliest years of colonial history, with strikingly consistent relationships to population growth, population movement, and changes in both the amount of opportunity and equality of access to it. Section V then seeks to explain how opportunity and certain demographic processes reinforced each other to sustain a pattern of such interrelated, highly cyclical fluctuations over long periods of our history. A few concluding comments in Section VI set forth what seem to be some of the implications of the findings summarized here for the future study of American history and social history in general.

1. Social Change in American History
and Historiography

THEY may not have labelled them as such, but writers on American history have usually based their work on explicit or implicit models of how our social structure has evolved over time. Patterns of social change assumed to result from the interworkings of social, political, or economic components have long been inherent in interpretations of critical events like the Great Awakening, the American Revolution, or the Civil War. These interpretations have brought to a sharp focus evaluations of more gradual yet persistent processes like the impact of New World life upon European people and the institutions which they tried to bring with them across the Atlantic, or the influence of the frontier upon a society chronically confronted with an open end of settlement. Similar hypothetical patterns of social change from point to point historically have kept cropping up in analyses of other significant determinants of our way of life such as the modernizing effects of market agriculture, the evolution of trans-oceanic trade, or the rise of manufacturing industry. They have figured liberally in discussions of the flowering of public education, the expansion of the electorate, or the emergence of high capitalism and the introduction of restraints to curb it.

Since the characteristics of leaders or their backgrounds are usually more readily specified or estimated than the changing everyday fortunes of the common man—and since many find leadership more exciting to discuss anyway—claims and arguments have often been set in terms of what kinds of men at this or that point in our history took the helm, or fixed the course, in the various ventures which contributed to the overall pattern of American development. Permeating the themes of great movements, specific conflicts, environmental influences, and cultural or institutional growth are suggestions that in a given segment of history, or at a particular point of time, our leadership became more openly recruited; or, conversely, that the social base from which it was derived became more narrow and selective. That is, at some juncture those with most opportunity to shape the society are supposed to have come in greater proportionate numbers from the families of fairly ordinary farmers, small traders, or artisans, or those of even humbler stations. At some other previous or subsequent time, in contrast, it is implied or stated specifically that American leadership—or some part of it—was drawn in noticeably larger proportion from families with positions already well situated in the social order.

To set the scene for the findings presented here and to demonstrate where they fit in with or challenge the existing literature which touches upon the history of American social structure, it is useful to begin by outlining various ways in which writings about the national and colonial past may be said to have conveyed or implied patterns of chronological change in the origins of leadership. The purpose of this effort is not to become involved in a critique of a given author or school of writers, but rather to illustrate the variety of patterns from among which the student of the American past has been invited to pick and choose. The fact that a particular scholar, for instance, has employed more than one scheme to describe change chronologically, or has shifted his ground and resorted to more than one model of how it came about, might be thought to subject him to charges of inconsistency and evasion while on the intellectual front line of trying to explain historical processes. In more carefully weighed judgment, however, such "cowardice in the face of the enemy" just when the real battle of scholarship has been joined can sometimes with equal accuracy and greater fairness be called a sign of strategic discretion, an awareness that change at all times and in all parts of a society need not follow a single rule. Even within this writer's own limited work on the development of American social structure, for instance, the central phenomenon summarized here only partly accounts for change, although the basic findings outlined in this presentation contain data from four centuries and relate to many different groups of people or types of leadership in the history of our society.

Thus the object of this brief reference to the literature—the word "review" would connote far more than intended—is simply to make more explicit the relevance of the present findings and their analysis to what has been offered before. The idea is neither to ignore nor hastily to discard existing interpretations, but to introduce some data which suggest their incompleteness. The task then becomes one of building upon, refining, and reordering what has been achieved previously toward understanding the development of our society.

One rather simple kind of pattern depicting the changing proportion of American leaders from homes that were fairly well placed in the socio-economic structure has sometimes been sketched in the literature as illustrated in Section A of Figure No. 1. This form of interpretation might be labelled the product of a "turning point" or "epochal" model of social change and variations in the sources of leadership. In this pattern it is maintained—or more vaguely left to be inferred from what is said about the structure of the society, the economy, or the polity—that at some critical juncture our leadership was quickly or decisively recruited from an appreciably broader or more democratic base.

"The American Revolution created a new kind of society" is the way in which school texts have too often coped with the question (cf. Pattern III of Section A in the figure). From a more scholarly and thoughtful stance, J. Franklin Jameson in the lectures he published in 1926 as *The American Revolution Considered as a Social Movement* maintained that "There are . . . some political changes that almost inevitably bring social changes in their wake." He went on to explain that while the fortunes and the influence of the most humble elements in the society were not directly altered by the Revolution, there was an appreciable democratization extending down into the middle ranges of the social structure.[1] More recently, Jackson Turner Main's treatment of the metamorphosis of the colonial legislatures into state legislatures suggests a significant shift in leadership at the same Revolutionary break in the course of our development.[2] In business life, Samuel Eliot Morison depicted the period after the Revolution as one exceptionally decorated with the personal histories of individuals who rose from fo'c'sle to quarterdeck and countinghouse.[3]

Another familiar argument suggests that long before—at the beginning, when the Pilgrims stepped off onto the rock, so to speak—settlers were at once initiating a style of life that because of the immediate impact of the uprooting for migration, the move itself, and the plunge into the new environment, led to departures from the ways of the Old

---

1. J. Franklin Jameson, *The American Revolution Considered as a Social Movement* (Princeton, 1926), pp. 25–26.
2. Main, *Upper House*, esp. pp. 269, 272, 276, 278.
3. Morison, *Maritime History*, esp. pp. 106–107, 112–113.

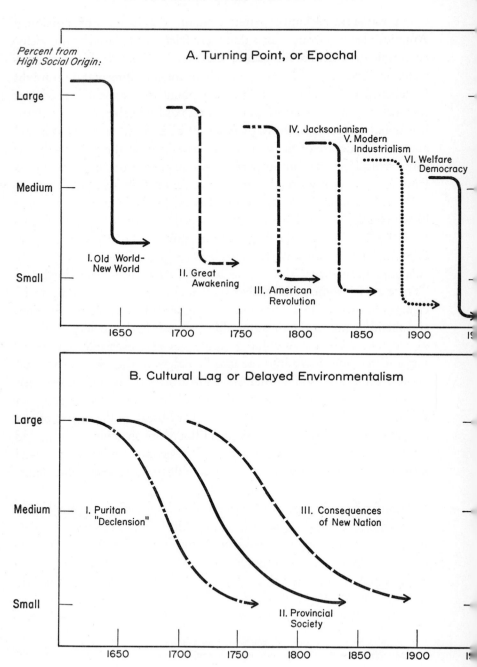

Figure No. I. Some Prevalent Interpretations of Chang

A. Turning Point, or Epochal

*Percent from
High Social Origin:*

Large

IV. Jacksonianism
V. Modern
Industrialism
VI. Welfare
Democracy

Medium

I. Old World-
New World

II. Great
Awakening

III. American
Revolution

Small

1650   1700   1750   1800   1850   1900   1

B. Cultural Lag or Delayed Environmentalism

Large

Medium

I. Puritan
"Declension"

III. Consequences
of New Nation

Small

II. Provincial
Society

1650   1700   1750   1800   1850   1900   1

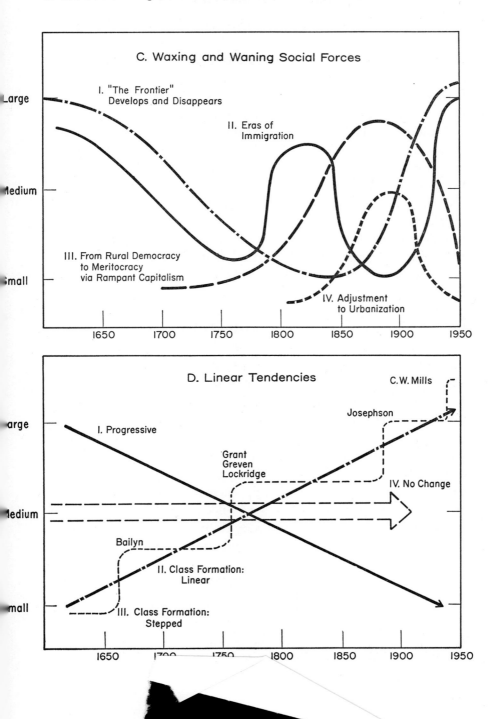

C. Waxing and Waning Social Forces

I. "The Frontier" Develops and Disappears

II. Eras of Immigration

III. From Rural Democracy to Meritocracy via Rampant Capitalism

IV. Adjustment to Urbanization

Large · Medium · Small

1650 · 1700 · 1750 · 1800 · 1850 · 1900 · 1950

D. Linear Tendencies

C.W. Mills

Josephson

I. Progressive

Grant
Greven
Lockridge

IV. No Change

Bailyn

II. Class Formation: Linear

III. Class Formation: Stepped

Large · Medium · Small

1650 · 1700 · 1750 · 1800 · 1850 · 1900 · 1950

World—including the manner in which leadership was derived (Pattern I of Section A of the figure).[4]

Other students of the American past have favored other 'giant steps' at which critical social change is purported to have taken place within a fairly short period. John C. Miller, in an early article written in the New Deal atmosphere of the 1930's, put all the eggs of religious, economic, and political conflict and change into the one basket of the Great Awakening era around 1740 (Pattern II).[5] Lately, Alan Heimert has once more underscored the connection of religious, social, and political thought at that time.[6] The era of Jackson, according to Arthur M. Schlesinger, Jr., was similarly one of multifaceted "revolution" which had economic, social, and intellectual sides as well as the political core that hardened in reaction to "a betrayal of the Jeffersonian promise of equal rights in favor of special benefits for a single class" (Pattern IV).[7] The New Deal, which as a contemporary cultural setting has colored interpretations of the past by both Miller and Schlesinger, could be called still another period in which opportunity as a whole, and the sources of leadership in particular, were fairly swiftly democratized—in this instance as the result of a fundamental reversal in the ascendancy of conflicting political ideologies and the advent of the welfare state (diagrammed as Pattern VI). In the late nineteenth century, meanwhile, the acceleration of urbanism and mass education, the creation of new occupational roles by the development of industry, the constant leavening of the labor force by a heavy infusion of immigrants at the bottom, the growth of city machines to exercise the political rights of the overlooked and exploited, could be considered as factors contributing toward a more open society and a more broadly based leadership under the misleading facade of class-conscious and wealth-conscious "Gilded Age" (Pattern V). One might argue, for example, that a Teddy Rooseveltian stress on individualism and self-reliance was no mere mystique or Horatio Alger opiate,

4. Oscar Handlin, "The Significance of the Seventeenth Century," *Seventeenth-Century America*, ed. James Morton Smith (Chapel Hill, 1959), pp. 3–12.

5. John C. Miller, "Religion, Finance and Democracy in Massachusetts," New England Quarterly, 6 (1933), 29–58.

6. Alan Heimert, *Religion and the American Mind: From the Great Awakening to the Revolution* (Cambridge, 1966). Page 12 gives a summary of this opinion.

7. Arthur M. Schlesinger, Jr., *The Age of Jackson* (Boston, 1945), p. 30.

but an ideology encouraged near the end of the century when, through the very confusion of society and the rapidity of change, it became relatively easier for many kinds of Americans to exercise their talents and energies and to "get ahead." Arthur Schlesinger, Sr., suggested this kind of improvement of conditions as a result of the developments of the 1870's and 1880's which he discussed in *The Rise of the City*.[8]

It is of course possible for students of American life to employ more complex conceptualizations of the changing nature of society or the sources of its leadership, thus incorporating two or more of these "steps" which have presumably carried us from the European institutions of the early seventeenth century to the far different way of life that characterizes twentieth-century America. Most of those who have written about long segments of our history, as in textbooks, or about the American past over long professional careers, have at least flirted with the idea of two or more successive stages, steps, or turning points at which our social structure shifted from its original condition toward the modern form. John C. Miller, for example, within the span of a single generation of American history from 1740 to 1775 treated first the Great Awakening, then the Revolution as social movements with such an effect.[9] In his brief discussion of politics and social structure in colonial Virginia, Bernard Bailyn distinguishes no fewer than three crises or pivot points within little more than a century that contributed significantly toward the opening up of Virginia leadership: the death, discouragement, and departure, within a relatively few years after the initiation of the Jamestown settlement, of those who had genuine aristocratic connections; the challenge in the 1670's of the "outs" to the "ins" who had become entrenched through a combination of patronage and family-building arising out of the immigration of new bourgeois leadership with gentry aspirations during the decades near the middle of the seventeenth century; and again, in the mid-eighteenth century, the pre-Revolutionary threat to the "established" mixture of social and political stature which had become the new synthesis in the decades following Bacon's rebellion.[10]

8. Arthur M. Schlesinger, Sr., *The Rise of the City* (New York, 1933).

9. Miller, "Religion, Finance, and Democracy"; Miller, *Origins of the American Revolution* (Boston, 1943).

10. Bernard Bailyn, "Politics and Social Structure," *Seventeenth-Century America*, ed. James M. Smith (Chapel Hill, 1959).

Environmental or ecological determinists among American historians have tended to use a gradualist modification of this type of thinking about social change. At times one does sense that the initial importation of European institutions to the New World is supposed to have produced a distinctly "American" society and sources of leadership from the start. The implications for leadership of this "instant environmentalism" could best be diagrammed approximately as already shown in Pattern I in Section A of Figure No. 1. Such crude Old World-New World differentiation, however, is now crumbling away as the English society from which the earliest settlers transplanted themselves is becoming better understood. Too much of the "Americanness" in this kind of thinking depends upon setting up a straw man of "Europeanness" preceding the migrations to the New World. If the too common stereotype of European society in American historical writing ever had much reality, it perhaps resembled the stagnant peasant communities of Ireland, Italy, or Eastern Europe, where later nineteenth-century immigrants originated, more than the sixteenth-, seventeenth-, and early eighteenth-century Britain where the vast majority of pre-Revolutionary Americans had their roots. Notions of the extended family, or of geographical and social immobility in England or much of Europe may have nurtured our egos by providing a favorable contrast of our present or recent condition to imagined Old World backwardness. But most of these exaggerations are now fast being discarded as overwhelming evidence piles up of nuclear family structure, internal migration, and social mobility in seventeenth- and even sixteenth-century Europe.[11]

Also employed in the literature, however, are modifications of the basic idea that Old World forms of social life changed immediately upon contact with the New World wilderness. Some of these more gradual or more complex models of social process incorporate the notion of a cultural lag in which Puritan institutions in New England, for example, broke up after a generation or two—say, in the late seventeenth or early eighteenth century—with implications for opening avenues to roles of leadership that might be portrayed as in Pattern I of Sec-

11. This literature of French, English, and now American "historical demography," summarized in Philip Greven, Jr., "Historical Demography and Colonial America," *William and Mary Quarterly*, 3rd ser., 24 (1967) 438–454, is, with related inquiries, putting much modern sociological study into badly needed perspective.

tion B of Figure No. 1. As long ago as 1933, Clifford K. Shipton pointed up some of the fundamental fallacies in this notion of crumbling institutions as applied to Puritan New England in the writings of James Truslow Adams, Thomas J. Wertenbaker, Marcus W. Jernegan, and Vernon L. Parrington, among others.[12] Such criticism, however, has not kept that concept of social change over time from being a resurgent theme in the literature. The notion of a metamorphosis in religion and the society that it served after a lag of one or two generations ran rampant through the second volume of Perry Miller's *New England Mind*.[13] Explicitly from Edmund Morgan's *Puritan Family*, and implicitly from Morgan's revised views on church membership and the covenant in *Visible Saints*, the reader derives the impression of a later seventeenth-century society in which family interests—and potentially class interests—had grown stronger, in which restraints imposed on social stratification by the universalistic application of religious values to worldly affairs had been weakened or lifted.[14]

In his *New England Merchants in the Seventeenth Century*, Bailyn, in treating the more secular sphere of life, adopts the notion that old forms of political and social control imported by the more staunchly Puritan of the founding fathers shattered under the pressures of "new men" who more successfully capitalized upon the economic potential of the New World environment. He contends that within the time period of a single change of generations in the leadership, these new figures had risen to influence, intermarried with and formed business partnerships and political coalitions with the initial leadership. The older group had had a stronger image of "gentry" from the start, in addition to more explicit religious objectives for the new society.[15] A similar viewpoint is applied by Bailyn to the Virginia scene in mid-century. He notes the supplanting of a few early aristocrats by self-made men; then, as in New

12. Clifford K. Shipton, "The New England Clergy of the Glacial Age," Colonial Society of Massachusetts, *Publications*, XXXII (1937), 24–54.

13. Perry Miller, *The New England Mind: From Colony to Province* (Cambridge, 1953). For his notion of a second "decay" or metamorphosis in the 1720's, see note 19 and preceding discussion.

14. Edmund Morgan, *The Puritan Family: Essays on Religion and Domestic Relations in Seventeenth-Century New England* (Boston, 1944); Edmund Morgan, *Visible Saints* (New York, 1963).

15. Bailyn, *New England Merchants*, esp. pp. 39ff, 105ff.

England after the Restoration, an amalgamation of some of these new individuals with men of capital attracted somewhat later to the New World. The new wave of political leadership had largely come westward across the Atlantic to turn middle-class fortunes or political connections into comfortable places within the English system of life—colonial, domestic, or both.[16] On the question of later seventeenth-century decay in early Puritan efforts to establish educational institutions and secure popular involvement in education (a point of ideology which has, for present purposes, important implications for changes in equality of opportunity), Bailyn in still another of his writings reserves judgment and does not accept either the claim of deterioration exemplified by Updegraff's Columbia monograph of the early 1900's or the rebuttal led by Shipton and others who have maintained that the educational ideal was not abandoned.[17] In another recent volume in line with this theme of changing institutions in the New World environment, Richard L. Bushman has discussed in helpful economic, religious, and political detail, how Connecticut society was transformed from "Puritan" to "Yankee" beginning about 1690.[18]

Other writers have stressed lagging changes in American life and social structure in response to the environment at later points of our history, where the nature of New World life finally "got to" and altered essentially Old World forms. Perry Miller, for example, saw not only the challenge to early Puritan ideals from the second and third generation in New England but a threat, in turn, to *their* compromise (personified by the interests and activities of Cotton Mather) in the years around the 1720's (Pattern II of Figure I, B).[19] Charles and Mary Beard in their *Basic History of the United States*, on the other hand, envisioned floodgates of change in American society being opened by the forming of the new nation.[20] At first this flow of new development was gradual. Soon, however, it became rapidly cumulative as the founding of new states

16. Bailyn, "Politics and Social Structure."

17. Bernard Bailyn, *Education in the Forming of American Society* (Chapel Hill, 1963), pp. 78–83.

18. Richard L. Bushman, *From Puritan to Yankee: Character and the Social Order in Connecticut, 1690–1765* (Cambridge, 1967).

19. Miller, *Colony To Province*, esp. Book III, "The Splintering of Society," pp. 303ff.

20. Charles and Mary Beard, *Basic History of the United States* (New York, 1944), pp. 212ff.

and the erosion of the class structure of old states by settlement of their interior, the consolidation of a new, distinctively American political ideology, the growth of industrial cities, the influx of waves of immigrants, and the search of industrial workers for trade unions and labor parties made, in their view, for the evolution of the American ideal and an accompanying reality of accessible opportunity during the period from about 1789 to 1840. Interest in public education, symbolized by Horace Mann, contributed to the process of democratization which was said to have proceeded in the seaboard states in spite of their originally non-democratic constitutions.[21] A diagram of the proportion of leadership coming from relatively well-placed homes that would accord with this mode of historic interpretation might follow Pattern III of Section B of the figure.

If one took the pure Turner thesis, on the other hand, and tried to relate American socio-political structure directly to the extent of the frontier at any given time and the westward retreat of the frontier away from the baneful influence of Europe,[22] then one might expect the social sources of leadership to have changed according to the chronological form outlined in Pattern I of Section C in Figure No. 1. This diagram tries to convey the image of a graded but fairly rapid democratization of the origins of our leadership during a few decades of experimentation with the open end of New World living, then a substantial era of comparatively equal opportunity accompanying prolonged frontier conditions through most of the eighteenth century and the nineteenth century as well, until some time after the Civil War when the frontier closed off fairly swiftly. In more recent years Billington and others of the Turner school have provided some details as to where the frontier was at a given time, and who went there. These particulars allow some finer specification of what the Turner thesis should have meant in social change if it worked as suggested.[23] For the colonial era, Robert E.

21. *Ibid.*, pp. 213–288.

22. See, for example, the various discussions and Turner's own key articles in George Rogers Taylor, ed., *The Turner Thesis Concerning the Role of the Frontier in American History* (Boston, 1956).

23. *Ibid.*; Ray Allen Billington, *Westward Expansion: A History of the American Frontier*, 3rd ed. (New York, 1967); Richard Hofstadter and Seymour Martin Lipset, eds., *Turner and the Sociology of the Frontier* (New York, 1968).

Brown has implied something like the Turner model of the timing of social development in contrasting the "middle class democracy" which he found in revolutionary Massachusetts with contemporary European social structure and the antecedents of colonial society, on the one hand, and with subsequent American conditions, on the other.[24]

The concept of an ebbing and flowing tide of immigrants who underwrote "improvement" for the population already resident in the New World, and from their own ambitions and energies more directly contributed further personal histories of opportunity to the American record, resembled the effort to relate the frontier to social structure in that both postulated long-term middle-range processes opening up access for members of ordinary families to positions of leadership but access that might be actually reversed.[25] The frontier, it is generally argued, closed in the 1880's.[26] Immigration, on the other hand, was less heavy relative to the size of the indigenous population between the Revolution and about 1840 than before, or afterwards until the restraints of the 1920's were imposed (Pattern II).[27]

Similar models of historical processes that might be expected to have produced patterns of *both* opening *and* closing opportunities for leadership have been employed by others. Arthur Schlesinger, Sr., for example, viewed the era of the 1870's and 1880's in his *Rise of the City* as a period of disintegrating, polarizing society followed by reintegration and reestablishment of some of the classic forms of American life. Urbanization, industrialization, new modes and new extremes of wealth and power, massive immigration, and cultural displacement produced a critical era of hard times, insecurity, and the building of social and political defenses against feared and uncomprehended change. But the process of institutional reorganization that was taking place all this time under the cover of uncertainty and unease soon produced a new era of confidence and opportunity.[28] (A likely effect of this interpretation in

24. Brown, *Middle-Class Democracy and the Revolution*, pp. 401–402.
25. Oscar Handlin, *The Americans* (Boston, 1963), esp. pp. 272ff, 282ff; Oscar Handlin, *Boston's Immigrants*, 2d. ed. (Cambridge, 1959), pp. 212ff.
26. Previously its development was also interrupted by several wars whose effects are omitted from Pattern I.
27. Marcus L. Hansen, *The Atlantic Migration, 1607–1860* (Cambridge, 1940), esp. pp. 53–119.
28. Schlesinger, Sr., *Rise of the City*.

terms of the social sources of leadership is outlined in Pattern IV). The argument which Elbridge Sibley made in the 1940's about the impact of social class differentials in fertility on social mobility in America was also in reversible form, indicating that the gap between typical small family size high in the social order and the usual incidence of larger families further down was closing up again in the mid-twentieth century and thereby helping to tighten up access to opportunity for those born outside the leadership classes.[29]

Over a much longer time span, Edmund Morgan—in the fashion of Pattern III of Section C—has proposed virtually the reverse of the effects of the Turner model illustrated in Pattern I. He has chastised those who project a nineteenth-century and early twentieth-century notion of property concentrated in the hands of a few back into the eighteenth century, where this was not the case. He also suggests that today, in the mid-twentieth century, property may be more equally distributed again, closer to the colonial situation (for different reasons) than to the conditions of the nineteenth century.[30] Morgan's argument introduces the important notion that *different processes* can produce *similar results* in terms of opportunity, equality, or the social sources of leadership. They can, to use one current terminology, serve as functional substitutes for each other. Readily accessible education in a bureaucratized and professionalized modern economy, for instance, could produce a comparatively equal distribution of wealth or other opportunity similar to that which was once underwritten in an earlier age by relatively free access to land and to the profits of market agriculture.

On the other hand, ideologically "progressive" views of our national destiny from George Bancroft to twentieth-century American meliorism might be said to have defined the evolution of our society and its sources of leadership as leading steadily to greater and greater democratization. In this conception—illustrated as Pattern I in Section D of Figure No. 1—over the years lower and lower percentages of the elite were

29. Elbridge Sibley, "Some Demographic Clues to Stratification," *American Sociological Review*, 7 (1942), 322–330.

30. Edmund Morgan, "The American Revolution: Revisions in Need of Revising," *William and Mary Quarterly*, 3rd ser., 14 (1957), 3–15.

recruited from better-than-average placed families as the national ideal unfolded historically. Some recent expressions of this point of view are to be found in the notion of evolving New World pragmatism or "muddling through" that infuses Boorstin's colonial volume (and for which he has been taken to task by Bailyn).[31] Moreover, in a revision of an earlier contention to the contrary in his Yankee City Series, W. Lloyd Warner with James C. Abegglen just over a decade ago concluded from their study of the origins of businessmen that mobility in America as a whole, and mobility to high positions in particular, had been increasing somewhat in the course of the present century, especially through its second quarter.[32] More recently Stephan Thernstrom has placed his own data on nineteenth-century Newburyport in the context of other studies that have dealt with the life chances of the sons of laborers in America, to argue that if there has been any long-term trend, it has been in the direction of increasing rather than decreasing opportunity.[33]

Other writers, often directly or indirectly influenced by the Marxist approach to economic classes, have held on the contrary that things have been going from bad to worse in American society. In terms of the recruitment of leadership from various social classes this means from open to shut, from a broad base of recruitment out of families at many different places in the social structure toward a more narrow source of new leaders, with growing replacement simply from the families of the existing elite. Beginning as a noble, pristine agrarianism, the more modern our society has become, the more its leadership has become self-recruiting and in fact, if not in ideology, closed to those of more ordinary upbringing as depicted in Pattern II of Section D. Such thinking has been popular among mid-twentieth-century sociologists. It appears most explicitly and elaborately in the writings of C. Wright Mills, through his study of businessmen in *White Collar* with later embellishments in *The Power Elite*.[34] Warner and Low in *The Social System of the*

31. Daniel J. Boorstin, *The Americans: The Colonial Experience* (New York, 1958); Bernard Bailyn, "History and the Distrust of Knowledge," *New Republic*, 139 (December, 1958), 17–18.

32. Warner and Abegglen, *Occupational Mobility*, pp. 44–51.

33. Thernstrom, *Poverty and Progress.*

34. C. Wright Mills, *White Collar* (New York, 1951); C. Wright Mills, *The Power Elite* (New York, 1956).

Modern Factory and Elbridge Sibley and J. O. Hertzler in their writings came to similar conclusions between the early 1940's and the early 1950's.[35]

Among historians, meanwhile, conceptions of a rigidifying social structure on the eve of the Revolution and a shortage of land in older settlements have recently led to comparable deductions about a tendency towards a closing society during earlier periods of our history. These changes were either gradual or growing more urgent with the multiplication of mouths to feed and more subtle needs to fill in the second and third generations after the initial development of farm settlements. From a variety of evidence Jackson Turner Main has spoken of the pre-Revolutionary era in these terms: "The long-term tendency seems to have been toward greater inequality, with more marked class distinctions."[36] Philip J. Greven, Jr., and Kenneth A. Lockridge, out of more systematic studies focused on farm communities, discovered even before the middle of the eighteenth century a shortage of land in the rural areas which they examined, accompanied by signs of decreasing flexibility in the social structure.[37] A similar conclusion about Kent, Connecticut, in the immediate post-Revolutionary period was reached by Charles S. Grant.[38] Henretta has demonstrated how urban property tended to come under the control of a relatively few large holders.[39] And among the critics of the Turner thesis, Louis M. Hacker as early as 1933 castigated the frontier school of thought for blindness to class antagonisms, the concentration of wealth in our society, and the rise of class influences in American life once early settlement had matured.[40] Both in the evolution of early agriculture or its marketing facilities, and in later urbanization and industrialization, forces have been seen at work, reducing opportunity and the equality of its distribution through

35. W. Lloyd Warner and J. O. Low, *The Social System of the Modern Factory* (New Haven, 1947); Sibley, "Demographic Clues;" J. O. Hertzler, "Some Tendencies Toward a Closed Class System in the United States," *Social Forces*, 30 (1952), 313–323.

36. Jackson Turner Main, *The Social Structure of Revolutionary America* (Princeton, 1965), p. 286.

37. See note 3 to introductory section.

38. Grant, *Democracy in Kent.*

39. Henretta, "Economic and Social Structure."

40. Louis M. Hacker, "Sections or Classes?" a review of Turner's *The Significance of Sections in American History*, reproduced in *The Turner Thesis.*

American society—and thereby restricting the access of youths from ordinary families to positions of leadership.

Another way in which the notion of economically generated class development and social crisis has pervaded the literature turns upon the invocation of successive—and implicitly unrelated—constrictive shocks in the social structure. Such interpretations of American social evolution, illustrated in Pattern III of Section D of the figure, are virtually antithetical to the schemes envisioning successive steps toward *greater* equality as outlined in Section A.

Bailyn has drawn attention early in the historical record to the emergence of a mercantile class in New England and a group of planter-speculators in Virginia, each of which blended English connections with colonial capitalism in the middle of the seventeenth century and rose to dominate provincial politics.[41] The third generation land crisis stressed by Greven or Lockridge in eastern Massachusetts—if the geometrically accumulated pressures they suggest prove to be general for the population as a whole—would call for a tightening of the social structure somewhat before the middle of the eighteenth century.[42] The Beardian implication is that certain propertied classes virtually "captured" the process of framing and ratifying the American constitution.[43]

Matthew Josephson's view of developments at the end of the nineteenth century, on the other hand, suggests a sharply intensified control of our society by big businessmen with their political allies in a fairly straightforward realization of Marxist predictions of the historical development of capitalism.[44] A recent repetition of this theme as applied

41. Bailyn, *New England Merchants*; Bailyn, "Politics and Social Structure."

42. The difficulty about their conclusions in the context of *general* trends in America, to which Lockridge for one extends the argument, is this: what proportion of the total number of citizens lived under these conditions and what other proportion, in contrast, moved westward or into the cities where life was not nearly so stagnant? Eugene Harper, for instance, is finding quite a different kind of opportunity environment in western Pennsylvania in the latter decades of the eighteenth century. See the apparent immunity of Dedham to both the ups and downs of the growth cycle in terms of annual births in Figure No. 9, below. Even neighboring Dorchester and Watertown both seem to have been more in the mainstream of New England life.

43. Charles A. Beard, *An Economic Interpretation of the Constitution of the United States* (New York, 1913).

44. Matthew Josephson, *The Robber Barons: The Great American Capitalists, 1861–1901* (New York, 1934); Matthew Josephson, *The Politicos, 1865–1896* (New York, 1938).

to conditions of the mid-twentieth century has been composed by C. Wright Mills and orchestrated by other critics of the contemporary "establishment" in America, ranging in radicalism from Mills' "New Left" legatees to the editorial staff of the Columbia Broadcasting System and the Senate Foreign Relations Committee.[45]

Some sociologists in the 1940's and 1950's joined Sibley, Mills, and the early Lloyd Warner in maintaining that American society was "closing" in either a largely linear pattern or a more broken or stepped one. This interpretation, however, was widely criticized. Though neither Ely Chinoy in 1955 nor William Petersen in 1953 advanced specific counter-conclusions, each warned of fallacies in the argument that assumed dwindling opportunity. Wealth, they said, was in fact less concentrated currently than it had been after the Civil War. Technological change was creating new jobs to be filled even if there were fewer farms to develop in the classic pattern of opportunity on the American frontier. Internal migration served some of the same functions of dispersing and circulating opportunity as had been performed by the recently curtailed immigration. And even after World War II, immigration from Canada, Puerto Rico, and Latin America was not insignificant for certain regions of the country. The augmented role of women in the labor force could have the effect of improving the relative position of the ordinary man, as the arrival of unskilled immigrants had once done, and education (where easily accessible) could open up avenues of mobility.[46] The channels through which mobility occurred might be changing; but that did not mean that there was less of it. Students of business leadership, meanwhile, were coming up with findings that purportedly contradicted the conclusions of C. Wright Mills in this particular area. American businessmen, they maintained, were not proportionately more often derived from privileged homes.[47] Allowing for the shift of the whole American population away from the farm, the

45. Mills, *Power Elite*, esp. pp. 3, 20–24.

46. Ely Chinoy, "Social Mobility Trends in the United States," *American Sociological Review*, 20 (1955), 180–186; William Petersen, "Is America Still the Land of Opportunity? What Recent Studies Show About Social Mobility," *Commentary*, 16 (1953), 477–486.

47. Most notably Keller, Newcomer, Bendix and Howton, and Warner with Abegglen contrary to his own earlier views. (See note 1 of the introductory section.)

social sources of business leaders were said to be relatively stable from the Civil War to the 1950's.

Natalie Rogoff's 1953 study of men taking out marriage licenses in Marion County, Indiana (mostly urban Indianapolis) around 1910 and then again around 1940 introduced carefully collected support for the contention that social mobility among people of modest origins had not changed over the long term any more than the origins of the business elite.[48] New studies of particular communities at different points of time, and systematic comparisons of recent work with older local studies and national samples[49] have led to a current preference for the opinion that social mobility in general, like the recruitment of leadership in particular, has altered very little over fairly substantial periods of time in the development of American society since the later nineteenth century (Pattern IV). A recent study of New England town government by Lockridge and Kreider comes to similar conclusions about the period from 1640 through 1740.[50]

The currently popular view of "no change"[51] has a blissfully tranquilizing effect in the mid-twentieth-century social sciences—for historians who have been plagued for two generations by the Turner controversy, and for sociologists who have long been caught between Marx and the American ideal.[52] It lets us off the hook ideologically, and also allows us to ease up our commitments to an area of research that not only has grown boring after intensive cultivation but has also become involved with increasingly difficult definition and research. The stage has passed in this field of inquiry where unsubstantiated generalization is acceptable.

48. Natalie Rogoff, *Recent Trends in Occupational Mobility* (Glencoe, Ill., 1953).

49. See, for instance, the studies reviewed in Thernstrom, *Poverty and Progress*, pp. 218–219.

50. Kenneth A. Lockridge and Alan Kreider, "The Evolution of Massachusetts Town Government, 1640 to 1740," *William and Mary Quarterly*, 3rd ser., 13 (1966), 549–574.

51. Or of very slight change toward greater mobility in the society and therefore a slightly more open recruitment of leadership.

52. Perhaps the classic case in sociology is Seymour Martin Lipset and Hans L. Zetterburg, "Social Mobility in Industrial Societies," Lipset and Bendix, eds., *Social Mobility in Industrial Society*, pp. 11–75, in which their own data nevertheless seem to belie their contention that social mobility is not related to rates of development or economic change.

In the midst of all this welcome newfound conventional wisdom, however, we remain faced with some uncomfortable findings that do not fit the assumption of stable levels of overall social mobility or constancy in the social foundations of American leadership. The third quarter of the seventeenth century *did* witness in several colonies comparatively intensive family-building and at least a temporary tendency to harden class lines and circumscribe the distribution of political office. The socio-economic characteristics of the new state legislatures following the Revolution *were* different from those of the provincial houses that preceded them. The origins of federal civil servants appointed by Andrew Jackson *did* differ from those of officials appointed by John Adams, though much of the change had already taken place by Thomas Jefferson's time.

Contemporary witnesses are important. Sometimes men have thought, and said, that they lived in a land of opportunity which surpassed and improved upon the conditions of former years. At other times other men have maintained that opportunity was not what it had once been. Neither view—whether it came from expert or man on the street— need be regarded from the safe detachment of hindsight as a mere figment of someone else's imagination. The very long-term trend of opportunity toward or away from an open social structure may, indeed, have been slight, therefore allegations of a tightening or loosening of the social order over several decades or even centuries could also be unfounded. Yet despite these general errors, contemporary opinions of what was transpiring might still have been right—even if for the wrong reasons. Erroneous historical conclusions about the nature of long-term trends can have served largely as rationalizations for an intuitive but fairly accurate sense of more current or recent social change. It will be seen, moreover, that occasional comments by contemporaries, or by observers in hindsight, that things were getting "worse" (i.e., socially tighter) at some point (or just the opposite) need not contradict the overall conclusion that from century to century, and from one broad historical era to the next, there has been much less change in the recruitment of American leadership and in general patterns of social mobility than has often been imagined. This long-term constancy, in other words, tells only part of the story. It does not obviate the possibility of significant and even systematic changes in opportunity in shorter ranges of time that have been largely masked by the way in which data have been collected.

To specify still further the problems of broad generalizations concerning the history of opportunity, it is also important to remember that the origins of one group of leaders could well be closing up while entry to another group became substantially democratized. One authority on what was happening in the society at a given point may have been focussing on one part of the social structure while a man of contrary opinions might be remarking primarily upon another part. What at first may seem "no change" could be the net result of the counter-workings of almost diametrically opposed changes of parts within the whole, just as the net difference over long periods of time could conceal sharp swings back and forth within relatively short segments of broader eras. In the prospectus for the studies of which this discussion describes part, Oscar Handlin very carefully specified that opportunity need not vary uniformly through the entire society at a given point of time or over the same span of time.[53]

The question arises therefore of discovering what common truth might exist among these many views of the history of opportunity, or of going beyond them to some new conclusion altogether. If some more meaningful and valid generalization about what actually happened can be established, we can then attempt to explain why.

II. Actual Chronological Variations in the Origins of American Leadership

THE actual pattern of historical variation in the social backgrounds of different kinds of leaders in the biographical collections which were used in this analysis in fact resembled *none* of the models outlined in Figure No. 1. Here and there a writer who supported a given direc-

53. Oscar and Mary Handlin, *The Dimensions of Liberty* (Cambridge, 1961), pp. 137–140.

tion of change at a given point of time might be correct; and underlying long-term trends or more sudden basic shifts towards more or less open recruitment did exist in particular groups of leadership within the whole. Yet all the familiar forms of description and explanation in the literature fail to cope with what seems to have been the essentially *cyclical* nature of opportunity in the chronological evolution of our society. That is, the predominant feature of the way in which the proportion of American leadership recruited from families of high or low social position[1] changed in the past involved not steps or linear trends, not growth curves or prolonged "U" curves, but fairly regularly recurring and highly predictable fluctuations. These repetitive swings in the percentages of American leaders of different sorts who came from ordinary homes (or, conversely, from favorably placed homes) usually exceeded in amount of change the net effects of trends lasting a century or even two centuries in the course of our social development. To restate this view: opportunity *did* alternately open up or close up significantly for young Americans born in succeeding groups of years (from one birth cohort to another, to use the terminology of demographers), and thus the presently popular idea of "no change" in equality of access to positions of leadership is an unacceptable one. But the most significant variation in the social backgrounds of our national leadership occurred not as a consequence of great events like the American Revolution or major processes like the advent of industrialism or the closing of the frontier, but at fairly regular intervals of just over twenty years on the average. This pattern of recurrent or repetitive social change can be observed from the earliest English settlement to the end of the nineteenth century, where the materials of the present study run out, covering men who reached maturity and began their careers over almost three hundred years of our history.

---

1. Different technical definitions of high or low position in the social structure to classify the parents or guardians of the Americans studied here yield virtually the same patterns of change over time. See my forthcoming *Opportunity, Equality, and Population* (of which the present discussion is a shortened version) for further details. The cutting points of groupings most frequently used in the present discussion are described in Appendix A for the colonial Harvard and Yale men; in Appendix B for men covered in the *D.A.B.*

THE LIFE CHANCES OF COLONIAL COLLEGE MEN

The first place in which this cyclical variation in opportunity among those who filled positions of leadership in American society came to light involved the Harvard and Yale men of 1642–1745 whose biographies appear in *Sibley* and *Dexter*. Figure No. 2 (whose details appear in Table 1) shows, among alumni of successive groups of three college years each[2] who enjoyed better than average "success" as adults, the changing percentages who had fathers, stepfathers, or guardians who were highly placed in the social structure to begin with.

Among the alumni of 1648–50, 1669–74, 1693–98, 1717–19, and 1738–40 the proportion of those college men who became major public or military officials, substantial merchants or landowners, or exceptional professionals, whose fathers or guardians had also held such a high place in society was regularly 20 to 30 percent lower than among alumni in other classes around them. (Further detail of who was categorized "upper class" under these more general headings will be found in Appendix A.) Meanwhile the long-range change in the social sources of the college-educated elite over as much as a century from the mid-1600's to the mid-1700's "opened up" to those born outside the families of the previous elite 25 to 30 percent, no more change, in effect, than could be found over and over again during the course of a few years and repeated approximately every two decades. Among those born at intervals of about twenty-two or twenty-three years on the average, there were evidently *recurrent* conditions under which the leadership families of New England were significantly less self-recruiting and self-perpetuating than usual.[3]

2. Originally the college classes were divided into groups admitted by different presidents in order to examine the social scope of the educational service offered by successive administrations. These and other findings specific to the early New England colleges are presented in my forthcoming monograph on the social foundations of early American higher education.

3. The variance is large for the classes of 1684–86; and of the college years 1666–68 there were only three alumni who attained high place in their careers. Table 1 gives the standard deviation for the percentage in each group of three classes so that the reader will have some means of evaluating variance and relating percentages to the numbers of men on which they are based. The figure denotes by arrows above and below the central plot the standard deviation for those groups of years where the variance is least or where the mean is most significantly high or low. Since it is three years that are involved in each

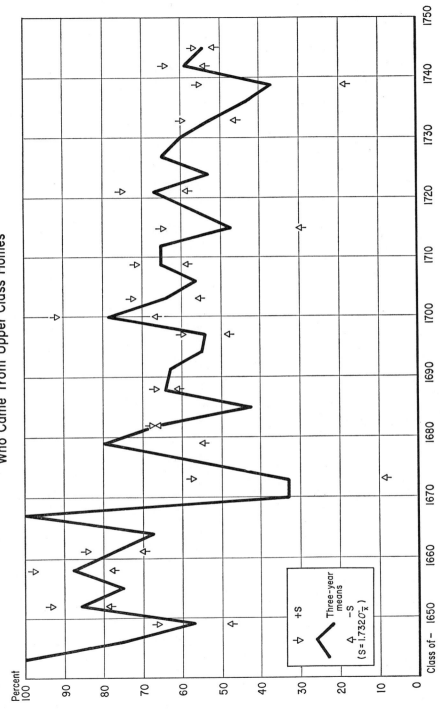

Figure No. 2. Percentages of Harvard and Yale Alumni Attaining Upper Class Positions Who Came from Upper Class Homes

TABLE 1

Percentages of Harvard and Yale Alumni Attaining Upper Class Positions Who Came from Upper Class Families*

College Years	No.	Percent from Upper Class Families	s†	Percent of All Known Students Who Had Upper Class Origins	% Upper Class from Upper Class / % All Students from Upper Class
1642–44	2	100	0	69	1.45
1645–47	4	75	43.2	36	2.08
1648–50	7	57	8.4	43	1.33
1651–53	7	86	6.3	47	1.83
1654–56	8	75	30.6	44	1.71
1657–59	8	88	9.7	41	2.15
1660–62	13	77	6.4	44	1.57
1663–65	3	67	47.1	41	1.63
1666–68	3	100	0	33	3.00
1669–71	3	33	47.1	38	.87
1672–74	3	33	23.6	17	1.94
1675–77	7	57	28.3	37	1.54
1678–80	5	80	24.5	67	1.19
1681–83	3	67	0	25	2.68
1684–86	12	42	26.2	37	1.14
1687–89	11	64	2.0	41	1.56
1690–92	8	63	37.5	39	1.62
1693–95	20	55	23.7	40	1.38
1696–98	13	54	4.9	33	1.63
1699–01	14	79	11.6	45	1.76
1702–04	14	64	7.6	33	1.94
1705–07	16	56	32.7	33	1.70
1708–10	17	65	5.4	35	1.86
1711–13	17	65	16.3	32	2.03
1714–16	17	47	16.8	29	1.62
1717–19	28	57	25.6	38	1.50
1720–22	39	67	7.3	31	2.16
1723–25	42	53	16.3	24	2.21
1726–28	45	65	17.9	31	2.10
1729–31	42	60	12.8	21	2.86
1732–34	49	53	5.7	28	1.89
1735–37	41	44	20.2	21	2.09
1738–40	38	37	17.8	20	1.85
1741–43	54	59	4.3 ⎫	35	ca. 1.62
1744–45	39	54	1.5 ⎭		

Sources: Sibley and Dexter

* For the types of positions of parents or alumni considered "upper class" see Appendix A.

† The standard deviation equals 1.732 times the standard error of the mean for a three–unit category and gives a confidence limit of 91.7 percent for the three-year means.

What these fluctuations of social origin mean—in terms of some names familiar to students of colonial life in New England—is that Samuel Sewall (H-1671), John Wise (H-1673), and their collegiate contemporaries seem to have entered a more "open" society when they set forth on their careers as young men in the 1670's than Joseph Dudley, Increase Mather, Solomon Stoddard, or Wait and Adam Winthrop from the college classes of the later 1650's and the early 1660's. And they also seem to have experienced a context of more equal opportunity than many alumni who came *after* them. Subsequently the classes of 1693–98, which contained leadership of the sort provided by Elisha Cooke, Jr., Josiah Willard, Josiah Cotton, Oliver Noyes, and Jonathan Law, produced a college-educated elite more openly recruited in their turn than the leadership from other years before and after. Both these two groups or college cohorts—Harvard men of the early 1670's and those of the mid-1690's—like the classes of 1648–50 before them, whatever their personal origins, their social thought, or the ideology of their times, appear to have faced a factually more egalitarian social structure than alumni of the surrounding years or those students in the "great" Leverett classes of the 1720's. President Leverett, who himself had been in the class of 1680, did not hinder this constrictive process of the 1720's when he put the final seal of approval upon the rather new custom of ranking incoming students by parental eminence, instead of academic promise.[4]

Yet the social hardening of Mother Harvard's arteries—of which the "backwoods" bitterly complained, yet the new college in Connecticut that the population of the interior helped to found was quick to emulate —did not last, either. College presidents came and went, affecting in different ways the careers of those whom they educated. More fundamentally, however, the conditions of opportunity in the society in

---

group, the standard error of the *mean* of the three years is $1/\sqrt{3}$ or $1/1.732$ times the standard deviation of the annual percentages which compose the group. Thus the figure given in Table 1, if added to and subtracted from the mean for the corresponding three years, shows the margins of almost twice the standard deviation of the mean. In other words, it sets the confidence limits of somewhat more than 90 per cent of the variability of the three-year averages plotted in Figure No. 2. These three-year averages, moreover, do not overlap and therefore do not present the probability problems of moving averages.

4. These particulars are made available in my forthcoming monograph on early Harvard and Yale.

which college men lived out their adult lives seem also to have changed once more. Samuel Adams, of the Harvard class of 1740, for instance, belonged to an age group that enjoyed the most open social conditions since the time of John Wise—far different from the environment that waited for the famous Harvard class of 1727, decorated with Thomas Hutchinson, Jonathan Trumbull, and many other leading men of pre- and post-Revolutionary America.

Nor did the process stop there. Breadth of recruitment continued to fluctuate among subsequent age groups as they had among the preceding. This fluctuation did, however, occur on top of a long-term trend towards greater egalitarianism. Yet this long-term trend, evident in Figure No. 2, had begun in the earliest years of settlement and moved as steadily in the Puritan society of the seventeenth century as it did in the more immediately pre-Revolutionary America in which our early national heroes matured. Even among the age groups who made the American Revolution, recruitment into leadership positions changed significantly from one college cohort to the next. John Adams of the Harvard class of 1755 sensed the reality of his environment when he wrote that the chance to get ahead when he came along was not what it once had been. He and his age peers like John Hancock (H-1754) not only created a new "establishment" which to some seemed a strange social result of the Revolution; they were also themselves the products of social conditions that were relatively "closed" compared to those faced by older men of different experience such as Samuel Adams and Meshech Weare, from whom they took the control and the honors of the new society.

At this point a possible objection should be noted. It might be thought that at the critical points of time, where Figure No. 2 indicates a high or low percentage of the most successful college men coming from upper class homes, simply an unusually large or an unusually small proportion of the *universe* of alumni in these age groups had high social origins. Did, in other words, a large proportion of those with highest place in society at the end of their careers who came from upper class homes in certain college cohorts merely reflect the exceptional makeup of the *total* college population in that period? On the contrary, Table 1 demonstrates that on the whole there was much less fluctuation in the social composition of the total New England college population (minus a few non-graduates who elude the surviving records) than in the social origins of those among them who reached highest status at the end of their careers. Furthermore, what variations there were did *not* follow the 22 ½ year pattern. Instead, the historical change in the overall percentages coming from upper class homes took the form of two long, largely linear segments of gradually broadening social origin from the class of 1642 through that of 1674, and then from about 1678 through 1740, with cuts or steps back to more "closed" total college student recruitment around 1675 and 1741. (These patterns and their causes are examined at length in a separate monograph on the two colleges, the lives of their alumni, and the apparent social functions of higher education in the first hundred years of American history.)

If, on the other hand, the percentage of the most successful alumni who came from upper class homes is expressed relative to the percentage of the same three-year college cohorts as a whole who had similar high social origins (in the final column of Table 1), then the classes around 1649, 1670, 1694, 1718, and 1743 had the lowest ratios while the classes around 1658, 1682, 1703, 1712, and 1730 had the highest proportion of upper class backgrounds among their elite members of high achievers relative to the weight of boys from upper class families in the original college intake. An analysis of variance employing Somers' d_{yx} using several layers or strata to describe the social positions of both parents and alumni further indicates that the eventual adult status of college groups around 1650, 1672, 1691–94, 1719, and 1739 was least of all connected with parental social position, while for the Harvard and Yale classes from around 1665, 1687, 1710, and 1729 "success" was most of all tied to social origin. These findings, reported in full elsewhere, use all alumni (not just the minority reaching upper class status) and measure downward as well as upward mobility. In the end, they strongly confirm the original impression of Figure No. 2 that the opportunities of colonial college men were "open" or "closed" at intervals of about 22 ½ years on the average in a way that did *not* reflect mere changes in the social sources of boys coming to college in the first place. The use of the universe of alumni to study the changing openness of opportunity in this fashion shows, furthermore, that patterns derived from the social back-

grounds of sometimes very small numbers of more than averagely successful alumni (for example, Table 1 shows N's of only three each for
the crucial class groups of 1669–71 and 1672–74) are *not* the result of
peculiarities attributable to small sample size.

Among college men of the colonial era there was some tendency for
the opportunities for leadership in the professions (primarily in the ministry) to open up, or to close down, for those from homes outside the
upper classes at slightly different intervals from those affecting merchants, statesmen, military leaders, or major landholders. Primarily
these distinctions seem to have resulted from somewhat different critical
ages for determining who went to the top in particular career lines.[5]
Generally speaking the upper reaches of the ministry were more open to
college men from homes outside the upper classes than were the higher
places of secular leadership. Though maintaining a parallel—if slightly
differently timed—pattern of undulation, the percentage of the professional elite who came from comparatively eminent origins usually
stayed below the comparable proportion for leaders whose primary
positions in the society depended more upon property and office. Many
propertied positions were inherited in spite of real difficulty in passing
on business wealth *per se* in the colonial era, and in spite of a striking list
of ministers' sons who became eminent merchants. There was also a
substantial amount of the more typically "American" transfusion of
new business blood, even via Cambridge and New Haven, by the sons
of lesser traders, artisans, and farmers who succeeded in economic affairs
and rose to places of wealth and political influence. Yet both professional
and secular leadership as enjoyed by college men, to restate the comparison, progressively opened up more to young men from fairly ordinary
homes over the century from the 1640's to the 1740's. Thus the two
long-term trends were parallel. And in both groups there appears to
have been a tendency for alumni about twenty-two years apart on the
average to benefit from more open or more equal opportunity conditions. Yet to experience comparably open or comparably closed life
chances, professional alumni had to be from three to six years ahead of
those who chose more secular routes to eminence.

Especially among the professionals, when the total alumni group is

5. Some examples are discussed below.

divided in this way the number of more successful men in any three college years becomes very small and the variance around the means becomes very large. Figure No. 3, however, shows how close-knit and substantial was the chronological fluctuation in the social backgrounds of those who grasped the better secular opportunities from among fifty years of alumni from 1696 through 1745. In this more homogeneous and still relatively numerous subdivision of the total alumni sample, there were almost always ten or more men in any three-year period who held a high place in property or office (or both) at the end of their careers— and often more than thirty in each such historical group or college cohort. There is little question that the percentages of these men who came from upper class homes in the college cohorts around 1715 and 1739 were significantly lower than in intervening or neighboring years.

In summary, the total group of college men who held better than average position in the socio-economic structure as adults can be separated according to the different kinds of careers they followed and substantial swings in the openness of the social origins of those who enjoyed the highest adult position found independently among professionals and non-professionals. And among the alumni of the first half of the eighteenth century who filled high secular positions as adults, where the sample numbers were largest and the career composition more homogeneous than in the total group, the pattern of fluctuating social change was in fact most clear. The curves are smoother, the dips and rises more marked, and the variance about the three-year means is more regularly low. These more particular findings, when the sample has been broken down into some of its parts, substantially strengthen the general argument that among the colonial alumni of New England the openness of high opportunity to young men who came from homes outside the upper classes (or conversely, the self-recruitment of these upper classes) did in fact vary chronologically in at least a quasi-cyclical fashion.

SIMILAR FLUCTUATIONS OF OPPORTUNITY IN SUBSEQUENT AMERICAN LEADERSHIP

The key questions now become: (1) whether this pattern of fairly regular chronological swings in the social recruitment of the most successful was a phenomenon just of families likely to have some mem-

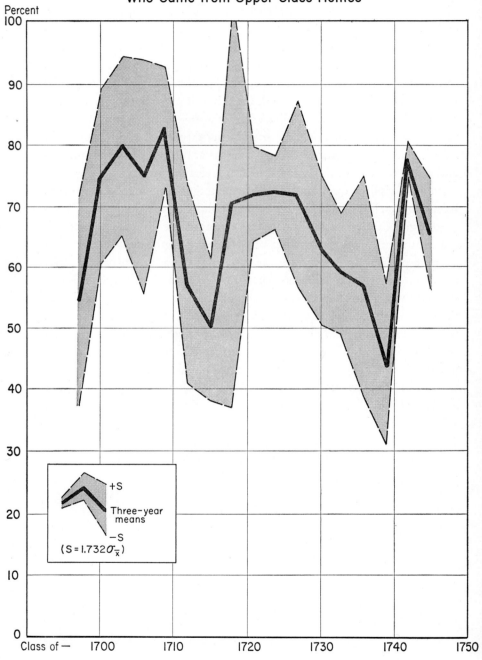

Figure No. 3. Percentages of Eminent Secular Alumni Who Came from Upper Class Homes

ber in college; (2) whether it was merely some peculiarity of the New England region; and, even if these two other limitations were transcended, (3) whether there was any generality to such fluctuations after the replacement of the first two or three generations of American leadership. The writer has been conducting simultaneously with the Sibley-Dexter investigation of the colonial college men of New England, a study of the origins and careers of 15,000 notable men and women of different educational and regional backgrounds for whom sketches appear in the *Dictionary of American Biography* (the *D.A.B.*). This second inquiry offered the prospect of slightly overlapping but predominantly independent evidence with which to test both the validity and the generality of regular fluctuations in the social sources of American leadership.

Overall fluctuations in the degree to which at various points of time (among various birth cohorts) the men of the whole *D.A.B.* sample came from what might be called upper class homes can be observed very much as would be indicated if the patterns among colonial Harvard and Yale alumni were carried forward to the end of the nineteenth century. But these overall oscillations, though significant in their own right, tell only part of the story of how relatively short-term changes in the social foundations from which American leadership was recruited usually exceeded long-term trends of a century or more in duration. The most clear and convincing evidence is to be had from types or categories of somewhat similar careers within the total *D.A.B.* sample and the way in which their variations of social origin chronologically fit on to, or can be extrapolated from, comparable leadership groups in the earlier college population. It has already been explained that the birth groups—there given in the approximate form of college classes—in which unusually open, or alternatively heavily "inherited," opportunity occurred were slightly different for ministers and physicians than for those attaining high places in nonprofessional careers anchored to various forms of property or public office. The typical gap among the early Harvard and Yale men was only three years; but that kind of "near miss" can begin very quickly to dampen down a cyclical effect whose timing from trough to peak, or vice versa, lasts eleven years or less.

Within the wide spectrum of notable people from many career lines who are sampled in the *D.A.B.*, the timing of fluctuations in the origins of religious and medical leaders according to birth cohorts once again usually precedes the comparable ups and downs in upper class recruitment among public officers of various types by about three years or more, as in the case of the colonial alumni in Sibley and Dexter. The *D.A.B.* sample, on the other hand, unlike the group of early New England college men, includes many educators and other academics. Their opportunity variations were timed among birth cohorts even further in advance of those most relevant for doctors and ministers. The *D.A.B.* also incorporates sketches for many businessmen. The ups and downs of their parental background pivoted among still earlier birth cohorts who came about a dozen years before, or almost in direct cyclical contrast to, the swings in the social origins of public officials. Thus much of the very real and quite large variation from age group to age group in individual occupations or types of occupations, with different length of training or with different critical age thresholds at which high ultimate advancement became possible or was blocked, is masked or obscured for the *D.A.B.* sample as a whole. Different kinds of leadership need to be examined separately if we are to say that 1800 was a "closed" point or 1812 an "open" point in American society for many varieties of men of different ages whose careers can be estimated from their birth dates to have reached in those years the most critical stage for determining eventual opportunity.

It might, first of all, be useful to examine the origins of public officials selected for inclusion in the *D.A.B.* Leaders in this area have often served to symbolize our nation as a social and political democracy. More than others they also have been in positions to change the rules for our socioeconomic development. There are basically three kinds of public leaders in the *D.A.B.*: elected and other civil officials, lawyers (who are mostly judges or public prosecutors and the like), and leaders of the military.[6] This combined sub-group of public officials can be compared with some

6. A separate volume will discuss differences within general occupational groups—for example, between elected and non-elected public officials; navy and army officers; judges and those who were primarily trial lawyers; business leaders in manufacture and those in finance or commerce.

consistency in occupation to early Harvard and Yale men who attained upper class status outside the professions, since there were relatively few college alumni in that colonial group who made their own fortunes in trade or land, or kept family resources of this sort going, without also participating in the public life of the colonies.[7]

Figure No. 4, the data for which appear in Table 2, shows how changes of the social backgrounds in the nonprofessional colonial alumni group and the sample of three kinds of public officers in the *D.A.B.* fit on to each other in two important ways to give the general argument about the historical development of opportunity in America greater strength than either source of evidence could provide separately. It is possible to demonstrate that the ups and downs of upper class recruitment of public figures continued to fall at about 22½-year intervals on the average, as in the sample of college men, and at virtually those very dates which an extrapolation of the chronology of such movements in the earlier group would predict or project.

It is not always so easy from the information given in the *D.A.B.*, however, to distinguish what might be called the local upper classes from the upper middle classes, to separate those fathers who were big businessmen or planters, or regionally eminent professionals, from average persons of these types. In the nature of the Harvard and Yale biographies, this had been a much surer distinction than that between the upper middle classes—particularly the nonprofessionals in the group—and those somewhat below them in the socio-economic structure. The "best" cutting point between high and low parental position for purposes of continuity of definition between the two samples of biographies is therefore not the most reliable threshold of separation to suit the materials in the *D.A.B.* With somewhat more certainty it is possible in that collection to distinguish fathers who were probably *minor* traders, manufacturers, and planter-farmers, lesser officials and military men, and low grade or semi-professionals—and those of still more humble station in life—from "upper middle class" parents who could fairly reliably be considered to be above them according to several different dimensions

7. The classic examples of men of great mercantile involvement and no major public office—Samuel Lilly, Thomas Brattle, Sr., and John Colman—were not college men. Cf. Bailyn and Bailyn, *Massachusetts Shipping*.

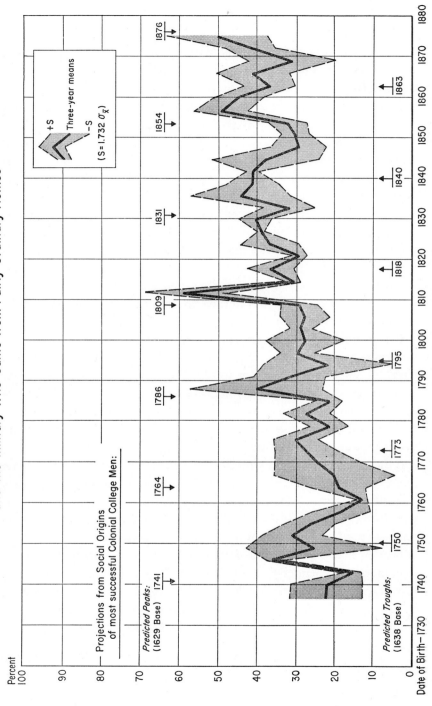

Figure No. 4. Percentages of <u>D.A.B.</u> Men with Main Careers in Government, Law, and the Military Who Came from Fairly Ordinary Homes

TABLE 2

Percentages of *D.A.B.* Men with Principal Careers in Government, Law, and the Military Who Came from Ordinary Homes*

Years of Birth	No.	Percent of Ordinary Origin†	s‡		Years of Birth	No.	Percent of Ordinary Origin†	s‡
1736–38	32	21.9	9.7	.	1808–10	86	29.1	4.6
1739–41	23	21.7	9.4	.	1811–13	93	59.1	9.7
1742–44	47	14.9	2.1	.	1814–16	99	30.3	2.0
1745–47	28	35.7	1.5	.	1817–19	94	36.2	6.1
1748–50	36	25.0	17.6	.	1820–22	99	29.3	1.5
1751–53	39	30.8	8.2	.	1823–25	112	36.6	7.7
1754–56	46	26.1	6.8	.	1826–28	103	38.8	0.9
1757–59	39	18.0	7.5	.	1829–31	92	40.2	4.3
1760–62	31	12.9	1.2	.	1832–34	111	31.5	6.6
1763–65	32	18.8	7.1	.	1835–37	93	44.1	12.6
1766–68	25	20.0	15.8	.	1838–40	69	40.6	7.0
1769–71	37	24.3	11.1	.	1841–43	59	40.7	1.7
1772–74	33	27.3	8.0	.	1844–46	58	37.9	13.6
1775–77	30	30.0	5.7	.	1847–49	51	29.4	6.8
1778–80	48	20.8	5.3	.	1850–52	50	30.0	4.0
1781–83	48	27.1	6.1	.	1853–55	50	32.0	5.0
1784–86	44	20.5	3.7	.	1856–58	55	49.1	7.1
1787–89	45	40.0	16.8	.	1859–61	54	44.4	6.3
1790–92	48	31.3	9.0	.	1862–64	41	36.6	6.6
1793–95	56	21.4	16.7	.	1865–67	27	40.7	9.5
1796–98	47	29.8	4.2	.	1868–70	36	30.6	11.4
1799–01	62	27.4	10.4	.	1871–73	29	41.4	6.7
1802–04	60	28.3	2.9	.	1874–76	16	50.0	13.4
1805–07	76	27.6	7.5	.				

Source: *Dictionary of American Biography*, 20 Vols., 2 Supp.

* For the kinds of parents or guardians considered "ordinary" ("lower middle class" or less) see Appendix B.

† Percentaged for those of known origin only. The unknowns quite regularly compose from one third to two fifths of the sample, and are *not* the source of the fluctuations.

‡ s=1.732 the standard error of the three-year means.

commonly used for defining a social structure, i.e., wealth, influence, probable prestige.[8]

Figure No. 4 turns the question of Figure No. 3 upside down, so to speak, to ask what percentage of notable public officers of the three basic sorts taken together—governmental, legal, and military—came from homes that were probably *outside* both the upper classes and the upper middle classes. Very much the same pattern emerges—in mirror image of Figure No. 3—of long-term democratization in the social sources of leadership accompanied by recurrent swings of opening or closing access to high civic and military positions among men coming from just about the very birth cohorts which would be indicated or "predicted" from the chronology of colonial college men.

In the first place, the long-term trend among public figures in the *D.A.B.* born from about 1700 through the Civil War displays the same slope towards broader and more open sources of leadership that was evident in Figure No. 3 among the non-professional colonial alumni born from the 1670's through the 1720's. The degree to which certain leading public figures in America have come from what could be called fairly ordinary homes increased steadily—that is, the social origins of this kind of leadership democratized—in fact for two and a half centuries of our history, from men born in England before the original heavy New World migration to those born during the Civil War who did not reach the political maturity of their forties until the early years of the twentieth century—in other words, through those men who governed our country between the two World Wars.

In the second place, however, relatively short-term fluctuations in the degree of upper class recruitment among notable civic officials, judges, and military leaders—which have swung back and forth on the average of somewhat over two decades per cycle—continued to occur and con-

---

8. Appendix B offers some details of how the division between "upper middle class" and "lower middle class" was executed operationally, including the kind of judgment that had to be made from the context of the biography rather than from hard, detailed information on wealth, business size, or professional eminence. For a convenient and hopefully not too misleading shorthand, all those of lower middle class or even plainer background are frequently referred to collectively as those who came from "fairly ordinary homes" or who had "quite ordinary social origins." These labels, that is, are used to stand for all men who came from *neither* upper class *nor* upper middle class families, as far as can be determined.

tinued to match or to exceed the 15 to 20 percent per century change typical of the long-term trend. The peaks of quite ordinary origin for these men, moreover, came very regularly, as the dates across the top of Figure No. 4 indicate, just a little after the expected periods if a 22½-year pattern of changes was extrapolated forward from the birth cohort of about 1651 (the college class of 1671 from the independent Harvard and Yale sample described in Figure No. 3). Maximum percentages in Figure No. 4, for example, occur in 1812 and 1836 rather than in the "predicted" years of 1809 and 1831. And while it is true that the birth cohorts of public officials with *lowest* percentages from lower middle class or even more ordinary homes tended to lag a few years behind the troughs expected from a simple extrapolation of the Harvard and Yale variations (based on the class of 1658, born on the average in 1638), nevertheless the spacing between the actual troughs (1761 and 1785, then 1803, 1821, 1848–51, and 1869) adheres closely to the familiar interval originally found among the early college men of New England.

Over and over again, in timing closely predictable from similar movements as much as two and a half centuries before, young men born ten years apart who rose to dominant positions in the society changed sharply in terms of their social origins—by differences as great as the ones between men born a hundred years apart. To say that leadership in public life in America has become increasingly accessible to those raised outside upper class homes over the full course of our history (or at least to where these data run out) may be true. This is not to deny, however, —to take one clear-cut example—that those in high positions who had turned forty in the years just after the Revolution (those born around 1746) came from substantially more ordinary backgrounds on the average than those *later* men who turned forty in the first years of the nineteenth century (born about 1761). To hark back to the preceding discussion of how the openness of American society has been handled in the literature, Schlesinger's Jacksonians apparently were complaining quite correctly of a recent tendency towards more closed political recruitment—it stands out clearly in the groups born from 1746 through 1761 who reached the forty-year-old mark from 1786 through 1801, and were firm in the saddle of American politics at age sixty from 1806 through 1821, while the future Jacksonian leadership was coming of age.

If we assume the pivotal age for getting on to the upper rungs of the ladder of ultimate political advancement to be about forty, we are then saying that when Sidney H. Aronson[9] found the federal officials appointed by Jackson (1829–36) to have fathers with high occupational places in the social structure just a little less frequently than those appointed by Jefferson (1801–08), who were in turn at least equally more "democratic" in this respect than the appointees of John Adams (1797–1800), we are comparing approximately the birth cohorts of 1789–96 with those of 1761–68 and 1757–60 respectively in Figure No. 4. One new or additional suggestion of the current data is that the government of James Madison may have been still more democratically recruited than that of Jefferson before it, while the Monroe administration may have been somewhat less "open" in this sense than both the Jacksonian and Madisonian eras of federal government.

In comparison with the information patterned in Figure No. 4, furthermore, it is important to note that almost identical cyclical movements or fluctuations appear in the proportion of important public figures whose fathers were laborers, skilled workers without employees or supervisory positions, military men from the ranks, seamen or overland transport workers, the most ordinary and routine level of office and sales clerks, or small farmers—those who in W. Lloyd Warner's parlance can be called "common men." (Appendix B). The same overall trend and the same rather cyclical short-term fluctuations that exceed long-range change over great segments of American history appear at this level of social origin as well. In general, moreover, from one occupational group in the *D.A.B.* to another, the use of different cutting points to delineate "high" or "low" origins for various types of leadership tends most of the time to produce very parallel chronological patterns from birth cohort to birth cohort.

A similar consistency, even when the terms of the definition are varied, applies to the choice between percentaging those known to have a given social origin on a base including individuals whose family position cannot be determined and percentaging with only those of fairly well known background as the base.[10] (Trends, moreover, cannot be

9. Aronson, *Status and Kinship*, pp. 56–83.
10. While in the process of preparing his study of the United States Senate (*Power and*

substantially affected by the weight of the unknowns since their proportion in the total in most cases remains very stable over long periods of
time, with the exception of very late birth cohorts, dying in the 1930's,
who are included in the second supplement of the *D.A.B.* Among this
last group a more systematic effort, benefiting from the help of close
living relatives, tracked down the parental positions of a higher proportion of the sample selected for coverage.)

The argument that the social origins of public officers selected for the
D.A.B. followed the kind of largely cyclical pattern described is strengthened, finally, by evidence that various subsections of the general category independently followed the pattern of the whole. First of all, public officers who attended a college of some sort and those who did not
experienced very much the same chronological pattern of movement
into leadership from one birth cohort to another down to the end of the
colonial period and on through the nineteenth century, though the
alumni were generally recruited from a somewhat less open social base
than those who had not been to college. In the second place, the careers
of government officials, judges, and lawyers, and army and navy leaders
all tended to mark peaks and troughs in the proportions recruited from
lower middle class or even more ordinary families among very much
the same birth cohorts. Thus, Figure No. 4 looks the way it does because the college and non-college men, and individuals in three different
occupational lines included in the broad public service category, all *independently* came more frequently or less frequently from fairly ordinary homes in approximately the same birth cohorts. The historical
variations of social origin in these five different sub-samples—two educational and three concerning more specific career lines—were not random or inclined to wash each other out. On the contrary, among the
related occupational groups, or the college and non-college members of
them—and including individuals who can be expected *a priori* to have
been affected by changes of party, policy, or events of state at about the
same time—the patterns for each distinct sub-group are similar enough

Politics), David J. Rothman generously made available information on the parents of senators covered in the *D.A.B.* which he found in all sources outside this collection of biographies. From this information it appears that parental status not accounted for properly
in the *D.A.B.* could be anything short of glaringly humble circumstances on the one end
and national eminence on the other.

so that when the whole category of public servants in the *D.A.B.* is assembled the more substantial numbers present in the total give even
clearer and statistically more convincing manifestations of the same
cyclicity than is evident in each of the parts examined separately.

Parallel fluctuations of the social origins of other leadership groups,
though located in somewhat different birth cohorts, also stand out from
the data of the *D.A.B.* As among the public officers the distinction between the upper middle and the lower middle classes (Appendix B)
serves readily to illustrate typical chronological changes which can also
be identified at other cutting points.

Figure No. 5 shows, first of all,—contrary to the situation among
public servants of various sorts (and also in contrast to the pattern for
divines and doctors among colonial Harvard and Yale men)—that the
proportion of ministers and medical leaders included in the *D.A.B.* who
came from rather ordinary families was on the whole *declining* slowly
among men born from the middle of the eighteenth century onwards.
More striking, however, are the marked fluctuations of a short-term
nature in the percentage coming from fairly simple backgrounds. These
more cyclical variations back and forth on the order of 20 to 30 percent
within only a decade during each swing from trough to peak or peak to
trough came in birth cohorts about three years before similar shifts already noted in the proportion of public servants who had been raised in
comparable homes (Figure No. 4). This is almost exactly the same temporal relationship in the career patterns of these two groups of professionals and those of men holding public office of some sort that was evident for colonial Harvard and Yale men in the earlier analysis.

In addition, the proportion of the *D.A.B.* doctors and divines who
came from even more humble or ordinary families (what might be
called "common man" social origins—cf. Appendix B) varied with
the same timing that was evident at the cutting point between the upper middle and the lower middle classes. The same consistency of chronological change between higher and lower thresholds in the social
structure as described for public officers was evident in these two professions as well. In fact, the fluctuation in the proportion of leaders in
medicine and religion who were the sons of small farmers, working

Figure No. 5. Percentages of D.A.B. Men with Main Careers in Medicine and the Ministry Who Came from Fairly Ordinary Homes

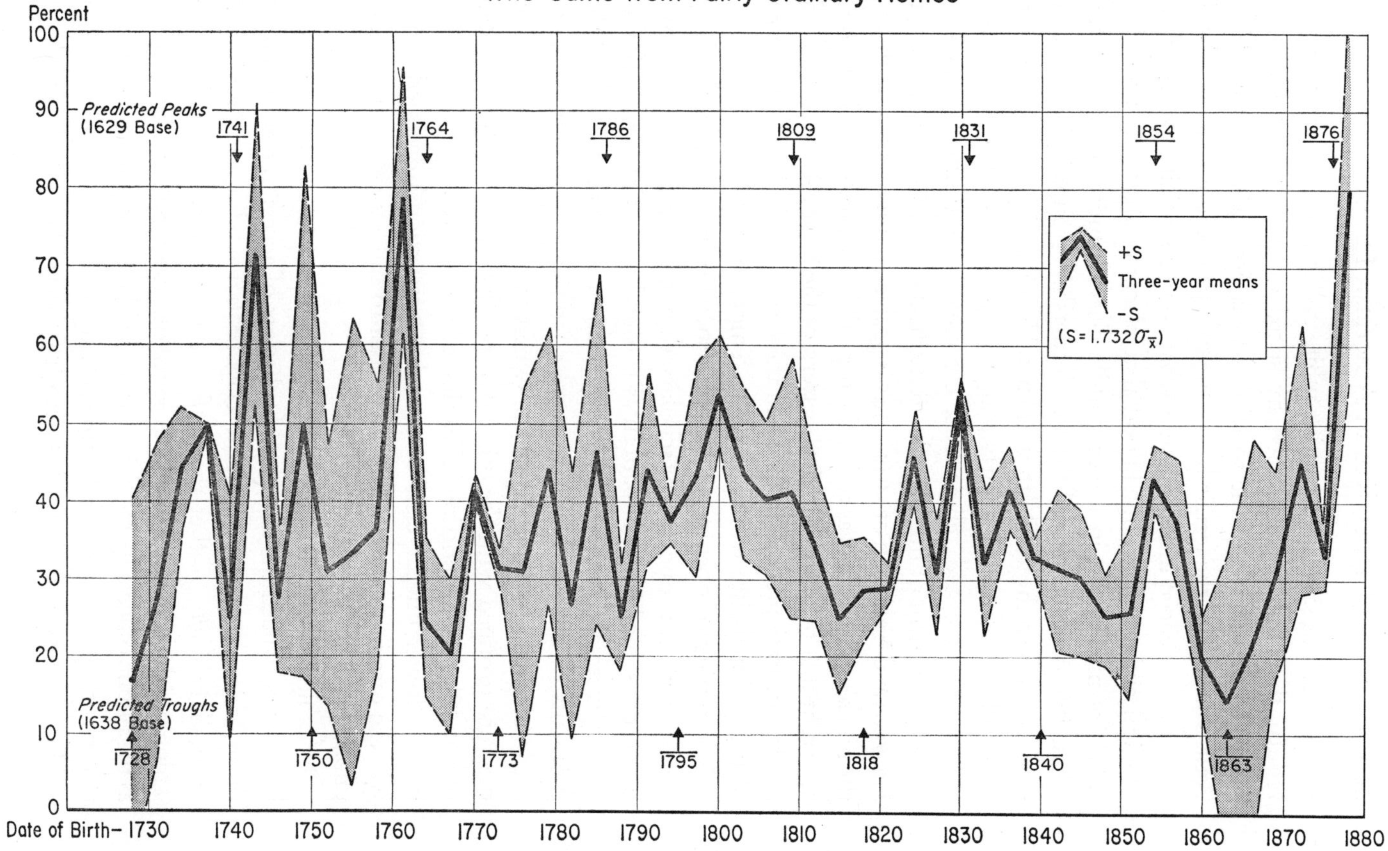

men of various sorts, and routine white collar workers was even more
regular than the cycles defined by social origins divided higher up,
nearer to the middle of the social order, as presented in Figure No. 5.
And, once again, the leadership of the two professions to a considerable
extent experienced independently what were essentially parallel chronological swings in the likelihood that places of distinction would be
filled by men raised in lower middle class or more ordinary homes.
These fluctuations affected the two leadership groups in just about the
same ways even though both the general levels and the long-term trends
of recruitment from such fairly plain families were quite different as between medicine and religion. If, moreover, the timing of unusually
open recruitment of ministerial and medical leadership from among the
Harvard and Yale men of 1642–1745 is projected hypothetically through
the nineteenth century, as across the top of Figure No. 5, it then becomes
apparent that the chronological pattern of the Sibley-Dexter data offers
a very accurate prediction of when these two professional components
of the national elite would be most democratically derived.

The timing of opening and closing social origins among those who
became eminent educators or scholars, shown in Figure No. 6, followed
much the same historical pattern as is found in Figure No. 5. But academics were apparently about nine years or more older in the crucial
moments of their careers than were doctors and ministers. Therefore
academics tend to damp down the swings in Figure No. 5 somewhat if
they are grouped with the other two professions. Over the long haul,
meanwhile, the proportion of leading educators coming from ordinary
homes (lower middle class or even less pretentious) declined—just as
was the case in medicine, but in contrast to the long-term tendency in
public life.

Notable individuals in the visual arts, drama, and music, on the other
hand, experienced the comparable changes of access to opportunity for
those of less than upper middle class background among age groups
born slightly *after*, rather then *before*, the ministers and medical men.
This gave them parallel swings in social origin in the same birth cohorts
as the public officers. (Or—as seems more likely—as young men in their
twenties they were affected by the same ups and downs that were hitting
public servants in their forties who had been born a full opportunity

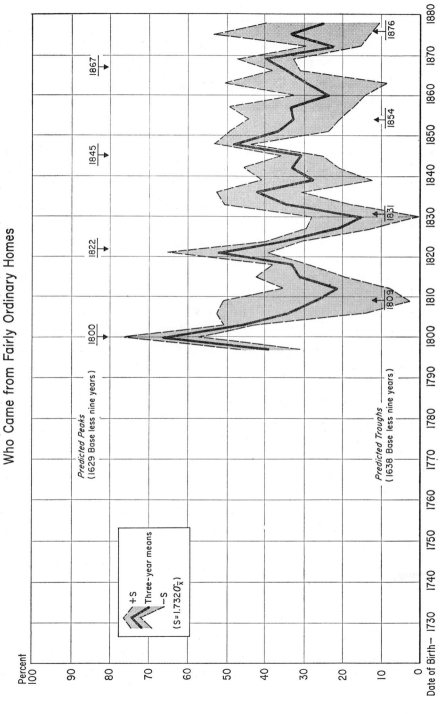

Figure No. 6. Percentages of Major D.A.B. Educators and Scholars Who Came from Fairly Ordinary Homes

cycle before.) In spite of the fact that such fluctuations synchronized with the pattern for public servants, however, the group of artists, like most of the professionals, displayed a gradual tendency for fewer and fewer of the most noted men in this area of activity to come from very plain families.

The remaining career category with substantial numbers of its leaders in the *D.A.B.* is composed of businessmen. To illustrate the typical underlying trend and the typical cyclical movements which occur in the social origins of this group when plotted according to many different definitions, Figure 7 demonstrates in its top line, first, how the proportion of businessmen covered by the *D.A.B.* who came from upper class homes varied over time. The percentage is inverted, or subtracted from 100 percent, for comparison with the lower parts of the figure. The definition of high social origin employed here is very similar to the categorization of "upper class" fathers of early Harvard and Yale men in Figures No. 2 and No. 3. It includes those parents or guardians who were men of substantial landed or business property, held high military or civil office, or were leaders in the professions or the arts. Significant fluctuations in the proportions of *D.A.B.* businessmen originating in such families occurred across successive birth cohorts—coming full cycle, as in other data, at intervals of somewhat more than twenty years on the average. The small variance through those birth groups in the figure where the sample numbers are largest makes it very unlikely that an attempt to describe the chronological changes in the social backgrounds of businessmen in the form of a straight line can be accepted as the most accurate or most informative description of the data. The basic underlying trend which ran beneath these fluctuations, on the other hand, moved towards a larger and larger role of upper class recruitment among the most noted businessmen selected for the *D.A.B.* The evidence suggests that entry to this elite was narrowing with time. Both the trend and the quite regularly spaced fluctuations, moreover, are confirmed— to take one of several possible illustrations—by five-year groups of data concerning the sub-category of *D.A.B.* businessmen whose main careers were in the limited area of manufacture, mining, and transportation (the industrialists as opposed to leaders in trade, finance, and communica-

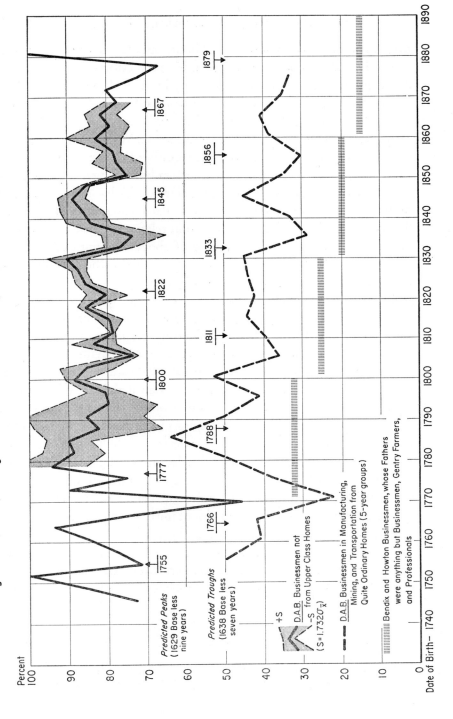

Figure No. 7. Percentages of Businessmen Coming from Certain Social Backgrounds

tions). This information is presented in the middle plot of Figure No. 7.

The *D.A.B.* sample of businessmen has been criticized for not being representative, and for having too many individuals who are included for reasons other than their business accomplishments.[11] In addition, a number of more recent analyses of the backgrounds of businessmen over time have questioned the contention of C. Wright Mills in 1945—based on the *D.A.B.*—that from men turning thirty near the War of 1812 onwards the recruitment of American businessmen has drawn increasingly upon individuals with comparatively high social origins. The findings of several of these studies were collated and commented upon a few years ago by Bendix and Howton in relation to their own further investigation based upon a sampling of about one-ninth of approximately 10,000 businessmen born from 1771 to 1920 who are covered in the *National Cyclopedia of American Biography*.[12]

In actual fact, a variety of evidence—not just the formulation used by Mills—illustrates how fluctuations in the social origins of *D.A.B.* businessmen obtained at a whole series of cutting-off points or definitions of parental standing. Whether an attempt is made to synthesize high or low social strata based on an array of parental characteristics or activities, or whether a stricter, narrower Marxian definition of economic class is adhered to—in terms, for example, of sons of manual workers or sons of business owners—the results are much the same. In each case, moreover, there is evident not only a decline in the proportion of the *D.A.B.* business group who came from the more ordinary kinds of families but a parallel decline in what seems to be the closest comparable classification of backgrounds in the data of Bendix and Howton themselves, as illustrated in the bottom plot of thirty-year data on Figure No. 7. There is no need to resort, as those authors do, to the role of the "lower middle classes" to explain the difference between the direction of change according to Mills and that in their own work. The "difference" in the direction of change just does not seem to exist by the test of several definitions.[13]

11. Bendix and Howton, "Social Mobility," 119.
12. *Ibid.*, esp. pp. 128ff.
13. *Ibid.*, p. 137. In Bendix and Howton's data (p. 122) not only does the long-term trend indicate a closing social background of business leadership on a slope similar to that

Furthermore, in all cases where similar parental classifications could be made from each of the two sources, the business group in the *D.A.B.* was more broadly or more democratically recruited than the larger *N.C.A.B.* group sampled by Bendix and Howton. These two investigators have already noted[14] that their own men and those of Mabel Newcomer had higher social origins than the group studied by Suzanne Keller. The Keller businessmen included leaders in banking and finance, wholesale distribution, entertainment, and mass communications, while Newcomer restricted her study to the top executives of the largest corporations in industry, public utilities, and railroads. The Keller sample is more like the *D.A.B.* selection in respect to the wider-ranging areas of business covered; and the two consistently show more socially variegated recruitment of leadership. The Keller study also indicated a 10 percent rise in the proportion of leading businessmen who were the sons of businessmen between individuals born around 1820 and those born around 1900. That 10 percent in eight decades is almost the same slope (just slightly less) that is indicated for the *D.A.B.* and which—at a much higher level of replacement from the families of already existing business leadership—characterizes the findings from the very *N.C.A.B.* sample used by Bendix and Howton.

Generally speaking, relative to the data from the *D.A.B.*—and probably also relative to Keller's study—the larger *N.C.A.B.* sample used by Bendix and Howton, by including more ordinary and less noted (or

---

found by Mills and confirmed in the present study of the *D.A.B.* as described in Figure No. 7 and its discussion, but the parallel holds up at other cutting points as well. Increasing over time are the proportions who are sons of substantial businessmen, of businessmen and gentry farmers, and of both these groups along with professionals and government officials. Decreasing, meanwhile, are the proportions whose fathers were farmers or manual workers, these categories or white collar, or all three along with master craftsmen and small businessmen. Those Bendix and Howton trends toward higher social origins for business leaders are quite consistent with findings using similar definitions in the *D.A.B.* materials, save that over and over again the *N.C.A.B.* sample as a whole has higher social origins for the group with known parental position. Some of that difference may, however, derive from the possibility that the *unknowns* in the *N.C.A.B.* are predominantly men of fairly *ordinary* social origin. To the extent that this is the case, the mode of percentaging and presenting the data misrepresents the significance of the *N.C.A.B.* materials. Ironically, the result is a *less open* image of the recruitment of American business leadership, an image which in their interpretation of trends Bendix and Howton lean over backwards to avoid. (p. 135).

14. *Ibid.*, p. 135.

notorious) businessmen, in fact encompasses a group whose social origins were more often fairly high. Their sample was more heavily weighted with individuals who were sons of other businessmen. The implication to be drawn from these comparisons seems to be that the "high flyers" of entrepreneurial history, the innovators, and the really outstanding managers of American business who are most likely to appear in *any* sample of economic leadership have long come more frequently from fairly simple homes than have more ordinary directors of business enterprise. Phrased differently, there is more than a mere suggestion here that, while being the son of a businessman or coming from the kind of family that stressed education and responsibility or could afford long training and career experimentation are social class factors which not only can be tolerated in the operations of large firms but can contribute positively to the fulfillment of certain executive functions, the creators of new businesses and other technical or commercial innovators and builders of enterprise have come with substantially greater frequency from the plainer families in our society. They have more often been self-made men.

To digress briefly into substance that will be presented in more detail elsewhere,[15] any social screening in executive recruitment, as in the growing emphasis on post-graduate business education[16] creates real dangers to the future of the American business system as it has been known in the past. A tendency to define the leading candidates for adult careers in terms of those who at various stages have the head start, rather than the greatest long-range potential, may be of relatively less concern and danger to the smoothly operating on-going bureaucracy. It may actually help such enterprises by providing new bureaucrats with useful middle class ambitions, values, and interpersonal skills. Yet at the same time these processes may work towards squeezing off the very kinds of men who historically made American business what it is today. That could be a very heavy price to pay for a thoughtless and complacent selection of who should be educated, or who should be hired. A certain

15. There will be a separate volume on the details of the career patterns of men in the *D.A.B.*

16. An advanced degree, of course, is not identical with advanced study—a fact we too often forget in our self-centered academic enthusiasm.

amount of calculated untidiness and waste may be required to keep business operations, and other fields of endeavor, healthily leavened with initiative and creative talent.

To summarize the findings on changes in the social origins of leadership from the end of the colonial era to the eve of the twentieth century, it is first important to note that among men included in the *D.A.B.* for their fame in several types of careers, the proportion who came from homes fairly low rather than fairly high in the social structure—by a variety of definitions—kept fluctuating in a pattern that on the average came full cycle about every 22 ½ years. Furthermore, the social origins of leaders of even very specific occupations within the five broader career categories—public office of various sorts; religion and medicine; education; business activity; and arts and letters—could also be observed to oscillate independently in basically the same chronological pattern that characterized the general sub-groups of leadership to which they belonged. And the timing of these fluctuations could be fairly accurately predicted by extrapolating hypothetically the swings of social origin among Harvard and Yale men of the classes of 1642–1745 who followed similar careers.

The social foundations of leadership in America did not alter, historically, in some grand, sweeping, overall conversion from an overwhelmingly class-dominated model to an image of the open society. Nor was there a long-term regression to a closed society. Intimations that either was at some time the case are at best literary exaggerations. The reality always lay somewhere in between the two extremes. Yet there were within the long-term span quite regular and significant variations back and forth in the degree to which American leadership came from the more usual kind of family in the society, rather than from the upper and the upper middle classes. Men who said or wrote that times were getting more difficult than they had been, or that America had become an exceptional land of opportunity, were not merely being tormented or tantalized by their own imaginations.

SOME RELEVANCE OF THE NEW FINDINGS FOR MORE FAMILIAR ARGUMENTS

Though the overall pattern of fluctuating opportunity through practically the whole history of American society is the essential and novel feature to be stressed, it is important to note that other kinds of changes in the social origins of leadership did occur underneath this pervasive and overriding pattern of cyclicity. Such variations could be crucial for particular types of leadership in particular periods of our history even though they made little difference to the overall shape of change or even in the patterns of other sub-groups of related careers.

In the first place, the base level in the proportion of leading lawyers who came from fairly ordinary homes dropped noticeably among those born after about 1815 (or of age forty-five at the time of the Civil War), even though the characteristic democratizing or opening trend which generally prevailed among the origins of all groups of public officers was resumed at once and continued to underlie short-term swings throughout the nineteenth century. In the military, on the other hand, beginning with those born in the 1780's and 1790's there was a substantial dip in the proportion coming from fairly plain social origins. Men who were of age to be the mature leaders of the American forces in the Mexican and Civil Wars—many of them were the early graduates of the military academies—came predominantly from upper and upper middle class homes, in contrast to military men raised and trained in the eighteenth century. Not just the Confederate dream but our most far-reaching imperialistic adventures south and west of the border were the projects of a military elite that was unusually aristocratic in origins compared with the leadership that preceded and followed them. Here, as among the judges, however, the democratizing trend resumed among those of age to reach high rank after the Civil War, so that men eminent in the forces during World War I came almost as frequently from "common" origins as did the colonial military leadership in the most open periods of its recruitment.[17] Among doctors, meanwhile, men

---

17. This phenomenon is very apparent in the families of colonial college men and in related analysis made of the membership of the New England legislatures. British officers serving temporarily in the colonies are not included in the *D.A.B.*

who turned twenty and received their training in the last years of the eighteenth century and the first years of the nineteenth, very seldom came from quite plain families, in contrast to a third or more among those medical leaders who were born a little sooner or a little later. And in the business group, finally, those who were about thirty or forty at the end of the War of 1812, as C. Wright Mills has already indicated,[18] were the birth cohorts in which leadership seemed quite suddenly to come from more ordinary origins, the most ordinary origins for any period of our history covered in the *D.A.B.* (Figure No. 7).

All changes in the social backgrounds of particular types of eminent Americans within the *D.A.B.* sample are important historical facts over and above any essentially cyclical variations in opportunity. Also significant are differences in underlying trend over the years. Government officials, judges, and military officers—and writers as well—with time increasingly came from more ordinary homes. In contrast, doctors, educators, artists, and businessmen from earlier to later birth cohorts in the sample appreciably *less* often had parents with quite plain station in the social structure. Religious leaders, meanwhile, displayed little or no long-term tendency of either sort through two centuries of American history. Finally, in overall *level* of recruitment from more varied and commonplace backgrounds some leadership groups remained throughout more "open" or more "closed" than others. These three generalizations about the differing derivations of particular kinds of American leadership are explored elsewhere in a detail that allows comparison by specific sub-categories within the occupational group (e.g., financiers as against manufacturers), by adult residence, and by education, community of origin, and early career stages as well as father's occupation. The current presentation, however, must stress the fact that from one end of our history to the other a largely cyclical pattern of changes in the social origins of American leadership overrode and was superimposed upon these other particulars in the recruitment of the national elite as a whole, and also in the backgrounds of many different occupational sub-groups within the total.

In concluding, it may be helpful to ask whether this argument for

18. Mills, "Business Elite."

substantial, relatively short-term, largely cyclical changes in recruitment reflected by the origins of American leaders in the two biographical collections is really very far out of step with the findings of other more conventional studies of leadership or more general investigations of social mobility and class formation in the American past. Did others unaware of the likelihood of such fluctuations in fact have such phenomena in their data?

In his *Politics and Power: The United States Senate 1869–1901*, David J. Rothman said

> In the decades after the Civil War, observers complained that the door to the Senate, like that to so many other institutions in America, was closing. The widespread lament, however, was inaccurate: the chamber was as open in 1901 as it had been in 1869.[19]

In addition to the tendency for the two extremes in the social origins of the senators to fatten at the expense of the middle, which Professor Rothman commented upon himself, what else lay beneath the surface of that generalization?

The conclusion quoted—besides underplaying what was probably a somewhat opening trend—masks substantial chronological swings of the now familiar sort in the proportion of senators who might be said to come from quite ordinary homes, as demonstrated in Table 3. Among later nineteenth-century senators who served long enough and made enough of a mark to appear in the *D.A.B.*, those born around 1812, 1836, and 1857—exactly where Figure No. 4 has already indicated similar conditions for *D.A.B.* government leaders as a whole—came appreciably more often (five times as often) from quite plain families. In contrast, nearly half of those born around 1821 and again in the later 1840's had fathers or guardians who might be classified as upper class or upper middle class. Table 3 also demonstrates that both the senators and the rest of the *D.A.B.* government leaders without the senators *independently* followed the familiar pattern of fluctuations in social background.[20] To talk of changing family origins among even as specific a group as U.S.

---

19. Rothman, *Politics and Power*, p. 132.
20. It is not clear yet what was happening in the 1832–34 birth cohort, but this will be pursued through a detailed study of the individuals involved.

TABLE 3

Percentages of United States Senators and Others with Main Careers in Government from the *D.A.B.* Who Came from Ordinary Homes*

Date of Birth	D.A.B. Senators		Others		All with Main Careers in Government		Hypothetical Peaks and Troughs‡
	No.	Percent†	No.	Percent†	No.	Percent†	
1796–98					28	39 %	T 1798–99
1799–01					30	33 %	
1802–04					34	24 %	(1803)
1805–07					41	37 %	
1808–10	4	75 %	38	29 %	42	33 %	
1811–13	13	85 %	40	58 %	53	64 %	P 1812
1814–16	11	73 %	45	33 %	56	41 %	
1817–19	10	60 %	34	47 %	44	50 %	
1820–22	14	57 %	26	15 %	40	30 %	T 1821
1823–25	24	63 %	27	37 %	51	49 %	
1826–28	22	68 %	26	39 %	48	52 %	
1829–31	23	78 %	28	32 %	51	54 %	
1832–34	19	47 %	36	28 %	55	34 %	P 1834–35
1835–37	14	86 %	37	46 %	51	57 %	
1838–40	9	67 %	31	32 %	40	45 %	
1841–43	9	67 %	27	41 %	36	47 %	T 1843–44
1844–46	5	60 %	24	54 %	29	55 %	
1847–49	7	43 %	27	33 %	34	35 %	(1849–50)
1850–52	6	67 %	18	22 %	24	33 %	
1853–55	4	75 %	28	36 %	32	41 %	
1856–58	2	100 %	31	52 %	33	55 %	P 1857
1859–61	3	67 %	36	50 %	39	51 %	
1862–64					28	36 %	
1865–67					20	40 %	T 1866
1868–70					21	29 %	(1869)
1871–73					27	44 %	

Sources: *D.A.B.* and researches of David J. Rothman for his *Politics and Power*.

* For the types of parents or guardians classified as having "ordinary" position in society ("lower middle class" or less) see Appendix B.

† Percentaged for those of known origin only.

‡ Predicted peaks and troughs of percentage from ordinary origin derived from backgrounds of secular leadership among colonial Harvard and Yale men (cf. Figure No. 3, above). In fact, the troughs in the *D.A.B.* group trail the peaks by twelve to fifteen years most of the time rather than the nine-year lag characteristic of the comparable men among the colonial alumni.

Note: parentheses indicate actual peak or trough somewhat out of line with expectations.

senators in terms of cyclical variations appearing in highly predictable birth cohorts fits the fact of historical change in the sources of American political leadership more fully and more precisely than other explanations. It is also of considerable interest to note from the table that federal senators—who on the whole rank rather high within the overall group of government leaders selected for the *D.A.B.*—came appreciably *more* frequently from ordinary families than the rest of the sample. As already observed among businessmen, those who rose to the *top* of American leadership have historically depended more than others upon the fact that the door to achievement in our society has been open to those lacking the most favored family setting for beginning their careers.

Lower down in the social scale, on the other hand—out of the realm of leadership altogether—a recent summary by Stephan Thernstrom in his *Poverty and Progress: Social Mobility in a Nineteenth-Century City*[21] of what is now a growing body of historical data on the life chances or social mobility of sons of common laborers in America allows some insight into at least the *potential* relevance of a cyclical pattern of chronological change there as well. The applicability of an interpretation of historical process in terms of fluctuations in the life chances of sons of urban workingmen cannot be demonstrated here but it is nevertheless possible to suggest that the proportion of sons of laborers in American cities who became a second-generation lower working class may well have tended to rise and fall in the timing evident in the social origins of American leadership as described above. Measures taken in 1952, 1933, 1910, and 1870 show smaller proportions of sons of unskilled urban workers becoming no more than unskilled or semi-skilled workers in their own careers. Evidence from these stages of our history, as summarized by Thernstrom from a variety of studies, indicates a more open society for the sons of very ordinary working men. The contrast of these points of time to other periods for which information is available offers somewhat more than a faint suggestion of movement back and forth through American history at intervals of slightly over two decades. In addition, rates of immigration and the incidence of recession with its implication for unemployment, both of which strongly condition the

21. Thernstrom, *Poverty and Progress*, pp. 218–219; and p. 106 for Thernstrom's own age or cohort classifications.

life of the working man, are known to have oscillated in this kind of temporal pattern.

At the end of his volume on the nineteenth-century working classes of Newburyport, Professor Thernstrom argued against "the pitfalls of ahistorical social science" as personified by W. Lloyd Warner's *Yankee City* study.[22] Perhaps a friendly riposte about "ahistorical history" might be in order, coupled with an appeal that future work be done with finer regard for chronology so that what seem to be significant patterns of change can be highlighted rather than obscured by the way in which the data were collected or grouped.[23] There seems to be a good deal of evidence to indicate that changes in opportunity throughout the society—and therefore quite possibly also many kinds of events or processes related to opportunity—adhered to quite a different kind of timing from anything the literature has invoked so far.

III. Sources of Cyclical Opportunity in Population Change, Community Development, and Institutional Expansion

IF such regularly recurrent, comparatively short-term shifts in the social origins of American leadership—and perhaps also in the life chances of ordinary men as well—were so important in the evolution of our society, what was their source or cause? To uncover fairly predictable fluctuations in the development of at least the upper reaches of our social structure over time, and to establish their generality and statistical significance, does not mean that we have adequately established the existence and the workings of some mechanism which, like a giant heart embedded at the center of the social system, pumps cyclical impulses

22. *Ibid.*, appendix, pp. 225–239.

23. This is not to suggest that sociologists do not keep on collecting and presenting data by decade if not by "generation," even in the recent, more sophisticated work by Blau and Duncan, *The American Occupational Structure* (New York, 1967), pp. 81ff. But then sociologists are not supposed to know anything about historical perspective.

throughout the body social as long as it lives. To turn an empirical observation about the widespread presence of quite regularly varying social change into a defensible and useful social theory of cyclical process in society, upon which further investigations of a variety of topics can be built, requires some testable explanation of what happened repeatedly in our past to create these effects.

SPURTS AND LAGS IN THE RATE OF POPULATION GROWTH

In the course of the present investigation the first indication of the sources of such historical variations in recruitment came from trying to explain why the numbers of students at the early New England colleges rose and fell as they did during the first century of American higher education between 1638 and 1745. Marked generational effects were evident in the college population. At certain points about thirty-five years apart, waves of sons of what had previously been large age groups or birth cohorts of English or American alumni inundated the little colonial institutions in college "booms" fully in proportion to what we know today. But sometimes coinciding with these generational influxes of students to Harvard and Yale, and sometimes falling in between these bulges, there appeared to be an additional pattern of changing numbers of students. At first it seemed as though this second set of academic bulges superimposed upon the recurrent generational effects came and went about every twenty-four years or in about four full cycles within the first century in the history of American student bodies.

In searching for an explanation for this second pattern, which differed from the generation by having considerably shorter frequency, the first hint of what was involved came from estimates of the New England population in the ground-breaking work of Greene and Harrington.[1] The number of students at college varied chronologically both with the interval at which bulges were created from one generation of alumni to their sons and with what appears—on the basis of very fragmentary

1. Evarts B. Greene and Virginia D. Harrington, *American Population before the Federal Census of 1790* (New York, 1932). Lockridge, in his demographic article on Dedham, drew a very similar "stepped" pattern of population growth in colonial Massachusetts independently from the same sources, though he did not comment upon the recurrence of spurts and lags at these intervals. Lockridge, "Land, Population, and Evolution," p. 321.

evidence—possibly to have been a rather uneven, alternately spurting and lagging, pattern of growth in the expansion of the total New England population. A larger number of boys came to college, in other words, when the number of people who lived in New England was growing more rapidly than usual.

Basically the very tenuous approximations offered by contemporary New Englanders, the early censuses, and modern scholars trying to reconstruct population from militia lists, tax or voting records, and numbers of households, indicate turning points from rather slow to appreciably more rapid growth in the population of New England in the 1630's, between 1655 and 1665, in the 1690's, soon after 1720, somewhere around 1740, and near 1761 and 1786. It is also very reasonable to expect an up-turn in the growth rate of the population in the later 1670's—where data are lacking—once the losses of King Philip's War (1675–76) had been sustained. What these gross demographic patterns summarized in the left-hand column of Table 4 (and given a "best fit" pattern of regular 22½-year fluctuations) depict is that even as late as the second half of the eighteenth century the population of New England increased from all sources perhaps only 3 percent in the seven years 1755–62 or 15 percent in the thirteen years 1749–62 (overflowing the limits of any war era explanation), in contrast to a burgeoning 30 percent in the decade 1765–75 leading up to the Revolution; that a mere 6 percent growth 1775–86 was followed by another 30 percent spurt to 1790, though in the succeeding decade the rate of expansion settled down once more to only 11 percent or so. We can imagine how seriously the prospect of such changes—especially if they were focussed at all in the most heavily consuming or job-hunting part of the population —would be viewed today in Detroit, on Madison Avenue, or at the Department of Health, Education, and Welfare.

These changes indeed appear to have had marked effects on the historical development of American society. For the composition of the alumni group that had higher than average career attainment and the degree of equality of opportunity among college men as a whole were both found to oscillate according to the type of pattern somewhat exceeding two decades that also characterized fluctuations in the rate of growth in the total New England population.

At this juncture in the research, when the early stages of an explanation of the pattern of leadership recruitment among colonial Harvard and Yale men were beginning to point towards demographic changes as a determining force, Daniel H. Calhoun, who was working with economic and demographic variables in studying the development of nineteenth-century American education, saw the connection and brought me into touch with the writings of those economists who for the past several years have been dealing intensively with the relation of migration and total population growth to economic activity.

The interest of some economists and sociologists in parallel, lagged, or inverted chronological fluctuations in social and economic phenomena dates well back into the nineteenth century. The early literature was evaluated and systematically advanced in 1925 by Dorothy Swaine Thomas in her classic *Social Aspects of the Business Cycle*.[2] Marriage and divorce, births and deaths, social problems and crime, and also emigration could be observed to vary historically somewhat in step with business conditions. Typically the British and American business cycles to which the social phenomena were related peaked and troughed at intervals of eleven years or less.[3] In the late 1920's, however, Simon Kuznets and C. A. R. Wardwell focussed attention on a different kind of historical business fluctuation.[4] These "long swings" or "trends cycles," as Arthur F. Burns later called them, have variously been assigned durations of from 15 to 30 years. Most specifically, Kuznets in 1930 saw American fluctuations in both prices and productivity in patterns of 22 or 23 years on the average. Writing more recently, Abramovitz and Easterlin have preferred durations of 15 to 20 years.[5]

2. Dorothy Swaine Thomas, *Social Aspects of the Business Cycle* (London, 1925).

3. *Ibid.*, p. 60. Cycles of this duration are sometimes called Juglar cycles. For a brief review of long, short, and medium length economic movements of this sort see Moses Abramovitz, "The Nature and Significance of the Kuznets Cycles," *Economic Development and Cultural Change*, 9 (April 1961), 225–248.

4. Simon S. Kuznets, *Secular Movements in Production and Prices* (New York, 1930); C. A. R. Wardwell, *An Investigation of Economic Data for Major Cycles* (Philadelphia, 1927). Also Arthur F. Burns, *Production Trends in the United States since 1870* (New York, 1934); Walter Isard, "A Neglected Cycle: The Transport-Building Cycle," *Review of Economics and Statistics*, 24 (Nov., 1942), 149–158; Walter Isard, "Transport Development and Building Cycles," *Quarterly Journal of Economics*, 57 (November 1942), 90–110.

5. Abramovitz, "Nature of Kuznets Cycles"; Richard Easterlin, "The American Baby

TABLE 4

Parallel Chronological Patterns in Population Growth, Immigration, and New Settlement or Internal Migration*

Population Growth, Shift from Slow to Fast†		Peaks in Immigration†		Peaks in New Settlement or Internal Migration†	
Theoretical‡	Actual	Theoretical‡	Actual	Theoretical‡	Actual
1627ff.	1630's fast G&H	1640	Civil War break 1641–42	1638	N.E., New Amsterdam, Md.; churches W. Indies Hansen
1650	1654–65 fast G&H to 1664, Va. & Md. Hansen	1663	merchants in 1660's Bailyn; returning ministers Weis, Sibley	1661	1664 N.Y. S.E. & S.W. Conn. Va. & Md. tidewater B, Hansen churches 1654 & later 1660's
1672	Va. and Md. ?	1685	early 1680's Pa. incl. Germans B; 1687 ? Shipton for N.E.	1683	Narragansett country Pennsylvania 1680 Charleston
1695	between 1688 and 1701 G&H	1708	1708 ? Shipton; New York seeks immigrants B	1706	1699–05 churches So. Carolina Delaware Valley Hudson Valley Inland Conn. B
1717	1720's fast G&H				

Population Growth, Shift from Slow to Fast†		Peaks in Immigration†		Peaks in New Settlement or Internal Migration†	
Theoretical‡	Actual	Theoretical‡	Actual	Theoretical‡	Actual
				1728	1729 churches northern N.E. Susquehanna & Great Valley, Pa. B
1740	1740–49 fast G&H	1730	1729 Shipton ca. 1730 German churches 1717 through 1720's Germans and Scotch-Irish build up B		
					1744–50 churches northern N.E. Berkshires Alleghany foothills Pa. N.C. piedmont, Shenandoah
1762	1761ff. G&H	1753	1749–53 Hansen		
				1773	1774 churches northern N.E. westernN.Y. & Pa. B southern piedmont
1785	1786ff. G&H	1775	1770–73 Hansen		
1807	1800–10 P	1798	to 1798 fifteen-year naturalization Hansen	1796	1796 western land bubble bursts Ky., Tenn., Ohio, western N.Y. B, Hansen
1830	1820–30 P	1820	1816–18 North 1819 poor reports Hansen	1818	1818 land sales North, S & C Ohio, Ind., Ill., Mich. Ga., Ala., Miss., Mo.
	1840–50 P	1843	1832–37 and 1842 North, census	1841	1835–36 land sales North, S & C Great Lakes, Wisc., Iowa Texas, La., Ark., Fla.

1875	1875–90 K	1865	1863
		1854 North, census	1854–55 land sales North, S & C to Great Plains, Oregon, Utah, Mexican Cession, California
1897	1900–10 K	1888	1886
	1898 E	1875–85 K	1880–90 land sales K filling in the West
		1884 E	1870–90 interstate migration Lee
		1887 C & Z	
		1882, 1888, 1892 census	
1920	1920–30 K	1910	1908
	1916 E	1900–10 K	1900–10 land sales K
		1909 E	1900–10 interstate migration Lee
		1910 C & Z	
		1907, 1910, 1914 census	
1942	1940–55 K	1933	1931
	1935 E	1920–30 K	1920–30 interstate migration Lee
		1925 E	
		drop 1930ff. census	
		1955	1953
		1957 census	1940–50 interstate migration Lee

* Does not exhaust evidence. See accompanying text for further detail.

† Sources:

G & H: Greene and Harrington.
P: Potter.
K: Kuznets, "Long Swings."
E: Easterlin, *Demography*, 1965.
Hansen: *Atlantic Migration*.
churches: cf. Figure No. 8 below.

Shipton: "Immigration."
C & Z: Coale and Zelnick.
Lee: Everett S. Lee.
B: Billington, *Westward Expansion*.
S & C: Smith and Cole.
census: *Historical Statistics*.

‡ Regular 22½-year intervals projected forward from the respective seventeenth-century base for each of the three kinds of data.

Professor Kuznets himself, on the other hand, has been very careful not to call his middle range "secular movements" or "long swings" "cycles" "since their periodic recurrence has not yet been demonstrated or explained."[6] Intensive work by Kuznets and several others in the past fifteen years, nevertheless, has carried forward substantially the understanding of the likely mechanisms behind the rather regular economic movements. In 1954 Brinley Thomas demonstrated fluctuations in the rate of emigration from Britain whose timing was related to various kinds of economic developments in the home country and in America. A. K. Cairncross defined the special role of domestic and foreign investment in these relationships.[7] Then in his 1958 paper for the American Philosophical Society[8] Kuznets put the search for an explanation of these rather long-term time series phenomena into the current form by showing how what he called "long swings in economic variables" were associated not just with immigration but also with more rapid or less rapid growth in the population as a whole. The role of increment from immigration was perhaps most important as a source of uneven overall population expansion in the period 1870–1925. The pattern of births and deaths, however, also was significant, increasingly so after 1930. Among subsequent contributers Moses Abramovitz pointed up the crucial role, via economic consumption or demand, of the formation of new households by recent immigrants or by unusually large (or small) birth cohorts of the indigenous population reaching the age to marry and setting up their own homes. Richard Easterlin then indicated that magnified variation in the native birth rate "took over" from massive changes in the flow of new immigrants as the prime source of demographic fluctuation once the latter had been politically restrained. He

---

Boom in Historical Perspective," *American Economic Review*, 51, 5 (December 1961), 869–911. A recent mathematical test for the possibilities of this kind of movement in the economy does not examine intervals which might be longer than eighteen years, and perhaps not surprisingly comes up with negative results. Irma Adelman, "Long Cycles— Fact or Artifact?" *American Economic Review*, 55, 3 (June 1965), 444–463.

6. National Bureau of Economic Research, *National Income: A Summary of Findings* (New York, 1946), p. 61, as quoted in Brinley Thomas, *Migration and Economic Growth* (Cambridge, England, 1954), p. 86.

7. *Ibid.*; A. K. Cairncross, *Home and Foreign Investment* (Cambridge, England, 1953).

8. Simon S. Kuznets, "Long Swings in the Growth of Population and in Related Economic Variables," American Philosophical Society, *Proceedings*, 102 (1958), 25–52.

has subsequently set out systematically to develop a model to explain how population change and many different business variations relate to each other in what some economists call the "Kuznets cycle."[9]

The present inquiry has benefited richly in the last seven years from the development of the data by the students of the Kuznets cycle and their search for the mechanisms that bind the data together—particularly from the work of Easterlin and of Everett S. Lee on migration. The analysis of the more numerous sample of biographies in the *D.A.B.* and of several other sources of information concerning how occupational places opened up or social places were filled, or how demographic processes operated, could be pursued from an early stage not only utilizing knowledge of the patterns among early Harvard and Yale men and their families but also drawing upon the vital and sophisticated economic literature. The particular contributions of that growing corpus to the present line of argument will be introduced where various aspects in the documentation and interpretation of "Kuznets cycles"—the economic side of growth cycles—bear upon specific data, or upon hypotheses invoked to explain cycles of more social or occupational opportunity in America through the first two and a half centuries of our history as well as in the period since the 1870's.

Most of the materials on which the economists have based their discussion become available in more conventionally acceptable form following the Civil War. Kuznets himself, however, made one of several connections that these scholars have seen to earlier phenomena when he pointed out that changes back and forth in the growth rate of the total U.S. population can be observed in alternate decades from the first census of 1790 onwards.[10] General data are available only once a decade that

9. Abramovitz, "Nature of Kuznets Cycles"; also Statement in U.S. Congress, Joint Economic Committee, *Employment, Growth, and Price Levels*, 86th Cong., 1 Sess., pt. II (1959), 411–466. Easterlin, "Baby Boom"; "Influences in European Overseas Emigration before World War I," *Economic Development and Cultural Change*, 9 (1961), 331–351; "Long Swings in U.S. Demographic and Economic Growth: Some Findings on the Historical Pattern," *Demography*, 2 (1965), 490–507; "On the Relation of Economic Factors to Recent and Projected Fertility Changes," *Demography*, 3 (1966), 131–153; "Economic-Demographic Interactions and Long Swings in Economic Growth," *American Economic Review*, 56 (1966), 1063–1104.

10. Kuznets, "Long Swings," p. 36.

far back. And a ten-year interval will tend rather soon to hide variation according to a pattern lasting about twenty-two years. Nevertheless, from 1790 through 1860 the population of the United States grew somewhat faster in every other decade than it did in the decades in between.

At first glance the materials from the census, as reviewed for example by J. Potter (though as late as 1965 he showed no knowledge of the economic discussion),[11] seem to challenge somewhat any hypothesis of continuing, regular fluctuations in population expansion extending or extrapolated from the constant chronology which best fit variations in colonial times at intervals which have also been encountered frequently in economic phenomena since 1870 (Table 4). Population changes may have been repeated about two decades apart, but they were not clearly where earlier timing would "predict" them to be in a straightforward cyclical projection. There are two cautions, however, before the theory of cyclical behavior in the expansion of the American population is discarded on the basis of possible contradictory evidence. In the first place, the spurts and lags in population growth that appear in the colonial materials are usually accentuated in, or concentrated into, a short span of about five years rather than a full decade. Overlaps of just a few years with decade evidence could produce the expected peak or trough in the growth rate; and a decade is long enough to include both a peak and a trough since fairly immediate "shelving out" after rapid growth seems to be a common sequence. Secondly, when the evidence on increments in population *after* the Civil War developed by Kuznets using overlapping decades every *five* years is held up against projections from colonial New England in the lower part of Table 4, the expected turning points to swift expansion beginning around 1875, 1897, 1920, and 1942 are matched very nicely with his conclusions concerning rapid growth in the years 1875–90, 1900–10, 1920–30, and 1940–55. Conversely, what from colonial patterns more than 300 years ago would be predicted to be slow periods of population expansion beginning about 1886, 1908, and 1931 fit with census data for 1885–1900, 1910–20, and 1925–35. The failure of available materials from about 1820 to the Civil War

11. J. Potter, "The Growth of Population in America 1700–1860," *Population in History*, ed. D. V. Glass and D. E. C. Eversley (London, 1965), pp. 631–688.

to match the expected dates of turning points may in part reflect the crudities of ten-year comparisons. The discrepancy may also involve a temporary set-over in the cycle where the typical intervals remain the same but the whole phasing shifts forwards or backwards by just a few years for two or three turns of the wheel, so to speak. Economic and social elements of the growth cycle "wobbled" in this era, too. This kind of off-movement can also be observed here and there with regard to the fluctuating proportions of various types of leaders who came from socially quite ordinary homes. As in those other cases, however, the temporary off-set in the phasing of rather cyclical rates of growth in total population does not mean that the projection of 22½-year interval loses its predictive value and potential explanatory power for related historical changes.

Beginning with the very earliest patterns of alternating spurts and lags in the development of the New England population, furthermore, there are several forms of evidence to indicate that these were real changes of pace, not a mere error of contemporary estimation or subsequent reconstruction. Section V, which follows, in exploring the demographic mechanisms of opportunity, will introduce supporting details on births, deaths, marriages, and family size applying to colonial New England and also to later national society as viewed through the family life of the individuals who appear in the *D.A.B.* But first, in addition to crude estimates of total population there are some other relatively simple indicators of immigration, the spread of new settlement, the growth of institutions, and the rate of entry of new personnel to existing positions of leadership which further encourage the conclusion that fluctuating opportunity was closely linked with demographic changes. On almost all sides, evidence found for the first two and a half centuries of our society can be demonstrated to fit the pattern of fluctuations found in more substantial and more sophisticated materials describing cyclical changes during the last hundred years of the American history.

PARALLEL PATTERNS OF IMMIGRATION AND SETTLEMENT TO 1775

In looking at some concomitants of opportunity changes and fluctuations in the growth rate of the population over the period preceding the

Revolution, it is simplest to examine together probable variations over time in the amounts of immigration and in the rate at which New World settlement spread up and down the Atlantic coast and westward toward the heart of the continent. The indicators available for estimating these two kinds of changes are inextricably interwoven and overlapping.

To summarize these kinds of data as outlined in Table 4, over the whole colonial era—and from northern to southern extremity—the English settlements on the North American mainland continued to multiply not according to some smooth exponential growth curve but in well definable fits and starts. Periodic surges of development opened up new areas and attracted both new sorts and greater numbers of immigrants. Meanwhile the native population expanded as well. Then, however, for the time being the new supply of people was worked into the system—digested into the body social, so to speak—before still more manpower was bred, or gathered into the colonies, to develop even farther-out regions of new land. The peopling of the American continent continued to push ahead throughout the pre-Revolutionary era, but in a rather pulsating motion.

How many Europeans[12] came across the ocean at various points of time is difficult to determine for the colonial era.[13] But it is possible to gather certain general impressions about the phases of heaviest immigration to the English colonies on the mainland of North America and the timing of the impact of fresh immigration and indigenous population pressure upon the development of new settlements. Clearly, to begin with, until the outbreak of the English Civil War there had been a heavy flow to all the British colonies on the North American continent: to New England, to Long Island, to Maryland, and of course to Virginia. New inhabitants poured in and the settlements which they founded spread inland: to the Nashua River Valley and overland to the Connecticut, or up that river, in the North, through the tidewater of the Chesapeake in the South. Meanwhile in New Amsterdam as well the

12. The vast majority of them still from the British Isles up to the end of the colonial period; but an increasingly significant number of Germans going into the southern and middle colonies in the last fifty years or so of the era.

13. Potter gives up rather quickly after just mentioning the 1720's, the 1760's, and the 1780's; "Growth of Population," p. 645.

dates of organization of new towns in eastern New Jersey and western Long Island indicate that this Dutch colony, too, experienced rapid growth in the same period.[14]

While all-engrossing civil strife at home brought colonization virtually to an end for the time being—if anything creating something of a reverse flow (certainly such a reverse flow of northern leadership) back across the Atlantic—in the later 1650's and early 1660's there is ample evidence of another boom of New World expansion. Settlement spread into southeastern Connecticut and Rhode Island, farther up the Connecticut than before and inland east and west of the river, in New York (seized by the English in 1664) and into New Jersey, filling out much of tidewater Virginia and Maryland,[15] and creating the first outpost in the Carolinas.

Thus just over twenty years after the spurt of settlement in the later 1630's and the early 1640's there are various signs up and down English-speaking North America—the organization of new colonies, the spread of new settlements, and related accounts or events of the times—that the population was growing rapidly, abetted by substantial new migration as well as indigenous increase.

In New England history it is conventional to identify a stagnation of settlement in the 1670's and for many years thereafter, and to blame it on King Philip's War (1675–76). Certainly this was a major crisis in the development of the region; but more economic discouragements to expansion are also evident even before the outbreak of hostilities. In addition, the political unrest stirred up by the effort of the restored monarchy to exert authority over excessively independent colonials across the Atlantic scarcely encouraged New World ventures. Troubles in the third Dutch War (1673) including the reseizure of New York, and conflict between those wishing further expansion and the older tidewater pow-

14. This was also a peak period for West Indian development according to Hansen, *Atlantic Migration*, p. 41. Later international aspects of the growth cycle, some of which are intimated in subsequent discussion here, suggest the possibility that at this time, too, the patterns cut across national borders. Materials on French Canadian and also Spanish American development at this and other relevant times would be most valuable to include in the present type of analysis.

15. Billington, *Westward Expansion*, pp. 67, 73; Hansen, *Atlantic Migration*, p. 33, discusses a rapid occupation of land in the period up to 1664 in the Chesapeake region, with a population of 10,000 in 1642 and one of 38,000 in 1664.

ers, accompanied by a tobacco depression in the southern colonies simultaneously, suggest that throughout the English settlements both the geographical spread of development and the growth of population to inhabit new regions were somewhat stifled for the time being.

The all-too-familiar argument that the dissemination of New England communities halted between King Philip's War (1675–76) and the Peace of Utrecht forty years later has misled two generations of scholars about the character of expansion in the northern colonies at this time. Contrary to the popular impression, many new settlements are evident soon after the critical conflict, but south of the concave perimeter of warfare, not moving northwestward for the time being, but filling out empty areas around Narragansett Bay, in the Connecticut interior, and in the hinterland of Cape Cod. Simultaneously families from older towns hived off to form new communities in still available farmlands scattered among the oldest settlements.[16] And down the Atlantic Coast growth was even more evident in the 1680's. Notably the Carolina settlements caught hold after a shaky start, Pennsylvania was established (and included the first German immigrants to the New World), and growth took place at this time in the more northern regions around Chesapeake Bay.[17] Yet once again colonial troubles, political and economic, can be seen within a few years to have cut back on what was probably a rapid rate of expansion in immigration as well as in new settlement.[18]

Faster colonial development reappeared, however, in the years around the turn of the century. In New England, settlement pushed into northeastern Connecticut, while still more towns were slipped in between and around the older communities in eastern Massachusetts and coastal

16. This process kept on very far into the colonial era. Lockridge, for example, notes a substantial group of towns founded in Suffolk County, Massachusetts, as late as the 1705–1739 period.

17. Discussion with advanced history students at The Johns Hopkins University has brought this growth to my attention. For particulars, see my forthcoming *Opportunity, Equality, and Population*.

18. By about 1687 Clifford K. Shipton sees immigrants no longer assimilated so quickly and completely into the Puritan society of Boston as they once had been because of their now more varied sources. "Immigration to New England, 1680–1740," *Journal of Political Economy*, 44 (1936), p. 226. For some other difficulties besides the well-known political upheavals of the late 1680's in several colonies see Billington, *Westward Expansion*, p. 85.

New Hampshire. Along with this growth behind the old frontier, so to speak, immigration apparently flourished also in spite of the intercontinental wars of the period. Enough new non-English immigrants of the "lower orders" had come to Boston by 1708 to cause the town fathers considerable concern.[19] Simultaneously, new people flowed into the Middle Atlantic region, perhaps rather slowly up the Hudson—hampered by the land policies of New York—but spreading out very rapidly in the Delaware Valley. And South Carolina began to find its permanent economic feet in this period.[20]

After some signs of slowing down in the last years of war just before the peace in 1713,[21] and even, surprisingly, in the years immediately following the termination of conflict, very rapid growth is evident everywhere in the 1720's: into central New Hampshire and down the Maine Coast, filling out central Massachusetts and the Connecticut interior, out of the Hudson Valley and into the Mohawk, into the Susquehanna region and the hinterland of Philadelphia. As part of this wave of expansion in the northern and middle colonies appeared the first major influx of Palatine Germans and Scots-Irish from Ulster, two groups who figured prominently in all further surges of development down to the Revolution. Then after a crest about 1730,[22] and some subsequent contraction in the flow of new citizens into the colonies, heavy immi-

19. Shipton, "Immigration," p. 229.

20. Billington, *Westward Expansion*, pp. 54–56.

21. New York authorities, for example, were out looking for settlers towards the end of the decade of the 1700's, expressing a concern for underpopulation. Some of their difficulties would seem to have stemmed from the land policies and patterns of large, speculative ownership which evolved in the early years of the new century. (Billington, *Westward Expansion*, pp. 85–87.)

22. Identifiable, among other means, by the dating of German churches in Pennsylvania. See below in this section. In the northern colonies Shipton ("Immigration," pp. 229–30) says that through Boston the intake of Scotch-Irish immigrants began to pick up from about 1711 and reached its peak in the 1720's. The flow of immigration as a whole via Boston, however, both declined and changed in quality in the 1730's. Proportionately more evident were groups such as criminals formerly sent out to the more southern colonies or aristocrats taking refuge from disturbances in the West Indies. He considers that beginning in the 1720's fighting in eastern New England (mostly Maine) pushed settlers back to Boston, bottling up new immigrants there, and led to a system of registration on the part of the town (p. 238). Low immigration was connected with the trade troubles evident in 1729. In the mid-1730's, also, the province took "the burden of caring for the unfortunate stranger" off the shoulders of the town, and local restrictions on immigration were relaxed (p. 238).

gration was renewed again. In the mid–Atlantic area the flood turned southward out of Pennsylvania into the hinterland of Virginia and on as far as the piedmont of North Carolina.[23] The population of the latter colony doubled between 1732 and 1754. Still further south, the new colony of Georgia expanded rapidly in this period.[24] Meanwhile, even though these were years in which New England began to become a backwater in the overall regional pattern of American development, a further burst of growth is evident at this time—eastward into Maine and northwestward in New Hampshire, that portion of Massachusetts across the Connecticut River, and also the upper and outer corner of Connecticut.

The final pre–Revolutionary surge of new settlement and new population, following the French and Indian War, brought into being as many as ninety-four new towns in Maine, one hundred in New Hampshire, and seventy-four in Vermont; and during this period of settlement Connecticut organizers took the first steps of what became, after the Revolution, a familiar pattern of New England colonization stretching across the northern part of the nation. Between 1762 and 1768 they sent out contingents to organize Wilkes-Barre and Plymouth in the Wyoming Valley of northeastern Pennsylvania. In New York, the thrust westward moved along the Mohawk Valley. More western parts of Pennsylvania began to be developed under the protective umbrella of militarily victorious English authority, and the great southward movement continued down the piedmont to fill out the interior of the Carolinas. Thus in both the spread of settlement and the inflow of new population via immigration no less than seven distinct waves of development, quite clearly separated from each other by intervening periods of appreciably slower expansion, can be seen to have given the growth of the English colonies in America a markedly cyclical pattern throughout the first century and a half of our history.[25]

23. This description follows Billington, *Westward Expansion*, pp. 87–93.

24. For peaks of expansion in both capitalizing and populating Georgia in the early 1730's, then in the early 1750's, see Paul S. Taylor, "Colonizing Georgia 1732–1752: A Statistical Note," *William and Mary Quarterly*, 3rd ser., 22 (1965), pp. 119–127 (especially p. 125).

25. Growth cycles can also be observed in Barbados, both before 1775 and afterwards: Otis P. Starkey, *The Economic Geography of Barbados* (New York, 1939), especially pp.

NEW TOWNS, NEW POLITICAL LEADERSHIP, NEW MINISTERS,
AND NEW MERCHANTS

These conclusions about the pulsating chronological pattern of new settlement and immigration in early America, linked in mutual relationship to the heartbeat of population growth, were often originally based on the most sketchy information culled at a considerable distance from the primary sources.[26] The validity of a fluctuating or spurting historical shape in population movement as well as population growth can, however, be substantiated by other kinds of evidence.

Table 5 begins to illustrate the cyclical character of the expansion of settlement more quantitatively by showing the number of new towns recognized by the Massachusetts legislature in successive periods of three years each from 1630–32 onward. Even in this, one of the earliest colonies, marked peaks and troughs in the rate of community development occurred not just through the colonial era but on into the post-Civil War period.

Clusters of new towns were recognized in the early 1640's, around 1670–73, then 1694, and again in the years near 1712–15. As a comparison with Table 4 indicates, this timing follows by a few years the peaks of immigration surges that have just been tentatively outlined for the colonial era. A cross-examination of the two tables also shows, however, that the authorization of new towns was concentrated just at the *beginning* of rapid spurts in population expansion, so that new immigration was followed by new town organization, which was followed by new gross population growth, which was in turn overlapped and followed by another wave of immigration. Whatever phase is chosen as starting point the sequence was repeated over and over again.

8–9, 67, 70, 72–93, 99–138, and 209–210; and for the British West Indies on a broader scale as late as 1763: Frank Wesley Pitman, *The Development of the British West Indies, 1700–1763* (New Haven, 1917). I am indebted to Patricia Molen of The Johns Hopkins University for an introduction to this material.

26. Further reading and discussion of the pattern of cyclical expansion with a number of persons now at work on a variety of projects (particularly with students of early American history at The Johns Hopkins University) has confirmed and enlarged upon the evidence for a fluctuating pattern of growth—not only in New England, where my own information is most particular and most varied, but in the southern colonies and the West Indies as well. Further details are included in my forthcoming *Opportunity, Equality, and Population*.

TABLE 5

Number of New Towns Recognized by Massachusetts Legislature in Successive Three-Year Periods 1630–1917

Years	No. Towns	Best Fit Regular 22½-Year Peaks	Years	No. Towns	22½-Year Peaks	Years	No. Towns	22½-Year Peaks
1630–32	10		1726–28	8		1822–24	4	
1633–35	5		1729–31	5		1825–27	1	
1636–38	4		1732–34	6		1828–30	0	(1829)
1639–41	9		1735–37	4		1831–33	1	
1642–44	8		1738–40	7	1739	1834–36	0	
1645–47	4		1741–43	4		1837–39	2	
1648–50	3	(1649)	1744–46	1		1840–42	2	
1651–53	3		1747–49	0		1843–45	1	
1654–56	5		1750–52	3		1846–48	6	
1657–59	0		1753–55	15		1849–51	8	1851
1660–62	3		1756–58	0		1852–54	6	
1663–65	0		1759–61	11	1761	1855–57	6	
1666–68	2		1762–64	15		1858–60	2	
1669–71	6	1671	1765–67	16		1861–63	0	
1672–74	5		1768–70	7		1864–66	2	
1675–77	3		1771–73	7		1867–69	0	
1678–80	1		1774–76	5		1870–72	6	
1681–83	3		1777–79	10		1873–75	2	1874
1684–86	2		1780–82	9		1876–78	3	
1687–89	2		1783–85	17	1784	1879–81	2	
1690–92	1		1786–88	4		1882–84	1	
1693–95	7	1694	1789–91	4		1885–87	3	
1696–98	0		1792–94	8		1888–90	1	
1699–01	0		1795–97	10		1891–93	1	
1702–04	0		1798–00	2		1894–96	1	(1896)
1705–07	2		1801–03	3		1897–99	1	
1708–10	3		1804–06	2	(1806)	1900–02	0	
1711–13	7		1807–09	3		1903–05	1	
1714–16	7	1716	1810–12	5		1906–08	0	
1717–19	3		1813–15	3		1909–11	0	
1720–22	1		1816–18	2		1912–14	0	
1723–25	5		1819–21	3		1915–17	1	

Note: parentheses indicate hypothetical date not met by actual peak.

Source: Frederic W. Cook, *Historical Data Relating to Counties, Cities, and Towns in Massachusetts,* Commonwealth of Massachusetts (1948).

Subsequent to these first four bulges of new communities, the years from 1726 through 1740 produced something of a "plateau" of active town organization in Massachusetts, judging from dates of political recognition in the table. The next spurt of population growth and immigration, however, to follow the same lag should have called for an extension of new towns right through the French and Indian War. In actual fact, quite contrary to a very plausible "war restricts new settlement" hypothesis, the bulge of new communities recognized from 1753 through 1767 was greater than any that had appeared before, in spite of the hostilities during most of these years. Only in the early war period of 1756–58, which was disastrous for the English forces from western Pennsylvania to upper New York just on the outer flank of Massachusetts, was the extension of new settlements apparently interrupted. The bulge clearly began before the war, furthermore, and was not just the result of it. But then town-founding actually fell off in the peaceful years preceding the Revolution. Less surprisingly, another flurry of town organization in Massachusetts followed the Revolution, reflecting both the fact of peace and another spurt of population growth which had occurred in the years preceding the war.

While bulges in the establishment of new towns that would be expected in Table 5 near 1806 and 1829—if the standard spacing at about twenty-two or twenty-three year intervals had continued—are missing, this does not mean that the recognition of new communities as an indicator of regular spurts in population growth loses its usefulness in Massachusetts henceforth. New Englanders flooded to western New York, Ohio, and the rest of the Old Northwest in the early part of the nineteenth century.[27] It is not unreasonable to expect that flow to have been interrupted by the War of 1812 and the business troubles of the following years, thus dividing into two likely separate historical bulges moving westward which were focussed chronologically just about where intensive town growth fails to appear as expected in the home state around 1806 and 1829. New Englanders also colonized southwards into Pennsylvania, North Carolina, and Mississippi. But as the frontier rolled out

27. Maine is not included in Cook's data plotted in Table 5. Its settlement—both before 1820 while part of Massachusetts and afterwards—involved many people from the mother state.

stage by stage, and New England became no longer so convenient a jumping-off point,[28] once again clusters of new communities were founded in the old state around 1850 and 1871. These points of relatively more frequent town organization before and after the Civil War— nearly two and a half centuries since the first settlements of Massachusetts were established—are almost exactly where an extrapolation of earlier intervals between peaks of community recognition in Table 5 would call for them.

New communities meant new opportunities of many kinds. These settlements needed new political representatives, new professionals, and new traders as well as the farm families who developed the land. Some details are in fact available concerning when new men became deputies to the General Court of the Massachusetts Bay Colony, when individuals for the first time became assistants or councillors in the upper branches of the legislatures of pre-Revolutionary New England, when new churches were established both in the northern colonies and in the Middle Atlantic and Southern regions as well, and when early American merchants were born. All these different kinds of historical particulars tend to corroborate the argument that recurrent spurts of population growth, indigenous and immigrant, kept occurring, and in turn themselves contributed "feed-back" towards re-creating largely cyclical patterns not just in the spread of new American towns but in the development of the specific *institutions* which grew to serve the people who filled the communities of the New World. The controlling roles in these institutions gave the colonial leadership most of their occupational opportunities. That is, not just overall population growth and redistribution—which at the bottom were the ultimate sources of changes in equality of access to leadership places in the society—but also the local communities and their institutions which more directly provided the openings, can be seen to have developed according to the familiar fluctuating pattern which quite regularly repeated itself at intervals slightly exceeding two decades on the average.

Figure No. 8 begins this new, more immediate analysis of how the

28. Though quite a few New Englanders were still going westward—for instance, to Wisconsin and Kansas—on the eve of the Civil War.

availability of opportunities changed historically by presenting the number of men who in given years became deputies to the General Court of
Massachusetts for the first time during the period of the old charter
government (1634–86).[29] Individuals who represented more than one
town, as several did in their careers, are counted only the first time they
came to the Court. At three points in the era there were noticeable
bulges of new members in the legislature. Virtually by definition there
were many new deputies as towns first sent representatives in the 1630's.
There was also, however, more turnover then than at many later times.
In part, the Antinomian (Hutchinsonian) crisis created factions which
went "in" and then "out." Over and above these results of that conflict,
nevertheless, there was a rather widespread tendency to try several men
before settling down to return certain favorites to the House over and
over again.[30] Subsequent to this early period, the numbers of men becoming deputies for the first time in the colony as a whole (which included Maine and New Hampshire for most of the era) were fairly high
once more around the years 1665 and 1680. Approximately twice as
many new deputies came to the Court in three-year periods around
those dates as in the mid-1650's or the mid-1670's.

A comparison of the different plots within this section of the figure,
however, demonstrates that the bulge of new deputies who came to the
Court for the first time in the years around 1665 had been elected primarily by towns *other than* the old Eastern Massachusetts coummunities
of Boston, Charlestown, Salem, Newbury, Rowley, Ipswich, Lynn,
Cambridge, Watertown, Dedham, Roxbury, Dorchester, Braintree,
Hingham, and Weymouth. Most towns in Massachusetts other than
these fifteen began to be represented in the General Court somewhat
later than they, and usually had only one deputy at a time, while the
listed towns had two or three legislators in office simultaneously for

29. This analysis is made possible by the very useful dissertation of Robert Emmet
Wall. See note 2 to the introductory section above.

30. Some towns had more closed representation, longer terms, and/or more family
succession than others. See Lockridge and Kreider, "Evolution of Town Government,"
for the example of Dedham, a community with relatively sluggish turnover compared to
many others except for its big break in 1683. For an analysis of what characteristics of
towns were associated with more, or less, flexibility in representation to the General
Court see my forthcoming *Recurring Reformation* which relates local religious, political,
educational, and economic cultures.

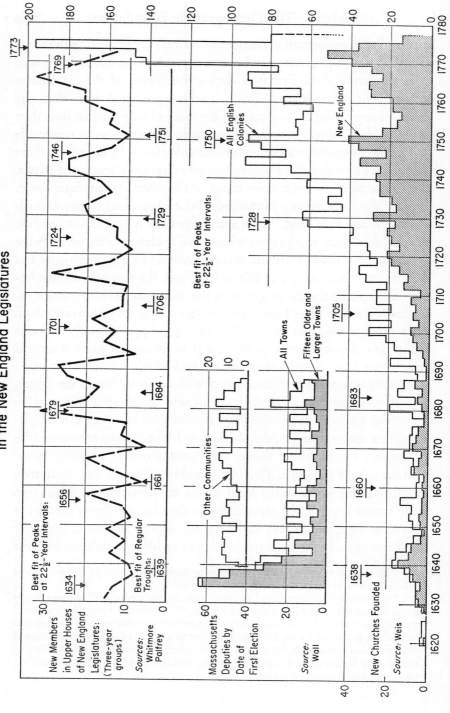

Figure No. 8. Dates of New Churches in All Colonies and Men Holding Office for the First Time
in the New England Legislatures

much of the 1634–86 era. Since the smaller and newer communities sent, on the average, their first group of representatives to the Court in the early 1640's, the next bulge of new men representing them for the first time around 1665 came at the familiar spacing of just over two decades later. The higher than usual turnover of representatives from the fifteen larger towns around 1680, on the other hand, came approximately forty-five years or two standard 22 ½-year cycles after their first representation in the mid-1630's. And a small but noticeable cluster of new men from these towns at the end of the 1650's came about half-way between those two points. Basically, it seems as though the fit of the two different sub-plots with each other reflects the early moving around after arriving in the New World that has been noted in the lives of many individual migrants and their families.[31] The second shuffling, which occurred within about a decade of the initial large migration of 1630 to New England, temporarily created a lagged pattern of community development and leadership, though that "late" timing among the second wave of original settlements quickly began to follow its own consistent cyclical interval. By 1680, however, the legislative representation of the later-established towns came back into step with openings for deputies in the earliest and biggest settlements as addition and turnover of political leadership in each group of communities fitted in with underlying spurts in the growth rate of the total population.[32] The pattern of the dates at which new towns were recognized in Table 5 shows—as it should, since recognition by the legislature and the first sending of deputies were not unrelated—somewhat the same distortion of the cyclical movements which should have come between 1630 and the early 1670's.

The tendency for the timing in creating new offices and in refilling existing ones to display bulges at the intervals of change which already have become familiar in the social origins of leadership and in the growth rate of the general population can be followed well after 1686, and on a

31. Greven, "Four Generations." See also my own *Recurring Reformation*, which shows the movements of all the first generation of ministers and relates them to the quest for not only better lands but also cultural congeniality between pastor and flock.

32. And that growth rate of the population itself settled down to a more regular pattern. Cf. Figure No. 9, on births, below.

broader canvas than that of the Massachusetts Bay Colony alone. In the upper houses of all the New England legislatures throughout the whole pre-Revolutionary era—the Boards of Assistants or the Councils as they were called—clusters of new men elected for the first time also often appear at intervals of just more than two decades on the average. According to the findings plotted at the top of Figure No. 8, beginning with the original membership in the 1630's further groups of men came into the upper branches of the New England legislatures for the first time at the typical 22½-year interval around 1658, 1679, 1703, rather late in the years 1730–33, but at 1742–45 and 1766 very much as would be expected from the early timing.[33]

The Councils and the Boards of Assistants, however, did not increase in membership as the number of towns in the colonies and their population grew. The total number of places was relatively stable for most of the time except that Massachusetts Bay in the 1680's was ordered by the Crown to elect the full eighteen assistants allowed in the charter, which had not been regularly done before. In part, the large number of new magistrates around 1680 reflects the result of that royal fiat. The extra peak on the figure a decade later, near 1690, on the other hand, in part reflects the entry of new men to higher office via the revolutionary Council of Safety in 1689 which overthrew Governor Andros. Many members of this group soon became participants in the new, regular Council under the charter of 1692. Even though some cronyism on the part of Increase Mather was also involved in the membership of the new upper house at that time, more generally what is showing near 1691— as showed around 1667 and would appear around 1715—is a generational "echo effect" of *previous* bulges of new men who had come into high office with the openings provided by the shorter cycle. That is, given an average father-son generation of about thirty-four years, the sons and nephews of magistrates created around 1632, 1658, and 1679, would on the average turn of age to hold high office themselves around 1666, 1692, and 1713.

    33. There is a peak at 1679 even without the effect of the new independent government created for New Hampshire about this time. The sources for this information are William H. Whitmore, *The Massachusetts Civil List for the Colonial and Provincial Periods* (Albany, 1870); John Gorham Palfrey, *History of New England*, 5 vols. (Boston, 1858–90).

From this and other evidence, there appears to have been some vacillation among the councillors or assistants between a tendency to honor families with the office over and over again (though except for Mather's original nominees at the charter change, members were elected) and another tendency for the choice to reflect forces of societal growth, expansion, and mobility of the sort which more clearly influenced turnover in the lower house in Massachusetts for the period 1634–86 as already described.[34] Beginning from about the 1720's onward—a century before the Age of Jackson—and taking over clearly in the period of the Great Awakening, the development cycle seems to have come to dominate the timing of new entry to the upper houses of New England as well, and to displace any generational "echo effect." *Then* it was, significantly, that the home government unwisely chose to precipitate issues of taxation and self-rule.

Bailyn has recently reminded us that the fundamentals of what became the ideology of the American Revolution had been present in the English colonies for some time. In the mid-eighteenth century that dormant fuse of principle was thrust into a bundle of social dynamics which produced a revolutionary explosion.[35] One part of the story of how this happened may be intimated here by the changing timing of new participation in the upper reaches of the colonial governments of New England. The implications, in this changing chronology of when new men arrived, are that the early role of family and social class in determining leadership had been displaced by the at least potentially more democratic effects of a periodic growth cycle well before the Revolution.

Finally, while the entry of new membership into the lower house was always timed (in the 1634–86 period observed in Massachusetts Bay) in step with the cycle of development, and while the introduction of new participants in the upper houses became so, the intake of new *appointed* magistrates (judges and J.P.'s) very clearly adhered to a pattern of *generational* bulges about three and a half decades apart—with no evidence

34. There were family networks in the lower house as well. See Wall and my forthcoming monograph on the careers of Harvard and Yale men for details. But these effects were, statistically speaking, overridden by the other context.

35. Bernard Bailyn, *The Ideological Origins of the American Revolution* (Cambridge, 1967); Bernard Bailyn, *The Origins of American Politics* (New York, 1968).

of effects of the shorter growth cycle of somewhat more than two decades which, in contrast, did set the historical shape for the access of new
men to *elective* office in New England.[36] The tendency of a Pynchon to
follow a Pynchon, an Appleton an Appleton, or a Hutchinson a Hutchinson was a characteristic primarily of the appointed amateur judiciary
and local magistracy in colonial New England, not the elected officialdom. It is no accident that, when the college classes at Harvard and Yale
became ranked by parental eminence in the eighteenth century, it was
the father's date of appointment as a J.P. which played such a critical
role in placing boys near the top of the class. It is also revealing, perhaps,
that the decision to arrange college classes permanently by such social
principles as opposed to merit or potential ability was made—after
three or four decades of conflict about placing principles—precisely in
the 1720's when the generational "echo effect" was disappearing in
election to the magistracy.[37] It is possible that some form of psychological
compensation was involved in the simultaneous changes away from
family influence in political power and towards family-conditioned
honor in academic life, where most major political leaders tended to
have at least one son.

Elective public office was not the only area of leadership or institutional
development within early American life where the total number of
openings becoming available year by year followed the same largely
cyclical pattern as the spurts of growth in the general population, in
spite of other influences on opportunity such as replacement from generation to generation.

In New England, at least, it is quite clear that the number of young
men from birth cohort to birth cohort who chose to become ministers
reflected a generational pattern, not some form of the societal growth
cycle. There tended to be bulges about three and a half decades apart of
college men who made up their minds to take pulpits. Since the very
large majority of ministers in colonial New England were college men,
the same clusters by date of birth dominate the historical pattern of re-

36. This evidence on J.P.'s has been derived from Whitmore, *Civil List,* and is presented in my forthcoming Harvard and Yale monograph.

37. A new discussion of ranking at Harvard and Yale is included in my study of their
alumni.

cruitment to the ministry as a whole. It is evident, further, that these un-usually large groups of would-be ministers came out of college years in which there were exceptionally plentiful numbers of sons of previous ministers.[38] There were several families, not all of them so well known as the Mathers or the Cottons, who sent generations of boys into the churches. But there were also larger than usual numbers of youths who were not the sons of existing pastors who took up the ministry from the same generationally loaded Harvard or Yale classes.

Obviously a good part of the problem of manning the ministry was replacing aging and dying incumbents. The generational bulge ob-served here tended to work in well with this aspect of sustaining a sup-ply of manpower. The rate at which *new churches* were created, how-ever, and new openings for young men that did not require waiting for an older man to relinquish the reins became available, followed *not* the generational pattern but the shorter cycle parallel to population growth and the formation of towns.[39] This expansion of new churches in spurts or steps was characteristic of the New England colonies and *also* of the mid-Atlantic and southern colonies taken separately. The upper plot in the bottom part of Figure No. 8, which refers to all regions from Maine to Georgia, indicates that the manning of new churches lagged around 1687–91, 1705–12, 1731–36, and 1755–58, while the years near 1679–84, 1699–1704, 1727–30, 1743–50, and 1769–74 saw an intensified pattern of church-founding, both in new towns and by doubling up or branching out in older communities. The timing of these new institutional open-ings followed the same interval but consistently the opposite phase about eleven or twelve years away from fluctuations in the rate at which new towns were recognized by the Massachusetts legislature (Table 5 above). But the dates at which new deputies and new members of the upper houses were elected for the first time moved in step with the dates at which new churches took their first minister (Figure No. 8). The lag seems to have been one of a few years between the authorization of new

38. See the same forthcoming monograph.
39. Dated from the first regular ministry. The sources for this information are two volumes by Frederick Lewis Weis, *The Colonial Clergy and the Colonial Churches of New England* (Lancaster, Mass., 1936); *The Colonial Churches and the Colonial Clergy of the Middle and Southern Colonies, 1607–1776* (Lancaster, Mass., 1938).

settlement and the time at which the new community actually produced new leadership and institutions to answer the needs stemming from the intensified population growth that began about the time at which more new towns than usual were organized.

Even in colonial business, meanwhile, some knowledge of the dates at which better-known merchants were born also suggests spurts in New England trade that created openings for more commercial figures than was ordinary among birth cohorts just over two decades apart. Table 6 takes all men identified by Bailyn as merchants in his two volumes on early New England trade whose date of birth can be determined.[40] There were more merchants than usual born around 1602–11, 1641–50, and perhaps again in the 1660's on the basis of Bailyn's identifications alone. For several purposes of keeping a control upon what could and could not be learned about New England society from college men and their families, the present writer has been maintaining a rough card file on all men described as "merchants" in the northern colonies, including all those mentioned by Bailyn in his study of the "seventeenth century" and among the investors in the Massachusetts shipping of 1697–1714, but also all others who have been encountered in a variety of ways while analyzing colonial families and lists of political leadership. There are some problems for present purposes for all the data used: Bailyn's seventeenth-century study does a lot to focus on successive generations of early business leadership and may overstress inheritance; the 1697–1714 sample, though derived very firmly from the actual details of who owned cargoes, embraces only a rather short period for any time series analysis; my own supplementary sources may be biased towards those merchants who were alumni or who were likely to send boys to college, intermarry with college families, or crop up in other activities besides business. The right-hand side of Table 6, however, uses the supplementary evidence as well to fill out some of the indications of the data taken strictly from Bailyn as they have already been presented in the left side of the table. The expanded fund of data shows that larger than usual groups of notable or identifiable New England merchants can be found

40. Bailyn, *New England Merchants*; Bailyn and Bailyn, *Massachusetts Shipping*.

TABLE 6

Number of Identifiable New England Merchants Born in Successive Three-Year Periods 1583–1720

Years of Birth	No. from Bailyn†	No. All Sources‡	Actual Clustering	22½-Year Fit	Years of Birth	No. from Bailyn†	No. All Sources‡	Actual Clustering	22½-Year Fit
1583–85	1	1			1652–54	4	6		
1586–88	1	1			1655–57	0	1		
1589–91	3	3			1658–60	1	4		
1592–94	3	3			1661–63	4	9 }		
1595–97	1	1			1664–66	2	3 }	± 1665	
1598–00	2	2		1601	1667–69	2	8 }		1668
1601–03	7	7 }			1670–72	1	5		
1604–06	2	3 }	± 1606–07		1673–75		3		
1607–09	3	4 }			1676–78		3		
1610–12	7	7 }			1679–81		3		
1613–15	2	3			1682–84		4 }		
1616–18	4	4			1685–87		2 }	? (± 1686)	
1619–21	0	0			1688–90		4 }		1690
1622–24	2	4 ?	(1623)	1623	1691–93		3		
1625–27	1	1			1694–96		3		
1628–30	0	0			1697–99		6		
1631–33	2	2			1700–02		8		
1634–36	3	5			1703–05		10 }		
1637–39	6	6			1706–08		6 }	± 1707	
1640–42	7	8 }			1709–11		10 }		
1643–45	3	4 }	± 1645–46 1646		1712–14		6		1713
1646–48	4	7 }			1715–17		8		
1649–51	7	9 }			1718–20		8		

† Bailyn, *New England Merchants*; Bailyn and Bailyn, *Massachusetts Shipping*.

‡ Also Sibley, Dexter, and other miscellaneous sources.

Note: parentheses indicate hypothetical date perhaps not met by actual peak.

not only in the birth cohorts of 1602–11 and 1641–50, but also in those
of the 1660's and the later 1700's as well.[41]

In conclusion, it may be said that quite consistently through the history
of society in colonial New England—and in some cases past these geographical boundaries—opportunities in trade, the extension of particular institutions like churches, and the actual turnover for new men in
specific roles of leadership, did not grow according to some smooth
curve of societal development but rather expanded in spurts or steps at
intervals similar to those of the numbers of people and the numbers of
communities which trade, the churches, and political leadership served.
Behind the tendency for certain birth cohorts in early America to enjoy access to opportunity that was more than usually free of who their
fathers happened to be, there operated a cyclical pulsation of societal
growth at all these different levels of human organization which significantly affected how many opportunities there would be for successive
groups of young men and thereby conditioned how open, how socially
equal, the competition for desirable places would be.

IMMIGRATION AND NEW SETTLEMENT OR
INTERNAL MOVEMENT AFTER 1775

Still other evidence shows that alternate spurts and lags of immigration and internal migration which founded new settlements and
enlarged older ones kept on occurring after the United States had become a nation. These changes in the geographical flow of population
were usually repeated at the same intervals as before 1775. And usually,
also, these variations in immigration and internal migration took place
in the same temporal relationship to each other—and relative to alterations in the rate of gross population growth—just as they had done in
the colonial period. Since both those consistencies continued, furthermore, new peaks and troughs of immigration and internal migration
can be "predicted" and actually verified by means of the more sophisticated data available for the nineteenth and even the twentieth centuries.

Marcus Hansen's survey of immigration to America, in addition to

41. My own extra data—obtained mostly from college families and their connections
—begin to tail off about one quarter of the way through the eighteenth century.

telling much about the sources and mechanisms of trans-Atlantic movement up to 1860, provides an approximate evaluation of when the inflow was heaviest between the mid-eighteenth century and the mid-nineteenth century. In his view the European wars from 1742 through 1760 (he notes that 1749–53 was an interlude of peace) held down trans-Atlantic movement; but from 1760 to the eve of the Revolution the flood of new settlers rose rapidly, probably cresting in the years 1770–73. Naturally the Revolution impeded migration to the New World, whatever forces at the time may have pushed men and women out of the Old World. Apparently, however, there was a levelling off, in what had been a growing trans-Atlantic movement, before fighting actually began. By 1784–85, however, the flow was moving rapidly again, abetted by the liberal naturalization regulations made for the new nation in 1790. The tide probably ran fairly strong until about 1793 when England became involved in the hostilities set off by the French Revolution. Lest warfare on the seas seem the prime regulatory force for the amount of immigration, however, it is important to note that in 1795 the waiting period for naturalization in this country was raised to five years, while the delay was extended to as much as *fourteen* years in 1798. Even before the bubble of speculation in western lands burst in 1796, resident Americans were finding it more to their interest to curb the intake of new citizenry. In sum, several factors affecting immigration took a downturn together. The reaction and attitude of 'natives' (many of them once immigrants themselves) played an important part in this process of stagnation in the trans-Atlantic flow—as they did again in the riot years of the 1830's and the 1850's.[42]

The influx began to revive in 1801 for a year or two. (Jefferson at this time returned to a five-year naturalization period from the unusually long wait imposed in the administration of John Adams). The intake of Europeans slackened during 1807–09, but picked up noticeably in the 1809–12 era. Then it spurted substantially beginning in 1815, when the War of 1812 came to an end and the European conflict around France was settled. Yet by 1819 immigration once more took a sharp turn downwards. In part, this reflected the difficulty recent immigrants were having in finding work. The first half of the 1820's became very slow

42. Hansen, *Atlantic Migration*, pp. 65–67.

years for trans-Atlantic migration. This change from high immigration in the late 1810's to very slow intake in the 1820's, as recorded by contemporary observers, has been underscored recently by Douglass C. North in his survey of the American economy from 1790 through 1860.[43] Beginning in 1827 and perhaps running through the stock market panic of 1837 to about 1842, however, another and still bigger spurt of immigration to America picked up momentum, according to Hansen. Following the figures provided by North from 1820 to 1860 one could argue either that this growth in immigration came to an end with the crisis of 1837 or that it terminated in 1843—where an extrapolation of the colonial peaks of immigration would project the crest in that era (Table 4).[44]

Then in the late 1840's, famine in Ireland and both famine and political troubles in Germany turned large numbers of Europeans towards the American shore. These forces provided a "push" factor. Meanwhile, the spaces of the new continent which opened to settlement as a consequence of acquisitions in the West and Southwest[45] and the employment opportunities of the industrial revolution in the East, "pulled" another surge of people across the ocean. However one evaluates the causes of immigration,[46] in the early 1850's a very heavy flow of individuals and families came across the Atlantic to settle. This flood tide was the biggest so far, not only in absolute size but also in relation to the indigenous population.

In terms of the timing of other probable peaks of immigration, as summarized in Table 4 for the period after 1790 as well as before that date, the accentuated inflow of the 1850's was early. It should have lasted approximately up to the end of the Civil War rather than tapering off a decade sooner, downward from a crest in 1854. Even compared with the earlier of two possible peak dates for the preceding wave of immigration of the 1830's (in 1836 rather than 1842), the next and much

43. North, *Economic Growth*, pp. 97, 245.

44. *Ibid.*, pp. 97–98.

45. North (p. 99) shows major steps of territorial expansion at 1803 and 1848—forty-five years or two growth cycles apart, from the Louisiana Purchase to the acquisitions of the Mexican War.

46. Everett Lee has recently provided a theoretical model to accommodate many elements in migration. "A Theory of Migration," *Demography*, 3 (1966), 47–57.

larger bulge came too soon afterwards to fit at all well with the usual pattern of intervals of 22 ½ years on the average. Since the exceptional intake was ebbing substantially for several years before the Civil War, the early timing cannot, moreover, be attributed to the effects of that disruptive historical event. More likely, peculiarities of the "push" factors in Europe at this time or unusually strong nativist reaction against immigration in America account for the fact that the curbing of this aspect of population growth took place before the recurrent pattern of ebb and flow would normally have placed it.[47]

This temporary advance forward in time of the usual resurgent crest of heaviest immigration during the decade before the Civil War, however, did not bring to an end the old pattern of essentially 22 ½-year cycles which continued regularly from the major intakes of new citizens in the early colonial era. An extension of that familiar pattern from the first crest in the numbers of new settlers around 1640, for example, would call for further peaks after the Civil War near 1888, 1910, 1933, and 1955. In actual fact, the measures of immigration worked up from overlapping decennial data for Kuznets by Everett S. Lee show that the net results of migration for population increase in this country were greatest in the periods 1875–85, 1900–10, 1920–30, and 1945–55 (Table 4).[48] Annual data provided more recently by Coale and Zelnick, moreover, show that two peaks of immigration centered on 1887 and 1910, while annual data since World War II offered by Rubin demonstrate a new top near 1952.[49] Thus a pattern of recurrent crests of immigration

47. Prof. David Grimsted of the University of Maryland is currently engaged in a promising analysis of these upheavals and also the troubles of the 1840's about halfway between. There are questions in the present writer's mind as to whether the disorders in all three periods stemmed from similar causes, or whether the roots of the disturbances of the mid-1840's may have been somewhat different.

48. Kuznets, "Long Swings in Growth of Population," pp. 25–31.

49. Ansley J. Coale and Melvin Zelnick, *New Estimates of Fertility and Population in the United States* (Princeton, 1963), p. 26. Their data are stated in terms of the deviation of the immigration rate of the previous five years from the trend. Stated in absolute numbers, however, years of high intake are focussed similarly between 1881 and 1892, and between 1905 and 1914, with the largest single annual movements in 1882 and 1907. Bureau of the Census, *Historical Statistics of the United States, 1789–1945* (Washington, 1949), p. 33; Ernest Rubin, "The United States," in Brinley Thomas, ed., *The Economics of International Migration* (London, 1958), pp. 133–145. The postwar peak for immigrants forty-four years old or younger came in 1957, in comparison with a 315-year or fourteen-cycle prediction of 1955. Cf. Table 4 and U.S. Census, *Statistical Abstracts*, for the 1950's and 1960's.

to this country that is projected forward at 22 ½-year intervals from the clearly established bulge which culminated around 1640 and that fits other fairly closely specifiable points prior to the Revolution, predicts with only one significant exception,[50] eight recurrences of maximum immigration from 1790 to the present, composing the seventh through the fourteenth repetitions of the pattern since the mid-seventeenth century.

Much the same kind of ex-post-facto "prediction," furthermore, with surprising accuracy relates what is known of pre-Revolutionary surges of new settlement or *internal* migration to similar movements in the modern era. In fact, waves of internal migration to the frontier to develop new settlements paralleled very closely in time those peaks of immigration that have just been noted from the mid-eighteenth century onwards (Table 4). The Appalachian Piedmont filled up in the 1760's and early 1770's from Virginia to South Carolina. Much of western Pennsylvania was settled, farmers pushed out along the Mohawk Valley towards the Great Lakes, and northern New England was populated. Following the Revolution the push was on into Kentucky and Tennessee, parts of Ohio, and western and northern New York. But by the mid-1790's speculation outran the ability to find purchasers, and a significant collapse hit many prominent land operators.

Though some belt-tightening and concern over the activities of land companies were evident in the later 1790's from western New York to Georgia, General Wayne's victory of 1795 and the removal of many Indians from the Ohio Valley made settlement there more attractive. Meanwhile the legacy of the New York land companies, however grandiose their ambitions had proved to be, left behind sound foundations for a transportation system to serve the next surge of migration to the interior, and the purchase of Louisiana in 1803 cut off the French restraint on westward movement in the South. During the years from about 1800 to the War of 1812 seekers of new land began once more to fill the routes which now pierced the Appalachian chains at several places. Trade and transport moved with them. Tonnage on the Poto-

---

50. In the 1850's, perhaps in the 1930's also.

mac, for instance, heightened significantly in 1807 and 1811.[51] Once
the war was concluded, and the English backing of hostilities by the
tribes south of the Great Lakes was lifted, the surge westward resumed.
North and south, treaties relieved the Indians east of the Mississippi
of their lands. In the South, large proportions of the moving settlers
sought new acreage as the introduction of a cotton economy encouraged the consolidation of small holdings and the extension of slavery
in the seaboard states, while at the same time the new technology
and the new market for the staple held forth the promise of prosperity
for all who could secure suitable lands somewhere else. Southerners
poured into western Georgia and Alabama during the years following
the war. Public land sales in Alabama, Mississippi, and Missouri reached
an all-time peak in 1818,[52] just where an extrapolation of the colonial
pattern of internal population distribution would call for another crest.
This movement, however, was interrupted by a serious financial panic
in 1819.[53]

The shift out of the Old South soon ran strong again, nevertheless,
reaching further across the Mississippi into Texas, Louisiana, and Arkansas, as well as Missouri, while southern expansion also did much to populate the Ohio Valley until the 1830's. The southern portion of the
country as a whole in 1835–36 saw a second boom in land sales that
rivaled the one that had culminated eighteen years before. Further transactions in Alabama, Mississippi, and Missouri were matched by those in
Arkansas and Louisiana, while Florida had its lesser boom.[54]

Early in the new century, meanwhile, New Englanders poured into
western New York, developed new lands, and by their agricultural
success drove eastern prices down and forced still more New England
farmers to move westward in search of new holdings. The first spurt in
the sale of public acreage in the region of Ohio, Indiana, Illinois, and
Michigan had come in 1818–19.[55] In the 1830's another surge of north-

51. North, *Economic Growth*, p. 33. The figures go up again in 1815, but there are no
later data with which to place the top accurately.
52. *Ibid.*, pp. 119 and 256; Walter Buckingham Smith and Arthur Harrison Cole,
Fluctuations in American Business, 1790–1860 (Cambridge, 1935), p. 57–58.
53. Billington, *Westward Expansion*, p. 323.
54 North, *Economic Growth*, pp. 119, 256; Smith and Cole, *Fluctuations*, pp. 57–58.
55. Smith and Cole, *Fluctuations*, p. 56; North, *Economic Growth*, pp. 120, 256.

ern migration across the Great Lakes region pushed land sales to the all-time high for that part of the country in 1836. The boom was repeated in the older territories but was extended now to Wisconsin and Iowa.[56] After some interference by the financial crisis of 1837 and the role of large speculators who set unrealistic prices for their lands,[57] the push was on again. Abetted by the growth of railroads and the introduction of large numbers of fresh immigrants directly to the West during the 1850's—especially across the Great Lakes as far as Minnesota, and also down the Ohio Valley—mid-America to the edge of the Great Plains was substantially populated by the outbreak of the Civil War. This shift still further West was keyed by yet another boom in land sales peaking at 1854–55. The new surge of settlement, for the United States as a whole, roughly equalled those of 1818 and 1836. Meanwhile the annexation of Texas and much other Mexican territory, the development of Oregon, the California rush, and the Mormon migration to Utah acquired the territory and planted the outposts for what, following the Civil War, would be the last great thrust to populate new land in the history of the American "West."[58] That frontier history had begun developing in this pattern of recurrent spurts at least two and a half centuries before, when discontented settlers of Cambridge, Roxbury, Dorchester, and Watertown picked up their worldly goods in the mid-1630's and walked to the Connecticut Valley where—literally—the grass looked greener for their cattle.

The grass did not cease to look greener somewhere else for many Americans from time to time well after the frontier "closed" following the last great surge of movement to new western lands after the Civil War. As indicated in Table 4, a continuation of cycles of internal migration at the interval that was most common up to the mid-nineteenth century—with somewhat early peaks in the 1830's and the 1850's, as in immigration—would have called for unusually heavy movement cresting around 1886, 1908, 1931, and 1953. In point of fact, Everett S. Lee, working with census materials available only at decennial intervals, has

56. North, *Economic Growth*, pp. 120, 256.

57. Billington, *Westward Expansion*, p. 306.

58. For the expansion of territory see North, *Economic Growth*, p. 99. In the years 1845–48 the size of the United States grew from 1.8 to 3.0 million square miles: Texas, 1845; Oregon, 1846; Mexican Cession, 1848.

shown that overall interstate migration in America—estimated by three different techniques—was heaviest for the modern era in the periods 1870–90, 1900–10, 1920–30, and 1940–50, and slowest or most slight in the decades 1890–1900, 1910–20, and 1930–40.[59] For this modern movement within American society since 1870, most of which has gone into California, Texas, and Washington, and secondarily into Oklahoma, Michigan, and Florida, it would be hard to find a better fit by means of decennial data to the timing suggested by the pattern of new settlement far back in the colonial era three centuries before.

In internal migration or the spread of new settlement, as in immigration and overall population growth, throughout more than three centuries of our history—with only an occasional exception in fourteen repetitions of the hypothetical cycle (Table 4)—quite regular and predictable changes can be observed which could be expected to serve as at least partial determinants of the different amounts of opportunity apparently available for men who belonged to successive birth cohorts.

iv. Growth Cycles in Several Aspects of the American Economy from the 1630's to the 1960's

BEFORE returning to various groups of leaders in the *D.A.B.* to show how their dates of birth, places of origin, and career locations reflect—like their social backgrounds—this historical pattern of growth and lag in American society, it may be helpful to show how, in the years before data are available of the quantity and quality which allowed Professor Kuznets to demonstrate fluctuations in prices and productivity at the 22 ½-year average interval, there is also *economic* evidence of long-term changes in trade and other forms of business activity to parallel

59. Hope T. Eldridge and Dorothy S. Thomas, eds., *Population Redistribution and Economic Growth, United States, 1870–1950, Demographic Analysis and Interrelations* (Philadelphia, 1964), III, p. 30.

varying rates of population growth and population movement. The modern ties between fluctuations in the economy and related demographic changes, that is, go back to the very beginnings of our society. The economists who have preoccupied themselves with this type of phenomenon have already suggested the existence of growth cycles before the Civil War; and Professor North in his recent economic history of the 1790–1860 period has integrated some of their ideas into his work by indicating several manifestations of "long swings" in various kinds of economic data after 1815.[1] From 1815 to the Civil War, North's work—and that done previously by Arthur H. Cole and Walter B. Smith[2]—will suffice in most instances to demonstrate how economic fluctuations accompanying changes of pace in population growth and movement relate to the kinds of opportunity cycles found in the social origins of American leaders. Yet there is some evidence even further back that the same kind of parallelism between the long-range business cycle, on the one hand, and population growth, immigration, and new settlement, on the other, was a genuine phenomenon existing from our earliest history and not something emerging in 1815 after a quarter century of revolution and foreign wars, as North implies.[3]

    Tables 7, 8, 9, and 10 outline and summarize some of the evidence available in the literature to support a preliminary contention that the American economy since its very inception—or at least as far back as the 1630's—has manifested in several crucial respects the long swings at intervals of 22 ½ years on the average such as those found by Kuznets four decades ago to permeate modern data on production and prices.[4] The principal forms of economic phenomena whose variations follow the familiar pattern of periodic fluctuations in the mid-nineteenth century are commodity prices, general levels of trade or production activity,

    1. North, *Economic Growth*, pp. 11–14. North, however, does not seem to absorb the role assigned to population changes as the source of long swings, and stresses prices instead. These variations are then explained on the basis of *supply* rather than demand, though Abramovitz (apparently North's main authority on the growth cycle—the 1958 Kuznets paper is not mentioned) actually emphasized the part played by the consumption involved in new household and family formation.

    2. Smith and Cole, *Fluctuations*; Arthur H. Cole, *Wholesale Commodity Prices in the United States, 1700–1861* (Cambridge, 1938).

    3. North, *Economic Growth*, p. 12.

    4. Kuznets, *Secular Movements in Production and Prices*.

finances, transport, and construction. Even in the earliest years it is occasionally possible to use something that approaches a partial or approximate series for a given commodity, market city, or component of the transportation system. At other times, the clue as to what changes were taking place is much cruder; yet the comment of informed contemporaries will say in so many words that economic matters had not been so bad in a long time. In general, it is easier to place depressions or recessions chronologically from the early information on business or trade conditions. Therefore the tables are shaped primarily to date the known crisis situations, or to designate the period over which the economic slide from top to bottom took place. The opposite information, identifying the best times in the economy, or certain parts of it, is readily available from the published sources out of which the materials for the tables are drawn. And in any case, in order to date declines, the timing of peak conditions is often cited.

PRICES AND THE VOLUME OF TRADE

Commodity prices, especially those of grains, are the economic data which are available the furthest back in any form approaching a time series. Prices for corn and wheat in New England from 1635 through 1694 were compiled by Ruth Crandall and published in Margery Somers Foster's very useful little book on the economics of early Harvard.[5] What these data show is sharp drops in the price of grain from 1636 to 1642, and again from a peak at 1681 down to another trough at 1688. A lesser dent in the price level is apparent in 1655 and 1656. There is little doubt that in every respect the early 1640's were what has been called "the first American depression."[6] Similarly, there is corroborating evidence from the Dudley-Andros Council, which governed the Dominion of New England from 1686 through 1689, that trade was in a sore state at that time also.[7] The lesser break in prices in the mid-1650's, on the other hand, did not come where the expectation of an intervening growth cycle timed at 22½ years would have placed

5. Margery Somers Foster, *"Out of Smalle Beginnings . . .": An Economic History of Harvard College in the Puritan Period (1636 to 1712)* (Cambridge, 1962), p. 49.

6. *Ibid.*, p. 38.

7. Foster, *Economic History of Harvard*, p. 82; Viola F. Barnes, *The Dominion of New England: A Study in British Colonial Policy* (New Haven, 1923), pp. 63–65.

it. Yet John Hull, the mintmaster and one of the premier merchants of New England at that time, wrote in his diary that 1664 was an unusually stagnant year for trade.[8]

In part the lesser 1655–56 recession in prices may have been just a let-down following the first Dutch War (1652–54). If, on the other hand, economic conditions did largely and consistently reflect patterns of population change, the indication from the timing of town founding in Table 5 and church formation in Figure No. 8 is that the real population decline or levelling off during this early era also took place in the later 1650's rather than in the 1660's. Thus several aspects of the whole developmental system of interrelated population growth, community establishment, economic strength, and social equality may all have come "early" before settling down into what henceforth proved to be a quite regular pattern of recurrence throughout the remainder of our history.

If the varying economic condition of New England, as suggested, subsequently continued to adhere to the timing of changes in the growth cycle, another recession should be evident culminating about 1710, or twenty-two years after 1688. The expectations and the evidence are set out in Tables 7 and 8. There is no price series available for this point of time, but we do know from Foster of some tendency for the credit allowed on grain and livestock against college bills by Harvard authorities to be rather low about 1705–1706.[9] Looking at still another fragment of New England economic life, the very helpful record which the Bailyns have made available concerning shipping in the 1697–1714 period also indicates that the number of vessels on the Massachusetts register and their total tonnage were both lower in the years 1700–08 than in the years preceding or following. One probably very significant role in this decline was played by the concentration of Massachusetts shipping on the single harbor city of Boston. More than 95 percent of the tonnage listed for home ports in Massachusetts was registered to Boston alone in 1705 and 1706, in contrast to less than 80 percent in the years 1697–17—

8. *The Diaries of John Hull, Mint-master and Treasurer of the Colony of Massachusetts Bay*, American Antiquarian Society, *Transactions and Collections*, III (1857). Page 215 contains the following evaluation amidst other commentary on the winter of 1664–65:

All employments, a smite upon them: at least, in general, all men are rather going backward than increasing their estates.

9. Foster, *Economic History of Harvard*, p. 52.

taken together. At about the same time, hitting a low in 1704, there was least tonnage registered in Massachusetts for home ports in the British Isles, the West Indies, and other places outside the colonies where the net of Anglo-American trade extended. And the proportion of Massachusetts shipping registered to such external home ports was appreciably lower in the period 1701–06 than before or after. Focussed around 1705, in other words—the hypothetical intervals in Table 8 would call for another slump in trade activity from 1703 down to 1710—there can be found simultaneous troughs of a few years each in Massachusetts shipping as a whole, in the percentage of colonial tonnage (or ships) registered to home ports other than Boston, and in the attraction of foreign carriers to the New England trade. The total level of the fleet fell, colonial commercial activity retreated to Boston from secondary ports, and foreign shipping dropped out of Massachusetts commerce altogether for a while during the first decade of the eighteenth century. Perhaps a military historian can adduce evidence to show that hostilities in the prolonged warfare of 1689–1713 were most restrictive on trade in the 1700–08 period. But the decline of shipping in the years around 1705 came just about where the growth cycle would have placed it without resort to any explanation based on warfare. Typically, as will be seen below, the nadir in transport in the growth cycle comes a little before the bottom in general business activity—expected here theoretically in 1710.

The next recession, if it were to fit the usual timing of the growth cycle, should have come about 1733—or forty-five years after 1688. In fact, from his work on New England families Clifford K. Shipton noted many years ago that there was a depression in the 1730's (Table 8).[10] Boston wheat prices, furthermore, can be seen to touch bottom for this era in 1731 and 1739, according to calculations made by Ruth Crandall,[11] while the hard-money price of molasses remained relatively weak in the years leading up to 1739 during a broad period over which the more usual pattern was noticeable annual increase in value (Table 7). In Philadelphia, which was competing with Boston to become the leading commercial center of the British American world, meanwhile, an index

10. Shipton, "Immigration," pp. 227, 232, 239.
11. Cole, *Wholesale Prices*, p. 5.

TABLE 7

Growth Cycles in American Prices from the Seventeenth to the Twentieth Century

A Theoretical Pattern of Regular Cycles at 22½-Year Intervals		Some Evidence of Actual Historical Movements in Prices*						North Import Price Index		North Export Price Index		Burns & Mitchell	
Peak	Trough	Peak	Trough	Peak	Trough	Peak	Trough	Peak	Trough	Peak	Trough	Peak	Trough
1636	1643	†Foster (grain) 1636	1642										
1658	1665	Foster 1656–57											
1681	1688	†Foster 1681	1688										
1703	1710	Foster (Harvard College accounts) low ca. 1705											
1726	1733	Cole Phila. 1725	1732	Cole Boston lows 1731 & 1739		Lester Pa. low 1732							
1748	1755	Cole cities 1748–49 peak (little fall)		Cole Boston low 1755									
1771	1778	Cole cities 1772	1775	Cole Boston 1770	1775								
1793	1800	Cole cities 1796	1802	Cole Boston				1798	1803	1799	1802		

	Cole cities	S & C	Cole Phila.	S & C / North				
1816 1823	Cole cities 1816 1821	S & C low 1821	Cole Phila. low 1825	S & C cotton 1818 1819 North wheat & corn low 1842–45	1815 1832	1818 1826	1814	1821–24
1838 1845	Cole cities 1836 1843	S & C 1836–39 1843	Cole Phila. low 1845		1836 1849	1843–45	1837–39	1843–44
1861 1868	Cole cities 1857 1860	S & C 1857 1861		North no break by 1860	1857–60 high	1857 going down	1857	1861
1883 1890	Burns non-agr. & all commodity 1880 1890						1864 1883	1878–79 1886 + 97
1906 1913	Burns 1900 1910 (or later)						1909–10	1914–15
1928 1935							1917–20 1925	1933
1951 1958								

* Sources:

Foster: Foster, *Economic History of Harvard.*

Cole: Cole, *Wholesale Prices.*

S & C: Smith and Cole, *Fluctuations in American Business, 1790–1860.*

Lester: Lester, "Currency Issues."

North: North, *Economic Growth.*

Burns: Burns, *Production Trends.*

Burns and Mitchell: Burns and Mitchell, *Measuring Business Cycles.*

For specifics of references see text and accompanying notes.

† These dates used as base for extrapolating the hypothetical timing of regular cycles.

TABLE 8

Growth Cycles in General Levels of American Trade and Production from the Seventeenth to the Twentieth Century

Theoretical Pattern of Regular Cycles at 22½-Year Intervals		Some Evidence of Actual Historical Levels														
Peak	*Trough*	*Peak*	*Trough*	*Peak*	*Trough*	*Peak*	*Trough*	*Peak*	*Trough*	*Peak*	*Trough*	*Peak*	*Trough*	*Peak*	*Trough*
1636	1643		ca. 1642												
1658	1665	Hull	1664												
1681	1688	Barnes	1686–89												
1703	1710	Mass. shipping low B & B	1700–08												
1726	1733	Shipton	1730's	Lester, exports and imports of several colonies low 1729–33											
1748	1755														
1771	1778	Morison, Mass. low to 1784													
1793	1800	North: exports & imports 1796–01	1803 +1808												
1816	1823	1816	1821												

			S & C	Kuznets: flow of goods to consumers	Kuznets: additions to GNP w/o services	Burns: manufactures growth rate	Hickman: growth rate production & GNP	Hickman: growth rate consumption	Williamson imports	Williamson exports
1838	1845	1836 1843	1836 1843							
1861	1868	1859–60	1855–56 / +1860 1861–62					low 1870–73		
1883	1890			1882 1893	1882 1893	1880 1890–95	1882–83 1891			
1906	1913			1908 1915	1908 1916	1900 1920	1902 1911	1899 1915		
1928	1935			1926 1932	1926 1934	1925	1918–24 1927–34	1922 1930		
1951	1958		1950	1950	1950		1939 1950 / 1951–52 1957ff.	1945	1951 1954 / +1958	1947 1950 / 1953–54 / 1957 1958–59

Sources (other than those already given for Table 7):

Hull: Hull, *Diaries*.

Barnes: Barnes, *Dominion of New England*.

B & B: Bailyn and Bailyn, *Massachusetts Shipping*.

Shipton: Shipton, "Immigration to New England."

Morison: Morison, *Maritime History*.

Kuznets: Kuznets, *Capital in the American Economy*.

Hickman: Hickman, "The Postwar Retardation."

Williamson: Williamson, "Dollar Scarcity."

For specifics of references see text and accompanying notes.

of wholesale prices for several commodities shows steady decline from a peak in 1725 to a trough in 1732.[12] Lester, in his article on Pennsylvania, saw the parallel between the price trough in that colony and the one in New England that also came in 1732. His data on imports and exports for Pennsylvania, New Jersey, New York, New England, and Virginia and Maryland all consistently confirm the existence of a general depression in America from the late 1720's into the early 1730's.

Philadelphia trade, as was probably also the case in Boston, enjoyed a brief fillip in 1741–42; but the next major crest in prices was reached in both port cities about 1749. Cole's data indicate a solid shoulder, or plateau edge, to the price pattern in New York and Charleston as well at this time.[13] No marked drop in prices occurred thereafter, but a change from a gradual downward trend to a gentle upward slope did appear in wholesale commodity prices at Philadelphia, New York, and Charleston about 1756 or 1757, while those in Boston rose rapidly up from 1755.[14] The theoretical pattern of cycles outlined in Table 7 would call for a peak of prices in 1748, followed by a decline to a trough in 1755. The actual changes at certain key cities do not fit at all badly with that outline. Similarly, subsequent commodity price information for Boston and for the other three centers displays a decline that set in after peaks in 1770 and 1772 respectively, while the hypothetical crest set forth in the table should have occurred in 1771.

The record of prices in America after 1775 is interrupted by the confusion of the Revolution. The projected low should have been reached about 1778, in the middle of hostilities. Clearly the war at sea did cause major depredations in American trade. And readjustments to compensate for the loss of familiar markets lasted into the early 1780's (Table 8). But recovery was on the way in the middle years of that decade, according to Morison—first in the market agriculture of the South, then a little later in the North where changes in the pattern of shipping caused special problems.[15] The next peak in the economy, as indicated by prices, should have been around 1793, if the pattern of recurring growth

12. Anne Bezanson, *ibid.*, p. 32.
13. *Ibid.*, p. 106.
14. *Ibid.*; for Boston, p. 7.
15. Morison, *Maritime History*, pp. 30–31.

cycles had any reality for the new national economy and survived the impact of the Revolution without losing step since the last pre-Revolutionary reference point in the high of 1771. The next trough of economic activity and prices should have occurred, then, about 1800 (Table 7). In fact, Cole's data on commodity prices in New York, Philadelphia, Charleston, and New Orleans take the form of a peak in 1796, while Boston prices topped out for the time being in about 1796 or 1798.[16] Morison's favorite heyday of New England maritime life, the development of the China trade in the decade following 1784, fairly well outlines the most rapid period of postwar recovery before the next plague of business troubles set in.[17]

Commodity prices did subsequently sink again in all five of the key cities covered by Cole and his research group, and reached a new low in 1802. Similarly, the import price index used by North slid from a top in 1798 to a bottom in 1803 while his export price measure deteriorated comparably from 1799 to 1802.[18] At each of these two successive turning points in prices, first the high and then the low, any lag in the projected timing of the growth cycle which might have been the consequence of the Revolution was progressively reduced—from about four years in the arrival of the postwar crest (1796–98 rather than 1793) to only two years in the next trough (1802 rather than 1800). A comparable timing of the gross *values* of exports and imports, climbing for several years to a high in 1796–1801 and then dropping to 1803,[19] is recorded in Table 8 and reinforces the conclusion that the fundamental growth cycle or economic "long swing" apparent throughout the colonial period did survive any disruptions which might have been the result of the War for Independence.

Jefferson's Embargo Act of December 1807 is reflected in a dip in prices in 1808, and an even more pronounced cut in the total values of exports and imports. The volume of external trade, furthermore, was highly sensitive to the sea warfare of 1812–14. The next peak of commodity prices evident for the five cities observed by Cole and his associ-

16. Cole, *Wholesale Prices*, pp. 5, 106; Smith and Cole, *Fluctuations*, p. 15.

17. Morison, "Pioneers of the Pacific, 1784–1792," *Maritime History*, pp. 41–51, and ensuing chapters.

18. North, *Economic Growth*, pp. 27, 30.

19. *Ibid.*, pp. 26, 30.

ates, and for Cincinnati as well, nevertheless clearly came in the years 1814–1817.[20] The "prediction" from the colonial timing of economic fluctuations would call for a crest in 1816. Subsequently, however, the next "bottom" to wholesale commodity prices in Cole's cities did not come until 1830, whereas the hypothetical pattern would mark 1823 as the relevant date. But Cincinnati, the only western city observed, had its low in 1821; and the Warren-Pearson quotient of the U.S. price index relative to the British dipped lowest in 1821 and 1825.[21] Burns and Mitchell time the decline in wholesale prices from 1814 to 1821–24; the indexes used by North indicate extremes in exports in 1818 and 1826, while import prices topped in 1815 and bottomed in 1832.[22] To cite some other specifics, the prices of pork, lard, whiskey, and corn in Philadelphia all reached their nadir for the period about 1825;[23] and national values for wheat and corn, which had topped out in 1816–18, fell rapidly to arrive at a bottom about 1820 and 1825.[24] The price of cotton at Charleston, which had been highest in early 1818, declined very rapidly and hit low in mid-1819.[25] In terms of general levels of trade, meanwhile, the values of both exports and imports for the United States as a whole are estimated by North to have touched their lowest point for the time being in 1821, after peaks in 1818 and 1816 respectively.[26] From a number of viewpoints there emerges a quite consistent impression that the peak at 1816 and the trough at 1823, which would be expected in prices and overall economic activity from the theoretical pattern of continuing 22½-year fluctuations projected from similar movements almost two centuries before, were facts of American life, realities that undoubtedly were somewhat shaped by the warfare on both sides of the Atlantic in the era but which could be anticipated without resort to this more conventional source of historical explanation.

Those who are tempted to rely upon wars to account for major re-

20. North's quotient of wholesale prices peaks in 1816 (p. 82).
21. Cole, *Wholesale Prices*, p. 106; North, *Economic Growth*, p. 82.
22. Arthur F. Burns and Wesley C. Mitchell, *Measuring Business Cycles* (National Bureau of Economic Research, *Studies in Business Cycles*, 2) (New York, 1946), p. 439; North, *Economic Growth*, pp. 87, 92.
23. Cole, *Wholesale Prices*, p. 138.
24. *Ibid.*, p. 139.
25. *Ibid.*, p. 183.
26. North, *Economic Growth*, p. 84.

cessions, or to create the population changes which may underlie them, should note that—according to the information on prices and trade levels just outlined—the timing of depressions and hostilities relative to each other was different virtually every time. While the French and Indian War (the Seven Years' War in Europe) may have helped to end a recession, or a period of levelling out after rapid growth, the Revolution probably can most accurately be said to have prolonged (and intensified) a price and trade decline which commenced a few years before the oncoming conflict could in any way be called obvious. A substantial drop in wheat values in fact did reach its bottom in *England* in 1779, just one year after the hypothetical trough which would be projected for America on the basis of regular growth cycles. This drop in English grain prices began from a top in 1772–74, or only a consistent year or two after the commodity price peak in American cities.[27] The next recession in the United States then occurred while this country had no major war at all. Relative to possible effects of European disruptions, on the other hand, the decline now only began along with, or even somewhat followed, the involvement of England, still our largest external market, in the continental hostilities during the 1790's; in contrast, the onset of recession or levelling out had *preceded* both the French and Indian War and the Revolution. In the subsequent growth cycle, finally, recession started as late as two years or more after the fighting ended in the war of 1812–14 in North America and on the seas, and after Napoleon had been sent off to Elba. In order to fit economic variation to military events there has to be a different, individualized explanation for the relevance of war in each of these four successive growth cycles involved between 1750 and 1830. Such intellectual gymnastics would seem to stretch the law of economy of explanation past its breaking point.

The next skid from a top to a bottom in the economy should have occurred over the period from 1838 to 1845, if the cyclical pattern continued to hold. There is a variety of evidence to show that such was

27. For these trans-Atlantic particulars and for more discussion on the *international* character of growth cycles so far back as we have information see the concluding comments of this presentation and, especially, my forthcoming *Opportunity, Equality, and Population.*

actually the case. Both domestic and foreign commodity indexes developed by Cole saw highs at the beginning of 1837 and lows in 1843—just a year or two at most away from the predicted pattern.[28] Prices in individual cities demonstrate the same drop from 1836–38 to 1843–45 independently.[29] North has compared the period of 1839–43 to that of 1929–33.[30] Wheat and corn prices fell from highs in 1836 and 1837 to lows in 1842–45. Cotton prices hit bottom in 1845.[31] At Philadelphia, the values of corn, whiskey, pork, and lard all reached a nadir from 1844 through 1846.[32] North's export price index shows an appropriate drop from 1836 to 1843–45; the fall in import prices, by his standards, also began in 1836 but continued until 1849.[33] Wholesale prices according to Burns and Mitchell were highest in 1837–39 and lowest in 1843–44.[34] In the worth of both exports and imports 1843 was the trough year (Table 8).[35] The flow of goods in and out of the country once more moved in step with prices. While immigration, and particularly land sales (Table 4), perhaps tended to peak in this era a few years sooner than would be expected from the pure or inflexible expectations of a growth cycle interval of 22½ years between comparable phases, changes in prices and in trade levels came almost exactly "on time" in both the upward and the downward movements.

In land sales and immigration the next crest of the putative growth cycle very definitely came before it would be expected. Prices in a half-dozen key cities can also be seen to have started falling from 1857 rather than from the theoretical peak at 1861.[36] Yet in general the price decline of this period was not so clearly 'early' as the drop in land sales and immigration. Wheat and corn prices did start to go down somewhat just after the crest of 1854–55 in land sales, but not very fast or very far. They were struggling back up on the eve of the Civil War.[37] Cotton prices

28. Smith and Cole, *Fluctuations*, p. 68.
29. Cole, *Wholesale Prices*, p. 106.
30. North, *Economic Growth*, p. 202.
31. Cole, *Wholesale Prices*, p. 137.
32. *Ibid.*, pp. 124, 138; North, *Economic Growth*, p. 87.
33. North, *Economic Growth*, pp. 87, 92.
34. Burns and Mitchell, *Measuring Business Cycles*, p. 439.
35. North, *Economic Growth*, pp. 84, 91.
36. Cole, *Wholesale Prices*, p. 106.
37. *Ibid.*, p. 137.

went off very little between 1857 and 1860.[38] The corn, whiskey, pork, and lard prices of Philadelphia kept going up into the early 1860's without a break before the war.[39] North's export price index does start down from 1857 to 1860; but import prices, in contrast, stay up.[40] The Burns and Mitchell series of wholesale prices dips from 1857 to 1861; in this measure, however, the big and lasting break downward begins in 1864.[41] The values of U.S. exports and imports were higher in 1860 than they had ever been (Table 8).[42] The measure of gross economic activity provided by the external trade of this developing nation, in other words, showed improvement up to the Civil War.

Aside from the clear-cut case in the sale of public lands, in all there is more evidence to suggest that the usual economic indicators were still moving upward toward the expected peak in 1861 than there is to prove that they were deteriorating prematurely from the mid-1850's onwards. The out-of-phase behavior of immigration and land sales in this era, already noted in Table 4 and its discussion, seems to be a phenomenon most characteristic of western development. Its effect is least evident in eastern and southern prices, in gross trade values, and in import prices. The last should have been less sensitive to western production changes than were export prices. Perhaps some effects of recently very intense railroad development, or some sponsored immigration tied specifically to transport—whose long swings tended consistently to run ahead of those in national prices and production (Table 10)—are at the bottom of this departure from the pattern of the regular growth cycle. There may also be involved some impact of the direct and indirect consequences of the gold rush of 1849, working toward putting certain aspects of the economy, including the attraction of immigrants, at their peak before the "natural" time. North sees the reopening of the Russian wheat trade following the Crimean War and a French run against the English gold supply as sources of the 1857 crisis. The economic activity of the East in this country, sustained by manufacturing, was not hit so hard this early.[43]

38. North, *Economic Growth*, p. 124.
39. Cole, *Wholesale Prices*, p. 138.
40. North, *Economic Growth*, p. 92.
41. Burns and Mitchell, *Measuring Business Cycles*, p. 439.
42. North, *Economic Growth*, pp. 76, 79.
43. *Ibid.*, pp. 210–214.

Whatever the reasons for certain aspects of the economy to peak out somewhat early in the mid-1850's, following the Civil War the main features of the recurrent growth pattern once more resumed regular phasing and continued to occur where they would be predicted by extrapolating 22½-year cycles from movements in the earliest available colonial data two and a half to three centuries before. Many different aspects of economic activity have been shown to follow this kind of timing since 1870, though the parts have varied somewhat in their relationships to each other and some points of dating are in dispute among the economists who concern themselves with these types of movement.[44] Tables 7 and 8 continue past the Civil War to present two kinds of evidence from this literature to demonstrate the actual existence of declines in the economy which should, hypothetically, have taken place from 1883 to 1890, from 1906 to 1913, from 1928 to 1935, and from 1951 to 1958 if the pattern of earlier cycles really did keep on going at 22½-year intervals into modern times, extrapolated from the economic changes of the 1630's and 1640's.

As summarized in Table 7, the wholesale price indexes used by Burns and Mitchell show a peak at 1883 after the post-Civil War slide. Prices then went down rapidly to 1886, and resumed a more gradual decline thereafter to reach an ultimate trough in 1896–97. Subsequently, prices rose to a high in 1909–10 (1907 in Europe), then levelled off through the first half of the next decade. World War I occasioned an unusual—and, in terms of the regular cycle, an "extra"—leap upward in prices. Following the war, however, a new hump in the price structure appeared, centered around 1925 (as it also did in Britain and France and—after the exceptional postwar inflation—probably in Germany as well). The bottom for wholesale prices during the Great Depression was in 1932–33.[45] Burns's quinquennial outline of "trend-cycles," meanwhile, indicates most rapidly rising non-agricultural prices and "all commodity" prices around 1880 and 1900, with most noticeably declining prices around 1890 and 1910.[46] In this fashion, wholesale price movements continue

44. For a review of this literature see Kuznets, "Long Swings"; Abramovitz, "Nature of Kuznets Cycles"; Easterlin, "Baby Boom," and his two 1966 papers cited above in note 9 to Section III.

45. Burns and Mitchell, *Measuring Business Cycles*, p. 439.

46. Burns, *Production Trends*, p. 241.

into the twentieth century to adhere largely to the long-range hypothetical pattern of the growth cycle.

Table 8 shows, moreover, that—according to Hickman—the growth rate of production, consumption, private investment, and the Gross National Product all have followed very closely through the modern era the pervasive historical pattern of fluctuation at 22 ½-year intervals.[47] These aspects of the economy were much less sensitive than prices to episodic events like the Napoleonic Wars, the Civil War, or World War I. The principal exception was in the growth rate of the GNP which hit bottom very early in the depression of the 1930's and also attained a peak rate of recovery in 1939 before World War II broke out, rather than as in consumption and investment, in 1945. In part, the stagnation of the early 1930's was so great that a *little* recovery made for a high growth *rate*. Burns's trend cycles in many different forms of non-agricultural production, including manufactures from agricultural materials, appropriately reached peaks near 1880, 1900, and 1925.[48] And Kuznets, in his *Capital in the American Economy*, indicates that additions to the GNP *stayed* high after 1939 through most if not all of the 1940's reaching toward the predicted peak of 1951 in Table 8. Any movements reflecting "earliness" in the onset of the Great Depression (probably in part at least occasioned by the arbitrary end to massive immigration in the mid-1920's) very quickly returned to place thereafter. Meanwhile the flow of goods to consumers grew fastest near 1877, 1902, 1925, and 1948 or later, with the most sluggishness on this side of development in the American economy near 1887, 1912, and 1931.[49] Williamson's recent data, finally, show a decline in the value of exports from 1947 to 1959 while imports atrophied most obviously from 1951 through 1954. It would seem that in spite of shocks to the system from events like worldwide military conflicts or radical reversals of immigration law, the timing of major changes in the state of the economy continues even now to fit closely very long-range "predictions" which can be made by extrapolating from the chronology of early American con-

47. Bert G. Hickman, "The Postwar Retardation: Another Long Swing in the Rate of Growth?," *American Economic Review*, 53 (1963), 490–507; especially pp. 493, 491.

48. Burns, "Cycles in the Growth of Industries," *Production Trends*, chap. v.

49. Simon S. Kuznets, *Capital in the American Economy* (Princeton, 1961), pp. 342, 347, 352.

ditions at 22 ½-year intervals as outlined on the left side of Tables 7 and 8 respectively for prices and general levels of trade or production.

Economic long swings at a spacing of twenty-two or twenty-three years on the average were in actual fact first discovered by Professor Kuznets approximately forty years ago in data on the *modern era*. Since then, however, there has been considerable disagreement concerning the mean interval between peaks or troughs in various economic ramifications of the cycle. The temptation has been to favor shorter periods, with some estimates running to as little as fourteen years.[50] The historical long view now very much throws the weight of the evidence back to the original conception of somewhat longer cycles as introduced by Kuznets in 1930.[51] In terms of the strength of the economy as in population growth on which the pattern of economic development has been said to depend, in the expansion of communities and institutions which served the population, and in the changing social origins of leaders conditioned by the number of roles created at various stages by the spurting extension of the social order—in all these phenomena it is the 22½-year interval that has the power of predicting very closely where changes would occur over periods of time as much as two or three centuries long, transcending any temporarily disequilibrating effects of wars, revolutions, legal and political changes, or gold rushes.

MONEY AND TRANSPORTATION

SOME other more specialized facts of economic development, besides prices and levels of production or trade, can also be shown to have varied in a cycle recurring at 22½ years on the average over long periods of our history. In the first place, two aspects of stocks in this essentially capitalistic society followed the cyclical timing closely. The number of stocks traded, as the left-hand column of Table 9,A indicates, tended to be high when production and prices were high, and low when these other dimensions of the economy also hit bottom. Historically, the volume of shares turning over was least in the mid-1870's or

50. Especially by Abramovitz and Easterlin; also earlier by Wardwell and by Brinley Thomas.

51. Some reasons why other intervals may stand out and catch attention are discussed below, and at some length in my *Opportunity, Equality, and Population*.

sooner, in the mid-1890's, around 1913–14, and in 1933 or sometime thereafter.[52] Burns's trend cycle analysis similarly shows the most unfavorable change downward in the activity of the securities market in the quinquennia around 1885–90 and 1910.[53] The prices of stocks, on the other hand, in modern times have tended to keep on going down after the volume traded has bottomed out, so that the troughs in rail stock values according to Burns and Mitchell occurred about 1877, 1896, and 1920–21.[54] Kuznets dates minimum prices for rail stocks near 1875, 1894, 1920, and 1940—maximum prices at 1885, 1910, 1926, and 1952 or later. He places the peak prices of all stocks—rails, utilities, and industrials together—at 1885, 1909, 1927, and 1952 or later, very close to the hypothetical crests in commodity prices and production in the pure or theoretical cycle reproduced at the left of the table.[55]

Prior to the Civil War, however, stock prices began to fall, typically, *before* production and commodity prices started their downturn, and reached bottom also somewhat preceding the trough in these other facets of the economy. This different, earlier historical phasing is evident, after Cole, in the value of U.S. three percent stocks at Boston, which were cheapest in 1798 and 1815,[56] and also in rail, canal, and bank stocks somewhat further into the nineteenth century. According to Cole once again, these latter security prices fell from 1835 to 1842 and then from 1853 to 1859.[57] This shift in the timing of stock prices relative to other aspects of the growth cycle from the earlier-phased pattern characteristic of the six decades before the Civil War to the later-timed pattern evident in the next nine decades raises some interesting questions about the possibly different relation of securities to the rest of the economy during these two distinct historical periods. Perhaps to the eye of an economist there is some obvious causal connection of this phenomenon with a change in the role of foreign financing, the native bullion supply after 1849, or the significance of transportation stocks even within the area of overall sales in securities which took place as the backbone

52. Burns and Mitchell, *Measuring Business Cycles*, p. 372.
53. Burns, *Production Trends*, p. 223.
54. Burns and Mitchell, *Measuring Business Cycles*, p. 372.
55. Kuznets, *Capital*, pp. 373–374.
56. Smith and Cole, *Fluctuations*, p. 22.
57. *Ibid.*

TABLE 9

Financial and Monetary Aspects of the Growth Cycle

Theoretical Pattern of Regular Cycles at 22½-Year Intervals		Burns & Mitchell Volume of Shares Traded		Stock Prices		Hickman: Money Supply Growth Rate		Burns: Monetary Stock of Gold and Money in Circulation (Growth Rates)	
Peak	Trough	Peak	Trough	Peak	Trough	Peak	Trough	Peak	Trough
1793	1800				S&C: 1798				
1816	1823			1810	1815				
1838	1845			1835	1842				
				*					
1861	1868		low 1875–76 or before	1853 S&C	1859				
				1863 B&M	1877				
				Kuz	1875				
1883	1890	1881–84	1894–96	1881–82 B&M	1896	1881	1893	1880	1890
				1885 Kuz	1894				
1906	1913	1905–06	1913–14	1906–09 B&M	1920–21	1900	1907	1900	1910
				1909 Kuz	1917				
1928	1935	1929	1933 or later	1929 B&M	—	1918	1931	1915	1925 or later
				1927 Kuz	1936				
1951	1958			1952 Kuz		1944	1949ff.		

* B&M: Burns and Mitchell rail stocks; Kuz: Kuznets all stocks.
For sources see Tables 7 and 8 and text with accompanying notes.

B. PRE-NATIONAL MOVEMENTS IN MONEY SUPPLY AND CURRENCY VALUES; AND MEASURES TO STIFFEN OR LOOSEN UP MONEY

Theoretical Pattern of Regular Cycles at 22½-Year Intervals		Supply of Money in the Colonies		Colonial Money Values		Measures to	
Peak	Trough	High	Low	Hard	Soft	Stiffen	Loosen
1636	1643		Foster, Bailyn 1640				corn made legal tender 1641
1658	1665	mint in 1652	Bailyn, chronic to 1663	Foster:	good money leaves N.E. 1654ff.	coinage devalued 1654	Winthrop, Jr., proposal for "banke without mony" 1663
1681	1688	corn repealed 1670	mint closed by charter loss 1684; much clipping of coinage 1680's	Harvard premium for English sterling low 1685–86	Harvard premium high 1697, 1700	corn repealed 1670; law sets low silver price 1682	land bank proposal 1686; bills of credit on taxes 1691ff.
1703	1710	bills of credit 1690's (Bank of England 1694)	Foster, silver rare by 1711	Harvard premium low 1702	Harvard premium high 1715	Queen Anne's law 1704	Mass. banks 1714, 1715, 1720; N.Y. long bills 1717
1726	1733	McKay: issues of money in several colonies 1717, ± 1724	Foster, 1732–34; usury complaints 1730	Lester: colonial money valued in London 1722–25	late 1730's		New London bank 1732; Mass. proposal 1740
1748	1755	1737–45	1754	1739–46	1748	Mass. change of tenor 1749; Parliamentary law 1751	
1771	1778	1760–64		1759 or later			

Source (in addition to those for Tables 7 and 8): McKay: McKay, *Early American Currency*.

TABLE 9 (cont.)

C. INTERNATIONAL FINANCIAL FACTORS IN THE GROWTH CYCLE SINCE 1790

Theoretical Pattern of Regular Cycles at 22½-Year Intervals		North: Terms of Trade		North: Balance of Payments		Kuznets: Claims Against Foreign Countries	
Peak	Trough	Favorable	Unfavorable	Low	High	Grow	Shrink
1793	1798	1798–99	1808–09				
			1814				
1816	1823	1816–18	1820–23	1816	±1825		
			1826–28				
1838	1845	1835–39	1843–45	1836	1840		
				1839	1843		
					1847		
1861	1868	1850–51	1860 or later	1853	1858–60		
		1857					
		Williamson: Trade Balance		*Net Capital Imports**			
		1860	1871		W, E 1871		
1883	1890	1879	1888	1879	W, E 1888	1880	1890
1906	1913	1900	1908	1900	W, E 1911	1901	1909
1928	1935			1918–19 E	1940	1919	1932
1951	1958	1947	1950	1948	1950–53	1942	
			1953		1959		
			1959				

* W: Williamson.
  E: Easterlin.

Theoretical Pattern of Regular Cycles at 22½-Year Intervals		Inventories		Foreign Claims		Private Construction* & Producers' Durables	
Peak	Trough	Grow	Shrink	Grow	Shrink	Peak	Trough
1883	1890	1881	1889	1880	1890	1876	1884
1906	1913	1901	1912	1901	1909	1906	1917
1928	1935	1920	1929	1919	1932	1926	1935
1951	1958	1941		1942		1948	

Source: Kuznets, *Capital*, p. 352.

* Excluding non-farm residential construction and railway expenditures (which Kuznets terms 'population-sensitive' capital formation).

Production and Prices: Theoretical Pattern of Regular Cycles at 22½-Year Intervals		Population Growth		Growth Rate of Inventories & Foreign Claims		Net Capital Imports		Private Construction & Producers' Durables		Residential Construction & Railroad Expenditures	
Peak	Trough	Fast	Slow	Peak	Trough	Trough	Peak	Peak	Trough	Peak	Trough
			1875								1875
1883	1890	1888	1895	1880	1889	1879	1888	1876	1884	1890	1899
1906	1913	1909	1917	1901	1909–12	1900	1911	1906	1917	1909	1917
1928	1935	1924	1935	1920	1929–32	1918–19	1940	1926	1935	1925	1935
1951	1958	1950		1942		1948	1950–53	1948		1948	
							1959				

of the American economy evolved from market agriculture to industrial production.

Besides the number of stocks being traded and the prices of stocks, some other aspects of finance followed the pattern of Kuznets intervals rather closely over long periods of our history.[58] According to Burns (Table 9,A)[59] the amount of money in circulation and the stock of gold fell from 1880 to 1890, from 1900 to 1910, and from 1915 to 1925—the last being an 'early' decline in terms of the expectations of intervals of 22 ½ years on the average. Hickman, meanwhile, places the most rapid *growth* in the supply of money near 1880, 1900, 1918–25, and 1944; and the most sluggish development of the money supply around 1893, 1907, 1931, and 1949–58.[60]

Using this modern timing of changes in the availability of money as a base of reference it is then possible to look backward in time and to see if historically—long before the Civil War and the arrival of industrial America on the scene—the amount of money in circulation, as one aspect of an economy generally following the fluctuations of the growth cycle, occurred where it "should have" as estimated by projections *in reverse* at intervals of 22 ½ years.

To begin with, if the growth of money supply was—as Hickman says—most rapid around 1900, it should have been near its most expansive phase also near 1652, or eleven cycles before (Table 9,B). In actual fact the Mint Act was passed in Massachusetts Bay in that very year to coin (without consulting the home government) "pine-tree" shillings for colonial use. This step to expand the money supply followed upon a well-known money shortage in the 1640's. In 1641, in the midst of depression, coin was so scarce that the General Court authorized the use of grain as legal tender.[61] Then in 1670, on the other hand, money was in apparently sufficient supply so that the law could be changed to prohibit further use of corn as currency. In contrast to this likely indicator of an

58. For further evidence from the modern era see Kuznets, *Capital*; Easterlin, "Relation of Economic Factors to Fertility Changes"; and Easterlin, "Economic-Demographic Interactions."

59. Burns, *Production Trends*, p. 241.

60. Hickman, "Postwar Retardation," p. 495.

61. Foster, *Economic History of Harvard*, pp. 41–43.

improved availability of money, however, conditions were seemingly quite "tight" once more by the mid-1680's. Not only was the New England mint closed by the abrogation of the Massachusetts Bay charter in 1684; it was from the 1680's onward that New England currency was generally discussed in relation to ounces of silver, and those who dealt in money prudently kept scales at hand.[62] To relieve this situation the first bank of credit was proposed in 1686, and increasing numbers of bills against future taxes were issued through the 1690's, especially to help pay the costs of the Quebec expedition at the opening of the decade. Even Cotton Mather in 1691 supported the issuing of bills of credit. It was in 1694, meanwhile, that the Bank of England was established at home. In the early years of the new century which followed, nevertheless, hard money rapidly fled from the colonies. Silver was generally out of use by 1711, and had virtually disappeared by 1718. Proposals for a private bank against land were heard in Massachusetts in 1714 to relieve the shortage of a medium of trade. In 1715 a public bank for bills of credit was put forth as a lesser of two evils in the eyes of conservatives; but by 1720 land bank agitation came to a head.[63] Outside Massachusetts, Connecticut issued paper money in 1709, 1710, 1711, and 1713. Rhode Island followed suit even more amply in 1715, 1721, and 1728. New York issued "long bills" in 1715 and 1717, then nothing in the period 1724–34. New Jersey and Pennsylvania both put out money in 1724, and another wave came from the latter colony in 1729. Subsequently, nevertheless, money was in noticeably shorter supply in the 1730's—in Massachusetts, New York, New Jersey, and Pennsylvania, while new issues in Rhode Island and Connecticut died down for the time being.[64] The dates of movements in the money supply in this era,

62. *Ibid.*, p. 44.

63. For Cotton Mather's position see Perry Miller, *Colony to Province*, p. 309. For details of the monetary acts see Andrew McFarland Davis, *Currency and Banking in the Province of Massachusetts-Bay*, 2 vols. (New York, 1901); and Foster, *Economic History of Harvard.*

64. Davis, *Currency and Banking*; George L. McKay, *Early American Currency* (New York, 1944); R. A. Lester, "Currency Issues to Overcome Depressions in Pennsylvania," *Journal of Political Economy*, 46 (1938), 324ff.: R. A. Lester, "Currency Issues to Overcome Depressions in Delaware, New Jersey, New York, and Maryland, 1715–1737," *Journal of Political Economy*, 47 (1939), 182–217.

as outlined in Table 9, B, did not deviate very far from the 'predicted' peak expansion about 1720 and greatest contraction about 1730.

The proposals of the New London Society for Trade and Commerce followed on the heels of the depression of the early 1730's. The Massachusetts land bank of 1740, on the other hand, was dated somewhat closer to the time when the supply of money grew rapidly again, as is evident in currency data from Massachusetts, New Jersey, Rhode Island, New York, and Connecticut about this time. New Hampshire joined the list of money issuers in 1743–45. Subsequently there is also some indication, as summarized in Table 9,B, that the early 1750's were years of comparatively scarce money while the early 1760's saw the supply rebound. Working back in hypothetical cycles from Hickman's modern chronology, one should find scarcity most evident in 1753 and the recovery most obvious about 1765. On the whole, from the first years of settlement down to the eve of the Revolution peaks and troughs in the rate of expansion in the money supply in most colonies came when they should have, in the light of the timing of movements of this sort since the Civil War, while well-known innovative proposals to expand the amount of money available—by accepting grain as currency (1641), by issuing bills of credit against future taxes (1686, 1691), and by establishing a land bank (1714, 1720 and 1733, 1740)—came during what should have been the slope upward between slumps and subsequent spurts in the expansion of currency.[65]

Typically, the temptation to issue money was not resisted very well or very long by the American colonists. The most rapid periods of increase in money supply were soon followed by points of time at which colonial money was worth the least, relative to silver or to the pound sterling, in America or on the London exchange. These crises of inflation, when good money took flight to Europe and the real value of colonial money was depressed, gave rise to efforts to bring the currency situation under control. Points of maximum inflation and the timing of efforts to regulate the issuing of money are also outlined in Table 9,B.

The Massachusetts mint in 1652 put out a purposely light shilling in hopes that the silver would remain in New England. In actual fact,

65. Miller, *Colony to Province*; Davis, *Currency and Banking*; McKay, *Early American Currency*.

further devaluation was needed by 1654. Thereafter New England money was traded at about the same level until 1704, when a long era of inflation began.[66] But in 1682 by law Massachusetts tried to set a somewhat "harder" value of local currency relative to sterling than had actually existed for some time. Then it was twenty-two years later, in 1704, when Queen Anne attempted by proclamation to bring the currencies of all colonies under control. In point of fact, in Massachusetts at least, a recession in the first years of the century may well have brought the relation of colonial currency to sterling more into line even before the proclamation was issued. Treasurer Brattle at Harvard required a 25 per cent premium on English debts paid in colonial funds in 1685–86 and as much as 36 per cent by 1697–98. But in January 1702, at the onset of the shipping recession apparent in the data of the Bailyns, the guardian of Harvard's funds asked only a 30 per cent "advance" as it was called. A year and a half later, however, the rate was back to 40 per cent; and it had climbed to 50 per cent by 1715.[67] In about 1719 New England money was harder once again, Pennsylvania currency had a strong value on the London exchange in 1722–23, and New Jersey money also received relatively courteous consideration there in 1716 and 1724–25. The early stages of the expansion of the money supply in each financial cycle, which tended to come somewhat before the peak in trade and prices, were periods when colonial currency was strong relative to the English pound. The lowest value of colonial currency, on the other hand, tended to appear about the time prices and trade peaked for the historical cycle then in progress. Thus once again the money of New England, New York, Pennsylvania, New Jersey, and Delaware claimed a comparatively good price on the London exchange in the period 1739–42, while the theoretical year for the crest in trade and prices, 1748, marked a low point in the value of colonial money in England.[68] The exception to this pattern came in the 1730's where the currency of the middle colonies in particular reached low value only well on through that decade rather than in the mid-1720's, as would be expected in relation to the crest of prices and production. In 1751, finally,

66. Foster, *Economic History of Harvard*, pp. 43–46.
67. *Ibid.*, p. 45.
68. Lester, "Currency Issues in Delaware, New Jersey."

the crown tried to bring matters under control by forbidding the issuance of paper money by the colonies. This restriction was often honored in the breach, but the attempt was made, at least, almost exactly two growth cycle intervals since the proclamation of Queen Anne in 1704 and three cycles since the Massachusetts law of 1682.

Variations in the terms of trade across the Atlantic, the balance of payments, and the import of foreign capital into America—as Table 9,c indicates—were, like the money supply, fiscal measures, and changes in the value of colonial currency, also related to overall movements of the growth cycle in the history of the American economy. According to North, the terms of trade for the United States were least favorable around 1792, 1814, 1826–28, and 1843–45, and best in 1798–99, 1817, 1835–39, and 1857.[69] According to Williamson, from the Civil War onwards the trade balance continued to be most favorable in periods of maximum expansion, highest production, and highest prices—at or near the crest of the pure or hypothetical growth cycle of the economy in 1860, 1879, and 1900, and recently in 1947.[70] Our net foreign claims, in the estimate of Kuznets, improved most rapidly near 1880, 1901, 1919, and 1942, and deteriorated most obviously near 1890, 1909, and 1932.[71] Meanwhile the net balance of payments, as indicated by North, also most favored the United States in 1816, 1836–39, and 1854. Similarly, Easterlin and Williamson have shown that capital imports kept in step with the crests of the growth cycle by attaining maxima around 1837 and 1852.

Following the Civil War, however, capital imports like the trade balance *inverted* in phase and the *minima* came near the crest of the growth cycle—in 1879, 1900, 1919, and 1948. Now the *least* foreign capital came to this country as we reached the top in production and prices for the time being. It would seem that this change about the time of the Civil War in the flow of capital in and out of the country, in the same period during which the phasing of fluctuations in stock prices (Table

69. North, *Economic Growth*, pp. 31, 94.
70. J. G. Williamson, "Dollar Scarcity and Surplus in Historical Perspective," *American Economic Review*, 53 (1963), 519–529, especially page 522.
71. Kuznets, *Capital*, pp. 336–337.

9,A and its discussion above) and in the trade balance also altered, reflects a metamorphosis of the role of America within the overall system of international financing, especially with regard to English sources of investment. Consistently, however, in both the prewar and postwar patterns stock prices were lowest and the trade balance most favorable when capital imports were lowest—around 1842 and 1859, then switching phase relative to the basic growth cycle to come in 1877–79, 1896–1900, and 1919–21. These three financial aspects of the American economy kept pace together, even when jointly they shifted position relative to the other components of the development cycle.

Kuznets, in addition, has gone further into the detail of capital formation in the recent history of the American economy to show how net changes in inventories fluctuated closely in step with American claims against foreign countries—with maximum rates of accumulation near 1881, 1901, 1920, and 1941.[72] Both foreign claims and inventories grew most rapidly a few years before production topped out, in a timing virtually inverse to that of stock prices and capital imports (Table 9,D). The troughs in inventory development which followed were located in 1889, 1912, and 1929. In contrast, private construction and the creation of producers' durables (excluding 'population-sensitive' railroad development and home building) grew most rapidly about 1906, 1926, and 1948, or at the crest of production and prices. In this boom period on the brink of depression, the most increases in investment were made. These commitments, several years hence, would help drive the *next* recovery of production up out from the trough that was about to set in when capital creation attained its highest rate. Contrary to Kuznets' effort to relate *inverse* movements of "population-sensitive" capital formation in housing and transport to private capital formation in producers' durables, moreover, his own data actually seem to show—as summarized in Table 9,E—that peak growth rates in both these forms of commitment shaping future production and consumption coincided near 1907, 1926, and 1948.[73] It was claims against foreign countries and domestic inventories which worked in a different phasing. Their chronological pattern of variation departed from that of *both* "population-

72. *Ibid.*, p. 336.
73. *Ibid.*, p. 336, 338, 340.

sensitive" and other types of capital formation, which were the forms of investment that would feed in most directly to change the quality and the quantity of future production.

Table 9,E is offered to suggest—at least prima facie from their relative timing—the way in which certain parts of the American economy appear to have worked to create and re-create the Kuznets cycle since the later years of the nineteenth century. Though much further exploration of these issues is required, it may be useful to summarize here the typical relative chronology of changes in certain relevant economic components whose historical movements have been described, because of the implications which this timing holds for any explanation of how the economic system for its own part kept contributing to the continuance of the growth cycle over and over again.

In the cycles since 1880, while production and prices were still somewhat short of their peak, inventories began to shrink and net claims on foreign countries started to subside. The rate of new private capital investment next began to fall, accompanied by more "population-sensitive" investment in housing and transportation. These two types of decline in the rate of new private capital formation were followed by the most familiar and obvious break downwards from the peak level, the one in production and prices. Once those most visible sides of the economy began to drag, stock prices also began to recede, followed by capital imports. By now, a varied group of economic components were taking the downslide together. But having started early, the slump in inventories also culminated early. This was before the ultimate trough in production and prices arrived.

It was just prior to that low in production and prices, however, that new additions to the population reached maximum rates. These most rapid population inputs preceded the deepest recession by just a couple of years as long as immigration was the main source of variations over time in the number of new people added to the society. The crest in immigration since 1880 has tended to "overshoot" somewhat the peak in production and prices. Later, after immigration was strictly regulated in the 1920's, peak increments to the population (now depending mostly on the indigenous birth rate) arrived closer to a dozen years before the trough in prices and productivity. Immigrant groups historically tended to be largely composed of young unmarried persons or families with children. Hence less time lag was needed to create new consumption by family-forming adults than was necessary subsequent to the take-over of major variations in the native birth rate as the principal source of new population, which occurred a quarter of the way through the present century. As Easterlin's brilliant "Baby Boom" article has shown, the result, both before and after the change in the *source* of new citizens, was that the most new people were ready to marry, and to capitalize and equip homes and families of their own, just as or just after the trough in production and prices arrived. These were also the times, moreover, at which inventories were lowest (Table 9,E). Therefore any increase in demand should have been most directly reflected in improving prices and production. Recovering production was facilitated by investment in plants, transportation, and other capital improvements like machinery that had been created *several years before*, and had been "waiting out" the recession under-employed for lack of a market to absorb their energies. At the other end of the cycle, the shorter lag from the slow-down in immigration, and the longer delayed reaction from the point of decline in the birth rate to the comparable economic stage, each in their own historical eras of predominance as demographic mechanisms of economic change, began to pull the stepladder out from under production and prices just as they neared their peak.

This chain of causation in the growth cycle—with demographic and socio-psychological, and even perhaps medical, components in addition to purely economic mechanisms—will be developed in further detail in later pages. First, however, in order to round out the picture of historical fluctuations in key aspects of the economy, Table 10 points up the timing of cyclical movements in transportation activity, transportation development, general construction, and homebuilding.

Transport activity (Table 10,A) tended historically to reach bottom about nine years on the average before the lowest point in prices and production. This means, looking at it in another way as in Table 10,B, that the utilization, earnings, and volume of major forms of transport such as shipping, canals, and railroads declined to their *lowest* point— typically—just before prices and production came to a *maximum*. The

trough in the movement of goods via the main systems of transportation, moreover, arrived at about the same time at which (or very soon
after) inventories were growing most rapidly. This paired backlogging
of goods and sluggishness in transport, on the other hand, in turn followed the low point in additions to the population by five years or
more, which suggests the following steps in the arrival of recession: cut-
backs in the growth rate of the heaviest consuming age groups of the
population reduced demand for goods, which piled up in manufacturers' and wholesalers' inventories while the transport system began to
operate sub-par; this backlog in the movement of goods was quickly
reflected in a downturn of prices and production, sometimes a stock-
market panic, and a general recession that dipped down to a bottom
within a few years.[74]

In reality there is considerable evidence to show that these were recurrent relative timings during the historical development of the American
economy. According to North, for instance, shipping activity was low
around 1790–91, tonnage in the coasting trade was slight near 1793, and
the earnings of the transoceanic carrying trade were down in 1790 (Table 10,A).[75] Morison's more impressionistic evaluation of post-revolutionary shipping indicates that sea transport was having its troubles at
least into the late 1780's.[76] Subsequently, Morison's actual statistics of
shipping owned in Boston and New York show a decline between his
observation points in 1810 and 1820, while by means of more time-
sensitive measures North indicates low levels in coasting tonnage, intra-
continental tonnage on the Potomac, and the earnings of the carrying
trade all focussed around 1814.[77] This date, of course, was the last year of
the War of 1812. Shipping might well be down for that reason alone.
In spite of the over-publicized victories of a few American frigates, these
were poor times for ocean traffic due to the effect of British naval might.
The earlier nadir of sea transport near 1790 could also be blamed on the
disruption of trade patterns by the Revolution, from which it took some
time to develop new markets. Yet once again in the 1830's—at the

74. This attempt to put together the pieces of an overall explanation is carried further
in my Opportunity, Equality, and Population.
75. North, Economic Growth, pp. 28, 34, 42.
76. Morison, Maritime History, pp. 30–31.
77. Ibid., p. 398.

proper growth cycle interval from 1814 and two such intervals from the early 1790's, but in a time of general peace—coasting tonnage was down, Erie canal traffic was slow, and the earnings of the carrying trade reached bottom.[78] Then in the 1850's, perhaps in the wake of the Crimean War in Europe but before the heavy disruption of the Civil War in this country, transport activity reached another low point. This is evident in river and canal traffic in continental America, and in the coasting trade along our shores, as well as in trans-Atlantic and trans-Pacific shipping.[79]

If such timing of fluctuations in the activity of transport continued after the Civil War, low levels should have been evident around 1881, 1904, and 1926 to sustain the regular spacing of the 22 ½-year cycle. In point of fact, Burns's data on "trend cycles" for railway ton miles in the modern era[80] display troughs of growth in the use of this form of transportation in 1885–90, 1905–10, and 1920–25—perhaps a few years later than would be expected by a pure extrapolation of earlier timing in water transport fluctuations (Table 10,A), but still keeping fairly well to the typical cyclical spacing and coming during the earliest years of the downturn in prices and production if not, as would be most proper, actually preceding that decline. On into the twentieth century the slump in transport led, rather than followed, the onset of another recession.

So did a decline in shipping activity somewhat precede more general depression in the early 1700's, over two centuries before. Working the growth cycle interval backwards in time from the nineteenth-century chronology, a low in shipping should have been present in colonial America about 1701. In fact, the nadir of tonnage registered for the port of Boston between 1697 and 1714 came in 1702, according to the materials of the Bailyns. What is known of troughs in prices, in the concentration of shipping on Boston at the expense of lesser home ports, and in the attraction of English vessels to the American trade indicates somewhat later low points in all these other aspects of economic process

78. North, *Economic Growth*, pp. 106–109. Morison's data taken at decade intervals show no low in shipping tonnage owned in Boston and New York in 1830 or 1840, but the dip should have come in between these points in the rather insensitive ten-year pattern of presentation.

79. North, *Economic Growth*, pp. 106–109.

80. Burns, *Production Trends*, p. 223.

than is apparent for the amount of potential carrying tonnage kept active on the register. In what was probably another such shipping crisis
prior to the recession of the early 1730's, moreover, it is known that
maritime trade *per se* was poor in the early 1720's, and Shipton's biographies of this period in *Sibley's Harvard Graduates* also seem to contain a
cluster of alumni and their family members who failed in shipping at
this time although economic activity in other senses was booming to
support the rapid population of the interior. It is in 1722, furthermore,
that Lester has demonstrated a low in shipping tonnage registered in
Pennsylvania prior to the 1729 depression there.[81] Casting both forwards and backwards in time, the recurring fluctuations in transport
activity which are evident from a variety of sources in the first seven
decades of American nationhood seem to be part of a fairly regular pattern in which a transportation slump typically preceded the downslide
of prices and production in the growth cycle of the American economy.

One result of this decline in transport use was that transport *building*
or *investment* soon began to recede. Isard demonstrated twenty-five
years ago that the construction of transportation facilities in the successive key forms of canals, railroads, street railways, and automobiles
ebbed to lows around 1822–23, and in the 1840's, in the war years of
1861–65 and an extra postwar trough at 1874–78, then back in step with
the hypothetical timing at 1893–98, 1915, and 1931 or later (Table
10,A).[82] Kuznets places the slowest growth rate in railroad capital investment in the years 1875, 1899, 1918, and 1935.[83] Though there is not
much evidence before the 1820's of patterns in transport development,
some data are available on shipbuilding in the early eighteenth century.
In this period a low in transport *construction* would be expected to have
come just before 1690 and another around 1710, working backwards at
22½-year intervals from the modern chronology of similar conditions.
In point of fact, the data of the Bailyns indicate decline in both tonnage
and number of vessels built from 1711 through 1714. Furthermore, instead of construction figures being somewhat higher in the late 1690's
than in the early 1700's, as was the case in the amount of shipping active

81. Lester, "Currency Issues."
82. Isard, "Transport Development."
83. Kuznets, *Capital*, p. 352.

TABLE 10 (cont.)

B. THE RELATION OF TRANSPORT TO OTHER ASPECTS OF THE GROWTH CYCLE

Production and Prices: Theoretical Pattern of Regular Cycles at 22½-Year Intervals		*Population Increase*	*Inventories Grow*	*Transport Activity**	*Actual Production†*
Peak	*Trough*	*Slow*	*Fast*	*Low*	*Falls*
1861	1868	1875	1881	1885–90 (1881)	1882–93
1883	1890	1895	1901	1905–10 (1904)	1908–16
1906	1913	1917	1920	1920–25 (1926)	1926–34
1928	1935	1935	1941	(1949)	1950ff.
1951	1958	(births 1960's)			

* Theoretical regular cycle from Table 10, A in parentheses ( ).

† Gross national product, Kuznets, *Capital in American Economy*, p. 352.

on the Boston registry, there is a hint that the years preceding 1697 also may not have been strong ones for shipbuilding. Further indication of the growth cycle in transport construction perhaps comes from Pennsylvania just a little later in the colonial era. There both the number and the tonnage of ships constructed was climbing rapidly through the early 1720's, as would be expected in those years, though the data of Lester do not cover enough points of time to show either the up-turn beginning this slope or the down-turn ending it.[84]

In contrast to construction specifically for transport, building as a whole tended to reach bottom a few years *later* than the trough in production and prices, carrying on to low points in 1878, 1900, 1918, and 1933 or afterwards (Table 10,A).[85] Easterlin places the slowest rate of growth or greatest decline in gross or aggregate construction in 1841, 1860, 1874, 1895, 1915, and "early" in 1930 but with an extra dip in 1939–40.[86] Residential construction, meanwhile, was most sluggish in absolute volume around 1861, 1879, 1918, and 1931 with an extra cut in 1945 (Table 10,A).[87] Burnham Campbell, however, places lows in non-farm housing starts and also in new household formations in the 1910's and the 1930's with another estimated drop in "required additions" to handle the needs of the population of the 1950's, which by the end of that decade had not yet been reflected in a decline of actual construction or family formation.[88] Kuznets puts the slowest additions to non-farm housing in the early 1870's, then at 1899, 1916, and 1934–41.[89] In all, residential housing has tended historically to come to a trough somewhat after the bottom in prices and production. Aggregate construction slumps sooner than residential activity because it includes the somewhat earlier-moving capital expenditure of transport and industrial building as well as personal housing.

Not only in prices (Table 7) and the volume of production and trade

---

84. Bailyn and Bailyn, *Massachusetts Shipping*, pp. 102–109; Lester, "Pennsylvania."

85. Isard, "Transport Development," p. 104.

86. Easterlin, "Long Swings," pp. 498, 491.

87. Easterlin, "Economic Demographic Interactions," p. 1065.

88. Burnham Campbell, "Long Swings in Residential Construction: The Postwar Experience," *American Economic Review*, 53 (1963), 508–518; here p. 510.

89. Kuznets, *Capital*, pp. 328, 330.

(Table 8), but in the sale and pricing of securities, the supply of money, international terms of trade, the balance of payments, and various types of capital formation (Table 9) and also in transportation activity, transport construction, aggregate building, and the erection of dwelling space (Table 10) the growth cycle can be shown to have been a fact of American economic life for long periods of time, even reaching back into the earliest colonial years. There was a typical temporal relationship of these different aspects of economic development to each other which was for the most part repeated over and over again. A few lasting shifts of relative chronological position that have been observed, on the other hand, probably indicate the emergence of America as a developed, industrial rather than agricultural participant in the international economy. They may also reflect some functional substitution between alternative mechanisms with n the whole system, as one aspect of the economy took over for another and carried more of the burden of cyclical movement —similar to the recent change from immigration to the birth rate as the prime source of twentieth-century variation in the amount of new additions to the population, as Easterlin has argued.[90]

Some of the current confusion in the economic literature, finally, about the spacing of the "Kuznets cycle," "long swings," or the "transport-building cycle" (after Isard), seems to reflect peculiarities of recent historical experiences like the ending of mass immigration or the timing of major wars. Judging from just a few cycles since 1870, or even (as is sometimes done) from a point as late as 1890, there are grounds for considerable disagreement as to how many cycles there were in a given period of time, or how far apart they were typically.[91] But over the long range of history, it appears that though such variations from war, discovery, or political action do occur occasionally in the more precise short-term chronology of particular parts as the total economic structure moves through the growth cycle pattern, the system—not only in its economic aspects but in its demographic and opportunity ramifications as well—does return with rather surprising dependability to the dates of turning points which would be projected very simple-mindedly

90. Easterlin, "Baby Boom."
91. Easterlin, "Economic-Demographic Interactions," has underscored this problem of typical cyclical interval.

from the "pure" 22½-year interval beginning from benchmarks in the first two or three decades of colonial settlement.

v. The Demographic Mechanisms of Opportunity Cycles

SURPRISINGLY regular and predictable fluctuations in general population growth, immigration, new settlement, institutional expansion, and various aspects of economic development can all be found to follow historical patterns of similar intervals over the course of American society since its earliest days. To think of these parallel movements in social and economic history as true and interacting products of a *cyclical* system of societal growth, however, it is necessary to demonstrate that the number of openings for leadership needed to cope with spurts of population did affect equality of opportunity or the social origins of elites; that the supply of new population from indigenous sources as well as from immigration responded to changes in the socio-economic environment; and that there were ways in which such a complex, interdependent system of processes could be re-started over and over again through three centuries and could adhere resiliently to the typical timing of 22½ years without being dissipated or upset by the practically limitless sources of variation that could bring an intricate cycle of this sort to an end.

A thorough pursuit of these particular pieces of critical evidence in so far as they are now in hand cannot be presented here. The relevant material is complex (it includes ties to contemporary data and non-American experience), and the appetite of most students of history for quantitative data is as yet a very limited one. A more complete interpretation is therefore published separately elsewhere. Yet to conclude the present discussion it is perhaps appropriate to provide some evidence of the effect which the numbers of openings available for successive birth cohorts seems to have had on the social origins of American leadership, on the ways in which native births as well as immigration fluctuated in step with conditions of opportunity and fed back new oscillations of population growth to keep the system advancing upon its consistently curvilinear track, and on the means by which the formation, development, and disruption of families parallel to socio-economic change over and over again created those fluctuations in the numbers of births at strikingly regular intervals.

PROBABLE NUMBERS OF OPENINGS IN AMERICAN LEADERSHIP
SINCE 1775 IN RELATION TO THE OBSERVED PATTERNS
OF NATIONAL GROWTH

In analyzing the historical relationship of the changing social origins of American leaders to various other manifestations of the development cycle, it is possible by examining comparative timing to secure at least some preliminary insights into the nature of the causal chains that have typically linked opportunity to rates of societal growth. The ultimate foundation for this kind of explanation must then come from following the workings of key parts of the recurring system through the lives of samples of particular individuals at many different vantage points in the society. Such a necessarily detailed pursuit of the mechanics of opportunity is presented elsewhere separately for early Harvard and Yale alumni and for those leaders included in the *D.A.B.* Working with only a more rudimentary level of information from an overview of the latter, larger sample and its major sub-groups, however, it is feasible here to begin, at least, to speak of the ways in which fluctuations in the social origins of leadership, in the number of openings for leaders, in migration, and in urbanization have fitted together in time with society-wide variations of the typical cyclical interval observed from other independent sources.

In the first place, of the men included in the *D.A.B.* for their notability in various principal types of main careers, certain birth cohorts were larger than others around them. Allowing for the basic curve of numbers in the sample by date of birth, which rises as far as the groups starting life about a quarter of the way through the nineteenth century and then falls off quite rapidly, in most major careers more men than might be expected from this underlying chronological sample shape were born around the early 1720's, the mid-1740's, near 1767, in the early 1790's, and in the periods 1809–15, 1833–39, and 1857–60.[1] Table 11 first of all shows the distribution by date of birth of all *D.A.B.* men with main careers in business (including communications and transportation as well as commerce, finance, and manufacturing or mining), and also the frequency in successive birth cohorts of three years each of those men of business who probably could with reasonable certainty be called "upper class"—omitting for the most part lesser newspaper editors, inventors of note but not distinction, other innovators like introducers of processes who did not become industrialists, finders of mineral resources whose careers did not keep pace with their discoveries, trail-blazing traders or sea captains who never became major merchants, and some miscellaneous individuals like well-known theater managers. There were, as the table depicts, bulges or peaks in the numbers of businessmen born around the period 1740–49, 1767, 1785, and 1794, 1809–12, 1836, and 1857. The extra peak among those born around 1821, or aged forty or so during the Civil War, was composed primarily of men who were figures of lesser ultimate stature in the social structure, not men of the greatest eminence. There is quite a similar pattern to the numbers of public officials in the *D.A.B.* including lawyers and judges, but not the military, when these are arrayed by date of birth as in the third column of Table 11. The particular variation from the basic cyclical pattern in this second major career category took the form of a rather early peak in the numbers born in the late 1750's, aged about twenty during the Revolution and in their forties during the Jeffersonian era (the crest should have come in the birth cohorts about six years later). There was also something of an extra-large sample born around 1731, the age bracket of John Adams, John Hancock, and George Washington—men in their forties during the Revolution. Among the public figures, though less evident than among the more ordinary businessmen, an extra peak in numbers shows up in the birth cohorts of the early 1820's. The probable source of this additional hump is indicated by the fourth column of the table, which arrays the military leaders in the *D.A.B.* by date of birth. In the early 1820's were born most of the leaders of the Civil War

1. Occasional variations in particular career categories within the total sample are described and explained below and in other discussions of these materials.

TABLE 11

Number of *D.A.B.* Men in Principal Career Groups Who Were Born in Certain Years

Three-Year Birth Cohorts Centered on:	All Business	Higher Business	Public Office (incl. Law)	Military	Ministry Medicine Education	Arts & Letters
1716	9	*	6	*	11	*
1719	5		8		11	
1722	8		20		18 P	
1725	9		24 P		12	
1728	11		19		14	
1731	11	7	38 X		21	
1734	16	7	34		20	
1737	19	10	34		17	
1740	19	13 P	36		18	
1743	14	5	46 P		17	
1746	15	5	31		30 P	
1749	22 P	10	44		25	
1752	14	8	48		30	
1755	15	5	52		18	
1758	15	7	56 X		23	
1761	22	7	45		25	
1764	24 ⎫	9	44		27	
1767	23 ⎬	10 P	36		22	
1770	26 ⎭	8	48		47 P	
1773	20	5	46		34	
1776	17	4	44		37	
1779	22	6	55		43	
1782	27	14	62 X ?	14	38	11
1785	48	25	63	15	45	16
1788	36	17	59	12	56	19
1791	49 ⎱	24	59	11	64	25 P
1794	51 ⎰ P	27 P	70 P	14	76 P ?	26
1797	46	23	68	14	76	34
1800	67	38	75	18	88	32
1803	82	41	84	14	94	28
1806	64	36	88	27	94	49
1809	102 ⎱ P	52	111	29	116	52
1812	100 ⎰	69 P	114	40 P ?	128 P	47
1815	75	46	123 P	38	97	59 P

Three-Year Birth Cohorts Centered on:	All Business	Higher Business	Public Office (incl. Law)	Military	Ministry Medicine Education	Arts & Letters
1818	105	69	108	54	125	51
1821	115 X	66	113	60	124	44
				Civil War leaders		
1824	90	64	118 X	69 X	135 X	66 X
1827	95	57	105	47	117	48
1830	98	64	105	39	132	46
1833	102	63	118 P	31	132	41
1836	121 P	77 ⎫ P	112	35 P ?	158	63 P
1839	114	77 ⎭	89	25	168 P	59
1842	99	67	80	21	158	49
1845	103	74	74	23	130	56
1848	92	68	70	12	154	61
1851	83	55	70	11	159 ?	56
1854	85	56	60	12	141	58
1857	104 P	75 P	70	13	150 P ?	77 P
1860	85	57	74 P	16 P	137	56
1863	62	46	48	14	100	42
1866	68	45	36	10	122	43
1869	53	39	37	6	81	40
1872	40	30	34	2	65	37
1875	19	16	22	4	60	24
1878	18	11	9	3	28	25

* Data exist throughout the time range, but numbers in these categories very small.

_____ Approximation of regular 22½-year peaks by 3-year groupings.

P Peak in the number in this career category, or shoulder where the number is rising or falling rapidly, which tends to follow that pattern.

X Extra peak at other times (see text for discussion).

era. But even in the military, where this Civil War effect was the dominant feature of the historical pattern of numbers selected for the *D.A.B.*, there are apparent "shoulders" on either side of the Civil War summit where additional men born around 1812 and 1836 rose to eminence in the Army and the Navy. These subsidiary bulges and the more modern hump of military leadership born around 1860, furthermore, are more obvious among the higher ranking figures than for all leaders of the armed services covered in the *D.A.B.*

Similarly, Table 11 displays humps or shoulders in the number of ministers, doctors, and educators born near 1722, 1746, 1770, 1794 (?), 1812, 1839, and 1857 (the last point before a sharp, permanent decline). Fairly consistent peaks in each of the three careers separately appear in the birth cohorts around these dates. The same is true in the law, if that is separated from public service—in spite of the preponderance of judges in the same sample—and grouped with the other "learned professions." Those who had their principal careers in what might be called arts and letters, too, came in largest numbers from the birth cohorts near 1815, 1836, and 1857—though an extra bulge, especially apparent for those in the visual and performing arts, came among the 1824 birth cohort, those in their forties during the Civil War.

Generally speaking, then, men from all major groups of careers who have sketches in the *D.A.B.* tended to be born more numerously in certain years than in others, over and above the basic chronological curve of the sample. Fluctuations at intervals of shortly over twenty years on the average were evident not just in the proportion of leadership groups who came from upper class homes (or, conversely, came from quite ordinary homes) as described above in Section II. They also characterized the *number* of men in relevant birth cohorts deemed important enough to be included in the *D.A.B.*[2] Both the social base of various forms of American leadership and the number of places in which men could attract attention varied at the same interval of timing which reflected the pulsating growth pattern of our society. And this was not all. From pre-Revolutionary days on through the nineteenth century the proportion of given groups of leaders who had been raised in different

2. The timing of these fluctuations from career group to career group was not the same, however, by date of birth.

kinds of communities and different regions of the country swung back and forth in a similar tempo. So did the proportions of those leaders who followed their careers as adults in various types of localities and parts of America. Both the community origins and the eventual career locations of those covered in the *D.A.B.*, that is, reflect the familiar timing of the development cycle. This does not mean, however, that for every occupational group the relative phasing of cyclical motions in openness of recruitment or equality of opportunity, in numbers of openings, in place of origin, and in place of career always was the same, that fluctuations in these variables moved in the same comparative temporal pattern for all key career categories. That was not the case. Some of the detail will have to be spelled out elsewhere, but Tables 12 through 15 show the outlines of these chronological relationships separately for men in four large sub-groupings of the *D.A.B.* sample: those whose main careers were in public office, all forms of business, the professions, and arts and letters.

From the chronological patterns in these tables at least several other tentative steps can be taken towards explaining the causes of sometimes more open than usual recruitment of leadership. Useful insights to this end can be gleaned from the timing of broad societal changes that have been outlined relative to more specialized historical changes in the composition or behavior of eminent men in different types of careers who were covered in the *D.A.B.*

To begin, the birth cohorts of *D.A.B.* men with principal careers in public office who came most frequently from ordinary origins were—as related in Table 12—about ten years old at one trough of the typical economic cycle and about twenty-five when the long climb up came to an end. The next time around in the swings of the economic environment, so to speak, they were approximately thirty-two at the bottom and forty-eight at the crest. Most lived long enough to enjoy a third boom from when they were about fifty-five until the time at which they reached seventy.[3] The table also demonstrates how, generally

3. It is the "pure" timing of economic peaks and troughs which are taken from Tables 7 and 8 for Table 12. For the actual dates of highs and lows in certain eras relative to the social and other origins of particular leadership groups see those two earlier tables.

TABLE 12

Some Social and Geographical Characteristics of the Careers of *D.A.B.* Men in Public Service* in Relation to Certain Aspects of the Growth Cycle

Pure 22½-Year Growth Cycle of Production & Prices:†		D.A.B. Birth Cohorts Centered on These Years:							Most Careers Peak in Washington
		Government:*		Government and Military:*					
Trough	Peak	Most Open Social Origins	Largest Numbers	Highest Percent Non-City Origin	National Crest in Internal Migration‡	Highest Percent Foreign Born	National Crest of Immigration‡	Highest Percent from Northeast§	
1755	1771	1746	1743	1740	1751	1746	1753	1737	
1778	1793	1770	1758	1767	1773	1767	1773	1764	
1800	1816	1788	1782–85	1785	1796	1797	1798	1785	1803
1823	1838	1812	1809–15	1815	1818	1815 ?	1818	1815	1830
1845	1861	1836	1833	1833	1835–36	1833 ?	1837 1843	1839	1854
1868	1883	1857	1860	1854 1866	1854–55	1860 ?	1854	1857	
1890	1906								1875

* Differences of category stem from initial grouping of particular analyses in *D.A.B.* study. Further refinement continues.
† From Tables 7 and 8 above.
‡ From Table 4 above.
§ "Northeast" includes New England, New York, Pennsylvania, Delaware, and New Jersey.

speaking, the birth cohorts which contained the largest numbers of notable public officials included in the *D.A.B.* were the same ones in which the highest proportion of such leaders came from homes in non-urban communities. Typically the greatest sample numbers and the maximum proportion not urban in origin arrived in about the same birth groups, followed by the greatest variety of social background among cohorts approximately three years later. While large numbers of political leaders were included in the *D.A.B.* from the birth cohorts near 1758, presumably as a consequence of the openings provided to them as young men by the Revolution and as middle-aged figures by the organization of the new nation, the birth group with most non-urban origins (1767) was still consistently just three years ahead of the birth cohort which came from the plainest social background (1770).

To underscore further the probable connection of the most rapid rates of growth in the society with the most democratic age groups of politi-cal leadership, a comparison of the life cycle of the birth cohorts who most frequently came from ordinary homes with the peak dates of in-ternal migration in the country, as transposed from Table 4 above, indi-cates that the groups most ordinary in origin were about five years old as the crest of a wave of internal (e.g., westward) movement swept over the American continent. They were of age to have been children in young families which sought to capitalize upon the surge to new areas of settlement. They would also have been of age to be the first crop of children raised in the historical bulge of new communities being popu-lated by that temporarily intensive migration. In the next such surge of internal movement in American society as a whole, on the other hand, the most openly recruited birth cohorts were, on the average, in their late twenties—about the usual age to be deciding upon a place in which to marry, settle down, and have families of their own.

The temptation here might well be to fall back on the full-blown Turner interpretation and to say that the frontier raised the most demo-cratic leadership. A look at the record, in Table 12, of which birth classes of public figures most frequently were raised in the northeastern states (New England, New York, Pennsylvania, New Jersey, and Delaware), however, points to the likelihood that the key move for more open op-portunity in this career category—if such transplantation was not just coincidental to, but a cause of, the social mobility of the age group—occurred with the *second* crest of national internal migration during the life cycle of the cohorts who came most frequently from fairly ordinary homes. This latter peak in nationwide relocation was the one which took place during the future leaders' late twenties. In other words, they probably did not move to new areas as immature, captive members of families but as individuals who in their early manhood followed the now hackneyed advice of Horace Greeley. Characteristically, moreover, the birth cohorts who were most often foreign-born were, in chronology, about the same as the groups which were largest in number, most openly recruited socially, most often products of rural areas, and most often raised in the Northeast.[4] Placing the location of adult men at the peaks of their careers, on the other hand, is difficult in these preliminary outlines because of the special role of Washington residence in politics and the military. Yet it is clear that among the most numerous, most socially open, most rurally rooted, most foreign-born birth cohorts also the highest proportion of public figures reached the culmination of their careers not in the Congress or the executive branches of the federal government, or in the central military departments, but in the state and territorial capitals and city halls of the nation.[5]

In summary, the opening of new settlements and the development of new concentrations of population as the result of internal migration and immigration contributed substantially towards shaping those birth cohorts of public officers who were most openly recruited in social terms. But the preliminary indication is that it was not those raised in the purportedly 'democratic' settlements of the Turnerian frontier who typified the opening social origins of political leadership in these age groups so much as it was those who made the move as young adults from farm areas of the older parts of the Northeast, or who had been born abroad and came in their young manhood to new rural areas or to growing cities. As throughout similar discussion in the following pages, these outlines can so far be only suggestive. Confirmation of such an ex-

---

4. Up to the eve of the Civil War the greatest evidence of foreign origins in political leadership was among those born about seven years on the average before the national flow of immigration came to a crest and began to recede.

5. Ambassadors are also involved in the distortion by a "capital city" classification.

planation of the sources of more open recruitment of leadership awaits a detailed pursuit of all the key variables cited here through the lives of specific individuals, not just the group of public officials as a whole in any given birth cohort. In the interim, nevertheless, certain interpretations of the source of the more socially democratic leadership which appeared in some periods rather than in others are strengthened, while alternative explanations are made less likely.

Among the business leadership included in the *D.A.B.*, in marked contrast to the closely parallel chronological patterns of the same two variables in the group of public officers, there was almost an *inverse* timing between recurrent cohorts with larger than usual numbers of businessmen and age groups with the highest proportion of businessmen who came from quite ordinary kinds of homes. This comparative chronology is outlined in Table 13 along with other relevant types of turning points, both for the development of American society as a whole and for the historical derivation of business leaders in particular. The numbers of businessmen were largest, however, in very much the same age groups as among public officers. That fact emerges from a comparison of Table 13 with Table 12. What this means in terms of the typical age of businessmen during the long swings of production and prices (the most pervasive and contemporaneously apparent aspects of the growth cycle in the economy historically) is that the birth cohorts producing the largest numbers of *D.A.B.* businessmen were about age twelve to twenty-seven, on the average, from the time the recovery began following a trough in business conditions to the point where the next boom developed to a head. That is, they received their education and entered upon their careers in improving years, years of expansion in the society and health in the economy. Typically they were about thirty-four at the bottom of the next recession, and spent their years from then until the age of fifty while the economy was, in general, on the upswing again.

In contrast, the smallest but *most openly recruited* birth cohorts of businessmen were about fifteen years old when the downturn into depression began (often starting with a very visible financial crash as, for example, in 1907 and 1929). They "learned the trade" when conditions

TABLE 13

Some Social and Geographical Characteristics of the Careers of *D.A.B.* Men in Business in Relation to the Growth Cycle

Pure 22½-Year Growth Cycle of Production & Prices*		*D.A.B.* Birth Cohorts Centered on These Years:							
Trough	Peak	Most Open Social Origins	Largest Numbers	Highest Percent from Northeast†	Highest Percent from Cities	Lowest Percent Rural Origin‡	Highest Percent Foreign Born	Most Careers Peak Outside Northeast†	Most Careers Peak in Major Cities
1755	1771		1746	1743			1740–46	1740	1755
1778	1793	1779	1764	1767 1779			1755–64	1761–64	1779
1800	1816	1800–03	1785	1794	1776–85	1788	1782	1776 1788	1803
1823	1838	1827–30	1809–12	–	1806	1809	1809	1806	1821
1845	1861	1845	1836	1833	1836	1836	1830	1830	1845–57
1868	1883	1866	1857	1860	1860	1860	1851	1857	1863–66
1890	1906		–	1881	1878ff.	1878	1875	1881	

* From Tables 7 and 8 above.

† "Northeast" includes New England, New York, Pennsylvania, Delaware, and New Jersey.

‡ Raised on farms and in villages or small towns of rural areas.

were hard and entry into business was not relatively attractive. But they were in their vital and flexible twenty-two- to thirty-seven-year-old segment of the life cycle, not overly encumbered by family or by long habits of business conduct, expectations, and attitudes, during the sustained climb out of the economic trough to the next crest. Then they were characteristically from forty-four to fifty-nine, in the prime years for moving into executive control or for expanding personal ownership, during the next upsurge of the economy following another "weed-out" period from age thirty-seven to forty-four while a new depression took its toll. Both their entry onto the business career ladder (at the ages fifteen to twenty-two) and what is probably a particularly sensitive age bracket for determining ultimate advancement in business (age thirty-seven through forty-four) were passed in "hard times."[6] The future D.A.B. businessmen who had the skills and determination (and the luck) to stay afloat through these crises at critical stages of their careers turned out to be more broadly recruited, though smaller, groups than intervening birth cohorts. In short, apparently there has been nothing like a good depression from time to time to keep entry to the higher ranks of American business leadership open, to make way for new men by pruning out inheritors, and to further the symbolic image of equality of opportunity in a society which is not only the leading industrial nation of the world but purports to be the leading democracy.

The birth cohorts with the largest numbers of D.A.B. businessmen in them, meanwhile, typically parallelled very closely in timing those whose business leadership came most frequently from the Northeast and from cities, and least of all from the more rural settlements of the country. Thus, the most socially open birth cohorts of D.A.B. businessmen, as in the political leadership, had rural origins—the difference being that these were not the birth cohorts which apparently enjoyed the most numerous openings to become notable businessmen. Also in contrast to the public office side of leadership, the most broadly recruited groups in business were not the most but the least often from the northeastern states in the early part of their lives. Yet it was these same cohorts of

6. The possibility of a different relevance of those age thresholds for building one's own business as opposed to advancing in a more bureaucratized organization is currently being tested.

most varied social origin and most rural origin and least northeastern origin who as a result of their careers ended by concentrating most of all in the biggest cities and the northeastern region of the country. This is to say that, recurrently, groups of future businessmen who were in their early twenties at the depths of a recession that had begun several years before were those among whom most movement out of relatively rural areas in the South and West to business careers in the big cities of the Northeast was apparent. The evidence is not yet direct, to prove without question that it was the same individuals within the birth cohorts who did all these things; but this was the net character of the age groups under examination. In placing these findings, finally, it is important to note that a business community in the largest, oldest centers of trade, fed by rural boys migrating to seek their fortunes, is no novelty of nineteenth-century America. W. K. Jordan, for one, has underscored the crucial parts which men of similar backgrounds played in the merchant community of London from 1480 through 1660.[7]

Turning to the professions, as in Table 14, it appears that among successive birth cohorts of *D.A.B.* men in these careers it was those who were about seventeen at the bottom of an economic trough, and about thirty-two at the peak following several years of subsequent recovery, who had the most widely varied social origins. Remembering the pattern of spreading professional opportunities as new communities were founded,[8] it is useful to note that these most openly recruited groups were on the average in their early thirties—a few years after the usual age to have a church of one's own, a medical practice or law practice, or an academic post with a future—when the rate of new settlement and internal migration came to a crest. In other words, they had their college and/or professional education during the first years of the long period of societal growth and improving economic environment, and also had the chance to set themselves up in the profession of their choice while the rate of expansion in opportunity was still coming to a peak. Typically these cohorts of professionals who came most frequently from the more ordinary families of the society, furthermore,

7. W. K. Jordan, *The Charities of London, 1480–1660* (London, 1960).
8. For example, the timing of the establishment of new churches, Figure No. 8, above.

TABLE 14

Some Social and Geographical Characteristics of the Careers of *D.A.B.* Men in the Professions* in Relation to the Growth Cycle

Pure 22½-Year Growth Cycle of Production & Prices†		D.A.B. Birth Cohorts Centered on These Years:						
Trough	Peak	Most Open Social Origins*	Largest Numbers	Highest Percent from Northeast‡	Lowest Percent from Cities	Highest Percent Rural Origin§	Most Careers Peak Within Northeast	Most Careers Peak in Major Cities
1733	1748	1737–43	1722	1743		1752	1740–46	
1755	1771	1761	1746	—	1776	1773	1755–61	1758–66
1778	1793	1779–85	1770	1788–94	1785	1785	1782	1773–82
1800	1816	1800	1794 ?	1815	1803	1800	1797	1800–15
1823	1838	1830	1812	1839	1830	1827–36	1839	1821–30
1845	1861	1854	1839	1869	1857	1860	1854 ?	1848–63
1868	1883	1872–78	1857–66		1878		1878 ?	
1890	1906							

* Includes lawyers and judges as well as physicians, ministers, educators.
† From Tables 7 and 8 above.
‡ "Northeast" includes New England, New York, Pennsylvania, Delaware, and New Jersey.
§ Raised on farms and in villages or small towns of rural areas.

most often had rural origins and least often had grown up in the north-eastern region of the country, though it was they who most of all *went* to the Northeast and to the biggest cities as the result of their careers. Among the professionals, as among the businessmen (whose birth co-horts with most numbers in the *D.A.B.* similarly tended to be diametri-cally opposite in cyclical phase to those groups most often coming from rather plain origins), the most rural groups were from outside the Northeast. In contrast, the rural, socially most open age groups of pub-lic officers came from *within* the Northeast. Subsequently the more plainly recruited professionals, once again like the same kind of business birth cohorts but unlike the public officials, clustered most of all in the Northeast and the bigger centers for their careers.[9]

In contrast, the most *numerous* though *least openly recruited* birth co-horts of professional leaders were typically only about eight years old in the depths of recession. They were hit during their training, however, by the next downslide of the economy which began when they were about twenty-three and reached bottom when they were, on the aver-age, about thirty. Just when they should have been getting ready to set up in their profession it was becoming difficult to sustain the usual semi-dependent training status, or "professional apprenticeship," of the early career years because of the poor conditions. Subsequently the improve-ment of the economy and the growth of institutions and communities which parallelled the fifteen-year recovery while the birth cohorts un-der discussion were typically age thirty-nine to fifty-four, however, created many openings for eminent doctors, bishops and other notable divines, and also distinguished educators to bring up the new baby booms which resulted from recurrent periods of brighter prospects in the history of the society. But those of more ordinary family resources, it seems, had to some extent already been diverted out of the main-stream of professional advancement by the previous hard times which had caught them located precariously in training and on the bottom rungs of the career ladder. The most numerous cohorts of leading pro-fessionals in American history as indicated by the *D.A.B.* sample, more-

---

9. Like Jordan's charitable bishops who came from country towns to the major sees and remembered the people of their early homes with schools, scholarships, hospitals, and poorhouses.

over, came most frequently from the Northeast and from cities, though they did not—relative to other age groups—noticeably concentrate as the result of their careers into the big centers and the Northeast. Perhaps here is an indicator that in the professions, as already noted in the business and public life,[10] the really top leadership was more likely to be drawn from plainer backgrounds than the somewhat distinguished but not so exceptional men selected for the *D.A.B.*[11]

In the career group included for distinction in arts and letters—Table 15 —the temporal relationships of changes in the key variables of numbers in the sample, broader social origins, rural background, and homes in the Northeast followed the pattern of figures in public life (Table 12) rather than the usual chronology for business and the professions (Tables 13 and 14).[12] The only slight difference from the public service pattern was that the birth cohorts with the highest proportions from the Northeast and the highest rural origins tended to precede slightly those with the biggest numbers and most varied social backgrounds. Also, as in the tendency for the birth cohorts of public figures with the most simple origins to be concentrated least of all in Washington at the height of their careers, the birth groups of writers and artists from the plainest homes were to be found least frequently in the Northeast as a result of their careers and least in the largest cities and regional centers. The career patterns of both public officers and artists or writers contrasted with those of businessmen and professionals in this respect.

These preliminary outlines relating, as group variables, the number of openings, the social origins, and the geographical and community mobility for men of key career categories in the *D.A.B.* suggest the value of systematic investigation of such factors in the lives of individuals. This must be done in both historical and contemporaneous research with particular sensitivity to the timing of changes of the variables and their

10. See above, Section II.

11. Critics of the *D.A.B.* for over-representation of New England and the East—often attributing undemocratic, anti-Turnerian failings to the editors, it would seem—may be on the wrong track.

12. Though in the business group the changes occurred in birth cohorts about five years later.

TABLE 15

Some Social and Geographical Characteristics of the Careers of *D.A.B.* Men in Arts and Letters in Relation to the Growth Cycle

Pure 22½-Year Growth Cycle of Production & Prices*		*D.A.B.* Birth Cohorts Centered on These Years:							
Trough	*Peak*	*Most Open Social Origins*	*Largest Numbers*	*Lowest Percent from Cities*	*Highest Percent Rural Origin†*	*Highest Percent from Northeast‡*	*Highest Percent Foreign Born*	*Least Careers Peak in Northeast*	*Least Careers Peak in Major Cities*
1773	1748				1737				
1755	1771			1761	1761	1761-64			
1778	1793	1788		1785-88	1788	1788		1788	1788
1800	1816	1810	1815	1803	1800-03	1800-03	1806	1809-15	1803-15
1823	1838	1836	1836	1833	1833	1827 1833	1827	1839	1833-39
1845	1861	1857	1857	1857	1857	1857	1845	1854	1854
1868	1883	1881			1878	1875	1866	1872	1872
1890	1906								

* From Tables 7 and 8.

† Raised on farms and in villages or small towns of rural areas.

‡ "Northeast" includes New England, New York, Pennsylvania, Delaware, and New Jersey.

relationships to each other in rather specific birth cohorts—better still in some instances, opportunity cohorts who passed (or did not pass) a given career threshold in a given year. This kind of approach is as essential for the study of the life chances of the common man as it is in the analysis of the origins of leadership. Clearly the interdependencies of social and geographical mobility (internal or international), community development, the growth of new institutions, and the turnover of leadership in old, established organizations or professions are not the same for all men in all careers. Important variations from one occupational type to another have been noted, and will be spelled out further elsewhere as the result of research that is still in progress. Yet already it is evident that for one or two, sometimes even three, centuries the temporal relationships of population growth, internal migration, immigration, community formation, institutional expansion, economic development and retrenchment, the number of particular types of leadership openings, and the breadth of the social base from which they were filled all display surprisingly consistent chronological patterns of a comparable cyclical nature in American history. Economists have concerned themselves for many years—intensively in the past decade—with the relationship of economic variables to population, and increasingly also to migration and regional change. It turns out that not just the bread and butter in our society since 1870 (where the economic argument for the most part begins) but the essence of American social structure—linking personal opportunity, community growth, institutional development, and societal change—since its very inception has always reflected, and re-created, cyclical fluctuations in the rate of expansion of our population.

FLUCTUATING NUMBERS OF BIRTHS KEEP RE-CREATING CYCLES OF SOCIETAL EXPANSION

It is possible to see, through long periods of American history, some fundamental alterations in the demographic processes of the family which have both reflected and helped to re-create over and over again this surprisingly regular and predictable pattern of growth and change in the social system. On the one hand, the kinds of fluctuation in several aspects of societal growth and in opportunity that have been described apparently stimulated variations in family patterns of reproduction. On the other hand, such variations in fertility kept feeding back cyclically new supplies of manpower and womanpower to sustain the oscillating nature of institutional expansion, proliferation in leadership roles, movement of the population, and long-term "booms and busts" in the economy.

Already it has been seen that immigration did much to shape the rate at which the American population, particularly the young adult population, grew. Reports of good opportunities in America pulled in larger numbers of new citizens than usual during certain years, and at other times—as in 1819 when reports of unemployment went back home, or as in the 1830's and 1850's after nativist riots in American cities—transoceanic migration was discouraged or even reversed. Yet immigration was not always as significant in proportion to the total population as it was in the 1850's, the 1880's, or around 1910, perhaps for a while near the middle of the eighteenth century, or in the 1630's when most people came from abroad and only very young children were "native born."

A second chief source of new population in fairly closely focussed age groups, however, the number of children born, also began to fluctuate very early in our history according to the typical 22½-year pattern found in so many aspects of American development. Figure No. 9 plots the totals of births recorded every two years in four towns of eastern Massachusetts—Dorchester, Dedham, Watertown, and Concord—during the colonial period. Dedham seems to have been a backwater largely untouched by the pulsating pattern of development; but births in the other three communities, both independently and jointly, adhered to the now familiar interval of recurrent change. Upward surges in the number of recorded births culminated around 1641 (Watertown and Dorchester were founded in 1630, Concord—like Dedham—about five years later), then at quite regular intervals near 1657, 1680, 1702, and 1725, with some shortening of both phase and amplitude for the cycle in the 1741–49 period, then around 1760 or 1769, and in double peaks at 1784 and 1796 on both sides of what should have been a crest in 1792 if the pure or theoretical 22½-year pattern were to be sustained. The "extra" peak of 1760–62, of course, marked the return of New England troops from the French and Indian War, while that of the early 1780's came just after the end of the Revolutionary mobilization. Meanwhile *low* numbers of births were recorded in the years beginning with 1644 and then around 1663–65, 1686, and 1713, with later troughs at 1737 and 1751–54, then in the period 1773–80 and at 1801, for the most part all very close to where 22½-year projections from 1644 would call for them.

As with the estimates of total colonial population, it is again possible to see the relevance of this kind of fluctuating pattern in the number of births further on into more modern American history. Birth data are hard to come by in the early nineteenth century, but the works of Spengler and Gutman[13] show a trough in Massachusetts births in the late 1840's and a crest on the eve of the Civil War to match predictions of 1846 and 1860, respectively, which would be made by extrapolating the chronology of Figure No. 9. Beginning in the mid-nineteenth century, however, the timing of peaks in the gross number of recorded births changed phase appreciably in Massachusetts—and in the nation as a whole, as Coale and Zelnick have recently demonstrated.[14] Yet the birth pattern kept the 22½-year interval in the new timing with highs at 1874, 1896, and 1918. Then after the loss of one whole cycle in the Great Depression, the new baby boom of recent memory gained most of its momentum by 1947, followed by more slowly continuing growth to 1957. The old pre-Civil War timing would call for a crest right in the middle of this period at 1952. The subsequent decline of births in the last several years has continued to go down past the theoretical terminal date of about 1959, extrapolating from the colonial and early nineteenth-century chronology; but the suddenly much more numerous girl babies of the late 1940's are now beginning to reach the most usual age for motherhood; and the gross number of births will start rising rapidly very soon if it has not already begun to do so, making the theoretical next peak or high step in total births at 1972 or 1973 not at all improbable in the reality of the near future.[15]

13. Joseph J. Spengler, *The Fecundity of Native and Foreign-Born Women* (Brookings Institution, Pamphlet Series, vol. II, no. 1, Washington, 1930); Robert Gutman, "The Birth Statistics of Massachusetts during the Nineteenth Century," *Population Studies*, 10 (1956), 69–94.

14. Coale and Zelnick, *New Estimates of Fertility*, pp. 21–23.

15. The number of potential mothers aged twenty-six will have increased 50 percent in seven years from 1966 to 1973.

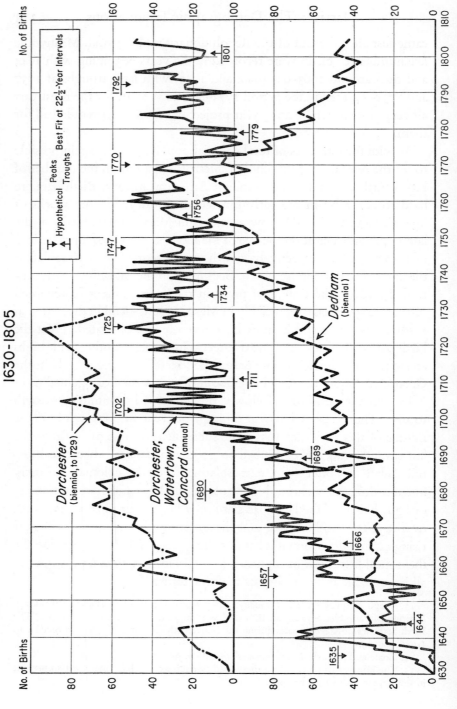

Figure No. 9. Number of Births in the Vital Records of Four Towns of Eastern Massachusetts 1630-1805

Some observable changes in typical family size, or in mean completed fertility per married woman or man confirm that the number of births did go up and down historically in quite different elements of the American population over substantial periods of time, and provide the first step of insight into *how* that cyclical pattern of fertility kept recurring. Figure No. 10 presents the average number of births known per ever-married Harvard or Yale alumnus, according to the year in which the man reached thirty-four—the mean interval from father to child in this era. The average college man whose average child was born about 1688, in other words, had 7.4 recorded births in his family in contrast to close to 5.0 births for the alumnus old enough to have had the mean of his family fall in the years 1699–1710. Confidence limits of about 92 percent for the three-year means are indicated on the figure. The data are presented in Table 16.

The most significantly large families were born to college men who typically had their average-aged child about 1667, 1688, 1712, 1727, and 1751 or 1754, while the smallest families were those whose average-aged child was born around 1662–65, 1676, 1700–09, 1715–21, and 1739. The best fit of a regular 22½-year pattern of large and small families to the data of Figure No. 10—as noted across the top and the bottom—would call for peaks around 1667, 1689, 1712, and 1757, and troughs about nine years later. The actual trough of 1739 is close to the theoretical low which such a pattern would call for at 1743, but the peaks of 1751–54 and especially 1727 are noticeably early in terms of a regular chronology projected forward from the seventeenth-century base.

Taking this hypothetical timing and looking backwards, on the other hand, historically *previous* periods of large families would be expected among those whose average child was born about 1644 and, before that, about 1622. In point of fact, as the far left of the figure indicates, the group of seventeenth-century merchants discussed by Bernard Bailyn[16] indeed had the largest number of births per man which can be identified for those aged thirty-seven almost exactly in these years, and the least children just about at the expected low points of 1631 and 1653. Merchants of thirty-seven are compared with college men of age thirty-four, not an unreasonable allowance for delay in family formation as the

16. Bailyn, *New England Merchants.*

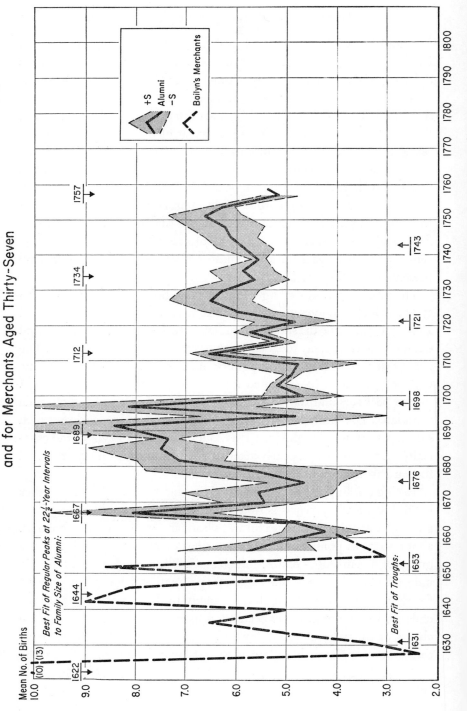

Figure No. 10. Mean Number of Recorded Births for College Alumni Aged Thirty-Four in Certain Years, and for Merchants Aged Thirty-Seven

TABLE 16

Mean Number of Recorded Births per Harvard or Yale Alumnus*

Alumni Age 34	No.	Mean No. Births	s†		Alumni Age 34	No.	Mean No. Births	s†
1656–57	5	5.80	1.39	.	1708–10	40	4.80	1.23
1658–60	5	5.20	.57	.	1711–13	37	6.54	.38
1661–63	5	4.20	.90	.	1714–16	47	5.03	.18
1664–66	11	4.83	.14	.	1717–19	34	5.74	.30
1667–68‡	12	8.08	1.62	.	1720–22	45	4.83	.83
1669–71	20	5.45	.84	.	1723–25	45	6.00	.71
1672–74	27	5.56	1.51	.	1726–28	40	6.53	.82
1675–77	30	4.67	.72	.	1729–31	51	6.32	.78
1678–80	15	5.60	2.20	.	1732–34	82	5.63	.67
1681–83	16	7.13	.86	.	1735–37	115	5.90	.64
1684–86	12	7.50	1.45	.	1738–40	134	5.55	.15
1687–89	11	7.37	.22	.	1741–43	113	5.84	.56
1690–92	9	8.44	3.14	.	1744–46	126	6.12	.52
1693–95	13	4.85	1.86	.	1747–49	115	6.22	.75
1696–98	11	8.18	2.54	.	1750–52	119	6.65	.73
1699–01	28	4.68	.83	.	1753–55	102	6.27	.22
1702–04	29	5.21	.10	.	1756–58	111	5.15	.37
1705–07	29	4.93	.11	.	1759	37	5.38	N.A.

* Omitting those who died young, were known bachelors, or left New England for their careers. Age thirty-four estimated from date of A.B. plus fourteen years.

† s = 1.732 times the standard error of the three-year means.

‡ There were two classes graduating in 1653, a three-year class and a four-year class.

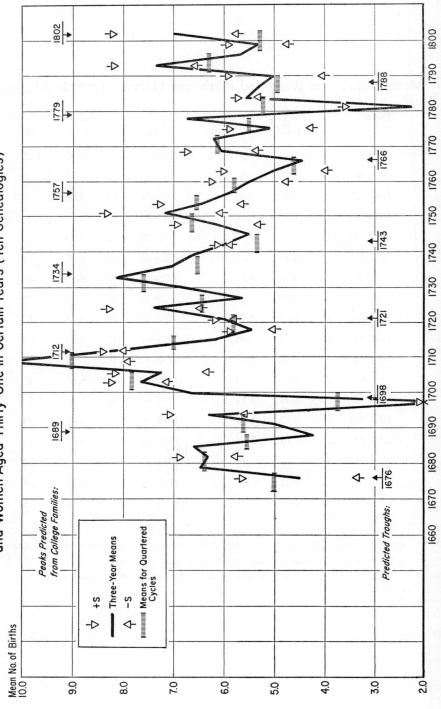

Figure No. II. Mean Number of Recorded Births for Watertown Men Aged Thirty-Four and Women Aged Thirty-One in Certain Years (Ten Genealogies)

TABLE 17

Mean Number of Recorded Births for a Sample
of Watertown Men and Women*

Mean Birth† Years of Children	No.	Mean No. Births	s‡	.	Mean Birth† Years of Children	No.	Mean No. Births	s‡
1675–77	4	4.50	1.06	.	1741–43	6	6.00	0
1678–80	2	6.50	2.50	.	1744–46	12	5.50	1.30
1681–83	3	6.33	.47	.	1747–49	14	6.14	.72
1684–86	5	6.60	2.33	.	1750–52	5	7.20	1.06
1687–89	5	4.20	2.14	.	1753–55	13	6.46	.71
1690–92	4	5.00	4.00	.	1756–58	17	5.88	1.48
1693–95	6	6.33	.67	.	1759–61	19	5.53	.65
1696–98	2	2.00	0	.	1762–64	8	5.00	.95
1699–01	3	6.67	1.55	.	1765–67	14	4.43	1.84
1702–04	3	7.67	.47	.	1768–70	12	6.08	.61
1705–07	4	7.25	.83	.	1771–73	10	6.20	2.48
1708–10	2	10.50	2.50	.	1774–76	11	5.09	.71
1711–13	5	8.20	.12	.	1777–79	11	6.73	2.00
1714–16	7	6.14	1.78	.	1780–82	4	2.25	1.25
1717–19	7	5.43	.35	.	1783–85	12	5.57	.11
1720–22	16	6.00	.10	.	1786–88	7	5.29	1.91
1723–25	5	7.40	.80	.	1789–91	14	5.00	.86
1726–28	6	5.67	1.84	.	1792–94	13	7.38	.73
1729–31	11	6.82	1.60	.	1795–97	14	5.68	1.39
1732–34	7	8.14	2.47	.	1798–00	18	5.33	.49
1735–37	11	7.00	1.90	.	1801–03	8	7.00	1.14
1738–40	6	6.67	2.02	.				

* All relevant data from ten family trees delineated by Bond (cf. note 18 to text).

† Estimated for men at age thirty-four and women at age thirty-one, the average generational gap respectively.

‡ s = 1.732 times the standard error of the three-year mean.

result of fairly regular time at sea during the early years of their careers.

Also in a sample of men and women from ten Watertown family trees or genealogies[17] described in Figure No. 11 and Table 17—most of them farm families in contrast to the college men and the merchants— reproduction times where the average number of children was small (estimating from the family dimensions of men age thirty-four and women age thirty-one, the mean generational intervals) are very accurately predicted by the hypothetical timing derived from Harvard and Yale families in Figure No. 10. Frequently, however, the points of the *largest* family size run somewhat earlier than such expectations. This was, of course, also the case with the college children themselves in the 1720's and the 1750's. In addition to the three-year means of family size and an estimate of their standard error where most relevant, averages are plotted in Figure No. 11 for broader blocks of years in the pattern 6, 6, 5, 6/6, 6, 5, 5 to quarter, in effect, each theoretical 22½-year cycle and to come out with an accurate total time of forty-five years every eight quarters or two full cycles.

Figure No. 12 then transfers (a) this summary pattern of the typical number of children born into Watertown families, (b) the three-year means for the family size of Harvard and Yale men, and (c) the data on Bailyn's merchants, for comparison with yet another source of insight into the fluctuations of fertility over large segments of American history. A third of the *D.A.B.* sketches, that is, describe the number of siblings in the family of orientation of the subject. Since the mean birth order of the *D.A.B.* men typically fell slightly below the middle of the average family size, the dates for that plot in the figure are moved two years earlier (e.g., 1701 to 1699) to describe families whose average child was born at the same time as the estimate for the average child in the other three kinds of homes. Families larger than nine are averaged in at that maximum value because of the way in which the material was coded; and the *D.A.B.* data are biassed toward surviving children. But offset-

17. Henry Bond, *Family Memorials, Genealogies of the Families and Descendants of the Early Settlers of Watertown, Massachusetts, including Waltham and Weston* (Boston, 1855). Some careful work by Nathaniel H. Smith while he was an undergraduate at Harvard made possible this and other analyses of Watertown families and of the vital records of several towns. The families are: Adams, Allen, Bond, Benjamin, Briscoe, Hagar, Learned, Parkhurst, Sanger, and Smith.

ting these strains towards underestimating family size is a probable tendency of biographers to note large families more faithfully than others. To summarize the evidence in spite of these problems, the general timing of changes in the means and of the most significant peaks and troughs of family size for the *D.A.B.* men in fact parallels very closely throughout the eighteenth century the patterns among the children of Harvard and Yale men and, later, the offspring of men and women from ten Watertown family trees. Among those born from the early 1800's to the 1860's, where the evidence runs out, the modern linear trend toward smaller family size set in. Yet fluctuations of a cyclical sort continued to appear in diminished, though still sometimes significant, degree.

Following upon a long period over which massive immigration provided the chief demographic response of cyclical movements of opportunity, short-term change in family size is once more very important today. Whelpton[18] has recently shown that women of age to have their average child in 1944 and 1949 had a mean of 3.0 offspring compared with 3.3 children for those of similar placement in the life cycle in 1959. By the time of the mean maternal cohort of 1964, however, the average likely completed fertility of married women in the United States had fallen back appreciably once again. A projection from the cyclical movement in Figure No. 10, beginning from the families of merchants and college alumni in the very first years of New England settlement, would call for smallest families among children born near 1946 and the largest number of siblings among those born around 1959—a rather striking fit with the present-day evidence.

In summary, over long periods of our history the domestic birth rate, as can be demonstrated both by the total number of births and by the typical family size of quite different particular groups of citizens, responded regularly in step with the growth cycle. Down to those years of the nineteenth and early twentieth century during which immigration periodically constituted an impressive intake relative to the size of the total population, changes of 25 to 35 percent (sometimes more) in the

18. Pascal K. Whelpton, "Trends and Differentials in the Spacing of Births," *Demography*, 1 (1964), 85.

total fertility of married persons were usual. We seem, furthermore, since the end of mass immigration early in this century to be entering an era of substantially varying fertility once again. Oscillations of this magnitude kept feeding back into the system of social and economic opportunity new impulses in the form of age groups who would need more goods, more places to live, more jobs, more institutions to serve their needs, more professionals to care for them and their families. The increased demands of these cohorts, in contrast to others coming in between, in many ways and on·many sides fostered more rapid growth in the society for the time being.

Such a direct, significant infusion of indigenous births back to sustain the familiar pattern of cyclical increase in the population can be followed for about two hundred years. Thereafter, the reality of massive waves of immigration taking over the task of providing a chronologically focussed input of new people in the 1830's, the 1850's, the 1880's, and the years leading up to World War I is beyond question. For the era since World War I Easterlin's exposition[19] and subsequent events since 1962 which have backed up his argument have together made very clear the reemergence of indigenous population change in the "right" places once more, taking over again the role of keeping the system periodically stimulated or deflated which immigration had principally filled for about a century.

OTHER DEMOGRAPHIC ELEMENTS IN THE CYCLICAL SYSTEM OF OPPORTUNITY

It is not necessary to leave the argument for a multi-sided cyclical system of growth throughout the course of American society without also understanding something about *how* the crucial recurrent changes of native-born input into the population took place. Analytically this is much more problematic than explaining variation in amounts of immigration. There exists some at least preliminary evidence, however, both as to the means by which typical family size fluctuated and as to other ways in which the creation of new indigenous population was stimulated or curbed.

19. Easterlin, "Baby Boom" and 1965–66 papers in *Demography* and the *American Economic Review*.

In the first place, it is possible to demonstrate how cohorts who would be reaching the most likely male or female child-producing ages in certain years were more prone to *delay* marriage. Such a delay was a very important influence on family size before the era of easy and widespread contraception, and still is significant today. Figure No. 13 presents the proportions of eventually married Watertown women turning twenty-two in given years (the mean age of marriage for the colonial era) who did not take a husband until they were twenty-six or older. It also gives the proportions of ever-married *D.A.B.* men reaching twenty-six in the same three-year periods who married after they reached thirty. Over and over again as the economy came to a crest and then began to slide into a depression—around 1726, 1748, and 1771, to take examples from the "pure" or theoretically regular timing in Table 7—the proportion marrying late touched a low point and then rose rapidly to a high. Once again, just as in the evidence on family size, the amount of chronological variation in the percentage marrying late among *D.A.B.* men who came of age to take a wife during the *nineteenth* century was greatly reduced—over a period in which large waves of immigration flowed and ebbed in response to the changing opportunities evident in American life. But among those aged twenty-six in 1892 a high proportion married late, while the level fell substantially once again to a low among those of comparable age in 1910. A projection from the timing of observed swings of this sort prior to 1800 would call for a peak of late marriage in Figure No. 13 at 1893 and a trough at 1907, a very close approximation to the real fluctuations as they reappeared once more.

Perhaps this reemergence of a key source of change in family size through variation in age of marriage itself contributed causally to the legal restriction of immigration a few years later. The immigrant, once the open end of the physical frontier was closed in the 1880's[20] and pressures to delay marriage from time to time seem to have reappeared on the American scene, became more of a threat—as he did in the years around World War I, the next point at which delayed marriage should have occurred based on the peak in 1893 (Figure No. 13).

20. It is not argued that the frontier was there to be exploited by any individual who felt the need (in a "safety-valve" theory), but that the society as a whole did enjoy some "elbow room" from having such an open end.

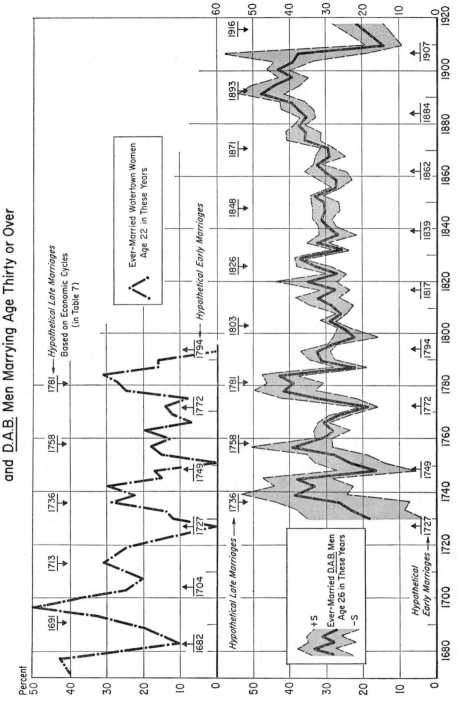

Figure No. 13. Percentages of Ever-Married Watertown Women Marrying Age Twenty-Six or Over, and D.A.B. Men Marrying Age Thirty or Over

Whatever the ultimate validity that can be demonstrated for this interpretation of changes near the turn of the twentieth century, it is clear that down to 1800 or so, at least, women in certain cohorts married about two years later on the average than did women in intervening birth groups. Since it was the early and most fertile years of marriage which were affected, such a delay could often mean that they had two children fewer—a rather strong variation, even taking into consideration the large average family size of six or seven which is apparent in the different groups depicted in Figure No. 12.

In addition to the tendency of larger proportions of men and women in certain cohorts to marry later than usual in years when the socio-economic environment was tight or difficult, several other factors affected the total number of native births. The details of these dynamics are currently being developed further from the several forms of colonial data which have already been introduced. But the outlines of these findings can be given here.

Among other forces which can be seen at work on family size and on the total number of births in the society, it can be seen that the proportion of men or women who did not ever marry was greater in about the same cohorts whose married members tended to have fewer children. And among alumni who did have children, histograms of the dates of seventeenth-century births show that typically those cohorts of reduced total fertility, at the end of their reproductive careers, in fact had most of all failed to have large numbers of children in the early years of marriage. This part of their life cycle, over and over again from one cohort with smallest family size to the next, was spent in years of recession. In contrast, men with the largest families had many more children in their early potential parental years (from about twenty-three to thirty-five) during the upswing of socio-economic conditions, then were still young enough to produce more children, sometimes by second wives, in the same phase of the next growth cycle. One of the characteristics of college cohorts with the most children was that they remarried most frequently. In short, not only did regularly spaced alumni birth cohorts have more children during the seventeenth century,[21] as would be ex-

21. This analysis is still being expanded.

pected from their chronological positioning relative to the opportunity cycle; it can also be shown directly that they actually had those extra children in the boom years. This is not, however, to say that socially mobile individuals always produced the largest families. Sometimes, rather, it seems as if having a large family may have been an alternative to enjoying mobility in "good times" rather than an accompaniment of opportunity in that particular form.

Death as well as birth helped to shape family size and the extent of total cohort replacement in early America. To begin with, potential parents of certain cohorts were more likely to die before their span of fertility had come to an end, cutting short family size in this way. Also young people at certain historical times were carried off more frequently before they could marry. Similarly, there was more infant or childhood mortality at some points of history than at others. This fact can be documented not only by the loss of children suffered by parents located in successive cohorts, but by the actual mortality of children with known date of birth. The loss of children born in specific years—hitting the later offspring of parents in some cohorts and the earlier offspring of others—can, furthermore, be demonstrated by histograms through at least part of the colonial era. One significant interaction of opportunity and societal growth with mortality in this period, finally, was that at certain times alumni moved into areas where mortality was high, while at other times opening or closing conditions of the socio-economic environment were likely to attract (or force) them into safer areas.

It can be shown, in this medical vein of explanation, that there was a certain periodicity of epidemics in early American history.[22] Such recurrent heavy mortality was not a simple matter of a single frightening attack of smallpox or diphtheria. Rather, several different kinds of disease—including measles, influenza, dysentery, scarlet fever, malaria, typhoid, and many unidentified "agues" and "fevers"—tended to follow each other through the population, with the next taking away those whom the previous had weakened.[23] It seems from what is available in

22. John Duffy, *Epidemics in Colonial America* (Baton Rouge, 1953), provides a useful consolidated source of this kind of information.

23. The dating of periods of mortality by a single shocking outbreak of, say, smallpox must be done cautiously. A very striking attack could be quite local (e.g., mostly in Boston) or really quite general in the colonies.

the way of material for dating colonial mortality[24] that disease tended to be most evident in the years around the baby booms which culminated in 1657, 1680, 1702, 1725, the 1740's, 1770, and 1792 (Figure No. 9). Heavy mortality caught the unusually concentrated population of as yet unexposed children, carried many of them off to speed the decline of the number of future adults surviving from the downward side of the birth bulge, and also undoubtedly gave parents second thoughts about the suitability of having more children for the time being. The chronology of colonial epidemics, moreover, if projected forward, "predicts" quite well the great urban health crises of the early 1830's and the mid-1850's, though these were perhaps a little "early" by such expectations.[25] There was in colonial America, however, often also evidence of epidemics at the mid-points between the clusters of illnesses which came in step with the peaks of "baby booms." Thus more than usually visible medical crisis occurred, in all, about every eleven years. It would seem that in these alternate periods the disease environment was also unfavorable, but typically the supply of unexposed children was not so dense as to spread mortality in the manner which characterized the other points of time.

There are, in fact, indications of a very long history of this kind of rather regularly recurrent chronology in mortality. And the relatively predictable spacing of clusters of epidemics over hundreds of years, along with the most likely interpretation of how they focussed in time in this way, suggests an explanation of how surprisingly persistent cycles of interdependent demographic and socio-economic phenomena could go on repeating themselves century after century, returning to high calculable points and not wobbling out of existence under the impact of a wide variety of sources of "error" or "deviation." A little variation will kill a cycle very quickly unless some form of "time clock" keeps working broken patterns or distorted cycles back into phase. In social phenomena such as mobility or economic "booms and busts" especially, it is hard to conceive of cyclical movement without constant imperfec-

24. See my *Opportunity, Equality, and Population* for an attempt to synthesize and summarize relevant information.

25. Early, that is, from the point of view of regular, theoretical long-range timing—like both immigration and new settlement in this period and also like certain economic characteristics.

tions of various sorts which must be brought back into line by some means if regular variations are to be preserved and restored.

The history of medical crises, however, suggests a way in which regular timing may have been reintroduced and reenforced in the growth cycle over very long periods of history. The evidence is so far most fragmentary and superficial, yet a *prima facie* case can be made—following Creighton in the English experience both before, and then parallel to, the American record just discussed—for repeated periods of unusually visible death from a variety of causes since well before the Norman Conquest.[26] In these chronological clusterings of mortality a succession of different principal epidemic killers were mixed with recurrent problems of crowding, sanitation, bad harvests, and harsh weather. Clearly to many such a claim for regularly recurrent environmental and disease components which are prone to create medical crises over and over again at largely predictable intervals will seem quite preposterous, but there is even contemporary experience to suggest this kind of timing in the incidence of illness.

Similarly, it would be easy to say that the traditionally famous killers like smallpox, diphtheria, cholera, the plague, yellow fever, and typhus can scarcely be considered dangers in developed countries in the modern era, and that they have not been replaced by other threats to life and health which might recur in fairly regular epidemic form. Yet the temptation to cloak ourselves in this comfortable assumption must be resisted for several reasons: 1) save for exceptional instances, these most striking sources of mortality did not necessarily do as much damage in history as compounded sieges of several less glamorous dangers including influenza, measles, dysentery, diarrhea, enteritis, malaria, and various "agues" and "fevers" which cannot be identified from this distance. 2) A long-known but modernly most prevalent disease like polio in this century seemed to step in and substitute at epidemic intervals for illnesses that had once been the principal killers of children but had been brought under control. Polio, of course, much more than killing, reduced chances of reproduction in its victims, principally through psycho-social consequences rather than insurmountable biological ones. 3) The crowding

26. Charles Creighton, *A History of Epidemics in Britain*, 2 vols. (Cambridge, England, 1891–94).

of our cities, the pollution of our air and water, and the problem of removing garbage and even more dangerous wastes are obviously aggra-
vated in periods of most acute population expansion and, as a result of
bulges in the age structure emanating from the growth cycle, at certain
times also find more young children or elderly people to prey upon.
The more intensely we let the relatively poorly serviced population concentrate in our cities the more likely we are to encounter high levels of
endemic disease, and also periodically accentuated outbursts of illness,
more like the situation of earlier history than the conditions of recent
years. 4) Even when potential mortality is controlled and lessened by
modern medicine, loss of work-time to the economy and inhibitions on
family formation and child bearing will nevertheless translate some
changes of the medical environment into further dynamics of the
growth cycle.

   In an effort to go one step further and try to explain how rather regular
waves of mortality might be expected to come about, it is necessary to
include what seem to be some essentially physical causes behind both
the biological and the socio-economic phenomena that have been encountered and described. It appears, that is, as though a line of explanation which has long been the butt of statistical humor may not be so
dead or so ludicrous after all. In a famous, perhaps notorious, paper to
the British Association in 1878 entitled "The Periodicity of Commercial
Crises and Its Physical Explanation," W. S. Jevons tried to develop the
idea that somewhat similar business and solar or "sun-spot" fluctuations
were related. The way he went about this was to argue that solar variations at the average interval of 11.11 years were the source of parallel
movements in agricultural prices, and that these in turn were the foundation of business cycles. The problem with his effort, first of all, was
that local metereological variations largely overlie and obscure those
world-wide weather movements which are regular enough to connect
with crop changes to produce or explain the hypothetical pattern. A
direct influence of weather on crops, crop prices, and from there on the
economy of a specific country (England) proved impossible to establish.
In addition, working with economic data from the South Sea Bubble of
1721 to the "collapse" of 1867, Jevons saw economic crises at the aver-

age of 10.43 years—not the same periodicity as evident in solar phenomena.

In actual fact, "sun-spots" and related solar changes in the long era from 1610 to 1913 displayed intervals of from 8.2 to 15.0 years to give an arithmetic average of 11.215 years.[27] On the other hand, more modern research on "long swings" or growth cycles at an average of 22 1/2 years in several aspects of economic development, in immigration, and in native births which is presented or reviewed here offers a new possibility of a connection with the solar series every other time around, so to speak.[28] Meanwhile, since Jevons' time knowledge of the ways in which solar variations affect the environment of human life has been expanded substantially, to include changes in the earth's magnetism, in radiation, in the thickness of skin on fur-bearing animals, and in the breadth of rings on trees.[29]

Yet are such findings relevant to the present discussion and not merely far from perfect coincidences? It would seem that the key is the very *limited* and *indirect* role of variation in the physical environment on the *quantity* or the *degree* of fluctuations in economic growth, personal opportunity, or demographic processes which have been examined here. That is, there is no direct reflection proposed by which the socio-economic opportunity system with its population aspects mirrors change in the solar environment through the impact of those physical forces on weather or crops as Jevons suggested, or for that matter—to use other reasoning—through solar effects in health, genetics, or sexuality. Instead, social opportunity, economic process, and demographic lags can

27. The Wolfer tables, as summarized in Carlos Garcia-Mata and Felix Shaffer, "Solar and Economic Relationships: A Preliminary Report," *Quarterly Journal of Economics*, 49 (1934), 8. Yule, examining crude data for the era 1749–1924, obtained an interval of 10.08 years by harmonic formula and 10.60 by regression equation; graduating the same data, he came up with intervals of 11.03 and 11.164 years by means of the same two techniques. G. U. Yule, "On a Method of Investigating Periodicities in Disturbed Series with Special Reference to Wolfer's Sunspot Numbers," Royal Society of London, *Philosophical Transactions*, 226 (1927), 267, as cited in the preceding. This literature is explored more fully in my *Opportunity, Equality, and Population*.

28. Most interestingly in 1929—the year before Kuznets published his *Secular Movements*—C. G. Abbot of the Smithsonian expressed the opinion that the average sunspot interval was 22.6 years with very little deviation. It was the intervening or alternate low point of solar activity which was not very clearly fixed in timing. Cited in Garcia-Mata and Shaffer, "Solar and Economic Relationships," p. 9.

29. *Ibid.*, pp. 7–8.

be demonstrated to carry most of the burden of cyclicity and to account largely for the 22 ½-year interval. But it is nevertheless possible that the environmental forces which Jevons discussed may yet prove to provide the "fine tuning" in the growth cycle system. That is, while the interval from one baby boom to the next, from one economic spurt to another, from an opening in opportunity to the subsequent one, together in their interdependence may most of all reflect the time it takes the men of the last baby boom to enter the labor market and the women to marry and bear children of their own, the long-term regularity of changes in the sun's activity on the health environment of man, on his food supply, on the virulence of disease and perhaps the mutation of new forms, and possibly also on the sexual urge may constitute the balance wheel which keeps returning chance variations in the other mechanisms back to the pure or theoretical timing of 22 ½ years on the average. The long-term timing of the solar or related physical movements, in other words, may keep demographic lags which tend to be approximately 22 ½ years long, or within a very narrow range of such regular chronology, actually coming back over and over again through centuries of history to that ideal or exact form of spacing.

THE WAY THE GROWTH SYSTEM SEEMS TO KEEP RETURNING TO PREDICTABLE INTERVALS

The more direct cause of regularity in the growth cycle, however, seems to have been a surprisingly stable average age at which—over the long haul, cutting across growth cycle variations—women have borne their first child. In colonial America as in this society today women had a mean age of just over twenty-two at this phase in their life cycle.[30] What this has meant is that there has been a rather constant tendency for a large bulge of girl babies born at any one time to be getting married, setting up a household, and having children of their own just about the typical growth cycle interval later. There is an "echo effect" or demographic lag, that is, from one baby boom to a focussing of marriages and household formation almost exactly one cyclical interval later.

30. Data on Sibley and Dexter wives of college men; Watertown families from Bond; for modern America, Paul C. Glick and Robert Parke, Jr., "New Approaches in Studying the Life Cycle of the Family," *Demography*, 2 (1965), 190.

From the standpoint of explaining the regularity of the growth cycle, that is all very well except that the extra large cohort of girls being followed through their life cycle would be bearing just the *first* of their children then. They would be having their *mean* or *average* child in the modern era about twenty-six years after their own baby boom, and in colonial times about thirty years later. What has to be explained is how all the births after their first ones are kept from creating a *generational* cycle with bulges something like twenty-six or thirty years apart.

This is where the interplay of economic change and demographic forces enter in. The lagged input of new population from a previous baby boom works in two ways in the economy. First of all, in consumption anyone who has set up a new home understands all too well the impact which this family act has on the market. When many girls are getting married within a short period of time, the economy enjoys a considerable uplift. Secondly, in the male lag or "echo effect" from the last baby boom the *labor supply* is increased periodically, with effects that Richard Easterlin has been developing in recent papers.[31] This line of argument about the effects of bulges of new labor upon the economy and their origins in "good times" goes back to the 'Law of Population' which Adam Smith put forth in *The Wealth of Nations* in 1776.[32] Fortunately we have done a little more with society-building since that turning point than we have with theory-building in the social sciences. Smith maintained that at about the time when economic growth forced labor costs so high that manufacturers had difficulty staying in business, the working population—stimulated by those high wages and accompanying conditions of opportunity—produced more children who augmented the labor supply and made wages manageable once more. Over and over again, he said, increases in the number of births would rescue the system from the brink of impossible labor costs. As wages fell, the birth rate would then drop back for the time being. This "law" is probably the first formulation of growth cycle theory. It survives the great attention commanded by Malthus, and the specific Malthusian attack

31. Easterlin, "Long Swings"; Easterlin, "Relations of Economic Factors to Fertility Changes"; and Easterlin, "Economic-Demographic Interactions."
32. For a simple summary of Smith's theory, see Robert L. Heilbroner, *The Worldly Philosophers* (New York, 1953), pp. 57–58.

on Smith's optimism about continuing growth with welfare, to supply us a way of coping with many characteristics of developed societies, and probably also developing societies, in the present era. What modern research has been doing, subsequently, is to demonstrate the average 22 ½-year lag before the new population created by "good times" comes to bear upon the labor market and the additional impact on consumption through the interval over which girl babies come to marry and have households and children of their own.

In an era of widespread effective contraception as well as the still relevant age-old alternative of delaying marriage, the response to improved socio-economic conditions stimulated by consumption and labor changes which reflect the previous baby boom can be translated very quickly into increased fertility not only for the young people coming of most typical age to beget and to go to work at this time, but also for other members of the society around them. Similarly, when the consumption impact of the bulge of girls getting married has come and passed, and a burst of young men seeking employment has left little room for their younger brothers in a levelling-out economy, demographic response to downturn can also be quick and general in the society. For example, all sorts and ages of women still capable of child bearing during the Depression of the 1930's—not just those most likely to be forming families —had fewer children than might be expected in those years, even if they "caught up" in their total fertility later.

Before modern contraception, mortality had much to do with cutting down what would have been the pattern-disrupting "tail" of later children in marriages. As has been stated, however, even in this early period families tended to have fewer children as socio-economic conditions worsened, over and above any losses to disease. Early Americans, like E. A. Wrigley's contemporary English men and women of the same period,[33] were not without means for controlling family size and the spacing of children. In this era when mortality played a key role along with more social responses to opportunity conditions in deter-

33. E. A. Wrigley, "Family Limitation in Pre-Industrial England," *Economic History Review*, 2nd ser., 19 (1966), 82–109. The apparent presence of growth cycles in several aspects of Wrigley's data (although he uses nine-year moving averages) is pointed up along with other international implications of this kind of theory in my *Opportunity, Equality, and Population.*

mining family size, any physically founded or solar-based regularity in the virulence of disease, or in weather conditions affecting man's resistance or food supply, could have provided the little touch of timing to keep the cyclical interval from falling off the edge at 22½ years, from wandering out of touch—either early or late—with the long-range projection. Mortality, timed ultimately by the interplay of biophysical determinants with demographic conditions such as scarcity of resources or crowding of susceptibles, could well have served to keep the growth cycle "on time"—or bring it back to time—over such long periods of history as have been observed.

VI. Some Implications for the Study of History and for the Understanding of Contemporary Society on the Basis of History

OBVIOUSLY there is much further work, in many different specialities, required before such an interpretation of how a complex of quasi-cyclical patterns of socio-economic developments can be accepted as a truly cyclical system of human life with the kinds of wide-ranging causal components which have just been suggested. Yet while we are waiting for the verdict to come in, so to speak, from investigations which are far beyond the competence of any individual person or any single discipline, we may profitably consider the general possibilities of this kind of recurrent pattern for the understanding of social as well as economic phenomena. It may be useful, in concluding, to examine some of the potential implications or applications of this type of analysis which uses an essentially cyclical model at the 22½-year interval.[1]

In the first place, concerning much of the current interest in historical demography and the history of the family, it would seem that many

1. There are other cyclical forces at work in social history, e.g., the generation (with a somewhat longer interval than the growth cycle) and also even more long-term processes.

tendencies which are labelled "European" or "American," or "early" or "modern" may, rather, involve reflections of oscillating socio-economic conditions in both Europe and America, both early and modern contexts. Already an awareness is growing, for instance, that the old distinctions about the degree of extended family forms will not hold up when studied over time or compared across the Atlantic. Similarities in age of marriage, number of children, other relevant structural characteristics of the family, and the processes in which they are involved are also becoming more apparent across the gaps of the old clichés. The notion of family forms and family dynamics which move in changing step with variations in the environment of family life may help to account for some of the ways in which similarities are combined or confused with differences.

It would seem, for example, that the need for the socio-economic functions of "extended" family patterns might well vary historically at least somewhat along with both fluctuations in the opportunity environment and oscillations of family size which have been observed to be part of the growth cycle historically. Clearly individuals are inclined to learn or to "inherit" the extended family form from the sub-culture or more personally idiosyncratic experience which characterized how they themselves were raised. Societies "pass on" family organization through their cultures as they transmit other patterns of social structure. But running across these tendencies of intergenerational transmission in family forms, there would also seem to be a possibility that the reinforcement of an extended pattern from the fact that it actually fulfilled useful functions for family members might well vary somewhat in response to the richness or barrenness of contextual conditions for finding work, getting married, raising children—life processes in which a felicitous socio-economic environment might be expected to offer more in the way of alternatives to the roles sometimes played by the family, and external attractions working against deeper involvement in the family and commitment to it. We should find, perhaps, more grandparents living in, more brothers and sisters or other relatives living together or helping each other out, at certain predictable points of history than at other times if this hypothesis holds true.

In the second place, the changing strains or temptations of certain phases of the development cycle in the opportunity environment of the family can be expected to encourage the dissolution of marriages or, conversely, the remarriage of divorced and widowed persons more than do conditions in other phases. In the colonial era, for instance, the known marital crises of Harvard and Yale men, and their tendency to remarry after the death of a spouse, both followed a largely cyclical timing. This hypothesis is also testable, provided—as always—we collect data not by decade or even longer intervals like generations but by more sensitive series of observation.[2] Third, the very serious contemporary writing about the young in our society today brings to mind the literature about the "lost generation" after World War I. Let us consider the possibility that these ties of the present back to earlier periods of time in American life are not coincidences of the historical experience, but rather, highly analogous cultural reflections of largely recurrent population conditions in which, (a) there are appreciably more young people than usual in the society, and (b) this age group has been raised in its later childhood and adolescence under fairly regular conditions of improvement or even boom in the socio-economic environment, and also probably in an aura of weakening family dynamics, bombarded and strained by the temptations and comforts of an easy life.

It is not too far fetched, on the other hand, to suggest that the different attitude of these young people towards material things and towards taking responsibility in or for society, and the penchant of commercial elements (or for that matter educators and politicians) to cater, even pander, to their desires, prejudices, and time horizons, provide important forces of a socio-cultural or psychological nature which do much to help *bring to an end* the more rapid than usual development of the society that has been going on for several years. Demographically, for instance, the idealization of romantic, highly individualized, socially uncluttered and uncompromised love—accompanied by technical advance and promotion in contraception (a technological and marketing change itself highly conditioned by the socio-psychological environment)—prob-

2. The problem with much of the English and French historical demography, as with work by American historians in this direction, is that it is—ironically—insensitive in the time dimension, i.e., insensitive to *history*. The development of more precise measurement has over and over again played a key role in the growth of science. Historical science can take important strides by introducing more precise and continuous dating.

ably has not increased promiscuity among young people; but it *is* apparently taking its toll of the birth rate. In a similar vein, religious revivalism has always been a threat to material society. Historians have not without cause tried to relate the fervor of the Great Awakening to a variety of demographic and economic behavior or concerns in that period.

Moreover, it may well be that the different external conditions under which the family shapes the personalities of the next generation in fact help to produce different kinds of people. That is, it is possible that the nature of the modal personality, or the distribution of certain kinds of personalities within the population, fluctuates according to cyclical variations in the environment under which socialization takes place. The psychic relationships of parents to each other, to themselves, and to their children which do so much to shape the early and most basic aspects of personality, seem subject to some variation in response to fluctuations in the age of marriage, in the ease of maintaining an independent or a comfortable household in the socio-economic environment, or in the degree to which the expectations of life which parents learned in one period of the cyclical history of societal development are being fulfilled or frustrated by subsequent and perhaps quite contrasting eras.

In later personality formation, on the other hand, the hold of the family for purposes of continued social training can be expected to be weakened during periods in which it is easier than usual for the young to leave home or to be accepted as adults by extra-parental definition. It is a matter of real, if statistically modest, record over and over again through the first century of American higher education, for instance, that those cohorts who were raised during a boom of general development, left college near its peak, but then had to adjust to adult life in much more depressing and demanding conditions were those in which alcoholism, marital instability, criminal activity, and also mental illness were clearly most prevalent. These college cohorts, on the average the familiar 22½ years apart, similarly as students were most frequently expelled or rusticated for causes ranging from inattention to studies and rowdiness to theft and bastardy. And projecting forward from the walk-out of the class of 1655 who refused to accept the extension of the Harvard course from three to four years, and from the student-junior faculty complicity in the conspiracy of 1676 which ejected and ruined President Leonard Hoar, not only can we very accurately "predict" at least the chronology of intervening events like the bitter fight over admissions and the evaluation of students which culminated at Harvard about 1721 (coterminous with the Cutler crisis at Yale), student agitation during the Great Awakening of the early 1740's, or—to take one of several later examples—the great spring rebellion of 1834 against President Quincy. In addition, the hypothetical pattern of this timing tells us that 1969 should mark the peak of a period of college student unrest and university disorder.

Across a broader scene outside the universities, it seems likely that the "mood of the nation" also goes through swings or cycles adhering closely to the familiar interval. Professor William Chambers of Washington University quite independently has come up with evidence from national election data of the nineteenth and twentieth centuries which shows changes of the party in power at rather regular intervals. Compare, for example, the mood of the electorate in 1968 with the political atmosphere and the results of 1946. To look at the sometimes violent consequences of popular mood, on the other hand, the city riots of the early 1940's and the mid-1960's fit together with the troubles at the end of World War I to produce recognizable chronological patterns and also hark back to the violence of the 1830's and the 1850's.[3] Those concerned with poverty rolls, school growth and change of clientele, unemployment, crime, and other related problems of the society, or institutional cures advanced to meet them, finally, should also find similar chronological variations.

There are obviously still many other ways of pointing the kinds of findings of cyclical change reported here toward understanding something more about the nature of the growth cycle and what it does. It should be added, perhaps, that evidence is accumulating very rapidly that this type of fluctuation in the socio-economic environment and in demographic behavior is in some degree, or in certain aspects, very

3. The draft riots of the Civil War would seem to be a different kind of phenomenon, though they are related to what has been going on in the past few years by another kind of recurrent phenomenon, what might be called moral history. (See my forthcoming *Recurring Reformation*.)

widespread among the societies of the world, including nations with "controlled" economies who experience their own resurgent baby booms, youth crises in "hooliganism" or in education and employment, and demands for consumer goods or for freer social organization.

Czechoslovakian reform may have given us a recent example, two cyclical intervals since the brief era of pre-Stalinist Soviet experimentation (the New Economic Policy was introduced in 1921) and one cycle since the Yugoslav "heresy" in the 1940's.[4] Similarly, it was a span of almost exactly two growth cycles from the English Civil War to the colonial revolts of the 1680's (and the Glorious Revolution at home), while the War for Independence broke out about four cycles later still. The hypothetical date for a crisis in the cyclical timing during this period would have been 1777.

By now historians have passed successfully through the one-dimensional explanation period of Turner and Beard (and also Marx) with a healthy skepticism about single-principle theories which take on the aura of dogma rather too easily and acquire disciples instead of testers and improvers. It is to be hoped, however, that having been once seduced and left abandoned by these interpretations, the profession does not then turn its back on the chances of a gratifying and enriching relationship with theory forever.

Clearly the kind of theory-building which has been presented here can have frivolous, even dangerous, results. It can become a game for its own sake rather than a means to the end of understanding how things happen in history—means which *can* be tested, and *must* constantly be tested, against the facts in every available relevant record. A few catchy conclusions or simple patterns for events can too easily substitute for badly needed thought. Yet if the type of interpretation offered here can be taken as *one* perhaps useful tool in the kit of explanation, and tried out as such and no more, there seem to be some interesting possibilities for understanding how many different kinds of social phenomena behave over the dimension of time, both historically and with the hope of developing a predictive social science for the future.

4. Hungary erupted in 1956, at the cyclical mid-point.

APPENDIX A

Social Groupings Included in the "Upper Class" Category
for College Men and Their Fathers or Guardians

"The Secular Upper Classes"

All magistrates, including elected members of the upper houses of the colonial legislatures and J.P.'s.

Military officers of the rank of colonel and above.

Men who seem to have been the more important merchants or landholders as indicated by whatever evidence was available in *Sibley* or *Dexter*, or in Bailyn's discussions of trade. No further research was conducted in inventories, tax rolls, etc. The cash figure for solvency of an estate at death, furthermore, though one of the hard quantitative pieces of evidence about property, could be quite misleading. There was a strong tendency over most of the colonial era for men of substantial property to hold high office of some sort, but there were always some exceptions; and the chances to have substantial property outran the limited supply of high offices toward the middle of the eighteenth century. (This effect shows up more in the careers of college men themselves than in the positions of their fathers.)

"The Professional Upper Classes"

Those ministers, doctors, and a handful of college presidents who stood out above the normal level of their professions. Considerable amount of judgment had to be used here, weighing for ministers, for example, both the nature of the pulpit they held and their own apparent personal influence and prestige. In theory, all ministers were equal in the Congregational system; in fact, a classification of this sort—making some "more equal than others"— is validated very well by the ways in which incoming students were ranked or placed by the colleges during those periods where social considerations are known to have been predominant. (The collegiate system of "precedence" also shows contemporary recognition of sons of leading merchants and landed gentlemen who held no high official position; and "old family" ties were not required for this—the college administration was willing to bet on "comers.")

For further details and examples, and for the fit of fairly standard sociological classifications to contemporary colonial evaluation, see my forthcoming monograph on the changing origins and careers of early Harvard and Yale men and the apparent social functions of these earliest collegiate institutions.

APPENDIX B

Cutting Points for the Classification of the Fathers of *D.A.B.* Men by Socio-Economic Position

"Upper Class"

Those in business, landed property, government, or the military who had responsibility for and control over large property holdings, large organizations, or major segments of them. Placing businessmen, planters, and government administrators—particularly from what little is said about the fathers of men in the biographies—sometimes required a fair amount of contextual judgment: but classification by a large number of coders proved to be usefully reliable in these terms. In the military: colonel and naval captain form the bottom layer of "upper class." In elective office: down through most congressmen and the top handful of state officials.

Those without a large number of subordinates or property control or power whose positions called for top educational, intellectual, or artistic achievement: most judges (including local judiciary and J.P.'s in the colonial era—cf. Appendix A); major university presidents; prominent teaching doctors and others of renown; best known lawyers in a region; bishops and other individual divines of broad influence and respect; what might be called "big time" college professors, scholars, scientists, and writers; best known artists and performers; and a few other persons such as leading philanthropists and particularly notable figures in sport. In these classifications, too, a considerable amount of judgment was required.

Throughout, the tendency of a father or guardian to *combine* major roles or assets in society could give him the benefit of the doubt for "upper class" placement. There was, however, no attempt to weigh in social prestige *per se*, or to transfer status from one family member to another except in the case of widowed mothers, who were given the classification appropriate to their late (or their next) husbands. Sheer wealth, where possible to determine, was coded alongside the largely occupational or functional system of stratification and occasionally was allowed to qualify ranking on that basis when other criteria were vague. There were relatively few cases in which substantial wealth was obvious and the father or guardian did not also have one of the above kinds of occupational or functional roles in society. But unrecorded wealth may have had something to do with problems of distinction between "upper class" and "upper middle class."

"Fairly Ordinary" or "Ordinary" Social Origin, "Lower Middle Class or More Humble Origins"

This cutting point, in the middle of the social order, so to speak, excludes all "upper class" parents or guardians as outlined above, and *also* those who might be called "upper middle class": that is, omitting the typical professional except the more ordinary schoolteacher, low-grade attorney, or marginal medical practitioner; captains or majors in the army, lieutenants and commanders in the navy; more ordinary artists, performers, and writers of some note; and men in business, land, or government who had some but not very many subordinates, a large but not impressive organizational or financial responsibility.

Once again, a considerable amount of judgment from the context was necessary to classify men at this level, particularly those whose position involved primarily property or intellectual performance.

"Common Man" or "Really Quite Humble" Social Origins

Those whose fathers or guardians were skilled or unskilled workers; routine clerks, bookkeepers, or sales personnel; small farmers or shopkeepers (usually with only the family as labor); military men in the ranks (excepting a few higher non-commissioned officers); seamen; and also the more extreme cases of the unemployed and institutionalized.

Further details are available in forthcoming publications focussing on the *D.A.B.* materials in their own right.

PRESIDENTIAL PLANNING AND SOCIAL SCIENCE RESEARCH: MR. HOOVER'S EXPERTS

Barry D. Karl

PRESIDENTIAL PLANNING AND SOCIAL SCIENCE RESEARCH: MR. HOOVER'S EXPERTS

BURIED in the rubble of the Hoover Administration was the beginning of a national program for social reform which had among its general purposes the abolition of poverty and the establishment of what progressives were already calling a "Great Society." Such a program was to be built on a comprehensive survey of American social needs, a national inventory scientifically constructed. Utilizing the brief but exhilarating experience of economists, sociologists, psychologists, and political scientists in the agencies of World War I, the survey was to bring together the leaders of the various segments of the social research movement to build a national reform system predicated on the use of the federal government as a central clearing house for social reform. The work of the President's Research Committee on Social Trends, appointed in 1929 and reporting in 1933, brought together many of the first rank of the new academics which the progressive era of university development had produced. Financed by the Rockefeller Foundation and operating under a mandate from the President of the United States, the Committee was to provide the data with which to draw up the blueprints for a peaceful revolution to make prosperity permanent.

Planned in September of 1929 and appointed in December—dates painfully parenthesizing the crash in October—the Committee collected its data and exercised its scientific mind amid the increasing din of the Depression. When *Recent Social Trends in the United States* appeared in January of 1933 it held in its fifteen hundred pages of text, charts, and tables, amassed over three years, the intended groundwork for the last

* The author's research has been aided by grants from the American Philosophical Society, the Charles Warren Center for Studies in American History, and Washington University in St. Louis. Grateful acknowledgment is made to the staffs of the Herbert Hoover Presidential Library at West Branch, Iowa, the Hoover Institute at Stanford, California, and the University of Chicago Libraries.

347

of a sequence of American utopias, while suggesting, however obliquely, the lines which a future tradition of distinctly anti-utopian reforms would follow. The last utopia of Herbert Hoover was not destined to retain all its elements intact; but its very failure would provide an important experience for the development of modern American social reform.

The questions raised by Hoover's appointment of a committee of social scientists are connected with a long history of problems in the relation between social science and social reform in American government, a history easily obscured by an emphasis upon the then unprecedented status of such a committee with so comprehensive a mandate. The President's Research Committee on Social Trends certainly entailed a break with various traditions by postulating that "social" behavior in the nation as a whole was to be placed within the overview of the federal government; that "science" could improve upon the experienced observations of legislators, executives, or the citizens themselves in the framing of national programs for reform; that social welfare deserved as much attention in the debates of the federal government as the older issues relating to currency, tariffs, railroads, and trusts. Yet the idea of applying scientific research to social reform was familiar on all levels of American government long before Hoover entered the White House.

As early as the 1830's and 40's survey studies of American cities by sanitary engineers had used collections of social statistics to suggest the complex of relationships involved in any discussion of systematic reform. By the time the Civil War broke out, reform groups had evolved relationships, nationally and internationally, with medical and bacteriological researchers, architects, engineers, transportation specialists, import-export business interests, insurance companies, and legislative drafting specialists to produce basic concepts of planning which laid the groundwork for the view of social reform and social research as comprising a system of related professional interests.[1] The United States Sanitary Commission during the Civil War was a privately-financed

---

1. See especially *Proceedings and Debates of the Third National Quarantine and Sanitary Convention* (New York, 1859). A brief history of the formation of the group is given in a letter from Wilson Jewell contained in that volume.

national organization to oversee conditions in army camps, hospitals, and prisons; but it was built on a federation of local reformers built up over the previous twenty years. The war expanded their interests and their numbers and made their methods of survey and research attractive to philanthropists like John D. Rockefeller, who named one of his first national medical corporations "The Rockefeller Sanitary Commission."

After the war, the interconnections of different reform perspectives in groups like the Civil Service Reform League, whose active membership included representatives of groups engaged in other reforms, as well as a key cadre of younger college and university presidents, paralleled the movements in the emerging social sciences for interrelationship among disciplines and the direct involvement of the latter in the reshaping of American society.

In 1887, only a few years after the famous manifesto of the young economists bound the newly-formed American Economic Association to action rather than to theory alone, Woodrow Wilson told his fellow political historians, "I suppose that no practical science is ever studied where there is no need to know it."[2] Such views of the essentially utilitarian role of the social sciences served increasingly important functions in defining the Progressive ideal of government. A closely related development was the rise of the modern foundation, with its characteristic immersion in systematized national reform interests. By 1900, the basic methodology of social reform and its particular vision of the relationship between scientific research and politics had also been established. The "method" consisted of variations upon three basic steps. The first involved a definition of the problem by a core group of interested specialists and influentials. Often the immediate circumstances were a meeting of one of the many professional associations to which such people belonged. The second step would be the calling of a conference to broaden the association of interested people, including three groups who might not have been involved centrally in the first stage: newspaper and magazine writers for publicity, philanthropists for financial support, and potentially concerned political leaders for the ultimate legal action. The third step would be the research survey in which ex-

2. Woodrow Wilson, "The Study of Administration," *Political Science Quarterly* 4 (1887), 197.

perts would study the multiple questions under consideration, introduce new ones if necessary, and produce, finally, a full document containing all the information and interpretation on which reasonable men, presumably in government, would base programs for reform.

Any one reform experience might dispense with some of the steps, or reverse their order; but one can find them in various permutations as early as 1841 in Lemuel Shattuck's study of Boston,[3] and in one of their first modern, national forms in the White House Conference on Conservation in May 1908. By World War I when Woodrow Wilson tried with limited government appropriations to create a functioning wartime system out of a willing private citizenry, he had a working pattern to turn to. Such agencies as the War Industries Board, the Committee on Public Information, and the Food Administration, to name only the obvious ones, brought a tradition of survey research and social-industrial reform to the service of the wartime government.

Even before the war the network of such groups was impressive. Private and public universities, state and municipal research groups, industrial and professional associations, philanthropic and welfare groups, all provided a trained cadre which moved into wartime government to struggle, some of them for the first time on a national scale, with problems of labor relations and employment, national and international shipping, science and industry, food distribution, and public health. But it was not the first time for all of them, at least as far as particular problems—public health, for example—were concerned. What was new was the sense of urgency in the national government about systematic scrutiny of the nation as a whole. Cloaked in the emergency of the war was a crisis of national knowledge which had been faced intermittently by presidents and Congresses seeking to judge labor disputes and railroad rates; but the cloak was thin. Economists like Edwin Gay and Wesley Mitchell, as well as politically-minded young lawyers like Felix Frankfurter, came through the war convinced of needs which extended well beyond the problems of a temporary war machine.

The war was an education for those who served in the wartime agencies, but that education did not teach the same lessons to all who studied

3. Lemuel Shattuck, *An Essay on the Vital Statistics of Boston from 1810 to 1841* (Philadelphia, 1841).

in Washington. Progressives who came out of the experience with their progressivism intact saw the need for national programs of information and advice far more extensive than the limited focus of pre-war issues where "conservation" could be used as a comprehensive term. Yet the commitment to the formulation of public policy by the public, not by the directors of a national wartime machine, required a transformation of major, not to say miraculous, proportions. The return to pre-war progressivism, armed with the experience of the war but not over-whelmed by it, called for a rational, scientific nationalism capable of energizing social progress. The recollection of pre-war localisms, super-imposed on the more immediate recollection of the brief attempt at cen-tral management, helped spark what was in effect a search for respon-sive national units of reform—regional, perhaps, but not local, effective in reform without being governmental. The concept of "voluntarism" has come to describe the programs evolved; but it does not describe the dream, nor the practical experience of half a century that fortified the dream.

Since 1919, many of his contemporaries had been looking to Herbert Clark Hoover as the man who would realize the dream, and for ten years he had retained his credibility in this role. When Hoover became president in 1928, he based his confidence in the future of his adminis-tration on convictions, shared as much by those who had opposed his candidacy as by those who supported it, that he could control at least three of the communities necessary to bringing about the domestic revolution to which progressives of every stripe had been committed. First, as a leading member of the engineering profession he was in a position to influence one of the country's oldest organized industrial reform groups. Engineers had financed and conducted surveys of American cities and states for almost a century, taking over the support of the conservation survey in 1908 when Congress refused to back it.[4] Secondly, as a fund-raising philanthropist who had spent the years from 1914 to 1919 engaged in tying together the interests of private philan-thropy and some of the interests of the wartime federal government, he had become closely acquainted with the new uses of old American fund-

4. See Samuel P. Hays' very full account of the conservation battle in *Conservation and the Gospel of Efficiency* (Cambridge, 1956).

raising techniques and their potential for arousing large-scale public response to reform needs.[5] Finally, as Secretary of Commerce from 1921 to 1928 he had established relationships with the country's industrial-banking network with the accompanying possibility of channelling information about national needs as a whole to modernizing business institutions in search of national markets.[6]

The basic components in Hoover's strategy were taken over from Theodore Roosevelt's concept of the White House Conference: involvement of experts, publicity, exchanges of information, and broadening of concepts. The idea that a heightened consciousness of problems coupled with the distribution of information about methods would produce effective improvements on a broad scale was nowhere better exhibited than in the Better Homes movement of 1921–32. This sought to rationalize urban development on a national scale by systematizing methods in the building trades, zoning commissions, mortgage procedures, and real estate salesmanship, while at the same time promoting through popular magazines and newspapers the virtues of social stability tied to home ownership.[7] The report of the President's Committee on Recent Economic Trends, assembled just before Hoover took office, was another example of the increasing emphasis upon scientific research as the basis for reorganization. Wesley Mitchell's work with that group represents the coordination of private and public sectors that Hoover had been working to perfect. A privately financed research group, the National Bureau of Economic Research, utilizing special funds from interested philanthropists, as well as the services of academic experts employed by private universities, was aiding the nation through the agency of the government. Like the wartime boards, the Committee on Recent Economic Trends used not only specialists but interested Cabinet officers as well as established figures like Owen D. Young who could represent

5. A useful history of these methods, particularly with respect to popular philanthropy of the 1920's, can be found in Scott M. Cutlip, *Fund-Raising in the United States* (New Brunswick, N.J., 1965).

6. See Joseph F. Bradley, *The Role of Trade Associations and Professional Business Societies in America* (University Park, Pa., 1965).

7. The papers of the Better Homes Commission are in the Hoover papers in the Herbert Hoover Presidential Library at West Branch, Iowa, to be referred to hereafter as Hoover Library, to distinguish it from the Hoover Institute at Stanford, where other papers used in this study are to be found.

the private community interested in the issue involved and sustain the interest and support of that community in the ensuing campaign to act upon the new information.

To those who had observed his management of his wartime responsibilities, Hoover's capacity to administer the complex relationships among such groups seemed to be of an unusually high order. Franklin Roosevelt, one of Hoover's wartime friends, wrote to Hugh Gibson, a common friend, that "I had some nice talks with Herbert Hoover before he went west for Christmas. He is certainly a wonder, and I wish we could make him President of the United States. There could not be a better one."[8] And Colonel House as early as December of 1918 had begun to consider the possibility of a Hoover presidency. House asked Hoover point blank the question which others were puzzling over at a distance: whether he considered himself a Democrat or a Republican. Hoover had spent most of the years before the war abroad, visiting the United States from 1908 to 1914 only at intervals. Though he joined the National Republican Club in 1909 and supported Theodore Roosevelt in 1912, his position in 1916 is not at all clear. His support of Wilson's position in the Congressional elections of 1918 alienated a significant group of Republicans and probably led to House's question. Hoover's answer was not calculated to clarify the issue. "Neither," he told House "I would be a Democrat if it were not for the reactionary element in the South. I would be a Republican if it were not for the reactionary element in the East. I shall give support to either of the parties which has a progressive program." He made it clear to House that he did not want the presidency, that he preferred to buy a newspaper in the United States and "see what he could do with it." House was still skeptical. "In my opinion, he is mistaken in believing he would not like to be President."[9]

Hoover's position here reflects one of the central and most critical elements of the reform mentality that evolved out of the Civil War and reached its peak in the Progressive era: the suspicion or outright rejection of partisan politics as a route to reform. In its public appeals for funds to support its work during the Civil War, the Sanitary Commis-

8. FDR to Gibson, January 2, 1920, Hoover Library. Gibson forwarded the letter to Hoover.

9. House Diaries, December 19, 1918. Yale University Library.

sion had claimed that "it has declined asking or receiving money from the government, for fear it might thus forfeit its independent position, and lose in moral strength what it gained by Government patronage."[10] Henry Bellows of the Commission had begun to work out a post-war plan for disabled veterans which he felt would also be damaged by direct political involvement, though he sought administrative support from the government.[11] Later conservationists, even in Congress itself, argued for a similar separation of reform from politics. "The time necessary to secure Congressional approval," Senator Newlands wrote in his plea for an adequate program to preserve natural resources, "and difference of view as to purpose or method, may result in indecision and delay, the worse enemies of effective development .... Unless some method of construction and development, insuring prompt decision and execution and continuous work by a body of experts is adopted, I fear that the best of projects may be wrecked in the shoals and quicksands of legislation."[12] If the necessity of utilizing "expert" knowledge involved the necessity, as well, of a divorce from politics, the carrying out of expert programs required the support of legislators who owed their position to politics. The shoals and quicksands of politics were going to have to be traversed by reformers whether they liked it or not.

By the 1920's there were alternatives, to be sure, and interested Americans were reading about them as they watched, with mixed enthusiasms, the emergence of Italian fascism and other examples of what W. Y. Elliott would label "the pragmatic revolt," the rebellion against constitutional liberalism and its concern for rights and the pursuit of a new order of political life adapted to industrial society. Groups concerned with such problems were not unaware of Hoover's commitment to the industrial state but were unsure of the form that commitment would take. On the eve of his inauguration, speakers at a meeting of the Anti-Fascist Alliance of North America described him as a "blood brother of

10. U.S. Sanitary Commission, *Documents* 5 (New York, 1866–71), June 21, 1861.

11. "If this matter be left to politicians, or be hurried through Congress by busy men, it will want all profound merits. It will be sure to violate our American principles, to wound political economy, and to botch the whole idea. If, on the other hand, we can slowly mature a wise, ripe plan, it may become a germ of the utmost beneficence to the soldiers and to the nation." *Documents* 49, p. 6.

12. U.S. Senate, *Document* 325, 60 Cong., 3 Sess., p. 32. Inland Waterways Commission, *Preliminary Report 1908*.

Mussolini,"[13] while some who had seen him in operation during the war feared his approach to the instruments of power.

An interest in scientific management tended to bring together the engineers, on the one hand, who had professional reasons to respect Hoover, and on the other, non-technical publicists and journalists whose fascination with the possible social extensions of Taylorism filtered through the articles they wrote for magazines like *The Survey*, *World's Work*, or the *Metropolitan Magazine*. French Strother, who, in addition to his career as a magazine writer, had served as assistant to Henry Morgenthau, Sr. in Greece and Turkey, met Hoover during the war and took to him immediately. A life-long Democrat, Strother served as an assistant to Hoover during most of the White House years, but he had already been part of an informal team of writers who planted popular articles on Hoover in national media throughout the Commerce Department years. The Hoover personality was one of the best-documented political phenomena of the 1920's. His travels about the country to speak to small groups of local leaders indicated a man who seemed able to use politics without becoming a politician.

In 1920 Strother wrote an article for *World's Work* in which he detailed Hoover's qualifications for the presidency: his "representative" Americanism, his power to command loyalty as "almost a form of worship," his distrust of the present distribution of American wealth, and his awareness of the necessity for using income and inheritance taxes to remedy the maldistribution. But even Strother found it necessary to explain his seeming rudeness as a "Quaker-intellectual honesty," a "passion of his mind to find truth," a driving search "to get usable knowledge."[14] For all of his career, and indeed all of his life, Hoover's impact as a personality had a divisive effect which left few neutrals. People were either for him or against him, not because he demanded it, although he was capable of that, but because the effect of involvement with him was to produce a sharp decision as immediate as it was irrevocable. His divisiveness was bound up with the characteristic progressive commitment to the most rigorous analysis of "facts" and the priority of scientific system over the loose compromises and shadowy motives of

13. *New York Herald Tribune*, February 11, 1929.
14. French Strother, "Herbert Hoover," *World's Work* 39 (1920), 578.

politics. Hoover did not have to become doctrinaire in the presidency. The brand of progressivism which he ably represented had been committed to a new scientific order of life from the beginning—one in which "American democracy" would be preserved, but in accordance with a definition of democracy that in some strange way omitted politics.

Morris Llewellyn Cooke, a consulting engineer and part-time urban reformer committed to scientific management, commented in July 1928 that, though he was not altogether sure that he would vote for Hoover, ". . . there is a possibility if he is elected, as he probably will be, that Herbert Hoover may show us how to shed politics in some large way in the demonstration of a democratic form of government." But, he continued, "if he only had Al Smith's personality and his own training I believe you might look forward to having a government-Pasteura."[15] What he meant by "government-Pasteura" he didn't explain, but one can wonder, perhaps, at what precise temperature the political bacteria in democracy would be killed, and what source would provide the heat: that democracy itself would survive the process he had no doubt.

Many men interested in the development of pure scientific research had watched their own respect for Hoover develop well beyond anything they would have anticipated, even during the hurried days of the war when Hoover seemed among the brightest of the young administrative stars which the emergency had brought into focus. As Secretary of Commerce, although with a sense of publicity which some found distasteful and all attributed to his presidential ambitions, Hoover had been able to restate the progressive ideal of commerce and industry as the real American contribution to Western civilization in fresh and promising terms. For men of science who had long suffered from the problem of financing their research apart from their teaching or their work in the relatively meager scientific areas of industry, Hoover promised a continuation and expansion of the sorts of cooperation between industry and science which the war had indicated might be possible; and Hoover's exhortations to his colleagues in the engineering field, his work with the National Research Council, and, most important of all, his obvious de-

15. M. L. Cooke to Charles E. Merriam, July 30, 1932. Charles Merriam Papers, University of Chicago Libraries.

sire to use the Department of Commerce as the chief clearing house for industrial-scientific intelligence, indicated the possibility of new and exciting directions in American research.[16]

By 1928 Hoover's active encouragement of trade associations and his use of the Washington conference as a device for the elaboration of industry-wide standards and voluntary agreements to abide by these had initiated changes in the building trades and injected the federal government as an advisory agency into many important industries. Aware of the hostilities generated between reformers and industry by reform enthusiasts, he sought to emphasize cooperation and education; but the battle was often uphill. In an era in which federal policy moved as quickly as possible not only to liquidate the involvements of industry and government during the war years but also to discourage future involvement, the Department of Commerce moved to invoke the useful relationships established by the experience of the War Industries Board in new areas like radio broadcasting and aviation. Nor did Hoover get much help from Cabinet colleagues like Andrew Mellon or Charles Evans Hughes, both of whom tended to find his search for overall systematic views of problems like foreign trade and investment an interference in their specialized provinces. Even there, the criticism Hoover evoked from colleagues was founded less on disagreement with his basic purposes than on his impatience with barriers he considered administratively unrealistic, or, worse still, political. He was committed to the formulation of methods of cooperation built upon the conclusions a rational man would be bound to reach when confronted with a scientific analysis of his own best interests. He walked a difficult and sometimes erratic course between administrative policies favoring far less regulation than he desired and the pressures from trades and industries seeking to use the power of government to support particular business interests.

Hoover's own interest in a return to private control of the national wartime agencies was founded on his belief that the use of philanthropic organizations and interested citizens during the war would operate as effectively in peacetime as in the war. Several important offices of the

16. "The Vital Need for Greater Financial Support of Pure Science Research," National Research Council, *Reprint and Circular Series*, no. 65.

expanded post-war Department of Commerce were wartime agencies shrewdly renamed for peacetime. His chairmanship of the President's Conference on Unemployment in 1923 began an expansion of his industrial management interests in directions which looked to the social effects of industry, the human side of scientific management. Edward Eyre Hunt, whose first association with Hoover had been on the Belgian Relief Committee, became his chief assistant in working out and implementing his new organization for governmental use of the social sciences.

Hunt was typical of the sort of assistant whom Hoover often sought. Class poet at Harvard, translator and adaptor of Middle English poetry, and one of the founders of the Harvard Socialist Club, Hunt had moved from an assistantship in the Harvard English department to an editorial post on the *American Magazine*. As a war correspondent in Europe on the eve of the war, he was in a position to aid in relief work and then with American entry, war work under Hoover. He became an enthusiast and publicist of scientific management in the post-war years, assisting Hoover in the Commerce Department and acting as secretary for the various industrial management committees, beginning with Waste in Industry, which Hoover, as President of the Federated American Engineering Council, had chaired and the Council had financed. Hunt was part of a generation in which the term "publicist" characterized a kind of transprofessional expert, a man often trained only by experience in his technical field rather than formal professional training, who conceived as part of his function the communication of ideas to professionals and the transmission of those ideas in popular form to the public. The reform methods of the late 19th century and Hoover's whole concept of the presidency rested on the existence and effectiveness of such men.[17] To the extent that scientific government would continue to depend upon the essential democratic support of public opinion, men like Hunt were central to the method. An extraordinary group, they had to be professional enough to speak authoritatively within the discipline, public enough to write interesting and entertaining popular prose, and subtle enough to handle the conflicts which were bound to arise.

The role which Hunt and Hoover played in the formation of the

17. Edward Eyre Hunt, *Scientific Management Since Taylor* (New York, 1925).

Social Trends group is interesting to trace, since it illustrates the function of men who communicated with representatives of the many separate communities who ultimately became involved in the presidential committee. Like many key figures in their generation, Hunt and Hoover prided themselves upon the useful accidents they produced by their shifting assemblage of sources of ideas which otherwise would have remained out of communication with one another. Such men, at their best, were uncommitted to specific results but deeply committed to the assurance that there would be useful results.

Initially, Hunt and the Secretary of Commerce were concerned with the problem of employment and the utility of social research for clarifying the problem. Through their interest in engineering research, both were aware of a set of projects being undertaken by the National Research Council to study the scientific aspects of human migration, a topic of some interest to European social scientists and of concern to a wide range of Americans. An industrial interest in migratory labor forces dated back to the progressive period where the possibility of a national clearing house to communicate national labor needs and supplies had been raised fairly frequently. The Russell Sage Foundation had attached to its particularistic concerns with urban social conditions, tenements, public health, and the like, an interest in the study of the effects of migration—a more acceptable post-war term than "immigration"—on social conditions. A growing group of anthropologists and sociologists were at least willing to accept funds from donors whose interest in problems of race and assimilation turned them to the new social sciences for answers.[18]

The National Research Council had been formed in 1916 to coordinate the work of American scientists during the war. It was reorganized on a permanent basis in 1919. Its financing during the war is obscure; but governmental funds, largely through the Navy, the Signal Corps, and the Council of National Defense, and private funds from such groups as the Engineering Foundation, kept it going. After 1919 support was transferred entirely to private sources. A $5,000,000 grant from

18. The Helen Culver Fund for Race Psychology financed W. I. Thomas and Florian Znaniecki, *The Polish Peasant in America*. Miss Culver's interest in racial assimilation went back to her Civil War work with the Sanitary Commission and post-Civil War experiences with Negroes in the South.

the Carnegie Foundation provided a building in Washington and maintained its administration. Its chief function through the twenties was to serve as an administrative agency for the distribution and management of scientific research funds for foundations—or indeed any source of money for supporting scientific research and having a group of national experts to make decisions and exercise control over the expenditure of grants.

In its post-war reorganization, the NRC had divided itself into a dozen divisions which now included psychology and anthropology as well as the natural and physical sciences. An awareness of the necessary conjunction of social science and natural science, the need for adjusting society to scientific change, expanded the NRC's interests parallel to the social expansion of post-war Taylorism. Industrial development and engineering also played a direct role in the Council's plans and debates. The complex relation between pure and applied ran through the debates of its various administrative boards; and the presence of industrial interests led to conflicts in the definition of the Council's purposes.

The Committee on Scientific Problems of Human Migration reflected the surge toward purity in social science. Its chairman, Robert M. Yerkes, represented a biological approach to psychology which had grown rapidly during the war period, as psychological testing by the government spurred the study of the mechanisms of the mind. E. G. Boring of Harvard and E. L. Thorndike of Columbia joined with Yerkes and others in the psychological aspects of the study. More than any other enterprise of the period, the work of the Committee on Human Migration illustrates the fundamental assumption of the universality and freedom from bias of "scientific" information. Yerkes was willing to argue, in effect, that the analysis of peoples by race, environment, and behavioral characteristics would yield universally useful data for further research by scientists, for social and political reform by government, for increased efficiency by industry. He felt that more of immigration regulations and procedures, shortages and surpluses of labor, the spread of disease and its treatment, the full range of social and physiological phenomena which could come under the rubric of "human migration," might grow from the same body of research.[19]

19. The Committee on Scientific problems of Human Migration, National Research Council, *Reprint and Circular Series*, no. 58.

Hunt and Hoover, then, turned to the NRC, to the National Bureau of Economic Research, and to the Social Science Research Council, warmed by the optimism which radiated from the purveyors of the new sciences of society. Government could serve as the agency for the distribution of the new knowledge and as the formulator of programs founded no longer upon the intuitions of neo-populist do-gooders whose well-meaning ignorance produced chaos, but upon the rigors of scientific study. By the time he became President, Hoover had established relationships with the working institutions of social research and with their sources of funds. He had surrounded himself with men capable of managing communication among the groups as well as presenting to the public in an acceptable form the results of research. He had good reason to feel, as he assumed the responsibilities of the presidency, that he had built a basic groundwork of relationships to provide him with the expert advice on which to base a social revolution in keeping with progressive ideals as he understood them. He had even devised a system of private financing of the continuing scientific study which that revolution required.

The technological optimism which Hoover took with him to the White House was characteristic of a successful publicity campaign to establish the image of engineering efficiency which an enthusiastic public had supported. "The first spokesman of a new dynasty in American politics took the oath of office yesterday," wrote the *New York World* on March 5, 1929. "For the first time since George Washington, a surveyor, was inaugurated as President in 1789, a man trained as an engineer became Chief Executive of the United States." His installation of a telephone on the desk of the president—previous telephone-age presidents had used a booth in an adjoining room—was taken as an indication of his new view of the modern presidency, a symbol of direct and efficient communication, complete with a desk set of push buttons. His inauguration was broadcast nationwide with announcers stationed at the head of Pennsylvania Avenue to describe the parade. The optimism seemed a bit strange to commentators like Will Rogers. Yet even his suspicions voiced the sense of change, the new mood of an active society to end unemployment, to join in an effective battle against poverty.

Mr. Coolidge came into office accidentally and we didn't expect anything. We just thought if this little, inoffensive fellow can keep some of the States from seceding we will all be thankful. But Hoover! Here is just a few things we look to be settled not later than Saturday:

Farm Relief—Now we have never had farm relief in all our history, but we look to him for it.

Prohibition Enforcement—Never had it since it was established, but we expect it from him.

Prosperity—Millions never had it under Coolidge, never had it under anybody, but expect it under Hoover.

And women think he will wash their dishes and look after their babies.

Nothing short of Heaven will we accept under Hoover. Good luck to you, Herb.[20]

Hoover's overtures to the working press had begun during the Commerce Department period when he instituted regular conferences. Those conferences were suspended during the campaign but reinstituted afterwards in a fashion which newsmen found sociable and informal. "Mr. Hoover's frankness," the *New York Times* correspondent wrote, "his assurance of a liberal system of furnishing worthwhile information for publication and his general attitude toward the press conferences brought an extremely favorable reaction likely to work to the benefit of both the Administration and the newspapers."[21] A literary secretary disseminated bits of information designed to amuse the public while it instructed them about the new President's efficient habits: the aforementioned telephone, of course, but also his arrival at his White House desk at the seemingly unprecedented hour of five minutes to nine, his ability to change suits in six minutes—the papers greedily consumed the details.

Underneath the fanfare ran a program: the shifting of the Commerce Department method to the presidency, the reorganization of the presidency—indeed, of the entire executive branch—to become the research clearing house which could modernize American government. The classic method of American social reform was to be brought to the nation as a whole, rather than confined to the local communities and regional associations which had created it in the first place. Surveys, financed by interested national associations of citizens, would collect data, organize it, and interpret it according to the principles and methods

20. To the editor of the *New York Times*, March 5, 1929. It might be worth noting that Rogers' regular correspondence with the editors of the *New York Times* forms a very cogent, Mr. Dooley-like commentary on the period.

21. Richard V. Oulahan, *New York Times*, March 17, 1929.

of the respective sciences they represented. The president would then use the rhetorical power of his office to persuade the public to acquaint itself with the assembled knowledge and to use the various associations which they had formed to implement the changes suggested. If self-interested business and industry could respond to the pressures of scientific analysis, so could citizens in need of hospitals, schools, and play-grounds. There could be a self-operating system of rational social control strikingly similar to the political communities described in 1927 by John Dewey in *The Public and Its Problems*. The Hoover strategy shares with that book an implicit view of party in politics which was current in much of the social science that Hoover's generation admired. The idea of a non-partisan president was more than a reform attitude shared by many progressives, although it was certainly that. American social scientists trained in the writings of James Bryce, acquainted with the views of Moisei Ostrogorski and Roberto Michels, were coming more and more to see a potentially anti-scientific role for party in government, and to single out aspects of industrial democracy which partisan debate could threaten.

If the new reform method resembled the animating philosophy in Dewey's self-governing communities of the rationally self-interested, it bore little resemblance to the political system that had elected President Hoover and might, in the last analysis, be called upon to give his programs practical effect. Morris Cooke's "government-Pasteura" required a purging of politics from the body politic. It is hard to see how Hoover's method could have entailed anything less than that. He was aiming at a rational revolution designed to create a Bellamy-like utopia.

The democratic commitment of American social research demanded that the community provide for its own examination so that it could sustain the programs recommended. The science on which that examination would be based would have to be publicly acceptable. Partisan politics would have to fall before the combined forces of accurate information and acknowledged social need. It was the joint culmination of the history of American reform, of the broadening base of American philanthropy, of the new social sciences, and of the lessons of progressivism. The war to end war was now to be succeeded by the politics to end politics. The only thing Hoover needed was time.

II

AT the heart of Hoover's elaborate plans for his presidency was a national program of social reform, based upon two major innovations. One was the first national survey of the nation's social resources —a counterpart in human terms to the famous survey of natural resources undertaken before the war to establish scientifically the appropriate national priorities concerning waterways and their uses, mineral resources, forests and recreation areas, and the other interests of the conservationists. The President's Research Committee on Social Trends was given a three-year mandate to survey the whole of American society, so that the issues of unemployment, education, old age, medicine, crime, the full panoply of both the new and the traditional reform concerns, could be dealt with in rational, scientifically organized form. Like the survey of natural resources, the social survey was to transcend the archaic boundaries of the states with their inevitably entrapping politics. The second major innovation involved a thoroughgoing reorganization of the executive branch of the government, focussing on the Department of the Interior as the new center of social reform and continuing social research. Hoover's appointment of Ray Lyman Wilbur, a university president and medical educator, as Secretary of the Interior signalled the beginning of that change.

That the intervention of the Depression effectively cancelled both innovations can easily divert the historian's attention from the fact that the plan posed problems in the politics of social research which were no more resolved by the energetic optimism of the New Deal than they were generated by the catastrophe that befell the Hoover Administration. Hoover had planned the whole program as part of a campaign for a second successful administration; yet the national scope of the program—its deliberately-designed bypassing of politics—put it on the same collision course with Congress which had destroyed generation after generation of national reformers and would continue even in times of prosperity to defeat the efforts of national-interest presidents to overcome the Congressional commitment to constituency interests. To the extent that the inundation of the Hoover strategy by the Depression consigns the program to the limbo of things that never came to be, the opportunity has been lost to examine a recurring set of problems triggered by Hoover's national survey.

The initial plans for the study of social trends were worked out by French Strother, the presidential assistant to whom Hoover had assigned the study of social issues and relations with the departments concerned.[22] According to Strother, the germ of the idea had come from Hoover himself as a result of inquiries he had made of social scientists that had revealed a shocking lack of data on which to base policies for coping with social problems.[23] Strother's contacts in the academic community led him to Howard W. Odum of the University of North Carolina, whose interest in the recently organized Social Science Research Council prompted him to suggest the forthcoming Hanover, New Hampshire, meetings of the Council as a possible forum for discussion of the problem. The Council's summer meetings had been, for several years, a center of communication and intellectual stimulation in the social sciences. Organized by Charles Merriam, professor of political science at the University of Chicago and the Council's founder and head, the summer meetings served many purposes. including the setting of policy for the coming year's distribution of grants, the bringing together of representatives of the foundations which provided the funds and the academics who profited, and the mixing of local, state, and federal officials who might provide useful ideas and benefit from the discussions. Held in a fraternity house in the isolation of the Dartmouth campus, the occasion provided recreation and a Chautauqua-like atmosphere—not unfamiliar to many participants—for reflection and inspiration.

William F. Ogburn, a sociologist in the process of moving from Columbia, where he had been closely associated with Wesley Mitchell, to Chicago, where he would become associated with Charles Merriam, was the man most immediately interested in the prospect of a genuine,

22. Undated memorandum. E. E. Hunt papers, Hoover Institute.

23. Minutes of March 14, 1932. Strother addressing the Committee, New York. These discussions are fully documented in the stenographic transcripts of the meetings, a sizeable body of material. Six sets were made. Those used here are in the Ogburn and Merriam papers in the University of Chicago Libraries, and in the Hunt papers at the Hoover Institute. The meetings were held in the Park Avenue offices of the Social Science Research Council.

scientific social survey. As a result of the Hanover discussions and at Odum's urging, Ogburn and Strother conferred in Washington on September 6. Plans for a dinner meeting with the President were already underway, with a guest list suggested by Odum. The assemblage was to include Merriam, Mitchell, Ogburn, Odum, Shelby Harrison of the Russell Sage Foundation, the new Secretary of the Interior Ray Lyman Wilbur, Strother, and the President. The device of a small dinner party was one which the President liked to use for bringing together members of such groups, informing himself about their programs, and persuading them to serve the government.[24]

Ogburn came out of his conference with Strother feeling that neither Strother nor the President had a clear idea of what he wanted. "Hoover wants us to tell him what he wants," was the impression Strother had communicated and which Ogburn related to Mitchell, "and that is why we are invited to dine." Hoover knew that he had been successful in his work in the field of commerce and production and wanted to set up programs having to do with such problems as "the family, housing, recreation, child welfare," according to Ogburn. "I think he has in mind the reconstruction of the Department of Interior . . . in such a way as to function largely in this field."[25]

Hoover's ideas on the subject were somewhat clearer than Ogburn had perceived, although there were inherent differences in point of view never to be adequately explored. Hoover, for example, assumed a unanimity on the meaning of "survey" which did not actually exist. Shelby Harrison, in his later history of the survey method, placed the beginning of the survey as a method of social reform in the 1890's at the earliest, with the Pittsburgh Survey of 1907 as the first true example.[26] The earlier ones—he didn't actually look much earlier than 1891—he dismissed as "engineering" surveys, not social. Yet the difference betwe n an engineering survey, which looked to the mechanical and industrial inefficiency of the city as the source of its social problems, and a philanthropic reform survey, which, in the work of Harrison's Russell Sage Foundation,

24. Memorandum of November 1, 1929. Hunt papers.

25. Ogburn to Mitchell, September 6, 1929. Ogburn papers, University of Chicago Libraries.

26. Shelby M. Harrison, "Development and Spread of Social Surveys," in Allen Eaton and Shelby M. Harrison, *A Bibliography of Social Survey* (New York, 1930).

at least, emphasized traditional problems like child welfare and education, was profound. In addition, the question remained whether social scientists like Ogburn, Merriam, and Odum accepted the tradition of the survey concept at all in their habitual emphasis upon the definition and measurement of the behavioral factors in American society rather than statistical correlations of disease, degrees of poverty, and the number and condition of tenement buildings or badly cultivated fields. The general optimism that brought the group together concealed differences in point of view that might not be easily resolved, even with Strother's enthusiasm and Hoover's working plan for government reorganization.

The Department of the Interior, according to this plan, would be divided into two parts, a "Division of Public Works" and a "Division of Education, Health, and Recreation," each under the direction of an Assistant Secretary.[27] The selection of his friend Ray Lyman Wilbur as Secretary indicates the approach Hoover intended to take.[28] Wilbur was quick to note the resemblances between a university president and Cabinet member. Approaching the Bureau of the Budget and the Congressional Appropriations Committees required some polishing up of the "art of extracting funds," but largely because, to Wilbur's way of thinking, "budgets and politics usually make no more successful mixture than do gasoline and alcohol."[29] Wilbur also noted the familiarity to a university administrator of private funds available to the Department for its public projects, and he was delighted to see the accustomed contributors: John D. Rockefeller, Julius Rosenwald, Carnegie, Brookings—in many respects, he need never have left home. Wilbur could provide the Hoover Administration with the classic talents of the turn-of-the-century university president: a persuasive familiarity with philanthropists willing to support education and an acceptable voice in the community of the new academics. Whether or not that era had passed was another matter.

A national academic community had begun to move beyond the walls of particular institutions, not only in intellectual interests—that

27. *The Memoirs of Ray Lyman Wilbur*, ed. Edgar Eugene Robinson and Paul Carroll Edwards (Palo Alto, Cal., 1960), p. 467.

28. See Strother to Edward Lowry, undated. Container 1–G /961 600, Hoover Library. Hoover's general reorganization plan.

29. Wilbur, *Memoirs*, p. 408.

development had begun in the 1880's—but in the search for funds for research and publication. The reorganizations of the foundations and the development of national academic associations with funds to manage had begun to change the role of the university president, leaving him the custodial manager of an institution whose "mind" was being managed within national professions. University administrators had traditionally concerned themselves with the mechanisms of education, not the mechanisms of research. Even the more enlightened—and Wilbur was certainly among them if compared, say, with his predecessor, David Starr Jordan—assumed a relatively simple, fixed content, a sturdy body of knowledge which was the basic subject matter of education. Like the Taylor industrial model which assumed that the products of the industrial process were stable enough to encourage emphasis upon efficiencies in the method of production, the intellectual system which Wilbur and Hoover sought to manage seemed to them to presuppose a relatively fixed body of material which could be collected and analyzed—and then administered.

Even men like Ogburn and Merriam who were engaged in violating that understanding by expanding research horizons so rapidly as to make the older methods of administering education obsolete shared with Hoover and Wilbur an optimism which was not to last through their generation. The optimism of the social science of the 1920's rested on a faith in the natural, rational limitations of the social process. It assumed the availability of finite bodies of data to which precise instruments of analysis could be applied, once those instruments had been perfected. Such analysis would yield programs of social and political behavior which would insure progress, at a sane and sedate pace, toward the ultimate human happiness. In that sense Hoover and his social scientists were of the same generation, riding in the same boat. But the question became whether Hoover's sense of the industrial engineering survey, Harrison's commitment to the social survey of the professional social worker, and the social science of Mitchell, Merriam, and Ogburn, provided them all with the same set of oars.

The organization of a great deal of social research during and after World War I made Interior a logical place for the development of scientific programs of social welfare. The "new conservationists" like John

Merriam had moved toward conceptions of the scientific relationship between land resources and social welfare as exemplified in the National Research Council's Migration Study. Indeed the whole reorganized program of the NRC represented the broadening of a tradition borne almost exclusively in the latter part of the 19th century by the Geological Survey. The chart for the social research program, prepared for preliminary discussion, reveals many of the essentials of the traditional method that Hoover sought to modernize. The President, through the Secretary of the Interior and his administrative assistant, would control a conference on "social objectives" charged with producing a program for the "national public." The public would be directly involved in the study through "group representation" and an "advisory group of specialists" would be given the responsibility of overseeing the "working personnel (research and planning)" engaged in the studies.[30] These are assumptions about the relationship between group representation and the general public traceable to the theory of interest groups and pressure groups that was evolving in the 1920's.

Ogburn and Odum urged on Charles Merriam and Mitchell an acceptance of the President's invitation. The latter were skeptical, but for different reasons: Mitchell, because he was not sure that so broad a study could be done in such a short period of time, Merriam, because he was doubtful about the readiness of the newly-organized Council for such a public role. The problems of relating the drive for objective social research to the politics of the presidency had a divisive effect on the four men. Ogburn and Odum were more deeply committed to the absolute objectivity of social research, yet far more willing to move directly to the service of the President as a non-partisan representative of the nation as a whole. Mitchell and Merriam, although in different degrees, respected political involvement as a part of social research, yet shied away from making the social science community an instrument of presidential policy-making. All four had come out of the generation that had fed liberally on James Bryce's injunction that the only source of real political understanding was politics itself, and action in politics the only true method of attaining that understanding. Yet how to promote the utility

30. Chart accompanying original memorandum, September 1929. Secretary's file. Container 1–G /964, Hoover Library.

of social science without tainting the purity of research with partisan-ship would play an increasingly divisive role.

On September 26 the advisory group had its first dinner with the President. For those who had not met Hoover before, it was a startling experience. In the after-dinner discussion of the purposes of the study, Hoover began by asking each man present to give him a ten-minute statement of his views of the importance of such a conference. He neither interrupted nor interspersed comments of his own as each man spoke, only nodding at the end of the statement to indicate that the next speaker was to begin. When the entire group had finished, Hoover, who had made no notes during the comments, delivered a summary of the various points made, asking at the end if that was indeed the group's interpretation of what had been said. There being no dissent from his summary, he announced his approval and his sponsorship of the confer-ence, and after a few brief remarks, he left the room. Several members of the group felt a school-boyish sense of having been involved in an examination. Anticipating their own response as citizens in the presence of the President of the United States, they had nonetheless expected to be put at their ease by a contemporary experienced in the wielding of authority and fundamentally humane. Hoover was both of these, but in response to his own shyness or aloofness—his critics would soon call it "coldness"—he had adopted a manner of executive distance which fitted the current image of the business leader: terse, efficiently crisp, analyti-cal, objectively detached, capable of grasping problems and demon-strating that grasp. The "bully" enthusiasm of Theodore Roosevelt, like the booster collegiality of Harding, was out of fashion. Yet as the response to Hoover's manner came more and more to indicate, even those who approved of his methods sensed the lack of something essen-tial to a president, however indefinable.

The weeks which separated the first dinner meeting with the Presi-dent from the formal public announcement in mid-December were filled with the work of organization, not only of a formal prospectus to be submitted first to the President and then to prospective financial backers, but also, within the White House, of the relation of the Com-mittee's work to the administration. Like the conferences of the Com-merce Department years, the social trends groups was to be an example of the new departure from the old presidential role of calling for public examination only after public demand had indicated the need. Men like Franklin Roosevelt had admired Wilson's organization of a wartime government "from the top down,"[31] the call for management and control from knowledgeable groups acting for the public in the public interest, but governed by their own understanding of that interest. The function of the executive was to analyze public need and articulate it to the public. Democracy would enter into the implementation of programs, but the initiative for analysis and explanation would have to come from the top.

The Committee submitted its plan to the President on October 21, less than a month after its first meeting and three days before the first crashing jolts the stock market gave the society which the Committee had been asked to examine. As a result, the Committee's work would take place against the background of a deepening Depression; and the submission of its report to President Hoover in January 1933 would document in its own academic fashion the destruction of hope of the Hoover administration.

The Committee informed the President in its initial proposal that "after some three weeks of investigation, [it] has found that there exist data in sufficient quantity and accuracy to give assurance that a survey of recent social changes in a number of important fields is possible."[32] They listed some twenty-four separate fields, from "population, food and natural resources," their first category, to "public administration," their last, and encompassing what was intended as a thorough analysis of the "kind of people" who inhabited the United States, and the nature and quality of their lives. Whether such data actually existed reflects a dilemma which social research groups continually faced in their effort to cope with the tension between the reform tradition of collecting information to support a position already obvious to the reformers, and the new aim of dispassionate objectivity. "To safeguard the conclusions against bias," the Committee informed readers in a foreword which

31. Quoted in Frank Freidel, *Franklin D. Roosevelt: The Apprenticeship* (Boston, 1952), p. 319.

32. *Report of the President's Committee on Social Research,* with letter of transmittal, Wesley C. Mitchell to French Strother, Oct. 21, 1929. Container 1-G/967, Hoover Library.

opened each of the supplemental monographs the Committee published,

the researches were restricted to the analysis of objective data. Since the available data do not cover all phases of the many subjects studied, it was often impossible to answer questions of deep interest. . . . Discussions which are not limited by the severe requirements of scientific method have their uses, which the Committee rates highly. Yet an investigation initiated by the President, in the hope that the findings may be of service in dealing with the national problems of today and tomorrow, should be kept as free as possible from emotional coloring and unverifiable conjectures. Accuracy and reliability are more important in such an undertaking than liveliness or zeal to do good. If men and women of all shades of opinion from extreme conservatism to extreme radicalism can find a common basis of secure knowledge to build upon, the social changes of the future may be brought in larger measure under the control of social intelligence.[33]

The freeing of data collection and interpretation from the pressures of reform did not preclude their use in reform; but it did complicate the Committee's sense of its own purpose. Being a social scientist was different from being a citizen.

To refrain from expressions of approval and disapproval, not to make propaganda for any cause, is difficult for the student of social changes, for as private citizens, the Committee's collaborators have their individual scales of value, and some are eager advocates of certain reforms. But, as sharers in this enterprise, one and all have striven faithfully to discover what is, and to report their findings uncolored by their personal likes and dislikes, or by their hopes and fears of what may be.[34]

Part of Wesley Mitchell's purpose in forming the National Bureau of Economic Research and much of the interest in the forming of a continuing research body like the Social Science Research Council was to facilitate the collection of social research information in an environment sufficiently aloof from problems of social reform and politics to give the collection a neutral comprehensiveness rendering it universally useful. Whether or not a move so obviously into government, into the White House itself, could damage the essential accumulation of data was obscured by the Committee's initial insistence that such data did indeed exist.

The initial proposal estimated a budget request of $550,000 to $560,000. The White House had first suggested a budget of $400,000, to be

33. Leonard D. White, *Trends in Public Administration* (New York, 1933), p. vi.
34. *Recent Social Trends in the United States* (New York, 1933), p. xciv.

divided \$200,000 for research, \$100,000 for conferences, and \$100,000 for "follow-up," in which was included the whole publicity campaign for the program: publication of the research, magazine and newspaper campaigns, and radio broadcasts. That such a campaign, scheduled presumably for early 1932, was not to be considered "political" was part of the interesting set of illusions about politics which surrounded the Committee's formative stages. Those more familiar with recent reorganizations in the Rockefeller Foundation, informed the White House that there had been increased effort to concentrate on research, leaving publication and conferences to other donors. The decision was made to request a lump sum, undefined except by the program's basic objective: social research.[35]

That the President had already stated specifically that he wished the request for funds to come from him, not from the Committee or the SSRC, points once again to the curiously non-political role which Hoover conceived of the Committee as playing. Those interested in the particular positions of Foundations in the 1920's were aware of the growing concern with the necessity of distinguishing "social" from "political," and of the desire among old-school philanthropists to remove themselves from whatever connection thay had once had with political reform itself. The changes in names—Laura Spelman Rockefeller Memorial to Spelman Fund—and the changes in vocabulary—the increasing use of and sharpening of the distinction between politics and administration—all raised questions about the extent to which social science had expanded the philanthropic concept of objective social research or, as it might be more critically put, the extent to which the anti-political commitments of the foundations had reshaped the vocabulary of the social sciences. In any event, it became clear that Hoover did not view his identification with the Committee as being "political" in any sense that would violate a philanthropist's interest in being non-political or a social scientist's desire to be objective.

Strother wrote George E. Vincent, president of the Rockefeller Foundation on the day the Committee's prospectus was received. Strother assured Vincent that President Hoover "long had in mind, as one of his chief opportunities for service to the country . . . the conscious organiza-

35. Ogburn to Odum, October 22, 1929. Ogburn papers.

tion of all possible practicable means by which the Government might inspire, promote, or guide both public and private thought and action of benefit in the field of social problems." In his search for method, Strother explained, Hoover had requested the advice of a "small group of eminent sociologists and social workers . . . . They were to provide a plan which, if carried through, would produce a rounded and explicit picture of the whole American social scene, with such a wealth of facts and statistics and conclusions as to form a new and unique basis of thought and action for social scientists, social workers, and those officers of government who, like himself, have a special responsibility in relation to such problems." Strother attached the Committee's report, and, in his effort to make Hoover's specific responsibility in the matter clear, continued: "The President would wish to assume responsibility for the prosecution of the researches, and to sponsor the reports and experiments supplementary to them. He regards them as of fundamental importance, and certain to be of the highest public as well as scientific value."[36]

In some respects, what Hoover was doing in sponsoring the Committee himself and requesting the funds for it in his own name was no different from what he had done in the Commerce Department where he had employed the same techniques, nor was it different from the sort of thing Wilson had done, during the war, as president. But to translate these methods to the presidency in peacetime might not be regarded as reasonable continuities. Certainly the question of sponsorship and its relation to financing were to prove more complex than Strother or the President seemed to see at that moment. Strother spoke with Edward Eyre Hunt, whose work on the Mitchell study of economic trends had led Hoover to want him directly involved in the new group. Hunt felt that Strother had "hastily transmitted" the proposal to the Rockefeller Foundation. He saw the missing element from the Wilsonian wartime method which Hoover had used for Commerce Department committees: the joint committee of representatives of interest groups. Although no one seemed to realize it at the time, the "experts" were in fact the central interest group. The plan, as Hunt pointed out, did not combine eminent but publicly unknown specialists in various fields with eminent

36. Strother to Vincent, October 22, 1929. Container 1-G/967, Hoover Library.

and well-known "practitioners" who had influence within the communities to be affected by the proposals. "In the case of the report on 'Business Cycles and Unemployment' in 1923," he wrote in obvious annoyance, "it was not the fact that Wesley C. Mitchell, a world authority on business cycles, said that there were business cycles, but that Owen D. Young as Chairman of the sponsoring committee, and Secretary Hoover as Chairman of the President's Conference on Unemployment said that there were business cycles . . . . Economists had talked about business cycles for at least a century, but the thought had not percolated into the business mind."[37] But he was willing to concede that the President's personal sponsorship of the committee might answer some of his criticisms.

Strother assured Hunt that the President wished to sponsor the Committee himself; but Hunt still pressed for a wider group: Root and Rosenwald as humanitarians, Owen D. Young as "an enlightened businessman," a trio of "representatives of the newest in modern technology," Robert M. Hutchins, Charles Lindbergh, and Orville Wright. But, as Strother reiterated, this was to be the President's own project. No others were to be named. No oversight had been committed.

Hunt's concept of a more public point of view and his persistent assertions of it were to have interesting consequences. Returning the list of projects to Mitchell late in November, he asked for a revision of it. "The President wants the various projects . . . reduced to a language 'understanded of the people.' Could you do this for him . . .?"[38] Mitchell made it clear that he had no intention of complying and that the request should have been sent to Ogburn, now designated "Director of Research." Hunt was going to become thoroughly familiar with the manners of the academic community before the project was done. "My note . . . should have been a little clearer," he apologized: "What [the President] asked us to do was to put the thing in shape for public announcement, and although I have not yet learned to take the President's suggestions as royal commands, I suppose that there was some reason for not handing the thing back to Mr. Ogburn."[39]

37. Hunt to Strother, November 2, 1929. Hunt papers.
38. Hunt to Ogburn, November 22, 1929. Ogburn papers.
39. Hunt to Mitchell, November 30, 1929. Hunt papers.

Members of the Committee, too, had begun to have misgivings about the nature and extent of the President's "sponsorship." Early in December—public announcement still not having been made—the Committee decided to incorporate itself as the President's Research Committee on Social Trends and to make the request to the Rockefeller Foundation directly themselves on their own behalf. The decision to take that step had undoubtedly been influenced by behind-the-scenes information, probably with Beardsley Ruml as the source, that the Rockefellers were uncertain about the appropriateness of their financing of a group so prominently "of" the federal government. The Foundation had on several occasions been attacked openly by Congress for what the Rockefellers considered a misunderstanding of their philanthropic interest in the way the country was governed. The first report of the Spelman Fund had warned of the danger of confusing political and administrative objectives. "The Spelman Fund has no political objectives; it is interested only in helping to provide experience and wisdom in executing public programs which have already been adopted and which are no longer matters of political controversy."[40] As the White House's involvement with the Committee would come more and more to indicate, the line was not so easy to define.

The Rockefeller Foundation delayed its decision until mid-December. E. E. Day had become the program's chief backer.[41] Day had been the main support of social and political research in the Foundation, fighting a tendency on the part of board members to withdraw into medical and scientific programs and leave the social field to the more limited Spelman Fund. Day, too, had been the man who continued to press for a more active international program. The decision to use Chicago as at least an initial center for the Committee's organization had helped in the Rockefeller decision. It was far enough away from Washington to allay fears of undue influence from the White House. Hoover had requested that the Committee locate in the Capital,[42] and some among the academics preferred Chicago as a center in order to avoid a bias dictated by "New York and Harvard."[43]

40. Spelman Fund of New York, *Report for 1929 and 1930* (New York, 1931), p. 12.
41. Odum to Ogburn, September 21, 1929. Ogburn papers.
42. Hunt to Mitchell, December 19, 1929. Hunt papers.
43. Odum to Ogburn, October 23, 1929. Ogburn papers.

The question of location was finally resolved and on December 14, at a Chicago meeting attended by members of the Committee, Day, Strother, and Ruml, a grant of $560,000 was announced. At that meeting, too, were established the basic ground rules of committee responsibility: that its editorial authority would be complete, that editors would have the power of revision and rejection, that authors would not be allowed to withdraw work once it had been submitted. Those stipulations were to lead to some interesting conflicts, but they were observed.

The relation between the administration and the Committee remained a source of confusion throughout the life of the project. Mitchell was made chairman, Merriam, vice-chairman. Shelby Harrison acted as secretary-treasurer, Ogburn as director of research, Odum as assistant director, and Edward Eyre Hunt as executive secretary. The fact that Hunt and Mitchell were familiar both to one another and to the President from the economic study of 1923 gave the administration a sense of involvement in the work of the Committee which somehow failed to allow for the differences between Secretary Hoover and President Hoover, and whether those differences might indicate the necessity of a different mode of approach on the part of everyone concerned. Whether as a deliberate plan or not, no Cabinet member had been named to the Committee, presumably because the President wanted it that way; and handwritten memoranda in the Hoover papers testify to his intention to involve himself directly in the Committee's deliberations. Hoover made several attempts to get some kind of "affiliation" between the Committee and several others of his study groups, all of which were rejected by the Committee. Still, it was *his* project, now, and he wanted to make certain that he could utilize it effectively.

Hoover's communications with the Committee were through Hunt and Strother. Hunt wrote to Ogburn on January 15, 1930, that the President wanted results to begin coming to his desk in a year, that he wanted very much to "*use*" the report. Two days later, the President communicated, again through Hunt, the information that he "wanted light" on the subject of old-age security. Ten days later Hunt reminded Ogburn that the President wanted material to be given directly to him as progress reports for action, and he cited Luther Gulick's report on old-age security problems in New York as an example of the sort of thing he expected.[44]

Hunt's position as mediator worked both ways; and he did his best to translate the Committee's academic sense of independence to the President. The conference with the President which produced Hunt's letter of January 15 had contained considerably more presidential impatience than Hunt elected to pass on to Ogburn. Hunt had had the problem of telling the President that the original schedule, which had called for the submission of preliminary reports by the end of 1931, was going to be held up by difficulties involved in obtaining and processing data from the census of 1930 in time. "The President said he hoped it was not going to be a job of rewarming Census data," Hunt confided to himself in a memorandum dictated after the meeting. "The President said that questions like old-age pensions were coming up and that action would be necessary. Couldn't this be explored without waiting for Census data?" he asked, concluding in a remarkably revelatory aside that "to be of use to him he must have the results of the study during his term . . . that he did not expect to be re-elected."[45]

The question of "use" was to pressure the study from the beginning to the end, with both sides, the Committee and the administration, undergoing extensive education and re-education in the essential politics of the undertaking. The fact of the Depression bore in, changing in its effect as the general attitude toward the Depression changed. It played the Banquo at every meeting, an increasingly threatening presence as a program begun to perfect prosperity became something entirely different. But *what* had it become? Could its objectives be redefined in the confusion which surrounded the search for a definition of the basic economic and social condition of the country itself? A commitment to scientific objectivity, like the commitment to a survey of "trends" over a given period of time, required the Committee to establish a position for itself far enough above the level of contemporary turbulence to steer a calm, considered course.

As the Committee would once again reiterate in its "Prefatory Note," "The chapters and monographs are prepared with the primary purpose

44. Letters in Hunt papers.
45. January 14, 1930. Hunt papers.

of revealing major social questions. They present records, not opinions; such substantial stuff as may serve as a basis for social action, rather than recommendations as to the form which action should take."[46] Such statements would form a continuing litany of near-apology. "Certain topics are excluded because for one reason or another they could not be fitted into the Committee's scheme. The current business depression is not explained."[47] And on it went. "We were not commissioned to lead the people into some new land of promise," concluded the "Findings," "but to retrace our recent wanderings, to indicate and interpret our ways and rates of change, to provide maps of progress, make observations of danger zones, point out hopeful roads of advance, helpful in finding a more intelligent course in our next phase of our progress . . . and we trust that our endeavors may contribute to the readier growth of the new ideals, ideas, and emotional values of the next period . . . ."[48]

Objectivity and distance, could they be sustained in the clutter of events? Some thought not. "Writing this preface in late 1932," Leonard White commented in his supplementary monograph, "and faced with the rapid march of events . . . the author feels at one and the same time the necessity of re-interpretation of the material gathered nearly two years ago, and the futility of such reconsideration until we have passed out of the whirling tempest in which we now exist."[49]

The question of utility can be seen, too, in the periodic debates over prose style which the White House could foresee would limit the public appeal of the report. Strother had suggested at the beginning that Mark Sullivan be called in as editor and given a place on the Committee, or Ray Stannard Baker, or anyone, for that matter, with an appreciation of prose.[50] The Committee considered a search among historians as a possible answer; but Arthur Schlesinger, who was approached first, thought his work on the History of American Life series with Dixon Ryan Fox would take all his spare time, although he was much interested in the Committee's work and attended periodic meetings as an ad-

---

46. *Recent Social Trends*, p. xciii.
47. *Ibid.*
48. *Ibid.*, p. lxxv.
49. White, *Trends*, p. vii.
50. Strother to Ogburn, May 21, 1930. Ogburn papers.

viser.[51] Other names were mentioned—Allan Nevins and Carl Becker —but in the final analysis, historians were excluded.

"Excluded" is not too strong a term. Inherent in the debates among social scientists in the 1920's, although rarely documentable in any clear form, was a continuing conflict with history, not only with historians that is evident—but in a subtler sense with history itself. The focus upon the objectivity of facts, the photographic present with its injunction to "capture and record," the necessity of producing through research "new ideals, ideas, and emotional values of the next period" carried with it an inevitable implication that previous values and ideals could distort an objective view of the present. In simple professional terms, too, many of the social sciences of the 1920's had been breakaways from history; and while that spawning process could be documented in the forming of the national associations, the intellectual import of it could be seen in the assertion of a positive independence of past doctrines and historical formalism. Charles Beard's presidential address to the political scientists was clouded with warnings articulated more fully in personal meetings where he could bristle undisguisedly. His position is clear enough in *The Nature of the Social Sciences*, published in 1934 as a result of his debates in the Commission on the Social Studies. Yet even he came close to a rejection of history by introducing a kind of revisionism which made the writing of history a tool of present-oriented historians seeking to further or obstruct reform.

Philosophically, the issue went to the heart of the social sciences of the 1920's. The writings of John Dewey had based the test of principles on their relevance to present experience, not on past doctrine. That sense of the present made history either the tool or the objective of social revolution. If history was to be made a social science, it would have to be both scientific and socially functional like all other social sciences. In history the potential contradictions inherent in an effort to bring science and social function together seemed clearest. A utilitarian political bias could be used as an attack upon the writing of history, a proof of its lack of objectivity. Yet for economists and political scientists from the 1880's forward, a social science which did not strive for utility was a contradiction in terms. The effort to relate history to the social sciences re-

51. Ogburn to Odum, May 1, 1930. Ogburn papers.

vealed the distinctly revolutionary flavor which the search for a union of objectivity and relevance tended to conceal.

The new social science, then, dominated the selection of staff and the direction of the report. Odum's social research institute at the University of North Carolina accounted for three chapters: T. J. Woofter, Jr.'s "The Status of Racial and Ethnic Groups," Clarence Heer's "Taxation and Public Finance," and Odum's "Public Welfare Activities." Mitchell's influence can be seen in the selection of Edwin F. Gay and Leo Wolman for "Trends in Economic Organization," as well as in Wolman's "Labor Groups in the Social Structure" (with Gustav Peck) and Robert S. Lynd's "The People as Consumers" (with Alice C. Hanson). Merriam, Ogburn, and the "Chicago School" are reflected in Leonard White's "Public Administration," Carroll Wooddy's "The Growth of Governmental Functions," Charles H. Judd's "Education," Edwin H. Sutherland and C. E. Gehlke's "Crime and Punishment," S. P. Breckinridge's "The Activities of Women Outside the Home," two chapters by Ogburn, "The Influence of Invention and Discovery" and "The Family and Its Functions" (with Clark Tibbitts) and, Merriam's concluding chapter, "Government and Society." A solid representation of the new foundation executives also appear: Lawrence K. Frank of the General Education Board of the Rockefeller Foundation ("Childhood and Youth"), Frederick P. Keppel of the Carnegie Corporation ("The Arts in Social Life"), and Sydnor H. Walker of the Rockefeller Foundation ("Privately Supported Social Work").

The interconnections with government are clear enough in the lengthy acknowledgments to government bureaus for their statistical and research aid; but the involvement of philanthropically-supported research institutions is also important. Warren S. Thompson and P. K. Whelpton of the Scripps Foundation for Research in Population Problems provided the basic essay, "The Population of the Nation," which opened the volume. The Brookings Institution, the Russell Sage Foundation, the Milbank Memorial Fund, and the various universities associated with those and other philanthropic agencies gave staff time and clerical assistance to the Committee.

The selection of staff and the assignment of chapters was done by the Committee itself at its meetings; but the actual research projects were under the direction of the individual authors. Nevertheless, they used Committee influence as well as Committee funds to establish relationships with the various agencies, governmental and private, which had research facilities or data which authors would find useful. The interlocking directorships represented just within the Committee itself gave useful leverage to requests for aid. Merriam and Mitchell virtually controlled the Social Science Research Council, while Merriam helped direct the Spelman Fund, and Mitchell the National Bureau of Economic Research. Odum, too, was influential in the SSRC while directing his own research institute at North Carolina. Shelby Harrison was another route of access to the foundations, while Hunt and Strother had considerable leeway in requesting aid from government agencies. The pages and pages of acknowledgment testify to the breadth of the net cast by the Committee in its search for information and active engagement in research. The report serves an interesting function as an inventory of the network of Americans and American institutions committed to social science.

The White House suggested in February 1930 that it would be a good idea to appoint a woman to the Committee and asked for a list of names. The Committee submitted a list of twenty-two prominent women, including Jane Addams, Frances Perkins, and Ida Tarbell, most of whom were pencilled off by the White House. After deliberation, the President informed the Committee that he had selected three: Lillian M. Gilbreth, Alice Hamilton, and Florence Cabot Thorne. Lillian Gilbreth, wife of the scientific management expert Frank Gilbreth, was a specialist in her own right in the field of industrial psychology. Dr. Hamilton, of the Harvard Medical School, was a leader in the field of public health. Florence Thorne, Secretary of the American Federation of Labor, was added at the White House and was as close to a "political" figure as the President seemed willing to get. By direction of the President, the Committee voted for one of the three, and Dr. Hamilton was elected to join the group.[52]

Ogburn had promised Hunt as early as January 1930 that the Committee could give material to the President beginning in 1931, possibly February, and extending throughout the year, as long as the President

52. Strother to Mitchell, February 21, 1930. Hunt papers.

did not want the material in final, published form. "I am pretty sure that the President will insist upon having a free hand as to the use of material turned over to him," Hunt wrote. "Plans should be made with the possibility in mind that anything given to him may be published."[53] Ogburn at first saw no difficulty in conceding to the President his right to any Committee information he wanted; but others, even Ogburn, would eventually find that view of the Committee's relationship highly questionable, to say the least. In April the President asked that the Committee's study of crime include material on the relation between organized crime and immigration. "This may be difficult," Ogburn wrote, "but I think it can be done."[54] Edwin H. Sutherland and C. E. Gehlke, who were preparing the report, apparently did not agree. Census figures on prisoners were available only through 1923, and they were scanty, even if they did show that the percentage of foreign-born white prisoners of both sexes had declined significantly between 1910 and 1923. A statement to that effect was put in to meet the President's request. The authors did not trust the information sufficiently to expand upon it or to include it in their own conclusions. They did seek, basically, to argue that there was no crime wave in the United States in 1930, that the tendency was toward more severe laws at all levels of government and more effective enforcement, and that isolated situations in Chicago or New York had been dramatized beyond their statistical significance.[55]

A copy of the Crime report went to the President in mid-September and he immediately requested an additional copy to present to the Commission on Law Enforcement. Ogburn refused the request, explaining to Strother as carefully as he could that "while the report was a scientific one in the sense that the conclusions were drawn from data . . . it would be a report which would be very easily misunderstood . . . a leak resulting in publicity would be bad."[56] Hunt in particular had difficulty understanding the Committee's position, not only with regard to its seeming efforts to guard the uses to which its work would be put—he thought he had made the President's desire to control the project abundantly

53. Hunt to Ogburn, January 27, 1930. Ogburn papers.
54. Ogburn to Odum, April 8, 1930. Ogburn papers.
55. *Recent Social Trends*, pp. 1114–1167.
56. Ogburn to Hunt, September 18, 1930. Ogburn to Odum, September 25, 1930. Ogburn papers.

clear—but even with regard to its insistence upon its "scientific" language and organization. He felt that the demand for technical detail had begun to override the ultimate function of the report, but even there his idea of function had begun to change and one begins to wonder if he and the Committee had ever really agreed. Odum was quick to inform him that he "of all people should not use the same tactics against us which the critics of Mr. Hoover use against him."[57] That the function of social science in the context of political life was at issue remained a point too critical for discussion between them, although the fact that it was recognized can be spelled out in the recurrent clashes between the Committee and the White House, as well as in the Committee itself.

Others were equally confused over the nature and purpose of the Committee. Members of Congress had taken the announcement as an opportunity to collect whatever drops of patronage might be encouraged to fall their way. Strother dutifully forwarded their letters listing deserving constituents, usually school teachers or social workers, who might serve the Committee, to Ogburn with notes appended recommending that he ignore them.[58] The White House received letters and telegrams from men like the President of the Metropolitan Insurance Company, the Marketing Managers of the Buick Motor Company, management executives of Sears Roebuck, and the National Association of Credit Men congratulating the President on the appointment of the Committee, which they assumed to be for purposes of guiding sales policy for their various enterprises.[59] The businessmen were not as far off the mark as many of the participants in the Committee's work might have thought. The Committee on Recent Economic Changes had been advertised to the business community on such a basis. The ideal of serving the business community so that the latter could serve the public through more efficient production, lower prices, and higher wages— the Taylorist canon that Hoover had adopted—was also shared by social scientists like Wesley Mitchell and other progressive social scientists whose commitment to free enterprise did not stifle their utopian dreams.

57. Odum to Ogburn, April 15, 1930. Ogburn papers.
58. Senator W. J. Harris, to Strother, December 26, 1929; Strother to Ogburn. Container 1E/232, Hoover Library.
59. Hunt papers. Box 32, Container 1E/232, Hoover Library.

Hoover's initial plea to Mitchell to join the Commerce Department in 1921 had expressed sentiments shared by many who, like Mitchell, had struggled with inadequate standards of measurement and sources of information in the war agencies. "If the Department is to become the economic interpreter to the American people (and they badly need one)," Hoover had written, "it has simply got to be stiffened up with stronger economic operators."[60] Mitchell, too, had expressed concern over the growing separation between business economics and academic research in economics. The question of what role the government would or should play in bringing them together was a restatement of a dilemma as old as the progressive movement itself. One of Mitchell's first responses to the early days of the financial crisis was to request directly of Hoover that he ask Congress for two million dollars to study family spending. Hoover responded, as he did to all such requests, that the funds would have to come from private sources.

Hoover's direct connection with many American philanthropists had led him to feel that he could press for such studies to be undertaken by privately financed groups of his choosing. It was the classic method of entrepreneurial philanthropy: the persuasive search by responsible agents for funds needed for research programs designed to benefit the public. It had served Hoover successfully for some fourteen years by the time he sought to bring it to the presidency. The White House acted as Julius Rosenwald's intermediary in his contribution to an illiteracy campaign. When Hoover debated a study of the abuses of British and German unemployment insurance as part of his fight for privately-financed programs in this country, he wrote Mitchell for advice on the sources of funds for such a study. Mitchell suggested the Schurz Foundation; but Hoover decided to wait for a study being made by a newly-appointed British commission. Edward A. Filene offered the White House $25,000 to study areas of waste in the American system of the distribution of consumer goods. The White House conceived of its role as middleman, an arranger of relationships and associations. Hoover was proud to reply to his critics that 20 of the 42 committees appointed during his presidency had been privately financed, a figure he compared with the 44 privately-financed groups of Coolidge's 118, and the 75 of Wilson's 150

60. Quoted in Lucy Sprague Mitchell, *Two Lives* (New York, 1953), p. 364.

wartime groups. In total number of study groups appointed, he felt his 42 also compared favorably with Theodore Roosevelt's 107 and Taft's 63, as well as Harding's 44.[61]

Before the end of his term Hoover's interest in "fact-finding" would become the basis of some of the severest criticisms of him. A *Harper's* article of February 1932 was typical, at least in its title, of the comments that could be made. "The Great Fact-Finding Farce" by Lillian Symes documented many of the criticisms, although her treatment emphasized the unwillingness of those who have the facts to give them to fact-finders rather than the differences between "facts" and "opinions," the dichotomy beloved of the social scientists, or the unwillingness of Hoover to act once he presumably had the facts, the criticism that would come down through the New Deal. Miss Symes' emphasis is much closer to the persistent progressive problem in searching for facts, and the problem as Hoover came to see it. She quotes John R. Commons' statement that "The economic investigator is usually permitted to investigate no more than a small part of the whole institution. He is controlled by somebody higher up. He is not like the physical scientist who hurts only the theologians. He hurts or helps politicians, or business, or labor, or agriculture."[62]

The problem was considerably more complex than the immediate critics of Hoover were inclined to acknowledge. Facts under public scrutiny rarely appeared objective. The illusion of such universal objectivity had played havoc with progressive politics for a generation and bedevilled much of the social science that Hoover was seeking to utilize. For a generation straining to transcend the wasteful ignorance that many of them had come to associate with the arbitrary and erratic reform policies of the progressive era, the concern with method was particularly serious: not simply the collection of data, but the methods of collection, the attitudes and purposes of the collectors. Americans inter-

---

61. Mitchell to Hoover, April 11, 1931. Hoover to Mitchell, April 22. Container 1E/232, Hoover Library. Memorandum of E. A. Filene to Hoover, November 30, 1930. Container 1E/114, Hoover Library. *New York Times*, July 30, 1930, is the public source of information concerning the number of commissions; but the memorandum containing the statistics circulated among White House staff and the members of the Committee to provide some comfort.

62. *Harper's Monthly Magazine*, 164 (1932), p. 356.

ested in the problem had begun to examine the contrast between British Parliamentary Commissions and German mixed governmental agencies. The British method depended upon a more or less *ad hoc* group which had advantages and disadvantages in the fact that, created in the heat of the controversy that led to its appointment, it had a closeness to a specific set of issues which could, however, become myopic. The reform descendants of American sanitary reformers still pressed the method, at the same time that they had learned to raise the question of continuity, of how to sustain the survey experience beyond the immediate problem. Hoover's commissions, like all the reform commissions which preceded them, were to suffer from the essential discontinuity of the method. Many institutions of American government were not sufficiently sustained from administration to administration to enable the method to work as well as in the administrative stability of the British system.

The German mixed governmental agency had more permanent status in an existing administrative structure and was more effective as a continuing research group. But it raised the question whether a fixed bureaucratic agency would tend to become inflexible or at least unwieldy in its approach to evolving public problems. The Hoover administration and the New Deal utilized both methods freely. Hoover emphasized the *ad hoc* character of the British example and the German use of federal administrators as agents in non-governmental groups. The New Deal emphasized the German mixed agency method in the effort to experiment with *ad hoc* agencies which could then, after testing, be included in a more or less permanent system. The problems faced by the two administrations were characteristic of the differences in the methods of collecting data appropriate to each form. The commission method with its loose connection to the administration and the legislature was obviously more suited to a parliamentary system but in the American government tended to produce little action or to make action difficult. The mixed commission method was much more suited to a strong executive system with its direct ties to the administration of programs; but it excluded legislators as participants in policy making and tended to produce conflict which could result in ultimately ineffective compromise programs.

Both methods tended to arouse conflict with Congress by excluding it from policy making. The first sought to surmount this difficulty by using the logic of the report and its facts as the basis for public pressure upon Congress to act. But the classic American problem of finding a way to make pressure on Congress effective limited the utility of the method. The second method translated the problem into a battle between president and Congress for the creation of new agencies to construct and administer new programs. This method was limited also by the power of the president-as-politician to manipulate and maneuver in Congress.

Objective social science and the presidency had ultimately to be viewed as involved in politics, progressive disdain to the contrary notwithstanding. A revolutionary program built upon any other premise would have been doomed to failure. In this instance, however, the crash, the Depression, and a willingness to accept the New Deal as a dramatic revolution obscured a continuing battle common to the Hoover administration and the New Deal. The assertion that one had lost and the other had won would serve only to block understanding of the continuing reality that social science and social reform in America shared a common base in politics.

By 1932, perhaps as early as January, some members of the Committee were becoming more deeply concerned about the relation of the process in which they found themselves engaged to the growing political debate around them. Ogburn's enthusiasm ran unchecked by any doubts except for the actual scheduling of manuscript delivery and editing; but even he felt some perplexity at the staff's response to its own work. "A substantial proportion of the chapters that had been turned in," he wrote in a memorandum of January 25, "have been criticized by a fairly large number of the staff and others as having *too optimistic a tone*"; and he underlined the phrase to make sure that it impressed everyone as much as it had impressed him. Optimism, he conceded, could not be measured scientifically; and there was also the fact that it might suggest "an interpretation in the mind of the reader rather than an exact determination in an objective manner." He was still willing to struggle with the problem. "Again, optimism and pessimism vary according to different persons." Fundamentally, however, he felt that "in so far . . . as the author sticks to the measurement of the trends without evaluation the optimism would seem to be read into it by the reader, except, of course, as to the selection of the data."[63] And so it went. Ogburn remained convinced of the basic objectivity of the enterprise. Others were unpersuaded. The winter of 1931–32 had been a hard one for the country; and the problem of objectivity was becoming ever more intensely involved in the prospect of a political campaign.

The problem had begun to take shape in August 1931 in a debate the edges of which can be found in carping exchanges among Committee members on the use the President would make of their work and the influence he would be likely to have in its final shape. Merriam began to object to Ogburn's plans to turn preliminary materials over to the President, although it seemed clear enough at the beginning that such a release of materials would pose no problem. Hunt delayed circulating the minutes of that debate until December, and when he did, he omitted Merriam's objections. Merriam wrote to him to clarify his point and to insist on its incorporation.

My position was that if the President asked to see the work in progress, he was entitled to. But that it would be better not to submit piecemeal or unfinished reports to the President for the following reasons: that the President would get a better impression of the comprehensive work of the Committee if he first saw the Report and the conclusions as a whole. That the President would be in the most favorable situation, if he could say that he had seen none of the Reports until they came to him as the finished product of the technicians selected for the task. That the committee would be saved the embarrassment arising from any suggestions for change, to which it could not agree, or from being charged with having made such changes, even if in fact not true.[64]

Merriam's view of the relation between the Committee and the President did not at all conform to the understanding that Hunt had had from the President or from Ogburn; and Merriam's apparent distinction between "work in progress," which could be turned over to the President, and "piecemeal or unfinished reports" did not help to clarify the matter. But there were other signs of restiveness. Hunt continued to snipe at the style. In March 1932 he began to suggest that a publicity campaign might be started, if only to hint that a report would be forth-

63. Committee memorandum, January 25, 1932. Mimeographed. Merriam papers.
64. Merriam to Hunt, December 10, 1931. Hunt papers.

coming during the winter of 1932–33. Odum cut down the suggestion immediately. For one thing, Hunt had sought in his statement to under-play the concept of "social welfare" by arguing that the term as used by the Committee had meanings quite different from those which critics of the President might attach to it. "We are certainly dealing with dyna-mite," Odum remarked irritably, "when we ourselves send out a state-ment negating the whole claim of social science for accurate terminology and interpretation . . . . At the present writing all evidence, as I see it, is against this preliminary publicity."[65]

A meeting of the Committee was called for mid-March of 1932 to clarify the issue—or at least to determine the relationship between the Committee's report to the President and the one problem which had not been anticipated at the beginning but was gradually engrossing the Committee's attention: the November election and the anticipated bit-ter campaign. The White House had apparently continued to entertain the possibility of using the Committee's materials in the campaign; but that would have necessitated beginning a publicity program early in the spring at the very latest. Committee manuscripts now would not be available for publication until October, which further emphasized the need for a long preliminary build-up. Both Strother and Hunt had been using their magazine and newspaper contacts to drop hints about a forth-coming great announcement; but the Committee's refusal to allow pub-licity that far in advance—or finally any publicity at all prior to publica-tion of the summary report—brought any such plans to a halt. Both sides could agree that a sudden bombshell approach in October or even September would do no one any good. From the President's point of view, it would look like a last-minute political gambit and only confirm the criticisms of those who saw such motives in his commissions and conferences. From the point of view of the social scientists it would label them all politicians, which, regardless of the fact that some of them were still ardent supporters of Hoover, would have violated totally the very scientific objectivity they were struggling to achieve. Yet, as many of them would have agreed, the campaign was growing ever more in-

---

65. Odum to Ogburn, March 5, 1932. Ogburn papers. Odum to Hunt, November 21, 1932, December 21, 1932. Hunt papers.

volved in the judgments they were beginning to make about the nature and the quality of their work.

As chairman of the Committee, it was Mitchell's responsibility to write the introductory materials. He spent the spring of 1932 in England, reading mimeographed drafts of the reports and supporting Ogburn against Hunt's critical remarks. "It will take a serious minded reader to go far with it," he wrote to Ogburn. "My guess is that you will go down in history as the editor of a good national inventory of value to future historians, and not as the chief author of a best seller. . . . My introduction might perhaps point out in advance as tactfully as possible the superior merits of such a job, and make a possible reader ashamed to acknowledge that he cannot get excited about sober statements of facts."[66] But the real difficulties were still ahead. By August when the staff gathered in the New York offices to hammer out the final documents the crises were fairly constant as authors delayed their commitments beyond long-established deadlines. Confidence ebbed and criticism mounted. Ogburn's attempts to maintain an olympian editorial pose above the battle, shaping and guiding, only sharpened issues, and the correspondence is filled with asides covering such details as "nervous" excuses, illness, secretarial inefficiency, and the like, as Ogburn threaded a careful path through complaints and lamentations.

Merriam had finished his chapter on government in May. Ogburn's criticisms of the draft pointed to differences between them reflecting a deep intellectual opposition between Ogburn's more positivistic approach and Merriam's commitment to reform. After praising Merriam's general tone and scope, he continued, "It seems to me, however, that you have paid a price for these high achievements and this price, I think, would be the outstanding criticism which I would make. It is a lack of equivalent richness and evidence and data to support your observations and statements." While many of the questions which Ogburn proceeded to raise led to useful revision, the important differences in tone could not be obscured.[67] Hunt added his own criticism, accusing Merriam of writing "a political essay," in which "the statement of

66. Mitchell to Ogburn, May 8, 1932. Ogburn papers.
67. Ogburn to Merriam, May 11, 1932. Merriam papers.

problems seems to rest on your authority, rather than on the data."[68]

Like optimism, the effects of the war, the deepening Depression, the swirling effects of the election campaign as it moved about them, Ogburn's concern with objectivity and evidence would join the panoply of confusing and conflicting criticisms which confronted the commitment to an assemblage of scientific data with the obvious and increasing need for some kind of program for action. Merriam complained about the sense of suspension above history and events which the report had come to have. "No one would ever suspect there was such a man as Dewey from reading this. You would never know there was any such person as Giddings or Small. You would never know except for a few pages . . . that there were men like Roosevelt and Wilson or any of the other thinkers who instituted these educational or other changes," he commented. The lack of reference to international relationships also struck him. "We take a rather provincial attitude as if there were no other country in the world except the United States."[69]

All of these concerns were voiced, in only slightly less irritated terms, by Hunt. "*Recent Social Trends*, like *Recent Economic Changes*, will suffer from the fact that it is too nationalistic. The method adopted implies an isolation of American society which, while a convenience for research purposes, falsifies the findings."[70] Hunt shared Hoover's fear of a return to what he considered the isolationism of 1920–21, a view which emphasizes a belief in the necessity of treating the Depression as an international problem and seeking its relief internationally. While Hoover is often criticized for blaming the Depression on international economic disorder, his aim was not to encourage isolationism as a response, but to promote economic internationalism involving the country more effectively in world leadership.

In addition to his uneasiness about the neglect of international issues by the Committee, Hunt also voiced the frequently heard criticism that the Report took too little account of the coming of the Depression. As he wrote to Mitchell: "Every reader has to wade to this document through the dark waters of his personal experience during the Depres-

68. Hunt to Merriam, May 1932. Hunt papers.
69. Committee Minutes, June 4, 1932; June 20, 1932. Ogburn papers.
70. Hunt to Mitchell, February 17, 1932. Hunt papers.

sion. He has to keep wading until page 50 to find anything bearing on this tragic setting . . . ."[71]

By August Hunt's letters to contributors threatened an open break which both Odum and Ogburn hastened to cover up. Hunt had been highly critical of the chapter on race by T. J. Woofter, possibly over the political implications of its position on racial issues.[72] Odum's efforts to mollify without re-writing were successful. "We do not want any open breaks between Hunt and the collaborators, do we?" he asked Ogburn.[73] Everyone was conscious of one potential criticism or another which the report would face from the public press, but each one seemed to have his own hierarchy of anxieties. The basic issue of relevance and utility rested on the extent to which one saw the Depression as a disaster requiring revolution or one requiring patience and forbearance. Odum and Ogburn tended to join Hunt and the President in the latter group. "I have an idea," Odum wrote Ogburn a week before the election, "that President Hoover is going to value these volumes about as much as anything he has done. Barring a miracle, it does seem now that the volumes will be the first of a series of factors which will start the historical estimates of his work as ex-president. It is certainly a great thing that studies can now be looked at as studies and not as something to be shot at by politicians."[74] Odum had made his decision not only about the report, but about the outcome of the election as well. His sense of a release from politics is an interesting point shared by many on the Committee. The inexorable four-year march to another election had led them on a course none of them had anticipated.

Merriam's optimism had continued through March. "I am more than ever encouraged to believe that the outcome of our long effort is likely to be made something socially significant and vital. Perhaps Mr. Strother is right in saying that we ought to have more faith in the outcome than some of us seem to have."[75] By August he thought it might be a good idea to survey the reviews of *Recent Economic Changes* to see if they had pointed to any pitfalls which might now be avoided. "I have heard

71. Hunt to Mitchell, September 6, 1932. Copy in Ogburn papers.
72. "The Status of Racial and Ethnic Groups," *Recent Social Trends*, pp. 553–501.
73. Odum to Ogburn, August 4, 1932. Ogburn papers.
74. Odum to Ogburn, October 28, 1932. Ogburn papers.
75. Merriam to Hunt, March 17, 1932. Hunt papers.

several times that *Recent Economic Changes*, particularly the introductory part by the Committee, was too optimistic in view of what had happened since, and that there was not enough warning of what was to come. No doubt the business depression was pretty hard to foresee," he wrote in the letter which accompanied the clippings Ogburn sent. "They are certainly very interesting," he wrote, "but also tend to make the Depression more depressing."[76] Underneath the questions and the comments was a point which had played an interesting obbligato in committee meetings: just how much responsibility for predicting the future social research had. Would Mitchell and his economists have predicted October 1929 and the events which followed? Many social trends researchers, for example, were convinced that immigration restriction would stabilize the population of the United States by 1960, and the certainty of that outlook required commitments on all issues related to it.[77]

The question of purpose and prediction—and the relation of both to the forthcoming election with its seemingly predictable outcome—took an increasingly central position. Committed originally to the belief that it was not their function to propose solutions but only to provide evidence of the problems, they had nonetheless come to see the presence of the Depression and its dynamic development throughout the election year as a demand upon them for something more. Ogburn did not and could not absorb the effect of so chaotic a sequence of changes in the carefully-worked-out structure with which he had begun and which his position as Director of Research continued to impose upon the Committee. The Committee, lacking any other focus to shift its direction, could do no more than move, somewhat disconcertedly, according to plans formulated in September and October 1929. If President Hoover had considered a shift in focus, he formulated it, at least through his assistants, more as a gigantic propaganda campaign designed to restore confidence than as a program of social legislation designed to relieve immediate conditions. The sense of immediacy was the element most obviously absent from the initial deliberations.

In the final drafting, Mitchell and Ogburn were left in utter disagree-

76. Merriam to Mitchell, August 12, 1932; August 19, 1932. Merriam papers.
77. Minutes of the meeting of March 14, 1932. Merriam papers.

ment. Ogburn rewrote substantially Mitchell's first draft of the basic Introduction and Findings, and Mitchell bridled. He disliked Ogburn's language and pressed him to return to the original draft, suggesting that he get good editors if he wanted to.[78] The debate continued to the end. Ogburn found others who would agree with him that Mitchell's statement was too long, not sufficiently interesting, diffuse, discursive—he sprayed adjectives like buckshot, charging finally that there were not enough facts. Even that blow glanced off the adamant Mitchell and the report went through as he wrote it, replete with the elegance and grace which were the mark of Mitchell's prose, facts or no facts.

Ogburn's problem was real and consonant with the progressive dilemma: how to bring science to the public without weakening the professional acceptability of the science or boring the public. While popularizers had always faced that problem, social science popularizers, if there was to be such a profession, were in an even worse position. If the result of a scientific program was to be political action by and on the behalf of the public, then the program would have to be translatable into publicly appealing terms, without violating the line between scientifically-based programs and politically-inspired propaganda. But, as the Committee's apparent rejection of such names as Ray Stannard Baker and Stuart Chase indicated, some kinds of popularization were not within the bounds of the new social science.

Hunt came closest to articulating for the administration the criticisms now levelled against the work the Committee had done. "If the economic and social system is sound, let the Committee say so in the first sentence," he wrote to Mitchell in September. "If it is unstable, let the Committee say so. Or to change the theme somewhat, if there are certain portions of our society toward which we should look for emerging problems, let the Committee stake out its claim in the first paragraph and say 'thou ailest here and here.' "[79]

Someone might have reminded him that even the ancient oracles had foresight enough to cloak their pronouncements in metaphor; but that was precisely the problem. The Committee had begun as a fact-finding

78. Mitchell to Ogburn, August 10, 1932. Ogburn to Mitchell, September 6 and 9, 1932. Ogburn papers.
79. Hunt to Mitchell, September 6, 1932. Copy in Ogburn papers.

agency, however subject to abuse that term had become by the time it issued its report. It had moved into an historical environment which demanded programs and plans. Yet its mandate had been built upon Hoover's conviction that decisions about planning rested with him and that to turn such a responsibility over to an advisory committee might have involved a surrender of the authority of his office. Had he requested it, he would have had the support of Committee members like Howard Odum who felt that it would be "contrary to the major emphasis which the Committee has placed upon the studies to begin now to recommend action. . . . The very nature of many of the chapters would have been different, as I understand it, had we contemplated recommending action. I am wondering whether Mr. Hunt's urging of this represented the Committee or represented his own wishes and perhaps one or two members of the Committee."[80]

Only in wartime had such an agency, if the Committee could be called that, been allowed to intervene between the president and the departments of government. The shadow of the war and the recollected suspicion of the war agencies still hung over Congress and the administration alike. Even under continued pressure, as Hunt wrote to Mitchell, there was still "no prospect in Washington of reviving the war control boards." Nevertheless, he felt, "a decentralized and yet an articulated operating organization now exists throughout the country; the Reconstruction Finance Corporation of vast proportions and possibilities is beginning to act and the union of business and government has never been so close and so filled with the possibilities of good and evil. . . . I felt that I held in my palm the realities of our system."[81]

The underlying problem of the relationship between research and reform would not be resolved in the New Deal. The ingredients of the debate would remain what they had been in the Hoover administration: a three-cornered battle among that intellectual, extra-governmental community which considered itself professional in the study of society, the President and his Cabinet as managers of government, and Congress with its responsibility to represent and serve a constituency defined as an electorate or an interest. Each of the three could be considered gov-

80. Odum to Ogburn, December 10, 1932. Ogburn papers.
81. Hunt to Mitchell, September 6, 1932. Copy in Ogburn papers.

ernmental specialists, by their own lights; and their disagreements with
the other groups would be matched only by the internal debates which
alternately raised and resolved disputes concerning the nature of their
own functions. That any of the three could from time to time consider
itself out of politics, non-political, or non-partisan was the illusion
marking the persistence of progressivism.

To the extent that any members of the Committee would have been
willing to admit it, politics broke out into the open over the question of
the coming presidential transition, and the future of the extensive report. But it is an interesting kind of politics to observe. The issues did
not divide the supporters of Hoover from those of Roosevelt, but rather
those who felt that aggressive measures must be taken to get the report
into the hands of the President-elect, to cleanse it of its association with
Hoover, from those who felt that such an effort would brand their
work political in every sense of the word and somehow despoil it of
scientific objectivity. The problem had first arisen in a relatively innocuous fashion. Impressed with what they took to be the extraordinary
experience of the committee work itself, members of the Committee
sought ways of suggesting their own continuity as a permanent social-
planning group. In a discussion that constituted the best rationalization
of the Hoover method, Charles Merriam suggested that some kind of
"quasi-governmental corporation" would emerge out of such groups
as trade associations, and that this would come about whether or not the
Committee made any recommendations. He suggested that that value
of a combination of "governmentalists, industrialists and technicians"
viewed as a "quasi-governmental agency" might well be deduced from
experiences of the National Research Council, the SSRC, and the various
trade and industrial associations that Hoover had helped to salvage
from the war experience.[82]

Odum suggested that the work of the Committee be continued under
the auspices of the Social Science Research Council. He had two purposes in mind: a study of regional culture, particularly of what he called
the "technological regions" like the Tennessee Valley and the Ohio Valley, and a countering of the attack then about to be launched by Charles

82. Minutes of June 29, July 1, 1932. Hunt papers.

Beard on the application of the social sciences to social reform.[83] Both points had interest beyond the immediate situation. The first translated Turner's social science sense of regionalism into more contemporary terms, freed of the over-the-shoulder romanticism of the authors of *I'll Take My Stand*. The second touched equally interesting questions concerning the relation between a social science view of life that sought to reshape behavior according to scientific programs of analysis and on the other hand the tradition of individual freedom assuming an inherent capacity to behave in accordance with a liberal social order. Both problems were to be submerged in the nationalist rhetoric of the New Deal, although they would continue to operate just beneath the surface of that rhetoric.

The question of how to create a scientific social order out of scientific social research remained intractable. Lost in the cultural hostilities of World War II are most of the remnants of the high respect for Benito Mussolini that touched American intellectuals and rested on a serious questioning of the relation between liberal democracy and an industrial social order. One need only lift the logic of *Recent Social Trends* far enough above the American progressive landscape to see it in the context of the post-World War I international dilemma.

A more immediate consideration was the question whether the Committee's report should be pressed upon Roosevelt in any form. By November apparently only Ogburn remained deeply committed to Hoover, and even he was reluctant to see the work of three years inundated by the politics of a campaign. "This is the dark hour for 'the Chief,' " he wrote Strother on the 10th, "and I am truly sorry. I doubt if we've ever had a man in the White House who ever labored more courageously or more intelligently, or who fought better than did Mr. Hoover. . . . I should say roughly that Mr. Hoover did 100 times as much against a depression as any other President has done before. The people were not voting against Mr. Hoover, they were voting against the business cycle . . . the only type of man who could have saved himself . . . would have been a man of spectacular histrionic ability—an actor, a 'gesticulator' . . . ."[84]

83. Odum to Ogburn, February 21, 1933. Ogburn papers.
84. Ogburn to Strother, November 10, 1932. Ogburn papers.

Nonetheless, four days later Ogburn decided to take advantage of his friendship with his former Columbia colleague Raymond Moley; and in a two page letter he outlined the purpose of *Recent Social Trends*, its potential uses, and offered to send Moley a copy. Eager to purify his documents of any taint of politics, Ogburn emphasized the fact that the report could have been finished in the early part of the summer, but that Mr. Hoover felt that it ought to be kept out of the election campaign. "Mr. Hoover seemed particularly concerned that we release it at a time when prejudices were calmer and the atmosphere would be the most favorable for such a significant scientific study." In an effort to nail down his point more firmly, Ogburn explained that "The data prepared are useful to either conservative or radical, to Republican or Democrat. . . . It is not a document, therefore, that is designed for a particular Congress. Out attempt has been to lay the basis for policy making on the broader national issues. . . ."[85]

Initially, of course, no one had seriously considered the possibility of continuity, even in the knowledge that the preparation of the report would take virtually the entirety of a four-year administration. Yet the value of such an enterprise rested on an incredible faith in the stability of politics permitting intellectual and economic resources to float serenely above the fray, moving from administration to administration, party to party, Congress to Congress, powered by the force of truth. Ogburn discovered his error in a complicated series of responses. He had, in the first place, absolutely no authorization to write to Moley as he did, either from his Committee or from the President. It was, after all, the President's committee, and he would have used its findings for his own purposes had the circumstances made them usable to him.

That Ogburn was not altogether wrong in his assumptions about the desirability of continuity might be indicated by the fact that the same idea had occurred to Hunt, an administrative intimate of the President, who added to Ogburn's suggestion his own urging that he and Ogburn talk with Moley on Ogburn's next visit to New York. Hunt also promised that he would suggest to the President that he formally transmit a copy of the report to Governor Roosevelt. Hunt's suggestion, however, was made without the knowledge that Ogburn had already written ex-

85. Ogburn to Moley, November 14, 1932. Ogburn papers.

tensively to Moley, and when he discovered that such had been the case, he pulled back slightly.

> I think there is a distinct problem in the critical attitude of the Democrats towards the Hoover commissions and committees. If I were in their shoes I should be reluctant to give much public credit to agencies about which I had expressed so much criticism. On the other hand, I should certainly make private use of the material, and this presumably they will do. How to get public comment on it and direct public attention under Democratic auspices is still a part of the problem of presentation and should not be allowed to go by default.[86]

Although Hunt had seemed eager enough to press the report on the incoming administration, he nevertheless spent the month of December on the edge of battle with Committee members who suddenly found it impossible to get copies of the report, despite the fact that it had been available in final mimeographed form for over a month. January 2 had been set as publication date; but Hunt refused even to release copies to the Rockefeller administrators who had financed it. A leak of information to Frederick Lewis Allen for *Only Yesterday* exacerbated the confusion. Nor, as Ogburn was to discover, was the Committee itself in complete agreement on the question of relations with the new administration. "Doesn't such a recommendation for a formal study made for the President lie entirely in the President's hands," Odum asked in scarcely concealed annoyance; "and would it come within the realm of our staff or even the Committee to take a formal series of studies made for President Hoover and present them to Governor Roosevelt?"[87]

As later letters of apology indicate, no one on the White House staff remembered to bring the subject to the President's attention until the New York *Herald Tribune* did it for them. Strother was particularly annoyed, Hunt wrote to Ogburn in January, to read that "with President Hoover soon to withdraw to private life, the Committee, it was learned, was considering the presentation of the report at a later date to President-elect Franklin D. Roosevelt, with definite recommendations as to how it can best be put to use."[88] And the following day Mitchell informed members of the committee that "the President feels that it would be

86. Hunt to Ogburn, November 25, 1932. Ogburn papers.
87. Odum to Ogburn, December 10, 1932. Ogburn papers.
88. Hunt to Ogburn, January 10, 1933. Ogburn papers.

impertinent of him to present a copy of our report to his successor . . .
he objects seriously to our presenting a copy as a committee."[89] By
then, of course, the report had appeared in summary in many American
newspapers, had been widely heralded by many, and would soon be
available for anyone who wished to wander through its 1500 or more
pages of text, presumably even the incoming President. Hoover's refusal to "present" a copy was rapidly becoming no more than a formal
consideration.

Committee members were enormously pleased with the seriousness
with which the report was taken by newspapers and magazines. The
story circulated, largely through an item in the *Literary Digest*, that the
report had used up a million dollars and the labors of five hundred researchers, and, of course, there were comments about "fact-finding."
John Dewey, however, called the two volumes "monumental" and "a
mine of information and a wealth of suggestions." And he went on to
address himself to critics who had found the volumes too conservative.

I believe the enduring influence of the report will be increased by its reserves. . . . I have
often been impatient with methods of mere "fact-finding" used by so-called social and
political science. But in these volumes we have something more than *mere* fact-finding.
The facts are presented—sometimes only implicitly, sometimes explicitly—so as to
make *problems* stand out, and that, in my judgment, is the proper function of statements of facts. Hence the volumes are an arsenal. And I would rather have an arsenal of
authoritative knowledge than such a premature firing-off of guns as would make a lot
of noise and emit great amounts of smoke.[90]

Although Dewey's suggestion of a distinction between facts and
problems plays through Committee discussions, it was never as explicit
for the Committee's purposes as it was for Dewey. In fact, the Committee's initial awareness of the distinction was absorbed, finally, by another, related pair of terms: problems and programs of action. In the
last analysis, the Committee had not begun its deliberations with a concern for finding a program of action; but that was precisely the point of
view which dominated its concluding deliberations. They had assumed
from the beginning that, as deliberators, they would be handing over
the results to a man of action, and now the problem was how to find
him.

89. Mitchell to Ogburn, January 11, 1933. Ogburn papers.
90. *International Journal of Ethics*, 43 (1933), 344.

A. A. Berle recognized the puzzle in his comments on the study, although his vantage point was clearly influenced by his commitment to the new administration. He thought the evidence irrevocably imbedded in 1929 and trapped, therefore, in a now irrelevant past. That was not, in fact, the case as the Committee's constant emphasis upon the most recent available data might have testified; but it does suggest one important point. The Committee report had deliberately played down the sense of a revolutionary atmosphere, referring to the reality of that in other parts of the world, but maintained a hopeful, optimistic calm about the United States. This had been a decision carefully planned in the last rewritings of the report. By the time Berle was reviewing it, the American version of that revolution had occurred, in a safe and orderly fashion. The sense of fear had passed.

Berle used his discussion of the report for a lengthy development of comparisons on the relation between the individual and government, old style and new.

... one is tempted to continue through the endless vistas which are opened up by this book. Space does not permit this; and it remains merely to say that here is a compilation of source material of the first importance. It has the authenticity of well conserved and well directed scholarship. It has the barrenness of quantitative theory and statistical measurement. It indicates what happened; makes a fair attempt to explain why it happened; and through sheer force of limitation stops short of the question of whether it must continue to happen.

And in a crucial critique Berle attacked the self-imposed limitation

under which academic students today place themselves—their endeavor to be objective, non-controversial; to state facts, rather than to interpret them or plead a cause. One may regret that the academic community has fallen out of the habit of interpreting its data; feel (as perhaps many academicians do feel) that the desire for objectivity has been carried entirely too far.

He went on to acknowledge the possibility, indeed the hope, that "a master who is not one of the authors, or who might perhaps be one of the authors acting in a different capacity, may perhaps reduce much of the work to a serviceable tool."[91]

Berle had touched the central issue: that the profit of the work would depend on a "master" acting in a capacity different from that of the au-

91. *The Saturday Review of Literature*, 9 (1933), 533–35.

thors. The question was who and in what way, and the Committee had assumed from the beginning that it need not determine that point. It was the President's Committee, and the image of the master had begun to fade so early in the project that in the end not even the smile remained. Dewey was right in pointing to the essentially conservative base of the report, its dependence upon the logic of planning; but in an era of revolution, an "arsenal of authoritative knowledge" which did not make a certain amount of noise and emit a reasonable degree of smoke might end up looking like a pop gun.

Even Hoover felt called upon to support his own doctrines of science and objectivity, issuing on the day of publication a supplement to his preface to the book.

The significance of this report lies primarily first, in the fact that it is a cooperative effort on a very broad scale to project into the field of social thought the scientific need and the scientific method as correctives to undiscriminating emotional approach and to insecure factual basis in seeking for constructive remedies for great social problems. . . . The effort has been to relate all the facts and present them under a common standard of measurement.[92]

"Facts, facts, facts," Bryce had said; and there they were. Dewey saw problems rather than "mere" facts; Berle saw an iron-handed objectivity committed to the past, not programs for working out the future. He called for a "Parsifal" to ask the questions. Both the searchers for facts and the seekers of questions looked ultimately to some "master" to provide the answers. At issue in many ways was a definition of that master. Berle's Parsifal saw the vision of the grail and responded by embarking upon its pursuit in the sphere of action. Hoover's vision, like that of the social science to which he had appealed for guidance, was built upon an escape from the pressures of action and a conviction that scientific method and the observation of facts afforded protection against the intense personalism and the emotional unreliabilities of intuition and politics.

The debate did not end with the new administration. If anything, it intensified thereafter. Many members of the staff, from Mitchell, Merriam, and Ogburn down to editorial staff and researchers, continued to influence social research in the federal government, and their students

92. News release, January 2, 1933. Container 1G/967, Hoover Library.

would succeed them. *Recent Social Trends* as a study ceased to be a model in the sense of providing an ideal of social research; but it shaped an understanding of the problematical relations between social research and government, not by establishing methods or suggesting solutions, but by raising the fundamental issues for a new generation of social scientists. The new social science had committed itself to objectivity and to utility, to achieving important social effects free from the traditional inhibitions of politics and emotion. But objectivity and utility were not oracular voices speaking in harmony, supporting one another through the reasonableness of men who, convinced by science of the truth, would be forced by the logic of pragmatism to give it effect. Hoover and those social scientists like Ogburn and Odum who were convinced of the rightness of his principles sought what Cooke had called "government Pasteura," the management of life according to scientific observation and clinical application. They were committed to the belief that politics and science were, in American practice at least, antitheses which could be reconciled only by a gradual revolution in the nature of politics bringing it closer to science.

Nonetheless, and in a sense which could not sustain its reputation, *Recent Social Trends in the United States* accomplished its purposes. It collected in one place and for the first time most of the data reliably available on national social problems. It stands today as the single most comprehensive contemporary self-study of any era of American social history. As an attempt at a photograph of a moment in time, it succeeded to a remarkable degree in the literate, often sensitive conveying of detail about problems which past generations had sought to resolve and future generations would face. The studies of race, the costs and methods of medical care, the education of children, rural life and the decline of agriculture, urban blight and metropolitan expansion, all supply intelligent insights into present and future problems which were destined however to find little place in the intense focus of the Depression and the emergency pragmatism of the New Deal. Nor was that aspect of the report's failure accidental to its basic purpose.

Modern social life is so closely integrated as a whole that no change can occur in any of its phases without affecting other phases in some measure. . . . The usual practice of concentrating attention upon one social problem at a time often betrays us into overlooking these intricate relations. Even when we find what appears to be a satisfactory solution of a single problem, we are likely to produce new problems by putting that solution into practice.[93]

So wrote the Committee in the Prefaces to the monograph series. That had been Hoover's point as well. Systematic interrelatedness required the calculation of scientific, industrial analysis, not emotional fervor, bold experimentation, or fear.

The Introduction established the framework which would connect the report with the history of the survey movement and indicate its future potential. The Committee divided the problems of the nation into three groups: the natural environment of earth and air, the biological inheritance of American races, and the cultural environment "called civilization."

The clarification of human values and their reformulation in order to give expression to them in terms of today's life and opportunities is a major task of social thinking [the Committee concluded]. In the formulation of these new and emergent values, in the construction of the new symbols to thrill men's souls, in the contrivance of the new institutions and adaptations useful in the fulfillment of the new aspirations, we trust that this review of recent social trends may prove of value to the American public.[94]

Firm in that faith they entered oblivion.

III

IF one could project the image of social research and its relation to government action forward from the Progressive era and backward from the present, one might find two images which meet in the period between the World Wars in an uncomfortable superimposition. One image might be constructed out of the Progressives' rebellion against party politics and pursuit of a scientific view of society. The other would be focussed upon the endeavor to define a relationship between the requirements of a free and objective system of social research and the

93. Carroll H. Wooddy, *The Growth of the Federal Government* (New York, 1934), p. v.
94. *Recent Social Trends*, p. lxxv.

urgent needs of a political system dealing with a continuous state of social crisis. *Recent Social Trends* projects both images.

In social science this juxtaposition of research and reform meant discarding outmoded principles and theories, establishing generally applicable methods, facilitating the collection of relevant data, and examining the facts of life for what they were, not for what outmoded moralisms said they ought to be. In politics it meant discarding vague generalities which concealed cupidity and ignorance, establishing general methods of governing which could be applied equally to all, informing the public accurately about the conditions of life, and building programs on a realistic appraisal of carefully observed facts.

For both the social sciences and American politics, this revolution was directed against the evils of an establishment which, in the case of the social sciences, could be accused of repeating social, economic, religious, or metaphysical generalities in support of old dogmas unbuttressed by research, and in the case of politics could be accused of protecting party regulars and their allies. In economics and law the two frequently seemed to move hand in glove to support the power of special groups. But the relationship between practical politics and social science was no less important whatever its manifestations. The conviction that these could be brought into a more fruitful relationship rested on two relatively unquestioned assumptions. The first was that social science, given time, money, and intelligent application, could solve all social problems if its practitioners could be assured of an opportunity to impress their findings upon the government. The second was that politics, as reflected in Congressional debate and legislation, represented an increasingly self-limiting function eventually destined to give way before the onslaught of a rationally informed concept of national interest.

Presidents of the United States would come more and more to face the confusions inherent in this progressive faith as they sought advice from the social science community to provide information for programs not yet formulated, or to support plans to which commitments had already been made. What such presidents shared with the social scientists —or came to share as they experienced the presidency—was the belief that social science represented what presidents represented: the welfare of the nation as a whole; whereas Congress represented what politics represented: the chaos of localism, regionalism, self-interest, and—though it would never have been put this way—the ignorance that barred the path to utopia.

The unresolved contradictions inherent in social science progressivism were concealed by its righteous claims to non-partisanship. Yet wherever social science advice moved into the planning of programs of action, even if only by outlining the alternatives, it touched the heart of politics. In the process of endeavoring to improve the human condition, the planners and executors of programs hired and fired someone's constituents, built buildings with publicly contributed funds, consumed goods and services provided by businessmen in local communities, jostled and nudged the nexus of local, state, and federal agencies already engaged in adjacent projects. For generations the often-criticized practice of patronage had built a relatively efficient political engine for redistributing national resources and producing social change. The alleged objectivity of social science was itself a political challenge to the existing mechanisms for social adjustment and accordingly a form of involvement in politics.

As the next ten years were to suggest, the President's Research Committee on Social Trends had been an interesting education for the American community of social scientists, both those who continued to support its methods and aims and those who came to question these. While the Committee achieved no satisfactory definition of the relationship between scientific objectivity and social responsibility, it nonetheless opened the debate by revealing the dangers inherent in self-imposed limitations like those which the Committee had sought and President Hoover, acting upon his own philosophy of government, had gladly enforced. Was it his committee, with the results to be used by him as he chose? He thought so, and so, at first, did they.

The election of a new President changed that—somewhat. Ogburn, who seems to have had the strongest personal commitment to Hoover, came to feel the necessity of keeping social research in non-governmental institutions. Its best function was that of providing government with the results of research carried on completely apart from the pressures and demands of politics. Merriam, in contrast, felt that research belonged at the center of administration, at the level of the White House itself. Yet

Merriam's later experience with the National Resources Planning Board could be taken to indicate that the closer to the pinnacles of government administration a planning agency approached, the more it was subjected to the pressures of politics. Congress could not forbid a president to consult with the personnel of universities or to request the services of philanthropic foundations for studies of government problems requiring no public funds. Even when the National Resources Planning group under Franklin Roosevelt lived off appropriations that were not specifically designated for the purpose, it was still relatively secure from Congressional attack. But when its proponents rendered it more and more conspicuous, it came under direct Congressional fire in 1943. Despite the later development of groups like the Council of Economic Advisers to the President, the reluctance of Congress to provide for planning agencies in the executive branch still leaves presidents dependent upon the network of foundations and universities for social science advice.

The basic problem is not confined to the executive branch. The Supreme Court has perhaps the longest tradition of adapting the doctrines of current social theory to political practice, but this tendency has been greatly accentuated by the Warren Court. As American constitutional history from Dred Scott to Brown v. Board of Education would indicate, the problem of imposing the results of social research upon a community which considers them either revolutionary or reactionary cannot be resolved by judicial orders alone. When the products of social research are programs of action which seek to overthrow regional or national traditions of any kind, the process of implementation is likely to entail resort to force. Hoover, however, had seen such action as grounded upon persuasion and education rather than force. If he had had a period of stability in which to try out his approach, we might have a different perspective upon his presidency.

Hoover was an American revolutionary of the 1920s, a utopian optimist, the old order's candidate for ushering in the new order painlessly. Like progressive reform in its earlier guise, the social science utopianism espoused by Hoover was to be a revolution against politics, committed to the rational, unemotional building of a new, scientific society. Social science entered the New Deal in a much more political form as the new experts sought to engage more actively in the political process itself.

While many of them belonged to the previous school, their transfer of allegiance often cost them their claims to the unity—or even the logic—of science. The New Deal used social scientists as though they were astrologers, playing their programs for daily action without regard for the mysteries of the system. Politics and social science emerged from the New Deal with their differences intact.

Those members of the social trends group who moved on into the New Deal, even wavering ones like Mitchell, were beginning to recognize for social research what the New Deal seemed to recognize for American society as a whole: that the network of local responsibility, public and private philanthropy, regional business and professional leadership—Hoover's "American system"—could not cope with the crisis of the Depression by providing either systematic research or rational programs of action. But the question of an effective program of national social research was not resolved by the National Resources Planning Board either. Making social science "useful" in the sense of producing legislative programs to effect social change required increasing amounts of political skill. The politics of social science in its New Deal form suggested the need for two kinds of manipulation—in converting political leaders to particular positions framed by social scientists, a kind of lobbying that did not come easy to the latter, and in educating voters to support scientifically-based programs of reform, a public relations enterprise that could be equally difficult.

In the years that followed and arguably as a result of continuing experience with the politics of crisis, American social scientists came to accept the proposition that a commitment to social reform meant a willingness to formulate programs, and that programs meant politics, though the term itself has never become fashionable in this context. Philanthropic foundations, universities, and the federal government have become increasingly frank in their interpenetration of one another's reform interests, and the research they support more candidly tied to the continuity of crisis. A social science that retains the dream of a "great society," even as a rhetorical flourish, staggers the intellect with the threat of an endless succession of epiphanies; but the context, if not the very nature, of utopianism has changed.

A CASE FOR "COURT HISTORIANS"

Ernest R. May

A CASE FOR "COURT HISTORIANS"*

MANY students demand nowadays more "relevant" scholarship. From historians they ask for history that will help
them understand present-day problems. Sometimes, their
appeals serve a purpose. Student demands have had something to do
with reminding American social historians that not all Americans are
white. In regard to some other special fields, however, the call for "relevance" is less well-placed. This is true of that in which I till a little plot
—the history of international politics in this century. For what scholars
in this field do—or try to do—is almost inescapably "relevant."

Nearly anything written or said about international relations in the
last sixty or seventy years has, or may have, some bearing on thought
about current world problems. It cannot be otherwise. No one has yet
come up with any useful way of thinking about such problems in mathematical or philosophical or other than historical terms. They can be
grasped only by extrapolation or by use of analogies, and much of the
necessary data inevitably comes from those who make it their business
to construe the past.

Obviously, work by historians of international relations has most

* Though no one else deserves blame for this essay, it owes a good deal to discussion
that took place during 1967–68 in a study group on historians and the policy-making
process sponsored by the Institute of Politics in the John F. Kennedy School of Government at Harvard.

I am grateful to all its members, especially Richard L. Berkman, who, in the summer of
1967, conducted interviews with several government historians and with a number of
officials at the policy and working levels of the State Department and the CIA. The essay
draws on his interview notes, on statements made to the group by former high U.S. government officials who consented to meet with it, and on interviews which I conducted in
London in the summer of 1966 with officials of the Foreign Office and the Cabinet Office.
I must express my indebtedness to all these individuals and also to certain relevant publications, particularly two essays in *Foreign Affairs*: Arthur M. Schlesinger, Jr., "The Historian and History" (April 1963) and Herbert Feis, "The Shackled Historian" (Jan.
1967); another article by Schlesinger, "On the Inscrutability of History," *Encounter* (Nov.
1966); and Francis L. Loewenheim, ed., *The Historian and the Diplomat: The Role of History and Historians in American Foreign Policy* (New York, 1967).

"relevance" for those who make decisions about current problems.

Men in policy-making posts must continually guess at trend-lines in other governments. Those in Washington watching Soviet behavior, for example, look for indicators forming one or another of the patterns observed in the past—that of pre-1949 Stalinism, that of 1949–1953 Stalinism, or that of some more recent period. Experts such as Charles E. Bohlen and Llewellyn Thompson carry in their heads a wide range of alternative patternings, some of which they derive from writers on pre-1945 Russian foreign policy such as Adam Ulam, E. H. Carr, and B. H. Sumner. One expert, George Kennan, is himself an accomplished historian. His considered estimate of Russia as relentlessly expansionistic, expressed not only in memoranda within the State Department but in a noteworthy article in *Foreign Affairs*, "The Sources of Soviet Conduct" (July 1947), supplied a basic organizing principle for post-war U.S. foreign policy.

When choosing among alternative courses of action as well as when judging trends abroad, men in government draw on history. They say, "This worked in the past" or "That failed in such and such a situation." Thus, belief that NATO had dammed the outrush of Soviet power encouraged formation of SEATO and CENTO; the Marshall Plan served as a model for subsequent aid programs; and expedients were adopted in Vietnam because they were said to have succeeded in Greece, Malaya, or the Philippines.

These examples, to be sure, concern a government that many student pleaders for "relevance" see as reactionary and imperialistic. But men in ministries elsewhere, even in Cuba and North Vietnam, must likewise look for trend-lines and place bets by reading past form. It is hard to imagine any government, however composed or ideologically complected, where foreign-policy making would not be profoundly influenced by history.

And the trends and events important to policy-makers are exactly those most interesting to historians of international politics. We, too, concern ourselves with patterns and continuities and with the relative success or failure of past efforts to deal with recurrent problems. Unlike some of our colleagues, we have no tradition of awaiting passage of time for the sake of perspective. Bernadotte Schmitt and Sidney Fay were at work on the origins of World War I before that war was over. Since that time, historians in the field have attacked any subject for which documents were available. Elsewhere, a gap may exist between what seems "relevant" to potential consumers and what scholars *qua* scholars want to study. In this field, the two conform almost perfectly.

Yet the men who ought to have most interest in learning the history of international relations—those who have to cope with current policy problems—do relatively little to encourage its writing. Every once in a while, a book appears in the Soviet Union or China, exhibiting use of official archives of relatively recent date. For the most part, these works are propaganda tracts. Probably, however, they indicate the existence of other, more substantial studies produced for restricted circulation. The British Cabinet Office has begun quite recently to commission histories on post-World War II subjects, though mostly on domestic topics such as housing policy. Now and then, in London or one of the Commonwealth capitals, a historian is given official assistance, as Hugh Thomas apparently was for his study of the Suez crisis. The same thing occurs in Paris and Bonn. It happens quite seldom in Washington.

Although hundreds of historians work in the American government, almost none occupy themselves with writing about the trends and events most important to men who must make policy. Historical offices in the State and Defense Departments and the armed services receive requests for specific pieces of information. Insofar as an outsider can determine, these requests normally have to do with factual details. Policy-level officials in the State Department concede, when interviewed, that they usually take historical information from their own files, turning occasionally to the Bureau of Intelligence and Research but rarely to the Historical Office. Similar statements are made by comparable officials in the Pentagon.

Such comments do not mean that government historians waste their time. On the contrary, they do important work. For the most part, however, it relates to agency advertising or morale-building rather than current policy. The State Department's Historical Office is under the Bureau of Public Affairs. Its chief products are documentary publications—an annual compendium of presidential and departmental releases and the distinguished *Foreign Relations* series, reproducing material from the archives. The counterpart in Defense, almost a one-man shop, preserves the Secretary's files and drafts his annual report to Congress. Navy and Air Force historians similarly serve primarily as records custodians. The Army's Office of the Chief of Military History, by far the strongest government historical agency, publishes detailed narratives, mostly on the Army's role in World War II. The Atomic Energy Commission has an official history in progress, with one volume so far in print. The Central Intelligence Agency reportedly has a similar project under way.

Teachers and students have reason to be grateful for such of this work as they are allowed to see. On the whole, the agencies invest relatively little. They get more than adequate return in good will. It seems the fact, however, that government historians seldom supply policy-makers with assistance in applying past experience in current affairs.

This observation is not meant to imply that historians belong in the policy-line. They can be so used, of course, and many men with historical training are in fact employed as intelligence analysts by the CIA or the State Department. Like lawyers, historians are educated in a kind of critical thinking that is applicable to problem-solving. Given the disproportionate number of administrative jobs they hold in universities, it is surprising that so few, as compared with economists and political scientists, figure at high levels in government. But one holding a staff or policy-level post would not, while in that post, be functioning as a historian.

A few government historians work near the borderline. They prepare background material for staff papers. This is done by some members of the Historical Division of the Joint Chiefs. So engaged, they may or may not act as historians. It depends on how their assignments are defined. A man detailed to work on a Berlin contingency plan, for example, would collect data on the crises of 1948, 1958, and 1961. He could adopt one of several approaches. He might seek information supporting a particular prescription for dealing with the next crisis. Alternatively, he might try to extract pointers as to how the next crisis might arise and what course it might follow. Either way, he might or might not perform good staff service, producing just what his principals wanted. He would not, however, serve as a historian.

For, as a historian, he would make it his object to understand each past crisis in its own terms. His recounting would not speak directly to the problem in hand. Though he might provide inputs for better staff work than might otherwise be produced, his product would not in itself constitute good staff work.

Within the government, historians' work—careful analysis of what was done, said, and thought in circumstances different from those of the present—has mostly concerned subjects and episodes now somewhat removed from the concerns of policy-makers and their staffs. World War II has been treated by the services, especially the Army, in exhaustive detail. Volumes in the Army series by Ray Cline, Stetson Conn, Richard Leighton and Robert Coakley, Maurice Matloff, Louis Morton, Howard M. Smyth, and Mark Watson supply as broad understanding of that war as anyone could wish. These volumes deal not only with the Army itself but, on the basis of thorough research, with the other services, the Joint Chiefs, intelligence organizations, civil departments and agencies, and the Presidency. Of course, they also draw on captured German, Italian, and Japanese records.

Little that is comparable has been published on post-World War II events. One volume of the Atomic Energy Commission's history covers the creation of the Commission and debates in 1946 on the Baruch Plan. The Army, Navy, and Air Force have all produced works on the Korean War, the Army's again being the most detailed. Confined for practical purposes to service operations, these volumes tell little, however, about policy issues and their compromise or resolution.

Studies on other postwar topics have been prepared either by official historians or, more often, by analysts employed under contract. How many can properly be labelled historical studies is hard to judge. For the most part, they have probably not been written by trained historians, for historians are scarce in contract research organizations. The RAND Corporation has only one on its permanent staff. However, political scientists and others not holding historians' union cards sometimes write good history.

A more severe limitation lies in the fact that most such studies carry high security classification. As a result, they do not have the usefulness of published histories. Many in government who might want to consult a particular volume do not belong to the agency that sponsored it. As a result, they may not even know of its existence. If they do, they may still have trouble borrowing it. Locked in a safe, it will be hunted out only when someone sees an immediate need for consulting it. Unlike a volume sitting openly on the shelf, it does not form part of the store of knowledge shared by men addressing themselves to current problems.

Moreover, insofar as an outsider can determine, few of these classified studies possess anything like the breadth of view found in the better Army volumes on World War II. Resting on formal records retained by one agency, or perhaps only one segment of an agency, they disclose little about the conflicting perceptions, perspectives, judgments, arguments, and interests that entered into major policy issues. Richard Neustadt's study of decisions and non-decisions relating to the SKYBOLT missile, commissioned by President Kennedy, appears to be the only contrary example. Historical works of such a nature as to contribute significantly to the policy process seem seldom to be commissioned by the government.

Nor are they being written by outside scholars. At one time, the situation was otherwise. During the late forties and early fifties, some in the United States and Britain produced major works on the late thirties. One thinks of Wheeler-Bennett, Namier, and Langer and Gleason. Soon afterward appeared studies of diplomatic relations among the great wartime allies—above all, the books of Herbert Feis. At the time, references to Munich, the Nazi-Soviet Pact, Lend-Lease, the Morgenthau Plan, Teheran, Yalta, and San Francisco occurred frequently in debates about what to do in immediate situations. Having themselves read the existing histories or at least being advised by men who had, officials at the policy level possessed some grasp of the complex reality which each of these symbols represented.

With the passage of time, these symbols have lost their currency. Now, those most likely to be invoked date from the Truman, Eisenhower, and Kennedy years. Almost the only ones about which officials at any level possess sophisticated understanding are in the Kennedy period, and this primarily because of the coincidences resulting in Schlesinger's *A Thousand Days*, Sorensen's *Kennedy*, and Hilsman's *To Move a Nation*. Concerning even such frequently instanced cases as aid to Greece, the Berlin blockade, the formation of NATO, the Indo-China crisis of 1954, the Quemoy-Matsu crises, Suez, Lebanon, and the "open skies" proposal, most men in government rely on their own fragmentary and probably erroneous recollections.

The reason is not that academic historians have found such topics unattractive. Quite the contrary. But, as Feis puts it, they have been "shackled" by lack of records. Practically speaking, academic historians interested in post-1945 events have had available no sources except writings by journalists, legislative and other public documents, and a handful of tendentious memoirs.

Insofar as work by historians of international politics lacks "relevance," the explanation lies not with them but with the men to whom their work might be relevant. During the past two decades, American officialdom has given almost no encouragement to research and writing that might provide policy-makers and their staffs with documented, analytical historical narratives dealing with the trends and events to which they themselves continually refer in discussion of current and future problems.

Why has this been so? Why have official or contract histories not been commissioned, or files opened so that scholarly private enterprise could produce such studies?

Answering this question requires a closer look at officialdom. It is easy to argue that the American government would benefit from there being on bookshelves in Washington offices reliable reference histories of post-World War II events. Discussion of how to terminate the Vietnamese war would surely have been sharpened if participants at all levels had had some agreed-upon knowledge concerning steps taken to end the Korean War. As it is, "hawks" have argued that a threat of nuclear escalation brought the enemy to terms, while "doves" have cited the slow progress at Panmunjon as evidence that patience can pay off. A good history of the subject would probably show the circumstances to have been so different as to make any simple analogies entirely false. Even so, that could in itself contribute to clarity of thought. Similarly, debate about how to react to the 1968 Russian invasion of Czechoslovakia would surely have been improved if those taking part had had some check on what old-timers alleged to have been the facts about and the lessons to be drawn from the coup of 1948 and the invasion of Hungary in 1956.

To contend that the government would profit is one thing. To say that any particular official, from the President on down, ought to arrange for histories being written is something else.

Men highly placed in our government probably cannot visualize themselves making use of the products of such research. They already have too much reading matter. The Department of State alone handles more telegraphic wordage than all newspaper wire services put together. The White House receives copies not only of this traffic but also of that flowing through the Pentagon and the CIA. Even after extensive sieving, enough of this deluge reaches the desks of policy officers so that they have daily to disregard seemingly urgent communications. Most have to budget their time among reading, memorandum-writing, and attendance at departmental or interdepartmental conferences, simply praying that they can leave some things undone without catastrophe resulting. Living so, they, as individuals, can scarcely imagine taking time to pore over some lengthy narrative of a past event.

Even one who saw need for some particular piece of knowledge would probably seek it in a different form. He would want a pointed summary of, for example, those aspects of Korean War experience that seem or are alleged to be relevant to the Vietnamese case. From a historian he would expect a circumstantial narrative, stressing the unique rather than the comparable. Putting bluntly what others voice more diplomatically, one State Department policy officer observes, "Historians refuse to generalize, . . . to give up detail and to give up shadings." Quite realistically, such officials assume that written history—or a live historian called in for consultation—would tell them more than they want to know.

The preoccupied man at the policy level ought to feel, to be sure, that the staff below him should have access to reliable history, regardless of encumbering detail and qualification. If aware that his staff lacks such a resource, however, he would not necessarily demand it. Given the rate at which historians produce, even a monograph on a sharply defined subject—say, Korean peace negotiations—could not materialize in short order. The odds favor current problems having by then taken new shapes. The monograph requested now would probably not be the one wanted then. Only comprehensive histories, covering cases of as yet unsuspected relevance, could serve future needs, and such histories would at best be many years in the writing. No high official, especially if a presidential appointee, would expect by then to be holding the same job. He would therefore see histories as possibly improving staff work for his successor. Altruistically, he might wish that successor well. He would be unlikely, however, to wish him so well as, in his interest, to divert a great deal of effort away from matters currently clamoring for attention.

And effort would be required. For in the way of any serious historical program stand obstacles which no official could easily remove.

First is the obvious fact that any serious historical program would entail risks of disclosing secret or sensitive information. Since "Top Secret" and similar markings serve in government as attention-getters, papers so labelled are those most apt to have been read by men making decisions. They are therefore ones which historians want to examine. Though most probably never deserved such labelling and many that did lost their importance within weeks or months, a few undoubtedly deserve not to become public. Some contain technical data which would help potentially aggressive minor powers—say, Cuba or the United Arab Republic—develop nuclear, radiological, chemical, biological, or other weapons. Others might compromise individuals subject to the police power of other states. And historians might not be good judges of what ought to remain secret. For example, an American cable of many years back, itself innocent enough, might, if partially quoted, give foreign cryptographers a key to decoding other messages in the same cipher. These messages in turn might give them clues to technical information or intelligence sources.

The materials needed by historians would also contain much information which, on other than security grounds, government officials would prefer not to see released. Even now, the editors of the *Foreign Relations* series meet objections to publication of documents nearly a quarter century out of date. Men who figure in these documents remain alive, and desk officers concerned about relations with de Gaulle, Chiang, Tito, and their like, see positive disadvantages in letting confirmation appear that harsh things were once thought about them in Washington.

Within the American government itself men live on. Secretary of State Rusk could conceivably have been embarrassed by revelations about advice he gave when an Assistant Secretary of State in the Truman administration. Ambassadors or service chiefs of staff could have reasons for not wanting others reminded of views they voiced when deputy country directors or members of planning staffs. Given concerns on these scores, many men who make careers of government have an understandable inclination to feel that histories should be written only after all the participants are long dead.

Even where individual reputations are not at stake, agency reputations may be. Officials have to be aware that, if histories appear, they may contain not only security leaks and disclosures of sensitive information but also material which could be used for criticism of a department's past performance.

Concern about such dangers would cause many in the permanent bureaucracy to oppose any new program for producing published histories. To be sure, the utility of such histories would probably be greatest for working-level officials in the most prestigious and powerful segments of the national security organization—the White House staff, the regional bureaus of the State Department, planning staffs in the Pentagon, and the Office of National Estimates in CIA. As drafters of critical cables and memoranda, they most need to have in their heads or conveniently at hand precise information about past events.

This does not mean, however, that these officers constitute an actual or potential lobby in favor of more historical research. In the White House, the State Department, and the Defense establishment, most men so placed are in the Foreign Service or one of the military services. They expect rotation to other posts. Like officials at the policy level, they know therefore that histories commissioned now would not arrive in time to help them perform their present jobs. Inwardly, many have mixed feelings about any measures conducive to strengthening permanently the offices with which they temporarily serve, for their careers are built on service in embassies and commands outside of Washington. Thus, even at levels where histories would be most useful, few advocates of serious historical programs can be expected.

One can forecast with some confidence the oral and written commentary that would reach a cabinet member who circulated an inquiry about a program designed to produce post-World War II studies similar to those of Langer and Gleason, Feis, or Matloff. Security officers would protest the danger of secrets being disclosed. Pointing to the sheer mass of classified documents involved and the technicality of many of them, they would represent as virtually impossible any effort at screening. Intelligence analysts would probably question the value of investment in such a program as compared with adding to their own office force. Except in one or two agencies, staff historians would almost certainly object, contending that the public information, record-keeping, or question-answering services they now perform possess much more usefulness and should have first claim on any new resources. Others in public relations posts would caution against the danger of information appearing which journalists or hostile Congressmen might misuse. Administrators would note probable costs, including drains on the time of security officers and file clerks, demand on office space, and possible harassment of busy officials by historians seeking interviews. And the key operating or planning officers, while acknowledging potential interest, would stress disadvantages. They would warn of disclosures giving offense to individuals in other governments. They would observe that advice might be less candidly given within the government if individuals had foreknowledge that what they said or wrote could eventually appear in print. Though most would concede the usefulness of solid histories of recent events, and mavericks here and there would urge that such histories be commissioned, hardly any segment of the bureaucracy would see its interests served. On balance, the advice given a cabinet officer would be overwhelmingly adverse.

One cabinet member could overcome opposition in his own agency by persevering and working out compromises concerning selection of historians, clearance of manuscripts, and other details. His greater problem would stem from the fact that he alone could not achieve the desired result. He could not commission historians to use records from or even write authoritatively about any other department or agency. To be sure, understanding of events after 1945 comparable to understanding of events before that date will come only when archives and private papers are available in many countries. Historians with access to *all*

American records would be able to tell less than half the story. With records of only one segment of the American government, they could reconstruct only a portion of that half. While one can argue that anything would be better than nothing, it is nevertheless questionable that works less broad in perspective and ample in scale than the Langer and Gleason or Feis volumes would be worth the requisite investment of effort by either an official sponsor or by the kinds of historians whose talents ought to be engaged.

Histories that would have the requisite perspective and scale could be written only with files from the State and Defense Departments, the CIA, the AEC, the Treasury, the Budget Bureau, and the White House and with some access to participants and, if possible, to some of their private papers. No single cabinet officer could open all the necessary doors. To launch an appropriate program, he would not only have to struggle with his own bureaucracy but persuade several of his colleagues to struggle with theirs.

The scenario would not be markedly different if the President himself were involved. In fact, any cabinet member taking an initiative would probably seek presidential support rather than try to negotiate individually with his colleagues. And the President would inevitably be conscious of probable resistance to be encountered within each agency. He would have to ask himself if the result were so much to be desired as to justify his inflicting pain throughout the bureaucracy and in consequence using up some of his relatively limited power to manage it. It seems highly unlikely that he would regard the distant pay-off as worth the initial price.

Especially is this so because the President or any other strategically placed official would have to recognize that arrangements necessary inside the government would probably arouse criticism outside. Any program involving research in classified and sensitive files would entail privileged access by a few historians. Those few would have to be men accepted not only as meeting requirements for high security clearance but also as possessing judiciousness and discretion. Looking upon those chosen as "court historians," an indeterminate number of scholars would undoubtedly view their work as positively harmful, arguing that it would communicate to the public an official, "establishment" interpretation which the rest of the scholarly world would be poorly placed to evaluate or challenge.

Criticism on similar grounds would undoubtedly come from some members of Congress. Clearly, the Congress as a whole would benefit from having any new knowledge about the recent past. Equally clearly, Congressmen would protest loudly any access policy that resulted in disclosure of secrets, compromise of relations with other governments, or needless injury to individual careers. But certain Representatives and Senators would surely take up the cry that any program involving privileged access was designed to produce propaganda for the executive branch. To the extent that federal funds were involved, key members of the two houses might be tempted to credit this charge, solely with a view to slicing something from the budget.

We have here a not uncommon paradox. The government, abstractly conceived, needs and could use carefully written histories of recent international relations. Historians who specialize in that field would be eager to write these histories. If they produced solid narratives, Congress, the scholarly world, and the public at large would benefit. People involved in policy-making would benefit even more. At the very least, some hard information would take the place of gossip and legend. Yet this large collection of interests seems unlikely to be served because the object in view does not have great importance for any of those who stand to gain. So long as this remains so, an accumulation of relatively minor administrative, bureaucratic, and political complications forms a seemingly unbreakable logjam.

There may, however, exist a lever to loosen this jam, and it is a lever with which many scholars would willingly bear a hand, even if they have divided views about the ultimate aim. Many changes in the situation might be effected if the scholarly community mobilized itself to lobby for the wholesale opening of records more than twenty years old.

At present, only one department has a clear policy regarding use of files. In the State Department, all records more than thirty years old, except personnel records, are completely open. Some less old may be used if the *Foreign Relations* series covers the year in question and if notes taken are reviewed by the Historical Office. All records of later date remain closed. Since *Foreign Relations* now extends into 1945, the State

Department's archives are, for practical purposes, open for research if twenty-three or more years old.

Records controlled by the Defense Department do not fall under equally clear rules. In practice, however, researchers may obtain almost anything up to 1945 by using footnotes in official World War II histories as guides and requesting materials by file number from the appropriate archivists. With the same finding aids, other sources can be located and used in the Roosevelt Library at Hyde Park.

The present twenty-three year gap will soon lengthen. The *Foreign Relations* series has fallen steadily behind. Without any official histories resembling those of World War II, researchers will have no ready means of seeking Defense documents or penetrating classified files in other agencies and in the newer presidential libraries.

Perhaps this prospect will alarm scholars. Herbert Feis has already attempted to call them to arms through his *Foreign Affairs* article, "The Shackled Historian." If they respond in significant numbers, some action might result.

Those interested probably ought to seek action by Congress. Relatively simple changes in Titles 5, 18, and 44 of the United States Code would achieve the desired result. Title 5, Section 301, authorizing department heads to prescribe regulations for custody and use of departmental records, already specifies that they are not to withhold information from the public or limit the availability of records. Title 18, Section 798, defines classified information. Title 44 regulates management and disposal of records and their transfer to the National Archives.

A single piece of new legislation could dictate that all departmental records over twenty years old fall to the control of the Archivist and that, with certain exceptions, all such records be automatically declassified and made available for scholarly research. Exceptions could be stipulated for three categories: (1) records containing information, the disclosure of which would constitute a breach of good faith with the individuals from whom the information was obtained (this would cover personnel files, criminal investigation records, tax returns, and raw intelligence); (2) cryptographic or cryptoanalytic materials which the Director of the National Security Agency certified as having been reexamined and found likely to compromise cryptographic or cryptoanalytic devices or techniques in use at a more recent date; and (3) other materials which a department head certified as having been reexamined and found to contain information which, if disclosed, would endanger the national security. For each document in category (2) and (3), the head of the National Security Agency or the appropriate department head should be required to specify a date for automatic declassification.

Such proposed legislation would unquestionably provoke opposition from the executive branch. In view of the staggering quantity of classified material, agency representatives would protest the administrative difficulty of annually examining all documents twenty years old. But the answer to these points, as to points about potential embarrassment to other governments and compromise of the confidentiality of advice, is that these documents must at some point come into the public domain. The quantities involved would be no less if automatic declassification occurred after fifty years or forty years or thirty years. The real issue concerns the point at which the dangers become so marginal that they are outweighed by the public's right to the complete record.

The British now have a thirty-year rule. Under the Public Records Act, as amended in 1967, all official records not still in current use go to the Public Records Office and may be examined by any qualified researchers. The only exceptions are documents covered by a "breach of good faith" clause. Since civil servants occupy most policy-making posts in Britain, a thirty-year line has a logic there not applicable in the United States. Indeed, with all but a handful of American policy-makers being presidential appointees and the Twenty-second Amendment limiting a presidency to eight years, a strong argument could be made for our having a twelve-year rule. Certainly, a twenty-year rule, especially with safeguard clauses, should satisfy any criterion of reasonableness in the United States. Were the Committees on Government Operations to take testimony concerning a twenty-year rule, executive branch witnesses should have a very hard time making out a realistic case against it.

Associations of historians, political scientists, and perhaps international lawyers could pass resolutions urging such legislation. Individual members could communicate their support of it to Senators and Representatives. Representative Moss's recent "Freedom of Information" bill suggests that some members of Congress are predisposed to believe that doubts should be resolved in favor of the public rather than the executive bureaucracy. Congress might act. Or fear of congressional action might prompt the President or individual department heads to promulgate something like a twenty-year rule. Were such a rule to go into effect, prospects would improve for additional steps. One can imagine men at various levels asking, "For God's sake! What is in those files?" One can also imagine office and bureau chiefs agreeing that those due to become public in future must be examined. And the simplest recourse would be to assign departmental historians the task.

In the State Department, historians already do such work. Those compiling the *Foreign Relations* series examine almost all classified files. They consult experts about specific documents possibly needing to be kept under lock and key until the Department's thirty-year rule takes effect. This task involves twelve professional historians. With three or four more, the Historical Office could bring *Foreign Relations* up to the twenty-year line, get ahead in document processing, and thus, while performing more efficiently its public information function, be in position to reassure the geographical bureaus and other powerful departmental interests regarding records about to be made public.

A twenty-year rule would force Defense, the Joint Chiefs, the Services, CIA, and other agencies to take similar precautionary measures. The Office of the Secretary of Defense, the Joint Chiefs, and CIA could issue documentary volumes. They would be comparable to *Foreign Relations* in importance and interest, and they would have even more public relations utility. Students, teachers, journalists, and others using them would learn how intelligent and high-minded is much of the work done by agencies that many now regard as neanderthal and somewhat sinister. But, because many of the documents are highly technical, these agencies would probably find it more economical to have the sorting of their files accompanied instead by the preparation of narrative agency histories. The Atomic Energy Commission's official history, largely the work of two scholars, provides an admirable model. The Joint Chiefs, the Army, and the Air Force at present budget for enough historians to permit their easily producing similar volumes. The same is probably true of the CIA. Only the Office of the Secretary of Defense and the

Navy lack personnel, and their new requirements might be met by transfers from other parts of the Defense establishment. Systematic preparation of publishable documentary compilations or narrative histories for all national security agencies could be accomplished, in other words, at negligible cost.

The State Department, the Army, the Air Force, and the AEC already acknowledge the value of such works for public information purposes. Under pressure to solve problems created by a mandatory twenty-year rule, departmental administrators might recognize more readily their potential usefulness for staff reference and hence for policy-making. Officials would not, as at present, face a choice between change and no change—a situation in which bureaucratic instincts always tend to be timid and conservative. A twenty-year rule would compel them to choose among kinds of change. In these circumstances, sensible historical programs might appear to represent system as opposed to chaos.

If a number of departments and agencies reacted to a twenty-year rule by devising such programs, opportunity would arise, at least momentarily, for another step. Before departmental plans crystallized, a forceful argument could be made for central coordination. Someone in the Executive Office of the President, perhaps under the Secretary to the Cabinet or the Executive Secretary of the National Security Council, could be charged with seeing that each agency made adequate preparations for conforming to the twenty-year rule. He could also oversee the distribution of historians among agencies and the consistency of the programs they planned. Thereafter, he could facilitate exchanges of information and to some extent prevent labor-wasteful duplication of effort.

Such central coordination would not be instituted unless some senior official or member of the White House staff took initiative in urging it on the President. The difficulty of winning presidential approval would, however, be considerably less than at present or than at a later period when new routines had created new vested interests within the various departments.

And if central coordination were once established, still another possibility would open up. Conceivably, a coordinator in the Executive Office might sponsor a separate publication program aimed at producing general histories comparable in scale and perspective to Langer and Gleason's work on 1938–1941 and Feis's on the war years. One can visualize substantial surveys covering two- or three-year periods—1945–1948 and 1948–1950, for example—complemented by topical surveys as, for example, one on foreign economic policy, 1945–1960.

Drawing on departmental histories and records in presidential libraries, such works might be prepared by historians on the Executive Office payroll. Alternatively and preferably, they could be written on commission by historians based in universities.

The British followed such procedure in their World War II histories. As a result, they obtained volumes from such distinguished scholars as J. R. M. Butler, Norman Gibbs, and Sir Charles Webster. The Cabinet Office is now doing the same for postwar studies. The Langer and Gleason volumes constitute a partial precedent on this side of the Atlantic. The President, at the prodding of the Secretary of State, authorized the undertaking and, though one author was in government employ, the other, Langer, was not.

The great advantage of following these precedents would lie in the undeniable fact that most of the best historians prefer being professors and simply would not accept appointments in the career civil service. Still another advantage would derive from the government's probably being able to use this talent without significant cost to itself. For purposes of status and access, academic historians could be given Executive Office appointments without compensation. Whatever they needed for time off from teaching, travel, and the like, could almost certainly be obtained from a public-spirited foundation. Only minor support costs would have to be borne by the government.

Some, though not all, potential objection to "court historians" might be met if the Social Science Research Council or a joint committee of the American Historical Association and the American Political Science Association were to manage a foundation grant for this purpose and thus have a hand in choosing the scholars to take part. In any case, objections ought to be partially muted by existence of a twenty-year rule. Given the ways in which historians define their undertakings, the slow pace of research, and the routine of clearance for publication, volumes dealing with events more recent than ten years back would seldom appear. Skeptical scholars could thus anticipate having access to the sources within a decade or less. Their own work would be easier in consequence of having the survey volumes as pointers to problems and, through their footnotes, as guides to otherwise labyrinthine records. One could at least hope that such considerations, added to safeguards concerning staffing and funding, would curb complaint from anti-establishment scholars and make less likely adverse comment on Capitol Hill.

The foregoing obviously involves some romancing. It is by no means certain that a scholars' lobby could move Congress. With events of the Vietnamese war fresh in mind, many Congressmen might regard agitation for a twenty-year rule as inspired by potential subversives. Even if Congress should budge, executive agencies might not respond creatively. One can conceive of their reacting by detailing unimaginative Foreign Service, military, and CIA officers to reclassify and lock up everything not perfectly innocuous. And something more than improvement in departmental historical programs would result only if, coincidentally with Congress' moving toward a twenty-year rule, someone high in the executive branch seized the opportunities thereby created. It is hard realistically to express optimism about any phase in the sequence outlined.

If, however, scholars could stir Congress, a twenty-year rule were to be adopted, and there followed systematization of departmental programs, central coordination, and publication under Executive Office sponsorship of surveys concerning events as recent as ten years in the past, the government, the historical profession, and the public would all be gainers. Policy-makers and their staffs would possess more reliable knowledge about events which they use as trend gauges and action indicators. Men talking across departmental boundaries would have common knowledge about such events. Legislators, journalists, and others commenting on current actions would have less excuse for basing comparisons on legend instead of reality. Historians would pursue their "relevant" research with more expectation of being read by those to whom their work should have greatest relevance. As teachers, they could deal more confidently than at present with events from the lifetime of their students, and students might leave the classroom with somewhat more awareness than now seems common that the world is a complicated place and that the color of truth is often gray. In the largest sense, the public interest would be served.

ESSAY REVIEWS

England and America

JOHN CLIVE

American Democracy in English Politics 1815–1850. By David Paul Crook. Oxford: Clarendon Press, 1965. Pp. xvi, 237. $5.60.

One great virtue of this book is its modesty. Some historians engaged in the study of American influence on England during the nineteenth century supplement a natural desire to look for such influence with an almost uncanny ability to find it. Not so Mr. Crook, who is fully aware of the fact that while the debate about the meaning of American democracy was certainly *one* of the touchstones of English politics during this period, it was by no means either the sole or the decisive one. Thus he is willing to tell us, when the occasion demands it, that American experience was not at all central to the formation of Benthamite opinion; that many Whigs undoubtedly lacked interest in American affairs; and that neither of the two chief conservative theorists of the period, Coleridge and Disraeli, concerned himself in any significant way with the United States.

These examples of the author's candor serve not merely to illustrate his unprejudiced approach, but also to reveal the scope of his endeavor. In examining the influence of American democracy upon English politics during the first half of the nineteenth century, he has not confined himself to one or the other extreme of opinion—Radical or Tory—but has tried to survey the entire spectrum of political attitudes, devoting special attention to its middle ranges. As a result, he has successfully avoided the dualistic mold into which some of the previous accounts of the subject have been cast. These accounts depicted on the one hand Radicals and reformers deriving courage, inspiration, and program from the American democratic example; on the other, hidebound reactionaries for whom the very same example seemed only to confirm their worst suspicions of that form of government.

Mr. Crook has not fallen into this Manichaean trap; and that is the second virtue of this book. Not only is his purview sufficiently broad to include within it Whig as well as Tory and Radical attitudes during this period. He takes particular care to isolate and to define shifts and nuances within the categories with which he deals. The principal chapter headings reveal what those categories are: "The Benthamite Millennium"; "Whiggery and America"; "The Conservative Response." A final chapter, somewhat different in scope, deals with the variety of responses to Tocqueville's *Democracy in America*. A very useful appendix entitled "The United States in British Periodicals: 1815–1860" identifies the authors of some of the more important anonymous articles on America to be found in the leading political periodicals.

But what chapter headings alone cannot reveal is the solid common sense of the author's approach. Any study of external influence emanating from another country confronts certain obvious difficulties. There is, first of all, the difficulty of estimating the precise role of that influence in events and developments that might have occurred without it, propelled by purely domestic factors. Then there is the danger of "freezing" the stream of history; of ignoring the fact that in both countries, the one that influences and the one that receives the influence, changes occur over a period of time in the realms of politics and society, changes not necessarily consonant in thrust and direction. What is considered important at one point may no longer be regarded as such a few years later. Meanwhile, not only have the needs of the "recipient" changed, whether in terms of reality or myth. Conditions and ideas of the "sender" have undergone changes as well. Moreover, it is possible in a study of this kind to support almost any position with selective quotations.

Mr. Crook is conscious of these dangers and pitfalls and successfully avoids them. It would, for example, have been easy (and not totally inaccurate) for him to have categorized Bentham and his followers as "pro-American," and to have found a series of quotations in support of this statement in relevant documents and periodicals. It is to his great credit that Mr. Crook does not rest content with that. He points out, correctly, that the emphasis in Benthamite thought falls far more heavily on the happiness of the greatest number than on the individuals who make up that number. Bentham and his followers, though favoring a democratically elected legislature, were far more bent on assigning to that body total sovereignty and making it into an effective instrument of government than on restraining it by means of an elaborate system of checks and balances. Moreover, Bentham himself had no use at all for concepts such as natural rights or the social contract—he dubbed them "nonsense on stilts." Here, as elsewhere, he was out of harmony with the major tradition of American political thought. Yet he and his followers, men like James Mill and George Grote, celebrated the virtues of American democracy. Why? Because the American example was useful to them, inasmuch as it lent support to their propaganda for the causes they had most at heart in the decade and a half before the first Reform Act: a free press; religious liberty; a wider franchise; above all, a government without benefit of aristocracy or church.

The Benthamites would not allow the argument postulating "propitious circumstances" in America, an argument brought forward by Sir James Mackintosh and other Whigs unwilling to press English franchise reform to the point of universal suffrage. This argument, part of the Whig canon for much of the century, had it that universal suffrage was appropriate to the United States, though not to England; since in America unlimited availability of land and an expanding frontier created the possibility of an entire nation of landed proprietors, thus averting the danger of democratic rule to the established order of property ownership. Against this argument, Bentham's disciple Grote maintained that American respect for property sprang not from the peculiar economic and geographic circumstances of the country but from universally valid democratic principles according to which the many, always and everywhere, had an interest in supporting the rights of property of all.

In the *Westminster Review* and other Benthamite publications of the 1820's was to be found wholesale praise of American institutions, manners, and values. The authors of articles in these publications were not overly upset by what others called the low state of culture in America; being convinced that this would improve, once the nation had developed. Nor were they unduly exercised by any thought of contradiction between their praise of Jeffersonian minimal government across the ocean and the affinity of their own system for centralized power and administrative regulation. They saw in America what they wanted to see, with more regard to what use they could make of it in the current English political situation—which they were trying to change—than either to its accuracy or to its absolute consistency with the rest of their beliefs and ideas.

Things changed after the passage of the first Reform Act in 1832. The United States still served as precept and example for those legal reforms which continued to remain dear to the hearts of the Benthamites. But in the course of the thirties and forties, as the Philosophic Radicals themselves lost their cohesiveness of aim and action, and as their attempts to form a democratic party in Parliament met with failure and they drifted away from their temporary alliance with the working class, their attitude toward American democracy also underwent significant modifications. Doctrinaire praise for trans-Atlantic democracy in all its aspects gave way to a more discriminating examination of American institutions. Some Utilitarians—such as Roebuck and Grote—held on to their idealized version of American democracy longer than others. But it was the Chartists and some of the leaders of the Radical working-class movements who tended to take over this line; whereas it was John Stuart Mill, influenced by Tocqueville, who set the tone for Liberal thinking in stressing the dangers and possible abuses rather than the achievements of democracy as it existed in America. What Mr. Crook has done, then, in his account of Benthamite attitudes, is not merely to chronicle a major change, but to relate that change in an integral way to corresponding changes in English politics and society.

Thus in some ways the tracing of English views of American democracy during the nineteenth century resembles a journey through a hall of mirrors. People see what they want to see, and use what they want to use for their own purposes from another country or culture. Up to 1832, for example, the Whig *Edinburgh Review* cited the American example to press for suffrage reform, without making doctrinaire statements about the universal victories of democracy. From the thirties onward, the journal's tone became more critical. Now Whigs and Liberals delighted in deriving gradualist lessons from the United States; regarding the American Revolution as the work of responsible and propertied men, recognizing Jefferson as a Whiggish democrat. Each group saw America in its own image, and drew from it the lessons it most needed for itself.

But for the historian to generalize about groups and interests and their attitudes, he must be reasonably sure about the homogeneity of the groups and interests involved. Otherwise, the labels lose their utility. Mr. Crook tends to employ the conventional labels. Thus he speaks of the Whigs as "traditionally the party of the financial interests." One begins to have doubts as one asks oneself whether this makes much sense as applied to the Whig party in the early Victorian context. And these doubts are reinforced by Mr. Crook's description of Nassau Senior, whose articles on America in the *Edinburgh Review* during the 1830's set the tone of that periodical's approach. Senior is described as "the architect of the Poor Law Amendment Act of 1834," and as one who labored at the center of Whig politics. "Although an associate of the Benthamites and a pioneer in political economy, he came from a prosperous family with Tory sympathies, and was strictly conservative in his approach to the problem of popular government." Does not this very description seriously put in doubt the use of labels such as "Whig" and "Tory" as organizing devices for the study of public opinion?

Scattered throughout the book are further instances that echo this question. Take John Stuart Mill, for instance, whose solution to the problem of the stagnation of the middle classes through excessive uniformity "was not unlike that suggested by Tories such as [David] Robinson"; and whose extreme solicitude for the security of person and property Mr. Crook quite rightly calls "more Whig than Radical." Or take John Wilson Croker, a leading Tory publicist, who for almost a generation (from 1831 to 1854) retained virtually sole control of the *Quarterly Review's* editorial policy. Croker hated abstract theories of democracy, yet considered it a political way of life natural to the American environment; and he had a sense of the necessity for economic partnership between the two nations that Mr. Crook deems worthy of the Manchester School. To be sure, Croker at the same time feared for the future of American democracy, and prophesied attacks on property "when democracy became industrial and institutions were exposed to trial from 'the pauperism of great towns or the vicissitudes of demand and supply.'" Can one call these fears typically Tory? They were, in fact, very similar to those expressed by that arch-Whig, Thomas Babington Macaulay, who in his turn predicted eventual spoliation of the rich by the discontented American masses. Mr. Crook calls Macaulay's attitude "on the whole more Tory than Whig." But as one ponders this and other instances of cross-party views, one begins to wonder whether traditional party labels are the proper framework within which English attitudes to America during the nineteenth century ought to be examined.

Mr. Crook himself is certainly aware of this problem. Conservative and Whig impressions of the Republic, he tells us at the very beginning of his book, were highly idiosyncratic. And in the course of it he distinguishes between hidebound "Eldonian" Toryism and "Liberal" Toryism; and fully recognizes the disagreement among the Whigs about the worth and viability of the American constitution. What he does not do—and, in a sense, it is really beyond the scope of his book—is to place his findings into the context of recent views of Victorian England. And since his categories of analysis conform to the traditional party labels, one receives to some extent the impression of clusters of paradox and anomaly, of numerous special cases departing from the norm. But the fact that his account contains so many instances which simply cannot be subsumed under those labels is, I believe, indicative of something more fundamental, confirmed by a look at recent scholarship on nineteenth-century English history; and that is an increasingly strong feeling that these old labels are no longer adequate, especially when employed as automatic indicators of distinct social and economic interests and attitudes.

Thus it is now clear that when it came to the crucial question of state intervention, for example the limitation by law of the number of hours worked daily in factories, one cannot accurately speak of a struggle between paternal-ist Tories eager to impose controls and laissez-faire Whigs equally eager to prevent their imposition. This, like many other social issues, transcended party lines. Adherents of both major parties were to be found in each camp. Even the battle over the Corn Laws, for so long thought to have been a text-book example of pro-repeal manufacturing interests (read "Liberal") locked in combat with anti-repeal landed interests (read "Tory") no longer appears to have been waged in so neat and clear-cut a manner. One of the funda-mental facts about Victorian England was the diversification of economic in-terests in the hands of the propertied and wealthy; which makes it difficult, if not impossible, to speak of "pure" landowners, financiers, and manufacturers, and to characterize the political interests of these groups in crudely Marxist terms.[1] E. P. Thompson, for one, has pointed to the attractive forces that tended to draw together gentry and industrial *bourgeoisie* at a time when they "should" have been fighting.[2]

Moreover, political allegiance, whether of Members of Parliament or of ordinary voters, was by no means determined by economic and class interest alone. John Vincent has shown, for example, that at the local level there was to be found a nearly equal division of votes between Liberal and Tory within each class and occupation.[3] And W. O. Aydelotte has reminded us that given individuals, then as now, could be conservative in some respects and radical in others. The multi-dimensional character of political attitudes and the spe-ciousness of a simple polarity of right and left are characteristic of the nine-teenth as well as of the twentieth century.[4] In other words, in dealing with English views of America during this period, it is well to take into account political as well as economic diversification of interests. One must be prepared not only for diversity, but also for apparent contradiction and actual overlap. That this applies to the intellectual as well as to the political landscape has been demonstrated by Raymond Williams, who lays special emphasis on the way in which the critique of the new industrial society was carried out by such seemingly incompatible figures as Cobbett, Burke, Coleridge, Marx, and the

1. See George Kitson Clark, *The Making of Victorian England: Being the Ford Lectures Delivered Before the University of Oxford* (London, 1962), pp. 1–27; William O. Ayde-lotte, "Parties and Issues in Early Victorian England," *Journal of British Studies*, 5 (1966), 95–114.

2. Edward P. Thompson, "The Peculiarities of the English," *The Socialist Register*, 2 (1965), 311–362.

3. John Vincent, *The Formation of the Liberal Party 1857–1868* (London, 1966).

4. Aydelotte, "The Conservative and Radical Interpretations of Early Victorian Social Legislation," *Victorian Studies*, 11 (1967), 225–236.

Utilitarians.[5] Keeping this in mind makes one less surprised to find the Tory *Blackwood's* as well as John Stuart Mill inveighing against the materialism of American culture in very similar terms.

Students of Victorian England, then, must be prepared to encounter complexity and confusion rather than tidy and clearly-delineated compartments. This makes any general statement hazardous. Yet there is room for at least one generalization, and it is one directly related to Mr. Crook's theme, and borne out by his book. England in the nineteenth century was not a democratic society. And one refers to it as a society *en route* to democracy at one's peril, unless one adds in the same breath that the journey was to be long and circuitous, and that the great majority of travelers were dragging their feet, held back either by their own reluctance or by the power and persuasion of their leaders.

That the Tories were not enamored of democracy goes without saying. But neither were Whigs and Liberals. Mr. Vincent has shown that it was not just the aristocratic Whigs but the Liberal party as a whole, including great reformers like Gladstone and Bright, whose posture toward numerical democracy on the American model was, like that of John Stuart Mill, primarily one of apprehension. Moreover, the idea that the middle classes triumphed in the middle of the nineteenth century, only to be themselves bested by the working classes at the century's end, bears little relation to the facts. When, in Oscar Wilde's *A Woman of No Importance* (1893) Lady Hunstanton meets Hester Worsley's assertion that "In America we have no lower classes" with the rejoinder "Really? What a very strange arrangement!", she is not speaking in jest. Noel Annan has pointed out—and this is a point not sufficiently emphasized by Mr. Crook—that John Stuart Mill, in trying to apply Tocqueville's analysis of democracy in America to England, underestimated the immense strength of continuing aristocratic and upper-middle-class power. He could not imagine that for the next hundred years the intellectual minority he was so concerned to protect would be in danger not of being stifled by the masses, but of being gelded by the upper class.[6]

Given this social situation, cemented by tradition and deference; given the gradual decline of democratic enthusiasm among the Radicals, one would not be far off in characterizing the impact of American democracy on England in the course of the nineteenth century as primarily one that called forth varying degrees of suspicion and fear. During the middle decades of the century, even

5. Raymond Williams, *Culture and Society 1780–1950* (New York, 1958).

6. Noel Annan, "John Stuart Mill," in *The English Mind: Studies in the English Moralists Presented to Basil Willey*, eds. Hugh Sykes Davies and George Watson (Cambridge, 1964), pp. 219–239.

sympathetic observers gradually became disillusioned with America—whether by the panic of 1837, by aggressive American foreign policies, or by the slavery problem. There were exceptions, of course; to be looked for among Chartists and Dissenters and, on occasion, among aristocratic mavericks like Bertrand Russell's parents, about whom a Liverpool newspaper reported in August, 1867:

Lord and Lady Amberley, who are about to visit the dreamland of their youth, the Great American Republic, have determined on substituting on their boxes the word "Mr." for that antiquated monosyllable "Lord", which might prove so offensive to Yankee prejudices.[7]

But on the whole nineteenth-century England hardly formed a congenial environment for genuine democratic sympathies. And, as Royden Harrison has recently shown in his treatment of English working-class attitudes to the American Civil War, by no means all champions of *English* popular causes were agreed on how favorably they viewed "the great experiment" across the Atlantic. Internal conflict about this was part of the English labor movement, just as it was part of the other major political movements of the period.[8]

Two conclusions, then, emerge from looking at early and mid-Victorian England in the light of recent scholarship: a strong conviction that the key to the period is "deference" rather than "approaching democracy" as well as an equally strong persuasion of how difficult it is to correlate political party allegiance with socio-economic attitudes in any straightforward or automatic fashion. There are two major consequences for future studies of nineteenth-century English opinion about American democracy. One, that it may henceforth be assumed that the principal area of study will not be a spectrum ranging from warm support on one side to outright enmity on the other; but rather a broad middle-ground of suspicion and apprehension, tempered by occasional and selective sympathy. The other, that these attitudes are best examined not in the expectation of finding them running in exactly or even approximately parallel lines to major political party and class divisions; but, rather, in the expectation of discovering a full range of opinion *within* the confines of each party or class. The next order of business for historians of England and of Anglo-American relations is to construct fresh categories which will take full account of these insights. Future students of the subject in search of a new framework will find in Mr. Crook's book a pioneer work of the greatest value.

7. *The Amberley Papers: Bertrand Russell's Family Background*, eds. Bertrand Russell and Patricia Russell (London, 1937), II, 49.

8. Royden Harrison, *Before the Socialists: Studies in Labour and Politics 1861–1881* (London, 1965).

Church, State, Calvinism, and Conscience

SIDNEY E. MEAD

Isaac Backus and the American Pietistic Tradition. By William G. McLoughlin. Boston: Little, Brown and Co., 1967. Pp. xii, 252. $5.00.

Isaac Backus on Church, State, and Calvinism, Pamphlets, 1754–1780. Edited by William G. McLoughlin. Cambridge: The John Harvard Library, Harvard University Press, 1968. Pp. 525. $11.95.

Roger Williams, The Church and the State. By Edmund S. Morgan. New York: Harcourt, Brace & World, 1967. Pp. 170. $4.50.

These books have been much reviewed in the historical journals, their virtues praised, their particular faults noted, their significance assessed, and their place in the swelling corpus of New England Puritan studies precisely indicated. And because of the severe limitation of length now commonly imposed on such reviews, even the academic who, like Alice, must run as fast as he can to stay in one place, can read them. My purpose is not to "review" them in this usual sense, but rather to try to place them in the context of my overall, and limited, perspective on religion in American history. Necessarily such an "essay to do good" must be more or less impressionistic and highly selective. But I trust, with Don Quixote, that the many "other things which [I might have said], although I am unable to recall them, we will look upon as understood." This I think is in keeping with the intent of the authors.

Both Edmund Morgan and William McLoughlin are specialists (as I am not), having published intensive studies of early and later-day Puritanism respectively which are marked by a high degree of scholarly competence and devotion. But neither is an antiquary or mere chronicler of what happened. Their works seem motivated by the urge to communicate the significance of the life and work of their subjects in the development of "the American way," and the work of both contributes (as I think such histories should) to our self-understanding as Americans. Both are teachers as well as scholars, and I can say, as I am sure many others can also, that they have instructed generations of my students.

Morgan's theme is *Roger Williams: [on] The Church and the State*, which I

443

have seen in the context of *The Puritan Dilemma*, in which he told *The Story of John Winthrop*. McLoughlin's theme in the *Backus Pamphlets, 1754–1789* is *On Church, State, and Calvinism*; in the biography it is *Isaac Backus and the American Pietistic Tradition*. Hence the works are explorations of (1) the contribution of pietistic or evangelical Calvinists to the spiritual and ideological impetus that brought on the Revolution, and (2) the sense in which the Great Awakening "foreshadowed the outlook of the nineteenth-century American mind."[1]

To this extent the purpose of the authors seems not essentially different from that of Alan Heimert in his massive study of *Religion and the American Mind from the Great Awakening to the Revolution*.[2] The difference is a matter of selection, emphasis, and approach. Heimert takes as his archetypal "Calvinists" Edwards, Whitefield, and their disciples, and makes his work a polemic against those who have effaced the "evangelical sources" of the Revolution by placing sole emphasis on the contribution of the "liberals" of the Chauncy-Mayhew line. In doing so he largely ignores the actualities of the struggle for religious freedom in Massachusetts carried primarily by the Separates and the Baptists. McLoughlin, perhaps, makes too great claims for Backus and his cohorts,[3] to the slighting of the evangelical Calvinists within the establishment that Heimert concentrates on. But by giving us a lifelike sketch of Backus and a major selection from his *Works*, he corrects Heimert's one-sided picture as Heimert's study corrects McLoughlin's emphasis.

We are all indebted to Henry F. May for reminding us so clearly and persuasively that "The Recovery of American Religious History"[4] provides us

1. McLoughlin, ed., *Backus Pamphlets*, p. 16.

2. Harvard University Press, 1966. See my review in *The Journal of Religion*, 48 (July, 1968), 274–287.

3. "In the writings of the Separates and Separate Baptists, and particularly in the tracts of Isaac Backus, we may see clearly delineated the most far-reaching and prophetic expositions of the ideas and the spirit animating 'the new reformation' which grew out of the Great Awakening in New England. In them lies the key to that pietistic temper which has done so much to shape the course of the American experiment in religious freedom ever since." McLoughlin, ed., *Backus Pamphlets*, p. 19.

So far as the issue was the practical and political one of religious freedom, and a delineation of the political coalition that brought it about, McLoughlin's emphasis seems closer to the mark. It seems clear that when Jefferson spoke of "our dissenting allies" (LeRoy Moore, Jr., "Religious Liberty: Roger Williams and the Revolutionary Era," *Church History*, 24 (1965), 70), he was hardly thinking of Edwards, Whitefield, and Bellamy, but of the Baptists. If Jefferson was aware of and thought about Edwards and his consistent Calvinist disciples it is most likely that he saw them as staunch defenders of establishment —which of course they were.

4. *American Historical Review*, 70 (1964), 79–92.

(among other things) with a direct way of studying the relation between ideas and institutions. The works here reviewed exemplify this. Although Morgan asserts that he attempted to "deal only with the way he [Williams] thought about the church, the state, and the relationship between them," he also asserts that "Williams did what he did because of what he thought."[5] What Williams thought certainly rocked the Massachusetts Bay civil and ecclesiastical institutions in his lifetime. And his approach and ideas, revived in substance by Backus a century later, were behind the final thrust that eventually overturned them in 1833.

Yet Williams, who promulgated several "intellectual novelties,"[6] was not actually an originator of new ideas. Morgan is right in saying that "his thinking progressed not by opposing accepted ideas but by pursuing them through their implications to conclusions that his contemporaries could not or would not accept."[7] On this there has been general agreement from John Cotton to the present.

This it was that made Williams so hard to deal with. For unlike the Quakers, for example, it was difficult, perhaps impossible, to convict him of outright heresy and, so far as I know, none of the New Englanders from John Cotton to Cotton Mather accused him of such.[8] Their emphasis followed that of Cotton who spoke of Williams' "violent and tumultuous carriage," his "heady . . . turbulent" and "offensive spirit . . . both in judgment and practice," and of the "weakness and slenderness of the grounds of his opinions, notions, and courses . . . ."[9] Morgan notes that even the ministers who tried to convince Williams of the error of his ways could accuse him only of opinions "whereby a church *might* run into heresy, apostasy, or tyranny."[10] This line culminated in Cotton Mather's famous figure of the Dutch windmill and the conclusion that Williams "had less light than fire in him," and offered a

---

5. Morgan, *Roger Williams*, pp. 5, 4.

6. *Ibid.*, p. 90.

7. *Ibid.*, p. 5, or, p. 62, "In thinking about the church, Williams took a number of accepted doctrines and pressed them to unaccepted conclusions."

8. I base this observation on a review of the material provided by *Roger Williams, John Cotton and Religious Freedom; A Controversy in New and Old England*, ed. Irwin H. Polishook (Englewood Cliffs, N.J., 1967); *Roger Williams and the Massachusetts Magistrates*, ed. Theodore P. Greene (Boston, 1964); and two articles by LeRoy Moore, Jr., "Roger Williams and the Historians," *Church History*, 32 (1963); and "Religious Liberty: Roger Williams and the Revolutionary Era," *Church History*, 34 (1965).

9. "A Reply to Mr. Williams His Examination" (1647), in Polishook ed., *Controversy*, pp. 55–57.

10. Edmund S. Morgan, *The Puritan Dilemma, The Story of John Winthrop* (Boston, 1958), p. 125. Emphasis added.

"sad example . . . of that evil which the apostle mentions in Romans x,2: 'They have a zeal, but not according to knowledge.' "[11]

Mather was right. Those who knew Williams personally in Massachusetts Bay generally agreed that he was an estimable exemplar of the Puritan virtues—as Morgan notes, "a charming, sweet-tempered, winning man, courageous, selfless, God-intoxicated—stubborn . . . ."[12] In brief, they said he had commendable zeal, but that his conclusions were not according to *their* knowledge.

Similarly Isaac Backus was no theological heretic. The content and spirit of the orthodox Calvinism of his day permeates his *Works*, and McLoughlin rightly sees his "The Doctrine of Particular Election and Final Perseverance" (1789) as a last-ditch stand "upon the brink of the Second Great Awakening in which Calvinism suffered its final defeat, even among the Baptists."[13] The Reverend Joseph Fish, a defender of the establishment against whom Backus wrote one of his longest pamphlets, paid implicit tribute to the orthodoxy of Backus and the Baptists in saying, "I know not one *principle* or *practice* among them, that is agreeable to the Gospel but what they learned in OUR churches . . . ."[14]

Inasmuch as the theology of Williams and Backus was orthodox according to the Calvinistic perspective of their respective centuries, these studies have to do with Calvinists' contribution to the acceptance of religious freedom and the American democratic way. And because the respective establishments Williams and Backus opposed rested on the same Calvinistic perspective they accepted, the studies illustrate how radically different conclusions regarding social and political structures can and did sprout from the same theological premises.[15] Recognition of this fact provides the guard against lumping all Puritans together as anti-democratic—the tendency of such earlier interpreters as Parrington and Wertenbaker. It may also serve as a notice to some churchmen that theological agreement does not necessarily bring ecclesiastical harmony and unity.

11. As quoted by LeRoy Moore, Jr., "Roger Williams and the Historians," pp. 437–438. Mather ended by commending Williams for defending orthodoxy against the Quakers.

12. Morgan, *The Puritan Dilemma*, p. 116.

13. McLoughlin, ed., *Backus Pamphlets*, p. 448.

14. As quoted by Backus in "A Fish Caught in His Own Net" (1768), in McLoughlin, ed., *Backus Pamphlets*, 257.

15. Joseph Blau's concept and definition of "Protestantism" as "openness as to conclusions" is useful at this point. See his article, "What is American about American Jewry?" *A Quarterly Journal of Jewish Life and Thought*, 7 (1958).

These studies bring out one difference between Williams and Backus that is very important because it reflects a basic change in the relationship between theology (ideas) and experience (institutions) that was becoming obvious in the second half of the eighteenth century. Morgan correctly notes that although "in his writings . . . Williams was more often concerned with ecclesiastical and political institutions," yet his "every thought took its rise from religion."[16] This is to say that his approach was deductive—that he deduced from the common premises conclusions respecting action, and practice followed as a consequence.

McLoughlin makes clear that Backus' approach was the opposite—that his experience and practice preceded Scriptural and historical justification;[17] that in general Backus "had already reached his own conclusions" before he "came to a self-conscious search for historical antecedents."[18]

Backus, then, reflects his era when theology was increasingly valued for its *utility* in defending the way of life emerging out of the American experience; history for its utility as an arsenal of useful precedents; and religion itself for its utility in inculcating the good morals necessary for sound republican and free government.[19] This development reached a peak in Timothy Dwight, who led the orthodox hosts against "Infidelity" and ushered in the Second Great Awakening in New England.

16. Morgan, *Roger Williams*, p. 86.

17. Backus wrote that "much of what I have here written, I knew experimentally before I did doctrinally" and "only later did I examine Scripture [there] to discover the proof of what I knew." McLoughlin concluded that even "his [Backus'] reliance on revelation was secondary to his direct personal perception of divine truth." McLoughlin, ed., *Backus Pamphlets*, p. 28

18. *Ibid.*, pp. 17–18. McLoughlin's summary on these pages is worth quoting at length: "Beginning with Biblical exegesis to suit their needs, they gradually adopted additional arguments based upon 'charter privilege,' the Toleration Act, the English constitution, and inalienable natural rights. It was only in seeking authorities to buttress their arguments against 'oppression' that the Separates and Separate-Baptists rediscovered the relevance of the writings of earlier dissenters, the political theory of John Locke, the practices of the other colonies, and eventually even the works of Roger Williams, which Backus himself unearthed in the early 1770's. The final important source for Backus' disestablishmentarianism was the Revolution rhetoric and logic of the patriots . . . ."

19. Although Backus complained that defenders of the establishment now tacitly admitted that "rulers have no right to establish any way of religious worship for its own sake, they [do] have a right to do it for the good of civil society," and that they argued that the proceedings against the Baptists "are entirely the acts of the civil state, done for its OWN utility," he also admitted that he was "as sensible of the importance of religion and of the utility of it to human society" as they were. The utilitarian argument is inherent in his defense of Calvinism against John Wesley and the Arminians in 1789, where he argued that the doctrines of the latter were inimical to the freedoms of the new nation. *Ibid.*, pp. 375, 338, 358, 467.

It is in this development that I think one finds the distinguishing mark of "the real break with the Old World, the medieval mind, and the Puritan ethos" which McLoughlin notes.[20] The "modern" world was ushered in when first the primacy, then the reality of the Bible-oriented invisible world of Winthrop's and Williams' day faded like Alice's Cheshire cat even in the minds of ardent Christians. What was changed was nothing less than the way of conceiving, apprehending, and representing reality—a change so fundamental that it almost defies description. Simply put, it meant that the meaning of events experienced in this life was no longer found in their relation to the invisible world of the Christian drama, but in their ascertainable chronological or causal connections.[21] It is this change in the culture's accepted way of apprehending reality—which the evangelicals, among others of course, unconsciously furthered—that seems to me to have created all the problems for traditional Christianity in the modern world. The end result in America was not inappropriately suggested by Henry Steele Commager when he wrote that "during the nineteenth century and well into the twentieth, [organized] religion prospered while theology went slowly bankrupt."[22] This is the deep shadow that hangs over the revivalists' almost successful thrust to convert "the new nation to their brand of Evangelical Christianity."[23]

In order to understand the nature of the archetypal conflict between Williams and his Massachusetts Bay opponents it is necessary to understand the latter's scheme of things, which in substance still persisted in Backus' day. Whitehead held that a commonwealth is a society guided by a master ideal.

20. *Ibid.*, p. 74.

21. A profound and extensive exploration of this change is found in Erich Auerbach's *Mimesis; The Representation of Reality in Western Literature,* translated by Willard Trask (Princeton, 1953). He writes that the Christian or "figural interpretation of history . . . implies that every occurrence in all its everyday reality is simultaneously a part in a world-historical context through which each part is related to every other, and thus is likewise to be regarded as being of all times, or above all time." P. 136.

"In this conception, an occurrence on earth signifies not only itself but at the same time another, which it predicts or confirms . . . . The connection between occurrences is not regarded as primarily a chronological or causal development but as a oneness within the divine plan, of which all the occurrences are parts and reflections. Their direct earthly connection is of secondary importance, and often their interpretation can altogether dispense with any knowledge of it." P. 490.

From the viewpoint of what Auerbach calls "modern realism," the "connection between occurrences" *is* "regarded as primarily a chronological or causal development" and "their direct earthly connection" *is* thought to be of primary importance in understanding and explaining them.

22. Henry Steele Commager, *The American Mind, An Interpretation of American Thought and Character Since the 1880's* (New Haven, 1950), p. 165.

23. McLoughlin, ed. *Backus Pamphlets,* p. 448.

According to Winthrop in "A Modell of Christian Charity" the master ideal of his group was to "bring into familiar and constant practice" what "the most in theire Churches maineteine as a truthe in profession onely."[24] The early Bay leaders seem to have been in substantial agreement regarding what was implied in their profession (essentially of the sovereignty of God) for the establishment of their "due forme of government both ciuill and ecclesiastical." As Morgan puts it, "they had undertaken to establish a society where the will of God would be observed in every detail, a kingdom of God on earth."[25] This endeavor to actualize their ideal of "a kingdom of God on earth" they held in the context of the common English ideas of a national covenant and the "elect nation," which defined, in Winthrop's words, how "stands the cause betweene God and us . . . ."[26] It defined their "errand into the wilderness."

Williams was a radical threat to the Bay system because, while appealing to the same Scriptures and the same Calvinistic theology as did those of the establishment, he came to different conclusions about practice. This was to undermine their system by appeal to their premises. Perhaps one reason this has often been overlooked is that Williams was banished by civil authority (something that Cotton made much of) and historians in assessing the reasons tended to follow the Bay apologists in directing attention to his conclusions rather than to his premises. Morgan's *Roger Williams* places the emphasis where it belongs.

The Bay authorities, because of their power structure, could dispose of Williams, and his ideas also, by banishing him to an area beyond their jurisdiction. This was a territorial solution made possible by the available space.

Morgan sees that a territorial resolution of their problem was inherent in the whole Bay movement. "The Puritan Dilemma" of which he writes, was how to live a holy life in an unholy world—"the paradox that required a man to live in the world without being of it."[27] In England the paradox meant that these Puritans found themselves impaled on the horns of their self-created dilemma. For while they thought that the ecclesiastical forms imposed on

24. This is a constant theme throughout the developments in New England. Backus' New Lights called upon the churches of the establishment to practice what they preached. *Ibid.*, p. 4.

25. Morgan, *The Puritan Dilemma*, p. 69. See also pp. 88, 180.

26. See Morgan, *Roger Williams*, chap. iv. As Morgan notes, this "orthodox position furnished a powerful motive for holding society as closely as possible within the laws of God, an incentive for good behavior more immediate than fear of hell or hope of Heaven." *Ibid.*, p. 114.

27. Morgan, *The Puritan Dilemma*, p. 31. This of course is the perennial paradox confronted by all Christians.

them there were wrong because contrary to Scripture, yet they were commanded to observe those unscriptural forms by "the powers that be" of Romans xiii, 1–2. And because those powers were ordained of God, to disobey them was to sin and call down judgment on themselves. They were, in brief, damned if they did and damned if they didn't. Morgan argues rightly that Winthrop and his cohorts followed a course "that enabled them to avoid the problem rather than solve it: to leave England altogether, yet leave it with the approbation of the King and without repudiating its churches and the Christians in them."[28] This explains why they so highly valued the Charter, as Backus did also.[29] It was their only legal basis.

Williams, cordially welcomed at first by the Bay clergy and magistrates as one of them, could not in conscience thus avoid the problem, and he would not permit them to avoid it so long as he was present. He faced it head-on, and his clear solution is epitomized in his advice to Winthrop to "abstract yourselfe with a holy violence from the Dung heape of this Earth." And he made it quite clear that the King and his claims to the American land, the English nation which called itself "Christian," its Church, worshipping with the unregenerate in administering an oath, and the use of coercion to enforce the first table of the Law, were all included in the "Dung heape."[30] But Winthrop believed "that there was no escape from the dung heap of this earth; and that those who sought one or thought they had found it acted with an unholy, not a holy violence."[31] The Christian, he held, "must not ayme at a condition retyred from the world and free from temptations"[32] as the Separatists tried to do.

As a leader responsible "for holding society as closely as possible within the laws of God," Winthrop tried to steer a middle and balanced course between "excessive liberality" and "excessive purity."[33] Of the two he considered the latter the greater threat in Massachusetts.[34]

28. *Ibid.*, pp. 32–33.

29. See McLoughlin, ed., *Backus Pamphlets*, pp. 321, 340–341.

30. To understand the Bay Puritans' treatment of Williams it should be kept in mind that at the time Winthrop supposed that Laud's Commission was sending "ships and soldiers . . . against us, to compel us, by force, to receive a new governor, and the discipline of the Church of England, and the laws of the commissioners, occasioned the magistrates and deputies to hasten our fortifications, and to discover our minds each to other . . . ." Polishook, ed., *Controversy*, p. 41, from Winthrop's *Journal*, Sept. 18, 1634.

31. Morgan, *The Puritan Dilemma*, pp. 130, 99.

32. *Ibid.*, p. 11.

33. Larzer Ziff notes that Cotton "agreed with Nye and Goodwin that his road was the 'middle way' between Presbyterianism and separatism." *The Career of John Cotton: Puritanism and the American Experience* (Princeton, 1962), p. 213.

34. Morgan, *The Puritan Dilemma*, pp. 28–100. Within the establishment there was

But in his day the Bay leaders could avoid meeting the *arguments* of the (to them) extremists on either side by banishing them as troublers of the commonwealth, which, Cotton suavely argued, "is not counted so much a confinement, as an enlargement, where a man does not so much lose civil comforts, as change them."[35]

However, in the next century when Backus and the Baptists confronted the establishment with what was essentially Williams' position, this territorial solution was no longer possible. Backus and the Baptists could not be banished, and they would not exercise the freedom Nathaniel Ward had granted all dissenters to be gone, the sooner the better. So while spokesmen for the establishment in Backus' day may have recognized (more clearly than Winthrop had a century before in dealing with Williams) the subversiveness of the Baptist position,[36] the problem had to be met as a direct confrontation of opposites within the confines of the commonwealth. On their premises the Baptists had no alternative but civil disobedience.

Backus elaborated the argument. Holding, like Williams before him, that "God always claimed it as his sole prerogative to determine by his own laws what his worship shall be, who shall minister in it, and how they shall be supported," he concluded that in order to obey God they must refuse "any active compliance with some laws about religious affairs that are laid upon us."[37] The Separates, he had said in 1768, were "such as choose to suffer spoiling of goods or imprisonment rather than to pay what is demanded in an ungospel way."[38] And, he asked, "how can we be blamed for refusing to pay . . . when

---

always tension between the two emphases—between, for example, Endecott and Dudley on the one hand and Winthrop on the other, although all agreed on a "philosophy of government to give their commands a superhuman sanction," *ibid.*, pp. 86–88—a claim "to divine authority [that] was not peculiar to Puritans or to Englishmen" (*Roger Williams*, p. 80). Endecott and Dudley represented "excessive purity" from Winthrop's perspective, as he represented "excessive liberality" from theirs. It is important to keep in mind this disagreement between the leaders *within* the establishment in order to guard against the supposition that as "the Puritan Oligarchy" they always presented a completely united front in opposition to deviants and the way they were to be treated—the error of Parrington and Wertenbaker. See Moore, "Roger Williams and the Historians," pp. 442 and 451, note 38.

35. "A Reply to Mr. Williams His Examination" (1647), in Polishook, ed., *Controversy*, p. 53.

36. McLoughlin, in *Isaac Backus*, p. 59, quotes a late seventeenth-century Puritan, who concluded that on the Baptist principles ". . . all our holsom lawes & orders [are] left open to state destroyers . . . so that our very fundaments of civil & scared [*sic*: "sacred"?] order, here in New England, are at once thereby . . . overturned."

37. McLoughlin, ed., *Backus Pamphlets*, p. 317.

38. *Ibid.*, p. 250.

... it is evident to us that God never allowed any civil state upon earth to impose religious taxes" and declared His vengence against those who did.[39]

Ratification of Article III of the new Massachusetts constitution in June, 1780, brought the issue to a head. Backus, in opposing it in 1779, had argued that if Establishment "should be engrafted into our new plan of government we should have no constitutional remedy against it left upon earth."[40] Defenders of the Establishment charged, correctly, that the Baptists schemed "to make void in part our new constitution of government, that part of it which respects the public worship of God,"[41] and were determined to prevent this. Backus, continuing to urge refusal of "any compliance" with the laws, pointed out that if their enforcement "is continued among us, it must be by naked violence."[42] For now he argued, the "*Standing Churches*" are in direct disobedience to the doctrines of Christ,[43] and "stand upon—civil authority" alone.[44]

Here he touched the heart of the matter of civil disobedience, which is the last resort of the free individual conscience against a determined establishment after discussion of the issues has broken down. Its purpose is to force the existing establishment into the appearance of having nothing but "naked violence" on its side—something as contemporary as this morning's newspaper.

It did not quite succeed in Massachusetts, and the freedom for which Backus stood was not made legal until 1833, twenty-seven years after his death on November 20, 1806. Ironically, the ideal of freedom that came widely to prevail in the United States during the following century was closer to that of John Cotton, Nathaniel Ward, and the defenders of the establishments—the freedom provided by space to move away from undesirable location, neighbors, or oppression. And now, in the second half of the twentieth century when such freedom is less and less possible in our increasingly crowded country, the nature of freedom itself has to be probed in a situation roughly analogous to that of Massachusetts in Backus' day.[45] It is this that makes McLoughlin's books so timely.

What finally triumphed in the United States is what we commonly call the

39. *Ibid.*, p. 359.

40. *Ibid.*, p. 382.

41. *Ibid.*, p. 408.

42. *Ibid.*, p. 380. In arguing against Article III in 1781, Backus gave "five reasons why we could not in conscience obey their certificate laws any longer." It is a classic summary of the premises on which the evangelicals based resort to civil disobedience. *Ibid.*, p. 421.

43. Backus summarized the doctrines in "An Appeal to the People" of 1780. *Ibid.*, pp. 390–391.

44. *Ibid.*, p. 189.

45. I developed this view in the essay, "The American People: Their Space, Time, and Religion," *The Lively Experiment* . . . (New York, 1963).

separation of church and state.[46] In Christian circles such separation is rooted in the doctrine suggested by Matthew xxii, 21, "Render therefore unto Caesar the things which are Caesar's; and unto God the things that are God's." But just what this implies for church-state relations, and how it is to be institutionalized has been subject to a multitude of interpretations. The Bay establishment interpreted it one way, Williams and Backus in another.

Both agreed of course that basic premises which provided guidelines for the conduct of all human affairs were to be found in the Bible. So the method of interpreting the Scriptures was of central importance. And *here* apparently Williams differed most from the Bay apologists, but, as Morgan makes clear, only in degree.[47]

To them, all Scripture being given by God, the guidelines could be derived equally from Old and New Testaments.[48] So far as personal religious piety was concerned, they were passionately New Testament Protestants, stressing the redemptive work of Christ in the elect individual's soul. However, when they looked for guidelines for their "due forme of government" they found them in the Old Testament nation-church of Israel. But like all Biblical Christians who have sought a model in Scripture, they had to reject some aspects of the original. The method of interpretation called typological provided them a rationale for doing so. According to this method, developed early in Christian history to ease the difficulty of reconciling Old and New Testaments, some Old Testament forms were seen as types, or figures, of which New Testament forms were the antitypes, or reality. It was a flexible instrument, usually applied only when Old Testament forms could not be taken literally. Thus John Cotton was quite sure that "ceremonial laws were generally typical," but "not so Moses his Judicials . . . ."[49] But it was always difficult to give a finally convincing reason for such choices. What is inherent in the method, however, is the suggestion of real discontinuity between the Testaments, *and* an intimation that what the Bible intends may not be what it appears to say.

Williams, as Morgan notes, applied typology more broadly, and while ad-

46. The inadequacy of the terms *church* and *state*, especially when imaged with Jefferson's "wall of separation" between them, to describe and understand the actual situation in the United States is increasingly recognized. See my "Neither State Nor Church—Reflections on James Madison's 'Line of Separation,' " in *A Journal of Church and State*, Autumn, 1968.

47. Morgan, *Roger Williams*, p. 90.

48. For example, Cotton argued that "Thus it was in the Old Testament, and why should it be changed in the New" in those matters which "the Lord Jesus . . . did expressly appoint . . . in the Old Testament; nor . . . ever abrogate . . . in the New." Quoted in Polishook, ed., *Controversy*, pp. 70, 85.

49. Quoted *ibid.*, p. 85.

mitting "that some of the precepts of the Old Testament retained a universal validity, his usual demand was that the Old Testament be read in a typological sense."[50] Thus he greatly enlarged the area of discontinuity between the Testaments and concluded "*that the Pattern of the National Church of Israel, was a None-such, unimitable by any Civil State, in all or any of the Nations of the World beside.*"[51] It "was merely figurative and typing out the Christian Churches" which are "the Israel of God now, the regenerate or newborn...."[52] Thus Williams undercut the whole Biblical basis of the Bay structure simply by applying almost universally the method that the Bay apologists used primarily to circumvent embarrassing Old Testament commands of Jehovah.

A century later Backus and the Baptists used the same typological approach to emphasize "the discontinuity, the antithetical nature of the two, the complete and distinct break between the past [O.T.] and the present [N.T.] dispensations."[53] "Our fathers," Backus wrote, "run [sic] into their error by attempting to form a Christian Commonwealth in imitation of the Theocracy of the Jews."[54] And, echoing Williams, he held that "in the new-testament we are confined to no place but the saints are God's house."[55]

Such rejection of the validity of Old Testament forms as models of direct application for Christians cleared the way for complete separation of the spiritual and civil realms and the image of "the wall of Separation between the Garden of the Church and the Wilderness of the World" of which Williams spoke. Each realm had its peculiar weapon, and they were mutually exclusive—the civil magistrate the sword of steel, the church "the two-edged Sword of the Word and the Spirit of God."[56]

Williams' position was given classic expression in his often-quoted "Letter to the Town of Providence" in January, 1655.[57] The captain is to command the ship, seeing to it that "justice, peace and sobriety, be kept and practiced, both among the seamen and all the passengers." But he has nothing to do with their religion—"none of the papists, protestants, Jews or Turks, [are to] be forced to come to the ship's prayers or worship, nor . . . compelled from their own particular prayers or worship, if they practice any." As Morgan

50. Morgan, *Roger Williams*, pp. 91–92.
51. *Ibid.*, p. 93.
52. Quoted from "The Bloody Tenent Yet More Bloody," in Polishook, ed., *Controversy*, pp. 81, 82.
53. McLoughlin, *Isaac Backus*, p. 74.
54. McLoughlin, ed., *Backus Pamphlets*, p. 436.
55. McLoughlin, *Isaac Backus*, p. 76.
56. Morgan, *Roger Williams*, p. 101.
57. Morgan, ed., *Puritan Political Ideas 1558–1794* (Indianapolis, 1965), pp. 222–223.

summarizes, "the government had no business with the church at all" and "any religion that could benefit from the use of force was by definition not Christian."[58] Backus took the same position:

The civil magistrates work is to promote order and peace among men in their moral behavior towards each other so that every person among all denominations who *doth that which is good* may *have praise of the same*, and that all contrary behavior may be restrained or forcibly punished.[59]

It was universally agreed by all parties "that [civil] government originates in an agreement—a covenant—of the people." To the Bay Puritans, God was a participant in the agreement. But, as Morgan expresses it, Williams, noting that as a matter of fact "states did exist, did exercise authority, and did prosper where the name of Christ was unknown,"[60] succeeded "in evicting God from the proceedings."[61]

In this scheme magistrates and people alike are constrained to live simultaneously in the two distinct realms of God and Caesar. If, as Williams held, "Christians are called out of the world, they still are in the world 'in civill things for a while here below.' The Jord Jesus Christ, 'the greatest Polititian that ever was,' forever made this plain in his parable of the wheat and the tares (Matthew xiii)."[62]

Backus' position is essentially indistinguishable from that of Williams. And McLoughlin argues, correctly I think, that "under their new definition of 'liberty of conscience' [which meant their right 'to act and conduct as they pleased'] the pietists of the Awakening would have succeeded in destroying the whole basis of the Puritan Christian commonwealth. And that is in essence what Backus accomplished."[63] This forces the historian to ask, what did he and they put in its place?

Clearly Christians were to be guided in the first realm by the Word of God, the commands of Christ. But where were they to find guidance "in civill things," or a reliable definition of what was involved in rendering unto Caesar his due? And where was the magistrate to turn for authoritative definition of the "justice, peace and sobriety" he was to enforce, and of the limita-

58. Morgan, *Roger Williams*, pp. 90, 94.

59. McLoughlin, ed., *Backus Pamphlets*, p. 191.

60. Morgan, *Roger Williams*, p. 115.

61. *Ibid.*, p. 90. This way of putting it seems to me an exaggeration, but the point is essentially sound.

62. Moore, "Religious Liberty," p. 61. The inner quotations are from Williams' writings.

63. McLoughlin, ed., *Backus Pamphlets*, pp. 24–25.

tions of his power? It seems to me that in the theory of such complete separation of the realms as one finds in this pietistic tradition, a vast ambiguity was created in this area that left the evangelicals open to easy alliance with, and thereby tacit approval of, the theory held by any political party that seemed to promise *them* the freedom of conscience and practice *they* desired. They were willing to let the captain command the ship so long as he did not interfere with their churches.[64] If, as Morgan says, they evicted God from the civil covenant, they at the same time confined Him in their perspective and institutions.

McLoughlin suggests several "good" reasons why "It is not so strange perhaps that Baptist pietists should have been the bulwark of the party of the deistic Thomas Jefferson."[65] It has often been noted that on several matters their basic ideas were similar.[66] Above I have suggested why the pietists could follow the deistic political leaders in spite of the great theological difference that existed between them.[67]

A more substantial reason is that the deists' great Mr. Locke "appropriated his own views on religious liberty almost wholly from that great milieu of Puritan thought of which Williams . . . was a most consequential part." But Locke formulated these views for his time "in *reasonable* terminology for eminently reasonable men." As Moore puts it, Locke "borrowed Puritan

---

64. This was inherent in Williams. As Morgan notes, "Government, as Williams saw it, required skills that had nothing to do with religion," Morgan, *Roger Williams*, p. 115; "Christ himself had given instructions to His followers that must make them good subjects of any government," *ibid.*, p. 116; and "Williams' view made all governments equal . . . ," *ibid.*, p. 120. McLoughlin notes that "liberty of conscience and freedom of religion represented for him [Backus], and for most Baptists prior to 1773, essentially a self-centered and denominationally oriented goal rather than an absolute or clearly enunciated principle. Nowhere did Backus argue on behalf of dissenters in general, as Williams and Jefferson so often did; nor did he join forces with other dissenting groups to work for separation on an interdenominational basis. Always the Baptists worked with and for the Baptists." "Isaac Backus and the Separation of Church and State in America," *American Historical Review*, 73 (1968), 1398.

65. McLoughlin, ed., *Backus Pamphlets*, p. 429.

66. See e.g., William Warren Sweet's "comparison . . . between the basic ideas of the popular religious bodies and those held by the intellectual liberals," in "Natural Religion and Religious Liberty in America," *The Journal of Religion*, 25 (1945), 54–55. Sweet's view of the alliance was similar to that of McLoughlin, "The Protestant Churches," *Annals of the American Academy of Political and Social Science*, 256 (1945), 45.

67. McLoughlin is right in noting that my "claim [*The Lively Experiment* . . . , pp. 19, 40–44] for a 'rationalist-Pietist alliance' is subject to serious qualifications, especially in New England." "Isaac Backus and the Separation of Church and State in America," *American Historical Review*, 73 (1968), 1400.

ideas . . . [that had been] formulated in the service of God . . . and pressed them into the service of men."[68]

It is true that Williams and Backus in separating the two realms came to about the same conclusions respecting separation as did the deists, albeit perhaps from the opposite direction.[69] But the argument that the former were theocentric while the latter were anthropocentric must not be pressed too far. It seems to me that the argument of Jefferson and Madison was, in its way, ultimately as theocentric as that of Williams and Backus. All four argued from the nature of God.[70]

Their big difference can be pinpointed by applying Joseph Blau's concepts of "protestantism" and "pluralism." "Protestantism" is "openness as to conclusions" that is, that different conclusions respecting practice can legitimately be arrived at from the same beginning premises. "Pluralism" on the other hand, is "openness as to beginnings," that is, that men may come to the same desirable and legitimate conclusions from a great variety of theological and philosophical perspectives.[71] In this sense, the pietists were "protestants" and the deists were "pluralists."

This explains what McLoughlin notes, that "the Baptists never came wholly to accept the Lockean theory of religious liberty in Jeffersonian rationalist terms." Backus, as "protestant," held of course that the only true beginning was Christianity, and on this premise he based his belief that what was being formed was "a Christian state."[72] This belief, widely prevalent, "explains why it was so easy . . . for the Evangelical inheritors of the Separate-Baptist viewpoint to ignore the rights of non-evangelicals (Catholics, Mor-

68. Moore, "Religious Liberty," pp. 65–66. Moore bases his conclusion on the article by Winthrop S. Hudson, "John Locke—Preparing the Way for the Revolution," *Journal of Presbyterian History*, 42 (1964), 19–38. This thesis throws light on McLoughlin's observation that "the Separate Baptists were slow in asserting anthropocentric claims for religious liberty in terms of the rights of man. Backus preferred to argue, as Roger Williams had done, for the divine rights of God rather than for the natural rights of man." McLoughlin, ed., *Backus Pamphlets*, p. 37.

69. Jefferson and Madison as political leaders wanted to keep "the machinations of priestcraft" out of government, while "Backus and the Baptists feared the persecution of the State and sought to keep Christian churches free from the machinations of officialdom . . . ." McLoughlin, *Isaac Backus*, p. xi. This difference is a matter of emphasis and should not be pressed too far. Madison and Jefferson seem to have been about as ardent as Backus for keeping the state from meddling with the internal life of the churches.

70. This seems to me clear in, e.g., Jefferson's "Act for Establishing Religious Freedom in Virginia" and Madison's "Memorial and Remonstrance on the Religious Rights of Man."

71. Joseph Blau, "American Jewry."

72. McLoughlin, ed., *Backus Pamphlets*, p. 429.

mons, the Indians, Atheists, Free-masons) in order to protect the moral order of a [that is, of their] Protestant nation."[73] I think it may be said that those in the Evangelical tradition never intellectually digested the premise of "pluralism" (in Blau's sense).[74] This is the "unfinished intellectual business" that they laid on the table during the flight from "Reason" that was carried on the wave of the Second Great Awakening.[75] "Evangelical religion" may have been all, and done everything, that McLoughlin claims for it "in the years 1800–1900."[76] But it never extensively dealt with the theological issue between its "protestantism" viewpoint and the "pluralism" viewpoint which is the foundation of the Republic.

Finally, there seems implicitly to be developing an argument between historians respecting who, or which party, contributed most to the forming of the "American" mind and democratic way.[77] Insofar these historians tacitly accept the "protestantism" (in Blau's sense) premise, which perhaps reflects the dominance of the evangelical perspective even in the most secular of contemporary scholars. Inclusive studies based on the "pluralism" premise are needed.

This premise, that the same end may be reached from a diversity of intellectual beginnings, requires a very general definition of the common end sought by *all* parties. Here I take my cues primarily from Parts I and II of Alfred North Whitehead's *Adventures of Ideas*. In this perspective the movement of history exhibits the slow incarnation in social and political arrangements of ideals—"metaphysical intuitions"—respecting the nature of things, the implications of which are gradually articulated in "specific notions." It is on the level of these specific notions that conflict within a culture takes place—as, for example, between Williams and Backus on the one hand and the Massachusetts establishment on the other.

The "metaphysical intuition" yeasting in all of Christianity has been that the essential nature of Deity, and hence the master ideal for all human relations, is persuasion and not coercion. This ideal was always inherent in Chris-

---

73. *Ibid.*, p. 37.

74. "In his life and writings Backus set forth the principles of separation of Church and State which were to predominate in American life until very recently. They were not, however, the same as those set forth by Jefferson and Madison . . . ." McLoughlin, *Isaac Backus*, p. xi.

75. Mead, *The Lively Experiment* . . . , p. 55.

76. *The American Evangelicals, 1800–1900: An Anthology*, ed. William G. McLoughlin (New York, 1968), p. 1.

77. This seems to me implicit in the respective emphases of Heimert and McLoughlin, noted above.

tianity. But, to adopt Herbert Butterfield's useful concepts of "majority" and "minority" reports in characterizing an era, it was only in the seventeenth and eighteenth centuries that it became a part of the majority report of powerful leaders and sparked the revolutions that ushered in modern democracy. During those centuries the great thrust was made to actualize the ideal of persuasion in all social and political arrangements—the ideal carried in the slogan, "government by the consent of the governed." The principle of "consent" reconciled the tension "between the rights of individual conscience and the compulsory power of the state" which McLoughlin notes.[78] During the last half of the eighteenth century the ideal was precisely articulated and its practical implications spelled out, by men of many different and often antagonistic theological perspectives.

Only when the discussion is moved to the level of such inclusive higher generality can the place and contribution of such men as Williams and Backus, who articulated the ideal in the specific notions of their evangelical Calvinistic position, be justly assessed while at the same time doing justice to the contributions of contemporaries who articulated it in the specific notions of different theological systems—for example, the "rational Christianity" or "Arminianism" of a Mayhew or a Chauncy, or the "deism" of a Paine or a Jefferson. In the context of such general concepts the historian does not get involved in fruitless argument over who or which party contributed most to the eventual outcome—for example, whether the American democracy that flowered in the Jacksonian era owes more to the Edwards line of establishment Calvinists, the Chauncy-Mayhew line of "liberals," the Separate Baptist line of Backus, or the Jefferson-Madison line of Deists. I suppose that each of these parties tended in opposition to the others on the level of specific notions to operate on the "protestantism" premise. But interpreters of the American mind and spirit need to operate on the "pluralism" premise.

78. McLoughlin, *Isaac Backus*, p. ix.

Slavery and Race

JAMES M. McPHERSON

The Political Economy of Slavery; Studies in the Economy of the Slave South. By
Eugene Genovese. New York: Pantheon Books, 1965. Pp. xiv, 304.
$5.95.

*Prelude to Civil War: The Nullification Controversy in South Carolina, 1816–
1836.* By William W. Freehling. New York: Harper & Row, 1966. Pp.
xiii, 395. $5.95.

Slavery Attacked: The Abolitionist Crusade. Edited by John L. Thomas. Englewood Cliffs, N.J.: Prentice-Hall, 1965. Pp. xi, 178. $1.95.

Since the publication in 1954 of Thomas J. Pressly's *Americans Interpret
Their Civil War*, there has been no lack of continuing effort to explain the
background and causes of the war. Recent studies lack the sweep and grandeur that distinguished the writings of Rhodes, Channing, Beard, Phillips,
Craven, Randall, and Nevins, but something approaching a consensus has
emerged in the last fifteen years, emphasizing slavery as the basic source of
conflict. This renewed accent on the peculiar institution goes beyond a mere
revival of Rhodes's assertion that slavery was the "single cause" of the war.
There have been increasingly sophisticated efforts to explain slavery as a complex social and economic institution with far-reaching moral and political
consequences. But we still do not have a full understanding of the social psychology of slavery and race in antebellum America.

Much of the recent writing on causes of the war has taken the form of essays and articles rather than the broad, multi-volume studies produced by
earlier generations, and has been characterized by caution and a recognition
of the intricacies of human motivation. There are of course some exceptions. Eugene Genovese's *The Political Economy of Slavery* cannot be described as a cautious book. Genovese advances two major arguments in this
volume: 1) Slavery was a costly, inefficient labor system that impeded the
adoption of progressive farming techniques, prevented agricultural diversification, generated a low level of productivity per man-hour, and imposed a
backward economy upon the South; 2) The Old South was a semi-feudal

society which differed so sharply from the bourgeois capitalism of the North that it constituted a virtually separate civilization. Slavery, though an economic liability, was socially and politically indispensable to the existence of this civilization. As Genovese sees it, the sectional conflict was irrepressible, a contest between two distinct social orders dominated by ruling classes with opposing "world views"—Northern capitalists and Southern planters. Because of the economic wastefulness of slavery and the impossibility of meaningful agricultural reform (outside the upper South), preservation of the planter's world was dependent on the constant expansion of slavery into virgin territory. The rise of the free soil movement and the victory of Lincoln in 1860 thus spelled the doom of the slaveholder's society within the Union. Submission would have meant "moral and political suicide," so the planters struck boldly for independence. In essence, Genovese's interpretation of the coming of war is a restatement of the aggressive slavocracy thesis, with this difference: the aggressiveness of the slave South, in Genovese's view, was a defensive measure to insure survival of its way of life rather than an attempt to impose Southern domination over the entire Union. To the planters "slavery was the foundation of a special civilization imprinted with their own character . . . the cornerstone of their way of life." When "the slaveholders rose in insurrection, they knew what they were about: in the fullest sense, they were fighting for their lives."[1]

Five years before the appearance of Genovese's book, Charles G. Sellers wrote that "no picture of the Old South as a section confident and united in its dedication to a neo-feudal social order, and no explanation of the Civil War as a conflict between 'two civilizations,' can encompass the complexity and pathos of antebellum reality."[2] Yet Genovese has drawn just such a picture. Though he concedes that slaveholders had occasional "doubts and inner conflicts" about the morality of slavery, Genovese portrays an essentially monolithic commitment to the peculiar institution as "the very foundation of a proper social order" and "the essence of morality in human relationships."[3] This portrait leaves out the tortured conscience and inner trauma that other historians have seen in the South's attitude toward slavery.

Building on the insights of Wilbur J. Cash, Sellers found ambivalence and tension in the Southern mind on the question of Negro bondage. Cash be-

1. Eugene D. Genovese, *The Political Economy of Slavery* (New York, 1965), pp. 247, 270.

2. Charles Grier Sellers, Jr., "The Travail of Slavery," in Sellers, ed., *The Southerner as American* (Chapel Hill, 1960), p. 40.

3. Genovese, *The Political Economy of Slavery*, p. 8.

lieved that "in its secret heart" the Old South "always carried a powerful and uneasy sense" that slavery was wrong. Haunted by "the specters of defeat, of shame, of guilt," driven by "the need to bolster its morale" and "justify itself in its own eyes and in those of the world," the South created "defense-mechanisms" that amounted to a "sentimentalized version of slavery."[4] Sellers elaborated these suggestions in a brilliant essay on "The Travail of Slavery," which argued that the irreconcilibility between slavery and the dominant ideals of Christianity and Americanism was a heavy burden on the Southern conscience. "This sir, is a Christian community," said a Virginian in 1832. Southerners "read in their Bibles, '*Do unto all men as you would have them do unto you*'; and this golden rule and slavery are hard to reconcile."[5] The liberal ideology of the Enlightenment and the Revolution did not die in the South, even after the passing of the Jeffersonian generation.

Thus, in the opinion of Sellers and of Ralph E. Morrow, the proslavery argument was directed first at the South itself and "had as its end the psychological adjustment of southerners—slaveholders perhaps more than non-slaveholders—to the external conditions of their existence."[6] In his study of antebellum Southern myths, William R. Taylor agrees with Sellers and Morrow that the antislavery crusade touched a raw nerve in the white Southerner and "left him more and more defensive and touchy." If the South's conscience had not been so troubled about slavery there would have been no need to counterattack so stridently against the abolitionists. In an effort to reassure themselves ("whistling in the dark," in Taylor's words), Southern writers created an "image of sunshine and happiness around the old plantation home," but "not far beneath the surface of most of these fleeting portrayals of Negro life lurks the uneasy sense that slavery is a wretched, insupportable" institution.[7] "We must satisfy the consciences, we must allay the fears of our own people," declared Calhoun's newspaper organ in 1835. "We must satisfy them that slavery is of itself right—that it is not a sin against God —that it is not an evil, moral or political. . . . In this way, and this way only, can we prepare our own people to defend their institutions."[8]

Most of the South's intellectual effort in the antebellum generation was

4. Wilbur J. Cash, *The Mind of the South* (Doubleday Anchor reprint, New York, n.d. [1941]), pp. 73, 95.

5. Quoted in Sellers, "The Travail of Slavery," p. 48.

6. Ralph E. Morrow, "The Proslavery Argument Revisited," *The Mississippi Valley Historical Review*, 48 (June 1961), 86.

7. William R. Taylor, *Cavalier and Yankee: The Old South and American National Character* (Doubleday Anchor reprint, New York, 1963 [1961]), pp. 279, 280, 284.

8. Quoted in Sellers, "The Travail of Slavery," p. 51.

devoted to this end. Theologians searched the Bible to construct a religious defense of slavery; philosophers rejected the "pernicious abstractions" of the Declaration of Independence and turned to ancient Greece and the Middle Ages for models of society based on slavery and a strict order of hierarchy; anthropologists "proved" the inferiority and unsuitability for freedom of the Negro race; political economists waxed lyrical about how much better off were Negro slaves than the "wage slaves" of Northern factories; novelists and poets described a paternal, kindly, happy plantation society in which all classes and races were harmonized in the best possible manner. All of these themes, and others, can be found in the excellent collection of proslavery documents edited by Eric McKitrick.[9]

In his introduction to this anthology, McKitrick notes that in recent years there has been a revival of scholarly interest in the writings of Fitzhugh, Calhoun, and others. "Yet that interest has centered not so much upon these thinkers' concern for preserving slavery as upon their critique of Northern and European capitalism."[10] Historians, including McKitrick, have not recognized that the significance of such attacks on capitalism probably rested not so much in their intrinsic merit or their kinship with Marxism as in the psychological compulsion that lay behind them. Just as an individual, goaded by outside criticism of what he guiltily realizes is his most vulnerable weakness, will retaliate angrily by blaming others or by accusing his critic of the same or greater faults, so the South collectively responded to Northern criticism of slavery with the *tu quoque* retort. In polemics, as in football, the best defense is a good offense. Proslavery advocates therefore defended Negro bondage by launching into a critique of wage slavery in the North. One needs only to dip into proslavery literature to discover a touching concern with the low pay and long hours of Northern (or British) factory workers and the miserable conditions in urban slums. The need to soothe troubled Southern consciences by proving the "positive good" of slavery and its superiority to all other labor systems was probably the main motive behind the critique of capitalism.

The same psychological compulsion produced "the affirmation of Southern perfection" described by Charles Sydnor. Probably suffering from some sort of collective inferiority complex and tortured by suppressed qualms about slavery, Southerners responded to outside criticism with an aggressive assertion that they were in every way better than the critics. The greater their inner doubts the more loudly they affirmed their perfection, for they were try-

9. *Slavery Defended: The Views of the Old South*, ed. Eric L. McKitrick (Englewood Cliffs, N.J., 1963).
10. *Ibid.*, p. 1.

ing desperately to convince themselves, as well as others, that their way of life was defensible. Other societies, wrote Sydnor, looked to the past or future for their golden age, but defenders of the Old South, because of "this curious, psychopathic condition," claimed that "their own age was the golden age" and that "its main foundation was Negro slavery."[11]

Sellers maintained that the ambiguities and tensions in the Southern attitude toward slavery must be studied as a problem in social psychology. "Especially rewarding to both historians and social scientists," he declared, would be a study "of antebellum southern radicalism and its peculiar locus, South Carolina."[12] William W. Freehling's *Prelude to Civil War: The Nullification Controversy in South Carolina, 1816–1836* goes a long way toward filling this need. According to Freehling's convincing interpretation, the nullification crisis resulted not only from opposition to the tariff, but, more important, from South Carolina's desperate effort to curb the federal government's potential power over slavery.

Of chief interest here is Freehling's discussion of South Carolina's internal anguish over slavery, which provides a case study and amplification of the concepts in Sellers' essay. Slaveowners in the Palmetto State were plagued by a "morbid sensitivity" about their "disturbing institution" in the 1820's, and overreacted hysterically to the relatively mild antislavery movement of that decade. The Missouri debate, the Ohio proposition of 1824 for gradual emancipation, the American Colonization Society's request in 1827 for federal aid, even the proposal to send a United States delegate to the Panama Congress of 1826 (where representatives of Haiti would be in attendance) spurred a "frenzied response" that was "a measure of the guilt and fear which made Negro slavery a profoundly disturbing institution in antebellum South Carolina."[13] Fear of slave revolts intensified the forebodings of an already distraught gentry, and the 1820's witnessed three major insurrection panics in South Carolina: the Denmark Vesey plot of 1822, the Charleston fire scare of 1826, and the Georgetown conspiracy of 1829. The Nat Turner massacre of 1831 also had profound repercussions in the haunted minds of South Carolinians. The significance of these conspiracies and revolts lay not only in the fear they aroused among whites, but in their impact on masters who already had doubts about the system. "A slave revolt had a unique capacity to sweep

11. Charles S. Sydnor, *The Development of Southern Sectionalism, 1819–1848* (Baton Rouge, 1948), p. 339.
12. Sellers, "The Travail of Slavery," p. 68n.
13. William W. Freehling, *Prelude to Civil War: The Nullification Controversy in South Carolina, 1816–1836* (New York, 1966), pp. 49–50.

away all illusions and to force planters to confront the ugliness in their system," wrote Freehling. "A number of revolts could slowly demoralize a community already plagued by grave misgivings about slavery."[14]

In the 1820's slavery was justified primarily as a "necessary evil." This argument was one of expediency only; it conceded that the institution was morally wrong and could be defended only on grounds of racial or economic necessity. This justification had little success in quieting disturbed consciences, for "no matter how much Carolinians wanted to believe that slavery should be supported because it was necessary, they could never escape the suspicion that bondage should be abolished because it violated natural rights." A South Carolina publicist deplored in 1828 the "womanish qualms of conscience which we so often witness among many of our own citizens, as to the justice and morality of keeping men in bondage."[15]

Because the state could no longer afford the "*apologetical whine*" of the necessary evil argument, which revealed "the false compunctions of an uninformed conscience," it became imperative to proclaim slavery and the way of life it supported as a positive good.[16] Especially was this true after the failure of nullification and the rise of militant abolitionism in the early 1830's. Unity in the face of external attack became mandatory. New and harsh restrictions were placed on both blacks and whites in the name of preserving order. The slave codes were tightened, religious missions to the slaves curtailed, the mails purged of antislavery literature, gag laws imposed on antislavery petitions, and a curtain dropped on freedom of discussion in South Carolina. As in all societies subjected to outside pressure and inner tension, South Carolina whites sought a scapegoat—and found it in the abolitionist movement. It was abolitionist propaganda that made it necessary to prevent the slaves from learning to read; it was abolitionist fanaticism that required the burning of antislavery literature at the Charleston post office; it was the abolitionists who were responsible for slave unrest and uprisings, and thus for the more repressive slave codes; in Washington it was really the abolitionists who were the cause of the gag law. Within South Carolina, mob justice was swift for anyone who questioned the system. A minister who merely *discussed*, without endorsing, the Colonization Society's Liberia colony was driven out of Columbia by a mob.[17] The Great Reaction had set in.

In 1858 James Henry Hammond of South Carolina proclaimed the success

14. *Ibid.*, p. 110.
15. *Ibid.*, pp. 78, 79.
16. *Ibid.*, pp. 327–328.
17. *Ibid.*, pp. 338, 301–303.

of the proslavery counterattack. Prior to the 1830's many Southerners, said Hammond, "believed slavery to be an evil—weakness—disgrace—nay a sin . . . and in fear and trembling [they] awaited a doom that [seemed] inevitable. But a few bold spirits took the question up; they compelled the South to investigate it anew and thoroughly, and what is the result? Why, it would be difficult to find a Southern man who feels the system to be the slightest burthen on his conscience."[18] Was this a case of whistling in the dark? Sellers and Morrow think it was. "The surface unanimity enforced on the South in the forties and fifties by the Great Reaction," wrote Sellers, "concealed a persistent hostility to slavery."[19] A proslavery writer conceded in 1856 that a "secret doubt of the morality of African slavery" continued to affect "many of our best citizens." A troubled planter confessed to his wife that "I sometimes think my feelings unfit me for a slaveholder." Another master, a Mississippian, said simply in 1850: "I fear I am near an abolition[i]st." Even George Fitzhugh admitted privately that "I see great evils in Slavery, but in a controversial work I ought not to admit them."[20]

Sellers believes that Southern "guilt feelings," far from being expiated by the positive good argument, actually "increased during the final years of the antebellum period." Just as an individual declaims the loudest when his cause is weakest, so the South affirmed the perfection of its society more aggressively than ever in the 1850's. A European traveler found few masters who could "openly and honestly look the thing in the face. They wind and turn about in all sorts of ways, and make use of every argument . . . to convince me that the slaves are the happiest people in the world." The widespread relief in the South at the abolition of slavery by the Civil War, Sellers maintains, was a measure of the pent-up guilt and strain finally released by destruction of the tormenting institution.[21]

If the South really was plagued by doubt and guilt concerning slavery, why did she go to war in 1861 to preserve the institution? Sellers does not evade this question. Indeed, he comes to grips with it in a suggestive exposition of crisis psychology. Secession cannot be explained, as Genovese sought to explain it, as a rational, calculated decision: "Southerners did not and could not rationally and deliberately choose slavery and its fruits over the values it warred against." On the contrary, it was "the very conflict of values,

18. Quoted in *ibid.*, p. 299.
19. Sellers, "The Travail of Slavery," p. 52.
20. Quoted in Morrow, "The Proslavery Argument Revisited," p. 85, and Sellers, "The Travail of Slavery," pp. 55, 60, 66.
21. Sellers, "The Travail of Slavery," pp. 61, 55.

rendered intolerable by constant criticism premised on values Southerners shared, which drove them to seek a violent resolution." The psychological tension created by the ambivalence toward slavery in the Southern mind finally snapped from the pressures created by John Brown's raid at Harper's Ferry, the campaign of 1860, and the ensuing political crisis. The advocates of drastic measures took advantage of the "near-hysteria" of 1859–1861, wrote Sellers, and "inflammatory agitation and revolutionary tactics succeeded only because Southerners had finally passed the point of rational self-control."[22] A Virginian who tried in vain to prevent secession lamented that "the desire of some for change, the greed of many for excitement, and the longing of more for anarchy and confusion, seems to have unthroned the reason of men, and left them at the mercy of passion and madness."[23]

The Cash-Sellers thesis is attractive and plausible, and goes a long way toward explaining the defensive-aggressive style of Southern behavior before the Civil War. But we need a great deal more intensive research, of the kind Freehling has done for a twenty-year period in South Carolina, before we can fully accept the thesis. Was the Southern ambivalence toward slavery actually so great as Sellers suggests, or has it been largely projected into the mind of the Old South by twentieth-century historians searching for a Southern liberal tradition? Members of the historical profession are constantly urging each other to make greater use of the tools and concepts of sister social sciences in their work; here is an opportunity to apply the insights of psychology to a fascinating and important problem in American history.

Even if we tentatively endorse Sellers' interpretation of the travail of slavery, one vital question still remains: if antislavery sentiment, overt or secret, was so widespread in the South, why was slavery not abolished long before its agonies tore the country apart? There is, of course, no easy answer to this question. It has been asserted that slavery was retained because "it paid."[24] But there is a great deal of dispute about the profitability of slavery, and in any case it is questionable whether the source of so much national trauma would be preserved, or justified, on such doubtful grounds alone. Of course an investment of two or three billion dollars would not have been easily given up, but it seems likely that even if the federal government had paid full market value for the slaves, the South would not have accepted emancipation.

22. *Ibid.*, pp. 67–69.

23. Quoted in *ibid.*, pp. 69–70.

24. Kenneth M. Stampp, *The Peculiar Institution: Slavery in the Ante-Bellum South* (New York, 1956), p. 422.

In 1862 the loyal border states flatly rejected Lincoln's suggestion of compensated emancipation.

Why, then, did the Gordian knot of slavery remain tied until sundered by the tragedy of civil war? Curiously, an answer that in one sense seems obvious has not of late been explored in depth by historians. In his multi-volume study of the coming of war, Allan Nevins asserted that "the main root of the conflict" was "the problem of slavery *with its complementary problem of race-adjustment.*" The italicized phrase contains a concept of great importance, yet historians have largely ignored it, perhaps because they have assumed, with Kenneth M. Stampp, that since Negroes are "only white men with black skins" there was no real problem of race adjustment. Nevins himself discussed only briefly what he called the "overshadowing spectre of race-relationship" which was a "lion in the path" of emancipation. And David Donald, in an otherwise trenchant and provocative essay, dismissed Nevins's emphasis on race adjustment with the comment that "virtually nobody, North or South, was concerned with such matters in the 1850's."[25]

One needs only to sample the antebellum literature on slavery to discover that the problem of race was not only a major, but a *dominant* theme in discussions of the institution. As a Northern apologist for slavery put it on the eve of actual emancipation: "Politicians and fanatic clergymen may prattle as they wish about the end of slavery being the end of strife. The great difficulty will then but begin! The question is the profound and awful one of race."[26] Two main stereotypes governed Southern attitudes toward the Negro: on the one hand he was a childlike Sambo, inferior to the white man in mental endowment, shiftless and immoral, incapable of taking care of himself in freedom; on the other he was a brute savage who would quickly revert to "African barbarism" if freed from the restraints of slavery, and would rise up and cut the white man's throat. In truth, Southern whites feared the violence that might follow emancipation even more than they feared *slave* insurrections—this was the meaning of constant references to the "horrors of St. Domingo," where the worst massacres of whites occurred *after* abolition. There were many variations and nuances in these two stereotypes, and mutually contradictory images of the Negro were often held by a single individual. Whatever the image, it usually led to the conviction that emancipation was impos-

25. Allan Nevins, *The Emergence of Lincoln* (New York, 1950), II, 468; Stampp, *Peculiar Institution*, p. vii; Nevins, *Ordeal of the Union* (New York, 1947), I, 422–423, 504–509; David Donald, "An Excess of Democracy: The American Civil War and the Social Process," in Donald, *Lincoln Reconsidered* (Vintage Books edition, New York, 1961), p. 214.

26. Boston *Post*, quoted in Boston *Commonwealth*, Oct. 18, 1862.

sible unless the freed Negroes were removed from the South. Humane and kindly masters who secretly hated slavery were blinded by their vision of the "profound and awful" question of race to any constructive alternative. Many Southerners, indeed many Americans, who refused to accept the positive good of slavery nevertheless concluded that it was a necessary evil.

Proslavery writers skillfully exploited these racial convictions. William Grayson warned:

> The negro freeman, thrifty while a slave,
> Loosed from restraint, becomes a drone or knave;
> Each effort to improve his nature foils,
> Begs, steals, or sleeps and starves, but never toils;
> For savage sloth mistakes the freedom won,
> And ends the mere barbarian he begun.[27]

John C. Calhoun declared that liberty was "not a boon to be bestowed on a people too ignorant, degraded and vicious, to be capable either of appreciating or of enjoying it." Freedom, "when forced on a people unfit for it, would, instead of a blessing, be a curse; as it would, in its reaction, lead directly to anarchy." Slavery was "indispensable to the peace and happiness" of both races and "cannot be subverted without drenching the country in blood, and extirpating one or the other of the races."[28] Samuel Cartwright said in 1851 that "the White population of the Southern States have no other alternative but to keep [the Negroes] in slavery, or drive them out, wage a war of extermination against them, or go out themselves, and leave their fair land to be converted into a free negro pandemonium."[29] Edward Pollard, Virginia journalist and chronicler of the Confederacy, regarded slavery primarily as "a barrier against a contention and war of races," while a New Orleans doctor rallied whites to the cause of secession with the cry: "The alternative: a separate nationality or the Africanization of the South."[30]

The race problem pervaded Northern as well as Southern discussions of slavery. In the Lincoln-Douglas debates, for example, Stephen Douglas repeatedly charged that Lincoln and the Republicans proposed to free the slaves and make them the equals of white men. This was an explosive issue in Illinois, and Lincoln felt compelled to make evasive replies to the charge. On the

27. McKitrick, ed., *Slavery Defended*, p. 61.
28. *Ibid.*, pp. 9, 8, 12.
29. *DeBow's Review*, 11 (August 1851), 189, quoted in Arthur Young Lloyd, *The Slavery Controversy, 1831–1860* (Chapel Hill, 1939), p. 249n.
30. Quoted in Ulrich B. Phillips, "The Central Theme of Southern History," *American Historical Review*, 34 (October 1928), 41, 35.

one hand he thought every man had the right to freedom and to the fruits of his own labor, but on the other he did not favor immediate emancipation or racial equality. A man of compassion and humanity, an opponent of slavery, Lincoln nevertheless believed until perhaps the end of his life that the two races could not coexist permanently in freedom on American soil. "I think your race suffer very greatly, many of them by living among us, while ours suffer from your presence," he told a delegation of Negroes in 1862. White Americans were unwilling "for you free colored people to remain with us. . . . I do not propose to discuss this, but to propose it as a fact with which we have to deal. I cannot alter it if I would. . . . It is better for us both, therefore, to be separated."[31]

Lincoln's unsuccessful attempts to colonize free Negroes in the Caribbean during the Civil War represented the best efforts to solve the dilemma of slavery and race that America's most eminent statesmen could devise. Thomas Jefferson, James Madison, John Marshall, Henry Clay, Daniel Webster, and Abraham Lincoln pinned their hopes on colonization as the ultimate solution of the race problem. They believed slavery wrong; but they also feared that what they saw as the great physical, cultural, and intellectual gulf between the races would make it impossible for emancipated slaves to be assimilated into American society. Colonization, they thought, would get rid of the evil of slavery and the nightmare of race adjustment at the same time. In an 1824 speech supporting colonization, Senator Theodore Frelinghuysen of New Jersey said that to ask the South to free the slaves "on the soil" was to ask them "to deluge their land with the horrid scenes that would certainly follow the liberation of a licentious, ignorant, and vitiated population."[32] "Painful as it is to express the opinion," wrote Henry Clay in 1830, "I have no doubt that it would be unwise to emancipate" the slaves "without their removal or colonization."[33] In the debate over slavery in the Virginia legislature of 1831–1832, emancipationists proposed to abolish slavery *only* on the condition that freed slaves be removed from the state. A white Missourian wrote in 1856 that "if slavery could be voted out of the State of Missouri without having the Negroes set free among us, a majority of our people would be found at any time favorable to such a measure." Frederick Law Olmsted reported a conversation with a Mississippi farmer, who said: "I reckon the majority would

31. *The Collected Works of Abraham Lincoln*, ed. Roy P. Basler (New Brunswick, N.J., 1955), V, 370–375.
32. Quoted in Clifford S. Griffin, *Their Brother's Keepers* (New Brunswick, N.J., 1960), p. 42.
33. Quoted in *Slavery Attacked: The Abolitionist Crusade*, ed. John L. Thomas (Englewood Cliffs, N.J., 1965), p. 8.

be right glad [to abolish slavery] if we could get rid of the niggers. But it wouldn't never do to free 'em and leave 'em here. I don't know anybody, hardly, in favor of that. Make 'em free and leave 'em here and they'd steal everything we made. Nobody couldn't live here then."[34] An Indiana editor warned in 1850 against "the danger of encouraging a distinct and inferior race to abide in the same community with us. They are aliens and enemies, and some mode should be adopted to rid the country of their presence."[35]

There were, of course, alternatives to the bleak choice between slavery and colonization. One alternative was the situation that has actually existed in the United States since 1865: segregated, second-class citizenship for the Negro in a free society. And there was the alternative advocated by abolitionists: freedom, education, and legal rights that would pave the way for full assimilation of all Negroes into American life as equal citizens. But these abolitionists were considered hopeless visionaries or dangerous fanatics in their own time, not the least because their ideas ran counter to the deep-rooted racial convictions and fears of most white Americans. Three recent collections of antislavery speeches and writings make abundantly clear the formidable obstacle in the abolitionist path posed by the "profound and awful" question of race.[36] Not only were anti-abolitionist mobs spurred on by frenzied fears of "social equality," but more significantly, abolitionists constantly faced the question asked by reasonable but skeptical men: "What will you *do* with the Negroes, if freed?" Abraham Lincoln, after rhetorically raising this question in 1854, stated: "Free them, and make them politically, and socially, our equals? My own feelings will not admit of this; and if mine would, we well know that those of the great mass of white people will not."[37]

Here was the rub. Abolitionists tried to meet the question with the weapons of logic and eloquence. They denied that they planned to "turn the slaves loose" to prey on society, as their critics charged; rather they wanted to bring the emancipated bondsmen under the influence of "salutary laws" and education. In reply to the assertion that Negroes were congenitally unfit for freedom, William Lloyd Garrison repudiated "the postulate, that God has made, by an irreversible decree, or any inherent qualities, one portion of the human race superior to another." Give the non-white races "the same chances to im-

34. Quoted in Nevins, *Ordeal of the Union*, pp. 422–423.
35. Quoted in Emma Lou Thornbrough, *The Negro in Indiana, a Study of a Minority* (Indianapolis, 1957), p. 65n.
36. Thomas, ed., *Slavery Attacked; The Abolitionists: A Collection of Their Writings*, ed. Louis Ruchames (New York, 1963); William H. Pease and Jane H. Pease, *The Antislavery Argument* (Indianapolis, 1965).
37. Basler, ed., *Collected Works of Lincoln*, pp. 255–256.

prove, and a fair start at the same time, and the result will be equally brilliant, equally productive." Proslavery apologists pointed to the miserable condition of most free Negroes in the North and South as proof that freedom was a curse to the black man. Not so, replied Lydia Maria Child. Their low estate was the result of prejudice and discrimination. "They are despised, and abused, and discouraged, at every turn." In the few cases where they "are well treated, and have the same inducements to industry as other people, they work as well and behave as well." What about the "horrors of St. Domingo?" Abolitionists pointed out that it was not emancipation itself, but the attempt to reimpose slavery several years *after* emancipation that caused most of the violence on the island of Hispaniola.[38]

In answer to the key question, "Do you believe that prejudice against color ever can be overcome?" Lydia Maria Child said: "Yes, I do; because I have faith that all things will pass away, which are not founded in reason and justice."[39] Here, indeed, was the tragic flaw of the abolitionist movement. In that pre-Freudian age of utopian idealism and ebullient optimism it was possible for reformers to believe that prejudices unfounded "in reason and justice" could be overcome, but we have learned a good deal since 1860 about the power of irrationality and the tenacity of racism. Abraham Lincoln had a deeper understanding of the human psyche than did Lydia Maria Child. White abolitionists failed to recognize that even some of themselves were infected by prejudice manifested in patronizing attitudes toward Negroes in their midst.[40]

Allowing for differences in rhetoric and style, there are disconcerting parallels between the abolitionist agitation of the antebellum period and the civil rights movement of the early 1960's. There was the same emphasis a century ago on "freedom now," on desegregation of schools and public facilities, on voting rights, a similar commitment (by most abolitionists) to non-violence even in the face of screaming mobs, the same middle-class orientation in values and tactics, and the same optimism that "we shall overcome" as prevailed in the days of the sit-ins, freedom rides, and mass demonstrations in the first half of the present decade. And just as the realities of racism, reaction, illiteracy, share-cropping, convict labor, and lynching in the post-Reconstruction period cast a pall over the victories abolitionists thought they had won between 1861 and 1870, so the realities today of poverty, unemployment, white

38. Thomas, *Slavery Attacked*, pp. 7, 63–65.
39. *Ibid.*, p. 67.
40. Pease and Pease, *The Antislavery Argument*, pp. lxxiii–lxxiv.

backlash, black separatism, and massive riots have clouded the dreams of a few years ago.

Ulrich B. Phillips' reputation as a student of slavery is currently enjoying a revival;[41] perhaps it is time also to dust off Phillips' hypothesis that the determination to maintain white supremacy is the central theme of Southern history. Slavery existed in the South, Phillips argued, "not merely to provide control of labor but also as a system of racial adjustment and social order." No matter how guilt-ridden some Southerners may have felt about the morality of bondage, they could see no alternative (except the chimera of colonization) to slavery as "a guarantee of white supremacy and civilization." Thus when the chips were down in 1861, most Southern whites opted for independence because " 'Southern rights' had come to mean racial security."[42] Many masters may have felt relief in 1865 that the great burden of slavery had been lifted from their backs, but they quickly set about to restore white supremacy in a new form.

Without sharing all the assumptions behind Phillips' argument, one must concede that white supremacy has been not only *the* central theme of Southern history, but *a* major theme in American history and wherever whites and non-whites have lived together in large numbers. Race has been a baleful, brooding presence in American life, plumbing the depths of irrationality, violence, and despair. Its impact must be explored if our past is to be made meaningful. Allan Nevins's "overshadowing spectre of race-relationship" is, in essence, the same thing as Phillips' central theme of Southern history. Nevins's assertion that the major cause of the Civil War was slavery *and* the complementary problem of race adjustment, inadequately documented in his own volumes, stands as an invitation and challenge to historians. Thus far the challenge has not been accepted, for historians in recent years have been reluctant to come to grips with the issue of race, for understandable reasons. This issue is one of the most delicate and explosive in American society, past and present, and efforts to deal with it are susceptible to great misapprehension or misinterpretation, as Stanley Elkins, Daniel Moynihan, and William Styron, for example, have discovered. It will take courage to probe the realities behind the travail of race in antebellum America, but the job must be done if we are to deepen our understanding of slavery and the causes of the Civil War.

41. See Eugene D. Genovese's Foreword to the paperback reprint of Phillips' *American Negro Slavery* (Baton Rouge, 1966 [1918]), pp. vii–xxi; and Genovese, "Race and Class in Southern History: An Appraisal of the Work of Ulrich Bonnell Phillips," *Agricultural History*, 41 (October 1967), 345–358.
42. Phillips, "The Central Theme of Southern History," pp. 31, 35.

The Origins of American Constitutional Thought

STANLEY N. KATZ

The Meaning of the Separation of Powers. By W. B. Gwyn. *Tulane Studies in Political Science*, IX. New Orleans: Tulane University, 1965. Pp. vii, 159. $3.00.

Sir Francis Dashwood: An Eighteenth-Century Independent. By Betty Kemp. New York: St. Martin's Press, 1967. Pp. 210. $9.00.

The Concept of Representation. By Hanna Fenichel Pitkin. Berkeley: University of California Press, 1967. Pp. vi, 323. $7.50.

The Origins of Political Stability: England, 1675–1725. By J. H. Plumb. Boston: Houghton Mifflin, 1967. Pp. xviii, 206. $6.00.

"Machiavelli, Harrington, and English Political Ideologies in the Eighteenth Century." By J. G. A. Pocock. *William and Mary Quarterly*, 3rd series, 22 (1965). Pp. 549–583.

Political Representation in England and the Origins of the American Republic. By J. R. Pole. New York: St. Martin's Press, 1966. Pp. xvi, 606. $16.50.

Constitutionalism and the Separation of Powers. By M. J. C. Vile. Oxford: Clarendon Press, 1967. Pp. vii, 359. $8.00.

Locke et praeterea nihil, it now appears, will no longer do as a motto for the study of eighteenth-century Anglo-American political thought. The state of nature, doctrine of consent, and theory of natural rights were not as important, before 1776, as the ideas of mixed government, separation of powers, and a balanced constitution. The preservation of individual liberty through careful engineering of governmental structure was the dominant concern of political theorists in the new world and the old. The relevance for American history of recent research into English political thought of the late seventeenth and eighteenth centuries has been suggested by Professor Bernard Bailyn, but it seems apparent that we are only in the opening phases of a major reassessment of our constitutional heritage.[1] It is increasingly likely, as the books under review show, that the most direct impact of English thought in America

1. Bernard Bailyn, *The Ideological Origins of the American Revolution* (Cambridge, Mass., 1967); *The Origins of American Politics* (New York, 1968).

came from the oddly compatible ideologies developed on the one hand by Whig-republican theorists and on the other by the Tory or "country" opponents of the Hanoverian ministries. Above all, it was from the out-party contribution to the continuing debate over the purposes of politics and the actual conduct of government in Great Britain that the colonists drew the concepts they needed to analyze their own political arrangements.

Seventeenth-century English constitutional thought was characterized by universal acceptance of the idea of mixed government, a combination of the beneficial aspects of monarchy, aristocracy, and democracy designed to avoid the evil results of the simple or unmixed forms. Translated into political terms, the idea of mixed government represented the interaction in legislation of the King, nobility, and common people (institutionalized in the Crown, the House of Lords, and the House of Commons). Since each group was limited by the claims of the other two, it was assumed that there was a balance of competing demands resulting in laws favorable to the common interest rather than to any of the three estates.

Mixed government was a comfortable theory, resting as it did on the authority of Plato, Aristotle, Polybius, and Machiavelli, but it proved hopelessly inadequate during an era of civil war. The tensions of the 1640's alerted men to the fact that the Stuart constitution provided no effective limitation upon the executive powers (as we would now call them) of the Crown. Ultimately, the execution of Charles I and the abolition of the House of Lords altogether destroyed the traditional framework, leaving the Long Parliament the sole constituent of the formerly balanced arrangement. When Parliament itself proved tyrannical, a new theory had to be developed that would express the limitation of governmental power in republican terms. The answer was separation of powers, an analysis according to which legislative and executive functions rather than socio-legal strata acted to check one another.

In their new books devoted to the theory of separation of powers, W. B. Gwyn and M. J. C. Vile agree that the doctrine originated in the Interregnum, when the idea of mixed government became intolerable, but they differ as to the chronology of the theory of separation of powers and its relationship to the concept of a balanced constitution. Gwyn finds that from the Restoration to the Glorious Revolution the doctrine of separation of powers, although probably widely taken for granted, was superseded by the earlier idea of mixed monarchy, not to regain currency until the "Old Whig" opponents of William III, especially John Trenchard, resurrected the argument in order to attack the ministries, at the turn of the century. Then, from 1700 until the famous statement of the doctrine in Montesquieu's *Esprit des lois*

(1748), separation of powers was seldom mentioned, although Gwyn discovers that Bolingbroke and his associates on *The Craftsman* used the idea in conjunction with that of the mixed constitution.

Vile agrees that mixed government replaced separation of powers as the dominant English constitutional theory after the Restoration of Charles II, and that separation of powers survived as an unstated premise of political thought, reappearing most notably in the works of Locke. It was the great achievement of the years 1660–1750, he says, that the potentially contradictory ideas of mixed government, legislative supremacy, and separation of powers were woven into the fabric of constitutional thought as the "balanced constitution." In particular, the result of application of the doctrine of separation of powers to the theory of mixed government was the novel idea of checks and balances, unheard of in mixed government, in which "the branches of the government were intended to share in the exercise of its functions." The eighteenth-century developments, which represent a retreat from the pure doctrine of separation of powers as it was conceived during the Civil War and by Locke, are epitomized in the writings of Bolingbroke. For Vile, as for Gwyn, it is through Montesquieu that the English doctrine of separation of powers reached America.

Both Gwyn and Vile are impressive in the analytical clarity of their discussion of constitutional ideas. While Gwyn's brief monograph is mainly philosophical (although in a historical context), Vile's long book has the added virtue of relating the doctrine of separation of powers to long-term political developments in Great Britain and America. He is especially concerned to point out the possibility of radically different conclusions which could be drawn from the theories of balanced constitution and separation of powers, for the "separation" theorist might well opt for an entirely functional view of governmental operation which would ignore the class basis of balanced government. In the end, Vile argues, the doctrine of separation of powers was ideally suited to the requirements of a rising middle class which desired to dominate the legislative process while at the same time maintaining limits to the exercise of governmental power. It was also, he maintains, perfectly adapted to revolutionary situations in which the claims of the popular element had to be satisfied at the expense of formerly ruling segments of society: in England, 1640–1660 and 1770–1832; America, 1765–1783; and France, 1789 and 1748.

J. G. A. Pocock's article, "Machiavelli, Harrington, and English Political Ideologies in the Eighteenth Century," written before the Gwyn and Vile books appeared, displays the limitation of a less analytical approach. Pocock's techniques are those of the history of ideas, and his argument is to some extent muddled by the interchangeable use of "mixed government," "separation of powers," and "balanced constitution." He speaks in terms of individuals and political commitment, however, and in so doing he gives us a remarkably sensitive picture of why the abstractions outlined by Gwyn and Vile were so compelling to political men.

Pocock reaches back to the Civil War to identify the origins of eighteenth-century English political ideology. He acknowledges that seventeenth-century Englishmen accepted the Polybian notion of the mixed or balanced constitution, and says that, in trying to explain how the crisis of the 1640's had come about, they turned to historical explanations of the evident imbalance in the constitution. James Harrington developed the idea of the "agrarian law," the notion of an equivalence between the distribution of political power and the distribution of land, as the fundamental principle of governmental analysis. Translated into historical terms, Harrington's theory claimed that the cause of instability in England was the perpetuation of remnants of the feudal system, in which inequitable distribution of property had led to an overbalance of power in the Crown and nobility. The solution, according to his theory, was a redistribution of land among the largest class, the gentry, which would result in the "immortal Commonwealth"—a perpetually stable republic. Thus Harrington's thought constituted an attack on England's feudal past, in contradiction to the prevailing seventeenth-century view that the "ancient constitution" was the source and protector of English civil liberties. Harrington's critique was radical and republican, of course, and thus unsuited to the problems of the late Stuart era.

Pocock's concern is not with Harrington, however, but with those opponents of the court who began, around 1675, to transform Harrington's ideas to suit the age. These men, whom Pocock calls "neo-Harringtonians," sought to construct an ideology which would express the country gentlemen's discontent with the court. The existing "country" political thought depended upon the idea that the property-owners of the countryside were the only truly independent figures in English government; that Parliament existed to protect the rights of property "on which is founded all human liberty and excellence"; that all political power corrupts; and that the political function of country gentlemen (and hence of Parliament) was to guard against encroachments of the Crown upon liberty and property. The country ideology accepted the notion of the balanced constitution, but it also came to embrace the Harringtonian concept of the relationship of property to political power. What it could not accept was Harrington's historical view, and the contribution of the neo-Harringtonians was to "reconcile Harrington with the historical complacency of the English, by arguing that the ancient constitution was itself an example of the Polybian-Harringtonian mixed constitution." The neo-Harringtonians justified the monarchical past by arguing that "The English constitution consists of an ideal balance between the powers of the Crown and those of Parliament, which stands for property and independence." But they recognized the tendency of the Crown to invade the prerogatives of Parliament by means of "influence," and they developed the notion of a "complete separation" of Parliament and administration.

Pocock thus finds that the country theorists accepted the doctrine of the separation of powers, but he argues that they desired to preserve the balance of the constitution "by preserving the parts in independence of each other," while apologists for the court "contended that the balance was between parts that were interdependent and must be preserved by keeping the interdependence properly adjusted." The country ideologists always felt, of course, that the existence of administrative corruption in the court required a return to the principle of independence, and the neo-Harringtonians among them founded their argument upon the innate political resources of the landowning classes as expressed in Parliament. Unlike Harrington, however, in attempting to reform the eighteenth-century constitution they reverted to an ideal notion of the English past in which "every man owned the means of his independence and fought for his liberty, and the King had to seek the consent of the freeholders or their representatives in assembly." They reconciled Harrington's balanced commonwealth of proprietors with an optimistic assessment of the ancient constitution.

Pocock says that the neo-Harringtonians flourished around and after 1698, and included Henry Neville, Andrew Fletcher of Saltoun, Walter Moyle, John Toland, John Trenchard, and Thomas Gordon. *Cato's Letters*, by Trenchard and Gordon, were therefore neo-Harringtonian. Pocock even goes so far as to argue that the ideas of Bolingbroke and other mid-eighteenth-century apologists for the court were remarkably similar to those of the neo-Harringtonians. In constructing a justification of the Crown's right to exert influence over Parliament in the name of preserving the interdependence of the parts of government, the court writers argued that destruction of the feudal, tenurial, relationship of the King to Parliament required the introduction of some new form of influence, if the constitutional balance was to be preserved, and the solution they discovered was the Civil List. But here, Pocock observes, we have come full circle. Both country and court accepted the necessity for constitutional balance, but the court party came to accept Harrington's radical rejection of the feudal past while the country theorists clung to the idea of the ancient constitution. Thus the conservative administration Harringtonians repudiated history while the opposition neo-Harringtonians appealed to it.

Pocock's conclusion is that the period of the first two Georges was an important era for constitutional speculation. For him, however, Locke stood outside the framework of "the commonly accepted ideas about the constitution" and was, therefore, most useful to those outside the established order. For the true constitutional debate was between "a country interpretation which blended Machiavelli and Harrington with the ancient constitution and a Court interpretation addicted to historical criticism and *de facto* empiricism." He admits from the outset that he intends his essay as a corrective to Caroline Robbins' preoccupation with the republican strain in eighteenth-century political thought, which slights the contribution of the court apologists and unwisely neglects the court-country frame of reference in its concern for Whiggism.[2] He also contends, of course, that ideological analysis must take into account the impact of political necessities upon intellectual stance.

Pocock's premise, that the crucial change in constitutional outlook from the seventeenth century to the eighteenth was from a preference for the ancient constitution to an idealization of the ancient-and-balanced constitution, is too vague. More important, "Harringtonianism" seems an arbitrary label. Clearly it was not Harrington's personal influence which led to the type of thinking which interests Pocock, but a pervasive concern for the independence and power of property, a phenomenon which deserves closer examination. The article is brilliant, however, in its exploitation of the uses of history in constitutional thinking, and in opening our eyes to the importance of the court-country debate over the balanced constitution. Taken together, Gwyn, Vile, and Pocock focus our attention on the central constitutional issue of the early eighteenth century: the adjustment of the machinery of government and the relationships of social groups so as to avoid those dislocations of power which, given human nature, inevitably threaten individual liberty unless the political system is so constructed as to combat them easily and continuously.

Ideas about government should always be interpreted in the light of the intentions of their framers, and the analyst of constitutional thought should have a thorough grounding in the history of the period which concerns him. In the early eighteenth century, English constitutional thought developed in response to bitter political conflict, and for those interested in the origins of

2. Caroline Robbins, *The Eighteenth-Century English Commonwealthman* (Cambridge, Mass., 1961).

eighteenth-century American political theory, the half century following the Glorious Revolution is clearly of critical importance. The question is, how did English socio-economic behavior after 1689 influence writers who opposed the ministerial authorities?

Professor J. H. Plumb's Ford Lectures on turn-of-the-century English politics, *The Origins of Political Stability*, imply that the constitution reacted to politics rather than to ideology. His brief account, supported by recent work on the reign of Queen Anne, strikes a devastating blow to the Namierite view of the early eighteenth century and provides a plausible account of the origins of political factionalism in the middle third of the century.[3] Plumb is particularly concerned to demonstrate the depth and reality of the disagreement between Whigs and Tories prior to the accession of George I. The parties divided ideologically on questions of the role of the Crown and the extent of religious toleration, but their essential characters depended upon social and economic factors. The Tories, a majority party from 1690 to 1715, took on the concerns of the independent country gentlemen. They stood for frequent elections, low taxation, punishment for corrupt administrative influence, place bills, and land qualification for members of Parliament; they opposed Continental wars and extensive toleration. The Whigs, on the other hand, became increasingly identified with aristocracy and government. "They were committed to full scale war and preoccupied by methods of financing it." Between 1689 and 1720 the political temperature of Parliament was elevated to an alarming degree by the increased costs of election of individual members, by the expansion of ministerial patronage, and by the proliferation of governmental corruption, and the situation was exacerbated by the inability of either party to achieve a decisive victory over the other.

For Plumb, the central feature of the period is the submission of Parliament to the resurgent executive government of Sir Robert Walpole. He interprets the Glorious Revolution as "one more" failure of the Crown to subdue Parliament and as the coincidental reassertion of the gentry's insistence upon local power and the preservation of Parliamentary independence. The immediate political result of this middle-class triumph was twenty-five years of intense party warfare within the legislature and throughout the country at large. The division between Whigs and Tories was partly along pre-Revolutionary ideological lines, but mainly for control of the constituencies. These parties, re-

3. In support of Plumb's view, see especially Geoffrey Holmes, *British Politics in the Age of Anne* (London, 1967). The object of Plumb's attack is Robert Walcott, Jr., *English Politics in the Early Eighteenth Century* (Cambridge, Mass, 1956).

flecting as they did basic social and economic divisions, fought one another for the disposition of "charities, jobs, property, real estate, and freeholds of all kinds, as well as Parliamentary influence." The constitutional victory of 1689 and the all pervasiveness of the Whig-Tory contest permitted Parliament to "ride rough-shod over the administration" until 1715 or so, when Sir Robert Walpole devised a system of control which brought the turbulence of the previous quarter century to an end. Walpole's success lay in his alliance with the by-then-dominant Whig aristocracy, which enabled him to control the House of Lords and helped him to manipulate the House of Commons through shrewd distribution of place and favor. The result was destruction of Parliamentary supremacy and the establishment of oligarchical control of English politics and society.

More original and controversial is Plumb's argument that the "party rage" of the years 1688–1720 was brought to an end by the emergence of one-party government, executive control of the legislature, and "a sense of common identity in those who wielded economic, social and political power." The "origins of political stability," he asserts, lay in the fantastically rapid expansion of the departments of state, which provided both undreamed-of resources of patronage and an executive capability outside of the court, and in the fusion of the interests of the predominant Whig aristocracy with those of high finance and the executive. By the mid-1730's, according to this analysis, Walpole had stigmatized the Tories (who were in any case immobilized by their "opposition" ideology), diminished the size and scope of the electorate, evolved a single-party system, and proscribed political opposition. Walpolean England was thus the antithesis of the revolutionary ideal of 1688 in its exclusion of the middle class from politics in favor of the domination of an aristocracy: "What Sir Robert Walpole and the Whigs did was to make certain that political and social authority should devolve by inheritance." The mechanism by which the system ran was patronage—the open, unabashed, and brutal dispensing of office for political purposes—for "Place was power; patronage was power; and power is what men in politics are after." Thus Walpole's England provides the prolegomenon for Namier's England.

Superficially, Plumb seems to be denying the pattern of constitutional development suggested by Gwyn, Vile, and Pocock, as if this were the response of Cambridge to Oxford constitutional history, but such is not the case. One of the difficulties with these lectures is that they underestimate the role of ideology in politics, although Professor Plumb goes to some lengths to deny the charge. He suggests at one point that national issues are inferior to "areas of bitter animosity in the structure of power" as indicators of party purpose, but then reassures the reader in a footnote that party strife was indeed related to "bitterly opposing attitudes not only to the nature of political power but also to its social function and purpose." At another point he contends that the Whigs, however conservative ideologically, were innovators in politics: "the most powerful groups in the Whig party became preoccupied with the processes rather than the principles of government." The difficulty would seem to be that for the period after 1700 Plumb excludes as Whig anything which did not emanate from the New Whig (aristocratic and governing) tradition, and identifies the country mentality exclusively with the Tories. Thus he underplays the role of those opposition Whigs whose radical ideology had so much in common with the independent country position, and makes the cleavage between the ruling Whigs seem intellectually more dominant than it was.

A further problem is Plumb's bold use of terminology. "Single-party government," "executive control" of the legislature, and "oligarchy" are simply too absolute as concepts and too anachronistic as nomenclature to meet the facts of the case. The contours of Plumb's argument are convincing, but the details are sometimes rudely forced into place. To demonstrate that the Tories ceased to represent a viable alternative does not prove that there was a single party during Walpole's supremacy. Even if one discounts the Whig dissidents in the years before 1733, the sizable contingents of Independents and Court adherents (not necessarily Whigs within Plumb's definition) created a situation more complex than that of modern single-party systems. Some more refined concept is wanted to explain what was happening in Parliament during these years. Executive development is likewise wrenched out of context, as one can learn from the arguments of contemporaries about the separation of powers. Once again, Plumb is probably on to something, but his intuition has outrun his historical analysis.

Professor Plumb is in fact working within the tradition of the balanced constitution, but he has ingeniously transposed the weights on the scales. What he very nearly suggests is that the consequence of political and social balance is violent party strife, whereas executive preponderance results in political stability. Nearly, but not quite, for he believes that the root cause of the rage of party in the years around the turn of the century was the lack of restraint on Parliament. What he has done is to offer a Harringtonian-Tory view of mid-eighteenth-century politics which would have done Bolingbroke proud. He accepts the identification of political and economic power, and argues that the constitution was saved by Crown-Whig aristocratic insistence upon interdependence of executive and legislature. It is as though

Bolingbroke and Walpole had at last got together to contrive the perfection of the constitution.

The activity of members of Parliament was a major factor in the achievement of orderly government under Walpole, whether the process is viewed as one of "balancing" the constitution or of "stabilizing" politics. Parliament was the institution in which the social estates mingled and it was the point at which legislature and executive converged. Both political theorists and historians recognize the point, but it is only by examining the actual conduct of the M.P.'s that we can understand the intimate interaction of ideology and behavior. How an "Independent" country gentleman handled himself in Parliament is the subject of Betty Kemp's excellent little volume on Sir Francis Dashwood.

Independency, Miss Kemp argues in an introductory essay, was based on the belief that the duty of Parliament was to criticize the government rather than support it. The legislature must remain independent of the Crown and the corrupt practices with which the government sought to subjugate it. In particular, Parliament must abjure party organization, which prevented members from acting freely in accordance with the dictates of constitutional principle, and through which the King could influence their corporate behavior. Only if there were a sufficient number of the House of Commons who were not committed to party could governments be put in doubt about their ability to carry every proposal they put to the House.

Miss Kemp estimates that there were nearly 200 Independents in Commons between 1741 and 1781, although she points out that they were frequently confused with "the current anti-government party." Their inherent political dilemma was that they were too disorganized to accomplish great deeds, but their principles were such that closer combination would have destroyed the end for which they stood: "a free, uncommitted House of Commons, scrutinizing government proposals on their merits and not automatically either supporting or opposing them." They felt that their mission was to restore the true balance of the constitution, and they developed a vague program toward that end. Independents supported place bills which would limit the influence of royal appointees in the House, and they stood for the repeal of the Septennial Act, which they hoped to replace with a rule of annual, or at least triennial parliaments. They also proposed other restrictions on executive influence: "free elections, the restoration of the clause in the Act of Settlement which had required privy councillors to sign the advice they gave to the monarch; the restoration of ministerial equality and the end for ever of 'sole' ministers; the murder of that 'midnight assembly' the cabinet; reliance on a militia instead of a standing army." The "period of independency" can be dated, Miss Kemp thinks, from the mid-1730's to about 1781, when, largely because of the rise of radicalism, it became outmoded. In the first half of the era, Independents tended to oppose the government, whereas after 1760 they frequently supported it, although their actions were at all times unpredictable.

Sir Francis Dashwood, Miss Kemp assures us, was an archetypal Independent. Although his contemporaries thought of him as a Tory and he was sometimes accused of Jacobitism, it is more accurate to think of him as an Independent, if only because "he thought Whig and Tory an outdated nomenclature, as Bolingbroke did." Even the term "independent Tory" will not do for Dashwood, who did not think of himself as a Tory at all. Dashwood voted for all the measures of the Independent program during his years in the House of Commons (1741–1761) and while holding office, both as Chancellor of the Exchequer (1762) and as Postmaster General (1766–1781), he maintained a devotion to his earlier principles in his concern "to free administration from the shackles of political interest." At bottom, however, his Independency was a function of his beliefs, which were those of Stanhope and Talbot's "real" whiggery.

Dashwood's constitutional doctrine was enunciated in a 1747 election "Address" which Miss Kemp reprints as Appendix I of her book. In it, he defined the goal of politics as the "Support and Preservation" of freedom:

a Right every Man has to do what he will with his own, conformable to Law; . . . a Right every Man has to be judged impartially by his Equals, and to have his Property secured to him and his Posterity.

The balanced constitution, designed to preserve liberty, was endangered by selfish factionalism:

when once each Particular shall consult only his own immediate paltry Covenience, then the Frame, the Spirit, the Beauty of this Constitution must moulder, wither, and decay, and all its Harmony to be lost.

The clear moral for his constituents, Dashwood contended, was that they must select those representatives devoted dispassionately to the common weal. The safety of the constitution lay in preventing legislation that was "merely Ministerial" rather than "National," and it behooved the voters, therefore, to select disinterested members rather than placemen under the control of a "dissolute, immoral, luxurious Ministry." For Dashwood, Independent political action was the only way to check the ambitions of the administration and promote the public interest.

Independent constitutional doctrine, as displayed in Dashwood's career, was clearly based upon the separation of powers tradition within the eighteenth-century understanding of the balanced constitution. The vital concern of the doctrine was to retain freedom of action for individual members in order to combat the encroachments upon the independence of the House which resulted from control of patronage by the Crown's ministries. The Independents fell within the neo-Harringtonian character of "country" thinking expounded by Pocock, although Miss Kemp would doubtless argue that after 1760 the ideology of the "Patriot King" was also persuasive to them. Independency, in its Old Whig origins, was also closely allied to the radical opposition thought of the early eighteenth century with its emphasis on personal liberty and legislative independence and its animus against the "influence" of the Crown and the corruption of placemen. Miss Kemp's research in political history thus squares with the findings of the political theorists even more closely than Professor Plumb's work does.

How can we relate this new scholarship to the problems of American history? One looks to J. R. Pole's *Political Representation in England and the Origins of the American Republic* for guidance, but in vain. Dr. Pole has written an enormous book about the relationship of majority representation to the development of republican government in an attempt to explain why republicanism should have triumphed so soon in America. He is particularly interested in the growth of geographical representation in the colonies, and he analyzes the emergence of this phenomenon in lengthy studies of Massachusetts, Pennsylvania, and Virginia. Other portions of the book are devoted to late seventeenth-century English political theory, the constitution-making era which followed the Revolution in America, and the transformation of English representation in the eighteenth and early nineteenth centuries.

It is impossible to sum up Pole's complex, lengthy, and sometimes unclear argument, but certain points stand out. He stands unashamedly in the line of Whig historians, proclaiming that the central theme of Anglo-American history is the emergence of the legislature as the dominant part of government, institutionalizing the will of the majority. He contends that Americans were peculiarly sensitive to the arguments of Harrington, Sydney, and Locke, and that both the observed discrepancies between Whig ideology and English government, and the practical requirements of the American environment led the colonists to the creation of truly representative, and ultimately republican, governments. With the ratification of the federal constitution, Americans had made it possible for individuals to be represented in the legislature and for the legislature to actualize the desires of the people. In England, progress toward representation of interests and individuals, rather than the ancient estates, was much slower. The problem of the unrepresentative character of Parliament was not well-articulated until Burke's critique at the time of the American Revolution, and even the agitation of Radicals and Utilitarians for parliamentary reform partially succeeded in 1832 only by dint of the efforts of poorly-motivated conservatives. The achievement of English reformers in the nineteenth century was, of course, a constitutional reality in America before 1800.

There is a good deal that is helpful in this view, but it is too literal-minded. Pole's discussion of the political theory of the post-Civil War era is in the tradition of Trevelyan and Carl Becker, and quite simply fails to take account of the modifications with which this essay has been concerned. There is a hint that Pole knows better, for he acknowledges that John Locke was a negligible influence upon American thought before 1776, but he excuses his Hartzian insistence upon the importance of Locke by the curious argument that he "epitomized certain doctrines, without which the American revolutionaries would have found it difficult to explain their activities either to the opinions of mankind or even to themselves."

The fact is that although Pole prefaces his book with the assertion that it "explores the borderland between political ideas and the history of politics," his narrow view of political ideas severely limits the scope of his inquiry. He argues, for instance, that initially Americans and Englishmen alike accepted the idea of the mixed constitution. Eighteenth-century American political experience, including the tyranny of royal governors, the decline of the council, the rise of the assembly, and the restrictiveness of imperial regulation, forced Americans to conclude that legislative supremacy was sufficient foundation for government. Radical notions of the distinction between legislature and executive then emerged, and were realized during the Revolutionary era. By 1787, however, the Whig concept of legislative supremacy had given way to a more intrinsically American commitment to the supremacy of the constitution. Thus Pole traces an ideological transition from mixed government to legislative supremacy to government by a written constitution. It is hard to see, though, that the written constitution is on a par with the other elements in the equation, and it seems altogether uncertain that the idea of legislative supremacy was so universally accepted or philosophically unqualified as we are asked to believe.

What is worse, even Pole's case for "representation" is too pat, as Hanna Fenichel Pitkin's The Concept of Representation indicates. Mrs. Pitkin is a philosopher and political scientist who is primarily interested in the historical dimensions of the problem. She is a linguistic analyst of the school of J. L. Austin, concerned with "ordinary language" meanings, and the bulk of her book is devoted to an explication of several different versions of the concept of representation. She argues that there are two formalistic senses of representation. One is *authorization*, in which the representative is specifically empowered to act for his constituents, and the other is *accountability*, in which the representative is held to account for his actions. The two concepts are in opposition, but they are formalistic in the sense that they speak of the act of representation in terms of formal arrangements which precede, initiate, follow, and terminate it. Mrs. Pitkin next analyzes two interpretations based upon *standing for* rather than *acting for*, one descriptive and the other symbolic. The final view, and the one which receives the most attention, considers representation as acting for others, but as the substance of the activity itself, rather than as a formalistic act.

The most immediately relevant chapter of the volume is the one on Edmund Burke. Succinctly and with great acuteness, Mrs. Pitkin discovers a multi-faceted conception of representation in Burke's writings: elite representation of the nation, and both actual and virtual representation of the constituencies. She shows how Burke made sense of these seemingly contradictory versions of representation by arguing that the legislative process requires both the careful deliberation characteristic of an elite and the accurate reflection of popular feelings provided by the presence of interested representatives. Thus for Burke the ancient method of representation could be synthesized with the concept of interest representation for the good of the nation as a whole.

Pole, on the contrary, interprets Burke as strictly an interest theorist, failing to see the importance of the elitist-deliberative aspect of his thought, and he applauds him for carrying the tradition of Harrington into the nineteenth century. Burke is not of course the test case, but the comparison is instructive, for it reveals Pole's normative use of Whig theory, according to which Englishmen and Americans ought to have believed in representative, legislative supremacy. At the very least, Mrs. Pitkin's book jars us to the awareness that historians must be considerably more analytical when tracing the historical development of political conceptions.

In the end, Vile and Plumb have more to tell us about American constitutional development than Pole does. Vile's contribution is to suggest the contours of Anglo-American constitutional development. As we have seen, he argues that although the concept of separation of powers was replaced by mixed government after the Restoration, it remained a common assumption of English political thought. It was the notion of separation of powers which transformed mixed government, in which the three social strata were set against one another, into balanced government, in which the functional branches of the government operated a system of checks and balances upon one another.

In Vile's view, American constitutional thought paralleled England's. He contends that the idea of balanced government also held sway here in the early eighteenth century, although it was apparent that the English theory was not perfectly suited to the American situation. Both the lack of a truly aristocratic segment in society and the fact that the governor exercised powers greater than those of the Crown, created difficulties for the assimilation of the doctrine. As the conflict with England deepened at mid-century, however, the revolutionary separation of powers component of the theory of balanced government came to occupy an independent role as the sole justification for constitutionalism, and American dissatisfaction with the existing structure of colonial governments was thereby intensified. At the time of the Revolution, just as during the English Civil War (and, later, the French Revolution) the pure doctrine of separation of powers came to dominate American constitutional thought. Later, as in the English Restoration era, the notion of balance (specifically, the concept of checks and balances) reasserted itself to temper the radical implications of the pure doctrine.

Plumb, although he nowhere specifically discusses the matter, suggests some politico-constitutional lines of inquiry, for the "stable" constitution which he describes is precisely the system which the American colonists at last found intolerable. Is it not true that Plumb's three causes of political stability —single-party politics, executive domination of the legislature, and oligarchical control of society and government—are in the forefront of the complaints of the revolutionary generation? Plumb after all concludes that in the early eighteenth century, "The power of the land and of commerce fused to create a paradise for gentlemen, for the aristocracy of birth; it thus became much easier for England to adopt an impartial authority, to rule alien peoples, and to train its ruling class for that purpose, rather than to adjust its institutions and its social system to the needs of an industrial society." Small wonder, then, that Americans derived their constitutional notions from the opposition, or from the radical components of the dominant theories.

To understand more fully the constitutional roots of our nationality, we must begin at the beginning. For a long time, American political theorists and constitutional historians have been looking at things the wrong way round. They have sought the origins of the Bill of Rights, judicial review, and federalism, but they have seldom asked how an organic American view of constitutional government emerged out of the society, politics, and thought of the colonial era. The ideas and institutions of the Revolution and the state-making era simply cannot be understood in isolation from the large historical process of which they were a part, for the formative era of modern American government is properly at least as early as the first part of the eighteenth century. And, needless to say, to speak of the colonies in the eighteenth century is also to speak of England.

The intellectual origins of American constitutional thought would now seem to be located in the English experience of the late seventeenth and early eighteenth centuries. No longer, it appears, is it possible to accord precedence to Magna Carta and Lancastrian parliamentarianism, nor even, perhaps, to Fortescue and Locke. The central ideological experience of the seventeenth century was the destruction of the mixed government idea by the political ravages of the Civil War and the consequent search for a viable basis of constitutional government which would balance individual liberty and governmental authority. The concepts of separation of power and balanced government provided new tools of political analysis in this period, and it was this way of thinking which eighteenth-century American colonists assimilated.

There were serious obstacles in the way of applying the test of balanced government to the colonial situation: the executive branch was obviously weak, class structure was not well-defined, and the colonial assembly did not have the historical, social, or economic prestige of the House of Commons. Nevertheless, until the middle of the eighteenth century these irregularities were generally ignored. Increasingly, however, political crises within particular colonies stimulated ideological attacks upon the establishment's conception of balanced government, and the colonial "outs" turned for help to their English counterparts—the opponents of the Whig hegemony. Concerned to further their immediate political ends, the Americans chose selectively from the arguments of both the Whig radicals and the Tory-Independent "country" party. The result was the gradual amalgamation of Trenchard and Gordon with Bolingbroke, and the creation of an American ideology which was deeply suspicious of governmental (especially executive) threats to individual political freedom, peculiarly attracted to the potentially revolutionary separation of powers theory, and deeply committed to legislative and judicial power.

The socio-political origins of our constitutional heritage are not, however, so easily explained. It seems clear that Americans picked and chose among English ideas according to their needs, and some of the more obvious requirements of the colonial situation have already been described. Our knowledge of the process of ideology-formulation will remain superficial, however, until the political processes of the eighteenth century are better understood. It is obvious, for instance, why the poor performance of royal governors should ultimately have brought the authority of the Crown into question. It is not clear, however, why Americans should have retained so manifest a respect for executive power in the republican era. It is even harder to follow the stages through which our ideological development progressed. It would seem that there was a gradual accretion of thinking opposed to the received constitutional theory, but the process advanced by fits and starts. The American ideology derived most obviously from a series of unconnected political crises, such as the Zenger trial, the Massachusetts Land Bank controversy, and the Pistole Fee episode. But surely it also owes a more important debt to changes in social stratification, religious orientation (in particular, the Great Awakening), and economic development. Scholars have begun to ask the right questions, but the roots of American constitutional thought have only begun to be laid bare. It is with the new approaches exemplified in the books and articles under review—linguistic analysis, precisely defined concepts, and the recognition of the close relationship between theory and the realities of politics—that the task should be undertaken.

The Lives of Philosophers

MORTON WHITE

William James: A Biography. By Gay Wilson Allen. New York: Viking
Press, 1967. Pp. 576. $10.00.

It is extremely difficult to write a biography of a philosopher when you don't
know much philosophy, and yet, as this book unfortunately demonstrates,
the temptation to do so can be irresistible. Distinguished philosophers like
Jonathan Edwards, Emerson, and James frequently attract biographers who
cannot follow a philosophical argument. Sometimes, of course, this deficiency
in a biographer may not be a defect. In fact, if his subject is Emerson, it may
be a virtue, since it may prevent him from seeking arguments where there
are no arguments to follow. And if his subject is William James, a biographer
may have enough work cut out for him without digging into what he may
think of as the catacombs of epistemology and metaphysics. I have no doubt
that a very interesting book could be written about James even if the author
of that book were to avoid discussion of his philosophy and his psychology. He
was a hero, as Elizabeth Hardwick has said in her thoughtful introduction to
a volume of his letters, "courteous, reasonable, liberal, witty, expressive, a
first-rate writer," and, one may add, a man with enough sickness in his soul to
provide most biographers with enough of their usual material. For this reason
Miss Hardwick shrewdly observes that James's pragmatism, his pluralism, and
his radical empiricism need not be her province, and she wisely remarks, as
she steers clear of metaphysics and epistemology: "Reworking the sod from
whence so many crops have come in their season seems profitless for the enjoyment of James's letters, letters that are nearly always personal, informal,
nontechnical."

Unfortunately, however, Professor Allen has not seen the possibilities of a
philosophy-free biography of James. Although Allen's irrepressibly human
subject is vividly presented in this book—no biographer, however ignorant
of philosophy, could quote some of his marvelous letters without introducing
us to that genial, warm-hearted, neurotic "Irishman among the Brahmins"—

491

wherever Professor Allen tries to connect, as the saying goes, the charmer and his philosophy, the result is really embarrassing.

In his Preface, where Professor Allen states his main concern, he writes:

James's son Henry was still alive when Ralph Barton Perry wrote his two-volume *Thought and Character of William James* (1935), and he refused to divulge any personal information about his mother, simply because he regarded the publication of such information as an invasion of the family's privacy. Consequently, Perry was not able to write a full account of William James's life, for he was forced to omit almost altogether the important role James's wife played in his biography. Perry's work, although it gives a masterly analysis of James's ideas and his relationships with other philosophers, was not intended primarily to be a biography. The strictly biographical account is confined to a few chapters in the first volume, preceded and followed by detailed discussions of James's work and his ideas. This plan not only subordinates James's private life to his professional life but obscures the *growth* of his mind and character, depriving the reader of a sense of participation in the experiences being narrated. The present biography is strictly chronological, and attempts to trace the relationship between James's emotional and intellectual life—certainly important for a man who enthroned *feeling* with *thought* in philosophy.

It is the last sentence which is crucial and damaging. For if it states Professor Allen's primary intention, his book must be judged a failure. It is true that because Perry's splendid book concentrates on James's ideas, it cries out for supplementation by a work that would link James the thinker with James the human being. But unfortunately Professor Allen has not forged that link. He has not traced the relationship between James's emotional and intellectual life, because it takes two terms to make such a relationship, and one of them is virtually missing from Allen's account. To be sure, he makes occasional efforts at describing the thought of James, his forerunners, and his contemporaries, but those efforts are so feeble, so skimpy, and so misleading as to be almost worthless.

Let me recite only some of the evidence for my conviction that Professor Allen shows little grasp of James's intellectual work or its background.

(1) Every student of James knows that Darwin influenced James enormously, and one might expect his biographer to reveal a deep understanding of the theory of natural selection. But how does Allen summarize Darwin's great contribution in the *one* sentence he devotes to it? In this misleading way: "Darwin's theory of mutability, whereby variations useful for survival had caused all living creatures to acquire and transmit new characteristics, accounted for the development and separation of species" (p. 95). And after referring to James's Darwinian view that the mind has operated so as to en-

able the human organism to adapt and survive, Allen writes: "Incidentally, if we extend this concept to all living organisms, then even the most primitive biological creatures have minds similar in kind though not in degree to those of higher organisms, and this raises the possibility that the processes of evolution have not been entirely fortuitous and blind—though this extension goes beyond James's purposes in his book. Yet it seems clearly implied by his words, and he would doubtless have approved of the statement of a twentieth-century biologist, John Langdon-Davies, in *Man and His Universe*, that even plants have survived not because they were lucky but because they were clever" (pp. 319–320). If this is what Allen thinks is "clearly implied" by James's words, and what he would "doubtless have approved of," then it seems to me that Allen fails to understand not only James but Darwin's influence on him.

(2) A fitting companion of Allen's one-sentence summary of Darwin's views is the following pointless statement about the significance of Ernst Mach: "Mach is best-known for his formula giving the ratio of the speed of an object to the speed of sound in the same atmosphere, but he was, as James said, a 'genius of all trades,' and had made important contributions to psychology" (p. 248). So much for Mach.

(3) Finally, consider this incredible remark on "pragmatism": "He [James] had borrowed the term from his old friend Charles Peirce, who, however, had used it in the sense of a rational well-ordered life, whereas James had made it a means of judging true from false by looking at results" (p. 392).

We have seen that Professor Allen thinks of his work as different in emphasis from Ralph Perry's, and this is quite true. But whereas Perry was more interested in James's ideas than in psychoanalyzing him, and hence concentrated on presenting a stunning account of James's thought, Allen's book consists of twenty-three superficial chapters on James's personality, sprinkled with misunderstood versions of James's ideas, and a final chapter and Epilogue that hardly compensate for the previous paucity of intelligent philosophical comment. Instead of being connected organically with the tree of James's life, Allen's comments on ideas resemble nothing so much as Christmas decorations that are loosely hooked on to it, feeble little bulbs that flash uncertainly and throw no sustained light on the material or the shape of the tree itself.

As one reflects on the shortcomings of this work one may ask why there are so many books of this kind. And if anybody doubts that there are such books besides Allen's let him try to extract from certain studies of Jonathan

Edwards a clear statement of what he meant by "philosophical necessity," or what he meant by saying that the will is determined by the strongest motive. Why do so many so-called profound interpreters of earlier American philosophy lack a philosophy undergraduate's insight into the meaning of the words they are interpreting?

Here I can only sketch an answer. Partly because of the great historical and literary interest in earlier American philosophers, books and articles on their thought are often written by scholars who are inadequately trained in philosophy. And they are inadequately trained in it partly because of the vacuum which sucks them into the task for which they are inadequately trained: philosophers themselves are not interested enough in the history of American philosophy. While this vicious circle rolls along, those who write on Edwards or James without a proper understanding of them try to transcend their ignorance by offering "deep" interpretations of their hero's thought. Hence they fail to communicate and analyze what the philosopher in question may have been most concerned to communicate, because the less one is able to expound the philosopher's thoughts, the more one is impelled to dilate on his feelings alone. One begins by trying to connect the ideas and the feelings but soon one loses one's grip on the ideas, and the whole enterprise collapses into the kind of thing represented by this book: an entertaining biography which is adorned with useless snippets about Peirce, Darwin, Mach, Bain, Stumpf, Renouvier, Bergson, Pillon, et al., about whom the author knows very little and about whom, I venture to say, he couldn't care less.

The basic failure, therefore, can often be attributed to a lack of education, but how shall we remedy the situation? How shall we train aspiring biographers of American philosophers to develop the requisite knowledge of their subject's intellectual accomplishments if they wish to deal with those accomplishments? It may be said that the answer is obvious: ask them to take courses in the history of American philosophy. But I am convinced that this is not the answer. For even if professional philosophers could be persuaded to abandon their indifference to the history of American philosophy, it won't do to send students who are trained in history and literature into such courses with the expectation that they will gain the skill that is necessary for writing the kind of book that Professor Allen has tried unsuccessfully to write. For what is wanted, I think, is an understanding of philosophy that can only be gained from the equivalent of at least one year of graduate study in a Philosophy Department. The history or literature student who has this kind of training not only does not need courses specifically devoted to the American philosophers, but where he has the opportunity he should almost always be advised first to seek training in philosophy as such and then to study the American philosophers on his own. Naturally, if he can manage both a year of graduate study in philosophy and courses in the history of American philosophy, he will be in an even better position to produce a successful biographical treatment of an American philosopher, but where he must choose, there is no doubt in my mind as to the courses he should take first. Would we be satisfied with anything less than the equivalent of a year of graduate study in physics if a biographer wished to discourse seriously on the connection between Einstein's physical thought and his emotional life? Why, then, do we suppose that a biographer who wished to do the corresponding thing on James could do it without analogous training in philosophy?

It is true that in principle a historian is entitled to study the history of any discipline, and if he is a very gifted man and lives a long life he will undoubtedly be able to master on his own the rudiments of the relevant discipline or disciplines. But I am confident that in this day and age it is unlikely that he will be able to produce a really exciting work in the history of philosophy or a life of a philosopher if he is an autodidact who reads philosophical works as if they were novels. I do not deny that some philosophers about whom one may wish to write historically or biographically may be less technically forbidding than others and hence require less philosophical training for understanding their thought. I have already suggested that Emerson is probably a case in point, and it is unfortunate that such an atypical figure as Emerson dominates the minds of Americanists who think that all one needs to know is the language in which a philosopher writes in order to write his biography. But they forget Edwards, James, Peirce, Dewey, Royce, and Santayana; and they may not realize that the study not only of Aristotle and Kant but even the study of certain philosophers of perhaps greater interest to historical and literary scholars—I have in mind what may be called the Pico-Vico axis—requires philosophical training if it is to be conducted fruitfully.

By this I certainly do not mean to say that the history of philosophy or the biographies of philosophers should be written only by philosophers. What I mean is that serious training in philosophy is an indispensable condition for writing its history and for writing the kind of biography that Professor Allen has sought to write. And I would emphasize that this is not asking too much of students of American matters. I can well imagine the comment of scholars who exhaust themselves learning remote languages and establishing texts: "What? Do you expect us to be philosophers, too?" But even scholars of Greek philosophy have come to recognize that they can not live on philology alone, and that illuminating work on the major Greek philosophers requires a care-

ful study of philosophy itself. Why, then, should we expect less of those who
have the language of William James and who have his legible words in books
that are indisputably his? Why shouldn't we ask them to take thought and
add several cubits to their intellectual stature?

Dewey in Process

MARSHALL J. COHEN

Psychology. By John Dewey. (Fredson Bowers, *et al.*, editors, *The Early Works of John Dewey, 1882–1898*, II: 1887). Carbondale and Edwardsville, Ill.: Southern Illinois University Press, 1967. Pp. xxvi, 366, xxix–cix. $10.00.

Lectures in the Philosophy of Education: 1899. By John Dewey. Edited by Reginald D. Archambault. New York: Random House, 1966. Pp. xxxv, 366. $7.95.

Writing about American philosophers and their cultural setting in 1929, George Herbert Mead concluded that "in the profoundest sense John Dewey is the philosopher of America."[1] Anticipating more recent commentators on American culture, Mead argued that the American was a product of immediate gratification in a permissive environment and felt no need for Europe's carefully contrived rationalizations of the relationship between the individual and society. The American was man acting, free from the complexities of tradition-bound societies; he did not emerge out of revered social arrangements, he created them. If the idealisms of Kant, Fichte, and Hegel were the products of their cultural settings—and Mead believed they were—such philosophies would fall on barren soil when imported to America. Mead thus dismissed the social philosophy of Josiah Royce as a brilliant example of un-American idealism. Interestingly, even William James's "lofty individualism" was too much a product of his personal skepticism to appeal to the confident spirit of the pioneer. In contrast, Dewey appealed to the essential practicality of America. He rooted his philosophy in the concrete act and thus celebrated the Americans' genius in their conduct of business and politics.

Mead's Dewey, the creator of instrumentalism, is the familiar Dewey. But, as Mead himself notes, Dewey had a questionable past. As a graduate student and young instructor, he was a disciple of Hegel and entered the philosophical ranks armed with the idealist's universal spirit and the dialectic. It is indeed

1. George Herbert Mead, "The Philosophies of Royce, James, and Dewey in their American Setting," *International Journal of Ethics*, 40 (1929–1930), 231. Reprinted in George Herbert Mead, *Selected Writings*, ed. Andrew J. Reck (Indianapolis, 1964), p. 391.

still a shock, long after knowing of this past, to return to a work like the *Psychology* of 1887 and find Dewey entertaining ideas about the individual soul, universal mind, and God. Yet, for better or worse, this was whence Dewey came and the central question of his early career is the relationship between his youthful commitment to idealism and his later creation of naturalistic instrumentalism. Moreover, an answer to this question bears on the historian's judgment as to the significance of idealism in general as a movement in the late nineteenth century. Was it simply a form of school philosophy, as we have thought for so long, surviving as the vestige of antebellum transcendentalism in an age dominated by a materialistic philosophy that eventually produced, in reaction, the pragmatism of James and Dewey? Or was it vital enough to leave its own traces in the twentieth century?

According to his own testimony, Dewey's enthusiasm for Hegel was motivated by a personal need to heal an "inward laceration" that was the "heritage of New England culture"—a culture ridden with "divisions by way of isolation of self from the world, of soul from body, of nature from God." Hegel's organic idealism, which rejected the dualisms of earlier empiricist and idealist philosophy, dissolved the "hard-and-fast dividing walls." Such organicism "had a special attraction for me" and "left a permanent deposit in my thinking."[2] The moot point is just how permanent this deposit was. Joseph Ratner, in his introduction to a collection of Dewey's early essays,[3] argues that it can be (and presumably has been) exaggerated. Once Dewey realized the futility of trying to fit Hegel's categories to the material of scientific psychology, he simply abandoned them to create his own. For Ratner, the drama of Dewey's intellectual biography lay in the courageous decision to turn his back on Hegel and face the task of interpreting the world alone.

In contrast, Morton White[4] finds the origins of Dewey's instrumentalism in the insights he derived from Hegel. The idealist's conception of universal consciousness as the ultimate unity of subject and object became, in White's view, the "schema" for Dewey's later conception of nature as an organic unity. The conversion to naturalism was not a radical break with his past but rather a fifteen year "drifting" away from it, as Dewey himself put it later.[5] The re-

2. John Dewey, "From Absolutism to Experimentalism," *Contemporary American Philosophy*, eds. George P. Adams and Wm. Pepperell Montague (New York, 1930), 11, 19, 21.

3. John Dewey, *Philosophy, Psychology, and Social Practice*, ed. Joseph Ratner (New York, 1963), pp. 9–15.

4. Morton G. White, *The Origin of Dewey's Instrumentalism* (New York, 1943). White's is still the best single volume on Dewey's thought.

5. Dewey, "From Absolution to Experimentalism," p. 21.

cent publication of two works from Dewey's two periods provides the occasion for a review of this question.

The *Psychology* of 1887 was written from an idealistic viewpoint, according to which individual minds partake of a universal mind and reproduce in knowledge and action the contents of that universal mind. The book was originally an attempt by the young Dewey to reconcile the two divergent emphases of his graduate work at Johns Hopkins, the experimental "new psychology" of G. Stanley Hall and the Hegelianism of George S. Morris. It is clear from the beginning, however, that Morris' influence took precedence over Hall's. Whatever experimental psychologists discovered about the physiological conditions of sensation, muscular coordination, or other details of individual psychology was gratefully accepted and incorporated into an Hegelian framework. Inevitably the experimental temper of the new psychology clashed with the certainties of Dewey's preconceived idealistic system.

The present edition of the *Psychology* dramatically reveals Dewey's struggle to be honest to both of these traditions and his increasing difficulty in reconciling them. This edition is part of a University of Southern Illinois project to publish, under the auspices of the Modern Language Association, definitive editions of Dewey's early works. The *Psychology*, although it has been issued first, is the second volume in a five-volume set, *John Dewey, The Early Works, 1882–1898*. Using the computerized techniques of modern textual criticism, the editors have produced an extremely convenient variorum edition, which notes all the major and minor (sometimes even trivial) emendations in the several editions of Dewey's first book. Since the revisions were written in the critical years (1887–1891) when Dewey was reexamining his Hegelian orientation, such a clear record of them is invaluable.

The *Lectures in the Philosophy of Education: 1899*, here published for the first time, clearly belong to Dewey's later period. Discovered in 1963 by Professor Archambault in the Grinnell College library, these lectures (delivered at the University of Chicago) are student notes that, with Dewey's permission, were duplicated and subscribed to by other students in his class. They incorporate all of the major changes Dewey had made in his thinking during the 1890's, including a complete rejection of the idealistic framework of universal mind in favor of a wholly naturalistic viewpoint. In the *Lectures* Dewey's new psychology of impulses and organized habits was the basis of the educational theory to which he devoted so much of his thinking during his tenure as Professor of Philosophy and Pedagogies at the University of Chicago. As a record of his strictly educational views,[6] they add little to his well-known lec-

6. This edition does contain some useful information for the historian of education, in-

tures, *The School and Society* (1899) and *The Child and the Curriculum* (1902). On the other hand, they are an important example of the psychological views that found their published expression only much later in *Democracy and Education* (1916) and *Human Nature and Conduct* (1922). Moreover, the *Lectures* provide us with a synthetic view of human psychology very early in Dewey's naturalistic period, which his psychological essays[7] of the 1890's do not provide. These critical essays were important steps in Dewey's retreat from the idealism of the *Psychology*, but, if taken alone, they do not accurately portray the emphasis Dewey places on the social dimension of human experience in his later period. The *Lectures*, dealing as they do with the total experience of the child in school, balance the picture. They serve very well, therefore, as a convenient measure of Dewey's intellectual progress since the *Psychology* and of the impact, if any, his idealism had.

The most significant difference between the *Psychology* and the *Lectures in the Philosophy of Education* was the product of Dewey's movement from an intellectualistic to an activistic view of individual psychology. In the *Psychology* Dewey defined his subject as "the science of the reproduction of some universal content or existence, whether of knowledge or of action, in the form of individual, unsharable consciousness."[8] While he believed that consciousness is a synthesis of knowledge, feeling, and will, fully two-thirds of the book concerned the mind in its intellectual capacity. This was psychology in its traditional garb, beginning with the epistemological question of the relationship between the mind and the external world. The *Lectures*, in contrast, take the individual as primarily an active being endowed with outgoing impulses. From this standpoint, the business of psychology is to explain how these impulses find expression in the external world, how they become organized into habits, and how knowledge functions instrumentally in this process. Psychology was the study of men's natural acts; epistemological questions as such were quite irrelevant.

The variorum edition of the *Psychology* documents Dewey's first steps towards his mature position. Dewey revised the *Psychology* twice, in 1889 and in 1891 (the latter being the text of the present edition). The second was the

cluding a complete bibliography of sources cited in the syllabus to Dewey's course, a copy of the catalogue of the Department of Pedagogy at the University of Chicago, and an 1897 memorandum by Dewey on the organization of such a department.

7. I am thinking especially of "The Ego as Cause" (1894), "The Theory of Emotion" (1894), and "The Reflex Arc Concept in Psychology" (1896). All of these and other important essays are reprinted in Ratner's collection of Dewey's early essays.

8. Dewey, *Psychology*, p. 11.

more substantial, and the critical event influencing it was the publication of William James's *Principles of Psychology* in 1890. Not that James worked a revolution in Dewey's thinking; he did not. Some of the changes in the 1891 edition were more of emphasis than substance. For example, on the question of emotions Dewey had leaned toward the James-Lange theory even in the first edition of 1887; in 1891 he was unambiguously for it. On other matters, however, the revisions were substantial and indicated serious doubts about his idealistic framework.

Even in 1889 Dewey seemed to be withdrawing from some of the more extreme Hegelianisms of the first edition. For instance, in 1887 when discussing apperception and retention, processes through which the self gained knowledge and was thereby permanently modified, Dewey wrote:

In retention the self comes to exist as real; the mind realizes or objectifies itself just to the extent to which the world is apprehended and taken into self. Apperception occurs through the self; retention through the universe. Each process necessitates the other. The universe gets conscious existence for us as the individual self becomes real as it finds itself in this universe. . . . In knowledge the world is taken into the mind and gets ideal meaning, and at the same time the self grows into likeness with the world.[9]

At the same point in the 1889 edition Dewey eliminated this conception of retention, substituting in its place a functional interpretation. Ideas, he argued, have no "independent, separate existence." An idea is rather a "function of the mind; that is, the mind considered in a certain mode of activity." Retention, therefore, is not the storing of ideas somewhere in the mind, but rather "consists in an alteration in the structure of the mind which affects the way in which it functions."[10]

In this and one other revision in 1889 Dewey dropped the idealistic conception of the relationship between individual minds and the universal mind. He did not, however, revise the second edition consistently, and even in the third edition when Dewey continued to deemphasize this notion and added other more substantive changes, he did not eliminate it altogether. It seems, nevertheless, that he was becoming uncomfortable with such metaphysical material in his psychology.

Dewey pointed out in a "Note to the Third Edition" that "the only change involving an alteration of standpoint is in the general treatment of sensation."[11] But the new treatment of sensation in 1891 did not completely jibe with his

9. *Ibid.*, p. lxxviii.
10. *Ibid.*, p. 134.
11. *Ibid.*, p. 5.

idealism. Eventually, the thrust of his new ideas led him to give up revising the *Psychology* and to turn to a different philosophical framework entirely.

The most significant change that Dewey introduced in 1891 was the idea of a "sensation continuum," or a "certain original continuous substratum of sensation out of which the various distinct sensations have been slowly differentiated."[12] Like James's stream of consciousness, Dewey's sensation continuum was his answer to English sensationalism, according to which sensations were simple, discrete atoms combined by the mind into more complex ideas. Both James and Dewey believed that consciousness was a continuous flow of sensations out of which the mind carved its own reality. And both emphasized the mind's activity in contrast to the passivity of the English empirical tradition.

From the first edition of the *Psychology* and before, Dewey had strenuously refuted a passive conception of mind. Even a sensation was for him a "virtual creation" of the soul, acting on an unconscious nervous impulse.[13] In the first and second editions, however, Dewey had been guilty of his own form of psychological atomism. For once the soul created its sensations they were themselves interpreted as the "elements of intelligence which, through their combinations, constitute knowledge. . . ."[14] Dewey had seen the job of the psychologist as comparable to that of the physicist or chemist, who analyzes his subject in terms of its most elementary units, atoms or molecules. Likewise, the psychologist "finds himself forced . . . to the supposition of a psychical unit beyond further analysis, and forming the basis and material out of which the concrete forms of knowledge are built up. . . ."[15] In the third edition, Dewey eliminated all of these references to sensations as elementary units and specifically indicted the atomistic theory.

In earlier editions, however, Dewey's idealistic atomism had played an important role in his analysis of mind. For there he argued that a sensation, while it is consciousness, is not knowledge. Knowledge has to do with the relationship among things in the world; of this sensations alone can tell us nothing. Because sensation is mere "excitation," or bare consciousness, it "requires comparison and association . . . [the] activity of intelligence" to become a significant sign of an object.[16] Thus, Dewey reserved to the higher, more active powers of the mind, the function of producing knowledge.

12. *Ibid.*, p. 35.
13. *Ibid.*, p. 42.
14. *Ibid.*, p. lx.
15. *Ibid.*, p. lxii.
16. *Ibid.*, p. lxi.

In the third edition Dewey undercut this conception of sensation as mere consciousness and the idealistic theory of mind it implied. The atomistic theory, he wrote, cannot account for the "unity of mental actions and of mental products" without recourse either to a process of "indissoluble association" or to "a *special* relating power of the mind." Then, significantly, Dewey went on to say: "More particularly examination shows that the discreteness and independence which we attribute to our sensations belong rather *to the objects to which we refer the sensory qualities.*"[17] First, we should note that while Dewey never advocated a theory of indissoluble association to explain the unity of knowledge, he always appealed to the special relating power of the mind. Sensations have to be related by the mind in order to become knowledge. Moreover, if the apparent discreteness of sensations corresponds to discrete qualities in objects themselves, then sensations tell us something about the world to which they refer; that is, sensations are simple forms of knowledge.

It seems that Dewey now accepted James's theory that a sensation was but a simple perception. Yet, as in the case of the second edition, he did not apply the implications of this idea consistently to his treatment of knowledge. He still maintained in 1891 that "sensations are not knowledge"[18] and interpreted mental activity in terms of the associating powers of the mind. But at several points in a persistently idealistic framework, Dewey slipped in some interesting changes that indicate the direction in which he was moving. For instance, apperception in 1887 was "the relating activity which combines the various sensuous elements presented to the mind at one time into a whole, and which unites these wholes, occurring at successive times, into a continuous mental life. . . ."[19] (Note the special mental power relating separate elements.) In 1891 apperception is "that activity of mind in which the *significance* of mental *events* is brought out, through becoming explicitly conscious of the relations involved in them."[20] Here the relations, if made explicit through apperception, must have been implicit in the sensations themselves. If sensation is a simple form of knowledge and if the relations between objects in the external world find their reflection in the self's direct experience of that world, perhaps the whole idealistic apparatus of the self's reproducing the universal mind was unnecessary.

When Dewey threw over the idealistic system to look at natural man di-

17. *Ibid.*, pp. 36–37.
18. *Ibid.*, p. 75.
19. *Ibid.*, p. lxxiv.
20. *Ibid.*, p. 81.

rectly, he did not abandon all of the insights he had gained from his Hegelian orientation. Indeed most of the elements in his later naturalistic psychology were apparent even in the first edition of the *Psychology*. Only there they were made subordinate to the idealistic analysis of knowledge. For instance, as a *dynamic* idealist, Dewey believed that in addition to knowledge, feeling and will were inseparable parts of consciousness. In a formula reminiscent of Hegel's dialectic, Dewey considered knowledge the universal element in consciousness, feeling the individual element, and will the relationship between them that "connects them into one concrete content."[21] Aside from such Hegelianisms, however, Dewey's discussion of feeling and will anticipated his later views of interest and impulse.

In the *Psychology*, feeling accompanies every conscious experience and serves the function of determining the self's interest in the particular fact of consciousness before it. Feeling as such exists because the "self is . . . *activity*."[22] Of course, in the idealistic system, the activity of the self is the gradual realization or objectification of its essential nature, just as the world of objects and actions is the complete realization of the universal, absolute self. The dynamic aspect of Dewey's idealism, however, did incline him towards conception of the individual as an object-oriented, active being. Dewey's treatment of impulse in the *Psychology* reinforced this active orientation. A sensation was not a "mere state of mind" but was an impulse as well. As an impulse, the sensation was "a disturbance of the equilibrium of the organism, setting free energy which must discharge itself in producing some change."[23] Indeed, Dewey maintained, without impulses knowledge would be impossible, for the impulse, or elementary will, to act induces the individual to attend to particular sensations, and attention is the basis of knowledge.

These ideas were all present in the first edition of the *Psychology* and co-existed with Dewey's theory of universal consciousness. It should be noted that Herbert W. Schneider, in his introduction to the variorum edition, makes significant errors of fact in his effort to emphasize the importance of the movement away from idealism in the third edition. He claims that the "doctrine of 'feeling or interest' . . . first enters in the 1891 printing and becomes central in his later work."[24] It is true that this "doctrine" becomes central later, but Dewey did not introduce it for the first time in 1891. Of the five examples Schneider cites, four appeared in the first edition and were never

21. *Ibid.*, p. 22.
22. *Ibid.*, p. 216.
23. *Ibid.*, pp. 301–302.
24. *Ibid.*, p. xxxv.

revised. Only one was part of a revised paragraph, but the revision had to do with the theory that the individual mind reproduces the universal mind, not with the self's natural interest in objects.

We can see just how central the ideas of impulse, interest, and attention became in the *Lectures in the Philosophy of Education*. There Dewey began his study of individual psychology with the "active impulse," which naturally expresses itself in bodily movement. This movement produces changes in the environment, which are observed by the self and then "associated, or rather fused," with the impulse and give it conscious meaning. On each occasion of the impulse's "discharging," new experiences are had, more impressions of its effects in the world are associated with it, and its meaning is amplified.[25] Increased meaning eventually brings control as the active self gathers knowledge of the conditions under which the impulse functions best. Knowledge is, therefore, instrumental to the goal of gaining control and the controlled impulse itself becomes habit. The problem of elementary education, for Dewey, was thus reduced to providing an environment, sufficiently varied and coherent, from which the child will receive an orderly "return wave" of impressions that can be built into integrated habits.[26] In secondary education the process is similar only more conscious, so that the child is more aware of the ends his habits might serve. "Voluntary attention" to the habits and materials that will allow him to reach these ends replaces the "non-voluntary attention" accompanying the development of controlled impulses.[27]

While we can find certain elements of Dewey's naturalistic psychology in his earlier work, the change in perspective from which he viewed the individual was so fundamental that we can attribute little or no direct influence to his idealism in this regard. Dewey based his theory of learning by experience on the "coordination" or "organic circuit," the psychological unit of behavior he had analyzed in "The Reflex Arc Concept in Psychology." The psychology of knowing, learning, or thinking, is implicit within the natural act. All recourse to the soul, or the universal mind, in explaining them, was eliminated. Dewey had finally brought his psychology down to earth.

When we seek to explain the emphasis Dewey placed on the social dimension of human experience in the later period, the case is rather different. This emphasis was Dewey's major contribution to educational theory at the turn of the century and later to the political discourse of American liberalism. Its source lay in his idealistic analysis of the relationship between universal and

25. John Dewey, *Lectures*, pp. 304–305.
26. *Ibid.*, p. 309.
27. *Ibid.*, p. 319.

individual consciousness. Indeed the form and substance of his naturalistic social psychology can be found in the first edition of the *Psychology*.

Certainly, if we put any faith at all in Dewey's own testimony, one of idealism's great attractions was its sense of the organic unity between a man and his world, a world of objects and of other men. As in the case of other American idealists at the end of the nineteenth century, notably Josiah Royce and James Mark Baldwin, the idealistic analysis of consciousness led Dewey to the view that the self was essentially a social product, that an individual's development cannot be understood apart from the social medium in which he lives. The young idealist found support for this theory in the environmentalism of the new psychology. No longer could "psychical life" be understood "as an individual, isolated thing developing in a vacuum."[28] Anticipating his naturalistic viewpoint, he went on to say in 1884 that "we know . . . [the individual's] life is bound up with the life of society. . . . We know that he is connected with all the past by the lines of education, tradition, and heredity."[29]

The "schema" of Dewey's later conception of the relationship between the individual and society, as well as his view of nature (which Morton White has examined), was the relationship between individual and universal consciousness in the *Psychology*. As we have seen, upon receiving sensations from the material world, the mind transmutes this meaningless data into knowledge by establishing connections between them and the rest of the mind's content. Since the external world, in this idealistic system, is but the universal mind in objective form, the individual in acquiring knowledge establishes his relationship to the universal mind itself:

One side of the process of knowledge makes the universe individual by giving it its conscious unified existence in the self; the other makes the individual self universal by realizing its capacities in concrete forms of knowledge.[30]

If we substitute "society" and "individual" for "universe" and "self" in this passage we have the essence of Dewey's later social theory, expressed in somewhat garbled Hegelianisms. The individual is rooted in and partakes of a society, just as the self partakes of the universal consciousness; society finds its expression in the socialized individual just as universal consciousness does in the individual mind. As the "individual reproduced the universal mind, and

28. John Dewey, "The New Psychology," *The Andover Review*, 2 (September 1884), 285.
29. *Ibid.*, pp. 278–279.
30. Dewey, *Psychology*, p. lxxviii.

hence makes real for himself the universe,"[31] he also reproduces society through education and makes society real for himself.

In the *Psychology* Dewey filled out this "schema" of the relationship between the individual and society in his discussion of social feelings. There we find a theory of the social nature of the self that remained unrevised in all editions, after Dewey had eliminated the Hegelian formulations of the relationship of individual and universal consciousness. Social feelings "*arise from the relations of self-conscious beings to each other*" and the individual "can truly develop himself only in self-conscious activity, in personality, and this is impossible without relations to other people."[32] Sympathy, the primary social feeling, is, for Dewey, the bond which "constitutes society as an organic whole, a whole permeated by a common life, where each individual still lives his own distinct life unabsorbed in that of the community."[33]

With respect to his idea of the social dimension of experience, Dewey's conversion from idealism to naturalism was incidental. Substantively the concept remained unchanged. In the 1899 lectures Dewey defined education as socialization, that is, as a process of bringing the child "to consciousness of himself in a social way as a social being. . . ."[34] The objects of the external world themselves are "saturated with the particular values which are put into them" by other people.[35] And the educator must deal with this social medium so that

the child . . . learn[s] to conceive, to feel, to appreciate himself, and to act himself as a social being. These social values which he is to realize, cannot be anything outside of himself; they would not be values, and would not be social. They must become a part of his own character, of his own way of looking at things, and of feeling things, and doing things.[36]

To realize this ideal in education the school itself must be organized as an organic social unit within the society at large so that the child comes to understand his membership to the larger community. And the curriculum must deal with the everyday experience of social life that the child has before and after his formal education.

Dewey's insight into the social nature of human existence was the "permanent deposit" of his early commitment to Hegel. It was for Dewey alone

31. *Ibid.*, p. lxxix.
32. *Ibid.*, p. 281. Original emphasis.
33. *Ibid.*, p. 286.
34. Dewey, *Lectures*, p. 97.
35. *Ibid.*, p. 47.
36. *Ibid.*, p. 96.

what the idealism of Royce, Baldwin, and Dewey himself was for the concept of the social self in early American social science. Neither can be understood without reference to its source in idealism. The continuity in Dewey's career is especially important, moreover, for his personal contribution to social and political thought in the twentieth century carried this insight into the discourse of American intellectual life.

NOTES ON CONTRIBUTORS

JOHN CLIVE (born Berlin, Germany 1924), professor of history and literature, Harvard University.

MARSHALL J. COHEN (born Newark, N.J. 1939), instructor in history, Harvard University.

P. M. G. HARRIS (born Ann Arbor, Mich. 1930), lecturer in sociology, Howard University, Washington, D.C.

BARRY D. KARL (born Louisville, Kentucky 1927), professor of history, Brown University, Providence.

STANLEY N. KATZ (born Chicago 1934), associate professor of history, University of Wisconsin, Madison.

ERNEST R. MAY (born Ft. Worth, Texas 1928), professor of history, Harvard University.

JAMES M. MCPHERSON (born Valley City, North Dakota 1936), associate professor of history, Princeton University.

SIDNEY E. MEAD (born Champlin, Minn. 1904), professor of American church history, Iowa State University, Iowa City.

MOSES RISCHIN (born New York, N.Y. 1925), professor of history, San Francisco State College.

CHARLES STRICKLAND (born Amarillo, Texas 1930), assistant professor of history and teacher education, Emory University.

MORTON WHITE (born New York, N.Y. 1917), professor of philosophy, Harvard University.

R. RICHARD WOHL (born New York, N.Y. 1921), at his death in 1957 was associate professor of the social sciences, member of the Committee on Human Development, University of Chicago.